MW00636859

Family Life Education

Working with Families across the Lifespan

Fourth Edition

Carol A. Darling, PhD, CFLE
Florida State University
University of Helsinki

Dawn Cassidy, MEd, CFLE
National Council on Family Relations

Sharon M. Ballard, PhD, CFLE
East Carolina University

WAVELAND PRESS, INC.
Long Grove, Illinois

For information about this book, contact:
Waveland Press, Inc.
4180 IL Route 83, Suite 101
Long Grove, IL 60047-9580
(847) 634-0081
info@waveland.com
www.waveland.com

10-digit ISBN 1-4786-4737-X
13-digit ISBN 978-1-4786-4737-9

Printed in the United States of America

7 6 5 4 3 2 1

Contents

PART II
Practice of Family Life Education

PART III
Content of Family Life Education

Preface

The ruin of a nation begins in the homes of its people.

—Ghanaian proverb

In the eyes of a family life educator, the above Ghanaian proverb may be looking at the issue in the wrong way. A version that is more representative of family life education would be "the success of a nation begins in the homes of its people." The foundation of family life education includes a positive, proactive approach to individual and family functioning. We believe that most family life educators are "glass half full" people. They believe in the key role that strong, healthy families play in supporting and strengthening society and the good that can come from providing individuals and families with the knowledge and skills needed to be happy, contributing members of their communities. It is our hope that this book will contribute to this effort.

Dr. Carol A. Darling, CFLE, and Dawn Cassidy, CFLE, are pleased to welcome a new author to this fourth edition. Dr. Sharon M. Ballard, CFLE, is the Department Chair at East Carolina University and co-editor of the book *Family Life Education with Diverse Populations*, now in its second edition. We have all worked together over the years on various family life education endeavors and collaborated to bring forth this revised, updated, and expanded edition. We are also excited about the addition to our team of Dr. Cynthia Wilson, CFLE, from Florida State University, who prepared PowerPoint slides for this edition of our book. We are all indebted to Dr. Lane Powell, CFLE, who co-authored the first two editions, as she perceived the need for this book and provided the vision, creativity, and commitment for the first two editions.

Although this book is written primarily with undergraduate majors in human development and family science in mind, it can be useful to persons in related fields of study who are preparing for careers in community education and outreach. Such careers will require the preparation, presentation, and evaluation of educational programs and workshops for persons at all stages of the lifespan. It is imperative that practitioners have a working knowledge of how to accomplish these tasks effectively. The text is a realistic blend of theory and praxis (action with reflection) designed to encourage the type of hands-on experience needed to interact comfortably with diverse groups and a variety of topics.

In this fourth edition, we retain our focus on presenting family life education (FLE) as a profession with a history and an exciting future. Persons seeking certification as family life educators through the certification program of the National Council on Family Relations will find this book a great assist in understanding and developing competency in the area of family life education. The chapters have been updated to include current demographics, issues, program options, and practice in planning, implementation, and evaluation of FLE programs. There is greater attention to the diversity of our audience and settings with the inclusion of personal reflections of current practice from family life educators in various settings. Additionally, the content and context of FLE have been expanded within Chapters 8 to 12, including Relating Theory to Practice and Approaches to Sexuality Education, Relationship and Marriage Education, Parenting Education, and International Family Life Education. These chapters have not only been updated and revised, but also contain various conceptual models and interactive classroom activities. Additionally, the chapter on International Family Life Education includes the results of an international qualitative study with responses from six continents and 27 countries including Australia, Brazil, Canada, China plus Hong Kong, Croatia, Denmark, Finland, Ghana, Iran, Ireland, Israel, Jamaica, Japan, Luxembourg, Mexico, Netherlands, Nigeria, Peru, Philippines, Russia, Senegal, Singapore, South Korea, Spain, Sweden, Taiwan, and the United Kingdom.

As in the first three editions, each chapter includes a series of questions and issues for class discussion, as well as research problems and activities for independent or auxiliary study. Class activities and case studies are included as they pertain to the content of the chapter. The activity suggestions are indicative of a problem-based learning focus, which many educational specialists now recommend as preferable to a lecture course based on a body of content. Certainly, it is more desirable for a class that emphasizes praxis. When students are challenged to figure things out for themselves, they tend to retain information and strengthen their personal skills.

Writing this book has been a tremendous learning experience and one that has left us better informed and further committed to family life education. We want to acknowledge and thank our friends and colleagues who have helped us with this fourth edition by reviewing chapters, contributing teaching activities, and providing guidance and moral support.

Alexis Askew, East Carolina University
Fiorella Carlos Chavez, PhD, Arizona State University
Ming Cui, PhD, Florida State University
Marsha Rehm, PhD, Florida State University
Bethanne Shriner, PhD, University of Wisconsin, Stout
Alan Taylor, PhD, East Carolina University
Deborah Tippett, PhD, Meredith College
Susan Walker, PhD, University of Minnesota
Janice Weber, PhD, University of Louisiana at Lafayette
Mari Wilhelm, PhD, University of Arizona
Cynthia Wilson, PhD, Florida State University

We truly appreciate the seventeen colleagues who contributed their personal insights about the joys and challenges of providing family life education in a variety of settings. Their names, affiliations, and statements are included in Chapter 4, Settings in Family Life Education. Thank you also to the 35 family professionals from six continents and 27 countries who responded to our survey on the status of family life education in their countries.

We are deeply indebted to the many family life educators, too numerous to mention, that have contributed to the evolution of the field and profession of family life education, as well as to our own personal development. Additionally, we would like to thank Waveland Press especially Don Rosso, Senior Editor/Production Manager, and Dakota West, Editor, for their support, guidance, and editorial assistance. We want to acknowledge our professors, teachers, and mentors who have shared so much of their time, energy, and wisdom. We greatly appreciate our colleagues, friends, and students who have accompanied us on this adventure. Most importantly, we would like to acknowledge and thank our encouraging and supporting spouses—Paul Anderson, Tom Cassidy, and Kevin Gross—who kept themselves occupied over many evenings and weekends while we worked on this book. They, and all our family members, including Dawn's children, Hamil and Elaina, and Sharon's son, Jamie, are evidence of the value of family.

About the Authors

Carol A. Darling, a Certified Family Life Educator, is the Florida State University's Margaret Sandels Professor of Health and Human Sciences as well as Professor Emerita in the Department Human Development and Family Science. She has also been on the faculty in the College of Behavioural Sciences at the University of Helsinki in Helsinki, Finland, as a Docent in Family and Consumer Sciences, and has twice been a Fulbright Scholar in teaching and research at the University of Helsinki. She has received the Excellence in College and University Teaching Award from the Association of Public and Land-grant Universities along with the Ernest G. Osborne Award for Outstanding Leadership and Excellence in Teaching Family Relations and the Margaret Arcus Outstanding Family Life Educator Award sponsored by the National Council on Family Relations. She has also received the Distinguished Teaching Award and other teaching awards from Florida State University. Her PhD is in Family Ecology from Michigan State University with emphases in family relations and child development.

Dr. Darling has a long history of commitment to the National Council on Family Relations (NCFR). She received NCFR Fellow status in 2002 and served as president from 2001–2003. One of her ongoing contributions nationally and internationally has been to NCFR's Certified Family Life Educator (CFLE) program. She was a member of the original Committee on Standards and Certification for Family Life Education, which developed and implemented this credentialing program. In addition she was a member of the CFLE Academic Program Review Committee, the CFLE Exam Committee, and a founding member and chair of the CFLE Advisory Board. She has received NCFR's Special Recognition Award for Outstanding and Dedicated Service to the Certified Family Life Educator Program.

Dr. Darling's research activities and numerous publications and presentations have been in the areas of family life education; parenting education; human sexuality and sexuality education; family stress and crises; women's health issues; and multicultural education and cultural diversity in relation to individuals, families, and educational programs. She has had a life-long commitment to family life education both locally at Florida State University, other universities, and the public schools; nationally through the NCFR and various state affiliates; and internationally through her research, presentations, and courses taught in various countries such as Australia, Costa Rica, Finland, South Korea, Switzerland, and Taiwan.

Dawn Cassidy, a Certified Family Life Educator, is the Director of Family Life Education for the National Council on Family Relations (NCFR). She has an MEd in Work, Family, and Community Education from the University of Minnesota and was a co-author of the first three editions of this book. In addition to authoring chapters in several NCFR publications, she has been a co-author for multiple journal articles. Dawn has served as a parent facilitator for the MELD program for two years and as a member of the Southwest Family Room Collaborative Council, a United Way community resource program for families with young children. As a member of the Ethics Committee of the Minnesota Council on Family Relations, she was involved in developing guidelines for ethical thinking and practice for parent and family educators.

As administrator of NCFR's Certified Family Life Educator credentialing program, Dawn was involved in the development of the CFLE exam, which included an extensive job analysis for the field of family life education. She has presented on the topic of family life education both nationally and internationally in China, Japan, and Singapore where she assisted the Singapore Ministry of Social and Family Development in the development of a certificate program for family life educators. In 2021, she organized NCFR's first virtual summit targeted specifically to family practitioners and the practice of family life education.

Sharon M. Ballard is Professor and Chair of the Department of Human Development and Family Science at East Carolina University. Prior to earning her MS and PhD in Child and Family Studies from The University of Tennessee, Knoxville, she taught Family and Consumer Sciences at the middle and high school levels for six years. Dr. Ballard has been a Certified Family Life Educator (CFLE) through the National Council on Family Relations (NCFR) since 1998 and has conducted a variety of family life education programs in community settings. Sharon was a founding member of the CFLE advisory committee, serving as chair of the committee from 2009–2011, and was awarded the Special Recognition Award for Outstanding and Dedicated Service to the Certified Family Life Educator Program in 2012 and the Margaret E. Arcus Outstanding Family Life Educator Award in 2016.

Dr. Ballard's research has primarily centered around family life education programming and practice, parent education, and sexuality education. She has numerous published journal articles, presentations, and book chapters, including her co-edited book *Family Life Education with Diverse Populations*.

Part I

Field of Family Life Education

1

What Is Family Life Education?

Understanding Family Life Education

As a student in a family life education class, you may have been asked: "What exactly *is* family life education?" The following parable might help provide some clarification.

> There was once a village built upon the edge of a river where the water churned roughly over the rocks. There were signs at the river's edge warning of the danger, but people often ignored the signs and fell into the river. They often drowned or flowed downstream to a waterfall and were never seen again. The villagers came up with a plan. A net was put downstream to catch those who had fallen in the river. A full-time crew was hired to watch for villagers floating downstream, pull them from the river, dry them off, and get them to ambulances. A new hospital was built closer to the river's edge. All these efforts increased the survival rate but many were still injured or drowned.
>
> A couple who moved to the village watched what was happening and asked if something more could be done to save people (*collaboration*). The villagers were resistant, explaining that they had developed a good system and while they weren't able to save everyone, they felt that things had improved. The couple wasn't satisfied and decided to take matters into their own hands by helping to build a large fence along the rough part of the river (*prevention*), offering swimming lessons, teaching people how to maneuver their boats around the rocks (*prevention and education*), and speaking to villagers about the dangers of going into the river without a life jacket (*prevention and education*). Soon fewer and fewer people were falling into the river and those that did fall in were better equipped to save themselves. (NCFR, n.d.-a)

Family life education is about working upstream. Rather than waiting to act until problems develop and individuals and families are suffering and struggling, family life education incorporates a *preventive*, *educational*, and *collaborative* approach to individual and family issues. This proactive approach can prevent problems and enhance potentials. It can take place in a variety of settings aimed at a varied audience dealing with a myriad of issues, interests, concerns, and situations. The following situations describe some of the family life education activities taking place in communities near you.

> The Liberty High School young mothers' class, composed of 10 pregnant teenagers, watch their teacher bathe and change a real baby. Questions underscore their nervousness and fear about their impending role as young mothers. In the next period they will be discussing infant development. In the afternoons they work in the nursery with the young children of other teen mothers, under the close attention of the nursery director or lab teacher, who will model, instruct, and guide their participation.

> At a local community center, parents of 9th and 10th grade students gather together for another in a series of talks on *Parenting Your Teen*. They are there to learn more about adolescent development and behavior. Last week's discussion on adolescent brain development was especially enlightening. Having the opportunity to hear from other parents who are facing the same issues was reassuring; it's helpful to know that they are not the only parents whose child's personality seems to have changed overnight!

> In a neighborhood apartment, a young college graduate completes an online financial literacy program offered by the local Extension Service. He's learning about insurance, retirement plans and investments, and how to create a household budget. One of the modules is on goal setting, another on making informed decisions. He's hoping to avoid the bankruptcy and foreclosure faced by his parents.

> A nearby church is holding a marriage education class for engaged couples. The facilitator is "walking them through" an exercise aimed at helping participants identify their expectations for marriage. Later they'll learn about active listening and practice some new communication skills.

> At a senior housing complex, a group of older adults are attending the first of a four-part series on *Planning for Retirement*. They are looking forward to learning more about how to budget their income, stay healthy and active, maintain social relationships, and adjust to life without a regular job.

> After school, an 8th grade student visits the new *Choices* app that she downloaded for free onto her smartphone. Once in the app, she chooses a scenario and moves through a series of realistic, conflicting decisions regarding sexuality and relationships. She sees that several of her friends are online too and chats with them as she works through the scenario. They compare notes on the choices they made and how they affected the outcome. Along the way, she clicks on links that take her to credible websites for more information on healthy relationships.

Family . . . life . . . education is a concept that encompasses a multitude of images and expectations. These scenarios describe only a few of the many topics and audiences addressed through family life education. All call for a combination of skills and expectations of the leader-educator and of the "student" group. How do we define family life education in a way that encompasses its multifaceted contexts? How do we even define "family"? And what value does family life education have in supporting and educating individuals for family life? How do you, as a professional or future professional who will be working with families, develop the skills to respond effectively to so many demands?

This book was written to address the many issues involved in the educational preparation of family life educators, using an approach that promotes the interactive teaching style that is typical of the family life education model. Chapter 1 provides an overview of the definitions, history, and future directions of family life education, setting the context and developing an understanding and appreciation for the profession. Chapter 2 discusses the evolution of the profession of family life education, including current challenges and strategies for growth, the personal skills and qualities of the family life educator, and the importance of ethical guidelines. Chapters 3 through 7 address the practice of family life education, from understanding the audience and settings of family life education to designing, implementing, and evaluating family life education programs. Chapters 8 through 11 become more specific and address four content areas of family life education that are the most developed and the most often presented within the profession: family theory, sexuality education, marriage and relationship education, and parent education. Chapter 12 discusses international perspectives of family life education including its need, status, and methods. This is truly designed to be a practitioner's handbook; so when you get the call "Will you help us start a group for . . . ?" you'll be ready!

Defining the Practice of Family Life Education

A definition for "family life education" identifying the content, purpose, audience, focus, and timing of the practice has been discussed in numerous articles and conversations over the past 50 years. The evolution of the definition was first examined in the *Handbook of Family Life Education, Volume 1* (Arcus, Schvaneveldt, & Moss, 1993) and updated in previous editions of this book (Darling & Cassidy, 2014, pp. 6–7). When considering an operational definition of family life education, Thomas and Arcus (1992) posed the question, "What features must something have in order to be called family life education?" After extensive review of the literature and program designs, Arcus et al. (1993) concluded that family life education generally:

- is relevant to individuals and families across the lifespan
- is based on the needs of individuals and families
- is a multidisciplinary area of study and multiprofessional in its practice
- is offered in many different settings
- is an educational rather than a therapeutic approach
- presents and respects differing family values
- requires qualified educators who are cognizant of the goals of family life education

Arcus et al. (1993) reduced the aims, or rationale, for family life education to three primary ones: (1) dealing with problems that impinge upon families, (2) preventing problems, and (3) developing potentials for individuals and families. In other words, family life education is a process designed to "strengthen and enrich individual and family well-being" (p. 12). Additionally, Arcus and Thomas (1993) identified a variety of goals and objectives relevant to the practice of family life education. The most common are (1) gaining insight into self and others, (2) learning about human development and behavior in the family setting over the life cycle, (3) learning about marriage and family patterns and processes, (4) acquiring skills essential for family life, (5) developing the individuals' potentials in their current and future roles, and (6) building strengths in families. "One of the assumptions in family life education appears to be that, if these and other similar objectives are met through family life education programs, then families will be better able to deal with problems, to prevent problems, and/or to develop their potentials" (Arcus & Thomas, 1993, p. 5). Family life education can in turn help to strengthen society because the development of more stable and functioning families results in a more stable and functioning society.

A review of family life education definitions over the years supports Arcus' rationale for the practice. Rather than include a lengthy chronology of definitions from 1962 to the current day, we have identified several evolving and recurring themes and concepts. These concepts include *relationships, the role of the learner as a family member, life cycle, a focus on strengths and developing potential, methods for providing family life education*, and the *goal of family life education*. Although there is variation in how FLE has been defined over the years, the definitions provide a clear consensus of the most relevant concepts.

- **Relationships**: Definitions often include consideration of relationships as a core focus of most family life education efforts (e.g., "Throughout the concept of family life education is woven the idea of relationships" [Kerckhoff, 1964, p. 883]; and "understanding of and capacity for forming and maintaining effective human interrelationships" [Kirkendall, 1973, p. 696]).
- **Role of the Learner as a Family Member**: The role of the learner as a family member was also included in most definitions (e.g., "Learners were frequently identified as present and future family members" [Avery, 1962, p. 28] and "assist families and family members with their family roles" [Arcus, 1995, p. 336]).
- **Life Cycle**: Many FLE definitions recognize the varying ages of the learner and issues experienced throughout the lifespan (e.g., "To help individuals and families learn what is known about human growth, development, and behavior *throughout the life cycle* is the main purpose of family life education" [National Commission on Family Life Education, 1968, p. 211] and "information is offered to *individuals of all ages*" [Gross, 1985, p. 6]).
- **A Focus on Strengths and Developing Potential**: A focus on developing potential and recognizing the learner's strengths and role in the learning process is clearly identified in multiple family life education definitions (e.g., "develop the potentials of individuals" [National Commission on Family Life Education, 1968, p. 211] and "so families may build on their strengths" [Myers-Walls et al., 2011, p. 370]).
- **Methods for Providing Family Life Education**: Many definitions include consideration of the planned and intentional nature of FLE (e.g., "It is a program of learning experiences *planned* and *guided*" [Smith, 1968, p. 55]). Additionally, some definitions clarified the setting in which FLE occurs as well as the provider. One of the earliest definitions identified FLE as involving "any and all *school* experiences deliberately and consciously used by *teachers* in helping to develop the personalities of *students* (Avery, 1962, p. 28). Conversely, Duncan and Goddard (2016) identify outreach FLE as educational activities occurring *outside a traditional school classroom setting*.
- **Goal of Family Life Education**: Finally, a review of the many definitions of family life education reflects a consistent focus on helping the learners *reach their full potential* and improve daily life (e.g., "Family life education (FLE) is an organized effort to enrich and improve the quality of individual and family life by providing people with information, skills, experiences, and resources intended to strengthen, improve, or enrich their family experience" [Kirby-Wilkins, Taner, Cassidy, & Cenizal, 2014] while also "enabling

adults to increase the effectiveness of their skills in daily living" and "realizing personal potential" [Tennant, 1989, p. 127]).

While not a formal definition, information regarding family life education provided on the National Council on Family Relations' website reflects many of these same concepts: *Family Life Education* is the professional practice of equipping and empowering family members to develop knowledge and skills that enhance well-being and strengthen interpersonal relationships through an educational, preventive, and strengths-based approach. The skills and knowledge needed for healthy family functioning are widely known:

- strong communication skills,
- knowledge of typical human development,
- good decision-making skills, positive self-esteem, and
- healthy interpersonal relationships.

The goal of family life education is to teach these skill and knowledge areas and provide learning experiences to family members across the lifespan and foster positive individual and family development so families can function optimally.

THE FRAMEWORK FOR LIFE SPAN FAMILY LIFE EDUCATION

The National Council on Family Relations' (NCFR) Framework for Life Span Family Life Education is a helpful tool for further definition and clarification of the content and context of family life education. NCFR (NCFR.org) is the primary professional organization for the field of family life education. It is an international multidisciplinary, nonpartisan professional membership organization focused on family research, practice, and education. It provides an educational forum for family researchers, educators, and practitioners to share in the development and dissemination of knowledge about families and family relationships, establish professional standards, and promote family well-being.

The Framework for Life Span Family Life Education, first developed by the NCFR in 1984 and revised in 1997 and 2011 (Bredehoft & Walcheski, 2011), provides a context for the many topics that can be addressed within the practice of family life education. It has gone through several revisions since 1984 (the 2011 revision was retitled the *Family Life Education Framework*), but the general concept remains. The *Framework* is organized around three major dimensions of family life education: *age or life stage* (broadly defined as childhood, adolescence, adulthood, and later adulthood), *content* (the areas of individual and family development to be addressed at each life stage through education including families and individuals in societal contexts, internal dynamics of families, human growth and development across the lifespan, human sexuality, interpersonal relationships, family resource management, parent education and guidance, family law and public policy, and professional ethics and practice), and *context* (the recognition that all FLE is conducted with consideration of the family system and the reciprocal interactions between family and the ecosystem). Also illustrated in the *Framework* is the inclusive perspective of the educator, which considers justice, value, and diverse cultures, communities, and individuals. The 2011 revision of the *Framework* included the addition of a wheel graphic which demonstrates the process involved in program planning, implementation, and evaluation and reflects the application of the educational process to the *Framework* (Clarke, 1998). Revisions to the 2011 *Framework* resulted from focus group meetings and outreach to family professionals. The changes over the years reflect the increasing clarification and evolution of the content and context of family life education. Appendix A presents the entire framework by age category. The NCFR has produced the *Framework* in a poster format with an accompanying PowerPoint presentation for use in the classroom.

Models of Family Life Education

Over the years there have been many attempts to conceptualize and clarify family life education (FLE) through the use of various tools and models. Some of these include the NCFR *Family Life Education Framework* (Bredehoft & Walcheski, 2011); the *Levels of Family Involvement Model (LFI)* (Doherty, 1995; Doherty & Lamson, 2015); the *Domains of Family Practice Model (DFP)* (Myers-Walls, Ballard, Darling, & Myers-Bowman, 2011); and the *Framework for Best Practices* (Ballard & Taylor, 2012). Because these models consider a specific aspect of FLE, such as *content* (Framework for FLE), *practice* (Framework for Best Practices and LFI Model), or *provider* (LFI and DFP Models), the *Foundations of Family Life Education Model (FFLE)* was developed to provide a cohesive, comprehensive, visual conceptualization of FLE.

The Foundations of Family Life Education Model (FFLE)

The Foundations of Family Life Education Model helps to identify and organize the fundamental concepts and features of family life education (FLE) with a goal of creating greater understanding of the practice. This visual illustration incorporates the foundational principles of FLE (education, prevention, strengths-based, and research and theory-based), with changes in culture, context, content, practice, and family well-being, across time. This graphic identity was designed to provide clarity and understanding of the nature of FLE in order to increase opportunities for implementation and best practices (Darling, Cassidy, & Rehm, 2020).

The FFLE Model focuses on the ultimate goal of FLE, which is to optimize *family well-being*. Although well-being is subjective, it is often described as positive emotions (e.g., contentment, happiness, joy), life satisfaction, life fulfillment, and/or positive functioning. While family life educators do not necessarily teach specifically about well-being, the general outcome of FLE is to enhance the well-being of the participants.

The *foundational principles* of FLE include education, prevention, and approaches to family issues that are strengths-based and grounded in research and theory. *Education* is the essence of FLE and includes techniques and approaches to impart knowledge and build skills to enable individuals and families to function at their optimal level. *Prevention* is critical to deal with issues before they become

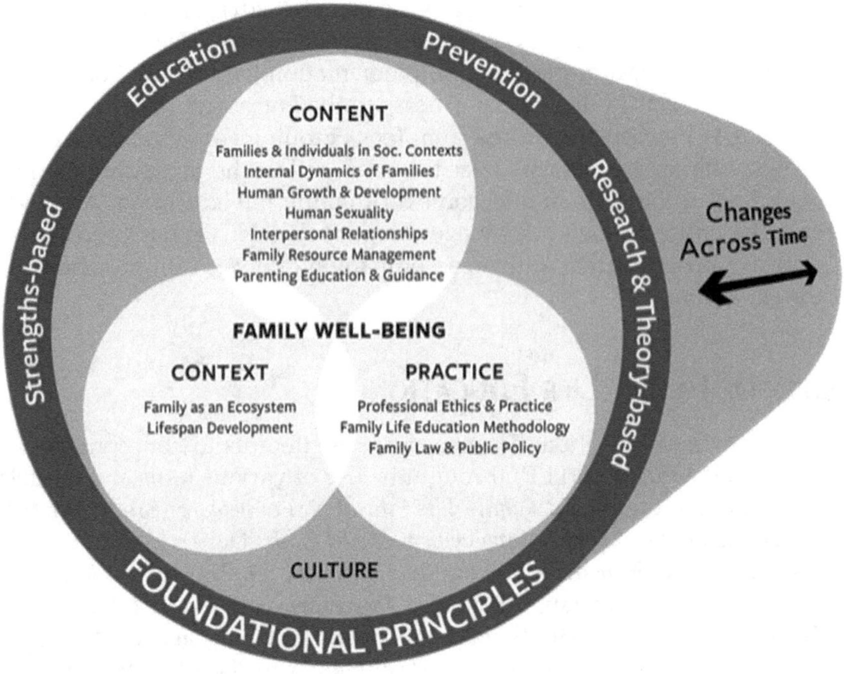

Figure 1.1 Foundations of Family Life Education Model

Source: Darling, C. A., Cassidy, D., & Rehm, M. (2020). The foundations of family life education model: Understanding the field. *Family Relations 69*(3), 427–441.

problematic and is a cornerstone of FLE. Family life education is *strengths-based* as it recognizes the inherent abilities of individuals to address problems and reach their full potential. The content and approaches of FLE are grounded in research that includes the infusion of theory. Frameworks that are *research and theory-based* can provide reasonable explanations of behaviors and family functioning and contribute to understanding the context of family life education.

Because of variations in family configurations and functions, *culture*, or overall way of life, is an important component of the FFLE Model, not only because of its role in program planning and implementation, but also because understanding culture is essential for family life educators who work with families whose race, ethnicity, or religion may differ from their own. Those who have ethnocentric views may judge others by the values and standards of their own culture. Therefore, it is important for family life educators to incorporate an ethnorelative approach to enhance the understanding of cultures relative to one another.

The integration of the foundational principles and culture undergird the three components of *context*, *content*, and *practice*. Family life educators need to understand the context of individuals and families which provides the background information and circumstances that affect an event or situation and the interrelated conditions in which it exists, such as where the information came from, what and who may be affected, and how. Family life educators need to understand not only the context of individuals and families, but also their students/learners, settings, and teaching methods to best meet situational needs. Thus, the use of theoretical frameworks can provide meaningful insight into the contexts of individual, family, and classroom behaviors

The content (or topic areas) within FLE largely focus on the life skills, relationships, and family functioning that promote well-being through the lifespan. One of the unique aspects of the FFLE Model is that it incorporates NCFR's Family Life Education Framework that references the 10 content areas of FLE (see Appendix A), but recognizes that not all 10 content areas are specifically about the *content* of FLE. As demonstrated in the visualization of the model, 7 of the 10 FLE areas focus specifically on topics that may be taught to families, (e.g., families and individuals in societal contexts, internal dynamics of families, human growth and development, human sexuality, interpersonal relationships, family resource management, and parenting education and guidance). Three of the "content" areas relate more to practice (professional ethics and practice, family life education methodology, and family law and public policy). A distinctive characteristic of FLE is the breadth of knowledge of family life educators, who are trained in all 10 content areas. Some may focus their work on an individual area such as parent education or human growth and development, but they still need to be generalists and draw on content from multiple areas in various ways.

In general, family life educators do not typically teach about ethics, public policy, or program planning and implementation when working with families. Rather, these are components of the practice of FLE and areas in which family life educators must be versed to meet best practices. Since family life educators deal with sensitive and personal issues, various ethical dilemmas may arise requiring an understanding of *professional ethics and practice*. The *family law* portion of the family law and public policy content area can involve topics taught to families such as when relevant legal issues like divorce education or family caregiving are incorporated into a variety of FLE programs, but other aspects are more relevant to the practice of the family life educator. As professionals, they must be aware of state laws affecting the children and families with whom they work, such as reporting child abuse or domestic violence. Furthermore, according to the Americans with Disabilities Act, family life educators also need to accommodate learners with special needs and disabilities to the extent possible. Additionally, *family life education methodology* does not reflect content taught to families but rather is about how the family life educator designs and implements the content. It includes selecting appropriate content and implementing various methods that are pertinent to the audience and then evaluating the programs to identify and confirm the content and approaches that are most effective—all part of the *practice* of FLE.

A final concept of the FFLE model is that it *changes across time*. Family well-being along with individuals, families, society, and FLE programs, have undergone multiple changes across time (e.g., changes in perceptions of gender diversity; effects of globalization; innovations in communication; use of technology in teaching; managing pandemic-related issues). Therefore, as the practice of FLE evolves, educators should be cognizant that the FFLE model is dynamic and will adapt accordingly.

The FFLE model provides a visual representation that can facilitate meaningful collaboration among FLE professionals and learners. By clarifying the core components of FLE, the model can enhance the understanding and promotion of FLE programs and their continuing evolution.

The Levels of Family Involvement Model (LFI)

The original LFI model (Doherty, 1995) considered the practice of family life education (FLE) in relation to family therapy (FT) and identified a five-level approach to clarify the professional boundaries between them. The original levels included (1) minimal emphasis on families, (2) information and advice, (3) feelings and support, (4) brief-focused intervention, and (5) family therapy. See Figure 1.2 for a depiction of these levels. The goal of the LFI model was to help family life educators avoid "crossing the boundary into family therapy" (p. 353).

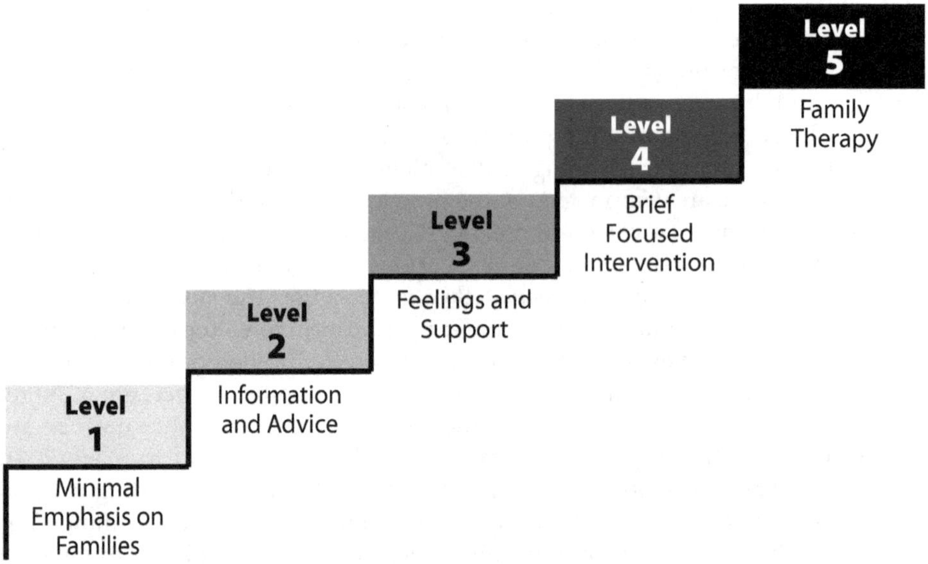

Figure 1.2 Levels of Family Involvement

Some of the concerns with this model included its conceptualization of FT and FLE in a hierarchical relationship, implying that only the first three levels were appropriate for FLE. While some advanced FLE professionals may occasionally function professionally in Level 4, if they are assisted by therapists to use Level 4 effectively, they should not enter the domain of family therapists. This model implied that family therapists would be able to professionally practice at all five levels. While educators do not possess the knowledge and skills of a therapist, it is also true that therapists do not necessarily have the knowledge and skills to provide educational experiences. Another concern with the LFI model is that the scope of the content for FLE and FT was unclear. For example, within the LFI model anger management is appropriate for family life educators in Level 4, but anger management with spouses or in-laws is not. There are also times that couples may benefit from both family life education courses and family therapy, although the methods would be different.

Based on feedback about the original model, Doherty and Lamson (2015) adapted it for family life educators for direct work with families who are dealing with common and complex issues. These five levels of increasing intensity include (p. 40):

- *Level 1: Institution-Centered*—"Communication is typically unidirectional with family members expected to cooperate with the norms, policies, and procedures of the institution" (p. 41). This type of program is usually found within contexts that are not family oriented, such as schools, medical settings, or company seminars on work–life balance. This level is considered outside FLE, but family life educators may interact with other professionals collaboratively.
- *Level 2: Collaborative Dissemination of Information*—Educational activities are related to family members regarding communication skills, knowledge of human development, decision making, and healthy interpersonal relationships. A family life educator can reach a large number of families in an educational setting such as online participation, but is limited in typical small-group learning environments where there would be little emphasis on sharing feelings and personal experiences.
- *Level 3: Working with Family Members' Feelings and Need for Support*—Content pertains to affective learning in groups and methods of culturally sensitive collaboration and problem solving. It is noted as the "*quintessential level for FLE*" and often deals with normative stresses of families compared to traumatic experiences (p. 41). Not only are activities, knowledge, and skills used in FLE incorporated at this level, but also feelings, experiences, and personal disclosure are elicited. However, a limitation of this level is that some families' needs and problems may be too intense to be adequately addressed in a group setting, because their concerns may go beyond normative family issues.
- *Level 4: Psychoeducational Intervention for Complex or Chronic Concerns*—More in-depth personal experiences are included along with personal problem solving. Most family situations at this level would be referred to other professionals. Family life educators would need training in complex and chronic concerns.
- *Level 5: Family Therapy*—This referral level is outside the scope of family life education as it involves the most intense family needs, assessment, diagnosis, and intervention. However, education may be a part of the treatment process.

While it is suggested that "the need for interprofessional collaboration is gaining momentum" (p. 45), the levels in this model still appear hierarchical with suggested limitations for involvement of family life educators. Since family science professionals and family life educators are employed in a variety of positions, roles, and settings, it is important for all professionals that work with families to have a clear understanding of their roles and responsibilities in the capacity in which they practice.

Domains of Family Practice Model (DFP)

In order to facilitate understanding the domains and boundaries of family life education, the DFP model incorporates a collaborative paradigm of family life education (FLE), family therapy (FT), and family case management (FCM), although FCM is only one kind of case management within social services (Myers-Walls, Ballard, Darling, & Myers-Bowman, 2011). In order to differentiate the domains and boundaries of these three professions, the following journalistic questions were incorporated: *Why? What? When? For whom?* and *How?*

The "Why" of family life education focuses on the purpose of each of these professions and why each profession works with families. While all three professions want to promote strong healthy families, FLE tries to help families build knowledge and skills, FT helps repair families and improve functioning, and FCS helps families comply with legal and policy systems and locate resources (see Figure 1.3).

The "What" element of the model refers to the content or research base that family professionals use for working with families. When examining the websites for NCFR, the American Association for Marriage and Family Therapy (AAMFT), and other organizations such as the American Institute of Health Care Professionals/American Academy of Case Management, family life education incorporated the 10 family life education content areas, family therapy had six core competencies, and family case management had various components found in multiple sources (DePanfilis, 2018; National Adult Protective Services, 2021). The specific

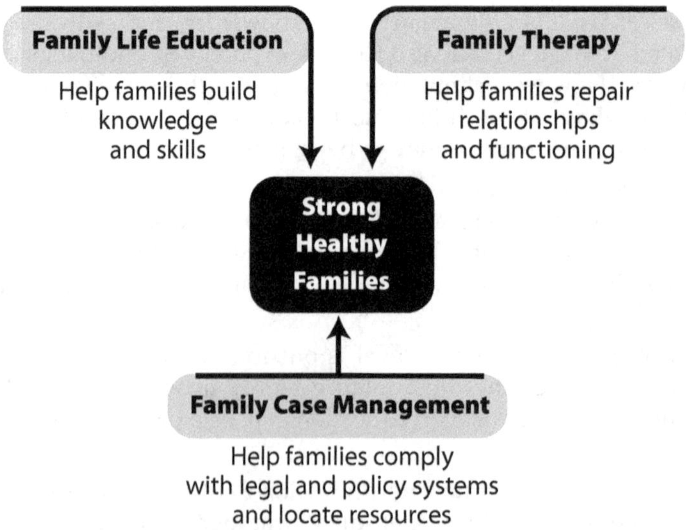

Figure 1.3 Why

components that comprise "What" can be seen in Figure 1.4 whereas the overlap of content from FLE, FT, and FCM can be seen in Figure 1.5. Certain elements can be found in all three professions, such as family systems theory and an ecosystems context, sensitivity to diversity, research-based practice, and values and ethics. However, the methodology of each varies.

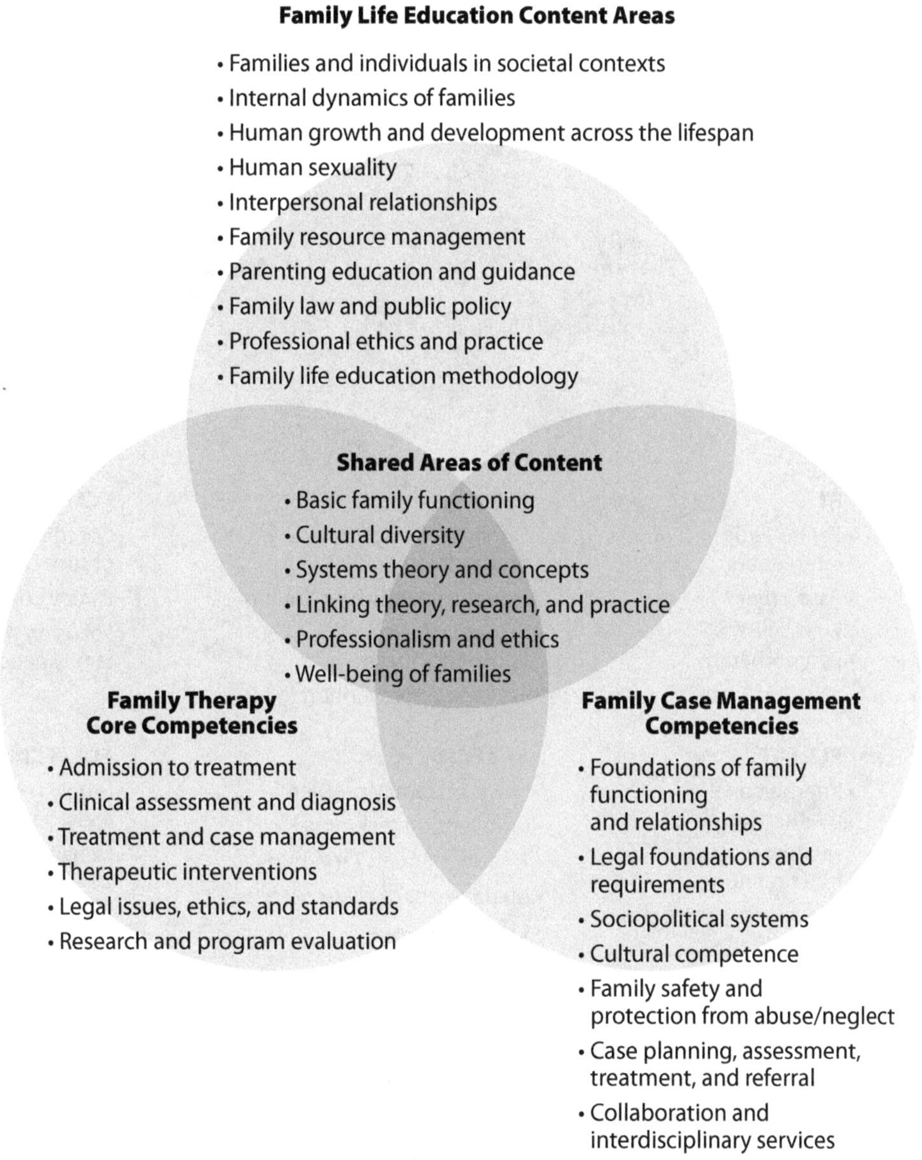
Family Life Education Content Areas
• Families and individuals in societal contexts
• Internal dynamics of families
• Human growth and development across the lifespan
• Human sexuality
• Interpersonal relationships
• Family resource management
• Parenting education and guidance
• Family law and public policy
• Professional ethics and practice
• Family life education methodology
Shared Areas of Content
• Basic family functioning
• Cultural diversity
• Systems theory and concepts
• Linking theory, research, and practice
• Professionalism and ethics
• Well-being of families
Family Therapy Core Competencies
• Admission to treatment
• Clinical assessment and diagnosis
• Treatment and case management
• Therapeutic interventions
• Legal issues, ethics, and standards
• Research and program evaluation
Family Case Management Competencies
• Foundations of family functioning and relationships
• Legal foundations and requirements
• Sociopolitical systems
• Cultural competence
• Family safety and protection from abuse/neglect
• Case planning, assessment, treatment, and referral
• Collaboration and interdisciplinary services

Figure 1.4 What—Content

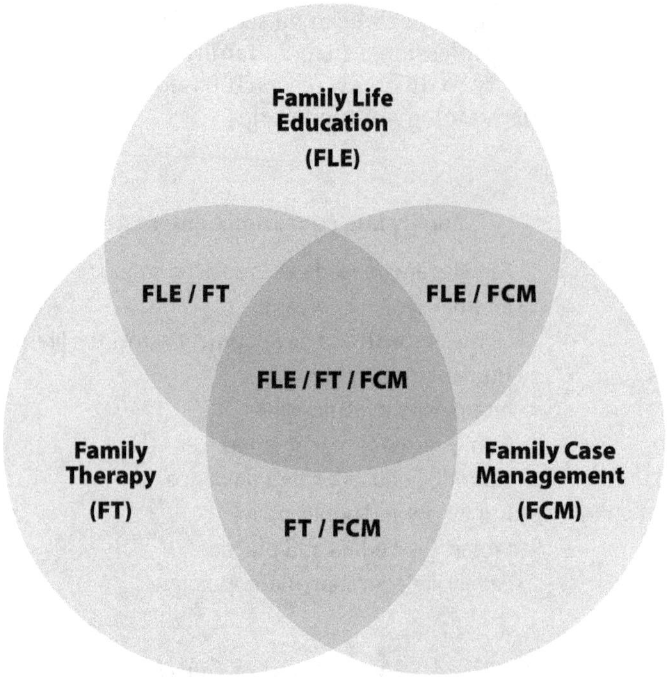

FT
- Therapeutic intervention
- Assessment and diagnosis
- Psychotherapy

FLE
- Family life education methodology
- Normal, healthy functioning
- Broad, inclusive knowledge base
- Education/ prevention focus

FCM
- Coordination of services
- Family advocacy
- Focus on meeting family needs

FLE / FT
- Interpersonal relationship skills
- Healthy sexual functioning
- Life course perspective

FT / FCM
- Focus on family problems
- Intervention techniques
- Treatment goals / methods
- Managment of client records
- Closure of cases

FLE / FT / FCM
- Family systems theory
- Sensitivity to diversity
- Research-based practice
- Ecological context
- Values and ethics

FLE / FCM
- Family resource management
- Family policy

Figure 1.5 What—Overlap

The "When" dimension focuses on when family practitioners in each role deliver services and the timing of those services. The timing of services is based on *primary prevention* (protection of healthy people from harm before something happens), *secondary prevention* (protection after problems, conflicts, or risks have occurred so the progress of the problem can be halted or slowed as early as possible), and *tertiary prevention* (helping people manage complicated, long-term problems to prevent further harm). Within Figure 1.6, FLE is noted as including primary and secondary prevention, FT manages secondary and tertiary prevention, and FCM focuses on tertiary prevention. In regard to timing of services, FT often focuses on the past to determine family background factors that may be affecting the family, on the present to help families manage their problems, and projects forward to prepare them for a future that minimalizes the issue of concern. FLE deals with the present with a goal to help families in the future, and FCM deals with the present by trying to find resources to manage their daily lives (see Figure 1.7).

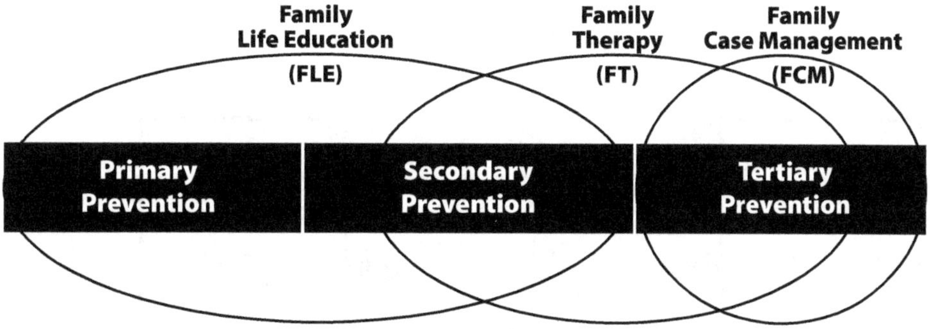

Figure 1.6 Timing of Services

"For whom" are the services of these three professions intended? There are two primary factors involved in determining for whom services are to be delivered—eligibility and motivation. *Eligibility* is determined by family professionals delivering services and often based on *ascribed needs*, which are identified by others as something a family needs. *Motivation* represents the participants' perceptions that a service is needed and appropriate, and is based on *felt needs*, which are personal and based on a learner's experiences. Whereas FLE and FT often deal with felt or ascribed needs, FT and FCS are often based on ascribed needs, referrals, or mandated attendance. For example, someone who wants to be a better parent might go to a family life education course on parenting or voluntarily seek a therapist (felt need), while parents whose child is in the juvenile justice system may be mandated to go to FT or see a FCM to help with their parenting issues (ascribed need) (see Figure 1.8).

The "How," or techniques and strategies of these three professions, is highly variable and dependent on the responses to the questions of *Why, What, When,*

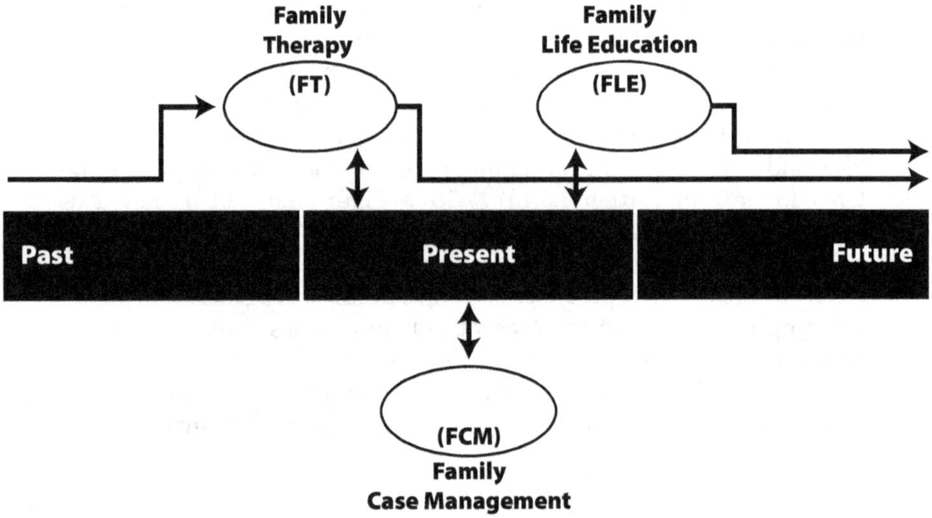

Figure 1.7 Orientation of Services

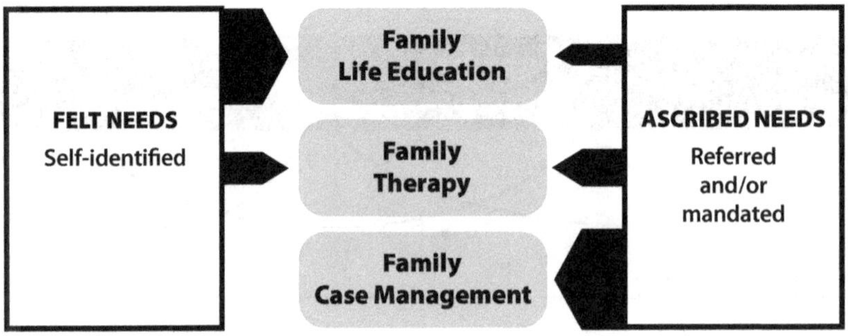

Figure 1.8
For Whom

and *For whom*. In other words, one has to examine the participant's needs, as well as the best delivery system. Are the needs felt or ascribed? What needs-assessment techniques can be used? How are services to be delivered and what methods will be used to best meet the family's needs? Do you use lesson plans, treatment plans, or case planning? What is the best setting (community, schools, institutions, or private offices) or mode (mass, distance learning, group, or individual)? Moreover, how are families involved in the services? Are learners active partners, therapeutic alliances, or involved in case planning?

Hopefully the diagrams have led to an understanding of Table 1.1, which contains the responses to the questions for these three family professions. There is not one profession that is better than the others as all three are interrelated and collaborative (see Figure 1.9). All have different purposes, methods, timing of services, and individuals and families that can benefit from the services provided. However, at times a family may benefit from being involved with one, two, or all three

Table 1.1 Domains of Family Practice Model

Question	Family Life Education's Responses	Family Therapy's Responses	Family Case Management's Responses
Why? Purpose and goals of work with families	To increase knowledge and develop skills so families may build on their strengths to function at their optimal levels.	To ameliorate relationship problems and mental or emotional disorders to achieve stable, long-term, emotionally enriching family relationships.	To help families negotiate systems, understand and comply with legal and regulatory requirements to increase family safety, permanence, and well-being.
What? Content base and foundation	Family and lifespan theory and research in the 10 content areas; learning, pedagogical or andragogical and educational philosophies and methodologies.	Family and relationship theory and research; therapy-focused philosophies and methodologies.	Case management theories and methodologies; research and information about social systems, resources, and policies; information about family dysfunction.
When? The timing of work with families	Deal with current family needs and challenges to prepare for and improve current and future family functioning.	Cope with past and current family problems focusing on past causes and patterns to improve current and future family functioning.	Deal with current problems and immediate crises.
For whom? Target population for services	Any individual or family willing and able to function in an educational environment and committed to learning.	Individuals, couples, and families who have been diagnosed with functional difficulties who are willing to participate in a therapeutic environment.	Families identified as being at risk or who demonstrate a need for assistance in meeting legal and societal regulations.
How? Techniques and methods used	Assess family-related educational needs; set goals on the basis of family needs and strengths; can occur in a variety of settings; teach about knowledge, attitudes, and skills; families—individually or in groups—are active in the learning process.	Diagnose family problems; identify a treatment plan guided by particular theories or philosophies; occurs in private settings; establish a therapeutic alliance with one family at a time; families have input but little or no interaction with other families.	Assess family functioning; set goals to fill gaps in family functioning; occurs in the field; coordinate community services while monitoring compliance, difficulties, and successes; families (may include extended family) participate in services but rarely interact with other families.

Source: Myers-Walls, J. Ballard, S., Darling, C., & Myers-Bowman, K. (2011). Reconceptualizing the domain and boundaries of family life education. *Family Relations* 60, 357–372.

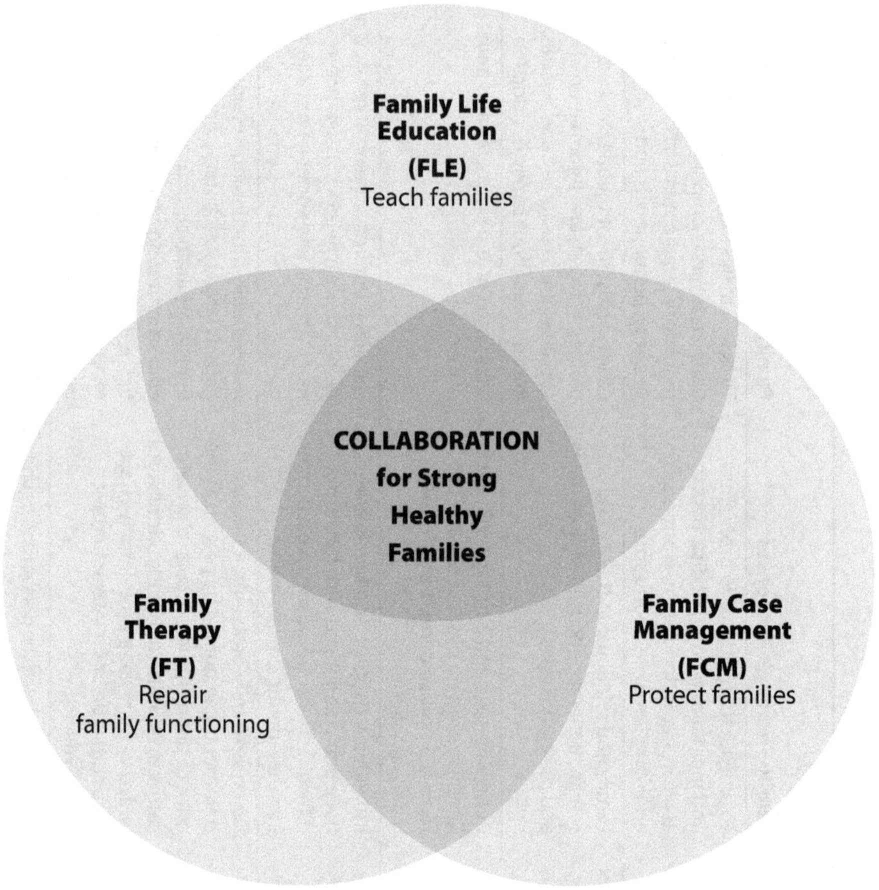

Figure 1.9 Professional Collaboration

of these family professionals. Understanding the domains and boundaries of these professions can be helpful when advising students and planning curricula, as well as when seeking and advertising positions for family professionals. Oftentimes family agencies have various persons who serve families in different ways. Understanding the DFP model may help both the employer and employee better define the roles and expectations of a professional position within that setting. Further, it can give service providers the flexibility needed to meet individual, family, and community needs.

The History of Family Life Education

The task of passing on knowledge about family life to the next generation has been part of the human experience since life began; but how and by whom it is done has varied among family groups, tribes, and cultures. It has also changed drastically over time and is, in fact, still evolving. However, at the beginning of the twenty-first century, one thing is agreed upon by all: The family—in all its different forms and circumstances—needs support and education.

Early Involvement in Family Education

Interest in parent education and family life has been ongoing for some time, as noted in the fourth century BC by the Greek philosopher Aristotle when he listed "the education of parents for raising their children" as one of his educational purposes. Even the famous educator Horace Mann (1796–1859) called for education to "meet the fulfillment of parental duties" (Dickinson, 1950, p. 5). During pioneer days, life was hard and children's lives were often short and tragic. At a survival level, the tasks needed for daily living have always taken precedence over the finer subtleties of excellence in parenting and family life. However, parents would still talk among themselves about issues they were facing in child rearing.

Family education in nineteenth-century America was of interest to various individuals, groups, and organizations. For example Catharine Beecher wrote *A Treatise on Domestic Economy* (1841), comparing women in low and high economic families and the differences in their stress and health. Another crusader was Jane Addams (1860–1935), who attempted to better the lives of poor families affiliated with Addams' Hull House, which developed a model of family intervention and education. Workers at Hull House cared for children of working mothers during the day and used the child as a "bridge" for education. New habits of hygiene and medical care were introduced and later weekly meetings for mothers were developed on making children's clothes and preparing food (Youcha, 1995). Their perspective on what can be done working together is at the heart of family life education.

Formalizing the Study of Families

Massachusetts became the first state to recognize and support FLE in a public school setting (Quigley, 1974). Other states soon followed, and between 1875 and 1890 domestic science and industrial education courses in public schools were widespread. By 1895, 16 colleges were offering courses in home economics (East, 1980). While their subject matter and focus varied, the recognition of training in family living skills was increasing. Based on the work of Ellen Richards and the Lake Placid conferences, the American Home Economics Association (AHEA) was established on January 1, 1909 to improve life conditions in the home and community (Baldwin, 1949, p. 2). Over the years other organizations and groups also contributed to the development of family studies, such as the White House Conference on Child Welfare, the Child Welfare Research Center, the Merrill Palmer Institute, the National Congress of Parents and Teachers, the American Social Hygiene Association, and the Cooperative Extension Service. In the first year of the Cooperative Extension Service, home economists visited 5,500 homes and trained 6,000 women to lead in educating others (Rasmussen, 1989).

Ernest Burgess, a professor of sociology, developed the first documented collegiate course on "Family" at the University of Chicago in 1917. However, due to home economics' ties to public education, books such as *When You Marry* (1945) by Reuben Hill and Evelyn Duvall, and *Family Living* (1950) by Evelyn Duvall, set the stage for home economics to replace sociology as the main discipline in FLE (Lewis-Rowley, Brasher, Moss, Duncan, & Stiles, 1993, p. 39). However, in the past few decades, many college and university home economics programs have been phased out or merged with other programs due to low enrollment of majors in the traditional home economics education area. Meanwhile, interest in human development and family science (HDFS) has expanded rapidly. Students see the HDFS major as a good foundation from which to launch careers in marriage and family counseling, family ministry, social work, child life, and early childhood education. The availability of family science degree programs is demonstrated through a comprehensive list of over 310 undergraduate and graduate programs in the United States and Canada, accessible through the "Degree Programs in Family Science" section of the NCFR website (www.ncfr.org/degree-programs). All of these careers could carry an expectation of expertise in conducting FLE classes in a variety of community settings and for diverse audiences.

The National Council on Family Relations (NCFR) was established in 1938 by Paul Sayre, a law professor at the University of Iowa; Ernest Burgess, professor of sociology at the University of Chicago; and Rabbi Sidney E. Goldstein (Walters & Jewson, 1988). This interdisciplinarity was a catalyst for cross fertilization of ideas from other disciplines and perceived to be an asset. NCFR's mission is to provide an educational forum for family researchers, educators, and practitioners to share in the development and dissemination of knowledge about families and family relationships, establish professional standards, and work to promote family well-being.

In the late 1960s, NCFR spearheaded the development of standards and certification for family life educators to define the content and context of the practice of FLE. As a result, in October 1982, NCFR's Board of Directors approved the *College/University Curriculum Guidelines, Standards and Criteria for the Certification of Family Life Educators*, and *An Overview of the Content in Family Life Education: A Framework for Planning Programs over the Lifespan.* NCFR began certifying family life educators through a portfolio process in 1985. In addition to sponsoring the CFLE credential, NCFR also provides recognition to universities and colleges that have incorporated content into their academic coursework for each of the 10 family life content areas needed for approved courses at their school. This has resulted in 142 NCFR-CFLE approved programs. A national exam is available to all other CFLE candidates (NCFR, 2013). Availability of national recognition has helped bring consistency to the academic content of the family degree and promote the field of family life education (NCFR, 2013).

Since the establishment of these guidelines and frameworks for FLE, there has been growing attention to advancing the field with increased research, promoting evidence-based programs, and furthering translational family science (Darling, Cassidy, & Rehm, 2017). FLE is rooted in the practice of family science and therefore inherently translational. Family life educators have a unique role to ensure that the programs and services provided to families are based on solid evidence and, in turn, that research is informed by practice. A noteworthy example of advancing the field through research is the publication of a special issue of *Family*

Relations (2020) on "Best Evidence-based Practices in Family Life Education." This special issue has a range of articles that focus on defining the field, examining FLE over the life course, and discussing critical topics and contexts in FLE. As the relationship between science and practice continues to evolve, translating and communicating successful practices, programs, and policies will need to take an increasingly prominent role in the future development, effectiveness, and promotion of FLE programs (Darling, Cassidy, & Rehm, 2017).

Future Directions

We continue to ask the same questions regarding the value of family life education. Why wait until children and families have suffered great emotional anguish when we know education could prevent many tragedies from occurring? Why do we invest so much time and energy into fixing people, families, and situations, rather than investing in prevention and providing education about the skills and knowledge needed to enhance individual and family life? Such solutions have always been the emphasis of visionary educators and social reformers. Unfortunately, society and the government has tended to focus efforts and funding on responding to crises rather than supporting preventive measures.

But the future of family life education is promising and there is reason for hope. In the recent past more attention has been focused on collaboration, definition, academic research and theory, and family life educator training and certification for the family field. Family life education is moving to a new level of appreciation among behavioral scientists, program developers, legislators, and the public. Issues of abuse, exploitation, and violence, long hidden from public view, have seen the light of celebrity confession and intense media coverage. Divorce and single parenthood are no longer squelched by social stigma. The sexual revolution has "outed" us all. Courts are mandating anger management and parent education programs. Pressure to transfer resources from the police to social programs and community-based efforts has brought renewed attention to prevention efforts providing increased employment opportunities for FLEs. Technology is taking us to new levels of involvement with one another, offering new opportunities for distance education and resources. Around the world, we are interacting with diverse cultures and discovering new ways of being family. And families, struggling to survive and to thrive, are becoming more willing to ask for help. It is time to bring knowledge and families together, and it can be done face-to-face and online with person-centered, trained professionals and effective programs. Chapter 2 addresses the growing field of family life education and the issue of professionalism.

■ SUMMARY

What is family life education (FLE)? There is no universally accepted definition, but we hope we have helped to clarify that it is multidimensional and exists in many formats and in various settings. For the most part it is education that is preventative and based on family strengths as well as research and theory. Various models have been used to help clarify what FLE is as a field including the content, how it is implemented, and by whom. A new comprehensive model called the *Foundations of Family Life Education Model (FFLE)* has been created to provide a cohesive, comprehensive, and visual conceptualization of FLE that includes its foundational principles along with changes in culture, context, content, practice, and family well-being across time. The *Levels of Family Involvement Model (LFI)* has been revised to help clarify the differences between family therapy (FT) and FLE, but mostly indicates in what situations family life educators should not practice. The *Domains of Family Practice Model (DFP)* aids in showing the *Why, What, When, For whom,* and *How* of three family professions as it compares FLE, FT, and FCM. The notion of boundaries, along with collaboration among these three professions, is notable. Professionals in each field are trained similarly, but also with some differences. Thus there are many opportunities to work together for the well-being of families.

The history of family life education is a long one, but its formalized study began in the public schools and universities in the twentieth century. The National Council on Family Relations had considerable influence on advancing the study of families and promotion of FLE through the development and publication of various guidelines and the creation of the Certified Family Life Educators program. Currently the research on families and family life education is making notable progress with increased research, promotion of evidenced-based programs, and furthering translational family science. The future of family life education can be viewed optimistically because of increased attention to collaboration and educational methodologies along with increased recognition of issues facing diverse families and their needs.

■ QUESTIONS AND ISSUES FOR DISCUSSION

1. How do the demands and stresses of family life today differ from those in the past? Consider particularly the dual-career family, single-parent low income family, and immigrant family.
2. What makes prevention and education programs hard to document in terms of effectiveness?
3. Should public school curricula include parenting courses? Why or why not?
4. What is the value of prevention/education programs in comparison to crisis intervention and remediation programs?

■ ACTIVITIES

1. Explain how a major prediction is or is not supported by the development of the "Domains of Family Practice Model": *Collaborative approaches to family life education will increase between generalists and specialists who value each other's contributions and realize that issues are too complex to be solved by one single organization or professional group.*
2. Identify a topical issue in family life education and analyze it using the FFLE Model (i.e., how is teaching about this topic affected by the foundational principles, culture, context, content, and practice as it affects family well-being over time).

2

Family Life Education as a Profession

> Carl has a baccalaureate degree in art history. He has worked for the past nine years as a youth coordinator for the YMCA and organizes activities and classes for neighborhood youth identified as high risk. He is a member of the National AfterSchool Association (NAA) and has served on their board of directors.
>
> Juanita has a degree in child development. She organizes a parent group in her neighborhood for other stay-at-home moms and dads with children under 2 years old. The group meets regularly and discusses a predetermined topic each time. Members rotate responsibility for researching the topic and presenting information. Much of the meeting is spent in casual conversation and support.
>
> Kathleen is the executive director of a neighborhood family resource center. She has a degree in human development and family science and is a Certified Family Life Educator (CFLE). Her responsibilities include overseeing the development and implementation of family activities, well-baby classes, parent-support groups, and a home-visiting program. She has worked in the field of family life education for more than 12 years.

Which of these people would you consider to be professional family life educators? What makes someone a professional? Chapter 1 clarified the conceptualization of family life education (FLE), its history and relationship to other professions, and the gradual recognition of its function in strengthening society. With the evolution of the field has come greater awareness of the importance of the individual's role in providing effective FLE programs and services.

This chapter looks at FLE as a profession and at issues of professionalism. How do we define a profession? What criteria are needed in order for an occupation to be considered a profession? Is family life education a profession? What is involved in becoming a competent professional? What skills and knowledge are needed to provide quality FLE experiences and to develop effective materials? Are there certain personal characteristics or traits that make someone a more effective family life educator? What ethical practices are necessary underpinnings of the profession?

Defining the Profession

The word *profession* means different things to different people, but at its core it is an indicator of trust and expertise. The following definitions help to clarify this concept and the meaning of professional, professionalism, and professionalization (Australian Council of Professions, 2003; Professional Standards Council, n.d.).

- A *profession* is a disciplined group of individuals who adhere to ethical standards. This group possesses special knowledge and skills in a widely recognized body of learning derived from research and education and is recognized by the public. A profession is also prepared to apply this knowledge and exercise these skills in the interest of others.
- A *professional* is a member of a profession. Professionals are governed by codes of ethics and professional commitment, competence, integrity, morality, altruism, and the promotion of public good within their expert domain. Professionals are accountable to those served and to society.

- *Professionalism* comprises the personally held beliefs about one's own conduct as a professional. It is often linked to upholding the principles, laws, ethics, and conditions of a profession as a way of practice.
- *Professionalization* is the pattern of how a profession develops, as well as the process of becoming a profession.

To facilitate understanding the professionalization of family life education, we have incorporated an adaptation of East's (1980) eight criteria that need to be in place for a field or occupation to be considered as a profession. Applying these criteria to the practice of FLE shows that FLE has definitely progressed as a profession. Table 2.1 provides a summary of the findings.

Table 2.1 Professionalization of Family Life Education

Professionalization Criteria	Progress Made	Room to Grow	Criterion 1 = No Progress 5 = Criterion—Fully Met
1. Activity Becomes a Full-time Paid Occupation	Though rarely called family life education, many professionals practice family life education on a full-time basis under such descriptions as parent education, sex education, marriage enrichment.	Family life education may only be part of a family life educator's job responsibilities as employment specifically in family life education may only be available on a part-time basis or incorporated into other job descriptions.	4
2. Academic Programs and Curricula Are Established	Family-related degrees have been offered since the 1960s. NCFR began recognizing academic programs that met the criteria needed for the CFLE designation, beginning in 1996. Currently there are over 140 approved programs.	Few degrees are called Family Life Education, but rather Child and Family Studies, Human Development and Family Studies, Human Services, Family Studies, Family and Child Science. The lack of consensus results in fragmented identity for the field.	4
3. Professional Associations Provide Leadership and Advocacy	Numerous family-related associations have been in existence since the early 1900s including NCFR and AAFCS. Associations focused specifically on parenting (NPEN), marriage education (NARME), and coaching (FLCA) have also been formed.	There are numerous family-related associations and organizations, which can cause a fragmented identity.	4
4. Standards and Competencies Are Developed	NCFR developed University and College Curriculum Guidelines and Standards and Criteria for the Certification of Family Life Educators in 1984.		5

(continued)

Table 2.1 *(continued)*

Professionalization Criteria	**Progress Made**	**Room to Grow**	**Criterion 1 = No Progress 5 = Criterion—Fully Met**
5. A Unique Role is Defined in Relation to Other Professions	Numerous organizations and credentials exist with some overlapping content, but development of NCFR Curriculum Guidelines and CFLE Criteria defines family life content areas. *Foundations of Family Life Education Model* and *Domains of Family Practice Model* help clarify the unique role of the FLE.	Employers and public are still unclear about what family life education is and how family life educators differ from social workers, therapists, counselors.	4
6. Recognition of the Profession by Those Served	Increased popularity of parenting, marriage, and sexuality education programs throughout the US reflects public's increased acceptance of education related to family issues.	Public is often unaware that specific credentials exist for family life educators.	3
7. Accreditation, Certification, and Licensure Provide Guidelines and Standards for Professional Practice	CFLE designation was developed to regulate qualifications of family life education providers. CFLEs must meet continuing education requirements to maintain designation.		5
8. A Code of Ethics Exists to Guide Ethical Practice and Protect the Public	The Family Science Section of NCFR established *Ethical Principles and Guidelines* in 1995. In 2009 NCFR formally adopted principles from the Minnesota Council on Family Relations' ethical guidelines process as the official CFLE Code of Ethics. In 2018, NCFR revised the CFLE Code to reflect the broader range of issues and situations faced by family life educators as the MCFR version was heavily focused on parenting education (NCFR, 2018a).		5

Adapted from Darling, C. & Cassidy, D. (2014). *Family life education: Working with families across the lifespan.* Long Grove, IL: Waveland Press.

1. Activity Becomes a Full-Time Paid Occupation

Although the title "family life educator" is not always used specifically, family life education is practiced by professionals in various settings throughout the world, including junior and senior high schools, Extension programs, the military, community education, health care, human services, faith communities, and higher education. FLE is carried out under such titles as parent education, sex education, health education, life coaching, marriage enrichment and education, life skills, prevention services, youth advocacy, and more.

In many cases, FLE is a full-time position, but it is also common for it to represent a percentage of the work carried out in settings with more focus on intervention. Many family life educators work in settings to help families that have been identified as at-risk or who have demonstrated difficulty with parenting, money-management, or relationship skills. Much of the professional's time might be spent in activities considered to be intervention or administration, but there are opportunities for providing family support within those settings through education. In another example, preschool directors might focus most of their time on administration of a preschool program, but they could also be responsible for identifying and implementing parenting education workshops. The time spent developing and/or offering parenting workshops would be considered FLE.

2. Academic Programs and Curricula Are Established

The first documented course on family was offered in 1917 by Ernest Burgess at the University of Chicago, but it was not until the 1960s that degrees focused on the family were more commonplace. The desirability of defining the necessary knowledge, skills, and abilities of family life educators resulted in the development of *Family Life Education Programs, Principles, Plans, Procedures: A Framework for Family Life Education* by the National Council on Family Relations (NCFR, 1968). In 1982, NCFR developed the *College/University Curriculum Guidelines*, and in 1984, the *Standards and Criteria for the Certification of Family Life Educators* and *An Overview of the Content in Family Life Education: A Framework for Planning Programs over the Life Span* (NCFR, 1984). NCFR approved the first Certified Family Life Educators (hereafter referred to as CFLE) in 1985.

In 1996, NCFR introduced the *Academic Program Review* and began to review university and college family degree programs for adherence to the standards and criteria needed for CFLE-approved programs. Numerous programs have sought this "industry" approval, which recognizes a defined and accepted curriculum content for the field. A list of degree programs in family science, which is available on the NCFR website (www.ncfr.org/degree-programs), includes information on over 700 family-specific or related degree programs, of which over 140 meet CFLE standards.

3. Professional Associations Provide Leadership and Advocacy

Professional associations can have significant influence on the public's perception of a profession by establishing standards of practice and advocating for the profession. Additionally, they provide opportunities for members to enhance their practice through networking and sharing information. A number of related professional organizations relevant to family life education exist, including the American Association of Family and Consumer Sciences (AAFCS) and the National Council on Family Relations. NCFR is widely recognized as the professional association for family life educators because of its involvement in the development of standards related to the content of family life education and its sponsorship of the Certified Family Life Educator (CFLE) program.

Professional associations like NCFR and AAFCS recognize a shared body of knowledge and common interests among a select group of professionals. Additionally, they offer membership at several levels of involvement and provide opportunities for continuing education and networking with others practicing in the family field.

4. Standards and Competencies Are Developed

As mentioned previously, NCFR identified standards of admission, the core body of knowledge, and competencies for the practice of family life education through the work of several task forces and committees working from the late 1960s to the early 1980s. This process resulted in the establishment of the CFLE credential.

The CFLE Standards and Criteria have continued to evolve over the years. They originally included nine family life content areas considered to represent the core of family life education. They were families in society, internal dynamics of families, human growth and development, human sexuality, interpersonal relationships, family resource management, parent education and guidance, family law and public policy, and ethics. FLE methodology was added as a 10th content area in 1991. Except for a few minor edits, these 10 content areas have remained essentially the same.

The process of becoming a Certified Family Life Educator (CFLE) has also progressed since first being introduced in 1985. From 1985 to 2007, professionals seeking CFLE certification provided documentation of academic preparation, professional development, and work experience in each of the 10 content areas via a portfolio application process. With the development of the Academic Program Review in 1996, (mentioned previously in this chapter), NCFR began approving university and college family degree programs for adherence to the criteria needed for the CFLE designation. The NCFR academic program review process recognizes the 10 content areas as the defined and accepted curriculum content for the field. Graduates of "CFLE-approved" academic programs can apply through an abbreviated application process (referred to as the CFLE-approved program process), as long as they have completed specific preapproved courses at their school. Inclusion and recognition of the CFLE Standards and Criteria within the curricula of university and college degree programs further supports the establishment of family life education as a profession. In 2007, NCFR replaced the portfolio application process with a national standardized multiple-choice exam. Development of the exam involved an extensive practice analysis that further identified and confirmed the knowledge, skills, and abilities needed for the effective practice of family life education (Darling, Fleming, & Cassidy, 2009). Another practice analysis was conducted in 2014 to update the scope of the practice and the exam. In 2020, the content outline was further revised to align content area objectives with Bloom's revised taxonomy (Krathwohl, 2002). Appendix B includes the NCFR Family Life Education Content Areas: Content and Practice Guidelines, which reflect the theory, research, and practice within the field of FLE.

5. A Unique Role Is Defined in Relation to Other Professions

There are a number of professional organizations relevant to families. As discussed, the National Council on Family Relations (NCFR) has been active in defining and developing family life education curriculum and certification criteria since the early 1960s. Additionally, the American Association of Family and Consumer Sciences (AAFCS) identified competencies and criteria for home economics and established the Certified Home Economist (CHE) designation, which was subsequently changed to being Certified in Family and Consumer Sciences (CFCS).

There are similarities and differences between the NCFR and AAFCS certification programs. Both require a minimum level of education and knowledge in the areas of human growth and development, family systems and dynamics, and family resource management. The redesign and expansion of the AAFCS credential in 2004 resulted in three separate credentials with a competency-based qualifying exam for each (AAFCS.org). AAFCS maintained the original broad CFCS credential, but also created a separate credential focused on Human Development and Family Studies (CFCS-HD). This credential more closely resembles the CFLE credential than did the original composite CFCS-HD credential, however, the overall focus of the HDFS credential is broader than that of the CFLE and focuses more on topics within the context of human development. The CFLE credential also considers issues relevant to human development, but approaches them from a lifespan and family systems perspective within the context of relationships. Additionally, the CFLE standards include greater emphasis on knowledge and skills relevant to human sexuality, parenting, and educational methods and techniques relevant to FLE.

Both CFLE and CFCS-HD designate work in government and human services settings and can focus on early childhood education, human development, family dynamics and relationships, and consumer economics and financial planning. However, many professionals carrying the CFCS-HD credential work in areas such as apparel and textile design and merchandising, food and nutrition science, hospitality, interior design, and in secondary and post-secondary settings which are clearly outside the realm of family life education. CFLEs work in a broader range of settings including faith communities, the military, health care, work-life programs, and in the private sector as consultants providing a range of family life education (FLE) programs and services relevant to family dynamics, parenting, relationships skills, resource management, and more.

Numerous other organizations exist with interests relevant to FLE. For example, professionals involved directly in sex education might join the American

Association of Sexuality Educators, Counselors, and Therapists (AASECT) or the Society for the Scientific Study of Sexuality (SSSS), and parent educators might be members of the National Parenting Education Network (NPEN). Couples or educators active in couples and marriage education may wish to join Better Marriages (formerly the Association for Couples in Marriage Enrichment, ACME) or the National Association for Relationship and Marriage Education (NARME) or become involved with the Coalition for Marriage, Family, and Couples Education (CMFCE). These organizations have formed to provide a professional forum for discussion of the many issues inherent in FLE. This abundance of related organizations reflects the multidisciplinary nature of FLE.

A proliferation of life and parent "coaches" has provided an opportunity to clarify the knowledge and skills needed to be a family life educator and has contributed to a unique role definition. Family coaching is a strengths-based approach to help families reach goals and improve family functioning through coaching techniques (Allen & Huff, 2015, p. 61). Family life education is also a strengths-based approach to help families reach their goals and improve family functioning. The approach used by family life coaches when helping families reach their goals is what provides a unique role definition that sets coaching apart from FLE. Family life educators can use coaching as an appropriate and effective method when working with families, but FLE can also be delivered through classroom settings, one-on-one interactions, publications, and online courses.

The popularity of coaching addresses the apparent need of individuals to seek guidance in dealing with daily life issues from a strengths-based perspective. While there is an increasing number of training programs, certifications, and organizations focused on coaching, it is still an emerging field. A search on the internet for the term *life coach* results in a plethora of companies and organizations offering certification and training. The lack of consensus regarding the criteria needed to be a coach creates opportunities for those without sufficient education, training, or oversight to offer coaching services. However, in 2015, the Family Life Coaching Association (FLCA) was founded to elevate and lend credibility to the practice of family life coaching and serve as the collaborative center for the field. Their mission is to create research-based, globally-recognized credentials, training standards, and networking opportunities for family life coaches (www.flcassociation.org). While FLCA is working on the development of a certification for family life coaches, there currently is not an identified national standard for the practice of family life coaching.

The Foundations of Family Life Education Model (FFLE) and the Domains of Family Practice Model (DFP), discussed in Chapter 1, represent advancements in the field of family life education by helping conceptualize the profession and identify the overlaps and contrasts among the fields of FLE, family therapy, and family case management (Darling, Cassidy, & Rehm, 2020; Myers-Walls et al., 2011). The development of the models has contributed to a unique role definition for family life educators that may help encourage collaboration among the fields. Ultimately the debate over role definition may subside as more widespread agreement evolves over the content and practice of FLE and its place in the continuum of services provided to families.

6. Recognition of the Profession by Those Served

As society faces increasing crises and challenges related to families (e.g., divorce, single parenting, blended families, economic recession, delinquency, substance abuse, and youth violence), there has been greater recognition of the value of prevention and education. Even health maintenance organizations are more frequently offering classes dealing with parenting, stress management, and balancing work and family, because they recognize the relationship between stress and health (CDC, 2013). Additionally more businesses are becoming aware that personal and family problems account for decreased productivity and attendance (Bond, Galinsky, & Hill, 2004) and are offering seminars, webinars, and other educational opportunities to increase employee well-being and productivity.

When groups or organizations offer family life education programs, they often seek someone to lead the experience who has expertise in an academic discipline or profession related to families. Family-specific degrees, as well as certification and experience, can enhance one's credibility as an expert in the area of family relationships. However, individuals and families seeking guidance related to relationships and parenting skills can find themselves choosing from a wide range of providers with varying training and expertise.

The increased interest in marriage and relationship education over the past years has led to a proliferation of "scripted" marriage and relationship education programs that can be taught "out of the box." These programs are designed to be presented by lay leaders who may not have specific academic training in marriage and family or educational methodology. Similar issues exist related to parenting education as seen by the explosion of "mommy and daddy" blogs and websites devoted to parenting. As with the relationship education field, there are a variety of parenting programs promoted to meet the needs of struggling parents. These approaches have created some tension between those who have specific education and training in family education and those who do not. While some feel it is possible to be an effective marriage, relationship, or parenting educator by following prescribed guidelines provided through specific curricula or approaches, others feel the most effective educators are those with formal training in family systems and dynamics, sexuality, interpersonal relationships, human development, and parenting, in addition to proven skills in program development and implementation.

Some would argue that formally trained family life educators are better able to draw from a variety of approaches and techniques that are more specifically adapted to the audience and situation, rather than applying a "one size fits all" approach. Persons trained in a specific approach or "out-of-the- box" curriculum may, in fact, be very effective, but they would not be considered "professionals" in that their expertise is limited to just one curriculum or setting. As long as they stay with the script, all is well, but questions can arise for which a certain level of expertise is needed.

Family life education professionals, as well as program participants, recognize that it takes more than being a "good parent" or a "happy couple" to facilitate effective learning experiences and the skill building that enhances interpersonal relationships. Adequate training and experience are imperative. However, the availability of such a variety of programs, learning opportunities, and the varying qualifications and training levels of the providers continues to challenge the solid establishment of FLE as a recognized profession.

7. Accreditation, Certification, and Licensure Provide Guidelines and Standards for Professional Practice

At times there is some confusion regarding the terms *accreditation* and *licensure* and the difference between a *certification* and a *certificate*. Therefore some clarification may be helpful when noting the use of certain terms below, such as voluntary versus mandatory, professional organization versus government or licensing bureau, and program versus individual.

- *Accreditation* is a voluntary process by which a professional agency or association recognizes that a program meets certain requirements. Most universities and colleges are regionally accredited.
- *Certification* is a voluntary process by which a professional agency or association grants recognition to an individual who has met certain predetermined qualifications or standards specified by that agency (e.g., CFLE, CFCS-HD). Certification is an ongoing credential that requires demonstration of continuing education in order to be maintained.
- *Licensure* is a mandatory process by which a government or licensing bureau permits individuals to practice in a designated profession (e.g., teachers, social workers, therapists). It gives qualified people the right to engage in a particular occupation or profession in that state, to use a specific title, or to perform a specific function. Licensure typically represents the minimum standard for practice (e.g., teachers, therapists).
- *Certificates* are offered by a professional agency, association, commercial enterprise, or university in response to the completion of a defined training program (e.g., gerontology, parent education). It is a terminal award, meaning that there is no ongoing requirement for continuing education or additional learning.

As has been discussed, the National Council on Family Relations offers a certification program for individuals, as does the American Association of Family and Consumer Sciences. AAFCS also accredits university degree programs in Family and Consumer Science. NCFR offers approval of degree programs for adherence to the CFLE standards, but does not provide accreditation, as that also involves review of program facilities and faculty.

The CFLE program was developed by NCFR for the purpose of regulating the qualifications of family life education providers and, indirectly, the quality of the materials presented. There is currently no state licensure requirement for family life educators, but since 1989 Minnesota has required early childhood and parent educators to be licensed in order to provide family education through the Early Childhood Family Education (ECFE) program. More recently, a few educational institutions including Adelphi University, North Carolina State University, and the University of Minnesota have begun offering graduate certificate programs in parenting education (NPEN, 2021). The National Parenting Education Network (NPEN) is continuing to pursue the option of a national parenting education credential. Likewise, there are specific certifications for focused areas of FLE including sexuality education (through AASECT), and personal and family finance (through AAFCS). These efforts reflect recognition of the importance of establishing some form of formal recognition of minimum standards for effective practice.

8. A Code of Ethics Exists to Guide Ethical Practice and Protect the Public

In 1995, the Family Science Section of the National Council on Family Relations approved *Ethical Principles and Guidelines* for use by family scientists. These guidelines dealt primarily with ethical issues inherent in teaching and research in academic settings. Two years later the Minnesota Council on Family Relations published *Ethical Thinking and Practice for Parent and Family Educators* (MCFR, 1997) for family life education (FLE) practitioners. NCFR in 2009 formally adopted the principles identified in the MCFR ethical guidelines process as the official Code of Ethics for the Certified Family Life Educator designation (NCFR, 2009a). In 2018, members of NCFR's CFLE Advisory Board revised the CFLE Code of Ethics to reflect the broader range of issues and situations faced by family life educators as the MCFR version was heavily focused on parenting education (NCFR, 2018). The most recent statement of the CFLE Code of Professional Ethics was noted in the fourth edition of *Tools of Ethical Thinking and Practice in Family Life Education* (NCFR, 2018a; NCFR 2018b). (See Appendix C.) The fact that a need was perceived for these ethical guidelines and codes provides further evidence of the recognition of FLE as a unique profession.

This step-by-step discussion of the criteria of professionalization shows that FLE is indeed an evolving profession that is moving toward maturity. Through the efforts of FLE pioneers and those currently working in the field, the profession continues to make progress toward the goal of recognition and participation on the same level as marriage and family therapy, counseling, and social work. Ultimately FLE will be the norm.

Challenges in the Field of Family Life Education

What needs to happen in order for family life education (FLE) to be a more recognized and valued approach to family issues and well-being? How can we get the CFLE credential and/or a degree in family science included as an employment requirement? Also, how do we get more people to participate in FLE? What if all expectant parents took parenting classes as part of childbirth preparation? Consider the impact on the divorce rate if all engaged couples participated in marriage education or if married couples regularly invested in their relationships by attending marriage enrichment programs? Imagine the personal and societal problems avoided if all high school students were required to complete a course in communication skills, money management, and conflict resolution? How many adolescent high-risk behaviors could be avoided with FLE at that critical developmental time?

FLE is making tremendous progress in advancing as a profession and an approach to daily life, but before FLE can become the norm a number of challenges need to be addressed. Some of the most readily identified challenges to the advancement of FLE include public awareness of the discipline and profession of FLE, the diversity of settings in which FLE takes place, and the unstable funding of FLE programs and services.

Public Awareness of the Academic Discipline

Although FLE has a unique role and clear academic standards, the lack of public awareness continues to be one of the biggest struggles faced by family life educators. As demonstrated, substantial progress has been made in establishing consensus on the content of FLE and the standards needed for effective practice. However, there is less agreement on what to call an academic degree meeting these standards. Very few degree programs are specifically titled "family life education." Rather, family-related degree programs carry a myriad of titles including family science; family studies; individual and family studies; family and consumer sciences; family and child development; human ecology; human development and family science, family, youth and community sciences; family and child science; child, adolescent, and family studies; family relations; and more. The overall field of family science has struggled with the issue of identity for many years, as noted by having over 700 academic programs in the US and Canada and a wide range of titles for family-related majors (www.ncfr.org/degree-programs). The graduates of these programs could possibly carry the expectation of expertise in conducting FLE classes in a variety of community settings and for diverse audiences. The establishment of a core body of knowledge and standards of practice has helped to create a clearer identity for FLE, but a more consistent name for the academic degree awarded to family professionals is needed. This would enable employers to more easily identify professionals qualified to apply a preventive, family-centered, lifespan approach to family well-being. Additionally, a consistent name for the academic degree would make it easier for family life educators to be recognized providers of mandated parent education or to have their services covered by insurance providers. NCFR has identified *Family Science* as the preferred name for the discipline. Their "Advancing Family Science" initiative is focused on strengthening the identity and visibility of the family science discipline. This effort will assist in bringing greater clarity to family life education which is identified as the *practice* of family science.

Diversity of Settings in Which Family Life Education Takes Place

There are probably numerous instances of family life education (FLE) occurring in your community on any given day. There are family life educators working in health care settings, community education, faith communities, junior and senior high schools, colleges and universities, social service agencies, corporate settings, government agencies, corrections, retirement communities, and the military. The multidisciplinary nature of FLE and the variety of settings in which it takes place can be both an asset and a liability. On the positive side, numerous opportunities fit the "generalist" training that is FLE. Negatively, the variety of settings makes it difficult to target efforts when seeking jobs. Do you apply with hospitals or through community education programs? Which job titles do you look for when searching the classified ads or the internet? The diversity of settings in which FLE occurs requires family life educators to be their own advocates. They must be able to articulate what family life educators do and what they have to offer. Appendix D includes a list of settings in which FLE can occur. As noted in an NCFR Infographic on *Career Opportunities in Family Science*, some additional opportunities include after-school programs, work-life balance, scouting programs, YMCA/YWCA, academic advising, vocational guidance, college student-life programs, program curriculum development, 4-H youth development, early childhood family education, health care, hospice, death and grief services, and blogging and social development (NCFR, n.d.-b).

As of early 2022, the *Occupational Outlook Handbook* (OOH) of the United States Department of Labor, Bureau of Labor Statistics (www.bls.gov/ooh) does not include "family life education" as an occupation. There are 21 occupations listed with "family" in the title such as various family-related medical professionals (e.g., family and general practitioners, family physicians, family practice nurse practitioners, family dentists), as well as family counselors, family childcare providers, family services social workers, family sociologists, and family therapists. The occupation of family services social worker only includes information on social work with no reference to any other family-related positions. As those involved in FLE know, the social work field has done an excellent job of branding itself and incorporating social work training (and in many cases social work licensure) into state and federal legislation. While this works well for jobs focusing on intervention and case management, it excludes a great many well-qualified family professionals who possess the skills and knowledge needed to help families through a preventive approach.

The National Council on Family Relations is working with the US Department of Labor (DOL) to include the occupation of *family life educator* in their official coding system. The first step for professional identification within the DOL is to get the term connected with an existing Standard Occupational Classification (SOC) system code that will at least alert DOL employees who gather occupational information to the existence of this profession. The more they see the title *family life educator* being used, the more likely the DOL will cite it within the SOC system and, eventually, within the *Occupational Outlook Handbook*.

The long-term goal is for employers, college students, and job-seekers to be able to go to the *Occupational Outlook Handbook*, enter the term *family life educator*, and pull up a page with information on the profession of family life educator similar to what would appear if the terms *social worker* or *counselor* were entered. This would include information on the nature of the work, working conditions, training, other qualifications, advancement, employment, job outlook, earnings, related occupations, and sources of additional information. Unfortunately, it could be a number of years before the title *family life educator* receives its own specific listing within the SOC system. A profession is added to the system when the title or position appears with a certain level of frequency. *Family life educator* does not yet appear often enough in the labor environment and will only do so when people identify themselves by this specific title or when employers identify their employees as such. This can be a challenge given the wide variety of settings and job titles represented within the field.

Family life educators should be encouraged to start this process by using the title *family life educator* on websites, business cards, and publications, and by encouraging employers to use the term in job postings when appropriate. Hopefully, with a collective and focused effort, the term *family life educator* will one day be recognized specifically by the Department of Labor, as well as others, which in turn will enhance family life education as a profession.

Unstable Funding of Family Life Education Programs

Many FLE programs are funded through federal and private grants. In most cases this funding is available for a specified period. Therefore, grantees often find themselves focusing much of their efforts on maintaining existing grants and obtaining new funding rather than carrying out the programs. Often, effective and proven FLE programs are discontinued due to the cessation of the funding period and a failure of funders to require inclusion of sustainability strategies into the original grant.

Additionally, the funding of FLE programs through grants typically involves administration of these programs through government and nonprofit agencies. This can result in a stigma for those attending these programs by sending a message that FLE is only for people and families that are having difficulties. No one questions the value of pregnant women taking classes to learn about the birthing process, but we have not yet reached the point where all parents attend parenting classes throughout their children's development. Funding of FLE by insurance providers and administration of programs through a variety of providers including employers, schools, faith communities, hospitals and clinics, private companies, and employee wellness programs could result in increased and consistent availability of opportunities and recognition of FLE as the norm.

Strategies for Growth

A number of strategies can be implemented to increase the visibility and value of educational and preventive efforts focused on the family that in turn will advance the profession. This includes the promotion and support of standards of practice, education of employers and the public, incorporation of family life education into intervention settings, recognition of family life educators as qualified providers in legislation, improved and stable funding, creation of niche markets, and promotion and normalization of FLE through the media.

Promote and Support Standards of Practice

CFLE and CFCS-HD certifications are perhaps the most relevant and appropriate credentials for those working in family life education. Family professionals can support the field of FLE by recognizing the need for established standards of practice. This might involve pursuing certification themselves or hiring or promoting those who carry the CFLE or CFCS-HD designation. Increasing the number of people who identify themselves as family life educators and are actively promoting this identification through the use of CFLE and CFCS-HD initials after their names in their promotional materials, on their resumes and vitae, and in job titles will help increase awareness of FLE as a profession. Likewise, increasing the number of qualified Certified Family Life Educators and professionals Certified in Family and Consumer Sciences is an important strategy in recognizing the value of FLE. The CFLE and CFCS-HD initials after a name bring attention to FLE as a practice with identified standards and requirements.

Educate Employers and the Public

Family life educators may find that they need to do a fair amount of educating about family life education (FLE) and its value. They often need to be creative and proactive in finding employment settings and willing to market themselves to potential employers. Employers may not really understand what a family degree or certification represents. They need to be educated on the fact that these credentials denote a solid understanding of families, a lifespan perspective, and the skills and knowledge needed to develop and present educational programs. Most family life educators trained specifically in family will work from a systems perspective, i.e., individual couple and family systems, as well as social service, business, and government systems. Graduates of family degree programs need to see themselves working as family life educators at *any* system level in *any* organization. They need to see themselves very broadly in terms of training and skills and encourage employers to do the same. Employers that benefit from hiring an employee with such skills and knowledge will be more likely to hire similar candidates in the future and to encourage others to do so as well.

Incorporate Family Life Education into Intervention Settings

Family life educators working in settings that focus primarily on intervention or counseling can often identify opportunities for offering family life education (FLE) within that same setting. For example, an agency that works primarily with families struggling with financial issues might want to offer money-management workshops to the community. Those offering home visits to parents identified as at-risk can incorporate family life education techniques into their work and might also sponsor evidence-based family education programs that provide opportunities for all families to gather together to share information, support, and friendship. Providing a family life education approach to home visiting can also highlight the appropriateness of *all* families (not just those identified as at-risk) to benefit from education and support of their parenting roles. While there will always be families needing the assistance of social workers or counselors, most family professionals recognize that preventing problems is best for families and society. The Domains of Family Practice Model discussed in Chapter 1 does an excellent job of identifying how family life educators can work in collaboration with family case managers and therapists to assist and strengthen families.

The events surrounding the death of George Floyd in 2020 led the way for a paradigm shift in how society chooses to deal with social problems. It provided an opportunity to advocate for the discipline of family science and to highlight the important role that family life educators can play in meeting the needs of society in a more effective and positive way. Family life educators are qualified to provide prevention and intervention services relative to social problems such as homelessness, domestic violence, substance abuse, and mental illness and there is merit in looking at how we as a society can focus more energy and resources on the prevention of problems by better supporting families and communities.

Increase Recognition of Family Life Educators as Providers in Legislation

The growing fields of marriage, relationship, and parenting education should expand opportunities to increase the legal recognition of family life educators as providers of services. A number of states have established or are considering legislation that mandates or offers incentives for people completing marriage or parent education classes. Typically this legislation includes a listing of recommended providers of these services. Unfortunately, legislators tend to favor bills that include a finite list of qualified providers. These providers are usually people who possess credentials, such as licensure, that are already sanctioned and recognized by state or federal bodies. It simplifies the passage of the bill, but may not provide the best measure of who is qualified to provide these services. For example, mandated parent education programs, required in some states for divorcing couples with children, often identify licensed social workers, counselors, therapists, or clergy as the only approved providers. While many of these providers may be well qualified to provide education regarding parenting, being licensed as a social worker, counselor, or therapist, or serving as a pastor, does not guarantee any specific knowledge in parenting or the ability to develop and implement educational workshops or work individually with parents in an educational capacity. Someone trained specifically in family life education (FLE) is more qualified to provide marriage or parenting education than social workers, therapists, or pastors who are identified as providers simply by virtue of their professional titles in that particular state. Additionally, family life educators can provide a more comprehensive, family-centered, strengths-based perspective compared to a singular focus on crisis management.

Fortunately, legislators, lawyers, and judges are beginning to recognize that professionals with family degrees and/or certification have the skills and knowledge needed to work with families, whereas in the past they automatically enlisted the services of therapists or social workers. For example, in the state of Utah, a bill was passed in 2018 that recognizes family life educators certified by a national organization (i.e., NCFR) as an approved provider of premarital counseling and education (NCFR, 2020). In Texas, Certified Family Life Educators and professionals with degrees in family are recognized as qualified providers for some parenting education programs mandated by judges. Parenting Coordinators that work with divorcing parents must also complete training in mediation, but their family degree and/or CFLE designation helps them to meet the minimum requirements.

Those interested in promoting FLE need to monitor applicable legislation and take the opportunity to educate those who introduce relevant bills to include family life educators among the list of approved or recommended providers. Inclusion of family life educators as "approved providers" in federal legislation would open the door for recognition by states and local entities in the public and private sectors.

Increase and Stabilize Funding for Evidence-Based Prevention Programs

Prevention is an important foundational principle of FLE. Many family problems are the result of a lack of knowledge or skills related to daily living. Thus, providing education about communication, human development, parenting, relationships, and management of resources can effectively minimize or avoid problems and enhance family functioning (Darling, Cassidy, & Rehm, 2017). Translational family science, which lies at the intersection of family research and the practice of FLE, is essential to facilitate the design and delivery of successful evidence-based FLE programs. However, funding for implementation and dissemination research is low. There is a wealth of data supporting the effectiveness of evidence-based family education programs. These reports consistently show a positive return on investment for funds provided to support preventive programs addressing early childhood education (Karoly, Kilburn, Cannon, Bigelow, & Christina, 2005), child maltreatment (Prinz et al., 2016), parenting, (McGroder & Hyra, 2009), teen pregnancy (Alford, 2008; Kirby, 2007), and juvenile delinquency and substance abuse (Miller & Hendrie, 2008; Spoth, Guyll, & Day, 2002), however, more research is needed.

The emotional costs of personal and family issues, such as intimate partner violence (IPV), are difficult to measure. However, a 2017 financial analysis indicated that the estimated per victim lifetime cost for IPV was nearly $103,767 for a female and $23,414 for a male, with a societal economic burden of $3.6 trillion based on 43 million US adults with a history of IPV victimization (Peterson et al., 2018). Examples of costs include attributable impaired health, lost productivity, and criminal justice costs. Governmental sources pay an estimated $1.3 trillion (37%) of the lifetime economic burden. Therefore, preventing sexual violence could avoid substantial financial costs for victims, employers, health care payers, and government payers. These findings can be used as an example to inform others of the potential benefit of prioritizing prevention education.

Child maltreatment is another issue of concern to US families and society, which results in a high lifetime cost per victim and creates a substantial US financial burden. Using the estimated incidence of investigated annual cases (2,368,000 nonfatal and 1,670 fatal victims), the estimated economic burden was $2 trillion which accounts for victim and intangible costs (Peterson, Florence, & Klevens, 2018). This economic burden is substantial, but could offset the cost of evidenced-based interventions that reduce the incidence of child maltreatment.

Adverse Childhood Experiences (ACEs) are potentially traumatic events occurring in childhood. One in six adults has approximately four or more types of ACEs, such as violence, abuse, and growing up in a family with mental health or substance-use problems. The repetitive stress of ACEs can result in changes in brain development and physical reactions to stress which are linked to chronic health problems, mental illness, and substance misuse in adulthood. Preventing ACES could decrease the number of adults with depression by 44% (CDC, 2019a). Education and prevention could avert or ameliorate many individual and societal problems, but funding for such programs is often grant-based, and therefore unstable especially in uncertain economic times. A more consistent funding stream is needed to ensure that family life education becomes the norm.

Carve a Niche

Family life education (FLE) takes place in a myriad of settings. Its multidisciplinary nature means that family life educators might find themselves competing for jobs or working alongside those trained in social work, psychology, child development, sexuality, or therapy. One approach to enhancing the visibility of FLE is to establish or identify a setting in which family life educators are uniquely qualified to provide services. Health care providers are increasingly offering workshops on parenting and stress management. Community education catalogs list numerous classes related to family life. Youth programs and faith communities are some of the most common settings for FLE.

The area of *work life* holds tremendous potential for family life educators who think of it more as "managing" work and family. It involves identifying personal values, being creative, and recognizing that everyone's solution is unique. Work-life programs have the potential to improve employee morale, reduce absenteeism, and retain organizational knowledge especially during stressful economic times (Quist, 2015). However, as the rates of work-life family imbalance and long work schedules increase, health costs rise accordingly (Salazar, Davenport, & Hancock, 2014). COVID-19 and the shift to remote work has had both positive and negative impacts on managing work-life and will likely impact how we work going forward. While for some families having parents work from home during the pandemic can create more time with family, it can also cause stress when children need help with online learning while parents are trying to work from home.

More corporations and businesses recognize the interconnectedness of work and family life. They understand that the personal lives of employees can have a detrimental effect on their work life, especially if their personal lives are riddled with substance abuse, domestic violence, family pressures, or serious financial difficulties. However, less serious or problematic issues can also affect work life, and can include issues related to normative family stressors, such as couple relationships, parenting, and elder care. Investment in online workshops or webinars on "communicating with your adolescent" or "time management" can result in increased productivity and/or decreased employee absence. Family life educators are uniquely qualified to provide these types of learning opportunities.

In many situations FLE can be incorporated into existing settings and provided as one of many services. For example, workshops focused on planning for retirement, estate planning, and caregiving issues can be offered in a retirement community or nursing home. Parenting education might be provided at a preschool or child care center through a published newsletter or a series of evening workshops. A doctor's office might find value in hiring a full or part-time parent educator to address parenting concerns often raised during medical appointments. These more specific efforts can be a way to introduce organizations to the value of FLE that could ultimately lead to more full-time services.

Few can argue with the merits of providing individuals and families with the knowledge and skills needed to lead satisfying and productive lives; but general acceptance of, or the lack of argument against, such efforts are not enough to ensure the advancement of the field. The challenge for advocates of FLE lies in increasing awareness of the research supporting the return on investment for evidence-based programs focused on primary, secondary, and tertiary prevention. We need societal awareness of parent education, marriage enrichment, and life skills training, along with recognition of the value of participating in these activities on a regular basis. When professionals in related fields recognize and value the knowledge and skills possessed by family life educators and understand the role that FLE can hold in a variety of settings and situations, we can work effectively as a team to assist families. FLE does not compete with social work, therapy, counseling, or ministry. Rather, it is a complement and part of a collaborative collection of resources and services available to help families function as effectively as possible (Myers-Walls et al., 2011).

Promote and Normalize Family Life Education through Media

Another strategy for advancing family life education (FLE) lies within the intentional use of media. *Cultivation theory* proposes that conceptions of the social world are shaped in part by exposure to images portrayed in the media (Gerbner, 2009). Television and movies have substantial influence in portraying and normalizing various family forms, including single parents, same-sex couples, cohabitation, and divorce. Television shows like *Modern Family* helped introduce and normalize gay characters. Media provide unlimited opportunities to incorporate FLE into story lines that can help educate the public about relationships, parenting, and sexuality. Other shows like *This Is Us* and *Black-ish* incorporate topics such as autism, teen pregnancy, cancer, substance abuse, single parenthood, dating, marriage, sexuality, adoption, and aging, and the influence these issues have on the family. The way in which the characters deal with their circumstances provides educational insights into both positive and negative strategies. The characters portrayed in television and movies can model the best practices for healthy parenting and relationships. FLE advocates can help advance and normalize FLE by influencing the producers of television and movies to incorporate FLE into their programming. Imagine the impact of having a character seek help from a parent educator when dealing with a troublesome teen, or if a couple struggling with communication problems attended a relationship education class rather than immediately consulting with a therapist.

Local news programs also have segments on family, parenting, and relationship issues. After one CFLE wrote a letter of concern about the quality of advice being provided on air, she was hired as the assistant producer and parenting expert for a new local program (see Chapter 4—personal statement by Jody Johnston Pawel). Like all worthy goals, the elevation of FLE to a recognized and valued profession will require the targeted, sustained efforts of all family education professionals and the organizations, businesses, schools, and governmental agencies whose missions and services stand to be enhanced by the profession.

The Professional Family Life Educator

Another important piece in elevating the field of family life education (FLE) is to ensure the professionalism of those who practice. The heart of professionalism lies in the skills and qualities of those who practice and/or deliver services to the public. By its nature, FLE often deals with personal and sensitive issues. A major component of FLE involves helping participants analyze, clarify, and determine their own values and value systems. Unlike an educator providing instruction in a hard science such as math or chemistry, the family life educator deals in matters of personal values, decision-making, and behavior, along with sensitive issues such as sexuality, communication skills, parenting, and money. Participants may respond with more emotion or defensiveness due to the personal nature of the topics discussed. In FLE, the feelings, motives, attitudes, and values of learners are central to the learning process.

Personal Attitudes and Biases

Because of the personal nature of the content and process of family life education (FLE), it is imperative that educators have a solid understanding of their own values, attitudes, and biases. Professional family life educators need to be comfortable with other people's feelings and accepting of various points of view. Many family degree programs require students to examine and study their own family of origin and family roles, rules, and values to increase awareness of the influence of their own family experiences. This helps to identify conflicts that may influence their ability to effectively practice FLE. Without critical self-reflection, educators could be unaware of what values, philosophies, or paradigms guide their personal and professional lives (Hennon, Radina, & Wilson, 2013).

In our increasingly diverse society it is important for FLE professionals to work toward cultural competence. Family life educators must move beyond knowledge about diversity and move toward culturally competent practice that includes recognition of structural inequalities and other unique challenges and opportunities that arise from developing and implementing programs specifically for diverse populations (Ballard & Taylor, 2022b). Awareness of one's biases toward such things as culture, race, physical ability, gender, sexual orientation, and socioeconomic status is necessary in order to practice effectively.

Family life educators must have the ability to function ethically and effectively in a variety of diverse settings. In order to do so, they must consider the following questions: How do I view differences among people? Are differences something to value, celebrate, ignore, or fear? Do I see my role as a helper, leader, advocate, or partner? How comfortable am I working with someone different from myself? Additionally, family life educators need to take time to seriously consider their perceptions and attitudes about such things as individual and societal responsibility. For example, are poor people poor because of the choices they have made or because of circumstances beyond their control? Is there a wealth inequality in our society? What is "privilege" and how does it exist in your community? Educators' perspectives on these issues can influence the ways in which they practice and interact with an audience. Expanding one's awareness of diversity and one's own cultural identities is a life-long journey (Allen & Blaisure, 2009, 2015).

Recognition and appreciation of the differences and similarities between cultures will enhance both the practice and personal life of the family life educator. One model to assist in understanding cultural competence is *LEADER: A strengths-based cultural competence model for FLE* (Mallette, Baugh, Ballard, & Taylor, 2022). This model is a holistic and strengths-based model that includes a reciprocal link between research and practice within the development of cultural competence. Knowledge, awareness, motivation, and reflective skills comprise the foundational components of cultural learning. These components are encircled by leadership competencies (learning, self-evaluation, assessment, development, engagement, and reflection) necessary for family life educators to move from learning to practice. FLE practice is captured in the model by seven tasks in which family life educators engage as they apply what they have learned in their culturally competent and strengths-based practice. These FLE practice outcomes or tasks include the following:

a. choose, adapt, and develop FLE curricula,

b. conduct needs assessment,

c. apply ethical principles,

d. advance social justice and public policy,

e. connect and engage with participants,

f. implement evidence-based programs and practices, and

g. monitor and evaluate effectiveness.

Often perceptions and attitudes are so ingrained that we do not even know we have them. It takes conscious effort and thought to examine the way in which we see the world. This can be uncomfortable and challenging, but if educators fail to face these issues they run the risk of compromising their ability to practice as effectively as possible, and cheat themselves out of a wealth of opportunities to grow and learn from those around them.

Personal Skills and Qualities

The National Council on Family Relations, as part of the Certified Family Life Educator program criteria, identified certain characteristics as crucial to the success of a family life educator (NCFR, 1984). They include general intellectual skills, self-awareness, emotional stability, maturity, awareness of one's own personal attitudes and cultural values, empathy, effective social skills, self-confidence, flexibility, understanding and appreciation of diversity, verbal and written communication skills, and the ability to relate well with all ages on a one-to-one basis, as well as in groups.

Clearly, personal traits and characteristics play an important role in the success of a family life educator. A self-assessment (Box 2.1) gives the reader an opportunity to evaluate personal attributes and identify areas that need improvement. Working with a mentor or supervisor, participating in peer evaluations, and observing experienced educators are some of the ways to enhance personal characteristics relevant to professional practice.

Developing a Personal Philosophy

Although certain personal qualities can enhance a family life educator's effectiveness, it is also important to develop a philosophical basis for teaching about families. Educators must thoroughly consider their beliefs in order to be effective. How do they define a family? What is the purpose of family life education (FLE)? They must be clear about the benefits of FLE and how it can be accomplished most effectively. A philosophy of FLE is important because it provides a sense of direction and purpose; allows educators to be in touch with themselves; enables assessment of educational problems; clarifies the relationship of FLE to the needs and activities of the larger society; and provides a basis for understanding the reality of the family, its value in society, the nature of family membership for the individual, and the role of FLE (Dail, 1984). Having a personal philosophy provides a deeper meaning to the educator's life.

Four beliefs that need to be addressed when constructing a philosophy of family life education include (Dail, 1984):

- beliefs about the family and the quality and nature of family life
- beliefs about the purpose of family life education
- beliefs about the content of family life education
- beliefs about the process of learning for families

Beliefs about the Family and the Quality and Nature of Family Life

Family life educators must look at their own beliefs about how they define family. Is a family defined by bloodlines, function, proximity, intention and/or legal recognition? Family life educators who do not consider a gay or lesbian couple to be a family, for example, need to be aware of this bias, as it could influence their ability to effectively work with such a couple.

See Box 2.2 for an exercise to consider the criteria used in defining family. Each example describes a different group formation. Students should independently

Box 2.1 Assessing Your Personal Qualities as a Family Life Educator

Listed below are qualities considered as critical for effectiveness as a family life educator. Rate yourself on the following scale:

1. Needs much improvement.
2. Needs some improvement.
3. Average, but not well developed.
4. Above average, moving toward competency.
5. Competent in this area.

- General intellectual skills. Ability to gather, read, and process information and to apply it to a topic and to group needs; to articulate concepts and ideas; to organize materials and stay on track when presenting them; to hear and incorporate ideas of others.
- Self-awareness. Ability to recognize and articulate one's own personal opinions, attitudes, and cultural values and not to assume that they are everyone's opinions, attitudes, and values; to understand personal tendencies to assume certain roles in a group, such as caretaker, controller, placater, dominant authority; to acknowledge one's own strengths and limitations.
- Emotional stability. Ability to recognize one's own level of emotional comfort or discomfort in a given situation; to express emotions in appropriate ways and at appropriate times; to maintain calmness in the face of crisis or confrontation and to refrain from personal attack on another person, either verbally or physically.
- Maturity. Ability to handle success, disappointment, frustration, or confrontation with dignity and understanding; to acknowledge one's own mistakes and weaknesses and not blame others; to move past grievances and continue to see each person as someone with value and potential.
- Empathy. Ability to put oneself in another person's place; to reflect the feeling to the other person; to understand her or his dilemma.
- Effective social skills. Ability to feel comfortable and enjoy the company of others; to share in group activities; to engage in conversation and to actively listen to others.
- Self-confidence. Ability to speak and act decisively in personal conversation or in front of a group; to accept the challenge of one's ideas without defensiveness and to state one's position with enthusiasm and documentation, not personal criticism or attack; to acknowledge personal strengths and accept words of appreciation graciously.
- Flexibility. Ability to adapt plans to suit a changing situation; to recognize when change is needed and be willing to try a new approach.
- Understanding and appreciation of diversity. Ability to acknowledge differences in others' values, attitudes, and lifestyles; to respect and appreciate cultural and ethnic differences in dress, customs, and language; to understand socioeconomic differences in income, education, and status and how these differences affect lifestyles and decision making; to actively resist gender, racial, and socioeconomic biases or stereotypes.
- Verbal and written communication skills. Ability to speak articulately, convincingly, and concisely; to write clearly in language that is not "over the head" of one's audience; to use illustrations and examples that support one's points; to know when an audience has been "overloaded" with information.
- Ability to relate well with all ages and groups and on a one-to-one basis. Ability to talk with and not down to any group or person; to resist judgment; to appreciate humor and sharing; to practice patience in listening and interacting.

determine if they would consider each grouping to be a family. Class discussion often reveals varying opinions about what does and does not constitute a family, often with fairly soft criteria.

In addition to how students define a family, educators need to have an understanding of how they think a family should function. What role does the family play in an individual's life? Where does the family fit within society? What needs to be in place for a family to function optimally? Understanding their beliefs about the role of a family and the characteristics needed for healthy functioning provides educators with a goal to strive for and a foundation on which to base their programs and other services.

Box 2.2 **What Makes a Family?**

Which of the following groups is a family?

1. A newly married couple moves into their first apartment together. They have both agreed that they do not want to have any children.
2. A man and a woman have shared an apartment for the past two years. They contribute equally to the maintenance and cost of the household. They have made a personal commitment to each other and plan to stay together for the rest of their lives, although they have no plans to marry.
3. A man and a woman have shared an apartment for the past two years. They contribute equally to the maintenance and cost of the household. They are good friends, but are dating other people.
4. A group of 10 people (5 men, 3 women, and 2 children) live together on a farm. They share responsibility for the maintenance of the household, including growing their own food. All household members take part in the care of the two children. The group is committed to living together harmoniously.
5. Two gay men live together in a house. They have made a personal commitment to each other.
6. Two gay women live together in a house. They have made a personal commitment to each other and were legally married in the state of Hawaii.
7. A divorced woman lives with her son from her marriage and her daughter from a relationship with another man whom she no longer sees.
8. A man and a woman share an apartment. They have a personal relationship and are committed to staying together as long as the relationship is beneficial to them both.
9. Two divorced heterosexual men live together in a house with their children and share the expense and maintenance of the household. Each man sometimes cares for the other's children while the other is working.
10. A woman lives alone, but speaks daily with her sister and brother who live in another state.
11. A brother and sister live with their grandparents while their divorced mother attends school in another city. The mother stays with the children and her parents on the weekends.
12. A widower moves in with his son and his wife.

Beliefs about the purpose of family life education

The family life educator must understand the purpose of family life education (FLE) in order to develop appropriate goals and objectives. Is the goal of FLE to change behavior? Is it to provide insight, skills, and knowledge? Is it proactive or reactive? Is it to provide support? Is it to promote a particular ideology or belief system? There are different perspectives through which FLE programs can be viewed and this outlook can vary depending on the FLE program that is being implemented. Is the family life educator focused on providing facts and information, engaging the learner in critical thinking and problem solving, or facilitating personal and social change? Family life educators must be clear about what they want to accomplish and why because assumptions regarding the purpose of FLE can influence program design.

Beliefs about the content of family life education

When developing a philosophy of practice, the family life educator should consider a variety of issues relevant to the content of family life education (FLE) programs including the appropriateness of certain content, the need to have program content that is free of bias or stereotypes, and the importance of supporting content with current research and sources.

For example, although issues of personal sexual or physical abuse may arise in FLE settings, continued discussion is not appropriate. In this case, a participant should be referred for counseling, therapy, or possibly to law enforcement. Professional family life educators should be familiar with appropriate sources of information and services so they can make referrals and research topics when necessary. A family life educator who attempts to deal with such issues directly or allows lengthy discussion in a group setting would not be acting professionally. The *Domains of Family Practice Model* provides a helpful framework for considering which professionals are best qualified to address particular issues in varying contexts.

In addition to being clear about what content and level of disclosure is appropriate for a FLE setting, family life educators want to be sure that their program content is culturally appropriate in order to be effective. Course content should consider family members of all ages; portray nonsexist roles for family members; include information about families of different racial, ethnic, and cultural groups; recognize the uniqueness of individuals and families regardless of age, sex, race, ethnicity, gender identity, sexual orientation, and cultural and socioeconomic backgrounds; recognize that the composition of families varies; and be based on current research (Ballard & Taylor, 2022b). The book *International Family Studies: Developing Curricula and Teaching Tools* (Hamon, 2006) includes discussion of numerous aspects of developing and teaching family content with cultural sensitivity and respect. Attention to program content needs to extend beyond program design and take into account the ways in which participants learn, barriers to participation, and environmental considerations that will vary depending on the population (Ballard & Taylor, 2022b).

Beliefs about the process of learning for families

Family life educators need to be concerned with how families learn and function as a group, as well as how the group affects the learning and thinking of individual members within it. Do groups learn differently than individuals? How can small groups be used most effectively? Are the developmental, social, and emotional needs of the group important? What is the role of learning goals and evaluation? How does the education of one family member affect others in the family?

An understanding of human development and the learning process enables the educator to use the most effective techniques for each audience and each individual. In addition, an educator who understands families as a system can recognize the value of including all family members in the learning process. When that is not possible, they consider the implications of introducing new information, such as parenting methods, into the family and are prepared to help other family members to adjust to new ways of thinking or acting. Chapter 6 discusses various teaching methods and learning experiences in more detail. The important methodology concept to consider in this chapter is awareness of one's own personal beliefs about how individuals and families best learn.

Constructing a personal philosophy can be a difficult process. It involves questioning, evaluating, and accepting and rejecting ideas. It is just that—a process—and it is continually evolving as the educator grows and learns. The time and effort spent in developing a personal philosophy of family life education (FLE) will be well worth the effort. Family life educators who have a solid understanding of their personal philosophies of FLE will be better equipped to assist individuals and families to lead more satisfying and productive lives.

Ethical Guidelines for Practice

Let's revisit two of the family life educators introduced earlier in this chapter in order to examine the issue of professional ethics.

> Carl has a baccalaureate degree in art history. He has worked for the past nine years as a youth coordinator for the YMCA and organizes activities and classes for neighborhood youth identified as high risk. Carl learns that Chris, a child with whom he has a close relationship, has become involved in gang activity. The child's parents have told Carl that they want him to keep close tabs on their son. They don't know about their son's involvement with the gang. Should Carl talk to the parents?

> Juanita has a degree in child development. She organizes a parent group in her neighborhood for other stay-at-home moms and dads with children under 2 years old. The group meets regularly and discusses a predetermined topic each time. Members rotate responsibility for researching the topic and presenting information. Much of the meeting is spent in casual conversation and support. Lately, one parent named Gretchen has been monopolizing the discussion and has disclosed information about her relationship with her husband. Some of the other group members appear to be uncomfortable with this level of disclosure, but Gretchen seems to be in need of the group's attention and input. What should Juanita do?

We often see ethical issues in the news, whether it relates to politicians, corporate executives, or Wall Street officials. While many professions have specific codes of ethics, there are some general rules of thumb to also consider. These include the *Golden Rule* (act in the way you expect others to act toward you); *Professional Rule* (take only actions that would be viewed as appropriate by an *impartial* panel of professional colleagues); and the *TV Rule* (a person should always ask, "Would I feel comfortable explaining to a national TV audience why I took this action?").

Professionals in fields ranging from medicine to law to auto mechanics are faced with ethical issues at one time or another. Family life education (FLE) is no exception and may, in fact, be more susceptible to ethical dilemmas due to the sensitive and personal nature of some of the issues faced in practice. Because FLE often deals with values and belief systems, it is imperative that professional family life educators have an understanding of the role of ethics in their professional lives.

Codes of ethics are designed to prevent harm to clients and professionals and to the professions themselves. For the helping professions, these codes commonly address five principles of ethical practice that are based on the teachings of Hippocrates (Brock, 1993). These are:

- Practice with competence.
- Do not exploit.
- Treat people with respect.
- Protect confidentiality.
- Do no harm.

Additionally, the values for family life education might consist of the following provisions (Brock, 1993):

- *Responsibility to Consumers.* Family life educators should respect the rights of their students, supervisees, and employees and promote the well-being of families.
- *Professional Competence.* Family life educators should maintain high standards of practice, stay abreast of new developments through continuing education, and keep within the boundaries of their profession.
- *Confidentiality.* Family life educators should protect the confidences shared by clients and students and not disclose them, except if required by law.
- *Discrimination.* Family life educators do not discriminate against or deny services to anyone based on race, gender, religion, national origin, or sexual orientation. If unable to provide services, they are to make referrals to other qualified professionals.
- *Dual Relationships.* Family life educators do not exploit the trust of clients or students with dual relationships.
- *Sexual Intimacy.* Family life educators should not be sexually intimate with their students or clients.
- *Harassment.* Family life educators should not engage in sexual or other harassment.
- *Personal Help.* Family life educators should seek assistance for their personal problems.

- *Responsibility to the Profession.* Family life educators should advance the goals of their profession (e.g., promote the incorporation of family life educators as providers of family knowledge in state legislation).

Developing a code of ethics, which is an important indicator of the evolution of a profession, can identify expectations for professional behavior and reflect important values. (Palm, 2015). One of the greatest professional challenges is to create a practical and relevant approach to decision-making when ethical issues arise. As professionals, family life educators need access to ethical guidelines for practice, as well as the capability to consider and act upon these guidelines. "Ethical codes guide our professional interactions with each other, as well as with our constituents. A code lets the public know what it can expect from those who call themselves professionals and helps us as practitioners face with confidence some of the difficult decisions that come with our work" (Freeman, 1997, p. 64).

The diversity and complexity of today's families require family life educators to expand and modify their roles. With these increasing challenges, the potential for doing harm also grows (Palm, 2018). This complexity inspired the Parent/Family Education section of the Minnesota Council on Family Relations (MCFR) to develop ethical guidelines over 20 years ago specifically for use by practitioners in parent and family education. They recognized that family life education was an emerging field and that many practitioners faced ethical dilemmas in relative isolation and with limited guidance (MCFR, 2018).

A multiperspective approach to ethics was developed that integrated the *relational ethics approach*, *principles approach to ethics*, and *virtues ethics* (MCFR, 2018). Relational ethics focuses on understanding relationships as a basis for making ethical decisions and developing caring and respectful relationships with family members. It asks, "Who are the stakeholders?" and considers the role of each person in relation to the other. The principles approach to ethics considers agreed-upon principles for professional practice along with such standards as "we will do no harm to children and insist on the same from others" and "we will define our role as family educators and practice within our level of competence." Previously, the way of defining professional behavior focused on technical competence and recognized the importance of considering the "greater good" for families and society, as opposed to only considering the aspirations of a single individual. However, now various organizations have codes of ethics and expectations of professional behavior. For example, marriage and family therapists use a medical model, and while family life educators may duplicate therapists in some ways, the relationship is not as intense. There are two approaches within the principles approach—*mandatory* (compliance with lay and specific codes of moral conduct for a profession) and *aspirational* (motivation to follow a set of ideal standards within one's practice).

The introduction of virtues ethics involves a more individualized lens that fills the gap of defining professional behavior and focuses more on technical competence than on moral character. In other words, do the right thing for the right reasons. There are three virtues noted for family life educators: *Caring*, which enhances the welfare of family members as agents in their own lives; *Practical Wisdom*, which is the ability to understand competing needs and make decisions based on reflection and consultation; and *Hope/Optimism*, which is a disposition to look at the strengths of family members and other individuals to see positive potential in situations. "These virtues provide family educators with internal strengths to think and behave in an ethical manner" (MCFR, 2018, p. 14).

When examining an ethical dilemma there are seven steps (NCFR, 2018; Palm & Cooke, 2021).

- Step 1: Identification of Relationships.
- Step 2: Identification of Principles.
- Step 3: Identification of Contradictions/Tensions.
- Step 4: Identification of Possible Solutions.
- Step 5: Select an Actions.
- Step 6: Skills, Virtues, and Resources Needed to Support Actions.
- Step 7: Plan for Review of Outcomes of Actions Taken.

The *Tools for Ethical Thinking and Practice in Family Life Education* (NCFR, 2018) publication provides a more detailed description of the principles, as well as a step-by-step process for their use when dealing with ethical dilemmas. NCFR adopted the principles identified in the MCFR guidelines for ethical thinking and practice as the official Code of Ethics for the Certified Family Life Educator program. All CFLE applicants must read and sign the CFLE Code of Ethics as part of the application process (see Appendix C for Code of Ethics).

Personal morals are not sufficient when dealing with ethical dilemmas in a work setting, as emotions can be triggered by challenging ethical situations. Professionals need to reflect on their own personal values and emotional responses to difficult situations, as well as consider the feelings of others in the situation and the ethics of their profession (Palm, 2018). Therefore, practitioners need to understand and internalize their profession's core values. Because of the nature of their work, family life educators are expected to balance the needs of a variety of clients. They have an ethical responsibility to children, parents, colleagues, employers, and society. Ethical dilemmas often arise out of the conflicting needs or interests of those involved. Consideration of ethical principles and the implementation of an ethical-guideline process can provide family life educators with guidance to help make a decision that is right for them and for the situation.

Importance of Professional Development

As you walk up to the stage to accept your degree and prepare to throw your mortarboard in the air, it is tempting to think that your time as a student is over. You have completed the course work needed for your degree, taken your last test, and submitted your final paper. Now it is time to get to work and put all your knowledge to good use. New professionals often give little thought to any need to continue their education beyond graduation (Darling & Cassidy, 1998), but it is an integral part of professionalism. Qualified professionals must stay current about research and developments within their field along with technology and best practices. Professional development refers to the ongoing training and education of individuals in regard to their careers. The goal is to keep current about the latest trends and research, as well as develop new skills to update oneself in order to renew certification or licensure and ensure professionals are up to standard. However, you can also pursue professional development on your own through programs offered by educational institutions, professional organizations, or even your own employer.

Continuing education and professional development can be accomplished through a number of avenues. Some examples include attending workshops, seminars, and professional conferences; completing online learning opportunities including webinars and self-paced learning modules; reviewing current research through professional publications, such as newsletters and journals; presenting research at professional meetings; and networking with others in the field through membership in professional organizations and associations. Most certification and licensing programs require professionals to earn a minimum number of continuing education credits or hours (CEs, sometimes called CEUs) or PDUs (professional development units), in order to maintain the designation or license. Therefore, professionals need to actively seek continuing education opportunities and maintain records that document attendance at meetings and professional activities. Membership in one or more professional organizations can provide numerous opportunities for continued growth.

■ SUMMARY

This chapter looked closely at the profession of family life education and issues of becoming or being a professional We have determined that the field of FLE meets many of the criteria set forth by experts in defining a profession. Challenges in getting the profession recognized and strategies for growth were considered. We acknowledged that developing a personal philosophy including personal insights, values, and beliefs about families and FLE is an important part of professionalism. Additionally, we explored the personal qualities and traits needed for effective practice. Finally, the importance of ethical guidelines in assuring best practices was addressed. These considerations provide the foundation for further discussion about the practice of family life education.

■ QUESTIONS AND ISSUES FOR DISCUSSION

1. Which people described on the first page of this chapter would you consider to be a "professional" family life educator? Why?
2. How do you define "family"?
3. What is the goal of family life education?
4. Can a person have a different set of values in their personal life than in their professional life? Why or why not?
5. How would you search for a position as a family life educator in your community?
6. What are some ways for family life educators to promote their services?
7. What current television shows are incorporating family life education story lines to help educate viewers about relationships, parenting, and sexuality?

■ ACTIVITIES

1. Trace the development of another social science profession (e.g., social work, marriage and family therapy) and apply the criteria of professionalization.
2. Interview a representative sample of family majors in your department and a sample of family life educators in your area. Compare their responses to the ethical dilemmas presented in the case studies in this chapter. On what bases do they make their judgments?
3. Using the *Case Study Process* in the NCFR publication *Tools for Ethical Thinking and Practice in Family Life Education*, determine the appropriate course of action for a family life educator when a parent in a parent education group reveals having been physically abused by his or her spouse.
4. Read through the two ethical dilemmas described on page 26. What should Carl do? What should Juanita do? (Additional ethical case studies can be found in *Tools for Ethical Thinking and Practice in Family Life Education* (4th ed.) (NCFR, 2018b).
5. Read the CFLE Code of Professional Ethics (Appendix C). Individually or in small groups select and provide examples for two to three Ethical Principles for Relationships with Individuals and Families, Relationships with Colleagues and the Profession, and Relationships with Community/ Society.

PART II

Practice of Family Life Education

3

Understanding Your Audience

Addressing the Needs of Your Audience

Family life education is relevant across the lifespan. Whether involving parents learning about their new babies, sex education with adolescents, college students making decisions about career options, newlyweds practicing communication and conflict resolution skills, or senior citizens preparing for retirement, family life educators need to be cognizant of the participants involved in their programs. This may include knowledge of the demographic data for your community, as well as learner backgrounds, needs, interests, and goals. Have they had any previous experiences with the subject matter and what do they want to accomplish by attending your class? In other words, what kinds of needs do they have?

Recognizing Types of Needs—Needs Assessment

Since family life education should be based on individual and family needs, a *needs assessment* can help to determine what those needs are. A needs assessment is a tool for making better decisions that can be used *proactively* to help you plan, *continuously* as an ongoing process of improving one's program, and *reactively* in response to some desirable or undesirable results (Watkins, Meirs, & Visson, 2012). By incorporating needs assessment strategies, you can plan your program priorities, curriculum, and modes of instruction to be more effective and better target your participants' needs, interests, and goals (Ballard, 2020).

The Domains of Family Practice (DFP) Model examines *for whom* family life education is designed and includes two primary factors—*motivation* and *eligibility* (Myers-Walls et al., 2011). *Motivation* represents the perceptions by participants that a service is necessary and appropriate according to their *felt needs* (Arcus et al., 1993). Felt needs are self-identified; evolve from their own experiences; and encompass the wants, desires, and wishes of the learner. Much of family life education is based on felt needs, which are usually normative and related to age or events, such as becoming a parent, being a parent of an adolescent, getting married, or retiring. New parents or parents of adolescents, along with engaged couples or newly retired persons, may desire some knowledge to help them in the role changes they are, or will be, experiencing. There are also some instances of family life education related to non-normative issues that result from job loss, financial difficulties, or health issues (Dew et al., 2020). Unfortunately, these are issues that became more normative during COVID-19 as families experienced increased stress and disruption to their daily lives (Goldberg, McCormick & Haylie, 2021). In comparison, *eligibility* is determined by the professionals delivering services and is often based on *ascribed needs,* which others identify as a need. Some parents may be mandated to attend family life education classes because of issues that arise from juvenile legal problems, abuse or neglect, or divorce. As an example, when someone says, "I'd like to be a better parent" they are expressing a felt need, but if someone was told that they "should" be a better parent, this would be an example of an ascribed need. Family life educators also consider *future needs,* as they often teach from a preventative paradigm regarding issues learners may have to face in the future. As a result, learners often enroll in family relations courses while in school to prepare them for future life changes or take classes prior to becoming new parents, having their last child leave home, or retirement.

Conducting an Assessment

The "how" question of the DFP model employs needs assessment techniques to determine the characteristics and needs of the target participants (Myers-Walls et al., 2011). It is a systematic process to determine the needs or "gaps" between current conditions and desired outcomes or "wants," and plan for improvements in individuals, education, or communities (Garst & McCawley, 2015). Knowledge of these needs can result from (1) examining the *demographic characteristics* of the target population and (2) pertinent *research findings* related to your audience, along with (3) participation of the learners in the planning process through a *needs assessment*.

To exemplify the process of determining the needs of your participants, consider offering a program on relationships for singles. *Demographic data* can tell you that 31% of those 18 years of age and older are single and that there is an equal number of males and females that are single (Brown, 2020). The number of people who lived alone in 2020 was about 36.2 million, which was an increase compared to 33.19 million in 2012 (Statista, 2021). This is due in part to the increasing age of marriage (29.8 for males and 27.8 years for females) and the increasing number of adults who choose not to marry (US Census Bureau, 2018b). However, many of these adults may be in committed relationships or are cohabitating. In 2018, 15% of young adults ages 25–34 lived with an unmarried partner as compared to 12% in 2008 (US Census Bureau, 2018b). Over half (52%) of young adults aged 18–29 now live with their parents, especially males (55%) compared to females (49%). The COVID-19 pandemic has contributed greatly to this increase (Fry et al., 2020). There can be many benefits of being single, such as freedom to choose how to spend money and time. Half of single adults say they are not currently looking for a relationship or a dating partner, citing more important priorities and enjoyment of the single life as reasons why they preferred to remain single (Brown, 2020).

Examining research related to your target population (e.g., singles) is another critical step in the assessment process. For example, research has indicated that there is a widespread form of bias towards singles that has evolved in our culture in that singles are targets of *singlism*—negative stereotypes and discrimination (DePaulo & Morris, 2013). Married persons are typically described positively, whereas singles are at times presumed to be lonely, miserable, and less warm and sociable than married persons (Slonim, Gur-Yaish, & Katz, 2015). While the "perceived" differences between married and single persons are large, the "actual" differences are not. One suggestion is to transition from a simple contrast of married versus single persons to thinking of singles as diverse and distinct groups that are unpartnered, cohabiting, widowed, or divorced. Some are single by choice and others may choose to have a partner one day, whereas some may face physical or psychological challenges that affect their ability to develop lasting relationships (Byrne & Carr, 2005). Other factors influencing the increased numbers of singles living at home are lack of employment prospects, and delays in marriage (Fry, 2013). Research has also indicated that as singles age they were willing to date people who are different from themselves. A majority of young adults report that they would consider a relationship with someone of a different religion, race or ethnicity, or who has an income significantly more or less than their income (Brown, 2020). These relationship decisions may mean that generic programs for singles may not meet their needs. Reviewing research literature can provide insight into issues that singles are facing and provide recommendations for practice that can facilitate understanding the needs of your target audience and designing a needs assessment measure.

While you can examine *demographic data* and *research* findings about your target audience (e.g., singles), it is also essential to make contact with potential participants as part of a *needs assessment*. A needs assessment is a systematic approach to studying the state of knowledge, ability, interests, or attitudes of a target audience in order to design an effective educational program. What does your audience know and think and what can you do to make your program more accessible, acceptable, and useful to potential learners? For example, what issues about relationships would singles want covered? What is their age and single status (never married and alone, divorced, separated, or partnered)? Are they single by choice? Are they seeking intimate relationships, close friendships, connections in the community, or assistance with family members who may be exerting pressure for a lasting relationship or seeking their services as a caregiver? Are they happy or unhappy with their single life? What are their issues of concern?

Whereas some needs assessments can be *indirect* through discussions with interested persons, such as an advisory committee, *direct needs assessments* are accomplished by gathering qualitative or quantitative data from potential participants. Direct needs assessment will involve greater resources to design, implement, and analyze the resulting data. In general, you want the best data possible within the constraints of your available resources (e.g., time and money). Whether or not you have conducted an in-depth needs assessment, during the first class session it is always good to ask participants their reasons for taking the class, what experiences they have with the topic, and what would they like to accomplish. It is important to share your plan for the class session(s) and determine if your strategy for the course will meet their needs. If not, ask them what changes they would recommend. You may not be able to accommodate all their suggestions, but at least you will have a chance to make some possible adjustments, if time and resources permit.

Steps in Conducting a Needs Assessment

Planning a Needs Assessment

Before actually beginning a needs assessment, it is best to create your objectives. In other words, what type of information would you like to gain? Do you want to know the learners' ages and interests in the topic; issues of concern; or best time, location, and format for the class? Who is your audience and how will you select your sample? Will you go to various singles groups affiliated with faith communities, schools, senior centers, or exercise facilities? Are there community stakeholders that can help you to gain the trust of your target audience? What methodology or instruments will you use and how will you collect your data?

Will you use online surveys or focus groups? How will you ensure that your methods are culturally appropriate for your intended audience? How will you analyze the data and use it in your decision making? (For specific details on conducting different types of needs assessment see Watson et al., 2012.)

Obtaining approval

Depending on your approach to needs assessment, you may need institutional approval, especially if the educational program or research project is funded through a university or grant. This might occur through a university human subjects review, Institutional Review Board (IRB), and/or additional permissions from schools, religious institutions, agencies, or parents that are involved. Make sure to allow time in your planning to get these approvals. If, however, you use secondary data that already exist, or a more informal method, such as discussions with advisory boards or other interested persons, you may not need to obtain IRB or other approvals.

Collection of data

There are several methods to collect data, including surveys, interviews, focus groups, and other creative approaches. Below is a brief overview of needs assessment techniques, along with some advantages and disadvantages of each method. Further examination of the procedures involved in each method is highly recommended. It is important to consider any cultural or linguistic differences of your target audience when designing data collection measures (Lopez et al., 2017). After you have designed the assessment method questions, it is good to pilot test your instrument and procedures with some selected potential participants (Donaldson & Franck, 2016).

- *Surveys*. Written surveys can be conducted by mail, email, online, phone, or in-person. While some methods of quantitative data collection are cost-effective (e.g., online or in-person groups), others are not, due to printing and postage charges. Data are anonymous and easy to summarize, but unless you ask the right questions, you may not gain the additional insights and details that you desire (Donaldson & Franck, 2016). During phone surveys you can get supplementary information without having to depend on the literacy skills of the participants, however, many people do not answer phone calls from an unknown number. Email and online surveys work well if you anticipate the participants will have computers, are internet savvy, and will respond to an email message from an unknown person prior to deleting it. Social media such as Facebook or Instagram may be another way to distribute a survey to your potential audience. At times you may be attending a group that has some potential participants in your target audience. If you have some surveys with you, it would be easy to get responses if the context of the environment facilitates this process. In other words, you might ask participants at a PTA meeting for their suggestions, but you will need to get prior permission to make this request.
- *Interviews*. Interviews involve conversations between two or more people to collect needs assessment data. They can be conducted face-to-face or

through the use of technology, such as phones, video conferencing, or online. Interviews are inexpensive to conduct and work well with open-ended questions. In addition, the interviewer can look for nonverbal cues and ask clarifying questions, as needed. However, it is important to respect interviewees' time. If resources allow, consider compensating participants for their time. The interviews can be taped with permission of the participants and then transcribed and coded, but this can be time intensive. One should develop statements to facilitate rapport and clarity about the intent and data needed by the interviewer (Donaldson & Franck, 2016). Again, as with surveys, some people do not respond to unknown callers unless they have some previous communication about an upcoming phone call to gather needs assessment data. This, however, may not be time and cost effective.

- *Focus Groups.* Focus groups involve a social experience of 6 to 8 persons who not only express their own opinions, perceptions, beliefs, and attitudes, but also listen to the opinions of others, which they may or may not incorporate into their comments. This format adds a "group dynamic" element that may produce more information than structured individual interviews (Krueger & Casey, 2015). Focus group methodology is not only a means to plan a needs assessment process, but also has the unique ability to facilitate understanding "reality" from the point of view of those involved in the group. Within the qualitative paradigm, focus group methods probe the attitudes and opinions of small groups, are stimulating to the respondents, and provide rich data through cumulative and elaborative responses often not obtained in individual interview settings (Krueger & Casey, 2015). Whereas focus groups are easy to establish, the data collection process can be intense with many different opinions and suggestions being offered in a rapid-fire sequence. With permission, recording the responses for later transcription is most helpful. Having a competent moderator, who is able to facilitate questioning and pursue major issues, is critical.
- *Other Creative Techniques.* Over the last 20 years, there have been many technological advances in conducting needs assessments (Garst & McCawley, 2015). Online surveys, social media, audience response systems (e.g., clickers), and mobile applications (apps) are just a few of the advances used in gathering data to better assess participant needs. Other creative techniques might include photovoice, in which participants use cameras to document relevant information, or data visualization techniques, such as GIS or other mapping devices, that can help examine needs at a community level (Garst & McCawley, 2015).

Your challenge as an educator is to design creative ways to do the assessment tasks of asking, studying, and observing. You may be visiting a home, office, or classroom; calling by phone; handing out questionnaires; or polling participants. If you are doing a webinar, you may want to send out a brief survey to participants as they register to determine their background, interests, and needs regarding the topic. You may also do something more innovative, such as posing a "three wishes" question to children about their family life or asking a group of pregnant teens to draw their greatest fears about becoming a mother. It may be asking a group of new parents to take a pretest about infant development at the beginning of class. This is an effective method because it gives the leader a chance to note knowledge gaps and provide accurate information while involving the group in a "kinetic" activity.

Interpretation of Data

Once you have collected and analyzed your needs assessment data, it is time to interpret them. This goes beyond simple tabulation by using various decision-making tools and techniques, such as prioritizing issues, engaging in consensus planning, using multiple criteria to make comparisons across options, and employing facilitator-led discussions to identify gaps (see Watkins et al., 2012, for further details). Next you have to decide the meaning of the results, determine if there are any patterns, and identify what actions will be most helpful to your target learners. It is often necessary to make difficult choices about which needs to address first, particularly if you have limited resources. Be careful not to overlook needs that might have emerged from your data because they do not align with what you want to offer or what you think is important (Donaldson & Franck, 2016). Share and discuss your results with others, as interpretations can vary. Results of needs assessments can also be used to raise awareness and to expand the reach of programs and services (Garst & McCawley, 2015).

Asset Mapping

Asset mapping is an approach to community development that focuses on the strengths and the capacities of the community rather than the deficits, and can help communities to solve problems, defeat challenges, and meet needs (Allar et al., 2017). Asset mapping does not take the place of a needs assessment, but it can complement a needs assessment and provide information at a community level. Community assets can include physical assets (space, equipment), economic assets, stories, people, associations, and institutions or agencies. Identifying strengths within these six categories to assess each community need will allow for a more creative, positive, and balanced approach to change.

Although generally used on larger scale community building projects of which family life education may be one piece, asset mapping has implications for planning an individual program. Are there assets within your target community such as relevant community agencies that might be meaningful partners in your family life education programming? Are there other resources that can help to support your programming? As you assess the needs of your target audience, do not focus just on what they are lacking, but assess their strengths. You can incorporate questions that focus on this type of information into whatever method you are using to collect your needs assessment data. What can these participants bring to the program? How can you capitalize on their existing strengths within your program? Pointing out areas of strength to participants can sometimes be important for improving self-esteem and motivation for continued learning. For example, when teaching a parenting class, assess what parenting skills or positive parenting characteristics your participants already possess. Focus your program content not only on what they lack for parenting skills, but also the strengths that they already have and build on those existing skills.

Role of Culture

In addition to assessing the needs of our participants, we should examine the concept of culture and how it can be applied. *Culture* is the total way of life of people—the customs, beliefs, values, attitudes, and communication patterns that characterize a group and provide a common sense of identity. Taken together, these components form a way of interpreting reality that is shared among members of a group. Individuals and families may align with multiple cultural groups or members of the same cultural group may have different levels of cultural identity (Allen & Blaisure, 2015). It is important for family life educators to determine the aspects of cultural identity that are most important to the families with whom they will be working. All cultural groups are valued for their unique qualities and dignity. Family life education programs will be more successful if they recognize and build on the strengths of cultural groups (Ballard & Taylor, 2022a). While we often think of culture in terms of race/ethnicity, culture extends beyond this paradigm to include age, gender, socioeconomic status, generational cohorts, immigration status, family structure (single parent, extended), sexual orientation, special circumstances (health issues, crises, military roles, incarceration), or combinations of various cultural lenses, such as a gay single parent or a mother serving in the military.

We often do not perceive the influence of culture, so one way to consider the multifaceted aspects of culture is to think about sunglasses as an analogy. How do sunglasses differ in shapes and sizes of the frames and lenses, including colors and types? In addition to the differences in the appearance of sunglasses, when looking through sunglasses, you see things differently. In relation to culture, what kinds of filters do people have that affect how they see individuals and families? Responses vary and may include race, ethnicity, sexual orientation, gender, religion, education, social class, political affiliation, geographical location, age, marital status, professional role, and living in a home or being homeless.

Implicit bias can play a role in culture. Implicit bias, also known as unconscious bias, refers to the attitudes and stereotypes that involuntarily affect your behavior without you realizing it (Staats, Capatosto, Tenney, & Mamo, 2017). Everyone is susceptible to implicit bias and one's individual implicit bias is often rooted in biases within one's environment (Vuletich & Payne, 2019). Therefore, it is important to take a contextual view of your own implicit bias and work to not only change implicit bias on an individual level, but also to think about how your environment might contribute or reinforce your implicit biases.

Stereotypes and Generalizations

Sometimes our biases are based on *stereotypes*. While we want to avoid stereotypes about people, we also need to understand how they differ from *generalizations*. Generalizations give insights into the tendencies of a particular group of people and often come from synthesizing available information from research and/or informed cultural experts and professionals. They can be a starting point for learning about different cultures. However, generalizations can become stereotypes if definitively applied to all members of a particular group. Stereotypes are oversimplified representations of a group of persons (e.g., race, nationality, sexual orientation, religion, age, family type) that are inflexible and can be inaccurate in terms of how they exaggerate real differences and the perceptions of these differences. Although stereotypes are often negative, they can also be positive. For example, you might say that a particular cultural group is good at math. The problem is that this is only a partial picture and an individual from this culture who is not good in math may feel undue pressure to perform. Generalizations may seem similar to stereotypes, but stereotypes are often taken to the extreme and become exaggerated beliefs that are applied to every member of a particular group. Which of the following examples are generalizations or stereotypes? (The answers are at the end of the chapter.)

1. Many people in the United States attend football games.
2. Everyone in the United States likes football.
3. Lots of Americans like fast food.
4. All Americans eat fast food every day.
5. Johan is going to be stubborn because he is from Country X.
6. Johan might be really stubborn because he is from Country X.
7. Many people from Country Z keep their feelings to themselves.
8. People from Country Z never share anything about themselves.
9. Maria will be late because women are never on time.
10. Maria might be late because some women are more likely not to be punctual.

Microaggressions

Microaggressions are based on implicit biases and stereotypes. Microaggressions are everyday verbal, behavioral, or environmental slights or insults toward marginalized groups that convey biases and can be delivered implicitly and explicitly. There are three types of microaggressions: microassault, microinsult, and microinvalidation (Nadal, 2008). *Microassaults* refer to overt and intentional acts of racism, bias, or discrimination intended to harm a person of a particular marginalized group. Examples might include using racist language or denying service to someone based on their race or sexual orientation. *Microinsults* are typically unintentional actions or verbal remarks that convey disrespect, insensitivity, and demean an individual's racial culture/identity, gender identity, sexual orientation/identity, religion, or ability. Examples of microinsults might be assuming a Black person is a service worker or assuming that someone of Asian descent was not born in the US. *Mircoinvalidations* refer to verbal expressions or behaviors that exclude, negate, or dismiss the marginalized group's psychological thoughts, feelings, or experiential reality (Torino et al., 2018). Examples of microinvalidations include statements like "I don't see color" or a claim that "All lives matter" in response to the Black Lives Matter movement.

Microaggressions cause harm, distress, and damage to people's humanity and social relationships (Thurber & DiAngelo, 2018). A person on the receiving end of the microaggression may experience a range of feelings from anger to self-doubt. Because they are continual and cumulative, mircroaggressions can take a significant psychological and physical toll on those who are the targets. For the person committing the microaggression, it can create distrust and inhibit relationships.

Cultural Competence

We all interact with other cultures whether we are in our home country, abroad, at work, or in our neighborhoods. Therefore, it is important to become more culturally aware and become more culturally competent in our FLE practice. *Cultural competence* is the ability to work effectively across cultural groups and is comprised of awareness, knowledge, and skills (Allen & Blaisure, 2015; Hanover Research, 2015). If we gain some knowledge about cultures (facts and traits) along with an awareness of others (their skills and behaviors), and ourselves, we can become more culturally sensitive and intelligent about other persons in our environmental context (Mallette et al., 2022). When we learn about different cultural groups within and beyond our own culture, we can see different points of view and better understand and address cultural differences.

LEADER: A strengths-based cultural competence model for FLE (Mallette et al., 2022) is a model of cultural competence that links learning to practice. The model starts with cultural learning and posits that culturally competent family life educators must have the necessary attitudes, skills, knowledge, and motivation in order to move toward a culturally competent practice. The leadership competencies of learning, self-evaluation, assessment, development, engagement, and reflection build on cultural learning and allow family life educators to move from learning to the behavior change needed to practice with diverse audiences. (See Chapter 12 for more on the LEADER model.)

A more nuanced understanding of culture is necessary for the development of cultural competence and an *iceberg* can be a useful analogy. An iceberg has a part that is above the waterline, or the *visible* part of culture such as the customs and language, but the vast majority is below the waterline and constitutes the *invisible* part of culture including values, cultural assumptions, nonverbal communications, thought patterns, and cognitive perceptions. Similarly we talk of the *Big C* of culture, which is what you see, and the *little c* of culture, which you do not see (see Figure 3.1).

We rarely get to know the essence of other cultural groups, so I (C. Darling) will use my own cultural heritage as an example as I am more familiar with it than other cultures. All four of my grandparents were born in Finland and came to the United States as young adults, so I lived within a culture of individuals in the US who had emigrated from Finland. Thus, I was immersed into the culture of Finnish-Americans. The *Big C* of culture contained the following:

- *Customs*—Traditions and holidays (e.g., I have participated in celebrating Finnish Midsummer, Independence Day, foods, clothing, arts, literature, politics, architecture and design, crafts, folk dances, and music. Having

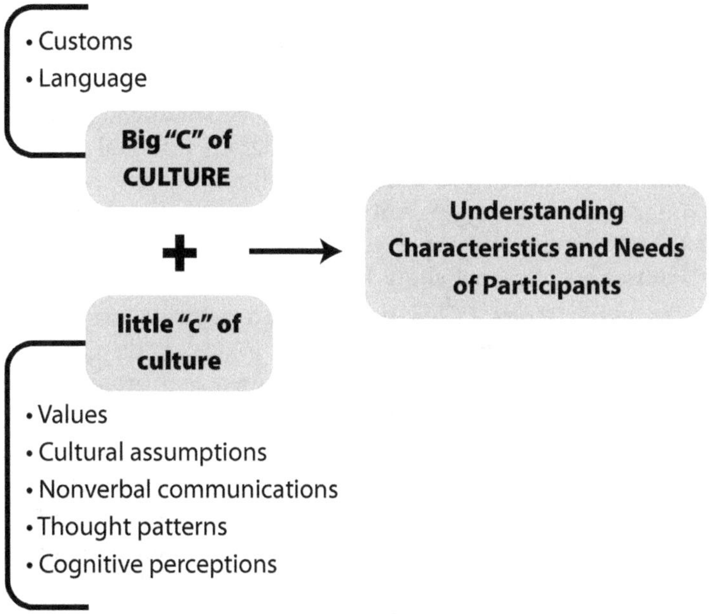

Figure 3.1 Role of Culture in Understanding Participants

attended a camp for Finnish youth as a child, I was able to learn about and participate in many examples of Finnish culture and appreciate the music of Jean Sibelius, the poetry of Johan Runeberg, and the architecture and design of Alvar Aalto and Eero Saarinen.)

- *Language*—Verbal and nonverbal (e.g., I learned some of the language from my parents and took courses both in the US and Finland to facilitate learning the Finnish language. I was also exposed to periods of silence, which spoke volumes, along with minimal facial expression and eye contact. Silence means privacy, personal thinking, or respectful listening. Finns may be quiet, but they are always thinking. Finland is more of a monologue culture compared to some other countries, such as the US, which is a dialogue culture.)

In addition, I assimilated elements of the *little c* (Tamminen, 2003) of Finnish-American culture, including:

- *Values*—Basis of how we act and what is right and wrong (e.g., many Finns have a strong sense of fairness, honesty, and trust. They have an ethic of hard work based on the need to survive. They also value promptness, the appreciation of women in politics, respect of nature, and the role of "sisu," which is a Finnish term for fortitude and perseverance.)
- *Cultural Assumptions*—Things taken for granted about a culture, which are not necessarily always true (possible stereotypes) (e.g., I learned that Finnish people are perceived to be hardworking, creative, and reliable, but they

also can be introverts, direct, and impatient. Additionally, because they have so many saunas in Finland, they are often perceived to be clean.)

- *Nonverbal Communications*—Touch, eye contact, finger symbols (e.g., I found that generally Finnish people tend to be somewhat shy, quiet, and use the phrase, "It goes without saying." There is minimal touching—in business, only handshakes are acceptable, although between good friends there might be some hugging, more often with women. Finns also keep their distance and are concerned about invading another person's private space. Houses and clothing should be modest.)
- *Thought Patterns*—Ways we think and process information (e.g., I learned that many Finns will often be direct, logical, and to the point, but extolling one's own virtues would be considered inappropriate. Finns should not boast about their education, money, status, or family background, and generally do not talk about it.)
- *Cognitive Perceptions*—Ways we understand knowledge (e.g., I was aware that Finland was a poor nation until the late 1950s and Finns worked hard for the collective good. They took pride in being the only country to pay back their war debt to the US after World War II. Prior hardships of family members in previous generations affected perceptions of one's country of heritage. Thus, my parents' generation in the US was taught that we had it better than our family members in Finland, so we should try to assist them in any way we could.)

When I taught in Finland, although I had been steeped in the Finnish culture through my US family, friends, and community, I still did not know all there was to know about the *little c* of the Finnish culture. However, because of my background, which is both American and Finnish, I am able to ask questions and get insightful answers. I am still learning and need to continue doing so, because culture both stays the same and changes. The *Big C* characteristics tend to remain the same, but the *little c* themes can change over months or years (Peterson, 2004). This example shows that there is no way we can know all the *Big C* and *little c* characteristics of our own culture and especially multiple cultures. However, by trying to learn as much as we can about other cultures, especially those represented in our classrooms, we will begin to understand how to design a class and implement it to best meet the needs of a specific culture or multicultural group. The *Big C* and *little c* of culture not only pertain to race and ethnicity, but can also apply to varying family structures, sexual orientations, and age-generations.

Characteristics and Needs of Various Groups

As family life educators we are dedicated to advancing the well-being and learning of our audience. Thus, we personalize our instruction as much as possible by trying to do our best for learners. We often identify groups by age, gender, or ethnicity; however, there are multiple diversities resulting in an intersection of characteristics, such as gay adolescent Latinos, single Asian mothers, Black parents of a disabled child, or White incarcerated females. While one cannot know the characteristics of all cultural groups, it is important to examine demographics, research, and theory relating to various cultural groups, while incorporating an ecosystems context (O-E Relationship, i.e., Organism Interacting with the Environment; see Chapter 8). When studying individuals or families, how would you characterize the environments within which they interact, including the legal, political, economic, religious, educational, and medical systems? If we can take existing data and think critically about any cultural grouping from an ecosystems perspective, we can create a better understanding to assist us in our teaching.

Developmental Stages and Generations

The developmental stages of your participants need to be understood as they relate to their individual and family needs. Moreover, people born at different times in varying generational cohorts will also have different personal needs, attitudes, and values that can influence their learning styles.

Developmental stages

While there are various stage-based theories of development, a commonly used one is that of Erik Erikson (1950, 1963), who proposed eight stages to clarify the developmental challenges faced at various times in people's lives. These stages and the approximate ages for each stage include: *Basic Trust vs. Mistrust* (0–1); *Autonomy vs. Shame and Doubt* (1–3); *Initiative vs. Guilt* (3–6); *Industry vs. Inferiority* (6–11); *Identity vs. Role Confusion* (adolescence); *Intimacy vs. Isolation* (early adulthood); *Generativity vs. Stagnation* (middle adulthood); and *Ego Identity vs. Despair* (late adulthood). While each stage builds on the successful completion of earlier stages, mastery of a stage is not required to advance to the next stage. Each stage has various components to negotiate, such as one's biological changes, sociocultural forces, and psychological crises (for further information see Harwood, Miller, & Vasta, 2008). Although we could be teaching all ages of the population, we more commonly work with adolescent and adult learners, whether they are young adults or seniors.

Adolescence is a time of profound changes in physical, cognitive, socioemotional, and moral development during which teens are making critical life choices (Santrock, 2019). This period is marked by tremendous growth, physical variability, and hormone changes, along with a focus on appearance, physical changes, and seeking self-identity. While in early adolescence same-sex friendships are predominant, maturation results in increased comfort with friends of both genders and an increased desire for independence from parents. There are also changes in brain development and cognition, as well as a shift from concrete to formal operations. This is tied to moral development and an adolescent transitioning from the desire to do something good because there is a reward, to doing good to maintain positive relations. As they become aware of themselves, adolescents not only become egocentric, but also aware of their skills and career potential that may help them focus on a future path. In order to facilitate learning in this age group, you may want to acknowledge the varying rate of growth and development, plan activities that build self-esteem, involve families, use a variety of teaching techniques to meet different learning styles, be responsive to diversity of all kinds, and give opportunities for development of critical thinking skills and evaluation of alternatives to various actions, especially those that involve risk taking (Santrock, 2019).

Young adults are strong, in good physical condition, and have stamina. Their memory and cognitive abilities are at their highest and they have a strong ambition to succeed, select a life partner, start a family, and accept responsibilities. Those in middle adulthood often are managing multiple roles such as employee, parent, partner, or caregiver for an older parent. It is during this period that adults may start to notice their own aging and are encouraged to stay active and take time for themselves during this busy phase of life. Some adults may have a midlife crisis, causing them to reevaluate their life goals and accomplishments and make some positive changes. *Later adulthood* can be marked by menopause, osteoporosis (a reduction of bone density), gray hair, less skin elasticity, and a loss of muscle mass. Memory and mobility tend to decrease as well. However, those older adults who stay mentally and physically active can more successfully negotiate these developmental changes.

Lifelong learning for adults is a function of their needs and wants based on societal changes that affect the complexity of their lives, such as increased life expectancy, shifts in caregiving to family members, concerns for health and wellness, use of technology, and expanding knowledge in all areas of life. Adult learners may have different reasons for engaging in family life education. They may have a desire to know more about a certain topic (*felt needs*) or have a mandated expectation of their need to know (*ascribed needs*). Maybe it is a way to connect with others with similar interests. An examination of the topics of high interest to adults aged 50 and older indicated that their highest-rated topics were nutrition and health, fitness and exercise, and positive aspects of aging (Ballard & Morris, 2003). Programs that help midlife and older adults to navigate shifting family roles and relationships may be of particular interest (Benson & Donehower, 2020). Family life educators should honor the life experience and collective wisdom of midlife and older adults by taking a collaborative approach in program facilitation (Benson & Donehower, 2020). They want real life situations that allow them to engage with the content and with other participants, and opportunities to practice skills with case studies or role-play (see Chapter 6).

Of course, some adults are no longer working because they have reached *retirement age* and beyond. The fastest growing segment of the US population is the group that is 65 years and older with a rapid increase in the "old-old" or those who are 85 years and older. Older women traditionally have outnumbered men because women tend to have a longer life expectancy. The population 65 years and older is projected to double between 2016 and 2060 from 49 million to 95 million. This growth will result in the 65 and older population increasing to almost 25% of the population in 2060. Within the 65 and older population, those 85 years and older are projected to nearly double to 11.8 million and by 2060 nearly triple to 19 million people (Vespa et al., 2020). The implications of living longer have some important considerations for older persons and their families (Benson & Donehower, 2020). Elder learners may want to attend classes to both learn and interact with others. Health issues are important along with financial planning and family relationships within the context of their advancing age. Remember that their hearing, sight, and physical abilities may no longer be as astute as when they were younger. Thus, educators need to pay attention to their physical abilities and limitations along with their issues of concern. To facilitate understanding the limitations faced by older learners, see the activity in Box 3.1.

Box 3.1 **Aging Changes**

An aging simulation activity can help students increase their knowledge about the physical changes in older adults related to sensory-motor functioning and their sensitivity to the feelings of older persons (Wood, 2003).

In small groups, have volunteer members modify one or more of their abilities to perform daily activities. These limitations could include the following:

- Put on glasses that cause blurred vision by coating the lenses with petroleum jelly (e.g., cataracts) or cover part of the outer edges of the lenses to simulate loss of peripheral vision (e.g., glaucoma).
- Insert ear plugs or absorbent cotton balls into both ears (e.g., hearing loss).
- Divide a cotton ball and insert into one nostril (diminished sense of smell and taste).
- Place transparent tape on the thumb, index, and middle finger joints of the dominant hand (e.g., stiffness due to arthritis).
- Insert dried split peas or sunflower seeds in the sole of each shoe (e.g., foot pain, loss of balance associated with bunions and corns).
- Restrict one knee with an ace bandage (arthritis).
- Use a straw to breathe while walking upstairs (e.g., respiratory problems).

Students who are not impaired will be designated caregivers and are responsible for the safety and assistance to those with aging impairments, along with observing their responses and the reactions of others. The groups of students will experience the effect of these limitations for about 30 to 60 minutes during which time they can move around campus and be involved in activities, such as going to the library, purchasing and consuming a snack, making a phone call, and/or using a computer, vending machine, and bathroom.

A debriefing discussion can include the following questions: what difficulties and feelings did they experience; what changes did they observe in themselves and others; did the experience stimulate any thoughts about older individuals and their impairments; what changes in feelings and behaviors toward older persons might evolve from this experience.

Generations

We frequently see terms in the news such as Greatest Generation; Baby Boomers; Millennials; and Generations X, Y, and Z, which are all used to describe groups of people of varying ages or generations of people who developed different value systems. Generational theory has become increasingly popular in recent years as a way to conceptualize individuals in a broad approach according to their birth generation. It seeks to facilitate understanding by characterizing cohorts of people according to their birth generation and how that time affected their values and views of the world. A *generation* is an average interval of time between the birth of one's parents and the birth of their offspring, typically about 20 to 22 years. Generations are not defined by a formal process, but by demographers, the media, popular culture, market researchers, and members of each generation (Dimok, 2019). Generations have their own defining experiences and identifiable sets of assumptions, values, attitudes, and approaches to life, along with shared aspirations about their role in society. During these periods there are significant events that tend to shape development and values, such as wars, terrorism, major political events, pandemics, and technological advances.

Studying generational similarities and differences is interesting, but tricky. There is no consensus about the calendar years associated with any particular generation, so most generations do not have precise beginning and end dates, with some generations overlapping, thus producing a group that may have characteristics of two generations. Dates that distinguish each generation are based on political, economic, and social factors and generally the majority of persons born between a tentative set of dates share many similar characteristics (Dimok, 2019). Table 3.1 has been developed to give an approximation of the generations, their characteristics, and the values of those born in that generation (Codrington, 2008; Mohr & Mohr, 2017; Pendergast, 2006, 2009; Rosen, 2010).

Four generations that comprise a majority of the learners in family life education programs are the Baby Boomers, Generation X, Millennials, and Generation Z, although a new Generation Alpha is emerging. To better understand these generations, some of their general characteristics and values are noted below (Barroso, Parker, & Bennett, 2020; Cilluffo & Cohn, 2019; McGregor & Toronyi, 2009; Mohr & Mohr, 2017; Pendergast, 2006; Ratnam, 2020; Zarra, 2017):

- *Baby Boomers* (born 1946–1964) value family, education, individualism, change, quality, inspiration and motivational support, conformance to team norms, success, conflict resolution, being open, freedom and choice, personal growth and fulfillment, and a mix of spontaneity and discipline. They try to balance materialism and generosity; are workaholics; are optimistic; need hands-on involvement; like loose structures, temporariness, task forces, and holding meetings; reject authority, but value sensitive authority figures; and work to get ahead and move up the ladder.
- *Generation X* (born 1965–1981) values independence, fun, challenges, creativity, access to lots of information, specific and focused feedback, and doing things their own way. They are resilient, independent, and economically conservative; have low perceived job security; appreciate directness and being up-front; accept diversity; are not civic minded; reject rules; are self-absorbed, aloof, isolated; perceive friends are not family; have varying interpersonal skills; and will not sacrifice life for work.
- *Millennials (Generation Y)* (born 1982–1996) value mentoring, nurturance, and guidance; education and skill building; and work as a means to personal fulfillment. They feel special; often considered as "me-centric"; live

for and through technology; are drawn to competence; like positive reinforcement; plan and are goal directed; are civic minded and social activists; celebrate diversity; perceive friends as equal to family; are marrying at a later age than other generations or are not marrying at all; are entrepreneurial and reinvent rules; need supervised environment and structure; are team oriented; and enjoy extreme fun. Millennials now outnumber Baby Boomers as the largest adult generation.

- *Generation Z* (born 1997–2010) do not know a world without technology and show expanded use of the internet, text messaging, cell phones, YouTube, Instagram, Twitter, and other social media platforms. However, they tend to be more private in what they share via social media than Millennials. They are multitaskers, have a short attention span, are impatient, and like Millennials, they often feel entitled. They are value-driven; identify with causes

Table 3.1 Generational Characteristics

Birth Years	Generation Name(s)	Notable Occurrences, Characteristics, and Values
1901–1924	Lost G.I. Greatest Generation (born)	WW1: technical practice with social mission; civic mindedness; public health; management and family with scientific base; frugal; male and female roles defined with first wave of feminism.
1925–1945	Silent Greatest Generation (served in WW2)	WW2: focus on management and thrift as result of decline of world economy from wars and Great Depression; hard work; law and order; self-sufficient; sacrifice; conformity; modesty; patience.
1946–1964	Baby Boomers (their parents were the Greatest Generation)	Civil Rights Movement; 1960s social revolution; anti-Vietnam rallies; focus on personal growth and self-expression; expanding consumerism; assassination of J. F. Kennedy; drugs, sex, rock 'n' roll; moon landing.
1965–1981	Generation X	Rise of media and consumerism; end of Cold War; feminist movement; widespread introduction of contraceptive pill; MTV; undefined/heterogeneous identity; global awareness; grew up as "latch-key kids."
1982–1996	Generation Y Millennials Echo Boomers	Globalization; information age/birth of WWW; use of communication, media, digital technology; increased peer orientation; culturally liberal; boomerang kids; trophy generation; school violence.
1997–2010	Generation Z iGeneration Homeland Net	Life-long use of communication and technology; expanded use of internet; social media, text messaging, smartphones, FaceTime, Twitter; dreamers; impatient; ADD; individualistic; have helicopter parents.
2011–2025	Generation Alpha	Technology-driven reality; affected by new avenues of social media, technology, change in family structure, climate debate, and the current COVID-19 pandemic; creating opportunities, adventure, and exploration for the future; have Millennial parents.

and support organizations that embrace social justice; and are becoming known as "we-centric." They are the most ethnically diverse and multicultural generation in history and embrace diversity.

- *Generation Alpha* (born 2011–2025) are predicted to be the most technologically savvy generation than any other generation before them. They are used to the accessibility of immediate information; many of their interactions and relationships now and in the future will be created through some form of technology; and they have Millennials for parents.

The last 30 to 40 years have been a period of an unprecedented transition from an industrial to an information-based culture and economy. Whereas Baby Boomers in general prefer face-to-face or phone communication, with many using email regularly, Generation X is more ambiguous and has embraced smart phones, email, and social media.

Gen Z, which began in 1997 (see Table 3.1), are true *digital natives* who do not know a life without the internet at their fingertips (Mohr & Mohr, 2017), with about 45% of teens reporting their internet use as "near constant." A majority of their waking hours are spent on media and technology, although they are even multitasking in their media usage. Digital natives are characterized as operating at "twitch speed" and not at conventional speed, as they employ random access, parallel processing, graphics, and generally get more screen time (television, computer, and phones) than fresh air. In other words they are connected, play-oriented, interactive, and graphics focused. They use many technologies and forms of social media, such as Facebook, Zoom, text messaging, FaceTime, Instagram, YouTube, and Twitter. About 95% of teenagers in the US indicate that they have access to a smartphone and this is fairly consistent across gender, race, and socioeconomic status. About 88% report having access to a computer at home, although this may vary across economic lines (Anderson & Jiang, 2018).

Understanding participants from different generations helps you plan your classes. If the teachers are digital immigrants, they need to realize that their students may be digital natives. Whereas past generations relied more on print media, both Millennials and Generation Z use digital media and are used to having information at their fingertips. For Millennials and Gen Zers, learning in an ideal world involves having it adapted to their needs, at a time and place they want it, with just enough detail, and on a device they have in front of them. All knowledge is connected to data and each other. Whereas students find, filter, and focus on content, teachers are perceived as guides, facilitators, and coaches (McGee, n.d.). Digital natives will respond better to graphics and visuals than to text. They are not just literate, but multiliterate and commonly use reading patterns associated with digital text browsing and scanning for meaning, preferring virtual texts to physical texts (Mohr & Mohr, 2017). The use of *tag clouds* (*word clouds* or *wordles*) or visualizations of term frequencies might be a meaningful learning tool. A tag cloud is a visual representation for text data using single words with the importance of each word shown with a font type, weighted font size, or color. They can be used as website navigation aids to tag resources by hyperlinking the term to digital information, such as web pages, photos, or video clips. Even before the COVID-19 pandemic, teachers were adapting to new technologies and using online learning platforms as a supplement to classroom activities. However, the move to remote instruction during the pandemic forced all educators to use technology and virtual classrooms as primary modes of delivery. Millennials, Gen Zers, and Gen Alphas who have been reared on evolving technologies, may also have little tolerance for lecture-style learning (Hughes, 2020; Mohr & Mohr, 2017; Zarra, 2017). Using personalized teaching activities and active learning is critical to maximize their understanding along with incorporating a "flipped" classroom model. Instructors adopting the flipped classroom assign electronic class lectures or instructional content as homework, and utilize class time to work through problems, advance concepts, and participate in collaborative learning (Mohr & Mohr, 2017; Roehl, Reddy, & Shannon, 2013).

Gen Z and Gen Alpha are poised to become the most well educated generations yet. Generations tend to get better educated, more diverse, and more tech savvy over time. Although Millennials and Gen Z take the lead with technology, previous generations also embrace technology. In addition, the COVID-19 pandemic has forced all generations to learn how to engage online. An online survey of 2,240 parents conducted in 2012 indicated that the internet is an important source of parenting information for them; yet, many found it difficult to find the information that they needed (Connell, 2012). More recent research indicates that parents are interested in online opportunities to learn more about parenting (Walker, 2017). With the surge in online learning and technology use, people still may have different skills, goals, needs, devices, and varying amounts of time available for online learning. The workforce is also affected by the technology practices of Millennials who prefer telecommuting (even before the increase in teleworking during COVID-19), but have an aversion to using the phone for conversations, which is important in some professions (Permenter, 2013). Not only should we address the characteristics and needs of different generations of people, but we also have to pay attention to how different generations use technology. This gives family life educators a greater opportunity to develop creative methods for reaching learners and give them access to the information that was previously difficult to obtain. To better reach our participants, we need to know them and understand their needs, as well as their technological abilities and resources.

Class, Gender, and Race/Ethnicity

Class, gender, and race/ethnicity influence family life through unequal distribution of resources and opportunities. Whatever the class, gender, or race/ethnicity group to which you belong, they all have characteristics of the Big C and little c of culture. We may perceive what it is like to be in the wealthy class or to be homeless, a person of a different race or ethnicity, or a person of another gender, but most of us do not know the values, cultural assumptions, nonverbal communications, thought patterns, and cognitive perceptions that comprise the little c of these cultural groupings. While this chapter will not go into depth on all the groups that might comprise the participants in your family life education program, a few groups will be highlighted.

Class

Whereas class focuses on the distribution of economic resources and a person or group's relative social position, there is disagreement on the meaning of *class* and how to define it. Often income, occupation, and education level are used as indicators of class, along with marital status, income of spouse and others in the home, and size of household. There are many family groupings related to class, such as families in poverty and homeless families. Poverty reduces the likelihood of marriage and makes the nuclear family difficult to sustain, but the extended network provides services, assistance, and coping support. In families of professionals, family life is often subordinate to the demands of one's profession, with corporate relocation being common. Little is known about wealthy families, who often have multiple residences and are connected to a web of institutions. A majority of Americans (52%) are considered middle class. This percentage has declined over the last several decades from 61% in 1971 (Cilluffo & Cohn, 2019). Although family income is increasing and is at the highest it has been in 50 years, income for the middle class has not grown as much as higher-income families, contributing to the increasing income inequality (Cilluffo & Cohn, 2019).

Families in the middle class often maintain this status due to the economic contributions of both partners and the support of social networks that help care for their children (Zinn et al., 2011). Needs assessments and program planning should consider financial, transportation, and time constraints to ensure that family life education be made affordable and accessible to all families.

Gender

Whereas sex is related to one's biology, gender refers to socially learned attitudes, behaviors, and expectations, as well as social and cultural meanings attached to men and women, which have links to class and race. There are two approaches to view gender. Whereas the *social roles approach* perceives gender differences as roles learned by individuals, the *gendered institutions approach* examines how gender is embedded in our society, resulting in advantages and disadvantages in various parts of our social and work realms (Zinn et al., 2011). Both approaches have implications for family life education. It is important to be inclusive of men and women in your programming and avoid making assumptions about gender roles within the family. Using the word "parent" rather than "mother" or "father" avoids a parent feeling excluded by gender-specific language. Some cultural groups may have gender-specific norms that will influence FLE programming. For example, Arab American women may prefer to have a female family life educator (Ads & Blume, 2022).

Race and Ethnicity

The US Census Bureau commonly uses the terms *race* and *ethnicity* to classify the population. Whereas race is a socially-constructed category based on a presumed common genetic heritage resulting in distinguishing physical characteristics, ethnicity refers to a broader group of people who share common origin and culture such as religion, language, history, dress, food, and other values (Zinn et al., 2011). Note: Census questions about race and ethnicity have evolved over time as have our views about racial and ethnic identification. While several different questions were tested, the 2020 Census asked respondents to identify their race and whether they are of Hispanic origin (Hispanic, Latino, or Spanish) in two separate questions. There are some critics to this approach because it classifies young people with mixed Hispanic and white origins only as Hispanic and therefore "non-white" in "census terminology," while most of them recognize and experience themselves as part of the white majority and are treated as such. The result of these census questions is perceived to overinflate the minority share of the population and ignore the assimilation process. As a result, Whites can become anxious because of the perceived decline of the white majority and thus they are less likely to support immigration (Scommegna, 2020).

The US population is comprised of over 331 million people belonging to various racial groups (see Figure 3.2), and is projected to become even more ethnically diverse in the next 50 years (US Census Bureau, 2020). In fact, estimates suggest that the US will become a *plurality nation* in which the non-Hispanic white population will continue to be the largest single group, but no group will be in the majority by 2045 (Vespa et al., 2020). The fastest-growing racial or ethnic group in the US is people who are of two or more races; this group is projected to increase 200% by 2060. The next fastest group is Asians, which is expected to double, followed by Hispanics and Blacks. The only group expected to decrease is the non-Hispanic White population, which is predicted to decline by 19 million people, yet will still be the largest racial group (Vespa et al., 2020). Hispanics remain our nation's second largest group (behind non-Hispanic whites), representing almost

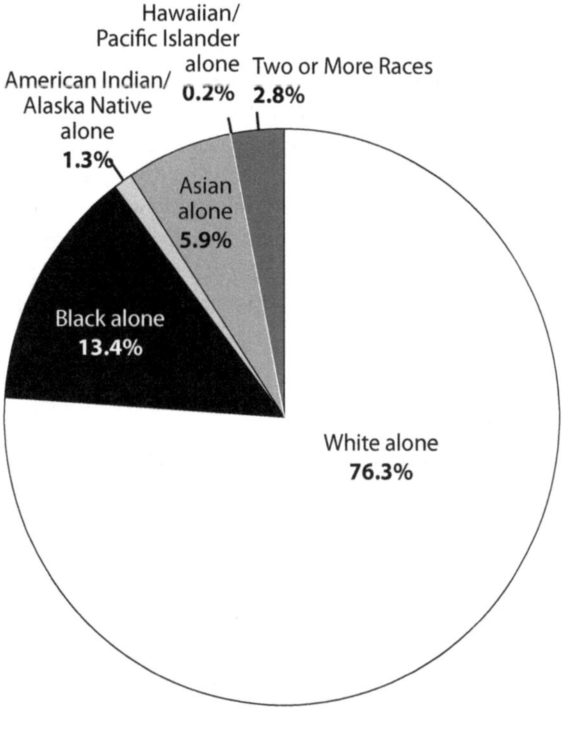

Figure 3.2 United States Population Characteristics

18% of the total population. White Americans are people of the US who "perceive" themselves as white. According to the US Census Bureau, Hispanics can be anyone who says they are (Lopez, Krogstad, & Passell, 2020).

Since race and ethnicity configurations within the US population are in flux, educators need to pay attention to the changing demographics, strengths, and needs of families. Many characteristics of racial/ethnic families are culturally unique, such as how members relate to each other, perceive family, spend leisure time, and worship, as well as their forms of entertainment, language use, and customs (Ballard & Taylor, 2022a).

Because a single chapter cannot convey all the information needed to understand the characteristics of multiple cultural groups, a few highlights have been noted below along with our recommendation to review other sources, such as Ballard and Taylor's (2022b) book on *Family Life Education with Diverse Populations.* This book provides insight about how family life educators can meet the needs of 12 diverse populations.

Black and African American Families are terms that are often used interchangeably and will be used to note those persons with African and non-African Black racial characteristics. The African American heritage emphasizes collectivism and importance of groups of people working together for the well-being of the family through raising children and pooling resources. Black families remain strong and resilient with extended family support networks, along with religion and spirituality as major assets that provide hope and resources to families. These resources include financial and emotional support, caregiving, help with household chores, and transportation, along with encouragement and advice (Baugh & Rajaei, 2022). Work and educational achievement are valued highly, as education is perceived as a pathway to success. Black families face undue challenges as a result of systemic racism and persistent discrimination. However, they are resilient so planning programs that highlight this quality as well as a strong racial identity is important for implementation of programs. Family life educators can partner with community leaders and the faith community to assist with the planning, implementation, and delivery of culturally relevant programs (Baugh & Rajaei, 2022).

Hispanic and Latino Families are terms that are used interchangeably, but there is a difference in that *Hispanic* refers to a person with ties to Spain, whereas *Latino* refers more to persons of Latin American origin, although there is an overlap between these two groups. As a result of criticism of both Hispanic and Latino, the term *Latinx* has emerged as a gender-neutral and inclusive term; however, many individuals of Latin American origin do not identify with the term Latinx (Noe-Bustamante, Mora, & Lopez, 2020; Schvaneveldt, 2022). Hispanic/Latino Americans are racially diverse and therefore constitute an ethnic category, rather than a race. Latinos value educational attainment, which may be related to level of acculturation or the level to which persons have developed a balance between their traditional culture and the majority culture. Family strengths include *familismo* (a strong emphasis and connection to family members and willingness to help them); *simpatia* (politeness and importance of pleasant interactions); *personalismo* (personal space and closeness expressed by shaking hands, hugs, a little kiss, and touching); *machismo* (males are patriarchal figures in the family who provide for and protect family members); and *marianismo* (females are sexually conservative and focused on children and family) (Schvaneveldt, 2022). Religion is also important to Latinos, especially Catholicism, which may be a factor in their low divorce rate (approximately 30% lower than the general population). Challenges include immigration, language barriers, transportation, and financial support and can be used to provide opportunities for family life educators to intervene and impact Latino families. Because there is considerable diversity in the Latino culture, programming should be developed for the characteristics of the cultural groups being served. Rather than using programs developed for the majority culture, family life educators should use some of the programs that have been developed or adapted for the Hispanic/Latino culture (Schvaneveldt, 2022).

Asian Families are quite diverse, with the five largest immigrant groups coming from China, India, the Philippines, Vietnam, and Korea, respectively. Some came to the US voluntarily as students and later sponsored additional family members, while others came because of political and/or unstable conditions in their countries of origin. Asian families value educational attainment and employment, with 49% of Asian Americans holding professional positions (Fong, 2008). However, some who were educated in their home countries have been unable to find employment in the US and had to take lower status positions due to language barriers (Paik et al., 2017). Women may have better language and job skills than their husbands. As a result, their employability may result in higher contributions to their family income than their husbands', which may create tension for their husbands who view their wives' earning abilities as a threat (Xia et al., 2013).

Family structures are often patriarchal, involve the extended family, and emphasize harmonious interpersonal relationships. In general, the family unit is valued along with family loyalty. Due to the periodic adjustments and changes of foreign-born Asian family members, they have learned to be highly resilient. Asian families desire a stable family for their children, but tend to keep family issues private within the family system and do not want to disclose any problems that would disgrace the family. Thus, they are more likely to become involved in family life education that is focused on parent-child relationships, rather than marriage relationships, and to participate in small groups in which they can ask questions that would not be perceived as challenging an authority figure (Hwang, 2022). Partnering with schools and planning programs for the whole family can be effective strategies that align with Asian family values (Hwang, 2022). Involving the entire family might also be a good option because of recent hate crime attacks on solo Asians as they engage in their communities. This has resulted in anxiety, fear, and anger which might be another topic for family life education programming (Petri & Slotnik, 2021). These attacks have been stressful on the Asian community and may influence the participation of Asian families in FLE programming.

Indigenous Families are diverse, as there are 574 federally recognized tribes in the US, as well as numerous other tribes that are not federally recognized (Allen, Duncan Perrote, & Feinman, 2022). Population estimates suggest that 60% to 65% of American Indians live in urban areas, but that may be skewed because recent economic difficulties have resulted in a migration back to reservations where the tribal communities and extended families can provide support (Hildebrand,

Phenice, Gray, & Hines, 2008). Population estimates may also vary because in some tribes American Indian women who marry non-American Indian men are removed of their tribal status (Krouse & Howard, 2009). Additionally, differing definitions of "urban" and flawed measurement strategies can result in under or over-counting Indigenous people living in urban areas (Lobo, 2009).

The primary strengths of Indigenous families are their extended family structures, humor, and resilience (Allen et al., 2022). While tribes have their unique features, a common characteristic is their sense of humor and telling of stories. Many Indigenous youth avoid problem behaviors; engage in prosocial behaviors, such as interacting with family and helping at home; and participate in school and community events. Resiliency in youth has evolved due to positive self-esteem, maternal warmth, family structure, and a sense of direction and tenacity (LaFromboise et al., 2006).

Challenges faced by Indigenous families include trauma from many sources (cultural, historical, intergenerational) and can range from a single event to multiple victimizations resulting from various forms of trauma over the years (Bigfoot, 2008). Some current issues faced by Indigenous families include health challenges such as chronic disease and mental health concerns (CDC, 2018a). Poverty has a wide range of negative impacts including graduation rates, teen pregnancy, gang involvement, mental disorders, suicide, substance abuse, incarceration rates (Cross & Cross, 2015), and intimate partner violence (Burnette & Renner, 2016; Weahkee, 2010).

Family life educators need to get tribal support and build on family strengths while paying attention to participation barriers including time, child care, transportation, and weather. Building trust is critical. Modes of learning include storytelling, shared experiences, observation, participation, discussion, and offering information either directly or indirectly with educators who are respectful, humble, and do not talk too much (Allen et al., 2022).

Family Structure

There are numerous configurations of families within our culture which, because of their family structure, have unique needs. In the US, a White, heterosexual, two-parent, married, nuclear family is often held as the standard and the ideal family form, also known as the Standard North American Family (SNAF). As a result of being thought of (often unknowingly) as being superior, the SNAF enjoy a level of *family privilege* that other family structures do not (Letiecq, 2019). Family privilege can be defined as the benefits that someone receives by belonging to a family system that has long been thought to be superior to all others (Letiecq, 2019). The concept of family privilege is connected to other forms of privilege such as *White privilege*. White privilege refers to the automatic advantage a White person has in our society as compared to a non-White person (Collins, 2018). The concept of privilege is not meant to impose guilt in those who hold privilege, but rather to recognize the role that both privilege and disadvantage can play in attitudes, opportunities, and resources for individuals and families. As family life educators, it is important to examine our own level of privilege and how that might impact our work with other families. Rather than perpetuate inequities and stereotypes, family life educators should value all families and provide equitable opportunities. Family life education is not just for the SNAF, but for all families of varying family structures such as unmarried parents, families with adopted children including transracial or transcultural adoptions, transnational families, foster care families, grandparents raising grandchildren, multigenerational families, older children (or so-called "boomerang" children) still living at home, and mixed-race families. Three family groups we will briefly highlight are single-parent families, stepfamilies, and same-sex or transgender-parent families.

Single-Parent Families constitute about a fourth of family households that contain children (Pew Research Center, 2015), with 23% of children living with only their mother and 4% living only with their father. A single parent does not live with a spouse or partner, but has daily responsibilities for raising a child or children and is considered the primary caregiver. Between 2010 and 2018, the percentage of children living in single-parent families increased slightly from 34% to 35% (Annie E. Casey Foundation, 2020a). Single parent families can result from separation, divorce, child abuse or neglect, adoption, death of a partner, or being an unmarried parent. While some single parents have never been married, most are divorced and report more negative life events, greater social isolation, more difficulties with parenting, more daily hassles, and lower levels of psychological well-being than when they were married (Amato, 2000). Single parents have new responsibilities, such as providing for their families, building new support networks, and incorporating aspects of the other parent into their parenting endeavors (Peterson, Hennon, & Knox, 2008).

Divorce is often associated with behavioral, psychological, and academic problems among the children. It is not just the marital dissolution, but also the number of transitions (e.g., multiple divorces, relocations, cohabitations of parents, and remarriages) that have affected the child's stability (Amato, 2010). However, children's adjustment after divorce can be facilitated by harmonious family relationships by both residential and nonresidential parents who are positively involved in their children's lives. Strong relationships with parents and other extended family members before and after the divorce can minimize negative effects of divorces on children (Jackson & Fife, 2017). Children benefit when they have close and supportive relationships with nonresidential parents, but more important than social contact is the involvement of both parents in authoritative interactions with their children, such as talking to them about their problems, providing emotional support, assisting with homework and everyday problems, setting rules, and monitoring behavior (Amato, Kane, & James, 2011). Additionally, the impact of parental divorce on children may vary depending on race, SES, and relationship with parents (Demir-Dagdas, Isik-Ercan, Intepe-Tingir, & Cava-Tadik, 2017). While co-parenting can be a challenge, some parents use technology (phone, email, and texting) to share information when living in separate households and needing to communicate asynchronously (messages are sent and received intermittently over periods of time). For couples in effective co-parenting relationships, communication makes it easier to plan and make joint decisions about their children. Divorce education programs focus on improving the co-parenting relationship and are often implemented by family life educators (Schramm & Becher, 2020).

Whereas couples generally negotiate responsibilities for work, caregiving, and housekeeping, single parents may be responsible for all of these tasks, resulting in work-family conflict. Lack of reliable transportation and adequate child care can make it difficult for single parents to maintain stable employment. Higher levels of parental education are strongly associated with better outcomes for children, however in 2017, 45% of single parents who were not cohabiting had a high school diploma or less (Livingston, 2018b). This work-family conflict contributes to poverty, unstable living arrangements, and family stress. In general, single parents are "time challenged" with their multifaceted roles and the lack of a "back-up" parent.

While single parents are often reported to be disadvantaged and do less well than two-parent families, there are different kinds of single-parent families, such as a teen mother or a mature professional who is a single parent by choice and design. In some families, a parent may be cohabiting with the father of the child or in a visiting relationship when parents date, but do not co-reside (Osborne, 2005). Additionally, using family structure to define single parenthood does not portray the processes that occur in parent-child relationships. When examining stable single mother-child relationships, it was found that mothers and children characterized their relationship as highly intense, exclusive, and interdependent. Because of limited resources, there were shifting dynamics of power and dependence where children adopted an ethic of care, although mothers worked to maintain boundaries (Nixon, Greene, & Hogan, 2012). Further attention is needed regarding father-child relationships because of the increasing percentage of fathers who are single-custodial parents.

While it is difficult for single parents to find the time to engage in family life or parent education classes, they can get information through pediatricians' or family physicians' offices; parents, friends, and relatives; and mass media, such as TV, books, magazines, and pamphlets. In addition, parents, relatives, and friends can provide not only support, but also information. Single parents need diverse sources of information and may benefit from online websites, programs, and webinars that they can schedule into their hectic lives.

Stepfamilies are families in which one or both adult partners bring children from a previous relationship. Terminology can be an issue for some families and professionals. The term *stepfamily* is problematic to some because of stereotypes of "wicked stepmothers" from fairy tales about Cinderella and Hansel and Gretel, along with Shakespearean plays, but it is the term of choice because it is consistent with the naming of other family types as defined by parent-child relationships. While some prefer the term *blended families,* it provides unrealistic expectations that a new family will quickly "blend" and mesh together to form a harmonious family group. Thus, this terminology may make some aspects of adjustment more difficult (NSRC, 2013). Other terms that have been used are reconstituted, combined, merged, remarried, extended, or expanded families. Children in stepfamilies are referred to as siblings (biologically related); *stepsiblings* (related through the marriage of their parents); *half siblings* (share one biological parent); *mutual children* (child born to the remarried couple); *residential stepchildren* (live with the remarried couple more than half the time); and *nonresidential stepchildren* (live with the remarried couple less than half the time).

Because the US Census Bureau discontinued providing estimates of marriage, divorce, and remarriages, it is difficult to estimate the number of stepfamilies. However, estimates of the percentage of children under 18 years of age who live in a stepfamily range from 9% (Payne, 2019) to 16% (Pew Research Center, 2015).

For adults, new partners are thrilling, but if there are children from a previous relationship there is minimal time for the couple to adjust and build a relationship because of the demands and needs of their children. One of the most difficult aspects of stepfamilies is the parenting of children who experienced loss and change with the addition of a stepparent into their lives. Forming a stepfamily with young children, who thrive on cohesive family relationships, may be easier than with adolescent children, who may be seeking to disengage from the family to form their own identity (Kemp, Segal, & Robinson, 2013).

Some challenges for stepparents include differences in parenting, discipline, and lifestyle, which can be frustrating for the children. Common differences in stepfamilies include (1) age differences in children in which step siblings may be close in age resulting in changes in roles, responsibilities, and birth order; (2) parental inexperience if a stepparent has never been a parent; (3) changes in family relationships especially if both parents remarry partners with existing families so children have different roles in each family; (4) difficulty in accepting a new parent especially if a child has spent a long time in a single-parent family; (5) coping with the demands of others when dealing with custody considerations and arrangements for family events, vacations, parties, or trips; (6) changes in family traditions as most families have different ideas about how holidays and special events should be celebrated; and (7) parenting insecurities of stepparents who may be anxious about how they compare to the biological parents (Kemp et al., 2013). Stepfamilies need clear and safe boundaries, especially when disciplining children. It is important to determine the role each parent will play in raising their respective children and dealing with household rules. Keeping all parents involved is essential among biological parents and stepparents, along with open and frequent communication. Creating new family routines and rituals helps to unite family members. While focusing on the needs of the children in a stepfamily is important, building a strong marital bond is also critical. If children see love, respect, and open communication, they will feel more secure. To better understand the complexity of stepfamilies, see the activity in Box 3.2.

With the increasing prevalence of stepfamilies and the family privilege held by "first families," stepfamily functioning is an important topic for family life education seminars for professionals that deal with families (e.g., teachers, school and family services personnel, counselors, psychologists, and attorneys). Some topics to include in these programs are effective co-parenting strategies with previous partners and the new parenting team; establishment of a support system; interhousehold relationships; empathy in adjusting to different family histories along with negotiation of roles and rules; the role of children in initiating or exacerbating conflicts; and navigating marital partner and parenting transitions, not-

Box 3.2 Changes in Family Structure and Complexity

Create several small groups of 3 to 7 members depending on the number of students in your class. This may result in 4 to 6 family groups.

These groups will become hypothetical families (e.g., intact nuclear families, extended families, and single parent families) with various assigned family incomes. Each family group will take a brief period of time to bond by creating a family name and describing some of the characteristics of their family, such as whether or not one or both parents work and in what kind of job/position they are employed; ages of the family members; the kind of house (number of bedrooms and bathrooms); chores for family members; and a favorite family activity, meal, and holiday including their traditions.

After the family groups are established, randomly assign each of them a difficulty such as divorce, remarriage, or the formation of a stepfamily. Some of the parents and children will be repositioned to join other family groups or have a family that is reduced in size.

Ask these new family groups to decide on a family name, if changed, and determine custody and visitation of children. How will they negotiate shared use of household space; expectations about chores; and participation in activities, rituals, meals, and holidays.

After discussing some of these changes, have the students share their feelings regarding the dissolution of their original families and changes in rules, roles, incomes, available household space, rituals, and holidays. How did they negotiate the incongruent lifestyles between their two families? What insights did they gain about the complexity of family changes?

ing that relationships evolve slowly and often dyadically rather than as a family unit (Adler-Baeder & Higginbotham, 2020). There are few family life education classes available for stepfamilies and many leaders do not initially have training in family life education, but have had personal experience in stepfamilies (Adler-Baeder, Robertson, & Schramm, 2010). When recruiting low-income participants for classes for stepfamilies, use of personal contacts can be the most effective strategy along with a curriculum that addresses the unique needs of stepfamilies. Incentives such as meals, monetary support, and prizes, as well as children's participation and their enthusiasm for attending also positively affect recruitment (Adler-Baeder & Higginbotham, 2020).

Lesbian, Gay, Bisexual, Transgender, and Queer or Questioning (LGBTQ) Families are often invisible in our culture. While heterosexual persons are attracted to people of a different sex, gays and lesbians are attracted to persons of the same sex, and bisexual persons are attracted to someone of both a different and the same sex (Maurer, 2022). Transgender is a general term that groups together people whose gender identity and/or expression is different from their birth sex. A transgender identity is not based on medical procedures and does not imply any specific form of sexual orientation, as transgender persons may identify themselves as heterosexual, gay, bisexual, or asexual (Pew Research Center, 2013a). While there is no precise determination of the size of LGBTQ population, estimates range from 4.5% to 6% (Goldberg et al., 2020; The Williams Institute, 2019). However, data are difficult to obtain because they exclude single gays and lesbians, some same sex couples who reside together, and those who do not self-identify as being transgender. There is an estimated 1.4 million American adults (0.6%) who are transgender people (Flores, Herman, Gates, & Brown, 2016), however, data for transgender persons are not often collected.

Whereas approximately 37% of LGBTQ-identified adults have had a child at some time in their lives, about 6 million children and adults have an LGBTQ parent (The Williams Institute, 2019). In the past decade there has been a surge in the amount of research conducted on LGBTQ families. LGBTQ family systems are vulnerable to many negative situations, such as job discrimination, harassment, isolation, stress, suicide, violence, and homelessness, as well as estrangement from family, friends, and places of worship (Bosley & Ranck, 2019; Movement Advancement Project & SAGE, 2017; Pew Research Center, 2013a).

A special aspect of LGBTQ families is their diversity, experiences, and unique legal status regarding discrimination and economic benefits (Maurer, 2022). They also have some family challenges related to negotiating family of origin concerns and issues of estrangement, building families of choice, and navigating in a complex world of peoples' reactions and assumptions of LGBTQ persons. Nevertheless, the wellbeing of children of LGBTQ parents is unrelated to parental sexual orientation, so children of LGBTQ parents are just as likely to flourish as children of heterosexual parents (Gartrell & Bos, 2010). LGBTQ families are perceived as resilient because of having to negotiate stressful situations throughout their lives. Transgender parents face the critical issue of disclosing their transition to their children. It is suggested that they be open and honest, discuss it in age-appropriate ways, and have continuing conversations (rather than just one) regarding this transition (Hines, 2006).

There are few family life education programs specifically for LGBTQ individuals and families and they may be hard to find. Checking with support organizations, mass media magazines for LGBTQ parents, and LGBTQ community centers is recommended, as well as engaging with LGBTQ leaders in the community (Maurer, 2022). Contacting groups can be helpful, such as *Parents, Family, and Friends of Lesbians and Gays* (*PFLAG.org*) or *Children of Lesbians and Gays Everywhere* (*COLAGE.org*), which includes their *Kids of Trans* (KOT) program. Since confidentiality is an issue, online courses may be a viable option. Educators should know general definitions and terminology; provide accurate, useful, and nonjudgmental content; establish a safe place (e.g., supportive, confidential, and knowledgeable); and incorporate appropriate terms (e.g., partner, parents), pronouns (e.g., based on the transgender person's gender expression and preference), and nongendered names (e.g., Chris, Pat, Leslie) into examples (Maurer, 2022). By attending to the social perceptions (e.g., stigma, discrimination, economic strain) and familial issues (e.g., boundary ambiguity, social support) of LGBTQ individuals and families, family life educators can provide meaningful programs for this cultural group.

Families of Children with Disabilities

Families of children with disabilities is a broad topic because children have many different kinds of disabilities that deal with physical movement, emotional issues, and sensory inabilities, such as sight or sound. Families of children with disabilities have unique parenting challenges. There has been considerable research on the stress associated with children's emotional, developmental, and behavioral disorders, which can have a substantial impact on the lives of family members (MacInnes, 2008). In the US, it is reported that 17% of children under the age of 18 have developmental disabilities, with males having twice the prevalence of developmental disabilities compared to females (Zablotsky et al., 2019). These disabilities can range from mild (e.g., asthma) to severe (e.g., cerebral palsy with extensive neurological complications). In 2018–2019, about 7.1 million American school-age children had a disability and 4.3 million had a disability that was seriously limiting (Woodworth, 2020). The US depends on families to provide medical care to their children with disabilities along with access to education in order to maximize their potential and equip them for adult life. However, the family's financial security, the parents' relationship, and the needs of other children in the home can all be stretched to the limit. Both mothers and fathers of children with disabilities report significantly greater amounts of parental and marital stress compared to parents of children without disabilities. In fact, couples that are together when their child is born are more likely to divorce than other parents and more likely to have a lower family income (Hodapp & Krasner, 2010; Hogan, 2012).

Mothers of children with disabilities often become the primary caregivers, whereas fathers are more likely to work longer hours, have two jobs, or continue working beyond retirement age to support their families. While we often focus on mothers because of their greater caregiving roles, fathers of children with disabilities also experience parenting stress, stress from family life events and changes, and a reduction in life satisfaction compared to fathers who do not have children with disabilities (Darling, Senatore, & Strachan, 2011). Siblings grow up in homes with fewer resources and greater expenses and while they learn to assist with personal care that results in developing more helpful attitudes and tolerance, siblings are at risk for health problems. They are three times more likely to experience poor health compared to children in homes where there is no child with a disability (Hogan, 2012).

While the birth of a child with a disability is often stressful (see Box 3.3), stress changes during the life cycle. As children with disabilities mature and develop over time, their families face multiplying needs, services, treatments, and costs. Additionally, their families are continually engaged with multiple systems (e.g., medical, legal, educational) and involved in Individualized Educational Program (IEP) meetings, which along with the parents may include teachers, school district personnel, and guidance counselors; psychologists or educational evaluators to explain test results; related professionals providing various types of therapy; and social workers, case managers, and others that the family wants to involve. While the IEP team has an annual review of each student, any member can call a special meeting of the team. All of this adds to the complexity of family life and the potential for feeling overwhelmed. Parents of older children with disabilities face significant challenges finding suitable training and employment for their adult children. Many of these parents continue to provide support for their adult child with disabilities, but wonder who will provide that support when they are no longer able to do so (Hogan, 2012).

Box 3.3 Parenting a Child with a Disability

To better understand the culture of parents who give birth to a child with a disability, this analogy can be helpful.

> There was a young woman who was going to France after she graduated from college. She took classes in French and studied about French history, geography, music, culture, and cooking. She had a Facebook friend in France, studied books about the best places to visit in France, bought clothes that would work in the French climate. She prepared and prepared and prepared. Finally the big day arrived and she boarded a plane to fly to Paris. However, en route to France there was a major transportation strike that resulted in an indefinite closing of airports, railroad stations, bus stations, and roads. So, the plane landed in Italy instead. She did not know the language, culture, or customs.

How do you think she feels?

> When a child is born with a disability, it is as if the parents plan to go to France and end up going to Italy instead. (Source unknown)

While there are many challenges to raising special needs children with several stressful demands, one cannot assume that this challenge is largely a negative experience. Some families perceive a positive benefit from parenting a child with disabilities. Fathers have reported learning some unique aspects of rearing their child with disabilities and that gaining new information from their child's condition was rewarding. Many families report being closer; resilient; engaging in more shared activities, such as games, television, and meals; and had a renewed outlook on life (Darling et al., 2011; Hogan, 2012).

Family life educators need to focus on the strengths of families with special needs children and understand how stress influences the entire family system and ecosystem. Each type of disability and its severity comes with its own unique challenges. At times educators may need to provide information about coping with stress, financial management, the couple relationship, and/or raising a child with special needs. Some parents, who may be isolated from the outside world and overwhelmed with childcare, may want some respite from daily tasks in order to find a balance in their lives. However, other parents may not only feel burdened by work responsibilities and competing demands to provide for the family, but also perceive personal challenges in raising a child with disabilities. Thus, family life education programs might provide what each parent needs, such as stress release for mothers and father-child sessions so fathers can interact with other fathers about their personal challenges and learn about parenting a child with disabilities, while sharing bonding experiences with their children and doing things together (Darling et al., 2011). In other words, family life educators may need to focus on mother, father, couple, and sibling needs separately or jointly in order to best provide for the family system.

Families with an Incarcerated Family Member

Families with an incarcerated family member are dealing with a complex and stressful situation. The term incarceration is used as an umbrella term related to incarceration in either a *jail* or *prison*. Whereas a *jail* is a local correctional facility used to confine persons before or after a judicial decision or a sentencing for primarily misdemeanors (usually one year or less); a *prison* sentence is mostly for felonies (usually more than one year) (Bureau of Justice Statistics, 2010). Approximately 2.3 million people were incarcerated in the US in 2018 (Sawyer & Wagner, 2020). With 698 per 100,000 individuals incarcerated, the US rate of incarceration is one of the highest in the world (Sawyer & Wagner, 2020). About 5.1 million (7%) of US children experience the incarceration of at least one parent during their childhood (Annie E. Casey Foundation, 2016). Because 60% (over 2 million) of these imprisoned men and women are parents of minor-age children, there are major implications for their family well-being (Charles et al., 2021; Harcourt-Medina & Mulroy, 2022). Most incarcerated parents report having some form of contact with their children either by telephone (71%), mail (76.5%), or personal visits (49.6%). If there is a positive relationship prior to being incarcerated, then continued contact and support is likely (Loper, Clarke, & Dallaire, 2019). Moreover, the family of a newly released prisoner often acts as a buffering agent, so including parent-child interaction opportunities is important for a parenting program to be effective (Loper et al., 2019; Purvis, 2013).

Incarcerated parents recognize the financial (e.g., loss of income, legal fees) and emotional hardships (e.g., feelings of abandonment, anger) associated with their incarceration (Correa et al., 2021). Prisoners' families and children also have to deal with feelings of shame and social stigma. To help with this situation, *Sesame Street* has developed a video and toolkit to explain incarceration to younger children (*Sesame Street*, 2013). Upon re-entry into society, there are additional challenges of supporting a family member who has been recently released, such as providing financial and emotional support, which can result in financial strain and increased anxiety for family members.

A primary concern is the care of prisoners' children. When parents go to prison, children often live with relatives who may be elderly. There is a marked absence of men in their lives, along with limited financial resources. Many grandparents become caregivers, but they may be elderly, may have health problems, and were not planning on new childcare responsibilities. Incarcerated parents want to maintain a relationship and communication with their children but often encounter barriers such as limited phone privileges, distance to the prison, lack of transportation, and conditions of the visitation such as visitor "pat downs" and long wait times (Correa et al., 2021; Harcourt-Medina & Mulroy, 2022). Furthermore, the children's guardians may limit or deny communication, so incarcerated parents fear their children will be taken from them or someone else will replace them in their children's lives (Hairston, 2002).

Children of incarcerated parents are at increased risk for internalizing behaviors (e.g., depression, anxiety, withdrawal) and externalizing behaviors (e.g., delinquency, substance abuse), along with cognitive delays, school difficulties, and increased risk for insecure attachment (Eddy & Poehlmann, 2010). Given the potential for long-term risks and consequences for these fragile families, evidence-informed prevention and intervention efforts are needed (Shlafer, Gerrity, Ruhland, & Wheeler, 2013).

While family life educators are professionally prepared to advocate for and develop multifaceted family programs, the term "family life education" has only recently been applied to the programs and initiatives designed for inmates and their families. Family life education programs include parenting classes for incarcerated parents, parent-child visitation programs, mentoring children of incarcerated parents, and relationship education. In recent years, there has also been an increase in reentry programs which provide education and support with integration back into society upon release from prison (Harcourt-Medina & Mulroy, 2021). While family life educators would be professionally qualified, they also need to be strong, determined, and confident individuals in order to teach these participants (e.g., correctional staff, volunteers, inmates, and family members) about parenting from a distance, stress and coping, and developmental characteristics of children (Harcourt-Medina & Mulroy, 2021). However, before beginning any program related to incarcerated individuals and their families, a needs assessment is essential.

We have included some brief comments about a few different family groups including their strengths, challenges, and suggestions for family life educators. As you can see, there is much to consider prior to teaching a diverse group of participants/learners. However, it would be impossible to know everything about multiple cultural groups, so to emphasize that point the following activity might be helpful. Blow up several balloons of different colors (with multiple balloons of each color) and have them in the classroom as participants enter. Explain that a certain color designates a particular group, such as Black families, Asian families, Hispanic/Latino families, Indigenous families, LGBTQ families, families of military service persons, single-parent families, families of incarcerated persons, and families of disabled children. Have the participants stand as you toss the balloons to them and ask them to keep the balloons in the air. Although all class members are trying to keep these multiple balloons in the air, it is logical that some will drop to the floor. Leave them on the floor and later discuss how it felt to keep all the balloons in the air at once and how it felt to have some "slip through the cracks" and fall to the floor. This experience is indicative of simultaneously dealing with multiple cultures. As hard as you try, you will not know all of the *little c* issues of cultures and may not be able to totally meet everyone's needs as you would desire, but it is important to work toward this goal.

■ SUMMARY

Within this chapter on understanding your audience in family life education, we have outlined the steps in conducting a needs assessment, paid attention to the role of culture and the *Big C* and *little c* of cultural paradigms, and examined the characteristics and needs of various groups based on developmental stages and generations. We introduced the concepts of implicit bias and microaggressions and the importance of interrupting these negative forms of communication if they occur in your FLE programming. It is important for teachers, as well as participants, to keep in mind that "words matter" whether we are talking about race, ethnicity, country of origin, physical or mental disabilities, physical characteristics (height, weight, birthmarks), or gender. Being an effective educator involves being careful, thoughtful, and deliberate about positive communication. It is so easy to speak without thinking. Words have the power to excite, inspire, anger, or give hope to others, so what you say matters. Paying attention to and understanding your audience and their needs is an important component of family life education.

Answers to the question on page 67: What items are generalizations vs. stereotypes? Numbers 2, 4, 5, 8, and 9 are stereotypes.

■ QUESTIONS AND ISSUES FOR DISCUSSION

1. Think of a time when you worked with someone of another culture or age group. What things did you or they do that facilitated a good working relationship?
2. What are examples of cultural groups in the US and what do you know about them (e.g., family, work, school, church, clubs, classes)?
3. What is a stereotype about your race or ethnicity that displeases you and why?
4. What are some generalizations and stereotypes related to various cultural groups?
5. What are some examples of microaggressions that you have observed? Did you or anyone else say anything to challenge the microaggression?
6. How would you manage a situation when a person says something negative about a race; ethnicity; physical disability; or other personal, familial, or group characteristic?
7. What are some common myths and stereotypes of stepmothers, stepfathers, and stepfamilies?
8. What stepfamily issues have you seen emerge with the people you know living in this type of family?
9. How well do you fit the characteristics listed for your generational group?
10. What single parents have you known and how did they manage their roles?
11. How would you handle a situation when some balloons (people of different backgrounds) "drop to the floor" and you could not handle all the various cultural issues that you are presented?

■ ACTIVITIES

1. Search the internet for popular articles on different generations (e.g., Baby Boomers, Generation X, Millennials/Generation Y, Generation Z, Generation Alpha).
2. Choose an ethnic group from your community to research in the library and on the internet, looking particularly at marriage, family experiences, and customs.

Then interview three or four persons from that ethnic group. Using the Family Life Education Framework in Appendix A, choose one of the categories (e.g., interpersonal relationships or families in society). Formulate a set of interview questions about the category across the lifespan that will help you examine how the chosen ethnic group experiences the developmental tasks articulated under that category.

3. Discuss how you would conduct a needs assessment for a parenting class (e.g., stepfamilies, single parents, incarcerated parents) using different methods (e.g., survey, interview, focus group, or other creative ideas). What generally can you learn about the participants (e.g., developmental needs, abilities, learning styles, and unique characteristics)?
4. Discuss the felt needs that were identified through the assessment process. What other needs (ascribed, future, developmental) should also be addressed in the program?
5. Watch a television program in a language that you do not speak. What do you think occurred in this program? What cues did you use to make your observations? How accurate do you think your observations were?
6. What do you think people from other countries perceive of American values, behaviors, and culture?

4

Settings in Family Life Education

Diverse Settings in Family Life Education

While the *Domains of Family Practice Model* examines the *Why, What, When, For whom,* and *How* of family life education, it does not address the issue of *Where* family life education is practiced (Myers-Walls et al., 2011). One reason is the variety of settings in which family life education (FLE) occurs. FLE is relevant to people where they live, work, and spend their time, such as within schools, faith-based organizations, health care, the military, and in the community. It can be an *approach* applied to address familial issues and topics and therefore can occur in a variety of settings and contexts. The almost endless potential for family life education venues creates both challenges and opportunities. In many settings, the nature of the work of persons practicing FLE may not be defined as FLE per se or recognized as such. As discussed in Chapter 2, this lack of a clear identity can make it difficult to find employment even though FLE often is or can be an appropriate and successful approach in a variety of settings. In order to understand the settings in which family life education occurs, this chapter will provide some examples of the variety of places in which family life educators and practitioners are employed, and will include some personal statements from family life educators working in these settings.

So where do family life educators work? It is important to profile family life educators due to the evolution of the profession and increasing student and academic interest in FLE. Therefore, in 2007 the National Council on Family Relations (NCFR), sponsored a "Job Analysis Study" (n=918 respondents) to examine the professional practice of Certified Family Life Educators (CFLE) (56.7%) compared to noncertified family professionals (43.1%) (Darling et al., 2009). A second study was conducted in 2014 (n=420 respondents) which included both CFLEs (80.6%) and other family professionals (19.4%) who were not certified (NCFR, 2014).

One element examined in both studies was the *organizational structure* of the employment settings of family professionals, which has not changed appreciably during this period (see Table 4.1). Most were involved in nonprofit settings followed by government and for-profit. The *primary focus of their organizations* was also similar and included education, intervention, and prevention. Both the 2007 and 2014 job analyses showed the *primary practice setting* of most respondents was in educational settings (post-secondary), with the *primary area of practice* being college/university education. However, these data may be less a reflection of where family life educators practice and more about the fact that, due to the academic nature of NCFR, respondents to the NCFR survey were more likely to practice in academic settings. Additionally, while family life educators and the CFLE program are known in the academic community, neither term is commonly used outside of NCFR and family science programs. Beyond education (48.7%; a combination of higher education and birth to secondary education), the second most frequently mentioned primary practice setting was community-based services (20.9%). Primary areas of practice were diverse, with formal education (colleges/universities and K–12) accounting for 23.5%, with the remaining 76.5% of the primary areas of practice attributed to a wide range of options including parenting education, counseling/therapy, child and family advocacy, health care and wellness, youth development programs, military family support, drug and alcohol prevention, employment assistance, along with a large array of other areas of practice. The variety of settings in which family life educators are employed indicates the multiple areas of practice in which they engage. The ages of the clients in these settings were predominantly young adults (ages 19–30) and adults (31–64), however the data also show that most respondents serve more than one age group (65.6%).

Although FLE focuses on education and not therapy or case management, many family life educators work in settings that combine more than one professional domain. As demonstrated through the Domains of Family Practice Model, intervention settings can provide opportunities for a preventative or educational approach. Providing student internship opportunities in a wide variety of employment settings and sharing strategies for obtaining positions can be helpful. In addition, promoting family life education within community and work settings can also advance the field. For further employment settings and career opportunities for family life educators, such as child life, work-life balance, youth development programs, after-school programs, academic advising, and college student-life programs, see Appendix D as well as NCFR's Career Opportunities in Family Science Infographic (NCFR, n.d.-b).

Table 4.1 Primary Practice Settings and Areas of Practice for Family Professionals: 2009 and 2014

Characteristic	2009 (n=891)	2014[a] (n=420)
Organizational Structure[a]		
Nonprofit	52.4%	54.5%
Government	32.7	31.6
For-profit	14.9	14.0
Primary Focus of Organization[a]		
Education	66.3%	65.6%
Intervention	13.6	15.1
Other	9.5	9.9
Prevention	10.6	9.4
Primary Practice Setting[a]		
Education (Post-Secondary)	35.9%	31.3%
Community-Based Services	20.9	20.9
University Extension/outreach	NA	11.1
Education (Birth through Secondary)	12.8	10.6
Other	6.5	8.4
Government/Military	5.1	6.7
Faith-Based Organization	6.5	4.1
Health Care & Family Wellness	4.0	3.9
Private Sector	8.1	3.6

(continued)

Table 4.1 *(cont'd.)*

Characteristic	2009 (n=891)	2014[a] (n=420)
Primary Area of Practice[b]		
College/University Education	19.3%	16.7%
Parenting Education	11.9	11.7
Other	7.2	10.5
Cooperative Extension/Community Ed.	4.9	8.1
Counseling/Therapy	8.8	6.4
Early Childhood Education	4.7	5.7
Marriage/Relationship Education	7.0	5.0
Child & Family Advocacy	3.9	4.3
Health Care & Wellness	1.9	3.1
K–12 Education	4.2	2.9
Aging/Gerontology	2.4	2.9
Ministry	1.5	2.4
Family Preservation	1.8	1.7
Youth Development Programs	1.4	1.7
Community Action/Service	1.4	1.4
Domestic Abuse/Violence Prevention	1.1	1.4
Child Care/Preschool	1.1	1.2
Nutrition Education & Counseling	.3	1.2
Sexuality Education	1.4	1.0
Work-Life Balance	1.4	1.0
Child Life Specialist	1.1	1.0
Drug & Alcohol Prevention	.9	1.0
Housing	.5	1.0
Military Family Support	1.1	.7
Family Law	.3	.7
Employment Assistance	.3	.7
Family Financial Planning & Counseling	.8	.7
Diversity/Cultural Awareness Education	.8	.7
Adoption/Foster Care	1.3	.5
Family Policy	1.3	.5
Criminal Justice	.6	.5
Crisis Hotline	.3	.5
Program Evaluation & Assessment	.3	.5
Head Start Programs	.8	.2
Victim/Witness Support Services	.3	.2
Pregnancy/Family Planning	.3	.2
Residential Treatment	.2	.2
Recreation	.1	.2
Peace Education	.3	.0
Communication & Writing	.3	.0
Media (TV, Radio, Internet, Film)	.1	.0
Hospice	.1	.0

Table 4.1 *(cont'd.)*

Characteristic	2009 (n=891)	2014[a] (n=420)
Age of Client[b]		
Newborns (less than 1 month)	6.6	14.3
Infants/children (1 month–12 years)	14.2	34.3
Adolescents (ages 13–18)	16.7	36.4
Young Adults (ages 19–30)	27.9	59.8
Adults (ages 31–64)	23.4	55.7
Elderly (ages 65–85)	8.0	22.1
Elderly (over age 85)	3.1	8.9
Do not work directly with families	NA	13.3
Number of Age Groups Served		
1	34.4%	
2	19.7	
3	18.0	
4	9.6	
5	12.3	
6	4.1	
7	1.9	

[a] Rank-ordered by 2014 data.
[b] Respondents could check all that apply. Some people work with multiple age groups.
NA: Data not available.

Adapted from Darling, Fleming, & Cassidy (2009) and NCFR (2014).

Personal Perceptions of Family Life Education Settings

In order to better understand family life education in a variety of settings, family life educators were asked to share how they integrate FLE into their work setting by providing examples of the types of programs they have developed, implemented, and/or taught, or that already exist within their settings; the challenges faced; and the trends that influence FLE programming. These personal statements relate to the primary practice settings noted in Table 4.1, including education, community-based services, private sector or being entrepreneurial, government/military, and health care and family wellness.

Educational Settings

Family life education can be found in various educational settings. Numerous college and university programs have courses pertaining to family life education with several undergraduate and graduate family sciences' programs providing curricula that qualify students for national certification. Family life educators in a university setting may also have unique roles such as teacher training or a director of online teaching. It is also frequently taught in middle and high schools within the Family and Consumer Sciences curriculum. A variety of topics that are becoming increasingly pertinent in school environments include relationships, domestic violence, bullying, character education, sexual health issues, and conflict management. Some components of family life education are also taught in preschool and elementary school environments. For example, early childhood educators often teach about self-esteem, as well as family and interpersonal relationships. In addition, some family life educators receive further training as high school counselors and even serve in international settings. Thus, family life educators within a school environment have opportunities to share new knowledge and skills to help students and families, as noted in the following personal statements.

Higher Education: Teacher Training

An important aspect of family life education (FLE) is the provision of high-quality training and professional development opportunities for educators (Content Areas 9 and 10). In my work for the Office for Faculty Excellence, I do just that. We provide professional development to faculty and graduate students on a university campus. Resources and support are primarily focused on increasing scholarly productivity, teaching effectiveness, and documenting efforts for the tenure and promotion process. In addition, we also assist our campus community with resources for work-life balance and self-care. Being a family life educator helps in this role as I understand that programming should be based on the felt needs of the community and driven by a needs and/or resource assessment.

The programming efforts that I have delivered in this role are aimed at providing mentoring resources and support for faculty. I developed a Faculty Academy in which faculty from all career stages engage with others across campus based on their areas of interest and expertise. Mentees select a primary mentor but have access to other campus mentors as well. A mid-career series was developed to address experiences that faculty encounter after receiving tenure or working for many years (e.g., promotion to full professor, faculty governance, transitioning to administration). With respect to teaching effectiveness, I developed an online course for faculty and graduate students to assess their teaching style and learn best practices for working with diverse student learners. My colleagues and I have also delivered parent education programming to faculty and staff on campus. Typically, there are few resources on campus focused on work-life balance and the impact that satisfaction with parenting has on productivity at work.

College and university faculty are extremely busy, so it can be difficult to schedule programs as there is no "right" time or day that will fit everyone's schedule. Availability changes each semester based on course schedules, required meetings, and other responsibilities. Technology can be a major factor in meeting this challenge. As most faculty and graduate students have access to university provided software, apps, and computer equipment, we are able to provide options for them to access content at any time.

The limited time that faculty have to devote to things outside of teaching, research, and service obligations makes institutional and administrative support and funding all the more important. It is imperative that university leadership find value in professional development opportunities for faculty, encourage them to participate, and provide financial support for faculty development initiatives. I am very lucky that our administrators are supportive and engaged in campus-wide efforts for faculty development.

Eboni J. Baugh, PhD, CFLE
Associate Professor, Human Development and Family Science
Faculty Fellow, Office for Faculty Excellence
East Carolina University
Greenville, North Carolina

Higher Education—Online Teaching

A family life educator in higher education can often experience a variety of interesting opportunities and challenges. I began teaching about families in a classroom setting on a campus that focused heavily on face-to-face interactions with college students in a typical lecture hall. In addition, I have worked in college lab settings with college students as they are taught to work with young children and parents. Currently, I am the director of an online college program preparing family life educators. This program is a degree completion program meaning that most of our students transfer from a community or technical college with a two-year degree. Our degree is offered entirely online which means that students who are enrolled in our program never need to visit campus unless they so choose. Typically, students only come to campus for their commencement ceremony.

This position has many roles such as teaching, service, and research, along with marketing of the program, reaching out to students who are struggling, preparing reports for the university about our major, and serving as the internship coordinator for our seniors. I teach a wide array of courses including Introduction to Human Development and Family Studies (HDFS); development courses (e.g., child, middle childhood and adolescent, lifespan); family theory courses; and professional development; as well as the internship course. Each of these settings is based on understanding the appropriate methodology to guide curriculum development, teaching, and evaluation, all while responding ethically to any challenges encountered.

One benefit of being a family life educator in higher education is the opportunity to not only teach, but also engage in research. Integrating theory, research, and practice through translational family science is paramount for me as a program director in online higher education. Currently, I am working with a team of colleagues to investigate the challenges that our online students face in their respective locations. We work on solutions to their problems one at a time. For example, we have found that instructor quality is the most important factor for students in regard to their perceived success, so we work with faculty to enhance quality engagement with their students.

In terms of challenges, many family life education (FLE) programs at the collegiate level, and particularly Family and Child Sciences (FCS), may experience lower enrollment due to a lack of emphasis on FLE topics at the K–12 levels. Thus, they do not perceive the breadth of future employment opportunities. As director of a program preparing HDFS and FCS majors, I facilitate exposing students to various work environments through internship experiences, organizations, and agencies in their own communities. After students select three settings in which they would like to complete an internship, I work as a liaison between the student and the internship site to secure that placement. These internship experiences are often parlayed into employment opportunities after graduation. As a result, I have had the opportunity to network with many service providers throughout the country. Being a family life educator helps me to not only place students in their internships, but also to make connections with other family life educators across the United States and experience pride in my students' professional accomplishments. When students are placed with supervisors who are also CFLEs, the mission of our program and the CFLE credential can be reinforced during their internship.

A final challenge (or strength depending on one's perception) of online higher education has to do with residency. In many online FLE programs, students are not restricted to living in a particular location and can earn their degrees from the comfort of their own home and community. Although some students struggle with not being in a more traditional face-to-face instructional setting, many find our platform to be engaging as they are able to work and talk with students from all parts of the world. Online learning provides a constant challenge, as well as opportunities for creative problem solving, but having the common interest of HDFS and FLE among these students is a way in which we all connect.

Bethanne Shriner, PhD, CFLE
Professor/Program Director
Human Development and Family Studies
University of Wisconsin–Stout
Menomonie, Wisconsin

Family Life Education in High School Family and Consumer Sciences (FCS) Classes

It is interesting to reflect on the integration of FLE into my current role as a high school FCS teacher. As a Certified Family Life Educator (CFLE) for over 15 years, I have experienced FLE programming from a variety of perspectives at various grade levels, such as the CFLE program at Crossroads College, a faith-based institution that integrated spirituality into its CFLE program. At Concordia University in St. Paul, MN, I taught graduate courses in Methods in Programming FLE and FLE Evaluation. In Oregon, I managed the CFLE program at Warner Pacific University and co-facilitated the development of a master's degree in a CFLE-approved Human Services program. After moving back to Minnesota, I began teaching high school FCS.

When I think about CFLE programming, I often reflect on the 10 content areas which have been deeply ingrained in various program reviews and courses I have taught. The courses we offer students are all electives, though we constantly hear from parents and teachers that "this course should be required." We offer several FLE-related courses such as Interpersonal Relationships and Communications, Child and Human Development, and Personal Finance and Investing. The content of these courses is focused on raising self-awareness for students and reflecting on their families of origin and the contexts in which they live and have developed.

Some high school students have difficulty seeing beyond their own developmental story, including their sexuality and conflicting racial, religious, and gendered contexts that can be experienced within the walls of a large high school. It can be challenging to teach students in an environment with rampant hormones, homelessness, mental and physical health needs, special needs, generalized dysfunction, and variations in parenting from parental abuse to helicopter parenting.

We excel in our focus on interpersonal relationships, which is a theme and priority in all of our classes. Sometimes students in our Interpersonal Relationships classes have complex needs. I don't mind the challenge of trying to love and nurture these troubled students because I feel it is part of our calling as FCS teachers, but it can be draining to try to handle so many different classroom challenges. Our classes can sometimes be more about practicing what we are trying to teach, and not necessarily witnessing students implementing and internalizing the content.

If students were to take all our courses, they would be well adept at understanding family resource management in terms of food, nutrition, clothing, finances, relationships, childcare, vocation, and housing. Given the variety of courses in this content area, students have the potential to gain greater depth in managing life skills as well as interpersonal relationships, which is arguably the foundation for all our classes. Although the curricula in public school programs follow state-mandated criteria, it is clear that FLE is integrated throughout the high school curriculum. The foundational strength and reputation of FCS programming is centered on nurturing human development and interpersonal relationships while teaching vocational skills that can equip them to excel in individual and family resource management.

Michael Jerpbak, PhD, CFLE
Family and Consumer Sciences Teacher
Mayo High School
Rochester, Minnesota

International High School Setting

School counselors are certified educators who can best be described as student advocates (often referred to as multitasking counseling ninjas or magicians, miracle workers, or the heart of the school). We utilize all areas of family life education in our work. School counselors design and deliver a comprehensive school counseling curriculum that improves student outcomes and promotes equity and access for all students. In the United States, we use the American School Counselor Association (ASCA) National Model that is intended to provide guidance in developing curriculum to help students in the areas of academic achievement, personal and social development, and career development. Our work is data driven and involves constant assessment to measure our effectiveness in helping all students succeed.

Counselors trained in the US are present in schools around the world. In order to reflect the international scope that includes best practices from multiple countries, the International School Counselor Association (ISCA) modified the ASCA National Model and added a global perspective. The global domain offers additional content standards that focus on encouraging mindful cross-cultural interaction and intercultural communication. Overall, the ISCA Model incorporates elements that better reflect school counseling programs in a foreign country and addresses the needs of both third-culture students, their family context, and host-country nationals. This is primarily the model I follow as I mostly work in international schools.

Using established standards-based mindsets and behaviors for student success, school counselors deliver developmentally appropriate activities and services that can incorporate family life education. This includes direct in-person interactions such as counseling, classroom activities, and advisement on future career plans. Indirect services are also provided on behalf of the student and include consultation, collaboration, and referrals. An example of an indirect service is giving presentations to parents on topics such as cyber safety, mental health awareness, or other current issues facing teenagers. Another example is maintaining an active database of community resources so that we can provide referral information to our families as needed.

In a perfect world, direct services with students would be about 80% of our time. However, one of the challenges we face is the appropriate use of our time and skills. Often, school counselors are given tasks that take away from our time with students. Examples are master scheduling, clerical work, and coordinating testing programs. This also leads to another challenge—too many students assigned to one counselor. In the US, a student to school counselor ratio of 250 to 1 is recommended. However, the national average is actually 430 to 1 for the 2018–2019 school year (the most recent year for which data are available). High ratios lead to counselors becoming "firefighters" who only have time to put out fires and handle crises. By keeping our ratios low, we can be more proactive and better able to build strong relationships that foster a more nurturing school climate.

I am grateful for the strong family life education foundation that my studies provided. The courses I took perfectly complement the work I do as a school counselor. I learned about typical human development, family dynamics, family stress, the basics of family law, and how to teach others to make good decisions and have healthy relationships. The courses allowed me to better understand larger societal issues such as domestic abuse, family legal issues, substance abuse, and work/family issues among others, as well as how to address them. For example, the course on Human Sexuality prepared me to be able to support students as they explore and question gender identity, gender roles, and their own sexuality. During the course, I also had an opportunity to teach group lessons so that I was comfortable openly discussing what many people would consider a taboo subject. Not only did these courses give me background knowledge, but also the confidence and skills necessary to be effective in my role. I have a more holistic approach in my work that allows me to view the student not only in their school environment, but also their family system, greater community, and society as a whole.

School counselors are leaders within schools, as well as change agents and advocates. We work hard every day to create a school culture of success that allows students to thrive. I am fortunate to have an FLE context within a career that allows me to inspire and empower others and make a difference in their lives.

Katherine Porter, MS, CFLE
High School Counselor

Community-Based Settings

Opportunities for family life education within the community are numerous. It may be offered by the Cooperative Extension Service through short programs, the internet, or media presentations. In addition, various agencies serve multi-need families and have a team of family professionals that work with these families to integrate family life education, family counseling, and family case management. Family life educators may work with foster-care families, the homeless population, or early childhood home-visitation programs. Other community-based family life education programs are offered within various faith-based institutions and can cover a range of topics from adolescent sexuality to marriage preparation and adjustment to aging. Family life educators may often be involved in multiple settings either simultaneously or consecutively as they find new challenges within their current setting or apply their creativity and knowledge in a new setting.

Extension

The mission of Extension within land-grant institutions is to take the research knowledge generated at the university and extend it across the state to benefit the general public. Family life educators are well-suited to serve as Family and Consumer Sciences (FCS) Extension Agents (referred to as Educators in some states) with county, regional, or state-level responsibilities in human development, family dynamics, or family life. Originally, Extension was one of the only sources of reliable, research-based information. However, in the information or digital age, people have access to an unprecedented amount of information. A shifting role for Extension personnel and family life educators is to disseminate research-based information in engaging and accessible ways; connect individuals and families to existing sources of valid and reliable (i.e., research-based) information; and help them become critical consumers of information. We must assist individuals to discern between fact and opinion by teaching them the *ABCs* of evaluating information resources—that is *A*uthoritative, *B*ias-Free, and from Current informational sources.

Unfortunately, in most states Extension is often referred to as "the best kept secret." A challenge for us is to broaden our outreach to meet families where they are, which increasingly occurs by embracing technology and digital outreach strategies. This involves moving beyond disseminating information through Extension publications, such as fact sheets, and instead incorporating dynamic mediums, such as video and audio messaging. It is vital to keep these messages short—one to five minutes each—and emphasize practical information that couples, parents, and others can readily incorporate into their lives. These micro-interventions can easily be shared on social media or pushed to individuals through apps on mobile devices. Digital outreach and micro-interventions should not replace traditional educational workshops or programs, but rather should supplement these approaches.

Another opportunity is to expand our educational efforts beyond solely focusing on direct education to include policy, systems, and environmental (PSE) change strategies. PSE change approaches, which originated in health promotion, have been integrated into Supplemental Nutrition Assistance Program (SNAP) Education sessions. PSE changes strive to affect systems that may act as barriers preventing families from making the changes we are promoting in educational programming. PSE change efforts are consistent with family life educators' knowledge and skills related to "individuals and families in societal contexts" as they address policies, systems, and environments across educational, governmental, religious, health care, and occupational institutions in society. Engaging in PSE change efforts is a great way to work on a local-level to promote family-centered policies and structure systems and environments that benefit families.

In my current work, I am implementing a comprehensive approach that incorporates educational programming with families, digital outreach strategies, and PSE change efforts to build the capacity of parents and professionals by equipping them to respond to the needs of trauma-exposed children and families. Trauma-Informed Parenting and Professional Strategies (TIPPS), is a coordinated program model that includes training workshops for parents (direct education), dissemination of educational messages through digital outreach (to both parents and professionals), and PSE change efforts with professionals resulting in the adoption of a trauma-informed approach to serving children, youth, and families. Family life educators are uniquely equipped with the knowledge and skills necessary to implement this kind of coordinated program model that includes educational programming, digital outreach strategies, and PSE change efforts, a comprehensive approach that meets the complex, dynamic needs of children and families in today's society.

Alisha M. Hardman, PhD, CFLE
Associate Professor, Extension Family Life Specialist
Mississippi State University
Starkville, Mississippi

Multi-Need Families in the Foster Care System

Post-adoption services support families who face the unique challenges of adoption, sometimes long after the adoption has been finalized. Adoption is a lifelong commitment requiring support for all members of the adoption constellation—the adoptive parent(s), the birth family, the child, and the siblings. Questions of identity, loss, and trauma can surface at various milestones throughout the lifespan. Family life education (FLE) continues to be a vital avenue to provide enrichment opportunities, build community supports, and help bridge the gaps toward ongoing adoptive family health. Trauma and evidence-based practices continue to guide curriculum development and are currently being utilized to obtain most funding and state contracts. Practitioners, like myself, work directly with a family to raise awareness of trauma over the lifespan, the impact on brain development, and the influence on attachment. By being with the family as knowledgeable guides, we can offer preventative support and guidance in navigating these difficult topics.

Many families self-refer for post-adoption services. This results in a double-edged sword, as the family is motivated toward services, but can be singularly focused on a felt or ascribed need. FLE practitioners balance the immediate needs of the family with their underlying stress. Utilizing an established assessment tool can help the family recognize underlying stress and identify effective services. For example, a family recently reached out regarding a specific child's need. After completing the assessment using a standardized assessment tool, underlying factors were identified contributing to the presenting need. The family worked to address these factors through a creative use of established community services, which in turn significantly reduced the initial concern. Post-adoption services are unique to each family. One family may need individual support to navigate the onset of puberty, another may require referrals for out-patient family therapy, and yet another may only need access to current training programs. Support groups, psychoeducational training, and special celebratory events help bring people together in the community and embrace their own adoption experience.

Perhaps the biggest challenge in providing post-adoption services is the lack of sustainable funding to develop and promote programming. Only a few states provide tax funds for post-adoption programs, even if adoption is a viable option for families in all states. Work is needed to advance evidence-based post-adoption services as the need continues to rise both domestically and internationally. Although there are challenges, it is personally rewarding as a family life educator to be able to assist these families during the transition after they adopt a child and to see these families succeed.

Jason P. Lehman, MS, CFLE
Post Permanency Specialist, Post-Adoption Support
Church and Community Engagement
Bethany Christian Services of Central Pennsylvania
Lancaster, Pennsylvania

Homeless Population

On an average night in January, the national homeless population exceeded half a million individuals (HUD, 2020). This statistic appears consistent from one year to the next even as efforts to address homelessness and poverty housing are increased. Family life educators, professional service providers, and community advocates are valuable contributors in a coordinated response for this vulnerable population. In my work with programs for individuals experiencing extreme poverty and homelessness, family life education (FLE) has been integrated into efforts that provide critical support in many settings.

Examples of outreach efforts include the following:

- Engaging in "just-in-time" education with homeless individuals in soup kitchens, domestic violence shelters, homeless day centers, city parks, and other locations in the field.
- Collaborating with local nonprofit, social service, and religious organizations to create and distribute laminated community resource cards to increase awareness of local resources and empower the homeless to advocate for their personal needs.
- Consulting with organizers of after-school money-management classes for high school students who live on a tribal reservation. Session topics include banking, savings, budgeting, credit building, and paying for college.
- Training community volunteers to conduct surveys during HUD's annual Point-In-Time count to establish a baseline of the magnitude and needs of the localized homeless community.
- Educating service providers and other community stakeholders regarding the diverse factors that contribute to experiences of homelessness. Providing foundational knowledge of the impact of poverty on protective and risk factors affecting lifetime outcomes from the perspective of key family theories.
- Facilitating a multiweek educational initiative to increase awareness of the causes and experiences of the homeless in order to inform outreach development.
- Guiding the organizational strategic planning process for community stakeholders using a strengths perspective to facilitate evidence-based, informed decision making for development of local outreach priorities and initiatives.

Outreach in the homeless community faces several unique challenges. Transience of client base is a reality that contributes to limited success of outreach efforts. The homeless tend to be distrustful of outsiders, including helping professionals and researchers. Relationship building is the most effective strategy for overcoming distrust but can be difficult to establish due to fluidity of residential tenure. Another challenge is created by limited availability or access to comprehensive support services for those wanting to exit homelessness. This challenge is often compounded by illiteracy or the presence of diagnosed or undiagnosed disabilities.

A general lack of awareness about homelessness is common in many communities. Outreach efforts are critical to establishing a network of informed advocates to provide evidence-based information to frontline advocates, as well as service providers, public policy makers, and those who are experiencing, or at risk of, homelessness. Without accurate knowledge of this social issue, communities are ill equipped to make progress in responding to, reducing, or eliminating experiences of extreme poverty.

While I have observed several trends that influence FLE among the homeless, I have found that a majority of frontline advocates, whether paid or volunteer, have minimal formal or academic preparation for their work. In many situations, on-the-job training is sufficient, but when there is no knowledge of family and developmental theories, advocates lack valuable insight that helps make sense of vulnerabilities present for the homeless. For this reason, it is critical that we prepare students in our FLE post-secondary programs with a strong foundation in translating family theories into real world contexts. With this knowledge, our students will be prepared to confidently enter careers strengthening vulnerable families through education, service, and advocacy.

Janeal M. White, PhD, CFLE, MIE
Coordinator, Southeast Texas Coalition for the Homeless
Southeast Texas Regional Planning Commission
Beaumont, Texas
Internship Coordinator and Visiting Lecturer, Family Science Program
McNeese State University
Lake Charles, Louisiana

Early Childhood Home Visitation

The Early Head Start (EHS) Home-Based Option (EHS-HBO) is a two-generation program, meaning that both parents and children are the focus. The theory of change in home visiting is that the home visitor or family life educator enhances the family's parenting to promote the child's development and health.

The EHS-HBO provides a range of family and child support services to economically disadvantaged families and pregnant women until the child is a preschooler. I provide support to early childhood home visitors through coaching, which is in addition to their regular reflective supervision and professional development activities. It is believed that when home visitors receive professional guidance, they are in a better position to support families. As a CFLE, I coach home visitors to help them reach their professional goals (e.g., earning a degree, supporting their practice) and to promote model fidelity. To coach home visitors regarding their practice, they often video record their home visits, and then we use observation measures to assess the quality of the home visit and parent-child interactions. During coaching, I engage home visitors in processes (e.g., reflective, strengths-based, responsive) that parallel those the home visitors provide to families.

I have helped home visitors to establish and achieve their goals through a myriad of techniques, such as appreciative inquiry, and in turn home visitors reported using these strategies to help families set goals. To coach families, home visitors are expected to have knowledge in a variety of domains; they need to teach families about a particular competency, and then coach parents to apply their knowledge and skills. Coaching is included in most national and some state home visitor competencies and helps parents learn new skills.

When home visitors coach families, they value the parent as the child's first teacher. This includes finding out what a parent knows about a topic and using materials in the home to help families reach their goals. For example, parents interested in doing relaxing and soothing activities with their infant may find infant massage techniques helpful. The home visitor can pose open-ended questions to find out what the parent knows and what materials (e.g., lotion) are in the family's home. The home visitor may use a baby doll to demonstrate infant massage and to help parents practice before engaging in infant massage with their baby. When the parent engages in infant massage, the home visitor can guide the parent in attending to the infant's cues. The home visitor can help the parent notice that the infant in the supine position is nonetheless active and may wiggle their body and lift their head upon having their feet rubbed. The home visitor can help prompt the parent to narrate, maintain, or adjust what they are doing based on the infant's responses. Home visitors set the stage to empower parents to provide developmental support to their child, which ultimately promotes positive child outcomes.

Although the EHS-HBO is effective at strengthening child and family well-being, the statistical results tend to be small to moderate. Home visitors' competencies likely play a part in how effective the model is, so generating more information about the types and effects of home visitors' competencies warrants further attention. Home visitors with the CFLE credential have advanced competencies in 10 FLE content areas, such as child development, parenting, family relationships, a strengths-based approach, cultural humility, and ethical processes to their work with families in the contexts of primary, secondary, and tertiary prevention efforts. One challenge is that the CFLE credential is not yet currently recognized at local and national levels as an advanced staff qualification and competency requirement for EHS home visitors. The CFLE is a long-standing credential that naturally fits with early childhood home visiting, aligns with many national home visitor competencies, and is an important subject deserving further attention from researchers and practitioners.

Bridget A. Walsh, PhD, CFLE
Human Development and Family Science
University of Nevada, Reno
Reno, Nevada

Faith-Based Settings

In faith communities, the rich tapestry woven by integrating spiritual wisdom with family life education (FLE) can be valuable for promoting healthy family relations, communication, and problem-solving in every stage of family life. Utilizing an approach to empower individuals and families to address life's difficulties with resilience and to educate them toward successful living is an important operation of faith-based fellowship. This culture promotes the strengthening of healthy personal relationships, and relationships with family members and others within our close circles of influence.

Within our local setting, we work to develop leadership in small, medium, and large groups. One-to-one, couple, and larger groups include FLE for premarital education and coaching; good communication and healthy relationship skills in marriage; child growth and development; wise child rearing education for parenting through the years; and healthy work–life balance. We attempt to create a sense of closeness as members learn together and from each other within the context of culture that operates as extended family for the many who benefit from such relational investments.

Our local outreach incorporates an FLE perspective for mentoring "at risk" children in local public schools. We provide support groups to help individuals deal with issues such as addiction and grief. We developed English as a Second Language classes to assist immigrant Latino families and initiated a Spanish-speaking church to promote the benefits of spiritual community.

Some of the greatest challenges that faith-based communities face in contemporary culture are related to work–life balance for families stressed by demands such as dual careers, single parenting, child disabilities, low income, and immigration issues. Added to these strains is the stress of increased participation in extracurricular activities outside of school and home that require adults and children to juggle limited time and energy with needed family, rest, and recreation time. Maintaining strong church-family relationships may also be seen as a pressure point within the context of diminished resources of time and energy.

Integration of FLE into the fabric of local faith communities is effective for influencing healthier work–life balance and lifestyle. Even when family relationships are unstable, strong belief systems and knowledge of family relationships can fill gaping holes during life's challenges and stresses. FLE increases parenting skills to lovingly attend to children's growth and development by creating teachable moments for nurturing truth and wisdom along with supporting healthy maturity and mindset development.

Utilizing strengths-based FLE to enhance resiliency skills and build on what is good and positive can empower members of faith communities to successfully manage their lives and increase the quality of their family relationships. Educational interventions intertwined within faith-based fellowship promote ever increasing spiritual growth; wisdom of family/faith-family cohesion and resiliency; and development of healthy personal, family, and faith-family values and beliefs. Weaving spiritual, relational, and missional growth and maturity into FLE content areas complements positive individual, family, and community functioning and successful living through the lifespan.

Kathleen Helgeson, MA, CFLE
Leadership Development
Village Church of Baldwin
Baldwin, Wisconsin

Faith-Based in Conjunction with Disaster Preparedness

"Braided streams" is the image that comes to mind when working in faith-based settings. This metaphor applies to my educational background, as well as my current work. My studies began with an interdisciplinary major in sociology, psychology, and theology. This was followed by an advanced degree in family life education (FLE), training and supervision as a marriage and family therapist, and graduation from a theological seminary. I have worked full and part-time in various positions such as a family life educator, preschool teacher, therapist, associate director of a family counseling agency, role specialist with a multidisciplinary church renewal center working with church professionals, and as the Lutheran Disaster Response coordinator for northeastern Pennsylvania.

Currently I am the part-time pastor of a small rural/suburban congregation and also serve as a volunteer to help rebuild the local county's community disaster response. In addition, I am an on-call intervention specialist for assisting with disruptions in the workplace. Being a family life educator facilitates working in multifaceted professional roles by providing me with an understanding of individuals and families through the lifespan. I find systems and ecosystems theories facilitate my appreciation of the interplay of economics, mental health, personality, community, and spirituality. Working to develop and support congregational health involves application of systems theory to communities of faith. Commitment to building on strengths, including family strengths, is also critical, along with staying aware of and sharing the perspectives of various professional groups. With my diverse background I am better able to look for many things that can impact people and situations, such as what to expect across the lifespan and how internal and external systems affect individuals and families.

I consider and refer to a broad range of possibilities and resources for response and assistance. For example, in dealing with serious illness and death, I listen for what ways a family might be prepared to handle a situation. What are likely understandings and reactions of various members? What is age appropriate? What is the best way to interact with the medical professionals and funeral directors? What are the pertinent cultural and economic factors? In other words, the integration of FLE into my current settings involves trying to be aware of the many different factors that interface with people's lives as they approach a particular situation.

At church I am continually asking how we can meet individual and family needs while building on their strengths. Besides programming, this concern is reflected in how we set up our newsletter. We have many elderly members who look forward to and really read our articles, so we search for topics that will address their needs and concerns and compose some that will include references to things they remember and cherish. In addition, over the years I have studied, developed, and presented a variety of programs on topics related to children of divorce, couples' groups, confirmation, Sunday School youth, and family finances.

When I served as a Lutheran Disaster Response coordinator for 14 counties, I was responsible for setting up systems for evaluation of situations, assessment of needs, case management, plans for rebuilding, and coordination of volunteer teams. We continually engaged in preventative and preparative work, as well as mental health services. An example of the latter was helping to deliver Camp Noah programs, developed by Lutheran Social Services Minnesota Camp Noah, in numerous locations around the country. These programs are for grade school children who have experienced trauma and disaster. I have also helped to develop a series of trainings for the general public and potential volunteers focused on relating to persons from an ecological perspective and had a major role in developing the current *Congregational Disaster Preparedness Guidebook* for the Evangelical Lutheran Church in America (elca.org).

All of these activities require knowledge of as well as sensitivity to family situations, individual and family development, modes of interaction, educational methods, preparation for future needs and situations, and collaboration with other agencies and government organizations. This approach also needs to be taught to staff and volunteers and shared with other response groups and government agencies.

Currently, all of these streams are being "braided together" as I seek to lead and cooperate with others when responding to the COVID pandemic. I continue to keep informed with the most accurate information about best practices from those who serve communities of faith, clinicians, health providers, family life educators, and other professionals. The use of technology is essential in my quest, along with building confidence in "common sense" and the wisdom gained through the years. Some "old" ways are useful, as are many of the new.

Ruth F. Doty, MS, MDiv, CFLE
Pastor, New Jerusalem Evangelical Lutheran Church
Fleetwood, Pennsylvania

Human Services—HIV Prevention and Reentry Workforce

When it comes to my career, I have learned that the days I go home and say "I love my job" are when I am educating individuals and groups. While working with underprivileged populations, we must not only provide knowledge and technical facts, but also available resources. It is very important to be nonjudgmental when it comes to convictions, homelessness, substance use, and health barriers. I welcome everyone to my classroom or office, and they leave with more knowledge.

Starting off my career in the world of HIV prevention, I met with individuals in testing/counseling sessions and taught workshops. There are not many professions in which you can perform a blood test on a client and provide results within minutes. I had to begin each appointment and class on the "right foot," often assuring clients that they came to the correct place and that our agency would be there for them. HIV treatment has evolved greatly during the past years and now is a diagnosis someone can live with if caught early and if they have the appropriate support, including education on safer sex and drug use practices, regular doctor visits, medication, food to help bodies process medication, and stable housing. The "Healthy Relationships" workshop I taught was an evidence-based program implemented by the Centers for Disease Control. Another favorite aspect of my work as a family life educator working in HIV Prevention was teaching LGBTQ Inclusive Sexuality Education. For a few years I advanced to an administrative position in fundraising and agency operations, and while I enjoyed it, I didn't love it as much as daily interaction with participants.

Currently, I'm working as a Workforce Development Instructor for Goodwill Industries. Goodwill's mission involves serving those who have employment challenges. When you shop or donate to Goodwill, you are helping people learn job skills. I work at the Goodwill Education Center and teach week-long classes to individuals reentering society from incarceration. When people returning to society are taught job skills and provided opportunities to earn certifications, they are more likely to find steady work and less likely to go back to jail or prison.

Students in my class have two objectives: to pass a nationally recognized Customer Service and Sales exam (earning a credential) and to enhance employability skills (e.g., creating resumes and cover letters, conquering interviews, addressing background, creating goals). After passing the exam and becoming Customer Service and Sales Specialists, qualified individuals have the option of completing a work experience with Goodwill. I meet with these individuals weekly to discuss their performance and suggest improvements for the next week.

Teaching and working with people are my strengths and there's nothing better than my students saying, "I couldn't have done this without you." Hopefully if I wasn't around, the participants would meet another family life educator or family professional who would be willing to give them similar respect, guidance, and knowledge.

Adrienne Lira, BS, CFLE
Workforce Development Instructor
Goodwill Industries of Greater Grand Rapids
Grand Rapids, Michigan

Previously HIV Prevention Specialist
CARES
Kalamazoo, Michigan

Private Sector: Entrepreneurs

Because stress and strain at home can negatively influence work performance, companies work to assure that men and women are able to succeed both at home and work. This means that companies are being more attentive to providing family life education programs for their diverse employees. In addition to corporations becoming more involved in family life education programs, some educators have seen the need for targeted services in their communities or states and have started their own consulting firms or educational organizations to provide services to families, corporations, and communities.

Entrepreneurship plays a vital role in the US economy, with 15 million Americans being self-employed (Simovic, 2019). Although it was projected that by 2020 there would be 27 million self-employed individuals, the data for the post-pandemic era are still unknown. Most entrepreneurs (86%) are motivated by opportunity rather than necessity, with 97% reporting that they would never go back to traditional employment. Approximately 67% of entrepreneurs attended college, but most do not have a business degree (Lange et al., 2018).

In the past few years there has been increasing interest by family professionals and FLEs in starting their own businesses. According to the 2014 NCFR Job Analysis Study, 11.9% of employed family professionals were self-employed (NCFR, 2014).

Entrepreneur—Personal and Professional Development

As the CEO of a personal and professional development company that focuses on trauma-informed education and resilience building, I seamlessly integrate family life education (FLE) into our planning, program development, and evaluation. The overarching goal in all our programs is referred to as a *Trauma-Informed Handle-with-Care Approach to Resilience.* In using this lens, we are intentional in our understanding of the interaction between individuals, families, communities, and broader social institutions in order to pinpoint opportunities to educate and support. Our programs target families as well as individuals in helping professions (i.e., social workers, therapists, educators, law enforcement, foster families, faith-based workers). Therefore, we are heavily influenced by current trends in mental health, social health, trauma, and resilience. We watch these trends very closely as they keep us informed of the latest research and help to focus and refine our programs with greater intention.

We have developed and implemented programs such as Exploring Secondary Trauma in Helping Professions, Overcoming Intimate Betrayal, and The Resilience Thread. We are also a part of a statewide collaborative that educates communities on the neurobiological impact of adverse childhood experiences (ACEs). Through collaborations we are learning that many individuals are unclear as to how they personally add value to building resilience and mitigating the impact of trauma both locally and abroad. This issue is proving to be a "tough nut to crack."

We are working hard to find tangible ways to highlight the importance of individual contributions for the collective good. For example, we have a Family Life course that explores the familial effects of individual decision making and its impact on family culture and cohesiveness. This particular course serves to give families tools needed to create a family culture conducive to well-being and togetherness. As an FLE, I have learned to take theoretical concepts and make them practical and user friendly for diverse populations in ways that resonate with family systems and professionals alike. I sincerely hope that through continued research and collaboration, we are able to view resilience as the norm instead of the need. When I look at the big picture of what we do and why we do it, everything from start to finish is saturated in family life education.

Naketta Lowery, BS, CEO, CFLE
Sustainable Life Solutions LLC
Rosedale, Maryland

Entrepreneur and Author: Parent Education

As a second-generation parent educator, I have been involved in family life education (FLE) since I was 8 years old and in professional FLE practice for over 40 years. During the first 20 years, I started and managed nonprofit FLE programs, while in the last 20 years I have been involved in government-funded FLE programs and created FLE programs and resources as a self-employed entrepreneur. I have developed several research-based outcome-evidenced curricula for parents and parent educators, including trauma-informed curricula for foster parents and caseworkers. I have also trained and supported FLEs worldwide who are either using my curricula or want to learn how to create their own programs and resources. Other than funding and income sources, there has been very little difference in the FLE activities I've conducted for nonprofits versus for-profits.

Everything I have done professionally relates to FLE. Obviously, the curriculum/program development, training trainers, and direct services I provide to parents and family life educators through training and coaching are clearly related. Whether starting a nonprofit organization, conducting an FLE program as a nonprofit employee, being a trainer consultant to the state, or operating my own private practice as an "entrepreneur," I use all the skills family life educators have (or need to have)—and more. Once, I recognized "bad" advice on a lunchtime news segment and wrote a letter of concern to the station. They called me to the station to meet with them and at the end they hired me as the assistant producer and parenting expert for a new local parenting tips TV show! That opened the door to literally hundreds of other media opportunities. So, you never know when your FLE training will be needed or where it might lead you.

When my nonprofit grant funding ended and I started my own private business, I saw myself as a social worker, so I sought out training and coaching with experts in the different areas I needed to succeed, such as publishing, speaking, marketing, and internet skills. I learned that the most effective business model focuses on relationship-building, and the most effective marketing strategies do not focus on sales. Instead, you want to use education-based marketing that informs people, builds a relationship with them, finds out what they need, and then helps them solve their problems, which is exactly what family life educators do. It was then I realized that being an FLE had prepared me well to be even more effective in reaching and serving families than a sales and marketing degree would have. They might know how to give a pitch or close a sale, but FLEs know how to connect, assess, and serve people, which are more important and effective long-term.

Although I had the right mindset and skills to succeed as a family life educator, figuring out how to transfer these skills to business and marketing tasks was still a huge challenge because of the social stigma that comes with "parenting classes" and other FLE programs. Many of the experts' strategies did not work as well with family life educators compared to clients in traditional business fields. I was repeatedly advised to change fields so I could succeed. Stubbornly, I refused and through years of expensive training and trial-and-error, I began to determine what worked. Fortunately, many of the family life educators I have trained and coached have the dedication and persistence needed to learn these new skills and take the fundamental prerequisite steps that would better ensure their success. As a result, they had gaps that caused a failure to launch, or they ended up spending a lot of money hiring people who could fill their gaps.

Self-employment and entrepreneurship are very real and viable options to earn one's living, especially given its family-friendly, work-from-home, flex-time options. Now, with so many people working from home and families facing many COVID-related challenges, it's a great time to try online methods of reaching and serving families. Since most every person in the world has a family or some related relationship, there is an almost endless supply of potential clients for family life educators. That is why more people with a passion for parenting or families are entering the FLE field wanting to start their own business/practice. If they approach it like a job, expecting others to magically come to them rather than taking charge of their own future and taking self-initiative, they often do not last long enough to launch. If they already have a "business mindset" and know-how and don't take the traditional college-degree path to the profession, they might succeed faster and better, but lack the needed FLE training and/or professional standards, ethics, and competencies, which is a concern.

Many family life educators who take the entrepreneur path will only focus on marketing strategies, which given the internet, has endless and ever-changing possibilities. That's only one area needed to succeed. The first and most important step is to have an evidence-based, proven-effective, top-quality service or program that is delivered through a well-run business. Then, use a relationship-building business model and education-based marketing to be more successful and feel more authentic in whatever FLE role you might have.

Jody Johnston Pawel, BSW, LSW, CFLE
President, Relationship Toolshop International Training Institute, LLC
Author, Speaker, Coach
Springboro, Ohio

Government and Military Settings

Government involvement in family life education can occur for many different reasons. At times, the courts are involved and may require certain courses such as mandated parent education. Additionally, the prison systems may offer various courses for prisoners or families to assist with their reentry. Various programs also exist for military personnel and their families.

There are three types of mandated family life education, although only two are mandated by the court system: *mandatory education for a "voluntary" role*, such as caring for a foster child, adopting a child, or accepting a foreign exchange student; *education for risky family situations*, such as mandated education for divorcing parents or parents taking a child home after a medical procedure; and *mandated education for parents or families judged as inadequate*, such as parents who have been found to be abusive and/or neglectful (Myers-Walls, 2022). It can be difficult to identify the strengths of some parents and families mandated to participate in family life education, but this can be a positive turning point for families and provide hope for making a difference. In addition, mandated programs have linkages among courts, agencies, and educators to assist families in need.

Because incarceration of a family member can result in a family crisis, family members of incarcerated individuals have often been referred to as "hidden victims" (Martin, 2017). Children of the incarcerated family member often face numerous problems. In fact, they are six times more likely to become incarcerated themselves. As a result, various programs, which are often voluntary, have been created for prisoners and families of prisoners.

Military members and their families comprise one of the largest workforces in the US. There are approximately 3.5 million military personnel with about 2.6 million family members (US DOD, 2018). These families face multiple challenges such as geographical separation, isolation, and relocation, which is particularly an issue for the children of military personnel. These changes affect family roles, spousal employment, stress, mental health, and social support networks, as well as children's education and relationships (Lucier-Greer & O'Neal, 2022). In addition, there is the risk of injury or death, traumatic brain injuries (TBI), and post-traumatic stress disorder (PTSD). Military families have the advantage of living within a system that values and supports individuals and families. Improved family policies and support have increased the level of commitment to the military of both the soldiers and their families (US DOD, 2009). Various programs exist for marriage and relationship education, family resource management, parenting education, and the development and education of children (Mancini, O'Neal, & Lucier-Greer, 2020).

Military Settings: Supporting PreK–12 Students of Military Personnel

School transitions and deployment support are Navy readiness and retention issues. The Navy benefits from having sailors who are able to focus on their duties, whether ashore or deployed. Relocating a school-aged child presents its own unique challenges and responsibilities. Some challenges include obtaining the correct course credits for graduation, understanding special education to include the Individualized Education Program (IEP) process and Section 504 of the Rehabilitation Act, and navigating school options. Even though military families move, on average, every 2.9 years and their children attend up to nine different schools by graduation, they are becoming more resilient individuals. This might be because local schools are increasing their understanding of military culture and implementing more social and emotional support resources, largely as part of the School Liaison Officer (SLO) Program.

The School Liaison Officer's primary function is to serve as a conduit between parents, educators, and the command so that military-connected children experience a seamless transition during the transfer between schools. SLOs assist with inbound/outbound school transfers, help to train parents and educators on state/local legislation, provide professional development training on military culture for school leadership/staff, and address concerns/questions of military families related to PreK–12 in local school districts. There are seven core services of the School Liaison Officer: School Transition; Deployment Support; Command, School, and Community Communications; Home School Linkage and Support; Partnership in Education (PIE); Post-Secondary Preparations; and Special Needs System Navigation.

In my work as a School Liaison Officer, I work collaboratively with area schools promoting positive school climates. I assist in the Youth Sponsorship Program, providing access to positive peer groups and social activities and help military children feel connected to their new community. When service members receive military orders for their next duty station, the first, and arguably the most important, question is "where will my child go to school?" SLOs work with families on how to successfully choose a school, integrate into their new school system, and develop "School-Based Programs" to help new students feel welcome and involved. I have had the opportunity to inform parents, educators, and the military command on military resources and support systems so that military-connected children experience a seamless transition during their transfer between schools.

It is my responsibility to understand the changing needs of the local military community and be familiar with the resources available to them. In this position, I have had the opportunity to work collaboratively with many local military leaders in a variety of settings to help them understand and address the current challenges (and highlights) of the military community. I also collaborate with many military-focused organizations and learn how they work together to support our service members.

As a CFLE in this position, I have established strong community connections to better serve families. I have learned to help equip and empower families to develop knowledge and skills that enhance their well-being, strengthen interpersonal relationships, and become their families' best advocate. (For a complete listing of the School Liaison Directories, please visit: www.dodea.edu/partnership/schoolliaisonofficers.cfm.)

Kelly D. Frisch, BA, CFLE
Regional School Liaison Officer
Command Navy Region Southwest
San Diego, California

Prison Settings

As a Certified Family Life Educator (CFLE), I have taught relationship education in several different prisons and currently implement relationship education in the Pitt County Detention Center for both men and women (in separate classes). With this current era of mass incarceration, we are seeing more and more families impacted by incarceration, and there is an increased focus on strategies to reduce recidivism. Healthy relationships are an important factor in reducing recidivism rates, but we rarely see prison programming with this focus. Family life educators are beginning to integrate the prison system (mostly by way of parenting education), but there is limited research on existing programs. In my experience, incarcerated individuals welcome relationship education classes with open arms. They are excited to learn how to better communicate, reduce stress, utilize positive co-parenting techniques, and often note that their family and partners on the outside can notice a difference in their behavior.

Teaching in a prison is not without its challenges. It can be difficult to get approval from individual wardens and/or the Department of Corrections, and there are often issues surrounding clearances and class schedules. Even when scheduled, there is the possibility of some sort of facility lockdown or other circumstance that will prevent the class from occurring (e.g., I once drove three hours to a class, only to find the prison was on lock down and there was no civilian entry for the day). Once in the prison or jails, you may also experience other disruptions such as medical emergencies, food trays arriving and resulting in an abrupt end to teaching, or officers entering to do checks. Participants may be pulled out of class at any point, or they may leave the facility all together (e.g., court appearances, transfers, release). While the facility may require training prior to the family life educator becoming involved, family life educators wanting to work with this population are encouraged to seek out additional training from other educators to prepare for what to expect, appropriate ways to respond, and effective modes of learning.

Even with the challenges, this continues to be the most rewarding family life education (FLE) experience I have yet to encounter. I can see the difference it is making in the lives of the participants and I hope that FLE will continue to expand across prisons and jails. As a participant in a previous class wrote, "I have never been more excited about something besides going home and it has been better for me since I've been in this class. I have learned so much about myself as a person that even I was surprised, and for that I am thankful. I do hope and pray that the healthy relationship class will continue." Offering FLE in prisons and jails has the long-term goal of providing incarcerated individuals the knowledge and skills to successfully reintegrate back into society with their families after release. As family life educators, we should support policies that expand the offerings of these types of programs to improve current and future quality of life at the individual and community level.

Kate Taylor Harcourt-Medina, PhD, CFLE
Family Life Educator, Pitt County Detention Center
Associate Professor
Department of Human Development and Family Science
East Carolina University
Greenville, North Carolina

Health Care Settings

There are a variety of health care settings that are amenable to family life education. Some of these may be collaborative with health professionals—such as nurses, health educators, and child life specialists—since family development and functioning are an integral part of health and wellness. Family life educators may work in public health programs and services, hospital-based family support, nutrition education programs, prenatal and maternity services, holistic health centers, long-term care settings, and hospice programs. There is a broad range of health-related topics pertinent to individuals and families, such as managing stress, learning about sexuality and contraception, and understanding death in the family. In addition, some hospitals offer programs for new parents and new grandparents.

Family Life Education in a Public Health Setting

Public health systems are commonly defined as all public, private, and voluntary entities that contribute to the delivery of essential public health services within a jurisdiction. The public health system includes public health agencies at state and local levels; health care providers; public safety agencies; human service and charity organizations; education and youth development organizations; recreation and arts-related organizations; economic and philanthropic organizations; and environmental agencies and organizations.

Family life education (FLE) is integrated into public health systems through family/professional partnerships which is a foundational strategy to promote family-centered care. Through this strategy, families have a primary decision-making role in the care of their own children as well as the policies and procedures governing care for all children in their community. Formal positions within public health systems such as Family Liaison Specialist and/or Parent Liaison ensure that family advisory boards or committees guide polices, programs, and quality improvement activities and offer family members training, mentoring, and reimbursement for their participation as active members.

The realization of how health disparities adversely affect groups of people who have systematically experienced greater obstacles to health and the principles of health equity have greatly influenced FLE in the public health setting. While health disparities pose many challenges, they also afford many opportunities for public health policy makers, health practitioners, and educators to increase opportunities to include the family voice in discussions of health and health disparities.

As a CFLE in North Carolina, I have worked in a variety of sectors including both local and state-level public instruction, a university setting, state-level early childhood education programming, and both local and state-level departments of public health. I firmly believe that FLE is a fundamental social determinant of health—an upstream cause of health, and thus representative of an important opportunity for improving health and reducing health disparities.

Heidi E. Austin, EdD, MCHES, CFLE
Project AWARE (Advancing Wellness and Resiliency in Education) Director
Exceptional Children Division
North Carolina Department of Public Instruction
Raleigh, North Carolina

Family Life Education in a Hospital Setting—Child Life Specialist

Child Life Specialists are educated and clinically trained in the developmental impact of illness and injury of pediatric patients. While the focus of my care is primarily the pediatric patient, I also serve the family as a whole. Pediatric patients usually have difficulty coping with stressful and/or traumatic events and gauge their response to an event by their parent's reactions. Serious injury, diagnosis, or death can cause a breakdown in communication and cloud decision making even in strong families. Other stressors like a recent divorce or financial strain along with the medical event can be the tipping point to put a family system into crisis. I rely on my education in Family Stress Adaptation Theory to help families manage both negative and positive stressors, which in turn greatly affects how their child copes with hospitalization and illness. My role helps improve patient and family care and satisfaction. The knowledge I gained from my Human Development and Family Studies (HDFS) degree and being a family life educator helps me do this effectively. In addition to starting the child life program in the children's ER, I coordinate our child-life team, have supervised HDFS interns for over 10 years, and teach an HDFS course on Health Issues in Families.

My training as a family life educator is woven throughout my role as a Child Life Specialist and the services we provide:

- Appreciating a family's culture and context allows for effective care, which is important during times of bereavement and complex medical care. Respecting a family's beliefs and incorporating them into the plan of care leads to a better outcome.
- Identifying factors that influence the relationship between work, personal, and family life relieves a family's stress. For example, providing parents with a medical note for their employers decreases the anxiety of parents regarding their workplace. Advocating for couples to take turns during long patient stays and sharing the burden alleviates some of the stress.
- Understanding the family's strengths and weaknesses in relating to one another is essential. Stress and conflict management become opportunities to help families cope in a more healthy manner. I try to strengthen the family's communication processes and reinforce strategies to help them function more effectively, especially when dealing with non-normative stressors that can cause ineffective family functioning.

- Focusing on the pediatric patients' siblings is important as they are the most often overlooked member of the family during an illness or trauma. If the patient's siblings are not at the hospital during the time of care, I still ask about them. I educate parents on strategies to include their other children and to explain what is going on in a developmentally appropriate manner. Parents often state this part of my care is what they appreciate most.
- Understanding the psychosocial aspects of human sexuality and addressing human sexuality from a value-respectful position is very important. Our region has seen a great increase in sex trafficking victims, so identifying these individuals is key to their recovery and well-being.
- Recognizing the influence of unhealthy coping strategies and the impact of violence in interpersonal relationships is critical. This helps me identify areas that the medical team can use to aid the patient and family in recovering. We have significant substance abuse issues with our teen population. Understanding that teens may be using substances to cope with unhealthy family situations is beneficial to addressing the problem.
- Identifying the family resources needed by parents in our pediatric emergency room is essential. Our pediatric emergency room helps to ascertain which families need resources during the triage screening by asking questions that allow us to connect families to resources that they probably had no idea existed (e.g., food).
- Educating parents constitutes a major part of my day. I provide guidance on helmet safety, car seat safety, safe sleep practices for newborns and infants, counseling resources for issues brought to our attention, and trauma reactions of children and adolescents.
- Understanding family laws and public policy are critical when dealing with divorced or divorcing families, custody issues, diverse family forms, and child abuse.
- Ethically practicing within my scope and collaborating with diverse team members are essential, along with maintaining appropriate personal and professional boundaries. In dealing with conflicting values, it is important to apply appropriate strategies. In my 22 years of experience, there have been many times when I have had to evaluate, differentiate, and apply diverse approaches to ethical issues and dilemmas.
- Knowing your audience is necessary when choosing strategies to identify and meet the needs of a particular audience. For example, I developed a pediatric course for Emergency Medical Services (EMS) and fire departments in our region. This came from a need of patients being unnecessarily traumatized in the field due to lack of education for that age population. The goal of the program was to educate EMS/and fire personnel about age-appropriate content and implement it for all battalions of a local fire department. The evaluations and measured outcomes supported its need. Prior to the class, many staff members identified lack of knowledge, stress, and guilt when providing care to pediatric patients. After the instruction they reported more confidence and knowledge for future pediatric calls.

As a Child Life Specialist during the COVID-19 pandemic I have had to rely on my training in FLE even more. For example, I identified factors that were influencing not only our staff, but also our patients and their families. Media was causing panic and fear. Parents were anxious and not aware that this was causing children/teens to be fearful and have misconceptions of the situation. With help from the Association of Child Life Professionals, I printed and laminated resources for staff on talking to children/teens about COVID-19. Age appropriate resources and a list of websites for families to access for support, tips, and education were a high priority. Within two weeks of children/teens being home full time because of the pandemic, we saw an increase in minor traumas (e.g., falls, lacerations, broken arms) and nonaccidental traumas.

One of the most difficult things to navigate during this pandemic is bereavement. Typically, family members are allowed at the bedside. During the pandemic, no visitors are allowed for adult patients, while pediatric patients can have one caregiver at their bedside. As Child Life Specialists, we work with our teams to provide support for families as a loved one dies. This includes setting up Zoom, Skype, or FaceTime for families to talk to their loved one and providing resources on talking to children about a family member in the hospital that may die soon. It is essential to acknowledge families' pain and frustration at not being with their loved one and give the family options to help children and teens feel connected during such a difficult time. While working during the COVID-19 pandemic, I have been able to advocate for children and their families by educating staff on family-centered care.

It is beneficial for patients and my students that I am both a Child Life Specialist and a family life educator. My students benefit from my experience with patients and their families in the HDFS courses that I teach at a university, and my patients and their families receive better care because of my education in FLE. The skills and knowledge I gained as a family life educator have also benefited the nonprofit organizations I have worked with in the past 12 years. I am grateful to be certified to work with both families and children. It is a win-win and I recommend this to any person working in these fields.

Angela McEvers, BS, CFLE, CCLS
Child Life Specialist for the Children's Emergency Room
Renown Children's Hospital
Reno, Nevada

SUMMARY

Family life education exists, or can exist, in a variety of settings and includes multiple job titles. This means it might be difficult to find employment unless you can understand the range and potential of these settings and how being a family life educator fits into the domain and practice of the profession. It may be necessary for you to articulate the nature and value of family life education as well as the unique skills and knowledge base provided by those with academic training in family science. Each setting has its specific characteristics and challenges, along with many opportunities for creative problem solving. Many times, you will need to "think out of the box" when seeking a position by creating a niche within an existing setting or becoming an entrepreneur to fill a void in services in your community. Family life education is an approach to enhancing the wellbeing of families that can be implemented in a multitude of settings.

■ QUESTIONS AND ISSUES FOR DISCUSSION

1. In what other settings could family life education be included? What content might be covered? How would you promote the inclusion of family life education within this setting?
2. In which institution/organization would leaders be most responsive to offering family life education programs: faith-based institutions, businesses, schools, military, or communities? What are the reasons for your response?
3. As family life education is becoming more collaborative with other professions, what additional preparation do you think family life educators need to be better equipped for their roles in this new paradigm?
4. Since family life educators are employed in a variety of settings, what kinds of job search strategies would you employ?
5. What types of profit or nonprofit organizations in your community offer programs to assist families? Do they provide any family life education or employ CFLEs?

5

Program Design in Family Life Education

Congratulations! You have been asked to teach a family life education program on a particular topic, and because you are qualified and have an interest to teach about this topic, you agree. Now what? Whenever you implement a new program, you engage in three related activities. First you design the program by gathering information and making decisions about the content and the way the program should be taught. You need to analyze the nature of the problem that needs to be addressed by your program, as well as information about your target audience in order to develop a conceptual foundation that is based on relevant theory, research, and teaching methodology. Second, you engage in teacher-student interactions as you implement the program. Third, you evaluate your program to see if it was effective in achieving the desired outcomes. Whereas this chapter will focus on the information you will gather and decisions you will make in designing the program, the following two chapters will deal with the options you have in implementing your program design and methods for evaluation.

Everyone is a teacher in some informal way, whether you teach a child to ride a bicycle, a neighbor to use the computer, or a friend to plant a garden. However, when you have a career involved in teaching others, you do so in a "planned" way and in a variety of contexts—from a traditional classroom or online course to a community seminar or individualized learning.

This chapter focuses on program design, which includes program format and features (e.g., number of sessions), mode of delivery, and the planned teaching strategies and techniques used to teach the content and meet learning objectives (Ballard & Taylor, 2022a). Family life educators may choose an existing program or curriculum and implement it as designed, adapt an existing program to fit the needs of the target audience, or design an original program.

Before you decide whether to design your program, adapt a program, or choose to implement an existing program, the first step is to understand what problem you are going to address. What do your participants want to learn? What are the desired outcomes of the program? Why are you conducting the program? What is your purpose? This will be based largely on the information gathered in the needs assessment (see Chapter 3 for more on conducting a needs assessment) and on the context of the program. For example, were you asked to conduct this program for a particular audience? Did you determine that there was a need that was important to fulfill? Did you discover evidence of an opportunity with this particular audience? What learning theories and learning styles are most applicable to your participants? Answers to these questions will help you to determine the reason and design for the program.

Overview of Learning Theories and Styles

> Tell me and I forget. Teach me and I remember. Involve me and I learn.
>
> —Xun Kuang

Learning Theories

Learning is a complex process that varies for different learners and can be viewed from a range of *theories/conceptual frameworks* that describe how information is absorbed, processed, and retained (Newman & Newman, 2007). There are three traditional categories of learning theory: (1) *Behaviorism* focuses on learning as reacting to external stimuli and is founded on the belief that behaviors can be trained, changed, and measured (Ertmer & Newby, 1993); (2) *Cognitivism* attempts to focus on the process of acquiring, storing, and constructing new information (Steele, 2005); and (3) *Constructivism* views learning as a process of creating new knowledge based on a learner's prior experience when information comes into contact with existing knowledge that has been developed by previous experiences—an approach that has worked well for adult learners (Adams, 2006; Koohang, Riley, Smith, & Schreurs, 2009; Ruey, 2010; Spigner-Littles & Anderson, 1999). *Social constructivism* is socially co-constructed learning that takes place through collaboration, interaction, participation, language, and social negotiation (Vygotsky, 1987). Since learning is considered to be a social endeavor, individuals learn from one another when engaged in the learning process (Jensen, & Frederick, 2003).

Other learning theories have also been developed, such as *connectivism*, which has evolved in the digital age to focus on learning by making connections between specialized information sources and interpreting patterns (Tschofen & Mackness, 2012). Learning theories have added to our understanding of change and how new learning is acquired and maintained. However, they do not consider the developmental level of the learner and his or her physical or cognitive maturation, changing values and goals, and capacity or motivation (Newman & Newman, 2007).

Learning Styles

Because people respond differently to the learning materials that are presented to them, a relevant approach for students and teachers has been the examination of learning styles. *Learning style* refers to an individual's natural or habitual pattern of acquiring and processing information. The focus is not on what participants learn, but how they choose to learn. Individuals have preferred learning styles that can be identified at an early age and remain relatively constant through time (Royse, 2001). Educators need to be aware that their selection of learning experiences may favor the bias of their own learning styles and thus, they should strive to create a variety of educational experiences that would not consistently disadvantage certain students. It is impossible to incorporate every student's favorite learning style, but by teaching in different ways, students can recognize their preferences while developing their ability to learn using other styles. Students need stimulation from many different dimensions. Everyone has a mix of multiple learning styles, but may favor some more than others or use certain ones in specific circumstances.

Incorporating learning experiences to engage multiple learning styles is becoming increasingly popular. Two such learning styles are included in this chapter with a sample application of each that can be used in a variety of settings. It should be noted that older learners, who have years of life experiences, are different from those who are younger, and thus learning styles and methods need to be adapted accordingly.

One seminal perspective is Kolb's (1984) Experiential Learning Theory and his learning styles model, which have helped educators understand human learning behavior and facilitate student learning through the lifespan, and have been particularly influential in the field of adult education (Newman & Newman, 2007; Stokes-Eley, 2007). According to Kolb, learning occurs in a cycle consisting of four modes. Learners can enter the learning cycle at any point and will learn best if they practice all four modes. These learning styles can be conceptualized as forming two intersecting axes (continua) that form a quadrant: the *Processing* continuum ranging from active experimentation (doing) to reflective observation (watching), and the *Perception* continuum ranging from concrete experience (feeling) to abstract conceptualization (thinking). A matrix containing these four modes is noted below (see Figure 5.1).

Kolb's learning theory incorporates the following four learning styles: (1) *Accommodators*, who are doers and feelers, rely heavily on concrete experiences and active experimentation and benefit most from group work and experiential methods, such as field trips, role-plays, and simulations; (2) *Divergers*, who are feelers and watchers, utilize concrete experiences and reflective observation and readily respond to discussions, emotionally moving lectures, and experiential methods such as case studies, service learning, and simulations; (3) *Convergers*, who are doers and thinkers, rely on their skills of abstract conceptualization and active experimentation and enjoy demonstrations, computer-aided instruction, and objective homework problems and exams; (4) *Assimilators*, who are watchers and thinkers, combine abstract conceptualization and reflective observations to excel in organization and synthesis and prefer logical factual lectures, textbook reading assignments, and independent or library research (Nilson, 2003). To assist with determining your learning style according to Kolb's conceptualization, an inventory of Kolb's learning styles can be found online in various locations. As with any learning style, this is a guide and not a strict set of learning strategies, but can be useful to educators as they design their courses and plan for varied learning experiences.

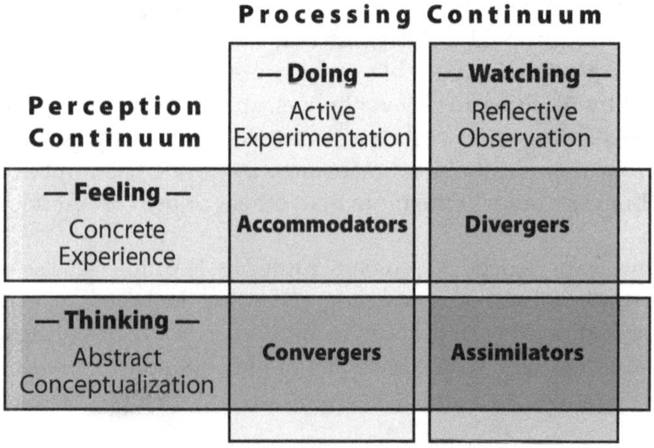

Processing Continuum
— Doing —
Active
Experimentation
— Watching —
Reflective
Observation
Perception
Continuum
— Feeling —
Concrete
Experience
Accommodators
Divergers
— Thinking —
Abstract
Conceptualization
Convergers
Assimilators

Figure 5.1 Experiential Learning Styles

Adapted from Kolb, D. (1984). *Experiential learning: Experience as the source of learning and development*. Upper Saddle River, NJ: Prentice-Hall, Inc.

An example of incorporating experiential learning styles into a parent education setting might focus on the topic of parent-child communication. After introducing a few general guidelines regarding communication, two parents would role-play being parent and adolescent who are attempting to resolve an issue in their relationship, such as getting a cell phone, driving a car, or sharing household responsibilities. The participants can portray these roles in various ways, displaying constructive and destructive communication styles. Afterward parents can discuss what they felt, thought, and learned playing these roles and what suggestions they might have for engaging in similar conversations with their own children. There could be a series of parents doing various scenarios. Since some parents would be playing the part of an adolescent, remembering similar conversations and roles from their own adolescence would provide insight and empathy to how their children feel. These practice sessions can facilitate better communication and reduce tension in the conversations they have with their own children. This activity involves the following:

- *concrete learning experience (feeling)*—learning from a specific experience and relating it to others' feelings.
- *reflective observation (watching)*—viewing the role-play and looking for meaning in the interactions.
- *abstract conceptualization (thinking)*—involving a logical analysis of ideas and acting on the intellectual understanding of the situation.
- *active experimentation (doing)*—getting things done by influencing people and their behaviors through action.

Another pertinent and accessible educational theory is Gardener's Multiple Intelligences (2006, 2011). He claims that rather than a singular measure of intelligence, there are multiple intelligences—we are all intelligent in different ways. While Gardener first reported on seven different kinds of intelligence, he later added an eighth and ninth. People generally possess all of these intelligences for solving problems, but these capacities vary for individuals. The kinds of intelligence are noted below along with some suggestions for teaching strategies.

- **Linguistic Intelligence** (Word smart): Language skills including sensitivity to the subtle meanings of words and written or verbal communications. Incorporating letters, poems, stories, and descriptions might be applicable.
- **Logical/Mathematical Intelligence** (Number smart): The ability to use mathematics and complex logical systems of thinking. Incorporating facts, data, and experiments might be applicable.
- **Musical/Rhythmic Intelligence** (Music smart): The expressive medium and ancient art form of music with its own rules, language, and thinking structures. Incorporating songs, musical games, and song titles might be applicable.
- **Bodily/Kinesthetic Intelligence** (Body smart): Bodily control and skilled handling of objects or tools involving fine or large motor skills. Incorporating dance, role-play, or movement exercises might be applicable.
- **Visual/Spatial Intelligence** (Picture smart): The ability to comprehend the visual world accurately. Incorporating charts, posters, videos/video clips, and cartoons might be applicable.

- **Intrapersonal Intelligence** (Self smart): Understanding one's own feelings and using these insights to guide behavior. Incorporating journals, diaries, and self-assessment measures might be applicable.
- **Interpersonal Intelligence** (People smart): Reading the moods and intentions of others, as well as working well with groups. Incorporating cooperative learning, interactive learning experiences, and giving feedback to others might be applicable.
- **Naturalistic Intelligence** (Nature smart): The ability to recognize and classify living things (plants, animals, and minerals) and sensitivity to other features of the natural world. Incorporating nature walks, plants, and animals, as well as observing changes in the weather might be applicable.
- **Existential Intelligence** ("Big Picture" smart): The ability to use collective values to understand others; see the world around them; and ponder questions about life, death, and ultimate realities. Incorporating different points of view, connections of classroom learning to the outside world, and teaching others might be applicable.

Because people have different styles of learning, there are numerous theories about how individuals learn. Some favor experiential learning, reading, writing, watching demonstrations, videos, or listening to lectures. While the research on learning styles is inconclusive regarding the effectiveness of any one style, knowing that teachers and students have different learning styles can facilitate program planning and enhance learning in your classroom. Students may prefer certain learning styles, but all participants learn better from the incorporation of multiple educational methods. By developing new approaches that will better meet the needs of learners, we can help a wide range of individuals understand their strengths and identify strategies that will stimulate their learning and feelings of success. An understanding of how people learn is essential to the program design process.

The Program Design Process

In previous chapters we have presented content on the diversity of participants (Chapter 3) and settings (Chapter 4) involved in family life education programming. This chapter can be a guide in planning one's course or program. In future chapters we cover information related to implementation, evaluation, and examples of content for family life education programs (see Figure 5.2).

Educational Settings

Before planning for your class it is important to consider if the structure of the class will be in a *formal, nonformal,* or *informal setting. Formal education* refers to teaching and learning in educational institutions, such as schools, universities, technical centers, or early childhood programs. It is systematic, structured, and administered according to certain laws, policies, and norms (Dib, 1988). There is usually a series of courses in a planned sequence, grades based on performance in

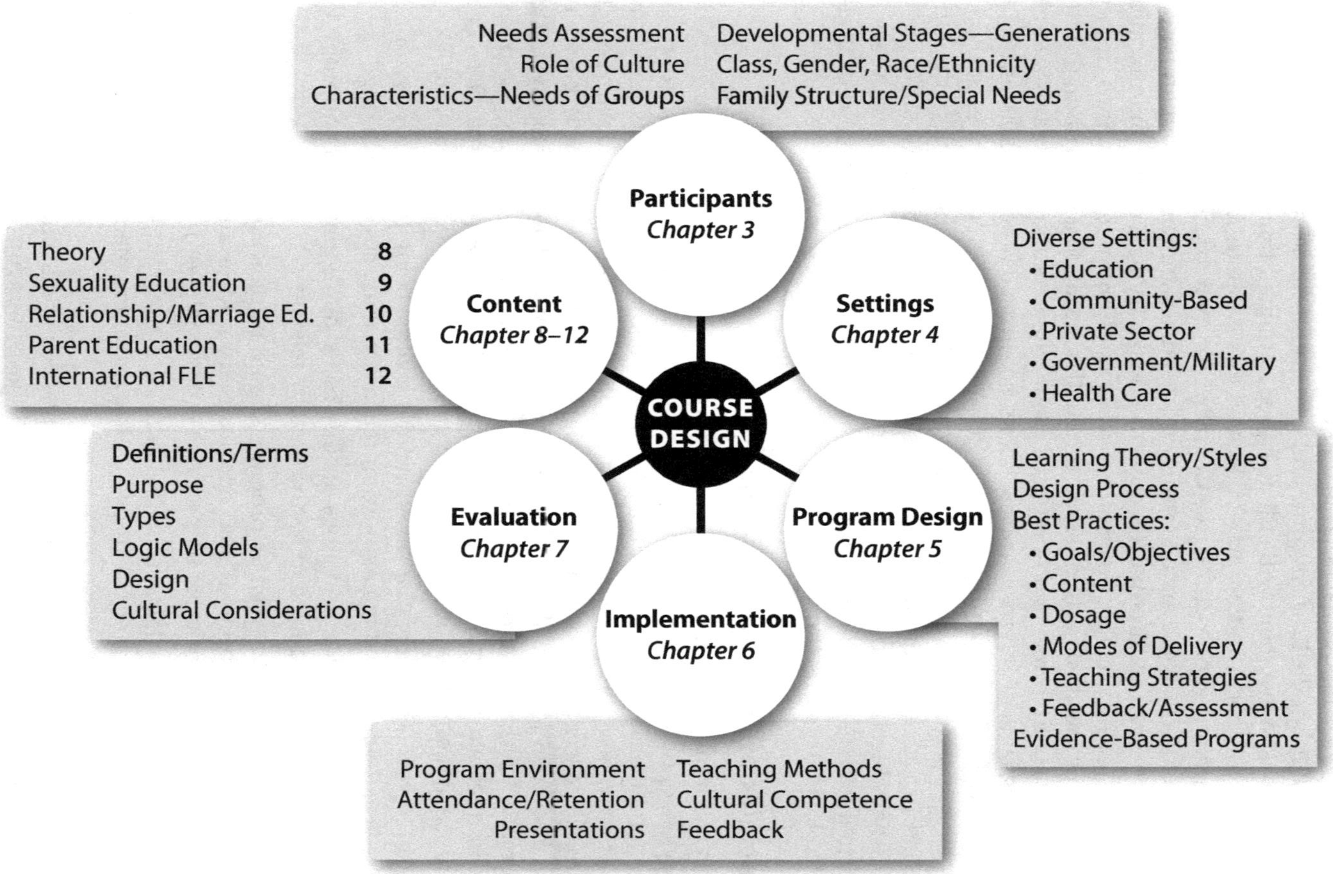
Needs Assessment
Role of Culture
Characteristics—Needs of Groups
Developmental Stages—Generations
Class, Gender, Race/Ethnicity
Family Structure/Special Needs
Participants
Chapter 3
Theory 8
Sexuality Education 9
Relationship/Marriage Ed. 10
Parent Education 11
International FLE 12
Content
Chapter 8–12
Settings
Chapter 4
Diverse Settings:
• Education
• Community-Based
• Private Sector
• Government/Military
• Health Care
COURSE DESIGN
Definitions/Terms
Purpose
Types
Logic Models
Design
Cultural Considerations
Evaluation
Chapter 7
Program Design
Chapter 5
Learning Theory/Styles
Design Process
Best Practices:
• Goals/Objectives
• Content
• Dosage
• Modes of Delivery
• Teaching Strategies
• Feedback/Assessment
Evidence-Based Programs
Implementation
Chapter 6
Program Environment
Attendance/Retention
Presentations
Teaching Methods
Cultural Competence
Feedback

Figure 5.2 Elements of Program Design

those courses, traditional scheduling, and the awarding of a certificate, diploma, license, or degree when the program is completed (Chamberlain & Cummings, 2003). A *nonformal educational* program has an organized session(s) facilitated by a professional(s), but the learners come and go because attending all sessions is typically optional. While there will still be a predetermined time to begin and end a session, the classroom setting may be located in a religious, health care, community, or after-hour school setting (see Chapter 4 for more on nonformal family life education settings). There are no exams or graded assignments, although participants may be given an informal assignment, such as trying a new communication skill with a family member. *Informal education* does not necessarily include subjects and "approved" objectives associated with a traditional curriculum. It often supplements both formal and nonformal family life education programs and can include magazine or internet articles, books, social media posts, blogs related to personal well-being, parenting, or other FLE-related topics. Informal education is a lifelong approach that may also occur when talking to another individual in a meeting or casual encounter. Nonformal education is the primary structure of family life education programs and since most people have experienced programs in formal settings, the following program design elements will just focus on issues related to nonformal settings.

Principles of Effective Programs

While it may be preferable to use a proven evidence-based program, it is not always an option, typically due to funding and staffing issues. Incorporating principles of established programs into new programs can provide a way to increase the effectiveness of prevention programs. Small et al. (2009) developed an approach called "evidence-informed program improvement" (EIPI) based on what had been learned about the common traits of evidence-based prevention programs. The EIPI approach provides a framework for considering the principles of effective programs. Eleven principles of effective programs have been identified and organized into the following four categories (Small et al., 2009):

1. *Program Design and Content.* Principles include being theory driven, of sufficient dosage and intensity, comprehensive, and actively engaging.
2. *Program Relevance.* Principles include being developmentally appropriate, appropriately timed, and socioculturally relevant.
3. *Program Implementation.* A program should be delivered by well-qualified, trained, and supported staff and focused on fostering good relationships (see Chapter 6 for more on program implementation).
4. *Program Assessment and Quality Assurance.* A program should be well-documented and committed to evaluation and refinement (see Chapter 7 for more on program evaluation).

Providers can incorporate these principles when developing new programs, even if the programs are not able to include measurements or be conducted in a way that would allow them to be defined as evidence-based. The principles can also be used as criteria to evaluate existing programs and influence program redesign. The application of the EIPI approach can enable family program practitioners to increase the effectiveness of the services they provide.

Framework for Best Practices in Family Life Education

Similar to the EIPI process, *The Framework for Best Practices in Family Life Education* moves beyond a focus on content and methods to include program format and features (Ballard & Taylor, 2022a). Best practices are informed by research, theory, cultural practices, and experience and can be used to design new programs or adapt existing programs (Ballard & Taylor, 2022a). Best practices can incorporate what is known about the audience and what will work for them in terms of cultural practices, content, and methods. The Framework considers program content, program design and delivery, program participants, as well as the family life educator who is presenting or developing the material. All components are considered within the context of culture and organizational setting and support.

> Therefore, effective FLE programs based on best practices are a combination of empirically-supported content that is relevant to the program participants, effective program design and delivery, and the experience and skill of the family life educator. The key to meeting the needs of a diverse audience is to pay attention to all framework components and to recognize that these components are interrelated and interdependent in high quality FLE programs. . . . these four components (program content, program design & delivery, program participants and the family life educator) set in the context of culture and organizational setting and support can provide a framework for FLE practices with diverse families. (Ballard & Taylor, 2022a, p. 5)

The following sections will discuss the program design process organized around these components.

Organizational Setting and Support

Before examining the specific content and activities that might be incorporated in a family life education course/program, there are contextual issues such as *culture*, *organizational setting*, and *support*. This is similar to what Fink (2005), in his model for *integrated course design*, called *situational factors* or *structural characteristics*. What do people expect of the course? Where will it be held? Is there community support? Are there similar existing programs in the community? What cultural considerations will be important to incorporate into your program? All of these contextual factors will influence your goals and objectives, which is the first step in the program design process.

Goals

What are current theories related to this content and what scholarly literature is available to address the audience, setting, and focus of the program? When you have a clearer perspective of what this program will entail, you may want to begin planning by using a backward design process and asking yourself the question, "What would you like your participants to have learned by the end of this course that will still be with them two to three years later" (Fink, 2005, p. 5). Your responses constitute the learning goals for the program. A *goal* is a broad general statement of intention or direction for the program describing what you want to achieve through your efforts. It may be somewhat abstract, hard to measure, and encompass a longer time frame. For example, a goal might be that you want participants to have a greater appreciation of the multiple roles of families.

When developing the goals for the course, ask yourself what you need to know to make the best teaching decisions. It is important to have information about the learners (demographics, backgrounds, needs, interests, and goals); the latest developments within the subject area (research and programs); available resources (material, financial, and human/personal); societal trends (local, national, and international, as well as state laws and policies); community contexts (attitudes, values, and resources); and learning theories (Chamberlain & Cummings, 2003).

Objectives

The next step in the planning process involves creating objectives for the course or program. An *objective*, compared to a goal, is specific, short term, and measurable. For some time, Bloom's taxonomy of educational objectives, which is probably the most widely known educational taxonomy, has been used to categorize learning. It encompasses the *Cognitive Domain* (knowledge), *Affective Domain* (attitude or self), and *Psychomotor Domain* (skills) (Bloom, 1956; Krathwohl, Bloom, & Masia, 1973; Simpson, 1972). Most attention has been focused on the Cognitive Domain, which involves behaviors concerned with intellectual pursuits, thinking, using one's mind, and relational learning that can be thought of as the goals of the learning process. In the original taxonomy, the behaviors were organized into levels from simple to more complex mental processes including *knowledge* (recalling information); *comprehension* (explaining information); *application* (using information); *analysis* (separating information); *synthesis* (combining information); and *evaluation* (making assessments). The taxonomy has been revised so that the new names of the six categories are parallel to the former names, but are changed from nouns to verbs (Krathwohl, 2002). Thus, the suggested terminology is *remember, understand, apply, analyze, evaluate,* and *create.* (Note that compared to Bloom's configuration, there is a reversal in the order of the last two categories.) Bloom's taxonomy has had a long history and popularity and is still widely used in creating curriculum objectives. Whether you use the original or revised taxonomy, the levels of cognitive domain should be considered when determining measurable course objectives for any course you design. See Table 5.1 for guidelines for these six levels of the cognitive domain regarding what is expected of learners, examples of objectives at each level, and verbs to reflect various levels of learning (Clauss, 2005; Krathwohl, 2002). This table can be very helpful in creating course objectives.

The customary practice in writing objectives is to specify the ultimate behavior of the learner. Behavior can be measured objectively because you have concrete evidence of achievement based on the wording of the objectives. Behavioral

Table 5.1 Creating Measurable Objectives Using Bloom's Revised Taxonomy

	Learners are expected to:	Examples—Students will:	Verbs to use when writing objectives reflecting this level of learning:
REMEMBER Can learners recognize and recall knowledge?	Remember a fact, idea, or phenomenon essentially in the same form in which they learned it.	**List** four functions of families. **Label** parts of the female and male sexual anatomy using the correct terminology. **Identify** pros and cons of having children.	Cite, count, define, find, identify, label, list, match, memorize, name, note, omit, point to, quote, recall, recite, repeat, say, spell, state.
UNDERSTAND Can learners interpret, exemplify, classify, summarize, infer, compare, or explain information?	Communicate an idea in their own words (translate); grasp the meaning of an idea to be able to explain it (interpret); or project the effect of things (extrapolate).	**Explain** the process of divorce. **Paraphrase** another's verbal and nonverbal message. **Infer** the effect of a pregnant woman's smoking a pack of cigarettes a day on the fetus. **Interpret** the phrase "You cannot not communicate."	Annotate, clarify, describe, elaborate, explain, generalize, translate, infer, interpret, restate, review, reword, summarize.
APPLY Can learners execute or implement procedures in a given situation?	Use abstractions such as concepts, principles, rules, and generalizations in specific and concrete situations.	**Use** active listening skills. **Survey** the needs of FLE program participants. **Demonstrate** an effective discipline technique for a toddler. **Implement** a family budget.	Apply, calculate, employ, give an example, illustrate, interview, operate, show, solve, survey, use, utilize, demonstrate.
ANALYZE Can learners differentiate, organize, attribute material into constituent parts?	Break things down into components; determine relationships among elements; distinguish factors; or classify information.	**Contrast** biological and environmental influences on human development. **Categorize** infant behaviors into domains of development. **Outline** the decision-making process.	Analyze, categorize, classify, compare, contrast, diagram, differentiate, distinguish, divide, examine, outline, relate, separate, take apart.

(continued)

Table 5.1 *(cont'd.)*

	Learners are expected to:	Examples—Students will:	Verbs to use when writing objectives reflecting this level of learning:
EVALUATE Can learners check or critique materials based on criteria and standards?	Judge the value of material based on definite criteria; rate ideas, conditions, or objects' or accept or reject ideas, things, or conditions based on standards.	**Choose** the best child-care option given a family's needs. **Justify** discipline strategies as parents of adolescents. **Evaluate** a plan to balance work and family. **Rank** characteristics of an effective family life educator.	Appraise, assess, choose, criticize, critique, debate, decide, defend, evaluate, grade, judge, prioritize, rank, rate, recommend, referee, reject, select, support, umpire, weigh, justify.
CREATE Can learners generate, plan, or produce information to make an original product?	Produce original plans; create new patterns or structures; or combine what is "known" into a new perspective.	**Integrate** professional literature reporting results of research on consumer behavior. **Develop** a personal anger management plan. **Propose** a family life education program for parents of "boomerang" children.	Blend, build, combine, compose, construct, create, design, form, formulate, generate, hypothesize, integrate, invent, modify, plan, predict, produce, pro-pose, rearrange, reconstruct, reorder, reorganize, revise, structure, write.

Note: Some scholars believe "evaluate" is a more complex intellectual effort than "create." Hence, the order of these two levels of learning can be interchanged. You decide!

(Clauss, 2005; Krathwohl, 2002)

objectives are applicable to learners in all settings and in a variety of contexts. One focus is to construct S.M.A.R.T. learning objectives (Drucker, 1954; Schmitt, Hu, & Bachrach, 2008). Consider whether or not your objective is:

S Specific—Does it say exactly what the learner will be able to do?

M Measurable—Is it quantifiable and can it be measured?

A Attainable—Can it be accomplished in the proposed framework with available resources?

R Relevant—Will it meet the needs of the participants and the organization?

T Time Frame—Can it be accomplished in the time available?

Program Content

Family life education programs must be based on research, as providing research-based information is one of the primary things that makes family life educators different than the "armchair" advice given by well-intentioned but unqualified people such as a family member. One of the foundational principles of family life education programs is "designed around and supported by research-based information" (Darling et al., 2020, p. 430). Part of the program design process is determining the scope of the program and the research-based content that is relevant and applicable to the target audience. But research-based information is not necessarily enough. Is the content needed by the target audience? Is it understandable? Is it culturally appropriate? As a family life educator, you must design your program in such a way that participants are receiving the information that they need in a manner which is understandable and relevant.

Theory

A theoretical foundation is important to consider when designing or selecting an FLE program. Theory should be intentional to help ensure the achievement of program outcomes (Futris, Mallette, & Richardson, 2016; Small et al., 2009). Family systems and ecological theories provide overarching theoretical frameworks for FLE programming by recognizing the entire family system and other contextual influences on the family (see Chapter 8 for more on theory). It is also important to identify a theory of change which may include the core components of the program that are essential in order to achieve program outcomes. In other words, what content and learning activities will be included that will help achieve the desired change in your participants. A logic model is often used to identify and illustrate the theory of change. Logic models are discussed in detail in Chapter 7. Regardless of specific theory used, all FLE programs should use a strength-based approach that recognizes and builds on the knowledge, skills, and capabilities present in families, invites participants to be part of their own learning, and promotes resiliency among family members (Ballard et al., 2016; Darling et al., 2017).

Program Participants

Family life education programs may be designed to be universal (for a general audience) or selective (for a specific subgroup) to accommodate varying levels of need. Whether your program is universal or selective, an understanding of participant strengths, needs, and interests as well as factors such as culture, learning styles, or ability levels will influence your program design or necessitate program adaptation to an existing program. What are the characteristics of the learners (e.g., amount of time involved in parenting, work expectations, achievement of personal and professional goals) and what kinds of past experiences might participants have had?

When thinking about your potential program participants, you need to consider physical/biological, social, and psychological differences. *Physically,* some participants may have physical limitations with their sight, hearing, or motor skills. When dealing with the location of the program, you may need to consider access to public transportation and handicapped parking. *Socially,* adults may have time and economic limitations that should be considered when determining the cost of any class. There may also be cultural factors, so attending a class may either be a status symbol, embarrassment, or a means to socialize. Previous negative or idealistic experiences with schools may also influence their willingness to participate. *Psychologically,* adult learners have high levels of personal and professional expectations of their learning experiences, but may want an informal learning environment. They want content that is practical, can be immediately applied, and will be relevant to their work or personal lives. Sharing the responsibility for learning and instruction with the instructor, as well as interacting with other participants will be of interest to them. Be aware of nonverbal cues regarding any confusion or lack of interest. This will allow you to vary the pace, change the activity, rephrase the question or statement, or regain the attention of the audience.

To entice people to attend the course, you may want to offer food. Either plan a dinner session where they can eat and learn or have some other kind of refreshments. Incorporating food can be a way to make the experience pleasant and provide opportunities for participants to connect with others in similar circumstances. Child care during the program, transportation to and from the program, or free parking are other incentives that can reduce barriers to attendance.

Program Features

After establishing goals and objectives, deciding on appropriate content, and considering the characteristics of your target audience, you are now ready to think about the specific format and features of your program. This includes the details of the program including dosage, mode of delivery, and teaching and learning strategies.

Dosage

Dosage refers to the number and length of sessions, the amount and quality of content that is provided, and/or the total length of the program (Nation et al., 2003). If designing your own program, you will be the person who decides how many sessions are needed, for what length of time, at what frequency, at what time of day, and what time of year. If you have adults in this class who work during the day, when is the best time to schedule these sessions? More people might prefer to come to a one-time session rather than commit to a long-term course with multiple sessions, although a one-time session may be a catalyst for their return to a longer program at a later date. If you have more than one session, you might also want to plan "backwards." Determine what you want students to reasonably achieve at the end of the course and then plan how many sessions are needed to reach this goal. The severity of the problem or level of risk may be an additional consideration as a higher level of risk requires more sessions or a higher dosage (Nygren et al., 2018).

Modes of Delivery

Another aspect of program design is deciding the actual format in which the program will be implemented or the mode of delivery. Modes of delivery include traditional face-to-face formats such as a classroom, seminar and home visits, or online delivery in either synchronous (i.e., real time) or asynchronous (i.e., self-paced) formats (McAllister, Duncan, & Hawkins, 2012). All delivery modes can be effective; however, choosing the appropriate mode of delivery is an important part of program design. You will want to consider things such as accessibility, cost, adequate time to process information and practice skills, and time constraints of your participants (Hughes et al., 2015; McAllister et al., 2012).

One way to view the delivery of family life education programs is to examine the options of incorporating mass, group, and individual modes. The *mass mode* involves educational information provided to the masses, but not just through mass media sources. The audience is anonymous because there is no direct contact between the educator and the participants. Anyone with the interest, access, and means (e.g., television, computer, reading ability) to participate can do so. This may be a special lecture by a knowledgeable person in the community, media presentation including radio or television (organizational promotional spots, educational programs), webinars, blogs, podcasts, the internet (news programs, access to government Extension sites, YouTube), and print media (books, magazines, newspapers, newsletters, bulletins, pamphlets). Social media sites and applications (apps), such as Facebook and Twitter, have emerged as other effective mass modes of delivery for family life educators and provide an opportunity to reach families "where they are" as well as help family life educators to promote their services (DeBoer-Moran, 2015, p. 285). You can even get creative and place short FLE messages on buses (Dooley, 2017), restaurant place mats (Consumer Financial Protection Bureau, n.d.), billboards (Baugh, et. al., 2017), or other prominent public places.

The *group mode* is oriented toward participants who are in learning groups organized around a particular topic. The group mode is *not* group therapy, but focuses on instructional goals. The structure of groups can be formal or nonformal and vary in size, composition, frequency of meeting, and duration. Small groups are often used for parent and relationship education programs with people of similar interests and goals. With increased use of Zoom or other virtual platforms during the COVID-19 pandemic, it has become more common for FLE programs implemented in the group mode to also be delivered virtually.

The *individual mode*, which involves one-on-one interaction, is often associated with counseling and guidance, which are outside the realm of family life educators. However, family life education does occur via the individual mode. Educators often talk to parents individually about the needs and accomplishments of their children or may do a home visit to both learn about the child and teach parents educational activities they can use with them. There are some parent education programs that use a home-visiting one-on-one model. At times educators may provide assistance or advice consisting of information and explanations to parents and families. Family life coaching—a collaborative and client-directed, strengths-based approach to working with families—is a good example of providing family life education in an individual mode.

Online and Virtual Programming

Online family life education can be defined as "any educational outreach primarily delivered via the internet that intentionally facilitates individual and family well-being by using online technologies that include programmatic educational strategies or structures" (Hughes et al., 2012, p. 712). Online FLE programming can be individual, group, or mass mode and can be synchronous or asynchronous.

Greater access to personal computers and the internet has increased family life education opportunities. These online opportunities expanded even more when COVID-19 necessitated most FLE programs to move to online or virtual delivery, with many using Zoom or other virtual platforms to provide programming. Although most family life educators had to make a fast pivot to online programming during COVID-19, simply transferring all materials and PowerPoint slides into an online course is not the easiest or most effective method of online programming. In general, it is best to redesign the course to meet the needs of participants within a virtual learning environment. However, virtual platforms such as Zoom and Teams better allow for synchronous interactive programming than do asynchronous methods. For example, chats, polling features, and break-out rooms can facilitate discussion, small group work, and other interactive techniques that are characteristic of in-person programs.

There are advantages and disadvantages to online teaching and learning. If the program is asynchronous, the material is available 24/7, so participants can engage with the materials at any time and can even go through materials multiple times if desired. Time is also saved because participants do not have to drive in rush-hour traffic if taking an evening class or find parking. There is also greater anonymity that can facilitate clarifying misconceptions and increase the honesty and quantity of class participation. While in-class discussions may be uncomfortable to participants because they may not want to speak in front of a group or need time to prepare a response, an online discussion allows time for thoughtful responses.

Some of the same issues for students are also relevant for family life educators, such as flexibility, convenience, and commuting times. Furthermore, there is greater global access and availability for participants and instructors in that you do not need to be in the same town or city. You can be in different parts of the country or even different parts of the globe and still participate in class.

If content is to be delivered in an online format, you must understand the online abilities and activities of your potential audience, as well as the way that families use the internet to learn about family issues. It is helpful to provide participants with brief and clear instructions at an appropriate reading level along with technical support to navigate the course, if needed. It is important to remember that the Internet and other technology can often highlight social inequality if people do not have access to the technology or the ability to use it effectively (Walker, 2016). Incorporating various forms of media is encouraged with the use of pictures, video, animations, music, and audio segments that add interest and educational value. It is often said, "A picture is worth a thousand words." Incorporating media can facilitate learning with fewer words, thereby providing knowledge about families and parenting to millions of people who are illiterate. According to the National Center for Educational Statistics, 23% of high school seniors and 21% of adults are classified as either illiterate or functionally illiterate (with a basic or below basic ability to read) (Rea, 2020). Because of this, making use of a variety of media sources is all the more important.

Teaching and learning strategies

Teaching and learning strategies or methods are the tools needed to deliver the educational programming to the intended audience. These strategies may differ based on the needs, learning style, culture, age, abilities, and preferences of the audience. As a family life educator, the ability to develop or adapt methods for diverse audiences is an essential component of cultural competence (Allen & Blaisure, 2015; Ballard et al., 2016; Mallette et al., 2022). It is important to be intentional and thoughtful about which strategies should be included in your program. Chapter 6 provides more information on different teaching and learning strategies and suggestions for effective implementation of them. However, in the next section, we provide considerations for choosing teaching strategies as part of the program design process.

Choosing teaching techniques

1. *Know your population.* Teaching techniques that work with a group of teenagers may not work with a group of adults. It is important to find out as much as possible about your population prior to planning your activities.
2. *Choose methods that maximize learner participation.* Everyone likes to get involved and family life education programs should include several activities that get participants talking, doing, moving, and thinking. Incorporating active learning strategies and providing opportunities for participants to practice skills through role-playing and other skill-based activities, rather than just receiving information, are characteristic of effective programs (Cotter et al., 2013; Small et al., 2009). Try to minimize lectures to about 10-minute segments and always make lectures two-way communication by allowing questions, comments, and discussion.
3. *Choose activities that will help students to achieve learning objectives.* The activities that you incorporate into your program should be directly linked with your learning objectives. What will the participants get out of this activity? Will it help them to achieve the learning objective?
4. *Be aware of the order in which you use different strategies.* It is a good idea to integrate different techniques. For example, following a mini-lecture, plan an active activity that allows the participants to talk and/or move about the room.
5. *Be sensitive to the timing when you use a technique.* Not only do you want to incorporate a variety of activities, but also think about the timing of the activity. Directly following lunch, you might want to choose something that will really get the participants involved. Do not forget to build breaks into your plans.
6. *Consider combining or adapting techniques.* Get creative when you are planning your program. Chapter 6 includes more on learning activities and tips for implementing them. However, these activities are just a guide. Feel free to combine them together or to develop your own! You may find that different teaching techniques work better with different types of groups. If so, adapt the techniques to fit the needs of the group.

7. *Consider what teaching strategy might be best given the size of your group or your mode of delivery.* Sometimes your group may be too big or too small for a particular activity. If you have a very large audience, a small group activity might not work. In this case, you may adapt the activity so that it is an individual activity. Other times the group may be too small. Perhaps you have planned a simulation activity and need at least ten participants for it to be effective and you only have seven. Your program plans should include instruction for either adapting the activity for a smaller number of participants or instructions for an alternative activity.
8. *Be sensitive to providing adequate discussion time following an activity.* Many learning activities require time to process the information. Therefore, build this processing and discussion time into your program design. For example, after a role-play activity, allow all of the participants to discuss their reactions and ideas regarding the role play. If you group your activities too close together, you may lose valuable learning opportunities. You might even write a few discussion or reflection questions into your program plans to ensure adequate processing time.
9. *Allow yourself to be flexible.* One of the most important traits of an effective family life educator is flexibility. Perhaps you find that your technology does not work, maybe your audience does not respond to an activity in the way that you thought that they would, or maybe the activity that you thought would take 30 minutes, only took 10 minutes. These are all examples of times when you need to think quickly and be flexible. It is imperative to go into the program with a plan, but be ready to deviate from this plan if necessary. Try to include additional activities, discussion questions, or content in your plans as options in the event that you find yourself with extra time.

Feedback, Assessment, and Evaluation

Throughout the program it is important to give formative feedback by providing information to participants about their learning. At times this feedback may need to be corrective, and not just about their strengths and weaknesses. Participants should also be given opportunities for self-assessment and reflection about their learning experiences.

In nonformal community education settings you will receive feedback from students in a variety of forms, such as casual comments; direct statements of praise or complaint; or nonverbal reactions such as facial cues, posture, or eye contact. Unfortunately, you may not accurately receive the messages that are being transmitted. One important form of feedback to pay attention to is whether or not learners return after the first class. In other words, the most important goal of a first class session is to create the desire for students to return for the next session.

You may also informally assess if participants are meeting the established objectives. Has there been a change in the participants' attitudes, knowledge, or skills? You might do this assessment through some of your planned activities. For example, if one of your objectives is for the parents in your parenting program to demonstrate three appropriate guidance strategies, you might assess whether they have met this objective through a role-play activity.

Evaluation does not occur at a single point in time in your program, but rather should be ongoing. Therefore it is important to include evaluation plans into your program design and not wait until you have implemented the program to decide how to evaluate it. Evaluation can be thought of as occurring on a continuum. A needs assessment, which establishes the needs of your target population, is at the beginning of the evaluation continuum (see Chapter 3 for more on conducting a needs assessment). Ideally, FLE programs are designed and implemented based on the results of a comprehensive needs assessment; however, resource constraints may result in an informal assessment of the target audience. At the first session of your program, you can do an initial assessment of who your audience is through introductions or icebreaker activities. You can quickly find out why they chose to attend your program and what they hope to learn. These types of informal activities should not replace a comprehensive needs assessment, but they can give you a sense of who you have in your program and how best to move forward with implementing your program plans. Knowing more about your audience may result in slight tweaks to your program design. For example, when you find out that all of the parents in your parenting class have toddlers, you may change some of your examples, role-play scenarios, or case studies to include toddlers as examples instead of children of other ages. Building this type of flexibility into your program plan will increase the chance that your program will meet your participants' needs and achieve the program objectives.

Evaluating participant satisfaction with a program may assess if participants would like more active learning strategies, increased opportunities to connect with other participants, or are experiencing barriers to continued attendance, such as lack of child care. Often called a process evaluation, it can be important in planning and improving program features, particularly if you are teaching a multisession program. Feedback that you receive after the first couple of sessions can be useful in tweaking the program to better meet participant needs.

Formative (conducted while the program is in progress) and summative (conducted at the end of the program) evaluations can generate information about whether or not your participants met the established objectives. Results of formative and summative evaluations may be used for improving the programs and to make decisions about offering the program again. See Chapter 7 for more on program evaluation.

Finally, evaluation using a control group or using a longitudinal design may determine a program's impact; programs that have been evaluated using these more rigorous methods are called evidence-based programs. There has been an increase in evidenced-based programs in recent years which can be an alternative to designing your own program. In the next section, we outline some of the pros and cons of using an EBP or other predeveloped program and how to find one that meets the needs of your target audience.

EVIDENCE-BASED PROGRAMS: BENEFITS AND CHALLENGES

Evidence-based programs are well-defined programs that have demonstrated through rigorous, peer-reviewed research, that they produce the desired outcomes if implemented as intended and have been endorsed by government agencies and well-respected research organizations (Small, Cooney, & O'Connor, 2009). EBPs have what is often referred to as core components which are those aspects of the program that are responsible for the program's effectiveness (Blase & Fixsen, 2013). These core components may include content, learning activities, or features such as dosage (length and number of sessions). Program fidelity, which refers to implementing the program as intended, is often determined by assessing adherence to the core components of a particular program.

Benefits of Evidence-Based Programs

There are numerous benefits to implementing an evidence-based program. It can help to ensure that the program is based on solid research and proven theories and increase the likelihood that the results or outcomes can be attributable to the services received from the program. Additionally, using a program that has been tried and tested adds to the likelihood of success. It can facilitate the most efficient use of resources because money is spent on proven programs rather than invested into the design of a new program. Another benefit of using evidence-based programs is that the program is likely to have undergone a cost–benefit analysis. This can demonstrate that the benefits of the program outweigh the costs, making it easier to obtain funding and support from policy makers, community leaders, and participants. Moreover, many evidence-based programs offer packaged materials, instruction, or staff training so that the program will be taught as intended by the developer. Finally, using well-implemented evidence-based programs can help assure that families receive the best services available.

Challenges for Evidence-Based Programs

While the value of implementing evidence-based programs is widely recognized, a number of challenges exist regarding their widespread and consistent use in real-world settings. First, the cost may be a barrier to using an EBP. It can be expensive to conduct the research needed to identify a program as evidence-based. As a result, there is often a cost to purchase the program materials and/or to receive training in how to implement the program with fidelity. Many smaller agencies and organizations may not have the funds necessary to purchase the rights to use the materials needed to implement an existing evidence-based program or receive the needed training, and may not have the capacity to conduct the program exactly as a developer intended, which could jeopardize the program outcomes.

An additional challenge may be a lack of programs that are suitable for your target population. You and your agency may have difficulty finding a program that meets the needs of its specific population, is a good fit for you as the family life educator, and aligns with its mission. A program that must be implemented exactly as designed may not allow adaptation for cultural values or local conditions compromising fidelity to the program model.

There is a lack of consensus over the criteria used to determine or define evidence-based programs which can make it difficult for a program developer or user to know what standard to pursue. However, there are a number of clearinghouses and registries that have established guidelines, standards, or criteria for inclusion. Many of these registries focus more on target populations and the prevention of negative outcomes over the promotion of positive ones (Cooney et al., 2007), but increased interest in primary prevention promises to result in advancements in the field. Box 5.1 includes a partial list of registries for evidence-based programs.

Box 5.1 Registries for Evidence-Based Programs and Practices

Arizona State University REACH Institute Evidenced-Based Programs
reachinstitute.asu.edu/programs

Blueprints for Healthy Youth Development (Annie E. Casey Foundation)
blueprintsprograms.org

Institute of Education Sciences (IES) What Works Clearinghouse—U.S. Department of Education
ies.ed.gov/ncee/wwc

Social Programs that Work, Coalition for Evidenced-Based Policy
evidencebasedprograms.org

What Works Wisconsin: Evidence-Based Parenting Program Directory
fyi.extension.wisc.edu/whatworkswisconsin

SUMMARY

Designing a family life education program has many interrelated elements, such as modes of instruction; organizational setting and support; choosing teaching strategies; and creating program/course goals, objectives, and evaluation. As noted in Figure 5.1, participants, organizational settings, content, and implementation need to be simultaneously incorporated into program planning. The selection of teaching and learning activities will be influenced by your original research into the program topic and the organizational support and setting, learning objectives, and assessment plans associated with your course design. However, "stay tuned" for the next chapter for some suggestions on various teaching methods. Once you have designed your program, you will continually refine it with new course objectives, teaching activities, resources, and assessment measures. You may also choose (or be asked) to use an evidence-based program which has already been designed. However, understanding the design process is important in order to determine fit with your target audience and to make allowable adaptations. Your goal is to develop the best possible class, course, or program that you can, but inevitably, there will be changes during the course and afterward. Program design involves the joy of creating and meeting the challenges of change.

QUESTIONS AND ISSUES FOR DISCUSSION

1. In what ways is understanding multiple intelligences important in the program design process?
2. What are some examples of mass, group, and individual modes that can be utilized in family life education?
3. What are some positive and negative teaching or learning environments that you have experienced and what contributed to your evaluations of that space?
4. What kind of experiences have you had with online courses? What contributes to a successful online course?
5. You have been asked to provide an 8-week relationship education program for teenagers in the community. Would you rather design your own original family life education program or choose an existing evidence-based program? Why or why not?

ACTIVITIES

1. Search online for an inventory of Kolb's learning styles, Gardner's multiple intelligences, or another learning style survey. Take the inventory or survey. What were the results? Do you agree with them? How can this information be helpful in your own educational experiences?
2. Have each student or a group of students explore an unfamiliar technological tool for use with online learning. Present this technique to the class describing its features, advantages, and disadvantages.
3. Give small groups of students an "in-class" experience of designing a course on an innocuous topic, such as basket weaving, building a birdhouse, or learning a foreign language that is not commonly taught in schools. What would be the "backwards" goal(s) for students? What would be the objectives of the course, content, learning experiences, and assessment?
4. Assign individuals or small groups of students to plan and teach a unit applicable to one of the content areas within the Certified Family Life Educator program. Students should also create exam questions and some type of program evaluation so they can analyze the effectiveness of their unit.

6

Implementation of Family Life Education

Now that you have learned about designing your program (Chapter 5), it is time to *implement* your plans. Implementation refers to how you actually conduct or teach the program. You may plan a fabulous family life education program, but poor implementation can prevent you from reaching your audience and helping your participants to achieve the learning objectives that you have set for them.

While you have planned which teaching and learning activities you might use as part of your program design, it is now time to take a deeper dive into different educational methods and how to effectively implement them in your family life education class or program. In this chapter we will present information relevant to a variety of family life education settings. To be continually thinking of each element as you plan and implement your class, it might be helpful to create a *worksheet* for this ongoing design process incorporating the following four columns (Fink 2005).

Learning Objectives for Course/Session	Teaching-Learning Activities	Assessment of Learning	Resources Needed (e.g., people, materials)

Family Life Education Implementation Framework

It does not matter if you are implementing a multisession program or a one-time workshop, there are common elements to the implementation process. The *Family Life Education Implementation Framework* (Ballard, 2020) provides a useful model that encompasses four main components of the implementation process: (1) program environment, (2) program participants, (3) program design and delivery, and (4) program facilitator. Once your program is designed, this framework can help you to successfully implement your plans. The components of the framework—as shown in Figure 6.1—overlap, reflecting how these different aspects of implementation are interconnected.

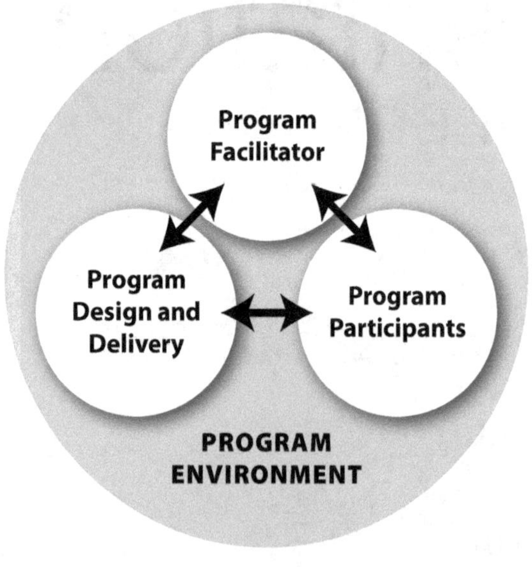

Figure 6.1 Family Life Education Implementation Framework

Source: Ballard, S. M. (2020). The practice of family life education: Toward an implementation framework. *Family Relations, 69*(3), 461–478.

PROGRAM ENVIRONMENT

Program environment includes the physical or virtual space where the program will be held as well as nontangible factors such as cultural context, organizational and community support, and current events or policies (Ballard, 2020). For example, if you are implementing a program at the local elementary school on parent involvement, the level of support from the school administration will influence your program and therefore is part of the environmental context of your program. Other characteristics of your community, such as a large immigrant population or a high poverty rate, also will influence the environmental context for your parent involvement program. You might assess what other similar programs are already offered in your community or if there are organizations or agencies with whom you can partner that might help you to reach your target audience. Societal trends and policies, as well as historical events such as the COVID-19 pandemic, impact both the setting for an FLE program (virtual instead of face to face) and the emotional climate as participants face new challenges associated with the pandemic (e.g., balancing teleworking with helping their children with remote learning). All of these macrolevel influences impact the microlevel, which is the actual space or setting in which the program will be held. Considerations for both the physical and virtual environments are outlined below.

Physical Environment

If you will be implementing your program in a face-to-face setting, the physical environment is an important consideration. It is good to visit this classroom before your program begins to determine the best arrangement of chairs/desks, lighting conditions, operational procedures for media equipment, and location of restrooms. Determine the optimal arrangement for the tables, chairs, or desks, so people can see and hear each other as much as possible. The number of participants and the arrangement of seating can greatly influence the educational setting. Even the temperature can have an effect on your program. If people are uncomfortable they will be unable to focus on the program and might not even stay for the entire session.

When doing a precheck of the classroom, note what supplies and equipment are available for your use. If you need technical equipment, you may have to request it in advance or bring your own equipment. It is essential to have a backup plan. At times a video file or computer will not work and you will need an alternate strategy. It is always good to have backup materials on a flash drive. This might mean you highlight the points of your presentation on the blackboard or white board. Furthermore, you may need paper and pencils for small group activities or other teaching supplies, such as toys if they are enhancements to your child development lesson; examples of books on topics that might be of additional interest to participants; or other handouts, objects, and props that may add to your class sessions. If providing handouts, think about when might be the best time for you to distribute them. It may be best to distribute them as your participants are entering the room, at some point during your program, or perhaps at the end as they are leaving. Be sure that handouts are easy to read, attractive, and relevant to the program content.

The following list of questions can be used as a guide to assess and plan the physical environment for your program.

1. Location
   a. Where will your program be held?
   b. Is this location convenient and easily accessible for potential participants?
   c. Are there rest rooms conveniently located nearby?
   d. Will participants need transportation to this location?
   e. If your program is in the evening, is it a safe location to be in after dark?
2. Room Arrangement
   a. Are the chairs comfortable?
   b. How will you arrange the chairs and/or tables?
   c. Where will you be located? Will you stand or sit?
   d. Does the room look inviting? Are there things that you can do to make it more inviting to participants?
   e. Do you need a microphone, and if so, is it stationary or portable?
3. Comfort
   a. Is the lighting appropriate?
   b. Is there proper ventilation in the room?
   c. Is the room too cool or too hot?
   d. Are there noises that could be disruptive (e.g., fans, traffic, other programs)?
   e. Where is/are the door(s) located and are you able to keep the door(s) open or will exterior noise affect student learning?
4. Special Accommodations
   a. Will you be able to accommodate participants who have mobility problems (e.g., wheelchairs, walkers)?
   b. Do you anticipate language barriers? How will you handle this?
   c. Will there be participants who have vision or hearing problems?
   d. Are your materials matched with the literacy level of your participants?
   e. What cultural considerations might be relevant to your participants?
5. Support Media/Teaching Materials
   a. What materials will you need for your program?
   b. Will you need to bring any of your own equipment (e.g., computer)?
   c. Will your support media work in the room? Do you have proper outlets, internet connections, etc.? If using the provided equipment, do you know how to operate it?

6. Food/Beverage
   a. Will you provide refreshments? Is there an appropriate place to set food and beverages?
   b. If people will be bringing food, is there an adequate place for people to eat?

Virtual Environment

Online FLE programs were becoming popular even before the COVID-19 pandemic forced many family life educators to move their programs to virtual environments. Family life educators now have many virtual learning platforms from which to choose. You will need to decide if your program will be asynchronous, where participants can access the content anytime and complete the program at their own pace, or if the program will be synchronous, or real-time. Many of the questions in the following list refer to synchronous programs but can still help you plan the virtual environment for any online program.

1. Learning Platform
   a. What learning platform will you use to deliver your program (e.g., Zoom, Teams)?
   b. Is this platform convenient and easily accessible for potential participants? Will they need to download anything prior to the program?
   c. Will you and your participants have sufficient bandwidth?
   d. Will you build breaks into your program?
2. Virtual Space
   a. Will you want participants to have their cameras on or off?
   b. What will be the preferred view—grid or speaker view?
   c. Will you use breakout rooms? Chat features?
   d. Does the virtual space look inviting?
   e. Will you use a virtual background?
3. Background Noise
   a. Are there background noises that could be disruptive (e.g., fans, traffic, pets) while you are speaking?
   b. Do you or your participants need a headset?
   c. Will you be able to mute participants when needed?
4. Special Accommodations
   a. Will you be able to accommodate participants who have vision or hearing problems?
   b. Do you anticipate language barriers? How will you handle this?
   c. Are your materials matched with the literacy level of your participants?
   d. What cultural considerations might be relevant to your participants?

5. Support Media/Teaching Materials
   a. How will you provide handouts and other materials to the participants?
   b. Will you be able to easily share your screen during the program?
   c. Will you be able to use video clips or other support media during your presentation?

Program Participants

Program participants are the individuals and families who attend an FLE program; their needs, wants, strengths, characteristics, culture and learning styles should be the primary consideration when planning and implementing your program (Ballard, 2020). Information about the needs of your audience was provided in Chapter 3, including the importance of conducting a needs assessment. This information is vital in both the program design and program implementation process. Marketing, recruitment, attendance, and retention are all related directly to your program participants and are important considerations in the implementation process.

Marketing and Recruitment

One of the most difficult aspects of family life education is marketing and recruiting people to attend your program. What good is a wonderful program if no one attends it? It is important to let potential participants know what your program is about, for whom it is intended, and what the benefits are. One way that you might choose to market your program is through a brochure or flyer that is print and/or digital. This should answer the following questions: what, why, how, when, where, and who. What will I learn during this program and what are the benefits of my attending? Why should I attend? How will I learn the information—what will the structure of the program be? When will the program be held? Where will the program be located? Who is going to conduct the program and what are his/her credentials? Although you want to answer all of these questions, keep marketing materials brief and easy to read. If it is too long, people won't bother to read it. Word of mouth is one of the most powerful marketing tools. If people like your program and benefit from it, they will tell others. If they do not like it, they will also tell others!

Attendance and Retention

People are more likely to attend a program if it will provide information that is relevant to their lives and will be useful to them. The best time for some people to attend a program is when they are going through a transition, such as the transition to parenthood, as learning new knowledge and skills may help make the transition smoother. Participants are often "program ready" or most receptive to change at these times of transition (Bakhurst et al., 2017; Small, Cooney, & O'Connor, 2009).

As you plan the implementation of your program, it will be important to try to remove barriers to attendance such as cost, time of day, or access to child care during the program. If participants do not attend all the program sessions, they are not receiving all the benefits of the program. Participant responsiveness, which is the extent to which they are engaged in the program, may help keep them coming back for all of the program sessions. Participants are engaged when they perceive that the program is relevant to their lives, they like the program facilitator, and when interactive learning strategies are used (Carroll et al., 2007). Conducting a formative evaluation (see Chapter 7 for more on evaluation) can help to determine if there are barriers to continued participation or things that could be changed to increase attendance and retention.

Program Design and Delivery

Selecting teaching methods that will help your participants achieve established learning objectives is part of the program design process and was discussed in Chapter 5. However, planning for a particular activity is different than actually implementing it! The sections below provide more detail on implementing teaching and learning activities that are commonly used in family life education programs, including presentations, multimedia, discussion, projective techniques, simulated learning, and games.

Presentations

Lecture

One of the common methods used by teachers is a lecture—a carefully prepared oral presentation of a subject by a qualified expert that at times may seem somewhat structured and formal. A lecture is used to present factual material in a direct and logical manner, entertain or inspire, or stimulate thinking and further study of a problem prior to opening the subject up for discussion. Furthermore, lectures can be used to reach many listeners at the same time, which is an advantage to those who learn well in this manner but may be problematic for others who learn better from different methods. If lectures primarily involve one-way communication with minimal feedback, they put students in a passive rather than active role. That is why it is better to consider this presentation type as facilitating a discourse, talk, and conversation rather than a one-way transmission of knowledge. Generally, lectures do not sustain attention, which diminishes in 15 to 25 minutes, and tend to be forgotten quickly. Therefore, plan mini-lectures of no more than 10 minutes and then break to involve students in some way, such as questions, anecdotes, personal experiences, problems, applicable current events, short quizzes, illustrations, discussion, and humor. Clickers or online polling features can be used to engage students and collect responses and can be incorporated in virtual as well as face-to-face programs. Retention will be enhanced the more you exercise their brains and involve their senses. Remember that as a presenter you are the primary ingredient in a successful learning experience. If you are enthusiastic, committed to the concepts you are presenting, and realize that class participation is also an essential element, you can be successful. Here are ten tips for effective mini-lectures.

1. Be sure that it truly is a *mini*-lecture. Keep it short!
2. Sprinkle mini-lectures in with other types of learning activities.
3. Make it two-way communication with your participants. Allow participants to ask questions and participate.
4. Be enthusiastic!
5. Keep to the point—be sure that the material is relevant to your program objectives.
6. Make the lecture relevant to the participants. Point out the relevance and the implications of the information.
7. Do not read your whole lecture verbatim—even if you are really nervous.
8. Use visual aids to support your message and add interest.
9. Include anecdotes and real-life stories to illustrate your points.
10. Summarize the main points at the end of the lecture.

Multimedia

Multimedia involves different forms of media that combine text, sound, animation, still images (e.g., cartoons, pictures, newspaper headlines), video (e.g., YouTube or news clips), or interactivity and can be accessed by computerized and electronic devices. In other words, this presentation mode encompasses all methods of instruction that utilize any form of media and can be combined with lectures, discussion, or other teaching methods. Family life educators are constantly looking for videos or print media to use in their classes to give examples or highlight certain concepts. Incorporating multimedia into your program adds interest, helps to provide examples or illustrate concepts, and helps to accommodate visual learners. Multimedia materials should be a systematic part of your program plan. They do not stand alone and need to be introduced and utilized as a part of the whole organized presentation. They may be used to stimulate other senses—hearing and sight, supply a concrete example for conceptual thinking, and provide experiences not easily obtained through other materials.

People are bombarded with so many visual images on a daily basis, from television to online videos to social media, that it is important to only incorporate visual stimuli into your sessions if they apply to the points you are trying to make, are followed by discussion, and are used in moderation. Full-length films or documentaries can be used but may involve greater time expenditures than are needed or available for your course objective(s). However, video clips can provide the examples you need and can be incorporated through PowerPoint or other presentation programs.

You can include music to illustrate different issues in relationships, whether they pertain to dating, parenting, or marriage. Music from previous eras can also be used to show how messages about relationships have changed over time.

Regardless of the type of media that you are using, it is important to be thoroughly prepared. Always test the media prior to the program. Be sure that the medium can be seen and/or heard. There is nothing more frustrating to both the presenter and the participant than to click on a video link and have it not work or have no sound. It also is good practice to incorporate a variety of media and not overuse any one type of medium. Mixing it up can help to create interest and keep your participants engaged.

Presentation tools

PowerPoint is a common presentation tool for family life educators but there are a growing number of other presentation tools such as Prezi (prezi.com) and Canva (canva.com). Regardless of the presentation tool that you choose, below are tips and best practices for your presentation.

- Begin by providing an outline of your presentation, possibly using bullets for your main points. This will give participants the intended direction of your presentation.
- Avoid wordiness by using only a few words, phrases, and dots. Make sure you proof your slides for spelling mistakes, use of repeated words, and grammatical errors.
- Use a readable font. Whereas some fonts are easy to read in printed documents (e.g., Times New Roman, Verdana), others are easy to see projected across a room (e.g., Arial, Helvetica). Depending on the room size, use at least a 24-point font and only capitalize letters when necessary, because CAPITALS ARE MORE DIFFICULT TO READ (McKeachie & Svinicki, 2006).
- Use a background that is simple and attractive. For a well-lit room, use a light background and dark text with the reverse for a dimly-lit room. If possible, keep the lights on in the classroom and avoid showing slides in a dark room for more than 15 minutes (McKeachie & Svinicki, 2006).
- Use a font color that is easy to read and has sharp contrast. Avoid red and green as people who are colorblind will have difficulty reading the content of your slides.
- Use color and graphics to add interest and emphasize a point. Check that the clips are not copyrighted and are free prior to using them.
- Horizontal arrangement of information is preferable to vertical arrangements. This is the default in PowerPoint.
- Use animation and transitions prudently to maintain a minimal level of visual disturbance. Overdoing can distract from your content.
- Use graphs and charts rather than tables to facilitate comprehension and retention of data.
- Incorporate multimedia clips to convey your message more effectively. Dynamic content from a brief video is a great way to engage your audience. Again, be careful not to overuse this format. Check that the clips are not copyrighted and are free to use.

- Talk about your slides without reading the content verbatim. Slides are used to enhance a presentation and are not "the presentation." Face your audience rather than turning to look at the screen.
- Pace the change of slides in your presentation to 1 to 2 slides per minute. If you change slides too quickly, learners have difficulty reading and assimilating the content, whereas if you change slides too slowly, learners have problems because the presentation drags.
- Having handouts of your PowerPoint slides available at the beginning of a presentation facilitates engagement while allowing participants to write additional notes on the handout. In all cases, one has to consider the cost of paper and ink and the effect on the environment of using multiple pieces of paper.
- Use note pages at the bottom of slides to facilitate your delivery and be prepared for technical issues, such as a computer failure or power outage. Have paper notes and a set of printed slides available as a backup.

PANEL

A panel presentation involves a group of four to six persons with special knowledge of a subject. It can be used to identify and explore a problem or issue, give learners an understanding of the various parts of the problem, and/or weigh the advantages and disadvantages of a particular course of action. As with a lecture, the goal of this type of presentation is to engage the audience in asking questions and giving comments. The panelists could each give a 5-minute introductory statement as to their current situation or position while being seated in a semicircle so they can see each other during the conversation and also be seen by the audience. Presenters then hold an unrehearsed, informal, and orderly conversation on an assigned topic in full view of the audience. This type of presentation has a moderator, who might be the instructor, whose tasks are to introduce the panelists, present the topic of conversation, incorporate prompting questions to begin the dialogue, keep the flow of communication moving, handle questions from the audience, manage disagreements, and bring the session to a close. A moderator may also have to deal with panelists who tend to ramble, are relatively silent, or are clearly wrong. If needed, the moderator can ask specific questions of some participants if they appear uncomfortable about speaking or have difficulty inserting themselves into the conversation. An example of a panel presentation that could be meaningful to an audience would be couples who are at various stages in the dating process or who have been married for varying lengths of time.

INTERVIEW

An interview is a presentation in which one or more resource persons respond to questioning by an interviewer. The purpose of an interview presentation mode is to share information. The interviewer serves as the moderator and before questioning begins, he or she can discuss with the resource person(s) the overall topic in order to reach agreement on the general line of questioning. Once the interview begins, the interviewer asks the resource person(s) questions that explore various aspects of the topic. An interview might be used to explore issues related to teen pregnancy and could involve a pregnant teen and her mother as resource persons. In this instance the informal dialogue is less threatening to the persons being interviewed because they do not have to prepare a presentation.

Workshop

A workshop consists of a group of persons with a common interest or problem who want to improve their ability or understanding of a subject. This method can be an effective means of explaining procedures, illustrating the learning process, and developing understanding by "doing," with the major ingredient being *active participation*. Although it is preferable to involve everyone, all members of the group may not need to be fully engaged in workshop activities and can observe others' participation. The workshop may be used to identify, explore, and seek a solution to a problem; permit extensive study of a situation; and provide a "hands-on" learning experience. It may range from one to several hours or to multiple sessions scheduled over several weeks. There may also be various centers to allow participants to rotate to different locations for a small group context within a larger setting. An example is a workshop for parents on creative learning experiences for their children that will involve the active participation of parents in various activities such as art, music, science, reading, mathematics, games, and outdoor activities.

Exhibits and displays

Using exhibits and displays allows groups of people to gather simultaneously in various areas of a room where they may see a demonstration, hear an explanation of an issue or program, or watch a media presentation. Exhibits and displays provide educational information to create interest in topics, as well as provide knowledge and resources. Visual media can help to attract attention, convey content, stimulate action and thinking, provide positive relations, and create affective changes (Chamberlain & Cummings, 2003). The variety within this style of presentation is limited only by imagination and productivity. Exhibits can be used to get attention; reach people who do not read and will not attend regular meetings; provide a dramatic impact; and/or create a casual, relaxed, and close environment in which to learn and potentially interact with others. Childhood safety in many different areas of the home, school, and near environment could be an example of an exhibit and display presentation.

Facilitating Interactions

Questioning

Skillful questioning is an important key to stimulating purposeful learning. Prior to class you might formulate some questions to remind you of the questions you intend to ask and help start the process. Thus, you can more competently guide students toward attaining the intended objectives and exploring conceptual skills at higher levels of the *cognitive domain*. For example, you can ask questions that deal with *Synthesis* (e.g., If you were given this responsibility, what actions would you consider taking?) or *Evaluation* (e.g., What decision would be the best for you and why?). You can also ask probing questions that focus on:

- clarification (asking for more information about what their response means);
- justification (asking students to defend their responses);

- refocusing (redirecting attention to related issues);
- prompting (providing hints to learners);
- redirecting (bringing additional learners into the discussion by asking for their reactions);
- connecting (involving attempts to link material and concepts that otherwise might not seem related);
- comparing (asking for similarities and differences related to various concepts, theories, communication styles, or teaching methods); and
- critical questioning (examining the validity of an author's or researcher's arguments) (Chamberlain & Cummings, 2003; McKeachie & Svinicki, 2006).

If you are asking questions, make sure that the learners have sufficient background for a response, word questions clearly and concisely, and direct questions to the entire group. You also need to allow them time to respond, at least 10 to 15 seconds (Nilson, 2003). A beginning teacher often asks questions but may be nervous and answer them before a student has an opportunity to react. If there is no response, give a hint or rephrase the question to make it easier to understand or incorporate a lower level of learning. Students may be hesitant to respond to questions if they do not know the answer and perceive they will be "put down." You want to establish a positive climate for participation.

How do you respond to questions that you are asked? First, it is important to *listen* to the question and ask for any clarification, if needed. Then *repeat* or *paraphrase* the question so you model this type of behavior to assist others in the class to hear the question. Watch students' *body language*, as this may also be part of their communication, and then *respond*. If you do not know the answer, *do not bluff* your response (Chamberlain & Cummings, 2003). Ask the class for their thoughts, brainstorm ways to determine the answer, and suggest that both you and the students attempt to determine the answer to share at the beginning of the next session, if there will be one. However, it is essential that you follow through with this suggestion during the next session. Use caution so that learners' questions and your responses do not extend too long or go beyond the interest of the entire class.

Discussion

Discussion is one of the key learning activities used in family life education programming. It is a great way to get participants involved, to assess their understanding of the material, and for participants to share knowledge and experiences with each other. It also acknowledges the strengths-based approach of family life education and the contribution that participants can make to the learning process. Discussion can be paired with lectures but can also be used as the primary mode of learning. In online learning environments, discussion can take place synchronously either via the chat feature or having participants unmute and speak, or asynchronously via discussion boards or forums. Whether in a face-to-face or virtual environment, effective facilitation of discussion can take practice. Here are some tips to keep in mind as you develop your discussion facilitation skills.

- After asking a question, wait—do not repeat it, rephrase it, or answer the question yourself.

- Ask open-ended questions rather than closed-ended and use a variety of probing questions.
- Prepare some discussion questions ahead of time but allow for impromptu questions that result from "teachable moments."
- Base your discussion questions on the goals and objectives that you have for the class.
- Arrange seating in a circle or other pattern that allows participants to clearly see each other.
- Be sure that all participants speak so they can be heard.
- Refrain from positioning yourself at the center of attention or otherwise in a position of authority.
- Be open minded; show respect and sensitivity to others.
- It is helpful to set some guidelines for discussion, such as being polite, respecting other points of view, letting one person talk at a time, limiting the time one speaks, and letting others finish without interrupting.
- Acknowledge and affirm each participant's contributions to the discussion.
- It is important to involve everyone, if possible, by noting who has not yet responded or might have difficulty entering into a conversation. However, do not force individuals to participate, particularly if you are discussing sensitive topics.
- Refrain from adding your own ideas until the end, if at all.
- Small group discussions may be a viable option for enhancing interactions that may not readily occur in large groups.

Other discussion techniques

Roundtable discussion groups involve a group of people that gather for a conference or session with each person having an equal status. The participants consider a specific issue and have a dialogue amongst themselves. The leader is usually the one who presides and moderates the discussion. He or she should have pertinent knowledge about the topic and may bring additional information, materials, and handouts. There may be a recorder to keep track of the group's deliberations and to report its progress, if this is a part of the intended purpose. Usually there are a variety of topics discussed in round tables, so that all individuals participate in the topic of their choice. At times, a person has the option of selecting to participate in two or more topics during the scheduled roundtable presentation. Thus, a bell or flash of lights could indicate the time to move to another group. An example might be a series of roundtable discussions on topics, such as childhood nutrition; reading activities; or safety in the home, school, or recreation activities.

Brainstorming is a technique for encouraging a large quantity of viable solutions to a problem by involving all members of moderate to large groups. Members can feel comfortable and supported when contributing their ideas, which can facilitate an interaction of ideas resulting in a synergistic effect. It is a process used to create an environment in which participants can offer suggestions without criticism resulting in the production of a plethora of creative ideas. It involves collaborative thinking to focus on a specific problem. There are certain guidelines for brainstorming: (1) the ideas are expressed openly, rapidly, and recorded on a black or whiteboard; (2) all ideas are welcome; (3) "free-wheeling" is invited—not paying attention to conventional norms; (4) "hitchhiking" is encouraged—improving on an idea by saying that you have an addition to a former idea; and (5) evaluation of ideas should be postponed until all possible ideas have been mentioned. After the flow of ideas has ceased, the group can examine the list to see if there are commonalities, themes to pursue, or ideas that seem prominent. While some of this scrutiny may occur immediately after the session, a smaller group of persons involved in organizing the session may meet to do so later. Brainstorming may be incorporated to create ideas for topics to be used in a series of family life education seminars in your community.

Buzz sessions directly involve every member of a large audience in the discussion process. The audience is divided into small groups (3 to 7 members) for a discussion that allows for all members to contribute their ideas. This method can be used to develop questions for a speaker, discover ideas for which the audience desires more information, determine areas of special interest for future programs, or evaluate a meeting regarding its value to the participants. If a speaker or panel was involved in a half or full-day session, buzz sessions might occur after an initial presentation and before a break. A written summary of points could be brought forth to the moderators of the session so that pertinent comments could be addressed in the time available for discussion and interaction with the speaker(s). Depending on the size of the group, a leader can circulate among the participants to provide encouragement to stay on task and provide assistance, if needed. When the leader senses that the groups are nearing completion of their task, a warning can be given such as "Take a minute or two to complete your task."

After a discussion, instructors need to evaluate its success in order to make improvements and plans for the future. Some questions to consider include the following:

- Was progress made toward meeting course objectives?
- Was the pace of the discussion fast enough to be interesting and slow enough to promote analytical thinking?
- Was the topic stimulating, challenging, realistic, relevant, and meaningful to the group?
- Did the participants have the background necessary to engage in the discussion?
- Were participants and their comments received in a positive manner and treated seriously?
- Did at least three-fourths of the group participate?
- Was the discussion summarized clearly and concisely?

Fishbowl is a discussion strategy that involves a small group of 6 to 8 people having a conversation while seated in a circle. These *fish* are surrounded by a similar or larger group of observers in an outer circle (the *bowl*). In other words there are two groups—one in the inner circle and the other in the outer circle. A facilitator gives a brief introduction that outlines this method prior to the members of the inner circle beginning their discussion. Participants in the outer circle listen and observe, but do not interrupt persons in the inner circle. If someone from the outer circle wants to participate and move to the inner circle, someone from the inner circle must vacate a chair. The purpose of this discussion method is to observe, analyze, and learn from other thought processes. An alternative is a closed fishbowl in which all chairs are filled. At some point after about 10 to 15 minutes, the facilitator can suggest that the observers in the outer circle discuss what they heard and understood about the views of the participants in the inner circle. The persons in the two circles can switch their positions and continue discussing some additional factors not previously considered or discuss a parallel issue (McKeachie & Svinicki, 2006). For example, this method can be used to discuss gender roles and expectations of males and females in dating, love, or marriage issues.

Projective Techniques

Projective techniques use stimuli to elicit spontaneous responses from participants about related topics or situations. Participants may complete sentences, stories, arguments, or other prompts. Summarizing and/or synthesizing should follow the sharing of participant responses.

Incomplete Sentences is a technique where participants complete one or more sentence stems (i.e., Teenage parenthood is . . . ; I feel that . . . ; I was surprised that . . .). It is helpful for participants to actually write their responses down. Their completions may be discussed in large or small groups, and/or they may be turned in to the educator to be tallied for evaluative or other purposes. Incomplete sentences can be used to summarize learning (i.e., "I Learned" statements), as feedback or evaluation, to elicit participants' feelings or views on a topic, as well as elicit their preferences and expectations (i.e., a needs assessment).

Word Association is another projective technique in which a list of words related to a specific topic are read orally. Participants either write down or respond orally to each of the words. This can be used as an opening activity to get participants thinking about a topic and as an informal assessment of what participants' thoughts are about a particular topic.

Carousel is an interactive technique that can provide an opportunity for everyone to provide input. Large pieces of paper or poster board are hung throughout the room, each with an open-ended statement or a brainstorming question on it. Depending on the size of the group, participants can work individually or in small groups to rotate through each of the papers. The key is each new group must come up with different responses than are already written on the sheet. This activity could be implemented using breakout rooms in synchronous online programs. After each group (or individual) has had a turn with each prompt, summarize and discuss the responses on each of them.

Simulated Learning

Incorporating simulated learning experiences into the program provides an opportunity to explore the paradigm of "real life" experiences. It promotes active learning and interest in the learning environment and motivates learners. Simulated learning experiences provide a common and enjoyable experience that can be a catalyst for meaningful discussion. Some of the benefits of a simulated learning experience include seeing something from another point of view, sharing emotions, developing insight into human relations, improving communication skills, and using higher-order thinking skills (Chamberlain & Cummings, 2003). Although there are a variety of simulated learning experiences, we will share only a few, including different kinds of role-play and case studies.

ROLE-PLAY

A role-play is an unrehearsed presentation during which participants act out a real-life situation in front of an audience of other program participants. There is no script or set dialogue since participants create their parts as they go along after receiving some prompts from a facilitator. The group then discusses the implications of the interactions. A role-play is especially effective when the situation acted out involves some type of interpersonal conflict. It can be used to examine a delicate problem in human relations and explore possible solutions to an emotion-laden issue. A role-play, which can be both educational and entertaining, can involve adults or adolescents in formal or nonformal settings. At some point, the facilitator will stop the role-play to begin discussion. The facilitator may ask each member of the pair how it felt playing that role. This is especially important if you have an adolescent playing a parent role and vice versa. Getting a different point of view may be insightful to some of the issues each is facing. An example might be a role-play between an adolescent son or daughter and a parent who finds drugs in the child's room. In addition to discussing the issue of drug use among adolescents, parent-child communication can be observed.

One problem with role-play is that some participants may feel uncomfortable being the center of attention and speaking in front of a group. Rather than run the risk of asking for volunteers and having no one respond, prior to class ask a few people to participate whom you perceive to be outgoing and might be willing to play various roles. At times, participants believe they have to play certain roles appropriately by saying and doing the right things. This adds pressure; so suggest that the roles can be played in any way that they choose. You can always ask the same pair or another pair of learners to role-play the scenario in a different way. Employing some other variations of role-play may be less stressful because more participants are involved and no one is the main focus.

CIRCULAR ROLE-PLAY

In this role-play format participants play two roles at the same time. Participants sit in a circle and respond in writing to a scenario that might take place between a parent and a child. They are asked to play the role of the parent with the person on their left and the role of the child in that same situation with the person on their right. In other words, any individual is simultaneously playing a parent and child in the same scenario, but with two different family pairs. After 4 to 6 or more exchanges between the parent and child, stop the interactions and begin discussing what was or was not effective in dealing with this situation and how simultaneously playing the parent and child gave insights into these two points of view. This activity leads to a lively discussion (see Chapter 12 for an example).

CASE STUDIES

Case studies can be used in many ways. You can read them aloud to promote group discussion, use them in an individualized assignment, or assign small groups to analyze a family's situation. Each group could have the same scenario or different ones. In either case, the conclusions of the group(s) can be shared with the entire class to elicit further discussion. Students can identify the problem, propose alternate solutions, examine and analyze the consequences of potential solutions, and decide on a course of action. See Box 8.1 for examples of case studies that can be used to better understand family theory.

Games

Educational games are designed to teach learners of various ages about certain subjects, expand concepts, understand a culture, and assist them in learning a skill. Conceptual play facilitates students' engagement and enjoyment in learning by actively involving them in some type of competition or achievement in relationship to a course objective. Make sure you clarify the objective(s) and rules for the game so that students understand what is expected, and only include a game if it fits the curriculum and learners have the necessary background information. In addition, provide all materials for the game, have reference materials available as needed, monitor the group while the game is progressing, and expect some noise. There are several types of games, including card games (e.g., BARNGA—explained in Chapter 12); board games based on class content (e.g., Bingo and commercial board games); word and pencil games (crossword puzzles and word searches); action games (e.g., charades and others that involve movement); and televised game shows (Chamberlain & Cummings, 2003). Television game shows such as *Jeopardy* or *Family Feud* can be replicated in a classroom setting to reinforce knowledge presented in a lecture or to review content for an exam.

Group Process

Groups are a "way of life" for educators. In addition to your entire class being a group that you will teach, you may be called upon to speak to all kinds of groups, become involved in various groups and committees to accomplish tasks, or use small group learning in your classroom. While groups are formed for various reasons, such as treatment groups, support groups, task groups or committees, subgroups, or internet groups, we will only be focusing on *educational groups* that are designed to increase knowledge, teach skills, make decisions, or all three.

Group processes are especially notable in classrooms where group projects and teamwork are the foundation of effective teaching. Group projects can help students develop multiple skills that are important in their professional lives, such as tackling more complex problems than they could do individually, sharing diverse perspectives, pooling knowledge and skills, and developing new approaches to resolving differences.

Generally group members come together to talk; listen to each other; and share values, expectations, and resources, and thus become interdependent. The intensity of the group can be low to moderate depending on the topic and the amount of time needed to complete its tasks. Groups can last for a few hours, days, or months and can range on a continuum from collaborative learning to cooperative learning groups (Royse, 2001). Collaborative and cooperative learning are similar in that they are both based on the educational advantages of a social experience; however, they also have some differences. Whereas *collaborative* learning focuses on communicative knowledge and involves a loosely structured small-group format in which students work on a task (e.g., projects, discussion groups), *cooperative learning* is a more structured group effort focusing on the subject matter in which students thrive on interdependence and individual accountability to accomplish a specific task. *Jigsaw* is a popular cooperative learning technique in which each member within the group reads and studies a different selection, then teaches what he/she has learned to the other members of the group.

One of the main tasks of an effective family life educator is to lead groups. You will be expected to (1) provide learning experiences that will aid participants in expanding their knowledge and developing their skills, (2) maintain a balance between the presentation of information and the activities needed to assimilate the information, and (3) cope with interpersonal problems that may arise in groups. For teachers it is important to continually reflect upon what did and did not work well in the group experience and why. An effective educator needs to be a good administrator (group management and task focused) with affective skills (person-centered, feelings focused, and emotional "climate controller"). Teachers, who are aware of these needs, can help group members ease tension and keep differences of opinion minimal during complex communication interactions.

Program Facilitator

The last component of the *FLE Implementation Framework* (Ballard, 2020) is the program facilitator and is all about you, the family life educator! The importance of the family life educator in successful program implementation is often overlooked, but there are many traits, characteristics, and skills needed to be an effective family life educator. Important skills for family life educators that make a difference in achieving positive program outcomes include empathy, active listening, problem-solving, the ability to develop a positive rapport and connection with program participants, enthusiasm, cultural competence, and clear verbal and nonverbal communication (Ballard, 2020; Bradford et al., 2012; Kumpfer et al., 2018).

Engaging with the Audience

To deliver your program effectively, you must be able to connect with your target audience, which requires good interpersonal skills. Depending on the length of the session or program, you will want to engage the participants as quickly as possible to "break the ice." Begin by introducing yourself. Briefly provide your credentials to support why you are qualified to teach this course, as well as a little personal background. It is sometimes good to match the facilitator and participants based on similar experiences or common traits (Bradford et al., 2012).

For example, if you are implementing a program specifically for military families, it might build credibility and trust if you are also part of a military family.

A multisession course can provide an opportunity for more involved introductions, However, if you only have a one-session class, time for extended introductions might be a luxury. Nevertheless, getting to know the participants and each other is essential. In a short seminar, at times you might ask students to raise their hands if they are members of certain groups or have certain qualities.

In the opening session you will set the stage for learning by creating interest in the content of the class and building rapport with your students. When students enter the classroom, ask questions, indicate an interest in them and their activities, and show a positive and enthusiastic attitude. Since style of communication is important, keep the amount of information low and digestible, especially if this is the first of multiple sessions. As you present new ideas, get feedback and request examples, while also taking time to respond to student input. In a relaxed mode, with a sense of humor, and through interactions that are respectful, send the message that you are a person with whom they can be comfortable and trust.

Verbal Communication Skills

Clear communication is one of the most important skills needed by a family life educator in order to effectively implement programs. There are five basic components of good verbal communication: volume, rate of delivery, clarity, vocal emphasis, and tone or pitch.

Volume

If you do not speak loud enough, participants will not be able to hear your presentation, no matter how good it is! Try to talk to participants who are sitting in the back of the room and reduce sound interference (e.g., fans).

Rate of delivery

How fast do you talk? In order to maintain interest, it is important to speak at a quick rate; however, you do not want to stumble over your words or slur syllables together. The ability to vary the rate and achieve change of pace is more important than the rate of speed itself. For example, when you are giving very important material or making an important point, slow down your rate of delivery. Use pauses before or after an important word or the revelation of important information. Pauses are also important to allow participants time to think, process information, or to catch up.

Clarity

Although you want to maintain a somewhat fast rate of delivery, you must maintain clarity too. Speak slowly enough to ensure that you get your words out clearly. Try to relax. Nervousness often leads to speaking too fast and stumbling over words. Articulate and pronounce words carefully. Avoid using slang terms and be aware of any accent that you may have.

Vocal emphasis

The way that you emphasize different words may contribute to misunderstanding when you think that you are being perfectly clear. For example, read the following sentence six times, each time emphasizing a different word. "I didn't say he stole the book." Do you see how the meaning of the sentence can change just by emphasizing one word in the sentence? Use emphasis to create interest, to make a point, and to clarify meanings.

Tone or pitch

There are two basic pitch problems: monotone and patterned. The monotone speaker does not vary his or her tone at all. This can be very difficult to listen to and can make it difficult to concentrate. The patterned speaker has a singsong voice in which his or her voice goes up and down at regular intervals. Listening to a recording of yourself speaking or having a friend watch and listen to your presentation are strategies that you can use to catch and ultimately correct any of these communication problems that you might have.

Nonverbal Communication

When presenting to a group, your nonverbal communication can be just as important as your verbal communication. Gestures, facial expressions, eye contact, and body movement are aspects of nonverbal communication of which you should be aware.

Gestures

Gestures should be a purposeful part of your presentation and they should be executed with ease, flexibility, and proper timing. Try to avoid meaningless and nervous gestures such as wringing hands; jingling keys or coins; fumbling with pen, notes, or a paper clip; or putting your hands in your pocket.

Facial expression

Your facial expressions should be consistent with your verbal message. Do not hesitate to smile at your participants. This can help them to feel at ease, and can encourage or reinforce their participation.

Eye contact

Eye contact is an important part of your nonverbal communication. Try to scan the room and sustain direct eye contact with participants for several seconds. Be sure to use "soft" eyes rather than "hard" or staring eyes. Avoid talking to your notes, the chalkboard, power point slides, or the wall. In other words, keep your eyes focused on the participants.

Body movement

If used properly, body movements can create interest during your presentation. However, some body movements, such as rocking back and forth, constantly shifting your weight, or leaning on a table or lecture stand, can detract from your presentation. Try circulating throughout the room, but avoid pacing back and forth or forcing the participants to continually shift in their seats. If you are using PowerPoint or other visual aids, position yourself in relation to your visuals so all of the participants can clearly see them.

Cultural Competence

Cultural competence is important for all family life educators and is comprised of knowledge, awareness, motivation, and reflective skills (Mallette et al., 2022). Reflection can help you to become more aware of yourself and the effect that your own cultural experiences have on how you relate to others. Knowledge of your audience can help you to implement programs based on identified strengths and challenges within individuals and families. Practicing with cultural competence also allows you as a family life educator to better address systems of structural inequality, which improves programming for a wide variety of audiences (Mallette et al., 2022).

Overall, as a family life educator you must be culturally competent and have the ability to practice in an ethical manner, in which you respect the culture, beliefs, and lived experiences of participants (Darling, Cassidy, & Rehm, 2017; NCFR, 2019). It is important for you to be enthusiastic, see the need for your program, and believe that it will make a positive difference in filling the needs of your audience. Competence as a family life educator comes with practice and experience and sometimes additional training, which may be needed to implement certain evidence-based programs. See Chapter 2 for more on the importance of cultural competence as well as other skills and qualities of effective family life educators.

Obtaining Feedback on Learning Experiences

Whenever you design and implement a program, you want to have some idea of participant satisfaction with your program. Your program evaluation will determine if learning outcomes were met. In other words, did your participants meet the objectives and is there behavior change based on the knowledge gained (see Chapter 7 for more on program evaluation). However, it is important to measure the effectiveness of the program implementation. If it is an Evidenced-Based Program (EBP), you will want to determine if you implemented the program with fidelity. You may also want to know if participants were satisfied with the program. Did they like the activities? Was the location or online platform convenient? Do they have suggestions for improvement? These are called *process* or *implementation outcomes* and can be important to assess along with program outcomes. You may get some sense of how well the program went from daily discussions or from an informal satisfaction survey. However, you might also consider soliciting additional feedback by asking participants to list and rank order five things (1 to 5 with "1" being the most memorable or valuable) from the program that they are most likely to remember in the future and explain why they chose each item. In addition, ask them what two new insights they gained about themselves, their families, or their profession and how these insights might influence them and their future interactions with others. The results are often quite varied but provide meaningful feedback on what impacted the lives of participants. It also indicates that different methods and content can engage different learners.

SUMMARY

There are many things to consider when preparing to implement a family life education program. The *FLE Implementation Framework* (Ballard, 2020) consisting of program environment, program design and delivery, program participants, and program facilitator can be an effective tool for thinking about the implementation process. Selecting and incorporating different teaching methods, such as varying the types of presentations (e.g., lecture, panel, interview, debate, workshop, multimedia, and exhibits and displays) adds variety and interest. Attention should be given to facilitating interactions through questioning, discussion, simulated learning experiences, games, and group process. During and after presenting course content in various ways, it is important to gain feedback on how you can improve your teaching and better involve learners.

QUESTIONS AND ISSUES FOR DISCUSSION

1. Should you use written notes when you present? If so, how should they be structured and used?
2. If you are a moderator, how will you deal with panelists or presenters who ramble, are mostly silent, or are sharing incorrect information? How will you deal with learners who are aggressive, defensive, or have personal problems and distract the flow of the presentation or question session?
3. When working with groups, how do you handle the discussion dominators, frequent interrupters, disruptive members, or persons in crisis who are dealing with deep emotions?
4. Would you be willing to participate in role-play? Which kind of role-play do you like the best or least and why?

ACTIVITIES

1. Have students find online video clips related to a content area in the Certified Family Life Educator program (Appendix B) and discuss how they could be integrated into their teaching.
2. Have students or groups of students demonstrate some of the teaching and learning activities mentioned in this chapter using subject matter from the content areas of the Certified Family Life Educator program (Appendix B).

7

Evaluation of Family Programs

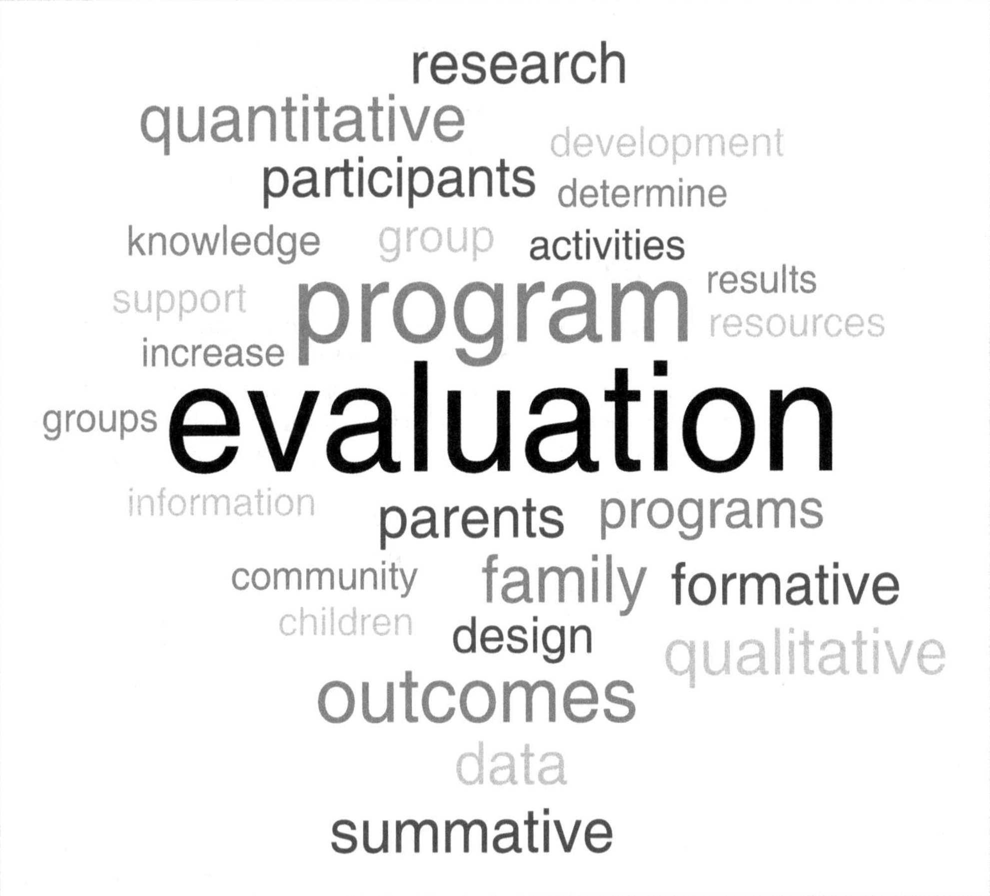

Imagine that you are the director of the Southwest Family Room, a neighborhood resource center located in a large metropolitan city. Funded by the United Way, the Southwest Family Room serves residents with children from before birth to age 6 living in the nine neighborhoods that make up the southwest section of the city.

The overall goal of the Southwest Family Room is to increase school readiness for children entering kindergarten. It was developed through the efforts of professionals at a lead agency and the input of community residents and business and service providers. The developers of the program have determined that one way to increase school readiness is to provide families with formal and informal support systems.

The Southwest Family Room provides this support through a number of activities, events, resources, and services. Activities and events include the Indoor Playground, Family Fun Night, numerous baby and toddler classes, and parenting education and support groups. They also offer a resource and toy library, make home visits, and produce a monthly newsletter and calendar of events for families with small children.

The Southwest Family Room has been operating for 5 years. Overall, things seem to be going well. But how do you know for sure? How do you and your staff know if you are meeting your goals? How do you know if you are making the best use of your limited staff and resources? How do those funding your program know if the program is effective and if it is making a difference?

Understanding Evaluation

A family agency or organization can spend a great deal of time and money promoting and carrying out programs designed to meet the various needs of families. But without conscious, systematic evaluation efforts, it might be time and money misspent. This chapter provides an *introduction* to the topic of evaluation. The intent is not to make you an evaluator, but rather to familiarize you with the concepts and steps that make up this sometimes complicated, but always important, aspect of family life education. Throughout this chapter we use the Southwest Family Room as an example to help you to understand and apply the concepts discussed.

The importance of evaluation cannot be overstated. Federal, state, and local governments and other funding organizations are showing increased interest in the effectiveness and accountability of the programs they support (Small & Huser, 2015). This increased pressure has resulted in more demand for evidence-based programs, which were introduced in Chapter 5 and will be discussed in more detail later in this chapter.

In recent years, the political climate in the United States has become more accepting and supportive of preventative efforts compared to the service and intervention approaches of the past. In fact, the Affordable Care Act of 2010 mandated the inclusion of a preventive approach to behavioral health and called for the development of a National Prevention Strategy to realize the benefits of prevention for the health of all Americans. The National Prevention Strategy recognizes that "many of the strongest predictors of health and well-being fall outside of the health care setting. Social, economic, and environmental factors all influence health" (National Prevention Council, 2011, p. 6). The National Prevention Strategy includes seven priorities: Tobacco Free Living, Preventing Drug Abuse and Excessive Alcohol Use, Healthy Eating, Active Living, Injury and Violence Free Living, Reproductive and Sexual Health, and Mental and Emotional Wellbeing. All of these priorities can be positively influenced by family life education.

In light of this, program evaluations need to be designed to measure individual program effectiveness, as well as to collectively address questions on the minds of policy makers about which family support and education programs work, for whom, how, when, where, and why (Jacobs, 2003). Especially where public tax revenues support parent and family education programs, taxpayers and legislators expect accountability and evidence of measurable benefit to the community. The development and recognition of effective prevention programs could serve to restructure the delivery of human services in this country. Although great strides have been made in recent years to increase the thoroughness and effectiveness of family program evaluation, there is still much to learn.

Beyond meeting the requirements of funders, evaluation is also important to those carrying out family programs and is an integral part of the program planning and implementation process. Without proper evaluation it is difficult to know if the programs being carried out are working. Family life educators must continue to conduct thoughtful and careful evaluations to ensure that family programs reach their goals in the most efficient manner possible.

Definitions

We begin the discussion by looking at the definition of *evaluation*, which is not an easy task. Rather than one shared definition which might limit the scope of evaluation (Poth et al., 2014), there are multiple definitions of evaluation. These multiple definitions capture the many facets of evaluation, including the various activities that are part of the process of evaluation, the questions that evaluation answers, and the outcomes that are achieved through evaluation.

However, there are commonalities among the following definitions articulated by several contributors to the literature on program evaluation. Jacobs (2003) defines evaluation as "a set of systematically planned and executed activities designed to determine the merit of a program, intervention, or policy or to describe aspects of its operation" (p. 63). Patton (2012) states that "evaluations . . . typically describe and assess what was intended (goals and objectives), what happened that was unintended, what was actually implemented, and what outcomes, and results were achieved" (p. 3). Finally, the Canadian Evaluation Society (CES) reviewed relevant literature and consulted with their members to develop this working definition: "Evaluation is the systematic assessment of the design, implementation, or results of an initiative for the purposes of learning or decision-making (2015)." The American Evaluation Association (AEA) also turned to its members and created a series of short videos in which AEA members explain their approach to evaluation in their work (AEA, n.d.).

Though the definitions vary, they all convey the key concept that evaluation is systematic and cannot be random or unplanned (Gross & Ballard, 2013). Casual observation of the program participants may suggest that the program is going well, but this is not evaluation. In other words, evaluation much be intentional with a specific plan for collecting and analyzing the information needed to assess effectiveness.

The goals of evaluation—to modify programs, increase effectiveness, and aid in decision making—are also consistent. Evaluation, which is different from research, is used to determine the value, quality, or effectiveness of a program. It is judgmental, and the results are usually program specific and often motivated by the program's needs. Information gathered can be subjective, however, the major reasons for conducting an evaluation are for planning, improving, or justification. An evaluation should result in some sort of recommendation.

Research, on the other hand, examines the relationships among variables and is nonjudgmental and conclusion oriented. One purpose for research is to contribute to knowledge building through the dissemination of findings. The intent is to have information that can be generalized, rather than specific to any one particular program. Evaluation answers the question of *what*, whereas research answers the question of *why*. Box 7.1 describes two scenarios; one involving research and the other, evaluation.

Box 7.1 Evaluation or Research?

The staff of the Southwest Family Room wants to know if toddlers who regularly attend a program like the Indoor Playground (which includes opportunities for climbing and exercise on playground equipment) show more advanced motor skills than toddlers who do not attend such a program. This type of study would be considered *research*. The staff of the Southwest Family Room also wants to know how the parents who attend the Indoor Playground feel about the program and if they find it to be a good opportunity to connect with other parents in their community. This type of study would be considered *evaluation*.

Reasons for Evaluation

For many family life educators, evaluation provides quite a challenge. Thorough evaluation takes planning, time, and money, often beyond the capabilities and resources of the average family education program and the technical expertise of the staff. Moreover, there can be resistance to evaluation. Program directors and staff may be concerned that evaluation will divert resources away from the program's activities, will increase the burden for program staff, and/or be too complicated. Some fear that it may produce negative results that will jeopardize program funding.

So why bother with evaluation? The reality is that evaluation is imperative to the success of a program. The results of an evaluation can do the following:

1. Verify and document program activities.
2. Increase effectiveness by identifying what is or is not working.
3. Modify and improve programs, services, and practices.
4. Assist with resource allocation.
5. Aid in planning and decision making.
6. Determine value, quality, or effectiveness of a program.
7. Justify the continuation of a program.
8. Demonstrate accountability to stakeholders.
9. Inform public policy.
10. Identify best practices and contribute to knowledge in the field.
11. Maintain satisfied clients/participants.
12. Determine program reach and whether or not the target audience is being reached.

Evaluation can provide a way to improve the efficiency and effectiveness of your staff's efforts by identifying strengths and weaknesses. You can increase the likelihood that resources are used effectively and goals are reached. Evaluation can show those who fund your program, as well as community members, how your program is benefiting its intended audience. Also, when results are shared with others running similar programs, it can contribute to knowledge in the field. If consciously incorporated into the design and ongoing operation of a program, evaluation does not need to be overly complicated or time-consuming and should never interfere with program activities.

TYPES OF EVALUATION

There was a time when evaluation was reserved for larger-scale programs and focused mainly on measuring long-term impact of established programs (Jacobs, 2003). However, the field has evolved and evaluation is an important component of all types of programming and can be performed for lots of different reasons. All programs should engage in evaluation regardless of size, stage of development, or access to resources (Jacobs, 2003). Programs go through different stages of development and effective programs evaluate at the right time (Small & Huser, 2015). But, not all evaluation focuses on end results. There are many different and valid evaluation questions to be answered, such as how well the program was implemented (Jacobs, 2003). Patton (2012) organized evaluation questions into three main questions: What? So What? Now What? "What?" answers the question of what happens in the program. This refers to the implementation or delivery of the program, such as activities, format, or participant engagement. "So What?" focuses on the results of the evaluation and examining what the evaluation findings mean. "Now What?" focuses on changes that should be made based on the evaluation findings. The questions that need to be answered drive the evaluation design, so it is important to think through these questions prior to beginning the evaluation process.

Evaluability Assessment

There is another step that can be implemented prior to an evaluation process: an *evaluability assessment* (EA). This is "a systematic process that helps identify whether program evaluation is justified, feasible, and likely to provide useful information" (Brunner, Craig, & Watson, 2019). An EA can include questions about both the design and the implementation of the program. Does the program have a design or model with clearly articulated, realistic, and measurable goals and objectives? An EA might compare the program design to the program that is actually being implemented. It could also ask if the program is serving the population for which it was designed. Are the resources identified in the program design actually in place? Is the program being carried out as originally planned and described? Are resources in place to provide for collection of data needed for program evaluation? Conducting an evaluability assessment prior to carrying out a full program evaluation can minimize the risk of determining part way through an evaluation that certain necessary components are missing or unobtainable.

Five-Tiered Approach to Program Evaluation

There are a number of methods and techniques involved in carrying out a program evaluation. The *Five-Tiered Approach to Program Evaluation* (see Appendix E) is a widely used evaluation approach (Jacobs, 2003). It provides a useful rubric for family life educators to ensure that a program is evaluated comprehensively. It prompts evaluators to think about the purpose of evaluation, its audience, and the procedures for collecting and analyzing data. The step-by-step tiers serve as a guide for a systematic strategy for evaluation. Tiers 1 through 3 guide users through assessing needs and ensuring accountability, quality, and clarity. Tiers 4 and 5 explain the process of translating data into new outcomes, applying findings to further research, enhancing the program, and determining areas for public policy action. In addition to Jacobs' Five-Tiered Approach to Program Evaluation there are many resources available to assist you in the evaluation of your family program. See the end of the chapter for a list of organizations and resources that can guide you in preparing for and conducting a program evaluation.

Assessing Needs and Assets

Perhaps one of the most important concepts about evaluation is the need to incorporate an evaluation plan *into the development and initial planning stages of a program.* A well-developed program begins with a ministudy (sometimes referred to as a needs assessment, a feasibility study, or an assets inventory; see Chapter 3 for a more detailed discussion of needs assessment). These ministudies often involve an examination of the current situation to determine if the proposed program is justified. A needs assessment can encompass both the target audience as well as the program environment. Who is the target audience for this program? What do these participants already know about the topic? What do they want to know? What resources are available? What are the strengths or assets of this community? Do similar programs exist in this community? Will the community support the program?

It also is important to assess characteristics of the target audience and how this might affect your program. Literacy level, socioeconomic status, and race are examples of characteristics that might be relevant. Other aspects of the program environment might include the context, culture, stakeholders, or organizational structure that might influence your program. Conducting a program in a low-income housing project would be very different than conducting one at a community center in an upper-class neighborhood. A stakeholder often may be the person who has asked you to conduct the program, such as the head of the company or the principal of the school. If you are working with children or teens, the parents also have a stake in what you are presenting in your program.

What benefits are likely to be produced through the program? It is important to be clear about the need for, and goals of, a program. If you do not have a clear picture of what the program is trying to accomplish, you will not know how to tell if you have been successful. Think seriously about what it is you want to learn from an evaluation. Consider its place in the continuing implementation of your program and integrate the evaluation into the ongoing activities. Remember that evaluation is a process, not an event.

Formative Evaluation

Evaluation efforts can have different goals and can be conducted at different points throughout the development and implementation of a program. Evaluations may be formative or summative in nature. *Formative evaluations* generate information for the purposes of planning, monitoring, and improving programs and are sometimes also referred to as *process evaluations* or *program monitoring*. Formative evaluations describe a program and provide feedback on how it is doing *while the program is still in progress*, often prompting changes in timing, approaches, etc. Formative evaluation can also assess progress toward objectives (Tier 4 of Jacobs' model). Therefore, formative evaluation might include surveying participants midway through a scheduled program to see if the program is meeting their expectations. If participants are not learning what they should, outcomes might not be reached. Formative evaluation can provide an opportunity to reteach or reinforce information.

As an example of formative evaluations, imagine that your agency holds a monthly meeting to provide education on infant development to mothers of newborns. Although the participants seem very enthusiastic about the meetings, attendance has been sporadic. By surveying the participants, you find that availability of transportation is a defining factor in whether or not they attend. Therefore, a car pool is arranged that provides rides for everyone who wants to attend the meeting, resulting in a dramatic increase in attendance. If surveying the participants had been delayed to the end of the program, it would have been too late to implement the car pool and a number of possible program participants would have missed out on the program. The use of formative evaluation throughout the program facilitates making changes that will increase the likelihood of better implementing the program and reaching intended goals.

Box 7.2 gives an example of a formative evaluation of the Indoor Playground program. With this information the staff can determine if the program is meeting

Box 7.2 **Formative Evaluation**

The Indoor Playground is held each Friday at the Southwest Family Room. Once each month, staff members distribute a survey to the attendees. The survey includes questions such as:

- How many times have you attended the Indoor Playground?
- What is your main reason for attending?
- Is this a convenient day for you to attend?
- Is this a convenient time for you to attend?
- If not, when would be better?
- What changes would you like to see in the Indoor Playground?
- How did you hear about the Indoor Playground?
- Do you attend any other Southwest Family Room events?

the needs of the participants and make any needed changes in scheduling and format. They can also determine which marketing efforts are working best. This formative evaluation will provide them information that can be used to modify the program while it is still in progress.

Summative Evaluation

Summative evaluations, sometimes referred to as *outcome evaluations*, are concerned with the end results of a program. How did the program affect the people it served? Were the program goals met? Summative evaluations can be used to determine if a program should be replicated, expanded, or perhaps discontinued. Summative evaluations can occur directly after the program is completed or it might also extend to measure long-term impact of the program. In other words, did the participants retain their new knowledge and skills six months after the program ended? Have participants changed their behavior as a result of their new knowledge and skill? In the example given in Box 7.3, a summative evaluation carried out at the end of the program cycle could determine if participants in the New Parents program had increased their knowledge of infant development. Another aspect of summative evaluation may measure the participants' satisfaction with the program. Did they like it? Were they happy with the presentation of it? Did they think the family life educator was effective?

Implementation Evaluation

In addition to assessing how much the participants are learning or if other program outcomes are being achieved, evaluation may also include how well the program was implemented. It is important to document what happens as a program is being implemented in order help demonstrate effectiveness, make revisions if needed, and to replicate the program (Small & Huser, 2015). There has been an increase in attention given to implementation evaluation. Aspects of implementa-

Box 7.3 **Summative Evaluation**

The Southwest Family Room sponsors a New Parents support group for parents of newborns. The meetings are facilitated by parents in the community who have completed a 16-hour group training program and provided with resource materials. Parents enter the program before their babies are born or just afterward. The program meets twice a month for two hours over a two-year period. A summative evaluation of the New Parents program would be conducted at the end of the two-year period with participants being interviewed or asked to complete a questionnaire. The intent of the survey or questionnaire would be to determine how the parents benefited from the program. Did they learn new knowledge about child development or new skills regarding parenting? Did their participation help them feel more confident about their abilities as parents? Did they feel less alone and less isolated? Do they feel more connected to their community, having met other families in a similar situation? Results of this summative evaluation will help the staff of the Southwest Family Room know if their goals have been met. The results may determine if the program will be replicated and/or may influence how future programs are conducted.

tion may relate to the program environment, program participants, program design and delivery, and program facilitator (Ballard, 2020). Implementation can include participant satisfaction, fidelity (teaching program as it was designed to be taught), retention and engagement of participants, quality of delivery, or program features such as length of the program. Evaluation of how well a program was implemented can occur at the end of the program or during the program.

Logic Models

Although the specific terminology varies, some common terms and concepts are used in the literature on evaluation. Both the W. K. Kellogg Foundation (2004) and United Way Worldwide (2009) offer publications that provide a conceptual framework for understanding evaluation called a logic model.

Programs can be developed and outcomes identified with a *logic model* or an *if-then* method of looking at a situation. Logic models can facilitate thinking through the progression of steps taken by program participants and provide a more realistic view of what to expect of the program. Logic models also help identify key components that must be considered in order to determine if the program is effective. Logic models include inputs, activities, outputs, and outcomes. An example of a logic model might be: *If* funding (input) can be provided, *then* parenting classes can be offered. *If* classes (activities) can teach about child development and parenting skills (output), *then* parents can acquire knowledge, gain skills, and change their attitudes about how to care for their children (initial outcomes). *If* they learn new approaches in dealing with their children, *then* they will change their behavior to reflect these new methods (intermediate outcomes). *If* they change their behavior, *then* they will increase the likelihood of positive childhood outcomes such as healthy emotional development. Applying this method can help identify the steps needed to reach intended goals and link activities to program outcomes.

Inputs

Inputs include resources dedicated to or consumed by the program. Examples are money, staff and their time, volunteers and their time, facilities, equipment, and supplies (see Box 7.4).

Box 7.4 **Inputs**

Inputs at the Southwest Family Room include financial support provided by the sponsoring agency, staff members and their time, and members of the community who volunteer their time to various programs and services that are offered. Additional inputs would be the site where the Southwest Family Room is located, including meeting space, materials, supplies, playground equipment, and toys available through the Indoor Playground.

Activities

A program uses inputs to fulfill its mission through *activities*. Activities include the strategies, techniques, and types of treatment that make up the program's service methodology. In our example of the Southwest Family Room, activities would center on providing education and support to families with small children. These activities would include the Family Fun Night, the Indoor Playground, the community calendar, and other events and services intended to provide education and support to parents of small children.

Outputs

Outputs are the direct products of program activities. They are usually measured in terms of the volume of work accomplished, such as the number of classes held, brochures distributed, and participants served (see Box 7.5).

Box 7.5 **Outputs**

How many people attended the Indoor Playground? How many sessions of the Family Fun Night were held? How many people used the toy library? How many brochures or flyers about the Southwest Family Room were distributed at neighborhood festivals and community events? These questions attempt to gather information about outputs. In addition to attendance, further quantitative information might reveal meaningful results. Program observers could tally specific parent-child behaviors.

Outcomes

Outcomes are the benefits or changes to individuals or groups that come during or after participation in program activities. Outcomes are influenced by outputs and reflected through modified behaviors, increased skills, new knowledge, changed attitudes or values, improved conditions, and other attributes. They represent changes in the participants from the time they started the program until the time they completed it. For example, outcomes of the program described in Box 7.6 would be a better understanding of toddler development and a resulting change in parenting behavior, such as the use of more appropriate discipline strategies. In some instances there is just one desired outcome for a program. However, in many cases there is a series of outcomes, each of which can contribute to the accomplishment of another and, ultimately, to the final outcome goals of the program. Different programs use various terms to describe these same levels but the most commonly used terms are *initial outcomes*, *intermediate outcomes*, and *long-term outcomes*.

INITIAL OUTCOMES

Initial outcomes are the first changes or benefits that a participant experiences as a result of the program. It may be a change in attitude, knowledge, skills, or all of these. In most programs these initial outcomes would not be ends themselves, but important steps toward reaching the desired ends.

INTERMEDIATE OUTCOMES

Intermediate outcomes connect a program's initial outcomes to longer-term outcomes intended for its participants. Intermediate outcomes are often exemplified by changes in behavior as a result of the new knowledge, skills, or attitudes.

LONGER-TERM OUTCOMES

Longer-term outcomes are the lasting outcomes that a program wants to achieve, and is sometimes referred to as "program impact." These are usually significant changes that are often longitudinally apparent and related to condition or

Box 7.6 **Outcomes**

Parents attending a monthly class, called "Discipline and Your Child," learn new techniques for directing the behavior of their toddlers. The staff hopes that providing comprehensive information about child development and discipline alternatives will expand parents' understanding of these topics. Staff members perceive that by increasing parents' knowledge, they will make better choices about discipline, including approaches to preventing misbehavior. The goal is for parents to use less punitive means and employ more appropriate choices with their children. By preventing misbehavior, parents can have a more positive attitude about discipline, feel more confident about being able to prevent misbehavior, feel more successful as parents, and enjoy their child even more. A positive change in the behavior of the parent will result in a better relationship with the child. Additionally, the child will be more likely to experience positive outcomes relevant to physical, social, and emotional development because he or she is being raised in an optimal environment. These are all examples of outcomes.

status. An example of a longer-term outcome might be that since the program began, parent attendance at parent-teacher conferences in the community has increased significantly. See Box 7.7 for an example of the various outcomes of a Southwest Family Room class. Unfortunately, many programs only have the resources to measure initial outcomes. The cost of conducting evaluations to include intermediate and longer-term outcomes is sometimes prohibitive for organizations operating on limited budgets. Measuring longer-term outcomes or program impact requires a more rigorous evaluation design.

Box 7.7 **Levels of Outcomes**

Initial Outcomes

After attending the "Terrific Threes" and "Fabulous Fours" parent education classes, there is a measurable increase in the number of minutes that most parents spend reading to their child in one-on-one parent-child time.

Intermediate Outcomes

Several months into the program, the staff member who oversees the program's lending library notes that the library is busier. When she checks her records, the librarian determines that library usage has more than doubled for most parents.

Longer-Term Outcomes

Two years into the future, as kindergarten teachers collect information about their students' preschool experience, they discover that children whose parents participated in "Terrific Threes" and "Fabulous Fours" scored significantly higher on all school readiness assessments.

Indicators

An *indicator* identifies the factors that are being measured to track the program's success of an outcome. An indicator is observable and measurable (see Box 7.8).

Qualitative Data

Qualitative data describe and interpret happenings or emotions. They are verbal or narrative comments that can be collected by observing or interviewing participants. Methods for collecting qualitative data include focus groups, interviews, questionnaires, case studies, and direct observation. Although qualitative data are difficult to analyze, they address what affects positive human behavior and what family programs hope to influence. Qualitative data might include descriptions of how parents teach children to play with a new toy; stories about how a support group changed a parent's perception of a crisis situation; or a series of excerpts from a parent's journal that describe what was learned during a year of being involved in a home visiting program. Qualitative data can be important for communicating with stakeholders and providing a way to share success stories (see Box 7.9).

Box 7.8 **Indicators**

One of the goals of the Indoor Playground is to provide opportunities for parents in the community to connect with each other. Staff at the Indoor Playground events might systematically observe parents to see if they are interacting with each other and if relationships are forming. This interaction between the parents, especially if the same parents sit together and talk to each other at subsequent events, could be considered an indicator of parents' connection with each other. Staff could also observe other Southwest Family Room events to see if some of the same parents attend and if they interact with other families.

An overall goal of the Southwest Family Room is to increase learning readiness of children entering kindergarten. One indicator of learning readiness is having received all recommended shots before entering kindergarten. Another indicator might be that children have been screened for hearing, vision, or speech problems and have received the appropriate intervention, if needed. If these problems are identified early enough for actions to be taken, children will be ready to learn by the time they enter kindergarten.

Box 7.9 **Qualitative Data/Evaluation**

If the staff of the Southwest Family Room wanted to gather *qualitative data* or carry out a qualitative evaluation, they could interview or survey the participants of the programs to collect information on how they feel about the programs and how they think they have benefited. Another option would be to observe parents at various events and record information about their interactions with their children or other parents. They could also hold a focus group meeting of parents of 4-year-olds to determine what issues are of most concern at this stage in their children's lives. This information could be used to help them design future classes or determine what resources might be most helpful.

Quantitative Data

Information gathered through quantitative methods is typically reported numerically and can take less time to analyze than qualitative data. Age, education level, and attendance records for various events would all be considered *quantitative data*. However, quantitative data can also include participant's perceptions, perhaps identified through a Likert-type scale (e.g., range of options from 1 strongly disagree to 5 strongly agree), regarding their perceived knowledge gains, comfort levels, or satisfaction. These data can be gathered through questionnaires, tests, surveys, counting the number of participants in the program, and/or observation (see Box 7.10). For example, one measurement of a quantifiable change in the parent-child relationship may be an improvement in parenting skills observed by the use of appropriate communication methods with the child or the correct implementation of guidance strategies.

Box 7.10 **Quantitative Data/Evaluation**

At each event held by the Southwest Family Room, a sign-in sheet with the participant's name is provided. Staff members use this information, in addition to attendance, to monitor how many people are attending each event—an example of an output in Tier 2 of Jacobs' model (see Appendix E). They may also collect data on how kindergarten children that have attended the program score on developmental assessments. These would be considered *quantitative data.*

Although evaluators are likely to continue to debate the best approach to evaluation, design, and data collection methods (i.e., qualitative vs. quantitative), many evaluators believe the questions that focus the evaluation study should lead to a discussion about which types of approaches are used. It is also important to note that many studies employ a mixed-methods approach, that is, a design using both qualitative and quantitative methods. The needs and interests of the stakeholders in your program may also influence the evaluation design and methodology. Stakeholders, which include anyone who is affected by the results of the evaluation, can include decision makers and policy makers as well as staff, people in the community, and the clients themselves (Ballard, 2020).

Evaluation Design

Not all programs are ready for an evaluation that measures program impact (Jacobs, 2003). Establishing impact (Tier 5 of Jacob's model) goes beyond measuring the achievement of short-term program outcomes and typically involves a more rigorous evaluation design that looks at long-term program impact. It is after this level of evaluation that programs may be determined to be *evidence-based programs.* A program can be identified as being evidence-based if "(a) evaluation research shows that the program produces expected positive results; (b) the results can be attributed to the program itself rather than to other extraneous factors or events; (c) the evaluation is peer-reviewed by experts in the field; and (d) the program is 'endorsed' by a federal agency or respected research organization and included in their list of effective programs" (Seibel, 2011).

The issue of evidence-based programs is increasingly prevalent when considering family life education programs and practices. As discussed earlier in this chapter and in Chapter 5, many funders are requiring that programs be identified as "evidence-based" in order to receive financial support (ASPE, 2013; Small & Huser, 2015). This attention and support has resulted in an increase in information and resources relevant to identifying, designing, and evaluating evidence-based programs. See Chapter 5 for more discussion on identifying and choosing an evidence-based program.

In order to be recognized as evidence-based, a program must undergo an evaluation study. There are a number of different ways to design an evaluation study with some designs considered to be more rigorous than others. Differences in design include the presence or absence of a control group, the method by which participants are assigned to groups, and the frequency with which outcomes are measured (SAMHSA, 2012). An *experimental design* (Tier 5 of Jacob's model) is considered the most rigorous, followed by *quasi-experimental* and *pre-experimental*.

Experimental Design

An experimental design, sometimes referred to as a *randomized controlled trial*, involves the comparison of a randomly assigned treatment and control group. Members of the treatment and control groups should have similar traits and characteristics. Both groups are measured or observed prior to implementation of a program, and after the program is completed the outcomes of the two groups are compared. The random assignment of the subjects to the groups helps to ensure that any differences in outcome are likely the result of the program. Repeating the experiment multiple times with several different control and treatment groups helps to increase confidence in the outcome of the study. While often the best way to accurately measure program effectiveness, experimental design is typically more expensive and can be more time-consuming. Box 7.11 provides an example of an experimental design.

Box 7.11 Experimental Design

Let's revisit the scenario in Box 7.3:

The Southwest Family Room sponsors a New Parents support group for parents of newborns. The meetings are facilitated by parents in the community who have completed a 16-hour small-group training program. Parents enter the program before their babies are born or just afterward. The program meets twice a month for two hours for a two-year period.

In this situation an experimental design would involve the random assignment of the parents of newborns born in a community hospital during an identified time frame into two groups. One group of parents would be enrolled in a "New Parents" support group and identified as the "treatment group." The other group would be identified as a "control group." Both groups would be given a pre-test measuring their knowledge of infant and toddler development. The treatment group would participate in the New Parent program over the course of the next two years. The parents in the control group would not participate in the program. At the end of the two-year program, both sets of parents would be given the same test again. If the parents in the New Parents support group demonstrated greater knowledge of infant and toddler development it could be concluded that participation in the program resulted in increased knowledge, especially if this same study was repeated with subsequent groups of parents and demonstrated the same results each time.

Quasi-Experimental Design

Given that it is not always practical or feasible to create a control group, a quasi-experimental design can be conducted (see Box 7.12). A quasi-experimental design uses two or more pre-existing or self-selected groups that share some common variable. The most important issue with a quasi-experimental design is the lack of a random assignment to treatment or control groups. Because of the lack of randomization, quasi-experimental designs tend to have lower internal validity than experimental designs because it is difficult to know for sure if the comparison groups differed in any important way that might account for differences in outcomes.

Box 7.12 Quasi-Experimental Design

A quasi-experimental design could be achieved through a delayed intervention. If all parents interested in attending a class could not be accommodated, a wait list could be created. Those on the wait list could complete the pre-test and post-test at the same time as those in the class but without the benefit of having completed the class. Initially those on the wait list would be part of a comparison group, but would eventually be able to attend the class. This can be a more ethical way to carry out a quasi-experimental design because it does not deny anyone the program or services that could be beneficial.

Pre-Experimental Design

A pre-experimental design is considered the least rigorous because it lacks a control group and does not involve random assignment. Only the people participating in the program are involved in any kind of measurement. There may be a pre-test and a post-test or just a post-test. Using just a post-test approach will only tell if the participants have reached a specific outcome, such as learning a new skill, since there will not be a baseline to assess. Incorporation of a pre-test and

Box 7.13 Pre-Experimental Design

Parents participating in a New Parents support program would be selected as the study group. All participants in the group would be given a pre-test about infant and toddler development upon entering the program. They would be given the same test at the end of the second year. It might be determined that the knowledge demonstrated on the post-test was the result of participation in the class. However, because there is no control group for comparison, it is difficult to say for sure if the increased knowledge was attributable specifically to participation in the class. There is no way of knowing if parents who did not participate in the class demonstrated a similar knowledge gain just by virtue of having been parents for the past two years.

post-test enables comparison of the participants' knowledge or attitudes before and after they enter the program, making it easier to measure how the participants have changed. However, because there is no control group it is difficult to attribute any change to the program itself.

CULTURAL CONSIDERATIONS IN EVALUATION

Regardless of the method of evaluation chosen, it is important to keep cultural contexts in mind. Most standardized instruments were designed for white, middle-class populations. These are often inappropriate when English is not the primary language of the individuals who will complete them or if Western cultural concepts would not be well understood or do not carry the same value. The issue of language is complex. For example, not everyone from a particular ethnic group can read and write even in their native language. Not only do dialects and regional language differences exist, but communication skill-levels also differ among generations, across socioeconomic groups, and among people with different educational histories.

Some Western concepts are difficult to translate and require data collectors to clarify survey items for study participants. For example, self-esteem is not only a concept that is challenging for US researchers to define and measure, but it may also be a concept unfamiliar to new or recently arrived immigrants. In addition, evaluators should be mindful of any participant's reluctance to fill out a form. In the situation of undocumented immigrants, participants may be fearful of revealing any identifying information that might be available to immigration enforcement. Carrying out pre-testing interviews and surveys or setting up advisory group review committees can determine the best approach for examining questionable words or concepts. This procedure is sometimes referred to as *pilot testing*.

It is important to be aware of *cultural response sets*. In some cultures, professionals may be seen as authority figures deserving of respect. Participants in this situation may feel uncomfortable or unwilling to provide any negative feedback even if encouraged. In some cultures, asking for help or appearing needy is inappropriate. Participants from such cultures may not feel comfortable revealing what they consider to be weaknesses. There may also be cultural taboos against revealing too much personal information. Other things to consider within varying cultures might be gender, age, and socioeconomic status. Are family programs experienced differently by men than by women or by people of different economic levels? Awareness and sensitivity to such factors will increase the effectiveness of your information-gathering strategies.

In order for family life educators to be successful they must have, in addition to knowledge and skills relevant to family life education topics, an understanding of the specific cultural beliefs and practices of the population with which they are working (Mallette et al., 2021; also see Chapter 3). It is important for this awareness to carry over into any evaluation processes put in place.

SUMMARY

This chapter has provided a brief overview of many concepts and issues involved in evaluation. As you have surmised, evaluation can be a complicated issue. However, its value and importance cannot be underestimated. If you find yourself involved in family programming in any way, you will be directly or indirectly involved in evaluation. It is imperative to take time to carefully carry out the necessary steps for an effective evaluation plan including assessing the needs and strengths of your audience, identifying existing resources, considering stakeholders and their expectations, and developing a logic model that thoughtfully considers the relationship between actions and results, along with program activities, inputs, outcomes, and indicators. It will be important to build formative and implementation evaluation into the design of your program, as well as summative evaluation at the end of your program or class to help you determine what worked and what can be improved. By following these important steps and considering the multiple aspects of evaluation, you will increase the likelihood that your program will improve and enhance the lives of its participants.

QUESTIONS AND ISSUES FOR DISCUSSION

1. How would you do a needs assessment, formative evaluation, and summative evaluation for a one-night, three-hour workshop called "Balancing Work and Family"?
2. What are some possible inputs, activities, outputs, outcomes, and indicators for the same program?
3. How would you gather qualitative and quantitative data in the above scenario?
4. What are the possible initial, intermediate, and long-term outcomes that could occur as a result of attending the "Balancing Work and Family" workshop? Could all outcomes be realized by the end of the workshop, that is, at the end of that same day?

ACTIVITIES

1. Identify a large federal grant opportunity that focuses on prevention rather than intervention. How would evaluation be different for a program that focuses on prevention?
2. Read Appendix E, "The Five-Tiered Approach to Program Evaluation," and provide examples of evaluations performed at each tier.
3. Your 6-week workshop, "Sexuality and Your Teen," has not been going as well as you had hoped. Attendance has been dropping, participants seem distracted, and it has been difficult to engage them in group discussion. How can you find out what the problem is and the reasons for their discontent?

WEB RESOURCES FOR PROGRAM EVALUATION

American Evaluation Association
www.eval.org

Centers for Disease Control Framework for Program Evaluation in Public Health
www.cdc.gov/eval/framework/index.htm

Community Toolbox (Work Group for Community Health and Development—University of Kansas)
www.ctb.ku.edu/en

FRIENDS—National Resource Center for Community-Based Child Abuse Prevention—Evaluation Toolkit Resources
www.friendsnrc.org/evaluation-toolkit

Harvard Family Research Project
Evaluation Exchange: www.hfrp.org/evaluation/the-evaluation-exchange
Evaluation Publications and Resources: www.hfrp.org/evaluation/publications-resources

United Way Worldwide—Focusing on Program Outcomes
www.unitedwaynems.org/wp-content/uploads/2018/02/Outcomes_Guide_Final-08.28.09.pdf

What Works Wisconsin—Effective Programs and Resources for Children, Youth, and Families
fyi.extension.wisc.edu/whatworkswisconsin

W. K. Kellogg Foundation Logic Model Development Guide
www.wkkf.org/resource-directory/resources/2004/01/logic-model-development-guide

Part III

Content of Family Life Education

8

Relating Theory to Practice

NEED FOR THEORY IN FAMILY LIFE EDUCATION

Theories contribute to our understanding of families by providing reasonable explanations of individual and family behaviors. Because families are so complex, there is no single theory that can explain all family behaviors, thus, we need several theories from various disciplines to understand family functioning. The incorporation and integration of multiple theories are essential because we are affected by many different elements within our childhood, family, gender, socialization experiences, and cultural beliefs. Moreover, the interaction of theory with research is essential for translational family science, which characterizes the process through which research findings are implemented in educational settings.

Theories can relate to examining families over time, families operating as a system, the interactions and exchanges within families, power within families, and individual family member perspectives (Allen & Henderson, 2017). Examples of some of the core theories and frameworks include family systems, ecosystems, individual and family development, social exchange, symbolic interaction, conflict, feminist, and stress theories. Family life education is founded in a systems perspective including both family systems and larger ecosystems, which are woven throughout the framework.

The Family Life Education Content Areas—Content and Practice Guidelines

Content and practice guidelines for the Certified Family Life Educator (CFLE) program include knowledge, skills, and abilities as well as consideration of theory, research, and practice within the field of family life education (see Appendix B). Teaching about families is grounded in the theoretical, methodological, and practical principles that integrate knowledge and praxis (Allen & Lavender-Stott, 2020; Darling, Cassidy, & Rehm, 2017). Family life educators often emphasize the importance of a strong theoretical foundation to guide programmatic development, however that perspective was not apparent in the results of job analysis surveys conducted to determine the competencies needed by CFLEs. Unfortunately, the importance of theory was not always recognized by those practicing in the field (Darling et al., 2009; NCFR 2014).

Although it is important for entry-level family life educators to have the knowledge and skills to be family life educators, it is apparent that a stronger theoretical basis is needed for family life educators to better practice their profession. Since theory is more abstract, applications of the theory need to be integrated to help participants go beyond facts and knowledge about families and think critically about how families function.

OVERVIEW OF THEORIES/FRAMEWORKS USED TO STUDY FAMILIES

Although the focus of this book does not include an in-depth description of all the theories relevant to family life educators, a general overview of some of the main theories will be shared. For some readers these highlights will be a review, whereas for others, it will introduce theoretical concepts for further exploration. Theories or frameworks can be macro or micro and be categorized into five domains: (1) examination of families over time, (2) families functioning within systems, (3) family interactions and exchanges, (4) power within families, and (5) perspectives of individual family members (Bailey & Gentry, 2013). In addition, Allen and Henderson (2017) noted four common assumptions related to all family theories: (1) developmental—families change over time, (2) diversity—families vary in composition and structure, (3) systemic—families are systems, and (4) process—families are dynamic.

A foundational principle of FLE is the value placed on evidence-based research and theory. Furthermore, including theory in the programming and content of FLE contributes to its effectiveness and credibility (Darling, Cassidy, & Rehm, 2019). When individuals have an opportunity to experience theoretical concepts in an applied manner, they can more readily incorporate that knowledge into their work with families. Thus, the second section of this chapter will provide examples of ways to incorporate the theories discussed when learning about and working with families.

Family Systems Theory

Evolving from general systems theory, viewing the family as a system provides an important paradigm when analyzing human and family behavior. The family as a whole is viewed as greater than the sum of its parts and as a social system with rules, roles, communication patterns, and a power structure (Allen & Henderson, 2017; White, Martin, & Adamsons, 2019). A *system* can be viewed as a collection of elements with interrelated and interdependent parts so what affects one person in a family also influences other members. The family system is maintained by a boundary that can be perceived as occurring on a continuum ranging from *open* (allowing elements outside the family to influence it) to *closed* (becoming self-contained and isolating the family from its environment). However, no family is completely open or closed. There are two key elements of family systems theory: (1) *structural characteristics* involving *boundaries* and their *permeability, subsystems,* and *hierarchies* and (2) *process characteristics* comprised of establishing boundaries; establishing connectedness and separateness; and establishing congruent images, themes, messages, and rules. There are a number of other key concepts, such as *inputs, outputs,* and *feedback; circular causality; family rules, routines,* and *rituals;* and *equilibrium* and *dynamic equilibrium.* A family systems perspective can be helpful in examining diverse families as it presents a uniform view of families and considers the ways in which race and culture affect both process and structural characteristics of families (James & Lewis, 2020).

Concepts from the *Couple and Family Map (Circumplex Model)* (Olson & DeFrain, 2006; Olson & Gorall, 2003; Olson, Russell, & Sprenkle, 1989) help us to understand (1) family *cohesion* or the emotional bonding within families ranging from *enmeshed* to *disengaged* and (2) family *flexibility* regarding the amount of change in its leadership, role relationships, and relational rules ranging from *chaotic* to *rigid* and how these characteristics can change through the family life cycle and across cultures.

The third element is *communication*, which is considered essential to facilitating movement on the other two dimensions. Having a balanced family system between the extremes of cohesion and flexibility tends to be more functional across the life cycle. The notion of cohesion can be further understood by examining *vertical attachment* to a previous or subsequent generation and *horizontal attachment*—connectedness within your same generation. Moreover, couples and families try to maintain their separateness and connectedness by balancing *centrifugal forces* that push family members away from the family and *centripetal forces* that pull family members together (Beavers & Hampson, 2000; Goldenberg & Goldenberg, 2013).

By using this model, theoretical clarifications can evolve from discussions of boundaries and distance regulation along with cohesion and flexibility. What types of boundaries exist for persons of varying ethnic, age, or gender backgrounds or when dealing with various crises? What kinds of expectations for family togetherness and flexibility exist for different ethnic and religious groups? For example, cohesion can have different meanings in cultures that value familism vs. individuality. A discussion of family stories, rituals, and rules can also provide understanding and meaning about differing families and groups.

Many FLE programs have a foundation in family systems theory and use the theory to guide content and delivery of programming. For example, the Strengthening Families Program (Kumpfer, 2020) includes both children and parents in the program recognizing the importance of including the whole family in order to effect lasting change in family processes. Additionally, inclusion of the whole family can increase participation. For example, a family focus in FLE programming aligns with the cultural value of *familismo* (family closeness and support) and is an important recruitment and retention strategy for Latino families (Schvaneveldt, 2022).

Family as an Ecosystem

An ecosystems approach is a broad contextual framework that can examine a wide range of issues related to individuals and families within various environments (Bubolz & Sontag, 1993; Darling, 1987; Darling, Cassidy, & Rehm, 2017, 2019; Darling & Turkki, 2009). Since it is not based on any particular family configuration, it can be used with families of diverse structures, backgrounds, and life circumstances. With individual and family issues becoming increasingly complex, a framework is needed that can handle the task of incorporating a broad view of multifaceted issues. Whereas human beings in interaction with their environments comprise the human ecosystem, a subset of the human ecosystem would be the family ecosystem, which focuses on the family's interaction with its environment (Allen & Henderson, 2017). There is increasing awareness that we are interdependent creatures and not independent organisms. This is not only true in our relationships with each other, but also with the total environment in which we live. Because family life education operates within the context of reciprocal relationships between the family and society, the *family ecosystems framework* can provide a holistic approach that adds understanding and context to family life education (Bubolz & Sontag, 1993; Darling, 1987; Darling, Cassidy, & Rehm, 2019; Darling & Turkki, 2009). While Bronfenbrenner's bioecological theory (2005) has been used for the scientific study of human development over time, the family ecosystem framework, which is similar in nature, is deemed more amenable to examining the complexity of families in an educational environment.

There are several basic premises that underlie the ecosystems framework. The first and most basic premise is that individuals and families are viewed as being in interaction with their environment, which constitutes an ecosystem (Darling, 1987; Darling & Turkki, 2009). In such an ecosystem, the parts and wholes are interrelated and interdependent. A second premise is that the family carries out certain essential physical, biological, economic, psychosocial, and nurturing functions for its members; for the family as a collective; and for the larger society. Thus, the unique and powerful value of an ecological perspective lies in its potential to examine these multilevel functions and systems in relation to each other over time. The third premise consists of the interdependence of all persons worldwide along with their resources. A core value in an ecosystems framework is the survival of humans, other living species, and the resources of our planet. The overall well-being and health of the planet and of all people cannot be viewed in isolation or outside the context of the whole ecosystem. Thus, the underlying value of an ecological framework is grounded in a balance between demands of the ecosystem for cooperation and integration versus demands of the individual for autonomy and freedom. The basic values of an ecosystems perspective focus on the complementary needs of the individual and the needs of the global ecosystem. Ideally, this complementarity facilitates the development and well-being of the individual and family, as well as the ecosystem.

The family ecosystem model is built on three major concepts: the *organism* or *human environed unit* (*HEU*), the *environments* encompassing societies' families, and the *interrelationships* between the family system and its surrounding environments (Darling, 1987; Darling & Turkki, 2009) (see Figure 8.1). The *organism* or *human environed unit* can be a single individual or plurality of individuals who have some feelings of unity; share some common resources, goals, values, and interests; and have some sense of identity. While many times the group of interest is the family, the focus of the human environed unit could be on an individual or any bonded group. The environments can be categorized into three types: (1) the *natural environment* (NE) is formed by nature and includes space-time, physical, and biological elements; (2) the *human-constructed environment* (HCE) is that which is altered or created by human beings and includes sociocultural, sociophysical, and sociobiological elements; (3) the *human-behavioral environment* (HBE) is socialized by human beings and their behaviors including psychological, biophysical, and social dimensions. The *regulatory systems*, which are part of the HCE, include the legal, political, economic, religious, educational, and medical systems. One should not forget the role of *worldwide natural resources and energy* supplies, as well as the *cosmos*. With our need for natural resources and energy, along with the influence of changing weather systems, these elements of the natural environment should be examined in context of the worldwide ecosystems of families. While the cosmos is not often part of common discussions about the ecosystem, recent attention to global warming, solar flares, and meteors falling to earth make us mindful of this environmental element. *Interaction* can occur within the environed unit, between environments, and between the environed unit and the environments. The family is continually adapting to changing social, economic, political, and biological elements in the environment.

The NE, HCE, and HBE and their interactions with individuals and families can occur at many levels, including the near environment, within the home, and externally in the neighborhood, community, state-country, world, or cosmos. Similarly, Bronfenbrenner (1979, 2005) in his ecological approach described the individual as influenced by a set of nested environmental structures. He incorporated levels of environmental systems based on their immediacy to developing persons in the ecological paradigm of the *microsystem* (setting nearest the individual involving direct and concrete interactions with the person and significant others); *mesosystem* (interactions among settings in the microsystem); *exosystem* (larger

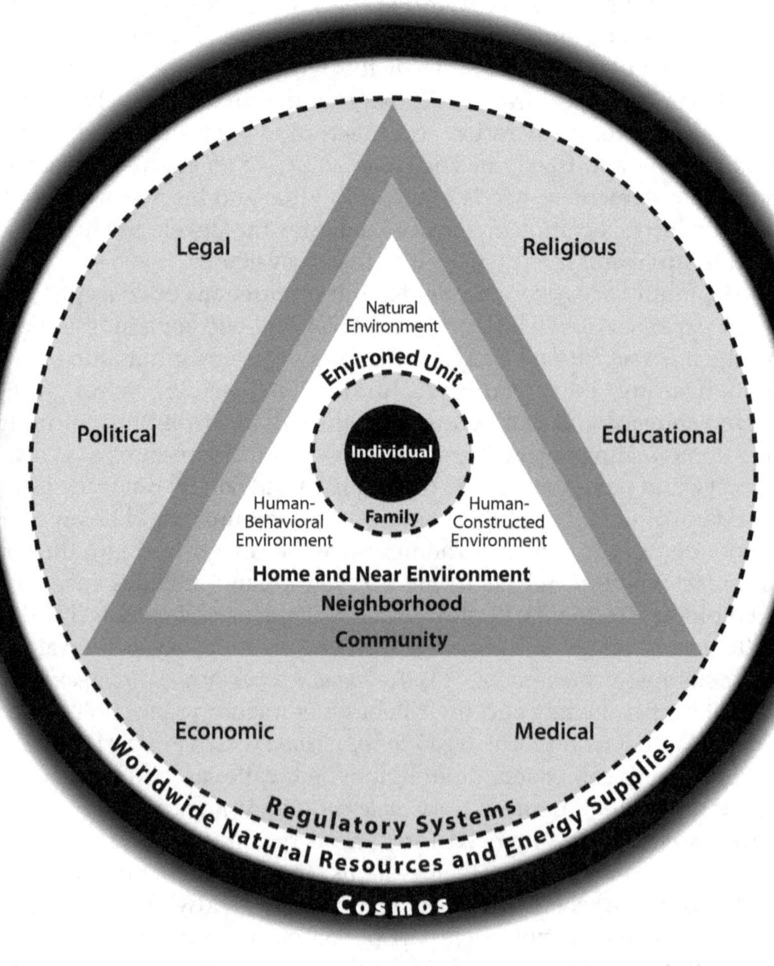

Figure 8.1 Family Ecosystem Model

social systems that have indirect effects on the person's micro- or mesosystem); and *macrosystem* (overarching cultural context and values). Later the *chronosystem* (systemic changes over time) was added to give greater attention to the developmental history of the individual (events and experiences) and its effects on development through the life course. Bronfenbrenner's (2005) move from ecology to bioecology signaled an approach that was more inclusive of biology and sociobiology and the role of the child's inherited biological qualities in the developmental process. His approach, which examined ways individuals and families are influenced by extrafamilial conditions and environments, has not fully promoted the interdependence among the natural, human-constructed, and human-behavioral environments (Bubolz & Sontag, 1993). Additionally, the theory does not address who controls the way in which laws and customs are defined. The resulting influence on families limits the theory's utility for examining Black and other marginalized families (Webb & Gonlin, 2019). While still in its youth, the ecological framework is evolving as an influential model in regard to theorizing about the family and the development of its members (White, Martin, & Adamsons, 2019).

Almost any issue can be examined from an ecosystems perspective incorporating the *human-environed unit* (HEU) in interaction with the *natural* (NE), *human-behavioral* (HBE), and *human-constructed* (HCE) environments, along with the nested ecological levels in which these environments exist. A pertinent and encompassing example for our current times is the application of the family ecosystems framework to the COVID-19 pandemic. While a natural disaster may affect parts of a community or country, the influence of the coronavirus is worldwide, although it has been handled differently in various countries. The virus can affect individuals of all ages and families (HEU), but they may react differently as various elements of the environment are encountered, such as the (1) human-constructed environment (HCE) (e.g., socially constructed policies such as social isolation, social distancing, testing guidelines; physical constructs such as homes, masks, ventilators, vaccine); (2) natural environment (NE) (e.g., the actual virus; the effect of length of time one is infected but asymptomatic; time in isolation and away from family, friends, and work; and the time needed to develop, produce, and disseminate a viable vaccine for emerging variants); and (3) human-behavioral environment (HBE) (e.g., close interactions with immediate family members on a daily basis; frustrations due to isolation and loss of income; the fear and anxiety that emerge about the past, present, and future). Many families thrive on family rituals such as birthdays, graduations, weddings, funerals, and anniversaries as punctuation points in their lives. However, changes have been necessary in how and when a family has had to modify their celebrations and care for their family members who are ill and dying.

Various regulatory systems are involved and interact with the HEU, including the following:

1. The *medical system* and health care workers have had a major role in this pandemic.
2. The *educational system* has had to create new ways to teach participants from a distance, provide school lunches, and manage graduations and other school events.

3. The *economic system* has experienced some major effects due to business closures, unemployment, and government financial support.
4. The *legal system* has had to deal with various directives from governors and mayors, as well as legislation for new policies and funding.
5. The *religious system* has had to find creative new ways to hold services and tend to the needs of their parishioners.
6. The *political system* at all levels has had a major influence on the management of this disease with different policies and results in various countries, states, and communities.

The worldwide natural resources and energy supplies have been influenced in regard to costs of fuel and transportation of resources from one country to another. Moreover the cosmos has been affected in a positive way due to the lack of flights and vehicle traffic reducing pollution and improving air quality.

Interactions between individuals within families (HEU) might bring them closer or result in tension and domestic violence. The HEU interacts with the HCU regarding the size of the home and its influence on crowding, isolating members who are ill, or conflicts with computer usage and virtual communications. The environment might also influence decisions about safety as people experience quarantine fatigue (HBE), visit restaurants (HBE and HCE), desire to be outside in the warmer weather, or go to beaches (NE). However, various regulatory systems (HCU) have created rules and policies that might restrict movement and cause further conflicts between safety and freedom (HBE). The tension regarding the wearing of masks during COVID-19 provides a clear example of the interaction between HCU and HBE.

Examples of programs that reflect a family ecosystems approach include FLE programs that have a home-visiting component such as Head Start Home Visiting (Petkus, 2015). Family life educators are able to observe the interaction of parents and children in their home environment and the ways in which the home environment may support or interfere with effective parenting practices. Other programs such as FAST (Families & Schools Together, 2020) facilitate connections between parents (HEU) and schools (HCE), two settings in the mesosystem (Bronfenbrenner, 1979), in an effort to positively influence child outcomes.

Family Life Course Development

Incorporating a developmental framework for both individuals and families can provide a longitudinal perspective to understanding families that incorporates time and history. A family life course development framework focuses on transitions of individuals during different periods of life within varying social contexts to explain the unique functions, processes, and changes associated with the family unit (Allen & Henderson, 2017; White, Martin, & Adamsons, 2019). Changes in families, like individuals, also focus on predictable stages of development and changes in internal development that occur across the lifespan through which most, but not all, individuals pass.

From the family development perspective, a *family* is an arena of interacting personalities organized into *roles* (expectations for a kinship position over time);

positions (role arrangement over time such as husband, wife, father, mother, son, daughter, brother, and sister); and *norms* (cultural expectations or guidelines that set behavioral limits). Examining the participants' current roles (e.g., caregiver of younger siblings, sharing in household responsibilities, contributor to family communication), positions (e.g., daughter, son, brother, sister), and cultural norms (e.g., cultural expectations of a son or daughter at current age) can help them relate to these concepts. While it may be difficult for participants to verbalize the cultural norms of various family members' roles, one might call attention to mothers and fathers in the news, who have violated the perceived cultural norms for parents so that their behavior became newsworthy.

We commonly refer to the family's life course as composed of all events and stages encountered and sequenced in a family. A long-used concept in family development is the *family life cycle* which is perceived as having eight stages. Families move to the next stage primarily based on the age of the oldest child except for the launching center which begins when the first child is launched and ends when the last child is launched. These stages and their approximate lengths include (Allen & Henderson, 2017; Duvall & Miller, 1984):

- *Married Couple: Establishment and Expectant Families* (begins at marriage—lasts about 1 to 2 years).
- *Childbearing Families* (oldest child from birth to 30 months—lasts about 2 years).
- *Families with Preschool Children* (oldest child from 2.5 to 6 years—lasts about 4 years).
- *Families with School-Age Children* (oldest child from 6 to 13 years—lasts about 7 years).
- *Families with Teenagers/Adult Trainees* (oldest child 13 to 20 years—lasts about 7 years).
- *Families as Launching Centers* (first child gone until last child leaves home—lasts about 8 years).
- *Middle Years* ("empty nest" to retirement—lasts about 14 years).
- *Aging Families* (retirement to death of both spouses—lasts about 7 to 13 years).

Stages evolve because of the addition or subtraction of a family member through birth (age of the oldest child), leaving home, and death. Research has indicated that when examining variables associated with the presence and ages of children, the family life cycle continues to be a useful predictive tool (Kapinus & Johnson, 2003). Furthermore, the transition to a new stage often marks a need for family life education programming, such as premarital education for couples planning to marry or parenting education for those transitioning into parenthood.

Within the stages of the life cycle, various *developmental tasks* are proposed based on normative expectations. These normative expectations are culturally bound and can vary based on race or ethnicity. If the task is completed, one will be adequately prepared to move to the next stage. However, failure at a task does not necessarily mean that an individual will not move to the next stage, but it may result in unhappiness, disapproval by society, and difficulty with optimal functioning in the next stage. Success or failure of task completion is often left to nonscientific value judgements, so it is often referred to as set of norms or role expectations for a particular stage in a family's life span (Allen & Henderson, 2017; White, Martin, & Adamsons, 2019). To apply the concept of "developmental task," you might consider an individual task that needs to be completed at a certain time in life (e.g., the task of learning to read). If children learn to read at the expected time in their lives, they have a sense of happiness and accomplishment, but if they do not accomplish this task and have reading problems compared to others, they may feel inadequate and embarrassed as reading is fundamental to moving forward with other school learning experiences. A family developmental task for a new married couple is to emotionally and financially separate from their parents and establish an independent residence. If this does not occur, independence as individuals and a couple may not take place. These illustrations can be used to stimulate discussion of other examples of individual or family developmental tasks, events, or stages that are milestones in one's development.

One criticism of family development theory is its assumption that all families develop in the same manner (Laszloffy, 2002). However, there have been several societal changes in norms from when this theory was first developed. Thus, you might ask participants if these family life cycle stages fit their families. Some will respond positively and some negatively, however, they may have to "think outside the box" to better understand their unique family circumstance. For example, in some families a child never launches. Moreover, it has become more common for young adults to live together before they get married. Thus, they could be working on some of the developmental tasks of newly married couples. There could also be a remarriage involving one person who is in the Aging Families stage with someone who is in the Families as Launching Centers stage, yet as a couple they are in the Establishment and Expectant stage. Realizing that this newly married couple is trying to accomplish the developmental tasks of three different stages simultaneously facilitates understanding the various complex issues this family is facing. No wonder this new stepfamily has some challenges. For various reasons many families may not progress through the family life cycle stages in an orderly manner. Moreover, while generally one focuses on the age of the oldest child, some researchers find the age of the youngest child should be considered, especially when dealing with single and blended families, as it provides information about the role and time demands facing parents with young children (Kapinus & Johnson, 2003). Another criticism of family development theory is its focus on a single generation or lack of consideration of culturally diverse families. Families are complex multigenerational units, so integrating systems theory with a multigenerational approach to family development theory can be helpful. (See Family Spiral Analysis in the application section of this chapter.)

Social Exchange Theory

Most gratifications, such as a happy family life, contentment in love, and need for acceptance, result from the actions of others. Thus, some of the rewards in life that people seek can only be obtained through social interaction. Whereas elements of social exchange theory can have various names, such as exchange theory, reciprocity theory, or equity theory, the basic premise is that humans form interpersonal relationships in light of the rewards, costs, or profits that they might be expected to bring. *Rewards* are anything that meet our needs, whether they are personal, familial, or community needs. We also obtain some general rewards from social approval, financial success, marital relationships, or children; however, these relationships can also have costs. *Costs,* which are the opposite of rewards, make a behavior less likely to occur. These costs may come from loss of opportunities as a result of any choice one makes. Within families, these costs may also come from additional responsibilities, as well as loss of autonomy, spontaneity, and/or freedom. When experiencing exchanges, the outcome of the exchange is based on the difference between the *rewards* and *costs* resulting in either a *profit* or *loss*.

Evaluations of social exchanges may also be conducted using *comparison levels*—the general standards upon which a person evaluates an outcome (rewards and costs) based on what is perceived to be deserved. One might consider comparison to other possible outcomes and relationships (past or present), along with comparisons to the other available alternatives. Other important concepts in exchange theory are *reciprocity,* the mutual giving and receiving involving the equalizing of exchanges, and *equity,* the fairness or justice of the exchange (Allen & Henderson, 2017; White, Martin, & Adamsons, 2019).

Exchange theory, which assumes that people are goal oriented and want to gain an advantage in social exchanges, is often used to study power within the family. Thus, the *resource hypothesis* may be employed in which the person with greater resources has more power and can gain the most benefit (Allen & Henderson, 2017). Through relationships people gain resources such as love, status, information, money, goods, and services (Foa & Foa, 1974). The *principle of least interest* suggests that the person with the least interest has more power (Buckley, 2016; White, Martin, & Adamsons, 2019). Exchanges in families are seldom clear due to the informality of family behavior. However, it is important to consider that family exchanges are not necessarily always returned in kind (same resource, such as money or services, is not mutually exchanged) and one can also build up equity over time. Children whose parents do things for them when they are young may reciprocate later in life by doing things for parents to meet their needs at that time of their lives. While the theory originally may sound calculating and manipulative, in actuality, the emergent quality of social exchange or successive social exchanges has been related to friendship intensity, satisfaction with interpersonal relationships, and intimacy.

Exchange theory can be applied to understand the rewards and costs of various decisions, especially related to the COVID-19 pandemic. Do you (1) wear a mask, what kind, and when; (2) travel using a plane or cruise ship; (3) socially distance and to what degree; (4) visit a restaurant; (5) send your children to school; and/or (6) attend college now or wait? Exchange theory assumes that individuals are generally rational about determining the costs and rewards of social exchanges in their lives, however that may not necessarily be the case. Culture and race may also be important factors in determining one's ability to achieve rewards or may influence the meaning given to rewards (Webb & Gonlin, 2019).

Applying the principle of least interest and resource hypothesis can also be useful when dealing with interpersonal, dating, marriage, and parental relationships. Analyzing relationships that may not have been successful regarding who had the most power in a relationship and who had the least interest can bring insight into current and future relationships. Costs and rewards are two additional concepts that are useful in teaching interpersonal skills. For example, John Gottman's (1994) research has found that a ratio of five positive interactions to every one negative interaction is the necessary balance to maintain a healthy relationship.

Family Stress Theory

> In this world nothing can be said to be certain, except for death and taxes.
>
> —Benjamin Franklin

In reality, a third thing that is certain is family stress. *Family stress* is a state of tension that arises when demands tax a family's resources. If adjustments do not come easily, family stress can lead to a *family crisis*, a situation in which typical coping strategies are ineffective and new ones are needed. Family crisis involves three interrelated ideas: a crisis involves change, a crisis is a turning point with the potential for positive or negative effects or both, and a crisis is a time of relative instability (Boss, 1999, 2006; Boss, Bryant, & Mancini, 2017; Weber & Branscum, 2020).

When dealing with family stress theory, the *ABC-X Model of Family Stress and Crisis* is often useful (Boss, Bryant, & Mancini, 2017; Weber & Branscum, 2020). Within this model "A" refers to the *stressor* or *crisis-precipitating event*. These events, which are influenced by the family's context, can be normative (expected during the life cycle) or nonnormative (unforeseen events or situations); internal or external to the family; brief or prolonged; ambiguous or clear; or can affect family configuration or status shifts in the family. There are several types of stressors, such as addition or loss of a family member, sudden change in family income or status, conflict over family roles, caring for a disabled or dependent family member, ambiguous loss, or stressor overload/pile-up. Small events may not be enough to cause any real stress, but can take a toll when they occur simultaneously or consecutively. Other stressors such as racial discrimination can be chronic stressors that compound overall family stress levels and affect the family's ability to cope (Bryant, 2020). The family's personal or collective strengths (ability to cope) at the time of the stressor event are referred to as *stressor/crisis-meeting resources* (B in the ABC-X Model) (Boss, Bryant, & Mancini, 2017; Weber & Branscum, 2020). Resources can be physical, economic, relational, social, or psychological characteristics that a family can use to respond to one or more stressors. How families *perceive*, *define*, and *assign meaning* to an event (C in the ABC-X Model) is key to understanding how they *manage the degree of these events* or *the crisis* (X in the ABC-X Model). The integration of stressor(s) (A), resources (B), and perception of the event (C) leads to the level of stress or crisis (X) and the response the family experiences ranging from bonadaptation to maladaptation. Family stress is not necessarily bad, but can become a problem when the status quo becomes overwhelming or a change occurs that is so acute that the family ceases to function and becomes debilitated.

Family life educators are instrumental in providing resources and helping families develop coping strategies (B) as well as helping to reframe the stressor and interpret the situation (C) in a positive way. For example, family life educators can teach individuals self-care techniques such as mindfulness or other calming techniques that can help them cope with stressors (Myers-Walls, 2020). Family life educators working with military families may provide resources and help forge a sense of community among families, both of which can help families cope with the situational stressors of the military (Mancini, O'Neal, & Lucier-Greer, 2020).

The *Roller Coaster Model* of family adjustment after a crisis is another important component of family stress theory (Boss, Bryant, & Mancini, 2017; Hill, 1949). According to this model, after a family experiences a stressor event it may go into a period of disorganization during which previous methods for managing and solving problems become inadequate. Depending on the amount of time needed for the family to reorganize, the family reaches a turning point and enters a period of recovery. This turning point can result from a change in the "stressor," availability of "coping resources," and/or change in the "perception" of the stressor and resources. The family will reach a new "level of organization," which may be lower, equal to, or higher than their previous level of functioning.

Ambiguous loss is an important stressor to highlight (Boss, 1999, 2006; Boss, Bryant, & Mancini, 2017; Weber & Branscum, 2020). Negotiating family boundaries is difficult when the loss of a family member is ambiguous—the facts about what happened are unclear. There are two types of ambiguous loss: One type is having a family member who is *physically absent* but *psychologically present* as exemplified by unexpected catastrophes, such as war, natural disasters, imprisonment, desertion, kidnappings, and more common types, such as migration, adoption, divorce, and family members leaving home or being institutionalized. The second type is *physical presence* but *psychological absence* as noted by some unexpected occurrences of brain injury, Alzheimer's and dementia, stroke, depression, and affairs, along with some more common types, such as preoccupation with work, computers and TV, or homesickness.

In dealing with the meaning of COVID-19, grief has become a common experience not only due to the loss of loved ones, but also the global sense of loss tied to changes in daily routines and separations from friends and family. This loss has no clear understanding and leaves a person searching for answers resulting in stress that is a reaction to the ambiguity of losing intangible parts of their lives. The boundaries of what we do or do not perceive as safe vs. what are scientific findings have become blurred. We have cancelled many things in our lives and cannot predict what the future will hold (Woods, 2020). In addition, many people may be experiencing ambiguous loss because of a loved one being physically absent due to COVID-19. Paying special attention to ambiguous loss is important, as youth and family members examine concerns being experienced about war, terrorism, and PTSD, as well as the aging of our society and the potential for a greater incidence of Alzheimer's disease and dementia and the multifaceted effects of COVID-19.

Cognizance of ambiguous loss can be meaningful for those who know someone who is experiencing these kinds of losses. According to Dr. Pauline Boss (www.ambiguousloss.com), "With ambiguous loss, there is no closure; the challenge is to learn how to live with ambiguity." Understanding family stress theory, the ABC-X Model, and the roller-coaster model as they apply to normative and nonnormative stressors, including ambiguous loss, can provide insight into family adaptability and resilience (Boss, Bryant, & Mancini, 2017).

Applying Family Theories in Family Life Education Settings

At times, learning about theory can be challenging because it is abstract, and participants do not necessarily perceive how it is connected to themselves personally or their environmental context. Thus, creating meaningful learning experiences can help participants better understand theory and how it applies to their lives. Examples include using analogies, personal reflections, news reports, "doing" theory, exploring life changes, reflecting on case studies, and family spiral analysis. Some of these experiences can provide clarity in both formal and nonformal classroom settings.

Integrating Analogies

To help participants understand the idea of developmental influences in one's life, a family life educator can use an analogy of baking chocolate chip cookies. This activity can also help to facilitate an understanding of diversity. As the process of making these cookies is discussed, one can find that people use different kinds of shortening, sugar, salt, nuts, chocolate chips, and eggs and may mix, bake, and store the cookies in a variety of ways. If each student were to bake a batch of chocolate chip cookies, they would all be tasty, but there would be similarities and differences in appearance, texture, and flavor. Using the cookie analogy, an educator can discuss cultural differences regarding prenatal development, early childhood experiences, adolescent changes, adult development, and family socialization experiences that can all influence the development of individuals and families (Darling & Howard, 2015). The cultural context can be incorporated by examining the role of different environments related to the analogy of baking cookies involving accessibility of ingredients (raw materials such as light or dark brown sugar or light and dark chocolate chips), using different ovens (temperature, time, and altitude), or values placed on foods for sustenance versus pleasure. Just as all people develop differently based on various values and conditions in their cultures, so do our cookies. While people and cookies may be quite different due to their development and culture, others may be similar, yet all have value.

Using Personal Reflections

While at first glance a theory may seem abstract and not applicable to one's life, asking reflective questions can provide personal insightful moments. For example, some of the concepts from exchange theory, such as rewards and costs, may seem to be cognitively based and not personally applicable. However, asking a simple question such as, "Have you ever felt 'used' or taken advantage of?" provides an "a-ha" moment. Most participants reply that they have had these feelings, so looking at the equity of exchanges becomes personally relevant.

Incorporating News Reports

A good way to understand the role of family ecosystems in one's life and family is to share video clips of news items in a classroom setting. Participants can get involved in discussions by finding examples of the human-environed unit (HEU)/organism, natural environment (NE), human-behavioral environment (HBE), or human-constructed environment (HCE) and the interactions between the HEU and its environments or interactions between various environmental elements. There are multiple examples in news clips involving weather and natural disasters, the economy, legal issues, and family or human interactions in the US or abroad that can lead to some insightful discussions and applications. By paying attention to news items from newspapers, magazines, television, and the internet, the educator and/or participants can frequently bring examples to the teaching environment that provide ongoing application and reinforcement of theoretical content.

"Doing" Theory

While family life educators often "teach" theoretical concepts, one suggestion is to have participants "do" theory by unobtrusively observing perceived family groups in public settings, such as a grocery store, sports events, restaurant, or mall to glean information about family systems (Whitchurch, 2005). When participants return to class, they report the locations of their observations, which can be used to show the ecosystems in which families are involved. They also can share the comments they may have overheard, which might pertain to finances, parenting, or interpersonal communication and can be used to exemplify concepts, such as boundaries, subsystems, feedback, family rules, cohesion, and or flexibility.

Exploring Life Changes

As a way for participants to recognize the interactions between themselves, others, and their environment, have them change a significant element of their life for three to five days and then ecosystemically analyze the results of this change. This can be done in an academic setting or modified to be used in a nonformal setting. After briefly orienting the participants about developing a research problem and potential methodology, participants can do a variety of things to alter their lives. However, caution should be given so they do nothing that is injurious to their health. Examples of changes might be to go without television, cell phones, email, tablets, social media, electricity, certain appliances, and certain cosmetics or grooming products; get 8 hours of sleep; change eating behaviors or clothing patterns; start exercising; study in a different environment; add or remove the use of a car, activity, or implement; share sincere compliments with others and/or try different interactional patterns with family members or friends in their lives. Participants should review pertinent literature, apply theoretical concepts, and analyze their findings. It is preferable to have them quantify their findings in some way (e.g., number of email messages received or missed, number of hours slept, cost of new eating pattern). Finally, ask the participants what they learned about their ecosystem from this exercise. Doing these projects as individuals or in small groups (two to three participants) and discussing them in class can provide further awareness of the application of the ecosystems framework in understanding how changes influence individuals, interactions, and families.

Reflecting on Case Studies

Participants may listen to presentations or get involved in discussions on theory, but applying these theories to family situations will add additional insights that can be transferred to one's own family situation to facilitate greater understanding. These case studies could also be used in a nonformal setting to become cognizant of the role of theories in understanding family dynamics. In an academic setting a case study can be provided to small groups of participants along with some general questions related to the theories to create an experience where group participants can work together cooperatively to better understand how families function. While a case study may be brief, participants can brainstorm what things might be like within this hypothetical family and then report back to the larger group how they applied the theories to these families. In an academic setting, this activity was positively received and not only facilitated application of theories, but also became a review of theories prior to an exam. These case studies could also be used in a nonformal setting to help understand the role of theories in understanding family dynamics.

Each case study in Box 8.1 represents a family at a different stage of the life cycle. (*Hint*—the families in the case studies have been given a color as their family name with handouts printed on colored sheets of paper to coincide with the family name. These sheets are collated by color so distributing them to the class helps to create groups of participants from different class locations.) Handouts might include some of the following examples of questions depending on what theories and concepts were incorporated into the class.

- **Family life course development theory**—Identify the developmental stage in which this family is currently involved, and the information used to determine the appropriate stage. Explain one task with which this family might be struggling and one that is being successfully completed.
- **Family systems theory**—Identify and discuss the permeability of one physical and one psychological boundary in this family. Describe a subsystem within this family and compare the rules and boundaries of this subsystem with those of the system as a whole. Where would this family be placed in the Circumplex Model (Cohesion—disengaged to enmeshed; Flexibility—chaotic to rigid)? Give one example of each of the following for this family: routine, ritual, relationship rule, and procedural rule.
- **Ecosystems framework**—What is an example of the natural environment, human-behavioral environment, and human-constructed environment related to this family? What are examples of two different interactions between the Human Environed Unit (HEU) and one of its environments (NE, HBE, or HCE) or between two environmental elements?

- **Exchange theory**—Select one family member and evaluate the hypothetical outcome of his/her relationship with another family member. What is a cost and reward associated with each member of this dyad? What is an example of reciprocity within this family?
- **Family stress theory and ABC-X Model**—What is the stressor (A) in the family and is it normative or nonnormative? What resources (B) does the family have for coping? How does the family perceive the stressor (C)? How is the family adapting to this stressor (X)?

It might be beneficial for groups to begin with a different theory and series of questions if the time is short and some groups cannot fully complete their group assignment in the allotted time. After most of the groups have completed their theory applications, the educator can facilitate a discussion of theories using some of their examples. Family groups would not need to present on all theoretical questions, but each group would present some insights about their families by demonstrating the application of theoretical concepts to their case studies.

Box 8.1 **Family Case Studies**

Provide each group with one case study and questions for application of the theories discussed in class.

The Green Family—Tom and Jeannie Green have been married for 27 years and are both employed full time. Tom is a car salesman, whereas Jeannie is an engineer. They have three grown children: Ken age 26, Kim age 21, and Jordan age 18. Kim and Jordan are both in college. In the past few years, Tom's father, Henry, who is 80 years old, has had some cardiac problems and has become weaker and less able to care for himself. Tom and Jeannie have noted that Tom's father can no longer care for himself and have reluctantly decided that Henry should come to live with them. What might affect how this family is functioning?

The Teal and Blue Family—Jake Teal and Chris Blue, a gay couple, have been married for two years. Because they always wanted to have children, they enlisted the help of a surrogate to give birth to their child. However, the ultrasound indicated a surprise because they are going to be parents of twins. Jake has been working as a mechanic, whereas Chris has been employed as an office manager. Chris had planned to take some family leave time to be with their newborn baby and was not supposed to go back to work until the baby was three months old. However, now with the birth of twins, they feel that Chris needs to stay at home with their newborn babies. What might affect how this family is functioning?

The Redmond Family—Sheila Redmond is a single mother with four children: Martin age 18, Jenny age 15, Kristin age 14, and Alex age 10. Jenny is pregnant and wants to keep the baby. While Sheila has mixed feelings about this pregnancy, she is insistent that Jenny should complete her education. What might affect how this family is functioning?

The Orange Family—Yang and Ming Orange graduated from college and married two weeks later. They had planned to work for a few years and then go to graduate school, but conceived a child on their honeymoon. They are seven months into their pregnancy and making plans for the future. What might affect how this family is functioning?

(continued)

The Gray Family—Juan and Maria Gray have been married for 10 years and have three children: Adriana age 8, Elena age 6, and Carlo age 4. Juan is a science teacher in the public high school. Maria, who used to be a nurse's aide, has stayed home taking care of their children since the oldest child was born. Now that their children are older, she wants to go back to school to become a registered nurse. What might affect how this family is functioning?

The Garnet and Gold Family—Eric Garnet and Lisa Gold fell in love on their very first date three months ago. They knew that they were right for each other and just got married. In two weeks they will graduate from college with Eric getting his degree in nursing and Lisa getting her degree in chemistry. Both Eric and Lisa want to move to another state away from their parents and are looking for positions elsewhere. They both definitely want a professional position in their respective fields since they have worked hard to get their degrees. What might affect how this family is functioning?

The LaVender Family—Rashid and Tonya LaVender have 3 children—Yolanda age 4, LaShanda age 3, and Dexter age 2. Since both Rashid and Tonya are elementary school teachers and wanted to be home with their children, they decided to share one teaching position after the children were born. Whereas Rashid teaches a third grade class in the morning, Tonya teaches the same third grade class in the afternoon. They also try to do various tasks for neighbors to help with their income, but the children take a great deal of time. What might affect how this family is functioning?

The Violet Family—Lamar and Latoya Violet have been experiencing some stress since they retired. Latoya makes trips twice a week to visit her mother in a nursing home 60 miles away and Lamar just had a mild stroke and is going through physical therapy. In the meantime their children and grandchildren want them to visit more often, but flying across the country is expensive. What might affect how this family is functioning?

The Beige Family—Luis and Teresa have three children who are grown, married, and living in three different cities. The two oldest children have children of their own, while the youngest is unmarried and in graduate school. Luis and Teresa have been looking forward to their retirement next year so they can travel, but their oldest daughter is thinking that they will be babysitting for the child they are expecting. What might affect how this family is functioning?

Incorporating Family Life Spiral Analysis

In order for participants to recognize that developmental theory and systems theory can be used simultaneously to gain meaningful insights into families, a family life spiral analysis can be used as the basis of an in-class demonstration, discussion, or assignment. Individuals place their extended families into two spiral diagrams: one is based on the ages of their family members and the other is based on their characteristics. They then analyze them according to the integration of two theories used as a basis of this assignment—development theory and systems theory. Further details about the incorporation of this analysis as a potential individual assignment, group activity, or voluntary demonstration can be noted in Box 8.2.

Box 8.2 Understanding the Family Life Spiral Diagram

- Figure 8.2 contains three concentric circles. The inner circle begins with stage 1 (birth/early childhood) and goes clockwise to stage 4 (mate selection). Then move out to the middle circle beginning with stage 5 (parenthood) and going to stage 8 (middle adulthood). Next, transition to the outer circle with stage 9 (grandparenthood) and go to Stage 12 (late adulthood). For some families with members who are living longer, extrapolate beyond stage 12 and add stage 13, which might be called "senior or elderly adulthood."
- Figure 8.2 is comprised of four quadrants. The top quadrant with stages 1, 5, and 9 is squeezed into a smaller formation to represent centripetal forces in a family system. In other words, when there is a birth of a baby in stage 1, the family boundaries are more closed and parents are focusing on their new child, as are grandparents, who are spending more time in family activities during the grandparenthood stage. There is a reconnection among family members across generations within this quadrant. In comparison, stages 3, 7, and 11 are spread further apart to represent centrifugal forces in the family system. Adolescents are becoming more involved with peers and looking forward to gaining independence. Their parents are renegotiating their marriage and dealing with career issues, while the older generation is newly retired and looking forward to travel, hobbies, and possibly a second honeymoon. The quadrant with 2, 6, and 10 represents movement toward centrifugal, whereas stages 4, 8, and 12 represent movement toward centripetal.
- At the bottom of Figure 8.2 are the approximate ages at which one transitions into any of these 12 stages. For example, the birth/early childhood stage is entered at birth or age 0, middle childhood/school stage at age 6, adolescence/puberty stage at age 12, and so forth.
- Table 8.1 contains a chart with six columns to accompany the spiral diagram. The two columns on the left indicate *Period* (centripetal to centrifugal) and its corresponding location within the Circumplex Model. For example, in stages 1, 5, and 9 one experiences centripetal forces, which in the Circumplex Model means high cohesion and low flexibility.
- The third column focuses on *Generations* or *Stages* in the life cycle.
- The fourth column contains some potential *Transitional Events*, which would be the events that mark entrance into a given period of the family life cycle.
- The fifth column has *Other Characteristics*, which are events or family traits that tend to occur during a given period of the family life cycle.
- The sixth column includes the approximate *Age Range* of the life cycle stage. Note that the age range for Stage 1 is years 1 to 6 with an 8 in parentheses. This includes the typical ages or social norms of individuals in a given period. The number in parentheses is for a two-year time lag. Thus, parenthood may begin at age 24 to 26 and end at age 30 to 32.

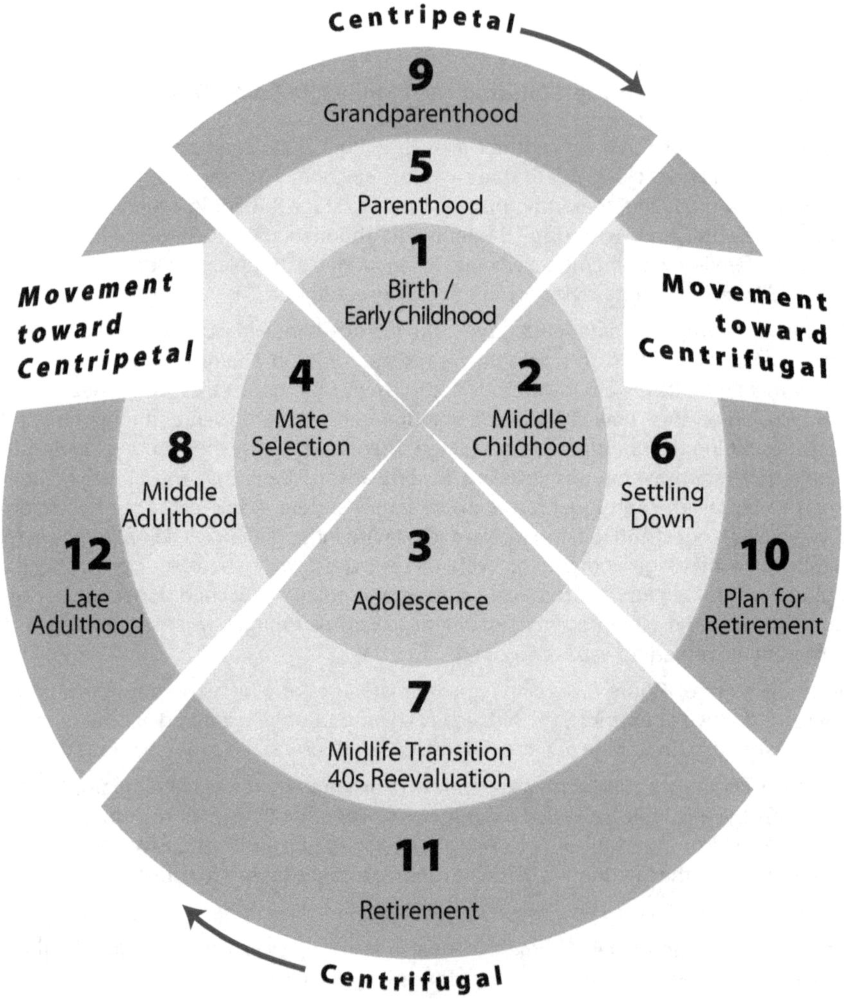

Transition Events (age)
1. Birth / Early childhood (0)
2. Middle childhood / School (6)
3. Adolescence / Puberty (12)
4. Mate selection / Independence (18)
5. Parenthood (24)
6. Settling down (30)

Transition Events (age)
7. Midlife transition / 40s reevaluation (36)
8. Middle adulthood / Empty nest (42)
9. Grandparenthood / Midlife changes (48)
10. Plan for retirement (54)
11. Retirement (60)
12. Late adulthoood / Pass the torch (66)

Figure 8.2 Family Life Spiral Diagram

Table 8.1 Family Life Spiral Analysis

Period	Circumplex	Generation	Transitional Event[1]	Other Characteristics[2]	Age Range[3]
Centripetal	Cohesion—high Flexibility—low	1	Birth/Early Childhood	Walking; talking; potty training; preschool	1–6 (8)
		5	Parenthood	Start career; religious exploration; graduate school; buy first house; mother/child love affair; establish traditions; seek advice from parents (reconnection)	24(26)–30(32)
		9	Grandparenthood/ Midlife Changes	Relived memories; menopause; focus on tradition; practical advice to generation 2 (reconnection)	48(50)–54(56)
Movement Toward Centrifugal	Cohesion—low Flexibility—low	2	Middle Childhood/ School	Reading, writing, arithmetic; separation anxiety; recognition of authority figures besides parents	6(8)–12(14)
		6	Settling Down	Career advancement; buy a house (2nd); religious commitment; routines set	30(32)–36(38)
		10	Plan for Retirement	Volunteer work; clubs; philanthropy; travel; retirement date set; assess/organize financial situation	54(56)–60(62)
Centrifugal	Cohesion—low Flexibility—high	3	Adolescence/Puberty	Cognitive/physical maturation (new mind/body); plan for independence; college/work exploration; values clarification	12(14)–18(20)
		7	Mid-life Transition/ 40s Reevaluation	Marriage renegotiation; affair; separation; divorce; second honeymoon; career reassessment; career change; back to school; hobbies	36(38)–42(44)
		11	Retirement	Third honeymoon or marital isolation; recreation/hobbies/travel; second career	60(62)–66(68)
Movement Toward Centripetal	Cohesion—high Flexibility—high	4	Mate Selection/ Independence	Dating/courtship; renegotiation of parent-child relations; more interests/peer-like; engagement/marriage	18(20)–24(26)
		8	Middle Adulthood/ Empty Nest	Reevaluation of marital relations (with stability); instilling values; loss of parents	42(44)–48(50)
		12	Late Adulthood/ Passing the Torch	Illness; widowhood; storytelling (archival function); instilling values	66(68)–72(74)

1 **Transitional Event**—Event which marks entrance into a given period of the family life cycle
2 **Other Characteristics**—Other events or family traits which tend to occur during a given period of the family life cycle.
3 **Age Range**—Typical ages (social norms) of individuals in a given period. Number in parentheses allows for two year lag.

Box 8.3 **Family Life Spiral Analysis**

To demonstrate spiral family analysis either use a volunteer in class or incorporate it as a student assignment by asking individual participants to plot their family members on two separate family life spiral diagrams: an Age Spiral and a Transitional Period Spiral.

1. **Age Spiral**: Place yourself and your family (your siblings, your parents, and your grandparents) into the family life spiral diagram based on your *current ages*. Insert a family member in only one segment of the age spiral diagram that most closely relates to his/her age. In other words, if a category ranges from age 6 to 11 and your family member is 7 years old, place him/her closer to the age 6 demarcation. Place an X in the diagram to represent the family member and include their name, family position, and age.
2. **Transitional Period Spiral**: Place yourself and your family (your siblings, your parents, and your grandparents) into the family life spiral diagram based on *current transitional events and other characteristics* (see the Family Life Spiral Analysis Chart, Table 8.1). Place a family member in only one segment of the transitional period spiral diagram. It might be that a family member has characteristics of more than one stage, so place that member in the stage that best describes what is most like him or her.

Participants may have questions about what to do if some family members are no longer living or if their parents have remarried. Have participants create diagrams involving the members of their family to describe as best they can their immediate and involved family system. If a grandparent has just died, he or she may or may not still be emotionally connected to the family and may or may not be included in the diagram. Depending on the student's perceptions of sibling and stepsibling relationships or living arrangements, the diagrams could be drawn in various ways.

Potential Discussion Points

- After completing these two diagrams, discuss and analyze what it is about *each* family member and his or her characteristics (within the chart) that caused placement of him/her in a particular transitional period? Did you have any difficulties placing family members according to the characteristics? What were these difficulties, if any? Discuss what changes in the characteristics column of the Family Life Spiral Analysis Chart (Table 8.1) should be made to accommodate these difficulties?
- To what degree do individual members compare to each other *within each spiral diagram* (compare age and transitional period spirals *separately*). Discuss issues related to any member(s) who are lagging behind or getting ahead of the general period of your family. Who is in or out of sync with the rest of the family and what does that mean for interpersonal relations and closeness in the family? You may have all members within the same quadrant, or you may have some members in one quadrant and a few that are in another quadrant. What does this mean for the functioning of your family?
- To what degree does the *"age spiral"* fit or match the occurrences of the "transitional period spiral"? (Compare *both diagrams together.*) For example, you may have a family member who has retired early. In other words, for his age, he is doing different things or has different characteristics compared to others of that same age. Therefore, he may be in different positions in the two diagrams. Discuss your family's positions in the spiral diagrams according to centripetal and centrifugal forces.
- How can you apply this family life spiral analysis to better understand your present or future family life? What have you learned about families?

Participants have perceived that this activity and subsequent discussions were not only meaningful and insightful, but also an enjoyable way to understand theory and obtain insights into their families. Here are some examples they reported.

Family change

- I can see that my family is changing dramatically. I have learned that different periods in the life of my family bring it together or spread it apart.
- Life changes are to a certain extent predictable. These diagrams provide a general picture for me to look at and notice how each family member's age and transition affect others in the family.
- The spiral diagrams helped me to see more clearly the reasons why our family seems to be constantly changing. We are all getting older and facing different problems and new challenges every day of our lives.

Closeness vs. separateness

- I have learned how my family functions and more importantly why it functions that way. I never understood before why at times one family member would not seem as close as the others, while at other times they would be very close to the rest of the family. I now know that one family member can feel detached from the family if they are a period ahead or behind the rest of the family.
- I have learned that pushing people away isn't always the answer, even though it may seem so at that stage of one's life.

Understanding others

- I can better understand why my father has become isolated. He has moved into a period much later than the societal norms for his age and the centrifugal forces in some ways are pulling him away from us.
- I realized how different families are if there are no children. My sister and I have often visited my father and stepmother. But, they have never had the responsibility of raising any children in their home. They are in one stage of the spiral, whereas my mother, stepfather, and siblings are in different stages. Not having children puts less stress on the marriage and on finances. This could be why my stepfather has not retired and why my father and stepmother have not had as many marital problems.
- I now understand why my grandparents are so involved in our family and why other members of the family are not as concerned with it. This spiral has also shown me that perhaps I should talk more often to my grandparents because of how they might be feeling at this time in their lives.

General family insights

- I have a tendency to see my family as being slightly messed up, but I learned that what I thought was messed up is really perfectly normal.
- I have learned that my family is pretty normal after all. The insight that this assignment has given me has proved most useful and definitely will be considered in the future.

SUMMARY

Using family theories in family life education programs can assist participants to better understand family behaviors and functioning. Rather than use one theory, it is good to consider the integration of various theories to gain a broader perspective of the topic being examined. Some basic theories/frameworks central to family studies include family systems, family ecosystem, family development, social exchange, and family stress theory, although there are others that can also be incorporated, such as symbolic interaction, feminist, and conflict theory. In addition to providing the basic concepts of the theory, being able to apply theories in classroom activities and assignments can facilitate student understanding.

QUESTIONS AND ISSUES FOR DISCUSSION

1. In your study of theories, which theory best helps you to understand your family and why?
2. What are examples of vertical and horizontal attachments in your life, as well as centripetal and centrifugal forces?
3. What is your life like today ecosystemically compared to your parents and grandparents when they were your age?
4. What kinds of changes in the ecosystem can be noted before COVID-19 until now? What changes may be long lasting?
5. How can using the ecosystem approach facilitate understanding current issues such as climate change and influence of environments on individual freedoms.
6. What stage of the family life cycle best fits your family and why? If your family does not fit any stage, why is this the case?
7. How have relationships with your siblings changed during various stages of the family's life cycle?
8. What are the rewards and costs of being male or female?
9. What have been some of the rewards and costs of living during the period of the COVID-19 pandemic?
10. How would your life change if your family experienced a natural disaster and your home, possessions, and livelihood were lost? Analyze this event using one of the theories/frameworks mentioned in this chapter (family systems, family ecosystem, family development, social exchange, or family stress).

9

Approaches to Sexuality Education

Everyone is a sexuality educator in some context, whether you are a teacher, parent, friend, or role model. Sexuality is an integral part of who we are, what we believe, and how we respond to others. It is a fundamental and dynamic aspect of the human experience that is worthy of dignity and respect. It encompasses physical, mental, and social well-being across the lifespan and is embedded within relationships and cultures (Russell, Mallory, Bishop, & Dorri, 2020; Satcher 2001). Sexuality is much more than body parts and sex; it includes biological sex, body image, gender identity, gender roles, gender orientation, and sexual practices, as well as our sexual experiences, thoughts, ideas, and fantasies (FoSE, 2020a). Sexuality is expressed in the way we speak, smile, sit, dress, dance, laugh, and cry (SRCP, 2020).

In the past, the meaning of the term *sex education* was unclear because the word "sex" is often used ambiguously to either indicate sexual behavior, reproduction, or being male or female. It all depends on the circumstance. If you are completing a survey, you might see a demographic question asking for your sex, but in reality the researcher wants to know if you are male or female. It is now more common to use the term *sex* to mean sexual anatomy that is biologically determined, whereas *gender* refers to being male or female, which is something we learn or construct for ourselves based on our social and cultural experiences. "Sex" is also used frequently to refer to the physical act of sexual expression.

Rather than use the term *sex education*, most educators now use the term *sexuality education*, because it is broader than what you do sexually with another person. Sexuality education is a lifelong process of acquiring information and forming attitudes, beliefs, and values about our identity, relationships, and intimacy (Bruess & Schroeder, 2018; SIECUS, 2004). It encompasses sexual development, sexual and reproductive health, interpersonal relationships, affection, intimacy, body image, sexual orientation, and gender identity and expression. It addresses the biological, cultural, psychological, and ethical dimensions of sexuality. Sexuality education should also recognize the diverse needs of people to facilitate their current and future sexual well-being.

The definition and scope of sexuality education evolved in the 1960s due to sociopolitical changes and public controversies regarding the inclusion of sexuality education in schools. Therefore, it was narrowly focused on adolescence, schools, and individuals' risky behaviors (Somerville, 1971). The terminology for "sex education" was often noted as "family life and sex education" to provide some political safety by incorporating a family context. In the late 1960s to 1970s, sexuality education received considerable attention in NCFR's journal, *Family Relations*, with such topics as premarital sexual relationships, homosexuality, and sexuality education for diverse populations (Russell, Mallory, Bishop, & Dorri, 2020). The focus on preventing pregnancy prevailed until the HIV/AIDS epidemic in the 1980s. The emphasis of sexuality education has been marginalized in the past 30 years, in part, due to conservative groups promoting educational decision-making by local governments, schools, and parents. In addition, researchers focused more on topics that could receive federal funding such as teenage pregnancy prevention and the effectiveness of abstinence-focused education in preventing HIV/AIDS.

Currently the focus of sexuality education has mostly been on parents as sexuality educators for their children along with an increased openness toward lesbian, gay, bisexual, transgendered, or queer (LGBTQ+) issues. While Human Sexuality is a required content area for the Certified Family Life Educator (CFLE) credential, it is one of the areas in which few CFLEs reported inclusion in their practice (Darling, Cassidy, & Rehm, 2020). This could be due to divergent cultural and professional values regarding sexuality along with a lack of comfort concerning their own knowledge and feelings of preparedness regarding a range of sexuality topics (Darling, Cassidy, & Rehm, 2017).

Adolescent Sexuality and Sexuality Education

Adolescence is a critical time in one's life for the development of sexuality. It is a period of physical and hormonal development associated with puberty, as well as other psychological, emotional, social, and cultural changes. Adolescents can also develop romantic and intimate relationships and engage in a range of sexual behaviors (Guttmacher Institute, 2019). As teenagers transition through adolescence, they receive many conflicting messages—more than any other age group. Whereas our cultural influences through movies, music, advertisements, and social media provide us with an allure and excitement about sexuality, the dangers and problems associated with sexual interactions are often communicated through news programs, public policies, school messages, and parents. Thus, the youth in our culture must find their way in a world of contradictions. While popular media scream "always say yes," many adults admonish "just say no," but the majority "just say nothing" (Brown & Taverner, 2001). To deal with this issue some parents, schools, churches, and politicians have encouraged abstinence, which means there should be no need for education about sexual behavior and interactions, sexually transmitted infections (STIs), or contraception. It is as if we live in a bipolar culture in which individuals and families are pulled in many directions, at times making it seem like we are walking on a tightrope when it comes to teaching about sexuality.

Sexuality has been a controversial issue in our schools, homes, and culture because it is closely tied to parental, social, and political concerns about the behaviors and well-being of our youth. Regarding the behaviors of adolescents, an estimated 55% of male and female teens have experienced sexual intercourse by age 18 and approximately 80% of sexually-active teens used some form of contraception (NNHS, 2017). While the US teen pregnancy rate has been declining in the past 20 years, the United States continues to have the highest teen pregnancy rate of all developed nations (World Population Review, 2020a). Moreover, the US has the highest STI rates in the industrialized world. Of the 37,823 new HIV diagnoses in the US in 2018, 21% were among youth (CDC, 2019b).

The goal of sexuality education is to help young people navigate sexual development and grow into sexually healthy adults (Sex Education Collaborative, 2018). Sexuality education programs are often tied to parental, social, and political perceptions of right and wrong and peoples' feelings about religion and personal freedoms. The issue is not if it will occur, but what kind of sexuality education is desired for yourself, your students, and your children at every stage of the lifespan. Most adults agree on what is "not" healthy for teenagers as they share a deep concern about coercive or violent sex, STIs including HIV/AIDS, and unintended adolescent pregnancy. However, the perception of health goes beyond the absence of disease to autonomy and the ability of individuals to integrate sexuality into their lives, derive satisfaction from it, and reproduce, if they so choose. Parents hope their children will have a good sex life in which they will be able to appreciate their bodies, express love and intimacy in appropriate ways, enjoy sexual feelings without necessarily acting on them, and practice health promotion. In other words, sexual satisfaction includes the ability to understand the risks, responsibilities, outcomes, and impacts of sexual interactions (McGee, 2004).

While most of our past efforts regarding sexuality education have been on risk prevention (e.g., avoiding pregnancy, STIs, HIV/AIDS) along with a trend toward the normalization of heterosexuality, the vision is changing to more fully incorporate the concept of pleasure. Inclusive and honest sexuality education goes beyond delivering information. It provides young people with opportunities to explore their own identities and values along with those of their families and communities. It also allows them to practice the communication, decision-making, and negotiation skills needed to create healthy relationships—both sexual and nonsexual—throughout their lives (FoSE, 2020a).

Approaches to School-Based Sexuality Education

School-based sexuality education for adolescents has generally promoted abstinence as a way to deal with sexual urges with some constraints on complete sexual freedom—it does not advocate that adolescent sexuality should mean abstaining from all sexual feelings, thoughts, and interactions. Adults do not want youth becoming prematurely involved in sexual interactions, but total abstention and over-control of sexual feelings and expression can create both current and future problems for adolescents in terms of repression, denial, and isolation from social interactions. Consequently, we need to examine if abstinence is being taught as a contraceptive method or a total avoidance of one's sexuality.

Through the years several programs have been created that are based to some degree on abstinence. These program names and funding sources change depending on political views that are applicable at that time. Box 9.1 highlights some of these programs and also the various names that have been used over time (KFF, 2018).

Abstinence-Only (Sexual Risk Avoidance) Programs

For approximately 40 years "abstinence-only sexuality education" has been the basis of school policy and curriculum decisions. Although decreasing in number, there are various types of programs that promote abstinence from all sexual behaviors as the only approach that is moral and safe in the belief that adolescents should be protected from the details of sexual interactions and told of harmful

Box 9.1 Types of Sexuality Education

Abstinence-Only Education (Also known as Sexual Risk Avoidance or Abstinence-Only-Until-Marriage Education)

Programs which have been recently rebranded as "Sexual Risk Avoidance Education," teach abstinence as the expected standard of behavior for teens and the sole means of preventing pregnancy and exposure to sexually transmitted diseases. They usually exclude any information about the effectiveness of contraception or condoms to prevent unintended pregnancy and STIs. Some rely on negative messages about sexuality, distort information, and promote biases about gender, sexual orientation, marriage, and pregnancy options. These programs are typically for teens and rarely mention LGBTQ+ individuals or relationships.

Sexual Risk Reduction (Also known as Abstinence Based, Abstinence-Plus, or Abstinence-Centered Education)

Programs stress the benefits of abstinence and include information about sexual behaviors other than intercourse, as well as contraception and disease-prevention methods. They typically focus only on teens to equip them to avoid or reduce the risks of STIs and pregnancy.

Comprehensive Sexuality Education (CSE)

Programs provide holistic, medically accurate, age-appropriate information about safer sex and safer sex practices including abstinence, as well as the use of contraception and condoms as effective ways to reduce unintended pregnancy and STIs. CSE programs also usually include information about healthy relationships, communication skills, and human development among other topics for students from kindergarten to 12th grade.

outcomes. Because these programs do not acknowledge that many teenagers will become sexually active, they do not include content about contraception or condom use, unless to emphasize their failure rates (KFF, 2018). These programs also exclude teenagers who may have already had sex whether by choice or as a result of sexual abuse. Therefore, students who become involved in intimate situations are left stranded regarding not knowing how to have safer sex. Some of these programs avoid certain discussions, such as same-gender sexual attraction, the sexual nature of persons with disabilities, diverse and nontraditional family structures, and pregnancy options. They promote gender stereotypes and fail to provide pertinent health information to sexually active adolescents or to those who are already pregnant or parenting (Guttmacher Institute, 2017; Santelli et al., 2017). Because the inaccurate communications of these programs are designed to control young people's behaviors, sexuality educators for all age groups need to be aware of these messages and be able to clarify misconceptions, remove stereotypes, and promote the use of medically accurate information.

Abstinence-only programs have been rebranded as Sexual Risk Avoidance Programs (Boyer 2018). They focus on teaching youth to voluntarily refrain from sexual activity. Interventions emphasize (1) the benefits of personal responsibility, self-regulation, and healthy decision making with a focus on the future; (2) the advantages of refraining from nonmarital sexual activity; (3) the increased likelihood of avoiding poverty when youth become self-sufficient and emotionally mature before sexual activity; (4) the foundational components of healthy relationships and their impact on healthy marriages and stable families; (5) the effect of other youth risk behaviors such as drugs and alcohol on increasing the risk for teen sex, and (6) strategies on how to resist or avoid sexual coercion and dating violence. These programs mandate the prohibition of teaching young people the benefits of condoms and contraception (SIECUS, 2018a). If some programs provide information on contraception, it must be medically accurate and complete to ensure that students understand that contraception offers risk reduction, but not risk elimination. The education cannot include demonstrations, simulations, or distribution of contraceptive devices (FYSB, 2020).

While some believe it is reasonable to wait until marriage before having a sexual relationship and then be faithful to that partner for life, this may be unrealistic for many young people because it fails to reflect the nature of modern societies in which people marry later in life, if at all. While the age that people first marry has been increasing, the age when they first have sexual intercourse has decreased. Over the years, this gap of time between first intercourse and first marriage has increased for both males (11.7 years) and females (8.7 years) (Santelli et al., 2017). Only a small percentage of young people wait until marriage for their first intercourse. With the high frequency of marital dissolution, people are also very likely to have several sexual partners over their lifetime. Moreover, these programs also do not account for LGBTQ+ relationships in which marriage may not be a viable option for some individuals.

Twenty years of research shows that abstinence-only education has failed to delay sexual activity or reduce risky behavior. Data also indicate that abstinence-only curricula are positively associated with higher adolescent pregnancy rates, especially in conservative states where spending on abstinence-only education is related to higher birth rates (Denford, 2017; Dorri et al., 2019; Stanger-Hall & Hall, 2011; Trenholm et al., 2007). Moreover, experts assert that government support of these programs has undermined sexuality education in the US, resulting in a decline in US adolescents who report receiving sexuality education on a range of topics including birth control (Guttmacher Institute, 2017).

Sexual Risk Reduction Programs

Sexual Risk Reduction Programs provide information about contraception and protection against STIs. Sometimes known as "Abstinence-Plus Programs," their emphasis is on abstinence and delayed initiation of sexual interaction in addition to broader risk-reduction components. The expected outcome is reduced risky sexual behavior, with some other potential benefits including increased contraception and condom use along with reduced sexual activity, teen pregnancy, and incidence of STIs. While these programs promote abstinence from sexual interaction, they acknowledge that adolescents may become sexually active. Thus, they include content on condom use and discussions of contraception, abortion, and STIs, such as HIV/AIDS (FYSB, 2020). Because abstinence has been long recommended as a basis for funding, without also including information on prevention, young people are in jeopardy of poor outcomes. Sexual Risk Reduction Programs can take place in schools or community settings (Robert Woods Johnson Foundation, 2017).

Comprehensive Sexuality Education Programs

Comprehensive sexuality education (CSE) goes beyond an abstinence focus to cover a broad range of issues related to the physical, biological, emotional, and social aspects of sexuality as well as sexual and reproductive health. It has been shown to reduce risky sexual behaviors and delay sexual activity (SIECUS, 2004; WHO, 2017). CSE recognizes and accepts all people as sexual beings and is adapted to the age and stage of development of the individual. Although CSE is aimed at school-age students, the concepts within the program can apply to people of any age. It encourages youth to value their health, well-being, and dignity; develop respectful social and sexual relationships; consider how their choices affect their own well-being and that of others; and understand and ensure the protection of their rights throughout their lives. Effective CSE, which is research-based and theory-driven, should teach essential knowledge, shape personal values and beliefs that support healthy behaviors, support norms for a healthy lifestyle, and develop the necessary skills to adopt, practice, and maintain health-enhancing behaviors (FoSE, 2020a).

The guidelines for CSE programs were developed by the Sexuality Information and Education Council of the United States (SIECUS, 2004) and updated in the *Sex Education Standards: Core Content and Skills, K–12* (FoSE, 2020a). These guidelines constitute a framework used in the US and several countries worldwide. Based on values that reflect the beliefs of most communities in a pluralistic society, there are four primary goals of CSE:

- To provide accurate *information* about sexuality.
- To provide an opportunity for people to *develop and understand* their values, attitudes, and insights about sexuality.
- To help young people develop *relationships* and *interpersonal skills.*
- To help people exercise *responsibility* regarding sexual relationships, including addressing abstinence, resisting pressures to prematurely become involved in sexual intercourse, and encouraging the use of contraception and other sexual health measures (SIECUS, 2004).

These guidelines focus on teaching seven key concepts including: Consent and Healthy Relationships, Anatomy and Physiology, Puberty and Adolescent Sexual Development, Gender Identity and Expression, Sexual Orientation and Identity, Sexual Health, and Interpersonal Violence. They can be taught with age-appropriate materials at developmental levels from kindergarten through high school: grades K–2, grades 3–5, grades 6–8, grades 9–10, and grades 11–12 (FoSE, 2020a). Sexuality education may also be introduced into preschool programs with content related to naming body parts and enhancing self-esteem. Within CSE, age-appropriate information is included on a broad range of topics related to sexuality, such as gender, sexual and reproductive health and HIV, sexual rights and sexual citizenship, pleasure, violence, diversity, and relationships (SIECUS, 2004).

Comprehensive sexuality education has become a mainstream value in the United States. Many parents believe that young people should be prepared for the healthy expression of their sexuality and given information about how to protect themselves from unintended pregnancies and STIs (SIECUS, 2018b). Abstinence is encouraged as the safer choice with sexuality being viewed as a natural and healthy part of living. There is respect for the diversity of beliefs about sexuality that exists in communities. Advocates of CSE believe youth should have the knowledge they need to make informed and responsible decisions about their lives. Moreover, more than 80% of Americans believe that CSE programs, which not only emphasize abstinence, but also encourage the use of condoms and contraception, should be taught in the schools (Kirby, 2007). In addition, young people should be learning about personal power, as well as negotiation, refusal, and communication skills to help them delay sexual interactions if they believe this is what they should do.

Effectiveness of Comprehensive Sexuality Education

A systematic review of three decades of research involving 218 articles indicated strong support for CSE. The findings provided evidence of the effectiveness of approaches that address a broad definition of sexual health and well-being and take positive, affirming, and inclusive approaches to sexuality across multiple grade levels (Goldfarb & Lieberman, 2020). Evaluations of CSE programs found they not only increased the use of contraceptives including condoms, but also did not hasten the initiation of sexual relations or increase its frequency. Youth who received information about contraception were at 50% lower risk of teen pregnancy than those in abstinence-only programs (Kohler, Manhart, & Lafferty, 2008). Approximately 40% of programs that focused on both abstinence and contraception delayed the initiation of sexual interaction and reduced the number of sexual partners and frequency of sexual activities, while more than 60% of the programs reduced the incidence of unprotected sex (Chin et al., 2012; Denford et al., 2017; Kirby, 2008; Santelli et al., 2017). Programs were effective for both genders, all major ethnic groups, sexually experienced and inexperienced teens, and in different settings and communities. In addition, some programs' positive impacts lasted for several years (Kirby, 2007). Nearly all CSE programs had a positive influence on one or more factors affecting sexual behavior, such as improved knowledge about the risks and consequences of pregnancy and STIs, values and attitudes about sexual involvement and use of condoms or contraception, perception of peer norms, confidence in the ability to say "no" to unwanted sex, insistence on using condoms and contraception, and communication with parents or adults. When studies were replicated in different communities, there were similar positive effects. However, if programs were shortened or had certain content removed (such as the use of condoms) the original positive results were not replicated.

Various public health and medical organizations support a comprehensive approach to sexuality education including the American Medical Association, the American Academy of Pediatrics, the American School Health Association, and the Society for Adolescent Health and Medicine. They are aware of the strong evidence that shows CSE helps teens make healthy decisions about sexuality and relationships (Santelli et al., 2017).

The Politics of Sexuality Education

Over the years public controversies have evolved regarding sexuality education resulting in the issue becoming politically contentious with respect to funding. Individuals who control the funding may have personal biases and beliefs that can influence which programs are promoted and implemented. The federal government has funded Abstinence-Only-Until-Marriage programs (AOUM) for almost four decades, despite overwhelming evidence they are ineffective and fail to achieve their stated goals. While funding bills may have rebranded these programs as "sexual risk avoidance education" (SRAE), the same stigmatizing and shame-based curricula continue. Although the new program names have been using the language of sexuality education proponents and public health programs, they still leave young people without the information to make decisions about their sexual health (SIECUS, 2018).

During the last decade there was a notable shift in abstinence funding to more evidenced-based sexuality education initiatives (KFF, 2018). The Personal Responsibility Education Program (PREP) was developed to provide grants to states in support of evidence-based sexuality education that teaches about both abstinence and contraception. In addition, the Teen Pregnancy Prevention Program (TPPP) was established to more narrowly focus on teen pregnancy prevention providing grants to replicate evidence-based program models, as well as funding for implementation and rigorous evaluation (KFF, 2018). Rather than rely on research and adhere to the congressional intent of the program, government officials have used TPPP to redirect additional funding into ineffective AOUM programs (SIECUS, 2019), even though a California judge had ruled that using an AOUM curriculum violated state laws on the grounds of medical inaccuracy and bias (*American Academy of Pediatrics et al. v. Clovis Unified School District*, 2015).

Because there is no federal law or policy requiring sexuality education, individual states, school districts, and schools decide which type of sexuality education will best meet the needs of their students. In some states there are *mandates*, which are *requirements* that all school districts provide sexuality or AIDS education to their students, usually with suggested curricula to be implemented at the local level (Guttmacher Institute, 2013). Other states have *recommendations*, which are provisions by state legislatures or state departments of education that *promote* sexuality and/or STI/HIV/AIDS education, but do not require it. While specific curricula may be suggested, it is up to the local school districts to design and implement these programs. It is important for all students, parents, educators, and voters to fully understand the characteristics of programs that use the term "abstinence." Do they mean abstinence-only (sexual risk avoidance), abstinence-only-until-marriage, abstinence-based (sex risk reduction), abstinence-plus, abstinence-centered, or abstinence-preferred for safer sex that will delay the onset of sexual intercourse (e.g., Comprehensive Sexuality Education)?

The federal government has funded a variety of sexuality education programs, although each state has its own curricula guidelines. For example most states have a policy requiring HIV education which is usually in conjunction with broader sexuality education. While there is a growing acknowledgement of the sexuality of youth, teaching about life skills has also become popular with most states requiring instruction on healthy relationships and violence prevention. Understanding the variability of state laws and policies for sexuality education is important for sexuality educators, as well as parent educators who help parents link what children learn in school to what they want their children to know (Guttmacher Institute, 2021). A summary of some of these laws and policies can be found in Box 9.2.

While CSE must be culturally responsive to the needs of LGBTQ+ youth and include instruction about gender identity and sexual orientation, only 11 states currently mandate this educational content. Ongoing advocacy is needed to promote the inclusive nature of sexuality education (SIECUS, 2020).

Box 9.2 State Laws and Policies for Sexuality Education

- **39** states and the District of Columbia (DC) mandate sex education and/or HIV education.
- **30** states and DC mandate that, when provided, sex and HIV education programs meet certain general requirements. Content should be medically accurate (n=18); instruction should be age appropriate (n=26 + DC); and instruction should be applicable for a student's cultural background and not biased against any race, sex, or ethnicity (n=9).
- **40** states and DC require school districts to involve parents in sexuality education, HIV education, or both.
- **20** states and DC require provision of information on contraception.
- **39** states and DC require provision of information on abstinence. Some states require that abstinence be stressed (n=29), while others require that it be covered (n=11 + DC).
- **19** states require that instruction is provided on the importance of engaging in sexual activity only within marriage.
- **17** states and DC require either an inclusive or discriminatory view of sexual orientation. Some states require inclusive content about sexual orientation (n=11+ DC), while others require that only negative information on homosexuality and/or a positive emphasis on heterosexuality (n=6) be provided.
- **19** states and DC require the inclusion of information on the negative outcomes of teen sex and pregnancy.
- **19** states and DC require inclusion of information on condoms or contraception when HIV education is provided.
- **37** states and DC require provision of information on abstinence when HIV education is provided.
- **35** states and DC require provision of information about skills for healthy romantic and sexual relationships.
- **38** states and DC require information about the prevention of teen dating violence and sexual violence. This includes information about asserting personal boundaries and refusing unwanted sexual advances (n=24 + DC); requiring the importance of consent to sexual activity (n=9), and requiring information on preventing, recognizing, and responding to teen dating violence and sexual violence (n=37 + DC).

Most states require school districts to involve parents in sexuality education, however, only a few require parental consent. It is important to understand the laws related to parental consent for sexuality education. These laws can have provisions that allow parents to "opt-in" or "opt-out" their children from sexuality education instruction. Under an "opt-in" policy, written permission is needed from a parent/guardian for a student to attend a sexuality education class. "Opt-out" policies require schools to send written notification to parents/guardians about what will be taught in a sexuality education class and who will be teaching it. It is the responsibility of the parents/guardians to review these materials, if they so choose, and respond to the school in writing if they do not want their child to attend these classes. Most states and school districts rely on opt-out policies, ensuring that a larger number of young people receive the benefits of sexuality education (SIECUS, 2018c).

Parents as Sexuality Educators

Sexuality education begins in the home with parents and caregivers as children's initial sexuality educators. The home is a continuous source of sexuality education where questions are answered or not, and sexuality is communicated verbally and nonverbally. Infants should receive as much approval for the discovery of their genitals as their nose and toes. Parents need to know that it is normal for a 5-year-old child to engage in sex play (e.g., playing doctor, watching others undress) and that how they respond to this kind of behavior can greatly influence the way the child will view his or her sexuality. Whether they like it or not, parents will have a strong influence on their children's sexuality. Silence may even speak louder than words (SRCP, 2020).

Raising sexually healthy children results from a combination of strong relationships, open communication, and clear messages regarding values and expectations between parents and their children (*It's That Easy!* Collaborative, 2016). Sexuality is not an event, but a process involving love and relationships. However, many parents do not communicate with their children about sexuality because they are embarrassed, do not want to think of their child as being sexual, are uncomfortable saying sexual words and phrases, use euphemisms, have no positive role models, and find there are a number of things about sexuality they do not know. Although some fear their communication might encourage sexual exploration, this is not supported by research (Flores & Barroso, 2017). Because parent-child communication results in the transmission of family expectations, societal values, and role modeling of sexual health reduction strategies, parents have an important role in shaping the sexual health of their children.

Some recommendations for parents to be positive sexuality educators and have productive conversations with their children include (SRCP 2020):

- It is never too late to start.
- Choose the right time and place.
- Listen more than you talk.
- Be aware of your body language.

- Forget the "big talk," as topics change as your child ages.
- Look for teachable moments.
- Make sure you and your child are talking about the same thing when discussing sexuality.
- It is ok to be embarrassed and tell your child how you feel.
- Books can be a great resource for both the parent and child.
- You do not need to know the answer to every question.
- Keep your responses simple until a child can understand a more complicated answer.
- Practice pays off; starting when they are young helps you gain confidence.
- Have a sense of humor.
- Ask your children for their opinions and feelings.
- Share your values.
- Teach your child that there is more to sexuality than having sex.

Sexuality education at home is not a substitute for sexuality education in the schools. In fact, many parents believe that having a program in the schools makes it easier to talk to their children about sexual issues. Many parents want to work collaboratively with schools to jointly facilitate the sexuality education of their children. However, depending on the state in which they live, the education can be widely different. Therefore, parents need to understand what content the sexuality programs in their states provide and how best to supplement that content, if needed. Parents typically do not know what is included in "abstinence-only" or "comprehensive" curricula. However, when informed about the content, most parents want more than "abstinence-only" education and prefer the inclusion of additional information about gender identity (Dorri et al., 2019). Many parent educators who want to help parents become more effective in the sexuality education of their children can refer to *It's That Easy: A Guide to Raising Sexually Healthy Children* (2010).

One of the issues facing parents as sexuality educators is the role of technology and media in sexual socialization. Parents need to be aware of the amount and accessibility of sexually explicit materials. Pornography has become a major industry that can shape attitudes about sexual behavior. It is easily accessed, sensationalized, and often inaccurate, and young people are exposed to it at earlier ages than in the past (Russell et al., 2020). There are also safety issues related to smart phones and camera devices installed to protect children that can be accessed by others outside the family. Therefore this issue needs to be included in parent education classes about sexuality so parents can be accessible and have ongoing conversations with their children.

Parents of an LGBTQ+ child may desire assistance in becoming an effective parental support person and sexuality educator. Sexual minorities "come out" at younger ages today than in past decades, with coming out to parents serving as a major part of their identification process (van Bergen et al., 2020). Increased positive media and legal attention for same-sex sexuality over the past decade may play a role in understanding the relative lower frequency of parental shock responses when children share that they are transgender. Parental validation of a child's sexual minority identity predicts greater self-acceptance and self-esteem along with less depression, substance abuse, and suicide ideation (Ryan et al., 2010). However, it is unclear that "coming out" and open communication about gender identity and sexual orientation with parents have become any easier. While validating communications from parents are increasing, it is premature to state that the tide has turned (van Bergen et al., 2020). Family rejection can have a long-lasting adverse impact on LGBTQ+ individuals (Puckett et al., 2015). LGBTQ+ youth desire to openly communicate with their parents about their sexual identities, but parents may need some guidance about how to successfully talk with their children. While it is desirable to have open communication about sexual identities, this is still an elusive process for many LGBTQ+ individuals and their families (van Bergen et al., 2020).

Diversity in Sexuality Education

Because sexuality education for certain groups has been neglected, it is important for educators to consider various kinds of diversity related to age; culture, race, and ethnicity; differing abilities; and gender. Whereas sexuality educators may develop specialized programs for diverse members of our society, all sexuality educators need to be aware of a range of diverse issues and differing needs.

Age

Everyone is a sexual being from birth to death, even if they do not have feelings of sexual desire. It is natural for young children to be curious about their bodies so how parents and caregivers react to their curiosity can have future impact of their sexuality. Questions such as "where did I come from," "what is that" (when pointing to a body part), "how did a baby get into your tummy," or "my friend says that a stork brought me," should be dealt with accurately and at their level of understanding. Children need to learn that while it is normal to be curious about their own and other's bodies, they decide who touches them. Thus, children can learn that sexuality is an acceptable topic for conversation, with a trusted adult and in appropriate places such as at home. If they feel safe discussing issues as children, they will be more likely to feel comfortable sharing information as they get older.

At the other end of the age spectrum, many people have not considered that seniors are sexual beings—their sexuality is invisible and often discounted by society. However, older adults are still interested in sex, have sex, and enjoy sex. They still have feelings, relationships, and see themselves as sexual beings. The topic of sexuality for seniors has often been neglected and treated comically in the media. Some of the attitudes about the sexuality of older people are partly due to our youth-oriented culture as we tend to focus on young people and their physical characteristics that can be perceived as sexy (e.g., trim bodies and smooth skin). Older adults often try to hide their sexual behaviors from their children. While sexual desire and behaviors may decline somewhat with age, there does not seem to be any specific age after which all people are sexually inactive (Das, Waite, & Lauman, 2012; Lindau et al., 2007). Each person and couple need to determine the kind and amount of sexual expression that best fits their health, relationship status, and desires. Seniors who have their health and opportunities for sexual interactions may be sexually active way past 70.

Sexuality education about seniors is needed to both help younger people understand the needs of older adults and help seniors with their specific sexual issues. Older persons need to understand the realities of the aging process, their changing sexuality, and new or different ways to engage in sexual activities (Fileborn et al., 2017). In addition, a range of STIs including chlamydia, gonorrhea, syphilis, and HIV have been reported by older adults, because many do not practice safer sex (Johnson, 2013). Others may fear the risk of heart attacks since the demands of sex on the heart may be reasonable to consider (Jackson, 2009). As people age, they may need to know how to negotiate new relationships with a partner who has lost interest in sexual interaction, as well as understand the effects of their changing bodies on sexual behaviors.

Sexuality education programs are not just for adolescents, but for people at all stages of the lifespan. Children and adults need sexuality education based on knowledge, self-awareness, and communication. Older people still have sexual feelings and desires even though their physiological responses may be a bit slower. Therefore, educators need to help those of different ages to have knowledge and healthy attitudes about sexuality.

Culture, Race, and Ethnicity

Differences in sexual attitudes and behaviors can be influenced by culture, race, and ethnicity as well as one's country of origin, geographical location (rural, urban, suburban, or area of the country), religion, and family membership. The role of ethnicity in sexual attitudes and behaviors has been overlooked until recently. Because there are so many differences among ethnicities based on economic status, the degree of acculturation, and adherence to traditional customs of one's heritage, it can be difficult to study various groups and develop educational programs. At times, sexuality educators assume if they read about various cultures or ethnicities, they can be effective teachers for these groups. However, sexuality educators need to also interact with their participants with openness and respect, so they can learn about their values and experiences related to intimate relationships and sexuality.

Understanding the cultural heritage of any group is essential to creating programs that are respectful and allow for interaction in meaningful ways. It is important to avoid using microaggressions, which are subtle everyday slights, snubs, or insults whether intentional or unintentional, to individuals in marginalized groups—racial and ethnic groups as well as groups based on sexual orientation and gender identity. Some examples include mispronouncing the names of participants after they have corrected you; anticipating emotional responses based on gender, sexual orientation, or race/ethnicity; expecting people of a particular group to represent the perspectives of others of their race/ethnicity, sexual orientation, or gender identity; using sexist language; assuming the gender of individuals; complimenting nonwhite students on their use of "good English"; and making assumptions about students and their backgrounds (Sue, 2010).

There are variations in sexuality within our culture that can be attributed to ethnic, social class, and economic differences. Ethnic groups are not homogeneous whether they are African Americans, Hispanics, Asian Americans, Native Americans, or Middle Eastern Americans. These differences and similarities are related to cultural contexts and practices such as premarital sexual interactions, cohabitation, marriage rates, role of religion, influence of education, gender roles, importance of family and extended family, use of certain contraceptives, and certain sexual behaviors such as oral sex and masturbation. Sexuality educators need to reflect on what they do not know about their participants and allow learners to join them in the learning process.

Differently-Abled

The sexual needs of differently-abled persons have often been neglected or misrepresented. Just because someone is in a wheelchair, is missing a limb, or has an intellectual disability does not mean they have no sexual interests. These individuals could have issues resulting from damage or deterioration of the central nervous system, neurological challenges, or chronic illness. Differently-abled individuals can be of any age. Since a wide range of disabilities and limitations can influence sexuality, differently-abled persons need support and education so they can enjoy their sexual potential. Depending on the situation, a variety of things may need to be addressed, such as physical loss of control over bodily functions, an inability to care for personal needs, a fear of being less of a person, and feelings of unacceptability.

Youth with disabilities (YWD) may wonder about being in an intimate relationship, having children, or being abused in some way. They are less likely to learn about sexuality from their parents or health care providers and are often excluded from informal learning that occurs in peer social networks (Holmes, 2021). Being left out of sex education makes YWD more vulnerable. Compared to youth with no disability, YWD were more likely to report coercive sex (18.6% vs. 12.1%); forced sex (13.2% vs. 7.9%); and sexual abuse (8.4% vs. 4.8%). Safety is a basic need for all youth but especially YWD. They must learn about their rights and responsibilities for communicating and respecting physical, emotional, and sexual boundaries. Disability inclusion benefits all persons. Although 5.6% of students 5 to 17 years old have disabilities, rates increase with age. According to the Centers for Disease Control, one in four US adults (61 million Americans) have disabilities (Holmes, 2021).

Programs need to assess the cognitive and emotional abilities of each person and then present developmentally appropriate materials. Dealing with romantic or sexual expression can also be important, as well as including behaviors that may or may not be appropriate in public settings. Teaching methodologies may have to be adjusted to reflect the individual's ability to learn by making the content more explicit. However, these materials may then be perceived as suggestive. People with chronic illnesses often have some sexual issues such as feelings of guilt about the effects of bodily changes on their sexuality or fears of a reoccurrence due to the physicality of a sexual relationship.

When dealing with children who have developmental disabilities, teachers and parents should consider the following questions submitted by teenagers 15 to 18 years old (SRCP, 2020):

- How can you tell if someone is interested in you?
- Is it ok if a boy holds my hand on the first date and I'm too nervous to say "no"?
- I really want to be married and I really want to be pregnant.
- How do you know if you are gay?
- What happens when you have sex?

Not all children with developmental disabilities can ask these kinds of questions, but low-functioning individuals still need information about their sexuality to help them understand opportunities for sexual expression, the importance of contraception, self-protection skills, and avoidance of showing their private parts in public.

Physical disabilities of children and adults cover a wide range of conditions, however people with physical disabilities may also desire to have sexual interactions. While some may decide to ignore sexuality issues because they believe these issues do not apply to them, others wonder if anyone will find them sexually desirable or if a partner will stay with them. Whatever the type of disability, do not assume that an adolescent will never be interested in romantic relationships. Most teens and young adults with disabilities desire to be in romantic relationships. They want to date, experience intimacy, and possibly marry. In order for children to make good choices, parents and educators need to teach them about these very personal topics. While some educators and parents may be apprehensive about talking to their children about sexuality, especially if they have a disability, the child will appreciate openness and come to view the parent or educator as someone they can turn to in a crisis (SRCP, 2020).

Gender

Discourse around LGBTQ+ individuals has changed over the past decades (Dunlap, 2016). Similarly, sexuality education has started to include and affirm gender-diverse groups based on one's *gender identity,* which is an internal understanding and experience of one's gender. Each person's experience with gender identity is unique and personal and is not the same as gender expression. We cannot assume that the way someone moves, talks, dresses, or styles their hair is indicative of how they identify their gender (The Trevor Project, 2020a). In the past, sexuality education programs either focused entirely on heterosexual or cisgender individuals and relationships or only included a casual mention of LGBTQ+ individuals by talking about gender neutral names and using the generic term partner rather than boyfriend or girlfriend (Bruess & Schroeder, 2018). There are several gender-related terms such as "gender nonconforming" (people who do not adhere to society's customs for dress and activities related to one's biological sex and gender assignment) or "nonbinary" (a gender category outside of gender binary in which only two genders exist). While "LGBTQ" is the commonly used term, it may not be inclusive so at times the term "LGBTQIA+" is incorporated. Although it is important to understand what these terms mean, it is best not to make assumptions, rather ask members of the LGBTQIA+ community how they identify themselves. Since language is constantly evolving, new terms are introduced while others fade from use or change their meaning over time. Box 9.3 helps to explain the meaning of letters in this acronym (FoSE, 2020a; Ginicola, Smith, & Filmore, 2017; Moor, 2019).

Box 9.3 **LGBTQIA+: Clarification of Terms**

- **Lesbian**: Person who identifies as a woman and is romantically, emotionally, and/or sexually attracted to other women.
- **Gay**: Umbrella term used for people who are romantically, emotionally, and/or sexually attracted to people of the same gender although most commonly associated with a person who identifies as a man who is romantically, emotionally, and/or sexually attracted to other men. At times it has also been used to describe the LGBTQIA+ community as a whole.
- **Bisexual**: Person who is emotionally, romantically, and/or sexually attracted to more than one gender, though not necessarily simultaneously in the same way or to the same degree. A bisexual orientation focuses on the potential for, but not requirement of, involvement with more than one gender. This is different from being attracted to only men or only women.
- **Transgender**: Person whose gender identity and/or expression is not limited by the sex they were assigned at birth. Transgender is often used as an umbrella term encompassing a large number of identities related to gender nonconformity.
- **Queer or Questioning**: Umbrella term used by people who do not conform to dominant societal norms and express fluid sexual orientation, gender identity, or sexual orientation. While used as a neutral or even a positive term among many LGBTQ+ people today, "queer" was historically used as a derogatory slur. Questioning refers to people who are exploring their sexual orientation and/or sexual identity and gender expression.
- **Intersex**: Person who is born with a reproductive and or sexual anatomy that does not fit the typical definitions of male or female. People with intersex bodies have an array of biological characteristics that straddle the two sexes. (Intersex is different from transgender.)
- **Asexual**: Person who does not experience sexual attraction, but may experience other forms of attraction (e.g., intellectual and/or emotional).
- **Ally**: Someone who is outside the LGBTQ+ community who supports the struggle for equality and rights.
- **+**: Symbol to represent self-identifying members of the community who are not included in the LGBTQIA acronym, such as pansexual or genderqueer individuals. The + can refer to anything a person wants it to be and also creates an opportunity for the LGBTQ+ community to expand its conceptualization.
- **Pansexual**: Person who has the potential to be romantically, emotionally, and/or sexually attracted to people regardless of gender or gender identity though not necessarily simultaneously, in the same way, or to the same degree. They have no sexual preference but are connected to people for who they are.
- **Genderqueer:** Gender identity label used by those who do not identify as man or woman and may combine aspects of each into their identity.

In 2015, national data indicated that 88.8% of high school students self-identified as heterosexual, 2% as gay or lesbian, 6% as bisexual, and 3.2% were unsure of their sexual orientation (Santelli et al., 2017). It is estimated that the prevalence of transgender individuals in the US is approximately 0.6%, which translates to 1.4 million adults. However, the prevalence is expected to increase in the next decade because "transgender" is now a more available label than it was previously (World Population Review, 2020b). Transgender is a broad, encompassing term for those whose gender identity is not similar to the gender assigned at birth. An even broader term is "trans" which includes those who identify as transsexual, transgender, cross-dressing, gender nonconforming, gender fluid, gender queer, and gender variant persons (Devor & Dominic, 2015). While some nations recognize transgender people as a third gender, other nations are not so open and require a mental health diagnosis before a transgender person can be legally recognized (World Population Review, 2020b).

Parents and educators need to be aware of mental health issues related to being LGBTQ+. Highlights from a survey of 40,000 LGBTQ+ youth ages 13–24 across the US include (The Trevor Project, 2020b):

- 40% of LGBTQ+ respondents seriously considered attempting suicide in the past 12 months, with more than half of transgender and nonbinary youth having seriously considered suicide.
- 68% of LGBTQ+ youth reported symptoms of generalized anxiety disorder in the past 2 weeks including more than 3 in 4 transgender and nonbinary youth.
- 48% of LGBTQ+ youth reported engaging in self-harm in the past 12 months including over 60% of transgender and nonbinary youth.
- 46% of LGBTQ+ youth reported they wanted psychological or emotional counseling from a mental health professional but were unable to receive it.
- 1 in 3 LGBTQ+ youth reported being physically threatened or harmed in their lifetime due to their LGBTQ+ identity.
- Transgender and nonbinary youth who reported having pronouns respected by all or most people in their lives attempted suicide at half the rate of those who did not have their pronouns respected.

A number of states have enacted legislation to protect students from bullying and discrimination based on their actual or perceived sexual orientation and gender identity. No matter how many positive steps have been taken, the experience in the LGBTQ+ community is still different as many face stereotypes, prejudice, and discrimination due to their sexuality. It is recommended that schools have enumerated policies for the health and well-being of LGBTQ+ and all students, so that students and school personnel have a clear understanding of rights and policies. Such schools would signal that LGBTQ+-based discrimination will not be tolerated. In addition, a recent Presidential Executive Order on preventing and combating discrimination on the basis of gender identity or sexual orientation has stated that "children should be able to learn without worrying about whether they will be denied access to the restroom, locker room, or school sports" (Biden, 2021). Training for teachers and school personnel is essential. While 26% of teachers indicate having no barriers to supporting LGBTQ+ students, 74% said they do not participate in supportive actions because of professional pressure.

Another important element within the school environment is extracurricular activities, LGBTQ+-focused, student-led, school-based clubs, which are often called *Gay-Straight Alliances* or *Genders and Sexualities Alliances* (GSAs). These students work together to promote social inclusion and a positive climate for LGBTQ+ individuals. In 2014, 37% of US high schools established GSAs. Experiences of bullying of LGBTQ youth can negatively impact their well-being. However, when schools had antibullying policies, LGBTQ+ resources, LGBTQ+ inclusive criteria, and GSAs, students felt safe and more connected to adults at school. A recent study showed that among transgender youth, many use a name that was different from the name given them at birth. When these young people were able to use their chosen name at school, home, work, and with friends, they reported 71% fewer symptoms of severe depression, 29% fewer thoughts of suicide, and 56% fewer suicidal attempts. Thus, other youth, parents, and school personnel can support transgender youth by referring to them by their preferred names (Bishop, Ioverno, & Russell, 2019).

Role of Research and Theory in Sexuality Education

Sexuality research faces many issues that other areas of scientific inquiry do not because human sexuality is often accompanied by fear, denial, guilt, and embarrassment. Since many people have personal opinions or experiences on topics related to sexuality, using current research and theory is essential to provide credibility to your program. Researchers use methods such as surveys, self-reports, behavioral measures, observations, and biological measures to learn about various elements of sexuality while incorporating the best possible sampling methods, measurement accuracy, statistical measures, and research ethics. It is important to be able to evaluate research findings from their original sources, because media often reports findings that are from both high- and low-quality research. In addition the medical field has become a major influence on sexuality, through what is referred to as the "medicalization of sexuality" (Stulhofer, 2015). Certain behaviors or conditions have been classified as problematic and needing medical treatment (e.g., drugs used for male erectile dysfunction). Therefore, sexuality educators need to be able to use credible sources and evaluate research prior to incorporating it into their programs.

Program evaluation is necessary for the continued improvement of sexuality education programs. Evaluation is not simply about measuring the acquisition of knowledge, but also changes in attitudes and behaviors and determining if the goals and objectives of a program were achieved. Program evaluation needs to move beyond assessment of learners to also consider the effectiveness of teachers and the educational process. Moreover, it is important to incorporate evidence-based sexuality education programs into program development. The evaluations of these programs have been published in peer-reviewed journals and demonstrated by research and evaluation to have had some kind of impact on participants.

Sexuality encompasses a broad range of topics and issues which can be better understood by providing reasonable explanations based not only on current research, but also theory. Although no single theory can explain all there is to know about sexuality, various theories and conceptual frameworks can be integrated to facilitate our understanding of sexual behaviors and interactions. A few theories and applicable examples are highlighted to provide a broad perspective for analyzing human sexuality.

- The *family ecosystems framework* can be used to provide an environmental context when analyzing issues (e.g., the influence of media in shaping our sexual thoughts, feelings, and behaviors). It can also help to understand the interaction and intersectionality of various overlapping factors influencing sexuality, such as gender, sex, race, class, religion, disability, and physical appearance. Sexuality does not exist in a void but interacts with dynamic overlapping contexts.
- *Family systems theory* can provide an understanding of relationship issues (e.g., the role of parents in providing sexuality education to their children, intergenerational communications about sexuality, physical and psychological boundaries related to sexuality, and feedback in partnered relationships).
- *Social exchange theory* can enhance understanding of the rewards and costs related to the potential outcomes of various sexual behaviors and interactions (e.g., the use of various methods of contraception, extra-relationship sexual interactions, or "coming out" with one's gender identity transition).
- *Developmental theories* can facilitate understanding sexuality from a perspective of change. Personal and sexual changes evolve through the lifespan from teens struggling during puberty to adults dealing with interpersonal relationships and family issues and seniors who continue to seek and enjoy sexual relationships as they continue to age.
- *Social learning theory* recognizes that learning occurs not only within the individual, but also in a particular social context, focusing on learning processes and social behavior (e.g., the learning experiences of children regarding sex and gender by observing and imitating their parents or scenes from television).

Model of Sexuality—Organizing Sexuality Concepts

The content covered in sexuality courses, which is based on research and theory, varies depending on the needs and ages of the participants, settings, and length of programs. There is an interaction between individuals and families with their social, psychological, cultural, and historical contexts. A *Model of Sexuality* (see Figure 9.1) can be used to identify and organize some fundamental concepts in the study of sexuality with the goal of providing greater understanding. This model can be incorporated in part or in total to help organize the content of a class or program and adjusted to meet the pertinent parameters of a course. This visual illustration focuses on health and well-being as it is influenced by the interaction

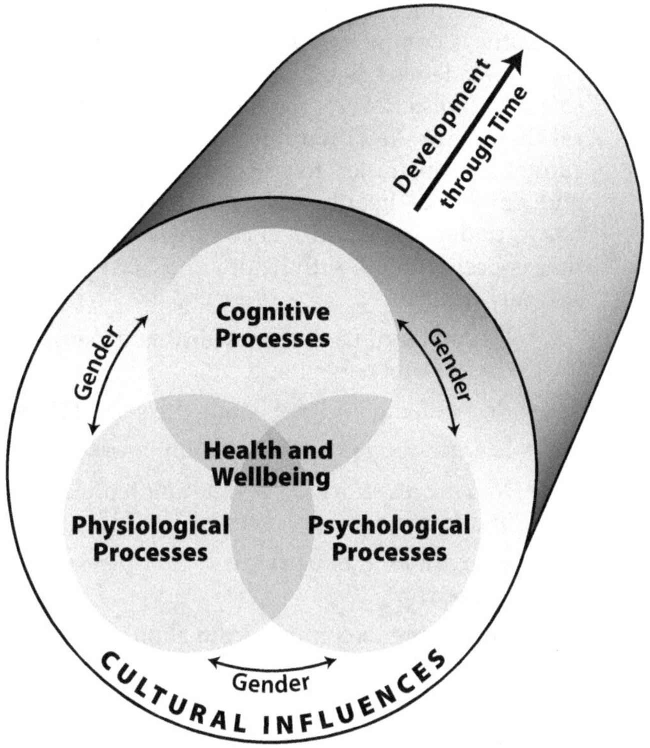

Figure 9.1
Model of Sexuality

of cognitive, psychological, and physiological processes; gender; and cultural influences that all change through time.

Health and Well-Being

The central focus of the Model of Sexuality is health and well-being. Sexual health—which is fundamental to the attainment of a state of well-being—involves physical, emotional, mental, and social dimensions (WHO, 2019b; Yarber & Sayad, 2019). While in the past sexual health discussions were focused on the absence of disease (e.g., HIV infections or STIs), dysfunction, or infirmity, sexual health is now viewed as a broader concept involving positive sexual health and well-being. Sexual health is relevant throughout the lifespan and is expressed through diverse sexualities and forms of sexual expression. It needs to be understood within specific social, economic, and political contexts. According to the Global Advisory Board for Sexual Health and Wellbeing (2020), sexual pleasure must be addressed in combination with sexual rights and sexual well-being. Only when approached in this way, can pleasure-inclusive education and research contribute to sexual understanding—otherwise, it serves only a specific, privileged population.

Focusing on health and well-being is essential because sexuality is an important component of an individual's and family's health, as well as public health. The interrelatedness of our physical and psychological health with our sexuality is complex. One example that demonstrates the effect physiological/clinical evidence has on well-being can be noted in the U = U concept (*Undetectable = Untransmittable*). If a person with HIV is on HIV medications (antiretroviral therapy or ART) with a consistently undetectable HIV viral load, the virus cannot be transmitted to a sex partner. This finding has implications for physical and emotional health and sexual well-being (NIH, 2019). It is important to know, understand, and feel comfortable with our bodies especially in a culture that is preoccupied with health and bodily perfection. What does it mean to be sexually healthy?

- Understanding that sexuality is a natural part of life and involves more than sexual behavior.
- Recognizing and respecting the sexual rights we all share.
- Having access to sexual health information, education, and care.
- Making an effort to prevent unintended pregnancies and STIs and seek care and treatment when needed.
- Being able to experience sexual pleasure, satisfaction, and intimacy when desired.
- Being able to communicate about sexual health with others including sexual partners and health care providers (ASHA, n.d.).

Although it often remains hidden, the promotion of sexual health is central to the attainment of wellness and well-being, however interpretations of sexual health may vary (WASH, 2008). Sexual health and well-being are multifaceted concepts. Therefore, examining relevant cognitive, psychological, and physiological processes in conjunction with gender and culture as they change over time can add to our understanding of this important dimension of individuals and their relationships.

Cognitive Processes

While we do not often talk about the cognitive dimensions of sexuality, the brain is nevertheless commonly perceived as our most important sex organ (Fournier, 2018). Cognitive processes pertain to acquiring knowledge and understanding through one's thoughts evolving from perception, memory, judgment, and reasoning as they relate to various decisions we make. We decide about sexual behavior regarding when to initiate a sexual relationship or interactions, with whom, and under what circumstances. Our thought processes can also affect our reasoning when dealing with moral and ethical decisions, such as sexual harassment or other issues related to "should I or shouldn't I, yes or no." Although sexual harassment can appear in diverse guises and in many different environments, it is quite common, widespread, and can occur at work or in educational settings. Approximately 4.5 million students have encountered some kind of sexual misconduct ranging from inappropriate sexual comments to molestation by a school employee (SafeSchools, 2019). About half the students have experienced sexual harassment with 87% indicating it had a negative effect on them. Moreover, 21%

of girls compared to 7% of boys report being cyberbullied online or via texts, with 75% of LGBTQ+ students being verbally harassed.

Within the cognitive dimension, ethical decisions about sexuality are important to consider. How does self-interest interact with moral demands when making life choices, especially regarding sexuality? In other words, what is "good for me" versus what is "good for all"? An ethical theory has two parts. The first part deals with elements that are fundamentally valuable, or the rationale behind decisions. In addition to some universal values such as honesty, fairness, freedom, tolerance, and helping others, we also have personal values related to love, pleasure, and feelings of self-esteem. Values not only serve as a basis for decision-making (with each person having his or her own hierarchy of values) but can also generate guilt if particular actions conflict with one's values and prioritization of values. The second part deals with morality or how we treat others, as we have some limits on what we can do to others. While we have some general rules to guide us, we also have specific situations for which no one set of rules applies. In these instances, we have to analyze and evaluate each situation to determine which ethical principles are relevant. Some principles that can be applied to different sexual and moral issues involving others include the following:

- *Principle of noncoercion*: People should not be forced to engage in sexual expression.
- *Principle of nondeceit*: People are not to be enticed into sexual expression based on deceit.
- *Principle of treatment of people as ends*: People are not to be treated as a means only; they should be treated as ends. In the sexual domain, this means that another person should never be viewed solely as a means of one's own sexual satisfaction.
- *Principle of respect for beliefs*: People must show respect for the sexual values and beliefs of others. This means that one person should not pressure another to act in a way not in accord with his or her sexual values and beliefs. This does not prevent one person from attempting to rationally persuade others that they are mistaken in their beliefs (Darling & Mabe, 1989).

Using these four principles can be enlightening when analyzing various sexual issues such as gay marriage, abstinence, sexual relations between a teacher and student, sexual violence, the use or nonuse of contraception, and the process of "coming out" to parents and friends.

Psychological Processes

Thoughts of sexual intimacy may produce a wide range of psychological and emotional reactions including excitement, love, pleasure, and joy. Additionally people have experienced emotions of fear, anxiety, guilt, jealousy, and embarrassment related to topics such as casual sex, infertility, childbirth, extra-relationship sex, gender dysphoria, sexual orientation, HIV/AIDS infections, sexual abuse, and/or sexual assault. Our attitudes and feelings about ourselves and others, as well as our emotional responses to sex and love, are primarily learned throughout one's life. *Social learning theory,* which identifies learning as a dynamic interplay between the person, environment, and behavior, proposes that societal reinforcements and punishments shape attitudes and behaviors that influence cognitions, observations, perceptions, ideas, beliefs, and attitudes about sexual behaviors (Bandura, 1977). As children, we use our siblings and parents as models of how we should interact with others, while later we incorporate teachers, peers, and social media as models and indicators of socially normative behaviors. However, for those youth who are questioning their gender identity, there are few role models.

Three words that have a great psychological impact on the lives of men and women in our culture are "I love you," although the word "love" may be often misunderstood. Love, which is a strong emotion or feeling arising without conscious mental or rational effort, motivates people to behave in certain ways. Moreover, it often provides the basis for pairs to commit themselves to each other. For some people, love is an essential ingredient for emotional survival and may be a prerequisite to engaging in sexual relationships. While there are several explanations of love, one frequently used model is the *Triangular Theory of Love*, which is comprised of three critical elements at three corners of the triangle—*intimacy, passion*, and *commitment* (Sternberg, 1986). A loving relationship can be composed of any one component, a combination of two, or all three to differing degrees, with individuals incorporating diverse combinations of the three elements at various times in the same love relationship (e.g., *liking*—intimacy alone; *companionate love*—intimacy + commitment; *empty love*—commitment alone; *fatuous love*—passion + commitment; *infatuation*—passion alone; *romantic love*—intimacy + passion, *nonlove*—absence of intimacy, passion, and commitment; *consummate love*—intimacy + passion + commitment). Love, which can bring pleasure and pain, at times results in some people feeling unhappy if any one of the three components is weak or missing. Both men and women may express their love for another person in different ways. Understanding the feelings, relational processes, and communication styles of men and women is essential to facilitate their interpersonal relationships and sexual interactions, along with the perception that the experience and meaning of love change over time.

Physiological Processes

Biological changes are only one aspect of sexuality, as it also involves our growth and development, reproductive functioning, and sexual arousal and response. It is important to remember sexual interaction is more than intercourse. Thus, there is a wide range of sexual behaviors and responses that can be included in the content of a specific program, as appropriate. A few of these topics may be uncomfortable for some educators, so they may rely solely on discussing human reproduction; however, the physiological processes of sexuality are much broader than puberty and reproduction. To ease these feelings of insecurity, sexuality educators may need to do some self-study and incorporate research findings to add a basis to what they teach. Journals such as the *Journal of Sex Research, Archives of Sexual Behavior, American Journal of Sexuality Education,* and *Journal of Sex & Marital*

Therapy are a few good sources for further research-based knowledge. Moreover, what one teaches about sexual physiology will vary according to age, developmental level, and the culture of your community. For example, the physiological curriculum for adolescents would be far different than that provided for senior adults. In addition to examining suggested content in the *Comprehensive Sexuality Education Guidelines for Kindergarten through 12th grade*, check out NCFR's Family Life Education Framework (see Appendix A) regarding sexuality, which suggests various topics to be covered during childhood, adolescence, adulthood, and later adulthood within the context of the family system (Darling & Howard, 2015).

Gender

Gender, which interacts with the cognitive, psychological, and physiological processes of sexuality, is a set of cultural identities and roles typically attached to a person's sex at birth and noted as feminine or masculine. These dimensions of self are assigned to people based on their bodies and their sexual and reproductive anatomy. Gender is socially constructed so it is possible to reject or modify the assignment made at birth and develop something that feels truer to oneself (FoSE, 2020a).

While we have often focused on gender differences based on stereotypical beliefs, research has indicated that some of these beliefs are true (e.g., generally males of all ages are more likely to engage in masturbation, especially during childhood and adolescence) (Peterson & Hyde, 2010). Other beliefs are false or changing (e.g., past research showed that males initiated sexual activity at younger ages and engaged in sexual behavior more frequently, but recent research has indicated that these differences are changing) (Fisher, 2012; Schick et al., 2010). When gender variations are found, the size of the difference varies based on factors such as age and culture. These differences result due to various reasons based on biology, social roles, and especially cultural influences, as many cultures still have some form of a double-standard and/or an interaction of biology and culture (Hyde & DeLamater, 2020). Because of changes in culture and time, there are currently fewer significant gender differences in recent research. Gender role expectations are not only culturally defined but depend on the era or historical time in which they occur. Unfortunately, much of the research is done with college students when males are at their peak of sexual development compared to women, which may exaggerate gender differences (Fisher, 2012).

Sexuality educators need to be sensitive and respectful to the way gender is approached in the classroom. As it states in President Biden's Executive Order, "every person should be treated with respect and dignity and should be able to live without fear, no matter who they are or whom they love" (Biden, 2021). All learners should be welcome no matter their gender identity, whether it is assigned at birth ("cisgender"), changed ("transgender"), gender free ("a-gender"), dual genders ("bi-gender"), or experienced in different ways at different times ("gender-fluid"). Moreover, some do not feel like their gender is a defining part of who they are. Use of pronouns (e.g., she, her, hers; he, him, his; they, them, their) behind one's name or in class introductions also needs to be considered. "Mx.," which is now included in the Oxford English Dictionary, is a gender-neutral prefix for people who do not identify as Mr., Ms., Mrs., or Miss (LGBTQ Nation, 2015). Moreover, "Mx." could be used when referring to a transgender person whose preferred pronouns (he or him, she or her) are not clear. Various ethnic groups are also changing gender designations in that "Latinx" is nonbinary compared to Latina or Latino. Incorporating gender pronouns and gender-neutral prefixes models intentionality about not assuming gender status based on one's name, gender expression, or presentation. This can help some learners feel that they are in a safe place.

Cultural Influences

A large part of our sexual learning occurs as defined by our cultural environment, which is the sum of our cultural influences both historical and current. These cultural influences could be from multiple sources such as family, friends, neighbors, school, laws, customs, advertising, and media. Within any cultural setting, we learn various sexual scripts, which are analogous to a script for a play or movie. *Sexual script theory* suggests that sexual interactions between partners are socialized not only through the behaviors of peers and family members, but also through the influence of mass media, such as books, television programs, websites, and social media. In other words, our sexual behaviors are learned from culturally desired normative outcomes that define what sex and sexuality are, how to recognize certain sexual situations, and how to behave in them. Additionally, sexual scripts are progressively learned throughout life and are always changing due to aging and social influences.

Scripts are ideas that people have about what they are doing and going to do (Gagnon, 1990; Gagnon & Simon, 1973). Whereas *cultural scripts* are based on collective meanings of a culture, *interpersonal scripts* relate to social interactions by individuals in a specific social context, and *intrapersonal scripts* involve the mental activity and management of the desires experienced by the individual (Simon & Gagnon, 1984). Scripts involve the *who, what, when, where,* and *why* of our sexual behaviors. The "who" part of our sexual script tells with whom we may or may not have sex and may involve limitations regarding age, gender, marital status, ethnicity, social characteristics, or blood relatives. The "what" provides us with the moral, immoral, normal, or abnormal guidelines of what cultures approve, such as an approved guideline in many cultures for heterosexual intercourse, but disapproval of sexual assault and evolving cultural and legal disapproval of marital and acquaintance sexual assault. "When" refers to the timing of sex related to time and age. Whereas time for sexual interaction is perceived as a private time when children are asleep or no one is in the house or apartment, age refers to the appropriate time to begin sexual relations, usually in adolescence or adulthood. "Where" focuses on the place where sexual activities occur and is often concerned with privacy. Traditional places in American culture for sexual relations are a bed in the bedroom or a hotel. "Why" refers to our motivations, explanations, or justifications for sexual activities, such as being in love or wanting to please oneself or someone else.

Our cultural scripts have traditionally placed more restrictions on women's sexuality than men's, although this has decreased over the years as exemplified by the lessening of some double standards. Many sexual scripts have portrayed males and females in traditional roles, but more contemporary scripts have evolved, such as the desire for both partners to take ownership in the couple's sexual experiences; communicate openly and honestly about their feelings; and meet each other's desires, needs, and wishes while trying to meet their own needs (Hammond & Cheney, 2009). The *who, what, when, where,* and *why* of sex need to be congruent with our values to engage in sexual behavior. An interesting example of scripting is a woman's visit to a gynecologist. While her genitals may be exposed and digitally penetrated, it is not necessarily arousing because one's cultural script of a visit to a doctor defines the setting (where), limited time of an office visit (when), individuals involved including a physician and nurse who is watching (who), activities (what), and reason (why).

Script theory can offer explanations for various sexual identities, but within our culture, there are more heteronormative scripts that have been portrayed in the media and social interactions. The norm of heterosexuality can impact parental expectations of a heterosexual future for their children. Thus parents may appear shocked or project silence, which is a complex response to "coming out." However, with the increasing professional and media portrayals of diverse gender options and increasing visibility of online LGBTQ+ communities, more alternative scripts are becoming apparent (van Bergen et al., 2020).

Learners in sexuality education settings may be from diverse cultural backgrounds that vary in many ways, such as the language they use for sexual practices and meanings attached to sexuality and sexual behaviors. Sexual activity can differ based on a culture's focus on reproduction, pleasure, or both. The US is composed of many ethnic groups and there are similarities and differences among and within these groups regarding sexual behaviors and beliefs. To be effective, sexuality programs need to address cultural variations and beliefs that might be influenced by views of gender, religion, and heteronormality. Cultural context is the key.

Understanding the role of culture in sexuality can be highlighted by examining sexual behaviors and beliefs of other cultures. They not only give us an indication of the wide variation that exists in human sexual behavior, but also emphasize the importance of culture in shaping our own behaviors. In other words, sexuality and sexual behaviors are not totally shaped by physiological drives and desires. Within cultures there are three main themes for sexual behaviors:

1. *Individualism* (emphasis on independence, autonomy, and individual rights—US and Canada).
2. *Collectivism* (interdependence and connections among people—Asian cultures).
3. *Honor* (reputation, respect, and honor toward others—Middle East and southern US) (Oyserman, 2017).

Societies regulate sexuality of certain behaviors in some manner, whether it is incest taboos, adultery, same-gender sexual behavior, or female genital mutilation.

Thoughtful observations from scholars in approximately 60 countries have provided some cross-cultural perspectives on the role of culture in our sexual lives (Francoeur & Noonan, 2004). Kissing, which is one of the most common intimate activities in most Western cultures, can be used to exemplify cultural scripts (Tiefer, 2004). While in some cultures, kissing accompanies sexual intercourse; in others it does not. There are also interesting variations of kissing such as sucking the lips and tongue of partners, kissing the nose and mouth at the same time, sticking one's tongue into a lovers' nose, or placing lips near a partner's face and inhaling. In Japan, intercourse is normal, but kissing can be perceived as pornographic. In Western cultures, a kiss can be a greeting or farewell, sign of affection, religious or ceremonial symbol, or deference to a person of higher status. There are cultural variations in meaning and practice for other sexual behaviors such as oral sex, masturbation, inflicting pain, or the frequency of intercourse, as well as the characteristics that constitute sexual attractiveness and the role and meaning of love in relationships.

When teaching about sexuality within the US, one needs to be aware that there may be different interpretations of cultural scripts among the diverse learners in your class. Because culture influences one's sexual behaviors, feelings, and interactions with others, sexuality education must reflect or at least accept the cultures of the participants. The educator needs to focus on the audience, content, methods, and context to meet the needs of the participants (Burnes, 2017). As we become more aware of diversity in the US and internationally, creating developmentally and culturally effective sexuality education programs needs to become a priority.

Development Through Time

Time, as it relates to sexuality, has two parallel dimensions—*historical time* and *personal time*. There have been numerous *historical* changes regarding our culture; interpersonal relationships; and science related to love, gender transitions, and understanding of the physiology of sexuality. Box 9.4 shows some of the changes in the last 175 years or so. Within our culture we have seen evolving laws and court decisions; increasing openness to LGBTQ+ issues; and technological/scientific advancements, such as new methods to facilitate conception and drugs for persons with HIV. Other changes that have infiltrated our cultural milieu include negotiating sexual relationships during the COVID-19 pandemic; the role of cell phones in relationships; social media; and "sexting," "hooking up," and "friends with benefits." These changes affect the age cohorts of people that are progressing through the life cycle during time periods when a particular cultural change is of interest to them developmentally and can affect their lives.

Personal time, as noted by aging and development, is another element of change. Participants in sexuality education courses are more interested in the issues affecting them at their particular personal age. For example, students in a college class on sexuality education may not be interested in the sexual activities, changes, and concerns of older people and vice versa. However, parents who have children in the home may not only be interested in their own sexuality and relationship issues related to being a parent or single parent, but also those issues their children are facing. These areas of sexual interest will change and evolve over time as individuals and families move through the life cycle.

Box 9.4 Timeline of Significant Events in the History of Sexuality

1846	US patent was issued for first diaphragm contraceptive device.
1873	US Congress passes Comstock Law, which prohibits distribution of contraceptives and information regarding contraception through the USPS.
1914–1921	Margaret Sanger opens first birth control clinic in New York City and starts the American Birth Control League, which was the precursor to Planned Parenthood.
1923	John Kellogg became president of Battle Creek Sanitarium and promoted plain foods (corn flakes) to prevent sexual feelings and discourage masturbation.
1948	*Sexual Behaviors in the Human Male*, a study with interviews of 5,300 males, was published (Kinsey, Pomeroy, & Martin).
1950	Existence of erogenous feeling on wall of vagina was suggested by Ernst Grafenberg, later became known as G-Spot.
1952	First sex reassignment surgery of a European-American, George Jorgensen, in Denmark —Lucille Ball, the first to play a pregnant woman on TV, was not allowed to say the word "pregnancy."
1953	*Sexual Behavior in the Human Female,* a study incorporating interviews of 5,940 females, was published (Kinsey, Pomeroy, & Martin). —Hugh Hefner published first issue of *Playboy* (first Playboy Club opened in 1960).
1957	Society for the Scientific Study of Sexuality (SSSS) was formed.
1960	Birth control pill was approved by the Food and Drug Administration.
1960s	Sexual Revolution began.
1964	Sex Information and Education Council of the United States (SIECUS) was founded.
1965	*Griswold v. Connecticut*—Supreme Court established the right to privacy and married women's right to contraception.
1966	*Human Sexual Response*, an observational study of the physiology of sexual response, was published (Masters & Johnson).
1967	American Association of Sexuality Educators and Therapists (AASECT) was founded.
1970	Title X Family Planning Program was established.
1972	Eisenstadt v. Baird—US Supreme Court case opening access to contraception to unmarried individuals and couples. —*The Joy of Sex* was published and on *New York Times* Best Sellers list for 8 years, longer than any other book in history (Alex Comfort). —Title IX establishes sex equity in education.
1973	*Roe v. Wade*—Supreme Court established women's right to abortion under certain circumstances.
1974	*American Psychiatric Association* removed homosexuality from list of mental illnesses.
1978	Birth of Louise Brown, first in vitro fertilization.
1979	Hysteria about herpes began with media campaign in late 1970s and peaked in early 1980s.
1981	First cases of unexplained infections (AIDS) among gay men in San Francisco.
1983	*Dr. Ruth's Guide to Good Sex* was published, followed by more than 40 other books (Ruth Westheimer).
1984	Identification of the virus causing AIDS results in explosion of research.
1986	Surgeon General C. Everett Koop publicly advocated that sex education, including AIDS education, be directed toward preadolescents and adolescents.
1990	*The Kinsey Institute New Report on Sex* was published based on national statistically representative sample (Reinisch & Beasley).

(continued)

1990	Title X of Health Service Act and Family Adolescent Family Life Act mandated that sex education content promote abstinence as the primary sexual value for adolescents and was required for agencies receiving federal funds for sex education.
1993	First female condom approved by Food and Drug Administration (FDA). —All US states have laws defining marital rape as a crime. —"Don't ask, don't tell" implemented by US military forces regarding sexual orientation.
1994	*Seventeen*, a teen magazine, first used the words "oral sex" and indicated "masturbation was a normal part of life." —Jocelyn Elders, Surgeon General of the US, was removed because of her positive comments about masturbation.
1996	Section 501b of Title V of the Social Security Act was passed, the state entitlement for abstinence-only-until-marriage programs in public schools. —The Defense of Marriage Act (DOMA) enacted, prohibiting the federal government from recognizing same-sex marriages and allowing each state to refuse recognition of same-sex marriages performed in other states.
1997	Ellen DeGeneres "comes out" to the media that she is a lesbian.
1998	AIDS public education mandated in 42 states; 23 states and the District of Columbia mandate sexuality education programs in public schools. —Viagra, an oral medication to treat impotence, approved by FDA. —Matthew Shepard was beaten to death in Wyoming for being gay. —*Will and Grace* premiered on TV; lead male character was gay.
1999	Human Papilloma Virus found to be leading cause of cervical cancer. —RU-486, a pill to facilitate abortions, became available in the US.
2000	Netherlands becomes the first nation to allow same-sex couples to marry, divorce, and adopt children.
2001	Surgeon General David Satcher issues *Call to Action to Promote Sexual Health and Responsible Sexual Behavior*, which underscored importance of comprehensive sexuality education programs.
2002	New forms of hormonal contraception (patch, vaginal ring, and monthly injections) entered the market.
2003	*Lawrence v. Texas* struck down the sodomy law making same-sex sexual activity legal in all states.
2004	Cialis and Levitra, two new male impotence drugs, approved by FDA. —Massachusetts became the first state to legalize same-sex marriages.
2006	House of Representatives Committee declared the majority of abstinence-only programs provided false and misleading information.
2010	End of "don't ask, don't tell" policy for gays in the military (began in 1993).
2013	US Supreme Court struck down the Defense of Marriage Act (DOMA) that prohibited the federal government from recognizing same-sex marriages.
2015	US Supreme Court rules that same-sex marriage is a legal right throughout the nation.
2017	"Me Too" movement began after Alyssa Milano encouraged the phrase to help reveal the extent of sexual harassment and assault.
2020	Same-sex marriages are performed and legally accepted in 29 countries worldwide. —US Supreme Court ruled that the 1964 Civil Rights Act protects gay, lesbian, and transgender employees from discrimination based on sex. —Pope Francis endorsed same-sex civil unions for the first time as head of the Catholic Church.
2021	Presidential Executive Order expanding federal nondiscrimination protections to LGBTQ+ people in many areas of their lives.

Application of Model

The Model of Sexuality can be used to understand the complexity of sexuality as it relates to sexual health and well-being. *Sexual health and well-being* are related to one's feelings of self-esteem and can vary based on one's cognitive, psychological, physiological, and social functioning while noting the integral role of culture and gender (Sakaluk et al., 2020).

The three overlapping circles of cognitive, psychological, and physical processes are portrayed as the same size, but at different times during one's life they may actually vary in size and importance. In other words, the *physiological processes* might be of greater interest to individuals who are beginning to explore various kinds of sexual interactions or seniors who are noting some changes in their physical responses. The *cognitive processes* may be more prominent with young people who are in peer groups that promote activities and interactions that might be in violation of their values. The *psychological processes* involved in love and companionship could also vary during the life cycle. An overlap of content from these processes can also exist. For example, love, which might be considered as a highly charged emotion, may also be a critical element for some people in their physiological interactions and cognitive processes. The emotion of love also involves certain chemicals in the brain such as oxytocin, adrenaline, and vasopressin that can be released when we see someone to whom we feel attraction (Fisher, 2004).

Gender and *culture* are essential components of the model and are continually changing through historical and personal time. The awareness of the complexity of gender has progressed beyond binary categorization and heteronormativity to incorporating an understanding of thoughts, beliefs, and decisions; feelings of love, pleasure, and excitement; and biological changes, arousal, and sexual responses. Cultural scripts have also evolved to become more contemporary with both partners taking responsibility in a couple's sexual pleasure.

The model can be incorporated as a visual means for participants to gain a broad perspective of sexuality, sexual health, and well-being, as well as an overview of the program to facilitate understanding the interrelationships of the content within the course. When designing a program, conceptually take a slice of this cylindrical model to match the development stage of your participants at a desired point in time. Developing a sexuality education curriculum is influenced by the setting, length of program, gender and age of participants, and cultural background. What is most important for them to learn at this point in history or time in their lives? Depending on the time available for teaching sexuality content, you may only be able to focus on a few elements within the model but understanding the full model can provide context for the program's curriculum.

SEXUALITY EDUCATORS

Sexuality educators can be teachers in educational settings (public schools, colleges, or universities), community groups, medical organizations, independent consultants, or nonprofit organizations that work with school districts, agencies, individuals, and other groups. Becoming a sexuality educator may sound exciting, interesting, scary, or challenging. Teaching young people about sexuality is different from teaching other topics. Educators must navigate the diverse views and lived experiences of their learners while being careful not to perpetuate fear and shame. Moreover, they must often do so with limited time and resources (Sex Education Collaborative, 2018). The next three sections offer some suggestions for gaining pertinent knowledge and assistance, as well as the importance of knowing oneself.

Training to Teach Sexuality

Teacher training is the most significant indicator in determining the quality of sexuality education programs, along with comfort for teaching this topic. Few academic programs, however, train sexuality educators (Cohen et al., 2004; FoSE, 2020a; Walters & Hayes, 2007). Because of its potential for controversy, people may feel vulnerable and be scared away from teaching sexuality courses. Although there are increasing numbers of sexuality programs in the public schools, educators may not have adequate preparation in the content and methods of teaching about sexuality and may be forced to teach content about which they are not personally knowledgeable or comfortable (Goldfarb, 2003). Most sexuality educators at the university level have advanced degrees, but no specialized training in the field of human sexuality. Some educators have taken a course in sexuality, but many have not because they were not offered in their departments. Some university departments such as psychology, sociology, social work, medicine, health, and family science have a single sexuality course; however they can vary considerably based on the perspectives of the discipline. This means there is little cross-fertilization among the disciplines on campus or in professional organizations regarding teaching strategies, collaborative research projects, and literature from other disciplines.

Sexuality content should be taught from an ecological context and be evidence-based and needs-driven. Because teacher preparation about sexuality is minimal, it is important to provide teachers with in-service training, applicable research, and clearly documented teaching activities that have been found to work well in classrooms. When these courses or programs are available, teachers learn from each other, develop camaraderie with other sexuality educators, and acquire the confidence and skills to teach this subject matter. Additional suggestions are to network with other sexuality educators, become well read, and engage in blogs and webinars with sexuality educators who can share information and teaching ideas (Taverner, 2006). Many teaching materials are available from the Sexuality Information and Education Council of the United States (SIECUS); Planned Parenthood; Center for Sex Education; Sex, Etc.; and AMAZE, along with other web resources at the end of this chapter. High-quality preparation is required for high-quality sexuality education.

The Certified Family Life Educator (CFLE) program does not take for granted that students can assimilate knowledge about sex and sexuality from portions of classes, such as family relations or human development. Therefore, the CFLE program includes human sexuality as one of the 10 content areas, with this content commonly covered within a course specifically in human sexuality. There is a wide range of subject matter within the CFLE content area including biological elements, such as sexual functioning, family planning, and health, along with psychosocial aspects of human sexuality, such as healthy and ethical sexual relations, dynamics of sexual intimacy, and risk factors, all addressed from a value-respectful position (see sexuality content in Appendices A and B). The American Association of Sex Educators, Counselors, and Therapists (AASECT) has also established a program to certify sexuality educators (see www.aasect.org/aasect-certification). Above all, the field of sexuality education is continually changing. If you feel there is room for growth and change in your knowledge, skills, and abilities to teach about sexuality, there are various organizations and courses that can help you to feel more comfortable in this role. Do not hesitate to seek information, insight, and self-understanding.

Standards for Teaching Sexuality Education

Effective teachers create a classroom environment with clear ground rules and expectations while acknowledging that there may be reactions to the content. They also encourage open, honest, and respectful communication in the classroom and facilitate discussions that engage learners. The most important qualifications of sexuality educators are that they are knowledgeable about sexuality, comfortable interacting with learners about a variety of topics, good listeners to determine what their learners know, and able to help learners relate the content to their lives (Hyde & DeLamater, 2020). To better understand the needed training and qualifications of sexuality educators, the National Teacher Preparation Standards for Sexuality Education were created to provide guidance to programs to better prepare undergraduate and preservice learners to deliver sexuality education (FoSE, 2020b):

- Professional Disposition: Teachers can demonstrate comfort with, commitment to, and self-efficacy in teaching sexuality education.
- Diversity and Equity: Teachers show respect for individual, family, and cultural characteristics and experiences that may influence student learning about sexuality.
- Content Knowledge: Teachers have accurate knowledge of the biological, emotional, and social aspects of sexuality and the laws relating to sexuality and youth.
- Legal and Professional Ethics: Teachers make decisions based on applicable federal, state, and local laws, regulations, and policies as well as professional ethics.
- Planning: Teachers plan age- and developmentally-appropriate sexuality education that is aligned with standards, policies, and laws and reflects the diversity of the community.
- Implementation: Teachers use a variety of effective strategies to teach sexuality education.
- Assessment: Teachers implement effective strategies to assess student knowledge, attitudes, and skills in order to improve sexuality education instruction.

Personal Traits

Those who teach human sexuality often have some similar characteristics. They tend to be open, interactive, able to teach within the affective domain, and take an interest in their participants (Bruess & Schroeder, 2018; Timmerman, 2009). Sexuality educators may not have had personal experiences associated with different groups, but they can still be effective as long as they are open and willing to learn about sexuality among married persons, singles, LGBTQ+ individuals, disabled persons, or within diverse cultures by studying the research and literature on these topics and communicating with participants to get insights into their lives and needs (Wilkenfeld & Ballan, 2011). It is particularly important to understand the cultural context of participants, especially if they come from another country. It is essential to be aware of same-gender sexual behavior, body image, religion, contraception, and/or sexual health that may be related to cultural socialization. Thus, a goal for sexuality educators is to be aware of and accept other cultural viewpoints while simultaneously representing the societal context of the culture in which they are teaching. An educator needs to assess the audience, intended messages, and context before developing an effective program. Programs that are incompatible with the participants' culture are doomed to failure.

Sexuality educators need to be comfortable with their own gender identity and sexual orientation. Since we have both feminine and masculine qualities, being aware of them and free of societal stereotypes and misperceptions are essential. It is also important for sexuality educators to have a positive body image and be accepting of their own appearance in order to discuss body development effectively. It is also hoped that sexuality educators have a sense of humor. At times, humorous situations will occur in educational settings, so a lighthearted and playful reaction to these circumstances will let participants know that you can relate to the real world. Humor heightens the learners' interest, makes it easier to discuss class topics, and provides a positive image of sexuality that at times results in some laughter, at no one's expense (Bruess & Schroeder, 2018; Timmerman, 2009).

Having good communication skills when dealing with groups and individuals is an essential quality. It is important for educators to role model the use of correct terms even though they may be cumbersome and awkward to participants and thus inhibit their comments in class. However, when people learn the appropriate words for private body parts, they are more likely to feel comfortable communicating about sexuality and reporting sexual abuse, if needed (SRCP, 2021). As long as the terminology is socially acceptable and understandable, you can proceed; however, there is a trend away from the use of euphemisms. If a term is used that is not acceptable, then it is the teacher's responsibility to identify the correct terminology without embarrassing the student (Bruess & Schroeder, 2018). At times the student may also state a misperception that is clearly inaccurate. For example, if a student said, "you cannot become pregnant the first time you have sexual intercourse," rather than publicly and emphatically telling the student that he or she is wrong, an educator could say this is something that many think is true, but actually, people can become pregnant the first time they have sexual intercourse. While educators do not want to embarrass any student, it is important to correct any myths.

Sexuality educators should be at ease when communicating with students or learners who come to talk to them about issues of concern. When a student is upset, a teacher or educator may be the person with whom they can share their feelings, such as distress over a mother just diagnosed as being HIV positive, anxiety over a personal diagnosis of breast cancer, or the trauma of abuse by a sexual partner. They may perceive a teacher or educator as approachable and feel comfortable sharing sensitive topics or concerns. In these situations it is important to spend time with the learner, listen, and refer him or her for help when needed. Students should be informed early in the course, possibly in the syllabus and first class, that at most educational institutions, instructors are considered mandatory reporters of sexual misconduct or assault. However, the policies on reporting are still evolving and are not totally clear or consistent across these institutions (Brown, 2018). Be prepared with a list of accessible therapists and relevant contact information to distribute for those who might need these services. Some teachers may also be therapists, but it is unethical to fulfill a dual role with students or clients.

Learning Strategies for Sexuality Education

Teaching about sexuality needs to be planned and thoughtful, yet spontaneous. Because of cultural and personal sensitivity related to the topic of sexuality, it is important to plan learning strategies that can facilitate creating a safe environment. In addition, it is helpful for learners to clarify their own values and for teachers to sensitively become aware of what they are thinking in ways that do not push them into self-revelation, unless they choose to do so. When teaching adolescents, providing learning experiences in which they can practice refusal skills can be meaningful, so that if they find themselves in situations that require them to say "no," they can do so with self-confidence. While these are planned activities, it is important to be alert for teachable moments, whether they occur in the classroom setting or in the media. Sexual issues are continuously evolving and becoming prominent in the media and surrounding environment, so being able to readily integrate learning opportunities into class discussions is essential.

Creating a Safe Environment

An emotionally safe environment is especially important when teaching about sexuality. People have so many issues and concerns about sexuality that feeling secure is critical. Because some students have experienced trauma, creating a trauma-informed environment recognizes that individuals, especially children, have gone through some serious events in their lives. Not only do they carry the memory of those events with them, but their brains may be different because of this trauma (Resilient Educator, 2020). To help participants deal with stress at home, many teachers are using innovative trauma-informed strategies, such as looking beyond the behavior, building relationships, meeting learners where they are, and creating a supportive environment. There are several ways to create a safe environment, such as providing *Class Guidelines* for participation and incorporating class activities such as the *One-Minute Squirm*, *Class Contract*, and *Question Box*.

Class guidelines

To help the participants feel at ease, class guidelines can be discussed or provided to the participants electronically or in a hard copy. The degree of incorporation of these guidelines depends on the nature of the course and its length—one hour, one week, several weeks, or one semester. Some of these guidelines include the following:

- Full participation is expected. Class will be successful if everyone participates; however you can only participate and share as openly as you feel comfortable doing.
- Any question is OK. Don't be afraid to ask a question during or after class.
- Use terminology that is socially acceptable. Some words can be offensive to others.
- Respect different values and points of view. It is OK to disagree, but not to tease someone.
- Do not use put-downs. Do not give anyone a negative label.
- Remember that everyone has feelings. We have feelings about topics and about what others may say about us.
- You do not have to speak. Everyone has a right to "pass" on a question or activity. No one has to say anything he/she does not want to share.
- The sessions will be confidential. Do not share what others have said outside of class.
- Do not use proper names during discussions. Use expressions such as "my friend," "a person I know," or "someone I saw."
- The teacher and participants should respect diverse views of sexuality and use inclusive language.
- Listen before you form an opinion. Have an open mind. No opinion deserves a put-down.
- Remember that no one's opinion is right or wrong. Everyone is entitled to his or her opinion.
- We all have a right to change our opinions. As we become more knowledgeable about a topic, we may change our minds. This is a sign of growth.
- Some topics are beyond the content of this course. Sexuality education covers a broad range of topics; however, we may not be able to cover them all.

One-minute squirm

Often times sexuality educators design activities, create assignments, or discuss topics that participants find embarrassing because they are expected to divulge more than they desire about their personal beliefs and behaviors. This could be due to their age, comfort with public speaking, religious beliefs, or level of sexual involvement and experience. While you can acknowledge this concern with students, experiential learning may have a more lasting effect.

Mention to your class in a beginning session that in a few minutes you are going to have them turn to the person sitting next to them to share about their first sexual experience. Then go on to discuss some general class information. Within a minute or two, return to this topic and tell them you will not be asking them to share personal information, but wanted them to experience what some students might feel if asked to communicate something that was too personal to share publicly. Ask how many "squirmed" when it was mentioned that they would be asked to share their early sexual experiences. How many would have refused if asked to do this and why? Then reaffirm that this is something that they will NOT have to do in this class. The participants' sigh of relief will be readily apparent. This experience is designed to help future or current teachers think about how their own students might feel if a learning experience was created that was not within their students' comfort zone.

Class contract

Participants may "hear" that the environment of a sexuality class is safe when class guidelines are discussed and they may "feel" a teacher's concern for their well-being by incorporating the "one-minute squirm" activity; however, integrating a class contract allows them to read and physically sign a statement that they have heard and understood a teacher's concern for their feelings of safety.

A contract, such as the one below, can be distributed to students to complete and sign on the same day the concept of safety is presented. This contract not only provides a safety net for the instructor in case someone later says that they had to do something against their values or beliefs, but also facilitates feelings of relief that the classroom is indeed a nonthreatening environment in which to learn about human sexuality.

Box 9.5 Human Sexuality Education: Class Content Disclosure Statement

I, *Name of Student*, hereby acknowledge that I have been told by *Name of Instructor* that this class will include explicit readings and discussions about sexual behaviors. Furthermore, I understand that my decision to participate in any of these pedagogical activities is voluntary, and I have the right to refuse to do any activity that is in conflict with my personal values, and that if I do, an alternative assignment will be designed for me. Furthermore, I realize I will not be penalized for exercising my rights as stated above.

Signed ____ Date ________________

Question box

Over the years using a "Question Box" has been a common strategy for providing a safe environment in which participants can ask questions. While some individuals have no problems asking questions, others may feel discomfort or embarrassment that they do not know the answer or that their question might reveal something too personal.

Distribute to the entire class identical pieces of paper or index cards. Instruct participants to anonymously write a question about sex/sexuality, or write something else, such as the words to their favorite song, if they do not have a question. Then, pass around the question box for them to insert what they have written or have them drop off the card as they leave class. Since all participants will be instructed to put their papers in the box, no one will know which question belongs to any individual student.

While some instructors may want to respond immediately, a suggestion is to read these questions after class and organize them according to the content to be covered in subsequent class sessions. Because many questions may be similar, respond to them all at one time and include related elements that may emerge. A question box may be included toward the middle or end of the program, because if incorporated too early most of the questions will relate to content planned for a later date. If the answer to a question is unknown, this delay gives time to prepare a response. Depending on the size of the class and the relevancy of questions, an instructor may not be able to respond to all questions. At times some questions may be inappropriate for an in-class response because they are too personal or out of the context of your class and would be better asked of a physician or sex therapist. Other individuals may submit questions that are outrageous just to get a reaction from the teacher. A question box can be integrated at various times during a program to stay attuned to emerging questions and issues of concern. If your program has only one session, you could do this at the very beginning of the session. You can then review the questions during a break to ensure that you are meeting participants' needs.

Values Clarification

Fundamental issues in sexuality are intertwined with personal value systems. Beyond needs and drives, sexual behavior reflects the individual values and attitudes toward self, peers, parents, and life. Understanding a person's values and value hierarchy is important in establishing relationships, sexual activities, and sexuality education. One can teach about values but introducing a variety of introspective exercises and discussion starters will enable participants to examine their values more critically, and therefore, potentially increase self-awareness, catalyze individual thought, and promote critical self-analysis. Although there is no single value or value hierarchy that educators are promoting, they are trying to have individuals identify their values and decide whether or not to keep these values and how to behave accordingly. Two examples of exercises to assist with value clarification include *Hierarchy of Perceptions* and *Values in Relationships*.

Hierarchy of Perceptions

Participants in sexuality education programs have perceptions and values related to many of the topics to be presented. This activity helps participants to understand their beliefs and values in relation to others in the class.

Create a list of terms, activities, and situations to distribute to class members. Without any identifying information on these papers, have them use a Likert-type scale from 1 to 5 to how they feel about each item (1 = completely unacceptable to 5 = completely acceptable). Suggestions for these items can be any of the following or others you might choose to add depending on the age, setting, and interests of your audience: abstinence; single parenthood; gay/lesbian marriage; transgender identity; sex without a condom; my body; female masturbation; male masturbation; oral sex; being a male virgin at age __; being a female virgin at age __; unmarried sex; sex between senior adults; sexting; sex relations between a teacher and student; best friend is single and pregnant.

After students indicate their opinions, have them fold their papers to give to the teacher. The teacher can randomly redistribute them back to class members who now speak for the individual whose paper they have before them and NOT their own paper. In a discussion, determine the items of highest and lowest ranks and what the values associated with those items might be. Note that some of these items may result in positive or negative reactions with the participants.

It can be enlightening to call attention to a few items for additional discussion. Ask participants to compare the responses for male and female masturbation or the age of male or female virginity as noted in the paired items. If there is a higher ranking for one gender, ask participants to raise their hands if this higher ranking applies to males (or females). Thus, a perspective can be gained about how their responses, which have been anonymous, compared to the beliefs of the other people in the group. Then discuss how far apart the paired responses might be because of gender. In other words, is there a gender issue related to the values associated with this behavior?

The last item of "best friend is single and pregnant" is also of interest and can prompt a discussion of their feelings about this issue. While many may feel concern for the young friend and indicate their support, others may feel sadness and empathy because being pregnant may negatively affect future plans. Then ask if age and circumstance would make a difference. In other words, if someone who was in their mid to late 30s and a professor in family life education chose in vitro fertilization (IVF) because she/he wanted a child, would that make a difference? Did participants perceive this was a female or male? This activity helps to clarify values, examine gender and context, and highlight value hierarchies. The instructor can suggest that there are many different value hierarchies displayed in this activity and, similarly, there will be different values and value hierarchies that will emerge when dealing with the content of the program. There are no right answers, just something to ponder as participants learn about themselves and from others.

Values in Relationships

This activity helps to identify, clarify, and verbalize personal values regarding relationship issues (adapted from Morrison & Price, 1974). Moreover, one can examine some of the assumptions underlying judgments and values and then compare them to the perceptions and value hierarchies of others. (See Box 9.6 for this activity.)

Box 9.6 **Value Differences in Relationships**

Write the following names for participants to view. Depending on the cultural context in which you are teaching, change the names as appropriate (e.g., John, José, or Johan) or gender neutral names (e.g., Blair, Morgan, Dana, or Dylan).

- John—Beth's fiancé
- Beth—John's fiancée
- Carl—Beth's classmate
- Anna—Beth's close friend
- Edward—Beth's new acquaintance

Explain that you will read a story and afterward you will ask them to rank these 5 persons from 1 (person you like best) to 5 (person you like least). There are no correct responses—only their opinions. Then read the following statement, which you may have to do twice or put it on a slide for participants to view.

> John and Beth are engaged to be married, but John is away in the service stationed in Alaska. Beth is still in school and shares a class with Carl. She and Carl become friends and sleep together. Beth decides she doesn't feel right about having intercourse with Carl and tells him they'll have to stop, and they do. Some time passes and Carl tells Beth he is driving to Alaska. Beth asks Carl to take her along so she can see John. Carl says, "OK, if you go to bed with me." Beth is uncertain what to do and asks her close friend Anna. Anna says, "Do what you think is best." So, Beth decides to go to bed with Carl. Meanwhile, John has been dating, on a casual basis, a nurse stationed near him in Alaska. When Beth gets to Alaska, she feels obliged to tell John about her relationship with Carl. John ends the engagement saying he can't trust Beth. Beth returns home and meets Edward. She is upset and tells him everything and Edward asks her to live with him.

When the participants have completed their rankings, form small groups of four to six individuals. Within these small groups, students are to discuss the issues involved in their rankings and come to a group consensus. This is not an average of individual rankings, but a thoughtful analysis of the factors needed to establish a group ranking.

While the small groups are working, create a grid on a board listing the names of the story participants on the vertical axis and the numbers from the groups on the horizontal axis. Have a member of each group report their rankings explaining why they ranked them in the manner they did or if they had problems in reaching consensus. The grid will most likely have a wide array of rankings for each of the story characters.

Discuss the issues that emerged such as:

- The role of honesty in a relationship.
- The relationship between emotional commitment and sexual intercourse.
- When intercourse is appropriate.
- The meaning of engagement.
- The meaning of "sleeping together" or "going to bed with."
- Exploitation in a personal relationship.
- The role of a friend.

Other points to discuss include what might be different if the names of the participants were changed to the other gender or being gender neutral. In other words, what would happen to their rankings if Beth would be Bob and John would be Diane, or Beth would be Blair and John would be Jaime. In addition, how might this values clarification exercise be applied to a current sexual issue in the media? To conclude this discussion, call attention to the variations in rankings for the story participants. We all have values, but we value things differently. Thus, these varying value hierarchies are an indication that they will also value class content differently during the remainder of the course. Depending on the gender of the people in the case study, were the value hierarchies different?

This activity could also be modified to deal with other groups such as an issue related to seniors. Maybe a couple is comprised of one member who has dementia while the other is the caregiver. A neighbor has a developing interest in the caregiver and things are progressing toward intimacy. The caregiver is perplexed and turns to a son/daughter and friend for advice. What values and value hierarchies would evolve from an activity and discussion of the persons in this group?

Refusal Skills

It is essential for people to understand that consent is complex and often nuanced. Not only should consent be freely given, but also all people in a sexual situation must feel they are able to say "yes" or "no" or stop the sexual activity at any point. Consent needs to be (1) clear and unambiguous, (2) understandable, (3) withdrawn at any point, and (4) voluntary (AASECT, 2019). Learning how to say "no" is an important skill for individuals of all ages. Resisting peer pressure at any age is not easy but is especially difficult among today's youth. Therefore, students may need some "practice" to implement refusal or resistance skills in a calm and positive manner so they can maintain their friendships with the person if they so choose.

Ask participants what kinds of sexual situations are problematic or uncomfortable and what factors are involved (e.g., alcohol/drugs, numbers of peers, perceived status in a group). A discussion might be helpful for dealing with the topic of assertiveness (and nonassertiveness) versus aggressiveness. You can ask participants for some sexuality pressure lines they have heard or experienced (e.g., if you love me, you'll have sex with me; I don't want to do anything except lie next to you; condoms are for people with diseases—do I look sick to you?). Structure some role play scenarios for your class but recognize that some people may be uncomfortable in front of a group. Therefore you might divide the class into small groups depending on the size of the class. Give each group in rotation a "pressure line" for their collective response and then have a participant panel score the responses using numbered cards from 1 to 5. Someone can keep score to see what group gains the greatest number of points. This activity helps students to practice saying "no," while maintaining a relationship with their friends and peers. At the end of this activity, they might discuss how comfortable they were when reacting to these statements. Did it become easier to respond as the activity progressed? Since alcohol consumption is frequently part of sexual encounters, ask them how alcohol or other substances would affect an individual's pressure for sexual interactions and the other individual's reactions to pressure lines?

A refusal skill suggested by a colleague dealt with his wife and daughter. If the daughter was with her peers and an activity or relocation to another event was suggested that was against her values, she would say she had to call her mother first to get permission to stay out later or move to another location. She would explain it to her mother and say, "Please, please can I _____." Saying "please" two times was the code for her mother to say, "No" and the daughter could ease out of a situation in which she did not want to be. Granted this does not work for all peer pressure situations and may not help this young woman to be direct in saying "no" to her peers, but it was effective for this mother and daughter. The young woman had considered her values and value hierarchies and acted upon that hierarchy. She might value honesty of peer friendship, but in this case it was of lower priority to her. In addition to leaving the situation, other things she could have done include suggesting an alternate activity, giving a reason why it was not a good idea, just saying "no," or saying "thanks, but no thanks."

Challenges of Teaching Human Sexuality

Teaching about sexuality is like walking a tightrope between school, parents, state, and federal mandates or recommendations, while also meeting the students' needs whether they are sexually active or not. Although sex and sexuality are almost everywhere in the media and school environments, honest and knowledgeable conversations about sexuality are not. Challenges include academic freedom, digital sexuality education, reading materials, emotions of participants, teaching in a vacuum, sensitivity about assignments, and perceptions of sexuality educators.

Academic Freedom

Whereas public colleges and universities often have academic freedom, some private colleges, which are funded by private foundations and tuition, may be concerned about the topics covered in courses. Curriculum may be more controlled in the public schools where elected school officials are held accountable for what might be taught about sexuality. One suggestion for teaching learners beyond high school age is to let them know that the human sexuality course will occur in a pluralistic setting in which multiple voices will be heard, so participants are allowed to make comments on all sides of an issue, but in no instance should they be disrespectful. The challenge is to keep an open dialogue, build bridges, and keep administrators and others informed.

Reading Materials

Selecting reading materials can be another challenge. Depending on the educational setting, the use of certain content, diagrams, and photos could be an issue. Some students say that they would not dare take their books home to their parents, while others say their sexuality books have been stolen from their dorm rooms or lockers. A few shared that this was the first time a significant other or spouse looked at their text and actually read it before the student did. In the current environment, it is easy to make readings available to class members along with a text or partial text. Some book companies are quite willing for teachers to select chapters from the texts they publish to create a reader that best meets the educational needs of the students.

Digital Sexuality Education

Young people are turning to digital sources for sexual and relationship advice in increasing numbers. The most common reasons youth look for sexual health information online are privacy and curiosity. Sexual minority youth are more likely to look for online information because they do not have anyone to ask. Since online information is most valuable to those persons who do not have alternative sources, care needs to be taken to ensure that the information is accurate and of interest to diverse groups (Mitchell et al., 2014). With the increasing number of apps, webpages, chat groups, and social media sites, there is a growing need to better understand how sexuality education can be delivered digitally (UNESCO, 2020). Sexuality educators need to navigate the options and scope of digital sexuality education where the content may be incomplete, poorly informed, or harmful. Some websites with reliable sexuality information are at the end of this chapter (e.g., Go Ask Alice, AMAZE, Advocates for Youth). This mode of providing sexuality education needs further exploration. We need to understand who is accessing it and how. If this is a new frontier in sexuality education, sexuality and family life educators need to examine its scope and be at the forefront of creating responsible programs with scientifically and medically accurate information.

Emotions of Participants

Another challenge when teaching about sexuality is having to navigate the emotional domain of participants. Some have experienced sexual violence, teen pregnancy, racist comments about sexuality, harassment, or have a nontraditional sexual orientation. Sexual orientation includes different forms of attraction, behaviors, and identities. However, this attraction can take different forms, such as sexual attraction, romantic attraction, or emotional attraction (The Trevor Project, 2020a).

Because it is important for teachers to understand the experiences and emotions of their participants, an anonymous activity called *Insight* can be beneficial. A range of responses from this activity can give instructors some anonymous insight into students' backgrounds and identify some of their needs and issues of concern.

Students are given a blank piece of paper, with no identifying marks, and instructed to inform you if there is anything you need to know about them regarding the topic of sexuality and/or if there is a question they particularly want answered during class sessions. Whether or not they have a response to these questions, they are to write something on the paper so others cannot identify who does or does not have an issue or question. Following are examples of responses received from an undergraduate class on human sexuality, which exhibit a wide variety of concerns, such as:

- I was date-raped and had to have an abortion. I am sensitive about this topic.
- I feel like I am promiscuous at times because I am not in a relationship and have sex with strangers. I am also kind of questioning my sexuality.
- When I was 6 years old, the carpenter/gardener took advantage of me.
- I think it is important for people to know that you can still get STIs when using condoms. Most sexuality education classes imply that by using a condom you are completely safe and that is simply not true.
- Sex was hardly discussed in my home at all. I would like to be more open with my family regarding sexuality.
- I want to learn more about sexual arousal.
- I think I am queer—how do I know and what should I do?
- How does being pregnant affect one's sex life?
- I have herpes and want to know if there is a treatment that can prevent my outbreaks from occurring as often as they do.
- My partner has never had an orgasm during sexual intercourse. How can I help change that? She enjoys intercourse, but I would like for her to enjoy it more.

Whereas the topics from some of these comments can be integrated into the content of the course depending on the length of time allotted, other topics may require professional assistance from alternate sources, such as referrals to counselors, therapists, or physicians.

Teaching in a Vacuum

When teaching about sexuality, the instructor is in a vacuum. It is difficult to be gone from class because there are usually no willing and qualified substitutes to teach this content. If you can find someone to teach while you are away, can they respond to questions in a knowledgeable and sensitive manner? Speakers can also be a problem if a teacher does not know what they will say, their presentation content cannot be readily integrated into the course, or they make an insensitive remark. Therefore, careful planning and preparation for speakers are essential.

Sensitivity About Assignments

Instructors need to be thoughtful and sensitive when creating assignments and activities and not ask participants to reveal their personal thoughts and feelings related to sexual issues or behaviors. They may volunteer these opinions in class, but some do not choose to share on certain topics. Moreover, it is important to never lose a set of papers, especially with student names on them. In fact, some teachers have students identify their papers with a preassigned number or submit assignments through online learning management systems. Some of these systems allow for anonymous grading, which may help students feel like they will be graded objectively and without bias or judgement.

Perceptions of Sexuality Educators

People often have a lot of misguided perceptions about sexuality educators. Some may perceive that sexuality educators are quite sexually liberal or adept. In addition, they may believe that sexuality educators would be capable of diagnosing and resolving sexual issues with a few well-chosen words or suggestions. If some class participants have had past experiences with unwanted sexual contact, violence, or harassment, they may be uncomfortable with the gender of the sexuality educator. Therefore, teaching across gender lines with both a male and female educator would be preferable, if it can be arranged and funded. In general, sexuality educators continually work to be beyond reproach in their demeanor, dress, and what they say. It is very easy for a student to share something that was said or done in a sexuality class that can be misperceived by the listener and passed to others as a rumor. In addition, some students may become distressed when teachers do not endorse or condemn certain behaviors about which the student may have a strong opinion.

JOYS OF TEACHING HUMAN SEXUALITY

Understanding the positive impact of sexuality education can help educators guide their teaching and maintain their enthusiasm (Sex Education Collaborative, 2018). One of the joys of teaching about human sexuality is the incredible range of topics that relate to so many different disciplines and aspects of life. There is always something new occurring in contemporary life that touches the area of sexuality. There are issues in the media and current events that can be added to class almost on a daily basis, so the elements of current relevance and creativity are always present. One does not become bored teaching about sexuality because new ideas are energizing. There is also camaraderie among colleagues who are teaching about sexuality. This may occur across fields, which facilitates an interdisciplinary excitement and sharing. A major joy is the opportunity to help others. Students are happy to find out what sexuality educators know while being given license to talk about sexual issues they have been thinking about for some time. This provides an opportunity to be involved in some life-altering situations, as shared by other colleagues:

- A victim of impotence from acquaintance rape had post-traumatic stress disorder (PTSD) and learned a lot about sexuality that helped her understand her situation and seek help.
- Within some individual's cultural backgrounds, sexuality was not discussed so one young woman came to the teacher after class to get more information on sexual pleasure.
- A student pondering her gender identity wanted some advice about where she could get some counselling about how to tell her parents.
- Following a lecture on "Why some young women don't use contraception," a woman informed the teacher that she had just made an appointment with her gynecologist.

- It is common that teaching about breast exams or various health exams results in preventing health problems.
- A discussion of testicular cancer resulted in one mother talking to her son about a self-exam. He found a nodule and needed to have one testicle removed, but it saved his life.

Educating people of all ages about sexuality within the context of family life education can advance sexuality education, sexual health, and well-being, as well as the field of FLE (Russell et al., 2020). Sexuality is an important area of human development and family relations, so please say "yes" to teaching in this field. While at times teaching about sexuality can be difficult, there are many who enjoy the challenge. In the words of Katharine Graham, "To love what you do and feel that it matters—how could anything be more fun?"

■ SUMMARY

Sexuality education is desired by youth, parents, and other adults for a variety of reasons, including gaining knowledge; enhancing relationships; and preventing premature, unprotected, and unwanted sexual involvement among young people. Many resources are available for information and education but getting them to the persons in need is not always easy. While there are several approaches to school-based sexuality education programs, they vary in effectiveness and availability in some states. Therefore parents often want to work in tandem with schools to facilitate the sexuality education of their children. Sexuality education is becoming less heteronormative and is more focused on diverse populations based on age; culture, race, and ethnicity; differently-abled; and gender.

Research and theory, which are essential to establish credibility for a sexuality education program, also provide context for the *Model of Sexuality.* The integration of cognitive, psychological, and physical processes, along with gender and cultural influences through time can facilitate understanding sexual health and well-being. Various teaching strategies can be incorporated that involve creating a safe environment, clarifying values, and learning refusal skills. While there is minimal training available in academic settings for sexuality educators, along with several challenges that other fields do not have, there are also some incredible joys, and opportunities, especially teaching content that can have considerable impact on the lives of others. Family life educators have knowledge of sexuality content and educational strategies, as well as opportunities to advance the profession and the sexual health and well-being of individuals, families, and communities.

■ QUESTIONS AND ISSUES FOR DISCUSSION

1. Why does sexuality education continue to be a controversial issue? What can students, teachers, parents, and administrators do to promote sexuality education?
2. How can family life educators promote nonschool programs and culturally diverse programs on sexuality education in the community?
3. What qualities do you perceive are important to being a sexuality educator?

4. What did you learn about sexuality when you were in grades K to 12? What changes would you have liked, if any?
5. How did you acquire sexual information as a child or teenager and what messages did you receive?
6. What should be taught about sexuality at different ages—young children, preteens, adolescents, young adults, mature adults, and seniors?
7. How can parents become more involved in teaching about sexuality to their children?
8. How as a parent, teacher, or friend would you assist a child or student who is questioning his/her gender identity?
9. What are some examples of websites for teens that have accurate and positive messages about sex and sexuality?
10. Are the four principles of sexual ethics adequate? Are they applicable to other areas beyond human sexuality? Are there any principles that should be rejected or additional principles that should be considered?
11. How does U = U change interpersonal relationships for those who are HIV positive?

■ ACTIVITIES

1. Using a specific entry or time period from the sexuality timeline (Box 9.3), how or why did that entry affect sexual attitudes and/or behaviors?
2. Find quotes, memes, or songs about love and analyze what they are saying and if it is part of today's culture.
3. Locate a popular press article to critique by examining named or unnamed sources, visual representations (if any), and research on the topic to refute or substantiate its claims.
4. Role-play in small groups how to respond to children's questions such as "Where do babies come from?"

■ WEB RESOURCES

Advocates for Youth

www.advocatesforyouth.org

Advocates for Youth promotes efforts to help young people make informed and responsible decisions about their reproductive and sexual health. Advocates for Youth believes it can best serve the field by advocating for a more positive and realistic approach to adolescent sexual health. They work with youth leaders to ensure that all young people's rights are respected and that they have the tools needed to protect themselves from STIs, HIV, and unintended pregnancy.

AMAZE

www.amaze.org

AMAZE uses the power of digital media to provide young adolescents around the globe with medically accurate, age-appropriate, and honest sex education they can access online, regardless of where they live or attend school. AMAZE also assists adults with communicating effectively and honestly about sex and sexuality with the children and adolescents in their lives. It incorporates the expertise of sexuality educators, animation professionals, and young people, along with the power of the internet. AMAZE provides age-appropriate, often humorous sex education videos, educational resources, toolkits, and lesson plans to help educators, health care providers, and parents.

American Association of Sexuality Educators, Counselors and Therapists (AASECT)

www.aasect.org

AASECT is a nonprofit interdisciplinary professional organization. In addition to sexuality educators, counselors, and therapists, AASECT members include physicians, nurses, social workers, psychologists, allied health professionals, clergy members, lawyers, sociologists, marriage and family counselors and therapists, family planning specialists, and researchers, as well as students in relevant professional disciplines. These individuals share an interest in promoting understanding of human sexuality and healthy sexual behavior.

Center for Sex Education (CSE)

www.sexedcenter.org

The CSE is the national education division of Planned Parenthood of Northern, Central, and Southern New Jersey. It is dedicated to all people having a right to education that will help them understand, appreciate, and take responsibility for their sexuality. It is primarily focused on writing and publishing sexuality learning activities and manuals that are used throughout the world. These written materials address all ages and nearly every topic in sexuality education. CSE also brings sexuality educators together for training and expansion of their skills.

ETR

www.etr.org

ETR (Education, Training, and Research) is a national nonprofit organization to improve health and increase opportunities for youth, families, and communities. They want all people to have the information, skills, and opportunities to lead healthy lives. It is the leading publisher of evidence-based programs for HIV/STI and teen pregnancy prevention and provides best-practices, professional development, and learning experiences on many topics of interest to sexuality educators. ETR has become a nationally recognized leader in the development and rigorous evaluation of effective sexual health programs for youth.

Go Ask Alice

www.goaskalice.columbia.edu

Go Ask Alice is a health question and answer internet service provided by Columbia University's Health Promotion Service and their team of health promotion specialists, health care providers, and other health professionals, along with a staff of information and research specialists. This site provides recently published inquiries and responses, allows you to find health information by subject, and gives the opportunity to ask and submit a question to Alice.

Guttmacher Institute

www.guttmacher.org

The Guttmacher Institute is a leading research and policy organization committed to advancing sexual and reproductive health and rights in the United States and globally. The institute produces a wide range of resources through an interrelated program of research, policy analysis, and public education designed to generate new ideas, encourage enlightened public debate, and promote sound policy and program development. The Institute's overarching goal is to ensure the highest standard of sexual and reproductive health for all people worldwide.

Kinsey Institute

www.kinseyinstitute.org

The mission of the Kinsey Institute is to foster and promote a greater understanding of human sexuality and relationships through research, outreach, education, and historical preservation. The Institute's goal is to be the premier research institute of human sexuality and relationships.

PFLAG

www.pflag.org

Parents and Friends of Lesbians and Gays (PFLAG) is the first and largest organization for lesbian, gay, bisexual, transgender, and queer (LGBTQ+) people, their parents and families, and allies. It provides peer support, education, and advocacy for those who care about sexual minorities.

Planned Parenthood

www.plannedparenthood.org

Planned Parenthood, a trusted provider of reproductive health care, believes in the fundamental right of each individual throughout the world to manage his or her fertility, regardless of the individual's income, marital status, race, ethnicity, sexual orientation, age, national origin, or residence. They believe that respect and value for diversity in all aspects of their organization are essential to their well-being and that reproductive self-determination must not only be voluntary, but also preserve the individual's right to privacy. They further believe that such self-determination will contribute to an enhanced quality of life and strong family relationships.

Sex, Etc.

www.sexetc.org

Sex, Etc.'s mission is to improve teen sexual health across the country. Each year five million young people visit sexetc.org, and over 45,000 read their magazine to get honest and accurate sexual health information. Sex, Etc. provides comprehensive sex education information including stories written by teens for teens. They have a blog and forums in which teens can participate in moderated discussions with other teens. Questions are answered about topics such as sex, relationships, pregnancy, STIs, birth control, and sexual orientation.

Sexuality and Disability

www.sexualityanddisability.org

Sexuality and disability begin with the premise that people with disabilities are sexual beings—just like anyone else. It is constructed as a series of questions a woman with a disability might have—about her body, the mechanics and dynamics of experiencing sexual intercourse, the complexities of being in an intimate relationship or having children, and the unvoiced fears or experiences of encountering abuse in some form.

Sexuality Information and Education Council of the United States (SIECUS)

www.siecus.org

SIECUS provides education and information about sexuality and sexual and reproductive health. Viewing sexuality as a fundamental part of being human and worthy of dignity and respect, they advocate for the rights of all people to accurate information, comprehensive sexuality education, and the full spectrum of sexual and reproductive health services. SIECUS provides countless resources to help educators, advocates, and parents secure supportive public policies, provide high quality education, and help our youth become sexually healthy.

Sexuality Resource Center for Parents

www.srcp.org

This resource is available to help parents do a better job teaching their children about sexuality by providing guidance in answering a child's questions about sex and sexuality, responding to comments and behaviors that seem sexual in nature, and assisting parents in being proactive in being effective teachers of their children. The content and quality of sexuality education varies by state, county, city, and school so parents need to be prepared to take responsibility to educate their children about sexuality.

Society for the Scientific Study of Sexuality (SSSS)

www.sexscience.org

SSSS is dedicated to advancing knowledge of sexuality and communicating scientifically-based sexuality research and scholarship to professionals, policy makers, and the general public. To acquire that knowledge the Society requires freedom of inquiry, support for research, and an interdisciplinary network of collaborating scholars. The Society believes in the importance of both the production of quality research and the application of sexual knowledge in educational, clinical, and other settings.

The Trevor Project—Saving Young LGBTQ+ Lives

www.thetrevorproject.org

The Trevor Project focuses on suicide prevention among lesbian, gay, bisexual, transgender, queer, and questioning (LGBTQ+) youth. It provides crisis intervention and suicide prevention services for young people under 25, as well as guidance and resources for parents and educators to foster safe, accepting, and inclusive environments for all youth, at home and at school. The project is committed to producing research that brings new knowledge and clinical implications to the field of suicidology. They provide crisis counseling, supportive counseling, a sense of community to young LGBTQ+ people, and advocate for laws and policies that will reduce suicide among LGBTQ+ young people.

World Association for Sexual Health (WAS)

www.worldsexology.org

WAS promotes sexual health through the world by developing and supporting sexology and sexual rights by developing, promoting, and supporting sexology and sexual rights for all. The focus of WAS is on advocacy, networking, and facilitation of information exchange of ideas and experiences through scientifically-based sexuality research, sexuality education, and clinical sexology with a transdisciplinary approach.

10

Approaches to Relationship and Marriage Education

Marriage Relationships and Well-Being

Healthy relationships can have positive effects on men, women, and children. Married couples are not only happier, healthier, wealthier, and better educated (Amato, 2010; Choi, Yorgason, & Johnson, 2016; Fincham & Beach, 2010), but also children who reside in married families tend to experience fewer behavior problems and have better educational outcomes (Amato & Cheadle, 2008; Fagan & Churchill, 2012). Although research has suggested that divorce may lead to negative outcomes for children, outcomes may vary based on culture, ethnicity, family structure, or special needs (Demir-Dagdas et al., 2018). Parenting practices might also help to mitigate negative consequences of divorce for children since relationship quality is also linked to parenting practices, which in turn affects child well-being (Adler-Baeder et al., 2013; Demir-Dagdas et al., 2018).

People who are married have greater financial well-being and accumulate more assets than those who are single, which could be attributed to a motivation to work in order to support others and/or the pooling of resources, health insurance, economy of scale, and/or retirement benefits (DeNavas-Walt, Proctor, & Smith, 2012; Fagan, 2009). When considering education, individuals with higher education have an increased probability of getting married. Moreover, persons with college degrees tend to have more stable marriages than those with high school degrees or less education (Fan & Qian, 2019).

As we age, positive marriage quality has a greater effect on adult health in that older married persons are more mentally and physically healthy with a delayed onset of physical limitations in carrying out their daily activities (Choi et al., 2016). Married couples live longer and are less likely to die from the leading causes of death. It is generally perceived that those who are married have a health advantage due to greater social support, decreased isolation, and incentives to act in healthier ways. However, it is not simply marriage that is associated with greater health, but a "satisfying" one. This is not limited to just marriage. Recent research suggests that those in cohabitating or other committed, high-quality relationships seem to have a similar association between relationship and well-being (Perelli-Harris et al., 2018; Zimmerman & Hameister, 2019). Although long-lasting relationships come in various forms, some of the core characteristics include the following (Staton & Ooms, 2012):

- long-term commitment
- positive communication
- nonviolent resolution of disagreements and conflicts
- emotional and physical safety
- sexual and psychological fidelity
- mutual respect
- enjoyment of time spent together
- provision of emotional support and companionship
- mutual commitment to children by parents

There is no clear blueprint for a happy marriage because people bring a number of personal and family background factors to their relationships. Nevertheless, Americans believe that spirituality and religion, shared interests, satisfying sexual relationships, commitment, intimacy, congruence in values and beliefs, and shared household chores are characteristics of a healthy and happy relationship (Geiger & Livingston, 2019; Karimi, Bakhtiyari, & Arani, 2019). The way couples communicate and spend time together also affects relationship satisfaction, as well as their compatibility.

The knowledge and skills needed for healthy marriage are widely known. Therefore, there has been increasing emphasis on providing relationship and marriage education to many people in a variety of settings. The benefits of marital health and satisfaction for couples, families, and children provide positive incentives for marriage and family life educators to continue developing programs as times and relationships change.

MARRIAGE: PAST AND PRESENT

Many changes in marriage have occurred over the years. For example, the term "traditional marriage" has often been mentioned, but we have to ask when, where, and how it is used. It has had many different meanings through time, such as heterosexual marriages or marriages in which the male partner worked outside the home while the female partner stayed home caring for the children. Now there are alternative configurations for marriage and relationships such as *peer marriages* (partners who have equal status in relationships, including finances, housework, and child-rearing roles), *alone together marriages* (couples whose mutual friends and activities together have declined, but still remain happy in their relationships), and *LAT relationships* (Living Apart Together—couples in committed marital or nonmarital intimate relationships, but living in separate homes) (Amato & Hayes, 2014; Amato et al., 2007; Lewin, 2017; Schwartz, 1994, 2001). Love, which has evolved for many as a basis for marriage, was originally condemned as too fragile of an emotion on which to base a marriage; however, as people took control of their destiny and love life, they began to demand the right to choose their own mate and to end unhappy marriages (Coontz, 2005). Love continues to be the number one reason that Americans choose to marry (Geiger & Livingston, 2019).

Marriage laws have continued to change over time based on shifting societal attitudes and needs of families (Thomas, 2020). These shifting attitudes and laws have led to increased diversity in marriage and committed partnerships including cohabitation, same-sex marriage, and interracial and interethnic marriage (Geiger & Livingston, 2019). Whereas 40 states once prohibited marrying outside one's race, in 1948 California became the first state to declare that a ban on interracial marriage was unconstitutional, followed by the United States Supreme Court striking down the remaining interracial marriage laws in 1967. For many centuries, women had no legal rights when they married, but over time laws have evolved at the state and federal levels to reflect the equality of spouses. Similarly, laws changed regarding same-sex couples' access to marriage when in 2015 the

US Supreme Court legalized same-sex marriages in all 50 states (*Obergefell v. Hodges*, 2015). Within just two years, the percentage of same-sex cohabitating couples who married rose from 38% to 61% (Masci, Brown, & Kiley, 2020).

As a culture, we are obsessed with marriage and all aspects leading up to a wedding, as evidenced by the myriad of television programs about finding the right partner, dress, or wedding venue. However, COVID-19 resulted in new wedding trends, experiences, and design elements with smaller weddings and more outdoor venues. Many couples took advantage of technology for wedding planning, such as trying on dresses virtually, sending virtual wedding invitations, keeping family and friends updated through wedding websites, and even having the actual wedding via Zoom (Lee, 2021a). The COVID-19 pandemic not only prompted change in wedding traditions, but also shifted the financial aspects of weddings. Social distancing and restrictions on the size of gatherings resulted in downsized celebrations and reduced costs. In 2020, the average cost of a wedding was $19,000, which was a decline from $28,000 in 2019 (Lee, 2021b).

Trends indicate that Americans have become more likely to delay marriage and less likely to marry. While roughly half of Americans 18 and older are married, there are differences based on socioeconomic levels and race/ethnicity with moderately educated couples less likely to marry (Parker & Stepler, 2017). In 2020, the US had its highest median age for first marriages, with 28.1 years for women and 30.5 years for men. The decline in marriage rates is partly due to people choosing to stay single, the increase in unmarried cohabitation, or reasons relating to jobs or careers (Graf, 2019; Parker & Barroso, 2021).

While stable, happy marriages are almost universally desired, almost half of marriages end in divorce or separation (Raley & Sweeney, 2020). However, divorce rates over the decades have declined and this trend has varied across age groups with rates higher for younger than for older adults. The economic disadvantages of relationship dissolution, whether divorce or cohabitation, continues to be greater for women than men (Raley & Sweeney, 2020). Among divorced men and women, men were more likely to remarry than women. A possible reason for this disparity is women are less interested than men in remarrying (Geiger & Livingston, 2019). While divorce is classified as a family stressor itself, the added stressors from the COVID-19 pandemic impacted family outcomes and transitions. For example, a study examining divorce in the midst of COVID-19 found that although divorce rates declined during the pandemic, thoughts about divorce increased, with constraints prohibiting couples from being able to follow through (Lebow, 2020).

Most children of divorced parents generally have lower levels of well-being, with some of these problems continuing into adulthood, such as poverty, troubled marriages, weak ties to parents, and symptoms of psychological distress (Amato, 2010; Demir-Dagdas et al., 2018). The effects of divorce for children vary depending on the context of the divorce. For some children there could be improvements in well-being, whereas others show little change or have problems that either improve or continue into adulthood (Amato, 2010). In addition, with divorce there could be long-term implications of family problems that persist across generations, as well as other problems related to risks for children and future grandchildren (Amato & Patterson, 2017). Divorce education for parents and children has become more prominent in the US in the past decade, with half of US states requiring some type of divorce and parent education (Speaks Law Firm, 2021). Co-parenting plays a vital role in children's outcomes when parents divorce. Therefore, researchers and educators have developed parenting and divorce education programs to promote healthy co-parenting and parenting practices among parents going through a divorce or separation (Schramm & Becher, 2020). Programs that were research-based, focused on skill development, and promoted co-parenting and positive parenting practices showed more promise for parents and children than those that were didactic or affect-based (Schramm & Becher, 2020).

RELATIONSHIP AND MARRIAGE EDUCATION

Due in part to a growing national marriage education movement, there are a number of resources and programs available to help couples have a happy, healthy marriage. Minimizing divorce with better education before and during marriage can potentially result in more stable relationships. Relationship and marriage education (RME) provides information to couples about relationship knowledge, attitudes, behaviors, and skills to assist individuals and couples in sustaining healthy, mutually satisfying relationships, and reducing relationship distress. This includes making wise partner choices, managing expectations, improving communication skills, and recognizing and preventing interpersonal violence (Stanley et al., 2020).

In the past, marriage enrichment programs were popular, such as the *Association for Couples in Marriage Enrichment* (*ACME*), developed by David and Vera Mace (Mace, 1982). Their goal was to take an educational rather than therapeutic approach and make a good marriage even better. Often there were weekend retreats devoted to revitalizing one's marriage within the context of spiritual renewal (Doherty & Anderson, 2004). Because of the perceived importance of stable marriages for children and families and the costs of marital instability to individuals and society, various efforts have been made to provide relationship and marriage education. In fact, the field of RME has experienced a notable resurgence since 1995, and especially in the last two decades when federal legislation allocated funds to support promising RME programs and initiatives targeted at lower-income couples (Hawkins & Ooms, 2010; Stanley et al., 2020). In many cases, RME takes a preventative approach before difficulties occur; however, many couples who attend RME may be distressed and struggling in their relationships (Stanley et al., 2020). Over time other RME programs have been established that are research-based, focus on couples' relationship skills, and are often of interest to premarital couples and couples with long lasting relationships. Although further research is still needed to determine the effectiveness of RME for diverse and disadvantaged populations, there is evidence that skills-based relationship education for couples enhances maintenance of healthy and committed relationships and should be disseminated (Halford et al., 2008; Hawkins et al., 2008; Stanley et al., 2020).

Relationship and marriage education can occur at many different times, settings, and circumstances in one's life, such as when one is single, either in one's youth or young adulthood, or returning to singlehood after being in a relationship. Although typically delivered to couples, RME also can be oriented to individuals. An individual focus might be warranted if only one person in the relationship is able or willing to attend or if the program is designed to strengthen skills for future relationships (Stanley et al., 2020). Couples can also engage in relationship or marriage education at any stage of their relationship. They may need to reconnect, understand what makes their relationship work, or learn practical skills to improve or enrich their relationship. Skills and insights can be learned in RME to avoid unhealthy relationships; build a healthy, committed, and growing relationship; maintain and enrich a marriage; and/or rescue a struggling marriage. Other key relationship skills include communication, conflict management, developing realistic and shared relationship expectations, and promoting positive connections and commitment (Halford et al., 2008; Stanley et al., 2020). Premarital prevention programs can produce immediate and short-term gains in interpersonal skills and relationship quality. While the findings from several evaluation studies have indicated mixed results, they are nevertheless encouraging. Because of the limitations and gaps within these studies, we need long-term data on family stability, child outcomes, parenting, and the spill-over effects of marriage relationships into the work place and vice versa (Ooms & Hawkins, 2012).

Research on the prevention of marital distress has led to evidenced-based programs that help alter the course of marriage and prevent divorce. If negative interactions can be improved, couples can enhance their odds of staying together. Examples of programs used to help strengthen relationships and marriages include the *Prevention and Relationship Enhancement Program* (*PREP*) (Stanley & Markman, n.d.); *Practical Application of Intimate Relationship Skills* (*PAIRS*) (DeMaria & Hannah, 2013); *ELEVATE* (Futris et al., 2014); and *Prepare/Enrich* (Olson, Olson, & Larson, 2012).

THE 5 CS OF RELATIONSHIP AND MARRIAGE EDUCATION MODEL

To better understand and show the breadth of the multifaceted elements of relationship and marriage education programs, one can incorporate the *5 Cs of Relationship and Marriage Education Model*: *Consumers*, *Content*, *Changes*, *Context*, and *Culture*. Although counseling and therapy can be implemented to strengthen or repair relationships and marriages, the 5 Cs Model stresses a preventive approach. The elements of the model include the Consumers (demographics and stages during the lifespan); Content of the program (theory, Relationship Assessment Questionnaires [RAQs], and the *Marriage Triangle* of factors related to marital satisfaction); Changes in circumstances that influence the marriage (e.g., remarriage and stepfamilies, military deployments, and family stress); the Context of the program (educator, setting, and educational strategies); and the influence of Culture on love, marriage, and divorce (see Figure 10.1).

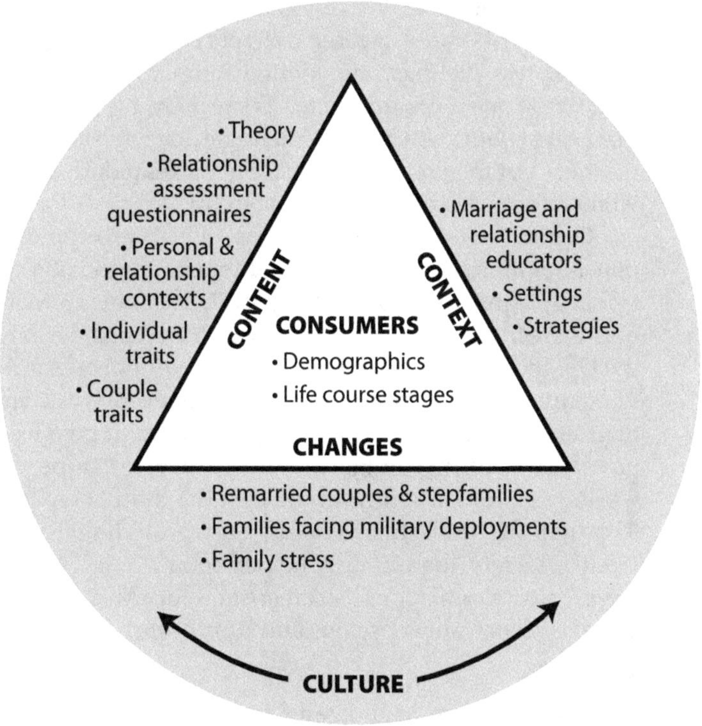

Figure 10.1 5 Cs of Relationship and Marriage Education

CONSUMERS—CHARACTERISTICS OF THE PARTICIPANTS

Understanding the characteristics of participants in RME programs can help educators more effectively plan, teach, and market their programs. In general, little is known about the individuals and couples who participate in relationship and marriage education programs. Whereas some participants are students in educational settings, others are couples in various developmental stages of their relationship. Pertinent elements to consider include *demographic characteristics* (e.g., *gender, age, income level,* and *race/ethnicity*) and *stage within the lifespan.*

Demographic Characteristics

GENDER

In a sample of 7,331 couples in a relationship formation, mate selection, and prediction of relationship quality study (Duncan, Holman, & Yang, 2007), gender was a factor regarding the likelihood of couples attending a marriage preparation course. In particular, the greater the value that females placed on marriage, the more likely the couple was to participate in a marriage preparation course. While some evidence of gender differences can be found in the research literature, they are outweighed by the similarities in gendered interests, abilities, and activities (Sahin & Yalcinkaya, 2020). The characteristics of men and women are not totally different or identical. We cannot say that all men and all women behave in a certain manner because gender differences are by degree (e.g., ability to communicate, express feelings, and define intimacy) and interact with the culture and context of one's environment. There may be gender differences in reasons for marrying. Both men and women cite love as being an important reason to get married, but men tend to focus more on shared ideas on raising children, whereas women focus more on financial stability (Wang & Parker, 2014).

Gender roles and expectations, which are typically determined by society, play an important role in couple interaction, decision making, and views of marital satisfaction (Allendorf et al., 2017; Williams & McBain, 2006). These shifting norms over the past several decades have considerably changed expectations in the US. Increasing similarity has occurred in gender roles, as couples become less structured and try to find a balance between work and home that better meets their needs. Whether it is a general freedom to be oneself or the result of the economic downturn, young adults do not want to be defined by gender and are working toward equality. In the past the term "help" was often used as it related to parenting, household chores, and providing for one's family. However, in today's society there is no "helper spouse" or "director of household management," nor is one spouse's career more or less important (Allendorf et al., 2017). Young adults want conscious and purposeful sharing of roles and responsibilities.

Age

The minimum legal age of marriage varies by country and state. Currently only two states (Delaware and New Jersey) have a minimum marriage age of 18 years with no exceptions (Hill & Elder, 2020). Many states have 18 as a minimum age but have exceptions for adolescents who have been court-emancipated. Additionally, the US does not have a ban on underage marriage partners that immigrate to the US (Hill & Elder, 2020). Child spouses often have few rights and little power in a marriage with an older spouse. Even if both marriage partners are 18 and meet the minimum eligible age to marry, it does not mean that they are ready for marriage (FindLaw, 2013; UNSD, 2008). Although some teen marriages are successful, early marriage can lead to negative outcomes, such as increased chances of violence, lower educational attainment and job earnings, increased likelihood of divorce, and poorer physical and mental health (ICRW, 2020).

Race/ethnicity

Research shows that Black couples and other marginalized populations experience racial disparities in employment and earning that are linked to forming and maintaining marriages (Sassler & Lichter, 2020). However, there is considerable diversity among Black marriages that needs to be considered, such as in African, Caribbean, Hispanic, and interracial marriages (Fincham & Beech, 2010). Overall, even after taking financial resources into account, compared with Whites, Blacks have a reduced likelihood to marry, if at all; lower quality marriages; more children outside marriage; higher levels of conflict; and if they marry, their marriages are more likely to end in divorce (Kanter et al., 2020). Gender roles are important in Black marriages. Black couples tend to be more egalitarian than

White couples, with both spouses sharing equitably in work outside and inside the family, as well as in child care. Most Black couples, however, would prefer a traditional division of labor, with husbands being the primary source of income and wives taking care of the family. Thus, there is a discrepancy between the ideals and realities that creates tension in many marriages. Black couples are less likely to support the lifelong norm of marriage and are also more likely to have experienced parental divorce and been part of a single-parent family while they were children.

Recent research has found that interest in RME may vary by age and race. For example, adolescent women and African Americans were more interested in participating in marriage education compared to adolescent men and European Americans (Kanter et al., 2020). Religiosity is a major strength upon which to build RME programs for Black couples. Having couples form social networks in which they participate together and also address gender roles may be important themes for relationship and marriage education (Amato, 2011a; Kanter et al., 2020).

Hispanics/Latinos are diverse in their countries of origin, level of acculturation, length of US residency, social class, religion, education, and other environmental factors that influence couples and families (Kanter et al., 2020). Because Hispanics/Latinos are the largest and fastest growing minority group in the US, it is important that marriage educators are prepared to work collaboratively with them (Bouchet, Torres, & Hyra, 2013). Whereas 45% of Hispanic women are married compared to 51% of White and 26% of Black women, overall Hispanic women have the highest cohabitation rates at 13% compared to 10% of African Americans and 8% of Whites (Bouchet et al., 2013). Hispanic/Latino family stability is influenced by immigration, with 13% of immigrant Hispanics/Latinos living apart from their spouses. Marriage among Hispanics/Latinos may also entail different cultural traditions. It is important to understand *familismo*, a cultural value in which family relations are held with high esteem, along with respect for father figures, which is based on the conceptualization of *machismo*. Generally, Hispanic families are more likely to have traditional gender roles and a patriarchal structure. It is wise for educators working with this population to be bilingual, if possible. Although Hispanics/Latinos function biculturally, their ability to be bilingual may vary. In addition, there are various groups of Hispanics/Latinos who speak indigenous languages and may not be proficient in Spanish or English. The heterogeneity of the Hispanic/Latino population reinforces the importance of conducting a needs assessment and involving members of your target audience when planning and delivering relationship and marriage education.

Income level

Some RME programs developed for middle-class committed couples may not be relevant for low-income populations. While marriage may be declining for those who have fewer economic resources, they still are interested in learning how to improve their relationships through educational programs. However, many lower-income couples decide not to marry so they will not lose their government assistance (Arnold & Beelmann, 2019). Regardless of race or cultural background, economic hardship adds considerable stress to relationships. Some of these stressors include shortage of finances, increasing debts, low levels of literacy, high unemployment, incarceration, substance abuse, depression, domestic violence, inadequate housing, and unsafe neighborhoods (Arnold & Beelmann, 2019). Since low-income individuals and couples encounter daily challenges that interfere with their ability to make progress in their relationships, comprehensive intensive economic and support services are needed to stabilize their marriages. These challenges must be addressed in a sensitive manner. Low-income populations are often disproportionately people of color, so programs should be designed to be relevant to many different populations. Low-income persons may also have difficulties with literacy, lectures, and reading, so activities should be understandable to all participants. Combining relationship education programs with other programs and services may be more feasible and could provide opportunities for honest dialogue, skill building, and enjoyment (Arnold & Beelmann, 2019). One of the best known skill-building programs is *Prevention and Relationship Enhancement Program* (PREP), which has been shown to have promising outcomes with lower-income, racially diverse couples (Owen et al., 2012).

Consumers of Relationship and Marriage Education Across the Lifespan

Various relationship and marriage education programs have been targeted for consumers at key *stages during the lifespan*. As people go through different stages of development, programs can be modified to meet their changing needs, while maintaining core values and principles. The following are some examples of issues and programs for adolescents, emerging adults, couples entering marriage, married couples, and older couples.

Adolescents

Adolescence is a time for involvement in relationship development including romantic attachments, coupled with an increasing independence from family influence. Romantic involvement during adolescence is an emerging developmental task that becomes salient in adulthood (Gómez-López et al., 2019). Although a majority of individuals do not marry until emerging adulthood, adolescents certainly think about marriage and divorce. If they are conscious of the dilemmas of marital distress and divorce, they may be more ambivalent toward relationships and marriage (Arocho, 2021). There are many influences on adolescent dating and sexual activity, including their parents' romantic relationships, which can impact beliefs and attitudes about relationships and provide tips on how to maintain satisfying relationships during adulthood (Jamison & Lo, 2021; Olmstead, 2020). Teens that live with both biological parents express strong support for marriage and also consider their parents' marriages to be high quality. In addition, they increasingly approve of cohabitation before marriage, support the delay of their own marriages, and have a greater acceptance of casual sex (Moreira et al., 2021). Male teenagers have more positive attitudes toward marriage than female teenagers and are more likely to want to delay marriage.

As adolescents enter their dating years, some will experience relationship problems including relationship violence (Moreira et al., 2021). Some conflict in adolescent relationships is common, so learning communication and relationships skills can help them negotiate a balance between closeness and independence. Healthy relationships can assist adolescents to develop self-confidence and self-esteem, provide opportunities for conflict resolution, and offer lessons on how to maintain and end relationships (McElwain, McGill, & Savasuk-Luxton, 2017). Therefore, many professionals argue that the promotion of healthy relationships should begin in adolescence before a committed relationship is started (Moreira et al., 2021).

Emerging adults

While traditionally relationship education has more commonly been provided to couples that are preparing to marry, focusing on emerging adults helps to link early parent-child relationships to later romantic relationships and healthy marriages. Emerging adults (those approximately between the ages of 18 and 29) are becoming more independent from their parents, but do not yet have adult roles and responsibilities (Arnett, 2014, 2015). This is also a period during which risky behaviors, such as increased alcohol and drug use, "hooking up," "friends with benefits," and involvement with multiple sexual partners can occur (Olmstead, 2021). Researchers have shown that individuals in committed relationships experienced fewer mental health problems and engaged in less risky behavior than those who were single (Gómez-López et al., 2019). Programs for emerging adults have the potential for long-term impacts in dealing with choice of partner and communication issues, which are easier to manage when being open to learning about relationships. Thus, providing relationship education to emerging adults may not only improve their current and future relationships, but also have long-term health benefits (Fincham, Stanley, & Rhoades, 2011). College students can participate in relationship education through academic course work, but it is also important to provide opportunities to emerging adults who do not pursue higher education.

An important topic in relationship education for emerging adults, as well as other adults, is commitment and its relationship to cohabitation, which has become widely accepted and an integral part of the marriage process (Manning & Cohen, 2015). In the US, cohabitation has become normative with more emerging adults cohabitating than living as a married couple (Gurrentz, 2018). Although often thought of as a precursor to marriage, fewer cohabitating couples are choosing to marry as compared to the past (Sasler & Lichter, 2020). Cohabitating couples who have at least four indicators of a higher socioeconomic status (e.g., steady income, health insurance, bank account) are more likely to transition into marriage than are those couples without these indicators (Gibson-Davis et al., 2018). Serial cohabitation, which is moving into a new cohabiting relationship soon after the dissolution of another, has increased over the past decade (Eickmeyer & Manning, 2018). Previous research on cohabitation before engagement has been associated with poorer martial outcomes including an increased risk of marital distress and divorce. However, as cohabitation prior to marriage is becoming more normative and given the complexity of pathways to marriage, the benefits of marriage and cohabitation are converging (Sasler & Lichter, 2020). The link between cohabitation and divorce is not as certain as once thought and there are many issues to consider. For example, did the marriage occur with their first cohabiting partner or did they engage in serial cohabitation? Did the couple enter into a cohabiting relationship with a strong commitment and intent to marry? How old was the couple when they began cohabiting?

The phenomenon of cohabitation has been described as "sliding versus deciding." In other words, some couples that may not have married without first living together do so because of the inertia of cohabitation; they "slide" into marriage without making a conscious decision to marry (Stanley, Rhoades, & Markman, 2006). When examining commitment there are forces that motivate connection: *dedication* or a strong sense of couple identity with a long-term view to maintain and improve the relationship for the mutual benefit of both partners, versus *constraint* or the costs or pressures of leaving, which helps explain why some people remain in unhappy relationships (Markman et al., 2010; Stanley, 2002; Stanley et al., 2006). Understanding relationships and commitment is important for emerging adults.

Couples entering marriage

Couples preparing to marry are often good candidates for marriage education and the need for premarital education is more important than ever. Couples are entering into marriage with more complex dating and sexual histories that may include cohabitation and childbearing without marriage (Clyde, Hawkins, & Willoughby, 2019). They are aware of the changes that are about to occur in their lives and motivated to make a smooth transition into their marriages. Premarital education can reduce the risk of divorce by 30%, yet, less than a third of couples entering a first marriage seek premarital preparation (Duncan, 2018). In order to meet the needs of contemporary couples entering marriage, Clyde et al. (2019) proposed that premarital education programs help couples to (1) transition from "me" to "we"; (2) clarify their attitudes and meanings of marriage; (3) address the complexities of sexual experience, cohabitation histories, and premarital childbearing; and (4) explore the effects of media on marital attitudes and behavior.

Although second marriages are more likely to result in divorce compared to first marriages, they represent an understudied population. Nevertheless, individuals in second marriages were less likely to receive premarital education (Dosset et al., 2009). Lower rates of premarital education for second marriages were attributed to a lower level of education and a lower probability of being married by a religious leader, along with a higher probability of cohabiting before marriage and having children from previous relationships. Thus, other types of support should be examined along with novel ways to recruit participants.

Married couples

Several marriage education programs encourage couples to understand and value the importance of spending time together. Economically disadvantaged couples, compared to nondisadvantaged couples, spend slightly more time together, mainly involved in leisure activities, such as watching television (Fein, 2009). While this advantage is lost when considering the differences in the number of hours they work, it persists after controlling for time devoted to work activities outside and inside the home. Couples with preschool children spend more time together, but less time alone compared to couples without young children (Fein, 2009). Thus, time use is an important factor in marriage education programs for married couples with and without children.

It is not just the quantity of time couples spend together, but the quality of time. With the natural rhythm of married lives, including busy schedules, endless tasks, and child care, it is easy to lose focus on one's marriage, resulting in less connection, spark, and intimacy. However, when partners are conscious, deliberate, and purposeful about maintaining and building a sense of connection over the years, they can create an *intentional marriage* (Doherty, 2000). *Rituals* of connection and intimacy have emotional meaning for both partners, such as romantic dinners, long talks, going for walks, and doing special activities together, and they are different from *routines*, which are things done repetitively with little emotional meaning. Rather than being on automatic pilot, Doherty suggests creating *rituals of intimacy* (e.g., dates for a special time together); *connection* (e.g., goodbyes in the morning and greetings in the evening); and *community* (e.g., couple activities involved in giving and receiving support in their larger world). Talk rituals are also important, as couples need time to talk every day—uninterrupted, nonlogistical, and nonproblem-solving communication. Marriage classes can also be intentional. In the busy lives of married couples that are working and caring for children, it can be challenging to find time to attend marriage classes. Thus, marriage education programs need to be fun, couple or family oriented, flexible, and provide quality child care, if needed.

Older couples

The proportion of older Americans who live in an intimate relationship without marriage has increased in past decades (Calasanti & Keicolt, 2007; King & Scott, 2005). This is in part because the benefits of marrying may not be as great for older couples due to the challenge of merging households, lack of support from adult children, and the potential loss of social security (Sassler, 2010).

Marriage programs for older and retired couples need to focus on the issues faced by this age group. Generally, older people rate their relationship quality as high, but experts disagree on the connection between relationship quality and retirement. Whereas retired couples have greater satisfaction because of reduced pressures from other roles, some perceive that increased marital interaction after retirement can result in a loss of privacy, resulting in tension or disruption. Although there may be some lifestyle changes with retirement, it does not typically disrupt long-term behavioral or communication patterns. However, having adult children at home is inversely related to marital satisfaction for both men and women (Chalmers & Milan, 2005). Overall, positive marital quality in midlife and older couples contributes to positive health outcomes in both spouses (Choi et al., 2016).

Content

The content of relationship and marriage programs can vary according to the age of consumers (e.g., adolescent, young adult, or senior citizen), circumstance (e.g., first marriage or remarriage), or the state in which they live. In 2009, Florida was the first state among many to enact legislation that reduces marriage license fees for couples that complete a premarital education course either separately or as a couple. Currently nine other states have joined Florida in offering incentives to attend premarital education and those that are implementing these programs well have seen a modest reduction in divorce rates (Hawkins & Clyde, 2019). The content of these courses can include instruction in conflict management, communication skills, financial responsibilities, children and parenting responsibilities, along with issues reported by married couples who seek marital or individual counseling.

Other suggestions for content include identified risk factors for relationship or marital distress. A greater number of risk factors means couples will need to work more on their relationships (Markman et al., 2010). Risk factors may include issues such as having children from a previous relationship, marrying at a very young age, or knowing each other for just a short time. An understanding of these types of risk factors is important for relationships, but they may not all be appropriate for marriage education settings. Some of the following issues are more amenable for marriage education programs:

- negative styles of talking and fighting
- difficulty communicating, especially in disagreements
- trouble working as a team
- unrealistic beliefs about relationships
- different attitudes and expectations about important elements in life
- low commitment to the relationship

The content in RME involves the integration of pertinent theories and *Relationship Assessment Questionnaires* (RAQs). Additionally, various *personal and relational contexts, individual traits,* and *couple traits* can be included (Larson, 2003).

Incorporation of Theory

An important component of RME is the incorporation of theory to guide program development. As noted in Chapter 8, theories contribute to our understanding of marriages by providing reasonable explanations of individual and family behaviors. Theories should guide the strategies utilized in relationship and marriage education courses and inform the interpretation of the outcomes of these strategies. Various theories can be integrated into marriage education programs such as the following:

- *Individual and family developmental theory* can examine the developmental tasks of both individuals and families through the life cycle as they pertain to relationships.
- *Systems theory* can facilitate understanding boundaries, equilibrium, and morphogenesis.
- An *ecosystems approach* can clarify environmental/contextual factors influencing individuals, couples, and families.
- *Social exchange theory* can be used to examine the rewards, costs, and equity involved in relationships, as well as family power and family violence.

- *Social learning theory* suggests that patterns of behavior can be acquired through direct experience or observing others.
- *Attachment theory* can facilitate understanding long-term relationships between parent and child and then later adult relationships. It is believed that those who do not initially experience secure attachments may develop sensitivity to rejection in later relationships. Thus, attachment theory can be used to understand the role of attachment style with mate selection choice, commitment, jealousy, separation, or divorce (Mikulincer & Shaver, 2012; Shaver, Mikulincer, & Cassidy, 2019).

Using Relationship Assessment Questionnaires (RAQs)

Often, relationship and marriage programs in academic, faith-based, or secular settings incorporate the use of RAQs, which based on the participant's results, can help guide the planning and selection of specific course content. Since early detection, prevention, and education are important for relationships, using RAQs and having partners share their results can facilitate understanding the factors influencing a relationship (Olson, Larson, & Olson-Sigg, 2009). These questionnaires enhance awareness and facilitate subsequent discussions between partners about their strengths and weaknesses, readiness for marriage, and goals to accomplish before marriage. Predictors of marital satisfaction and stability include (1) *background and contextual factors*, such as family of origin issues, education and income, and relationship support from parents and friends; (2) *individual traits and behaviors*, such as self-esteem, interpersonal skills, and physical and emotional health; and (3) *couple interactional processes*, such as similarity of race, religion, socioeconomic status, values and attitudes, and couple communication and conflict resolution skills (Larson, 2004b). One of the biggest predictors of marital success is the compatibility of shared meaning, core values, and goals (Gottman & Gottman, 2017). Examples of widely used surveys include:

- Couple Checkup (Olson et al., 2009)
- Premarital Preparation and Relationship Enhancement (PREPARE) (Olson, Olson, & Larson, 2012)
- Relationship Evaluation (RELATE) (Busby, Holman, & Taniguchi, 2001)

These questionnaires measure 85% or more of the relationship factors previously mentioned, can be completed in about an hour, and provide detailed reports on individual traits, couple traits, and relationship issues. RAQs also include information about remarriage issues. Some can be completed online or with the assistance of someone trained in using these instruments. Factors to consider in using RAQs include how you plan to use the results, the financial cost of the survey, number of class sessions for inclusion of survey findings, settings for the course, supplementary materials to be used, and the need for instructor training.

Personal and Relational Contexts

While using RAQs can show areas of similarity and dissimilarity between partners, to facilitate understanding these issues within a relationship or marriage education program, the *Marriage Triangle* can be incorporated to examine three factors that can predict future marital satisfaction. These three factors deal with *personal and relationship contexts, individual traits,* and *couple traits* (Larson, 2002, 2003).

Personal and relational contexts that can affect marriage relationships include age at marriage, parents' and friends' approval of the relationship, the quality of an individual's parents' relationship and other family relationships, previous marriages, children, parenting stress, and in-laws. However, we will only briefly highlight a few family of origin issues as an illustration.

Relationships are influenced by role models, particularly parents, who helped shape views about marriage. We bring past experiences into a marriage setting (e.g., happy marriage, bitter divorce); functional or dysfunctional family dynamics (e.g., abuse, neglect, poor communication); extended family dynamics (e.g., grandparents, in-laws); and/or family stresses (e.g., death, financial difficulties, stepfamilies). Other family issues to consider include: Was the parent-child relationship satisfying, affectionate, and close, or cold, detached, and neglectful? Was family communication open and honest without being hurtful? Does an adult have a healthy sense of independence from his or her parents? Some of these situations can have more indirect than direct effects on marital satisfaction. In other words, family of origin processes (A) influence personality, self-esteem, and communication skills (B) that subsequently influence marital satisfaction in the next generation (C) (A → B → C) (Larson, 2003). More recent research also found that family of origin made a difference in marital outcomes with those whose parents had an unstable marriage more likely to have unstable relationships themselves (Amato & Patterson, 2016). Gaining a deeper understanding of one's family of origin can assist in understanding oneself and a partner better and is essential to building and maintaining a relationship. A good beginning can include sharing each partner's preferences for leisure activities; who their friends are; and how they felt in their families, schools, and communities. Further discussions could involve views about work and family, financial management, and how couples will manage the addition of children to their relationship.

Individual Traits

Individual traits can include personality and emotional health, as well as the values, beliefs, and attitudes of each partner in a relationship. Understanding oneself facilitates real sharing with a partner that can be helpful in the ongoing development of the relationship.

Personality and Emotional Health

Personality traits influence behaviors in relationships across one's entire lifetime, and while some traits can be relatively enduring, others may change over time (Allemand, Steiger, & Hill, 2013). Generally, as people age they have increased self-confidence, warmth, self-control, and emotional stability. These changes predominate in young adulthood (age 20–40), but can also change at any age. The *Big Five Personality Traits* appear to be influential in intimate relationships. They include (1) *Extraversion*—being outgoing, enthusiastic, and social; (2) *Agreeableness*—being compassionate, cooperative, and trusting; (3) *Conscientiousness*—

being industrious, dependable, and orderly; (4) *Neuroticism*—being volatile and prone to worry, anxiety, and anger; and (5) *Openness to experience*—being imaginative, unconventional, and artistic. While the first four traits make a difference in relationships, the last one seems to have little to do with success and satisfaction in close relationships (Costa & McCrae, 2003; DeYoung, Quilty, & Peterson, 2007).

In addition to using scales from the *Big Five Personality Traits*, other personality measures can be incorporated into both formal and nonformal settings, such as the *Primary Colors Personality Test*, which has been adapted and published by PREP for individuals (Billings, 2004; www.prepinc.com). Along with personality, partners should consider emotional health (e.g., presence or absence of high anxiety, depression, and anger) for which insight can be gained by incorporating results from the RAQs subscales (Larson, 2003). As in personality determinants, a mutual discussion to compare similarities in personality traits and health issues can open a dialogue on what needs to be faced in the future and how to best deal with these issues.

Values, beliefs, and attitudes

A *value* is a measure of the worth or importance we attach to something that often is reflected in the way we live our lives. Values cannot be seen but can be recognized in behaviors and actions and used to set standards of conduct, make decisions, resolve conflicts, motivate behaviors, and judge the behavior of others (Moore & Asay, 2017). Values develop slowly throughout the lifespan and are influenced by many things, including one's culture, leaders, family members, friends, television, media, and more. While some values can change, core values do not shift much after our early twenties. Not having common core values can be a major problem for a relationship (e.g., one partner values having children and the other thinks children will impose on their lifestyle, or one partner believes that a successful career is highly desirable, whereas the other has family as a top priority [Vogt, n.d.]). While talking about differences is vital, if each partner's values are vastly different, communication may not be enough. Having these discussions before marriage is essential, because value differences are not easy to resolve after marriage. However, at times values may change due to a personal or familial experience with stress or crisis, such as a serious illness or accident that can elevate health and/or family to be a main priority and value. Values are often rank-ordered in importance, consciously or subconsciously, although one's hierarchy of values can change over time. Values that can benefit relationships are commitment, respect, intimacy, and forgiveness (Markman et al., 2010).

A *belief* is an internal feeling that something is true, even though it may be unproven or irrational. Some beliefs are dysfunctional, such as that disagreement is destructive, partners should be mind readers, a partner cannot change, sexual perfection is possible, and men and women are completely different (Larson, 2003). Core beliefs about oneself, marriage, and families can be valuable to a relationship or a risk factor if each partner has divergent beliefs (Markman et al., 2010). Individuals apply their beliefs and values through their attitudes, which can be expressed through their words and behaviors.

Participating in values clarification activities can help individuals and their partners better understand each other. Examining personal values and sharing the results with a partner who has completed the same exercise can be an opportunity to compare similarities and differences and then discuss what is important. Finding shared meaning can help couples discover deeper and more meaningful relationships. See Box 10.1 for *20 Things I Like to Do* and Box 10.2 for *Comparing Couple Values in Relationships.*

Box 10.1 Value Clarification Activity: 20 Things I Like to Do

Very few persons can overtly express what they value, so incorporating value clarification activities and sharing the results with a partner can provide for meaningful communication. One activity is to list *20 Things You Like to Do.* Then make a grid to one side of your list with the following headings indicating on the grid if any of the activities matches one of these categories:

$ An item or activity that *costs* more than $25

A An activity done *alone*

P A *people*-oriented activity

I An activity that involves *intimacy*

3 An activity that would not have been on your list *3 years ago*

R An activity that requires some kind of *risk* (physical, mental, or emotional)

F An item that would not have been on your *father's* list at your age

M An item that would not have been on your *mother's* list at your age

D *Date* (approximate) when you last did this activity

After completing the list and grid, contemplate how readily you were able to list 20 things you like to do. What activities are similar to your mother and/or father, or what do you do alone, with others, or with an intimate partner? Do you participate in activities that cost money or involve risks? Have you done any of these activities recently? If not, what does that mean for you? How have the activities you value changed over time and why do you think that is the case? After you contemplate your list, share it with a partner and examine what values these activities express and what you have in common.

Adapted from Simon, Howe, & Kirschenbaum, 1972.

Box 10.2 Value Clarification Activity: Comparing Couple Values in Relationships

To understand your values and those of your partner, separately draw two concentric circles. In the inside circle list the beliefs and values that you hold dear or your core values. In the outer circle, list the beliefs and values for which you might be flexible when dealing with issues in your relationship. Think of this diagram as an egg with the inner circle as the yolk and the outer circle as the white. After you have individually completed this diagram, share it with your partner. Where do you have some commonalities and agreements? What feelings and goals do you have in common? Can you honor each other's point of view? Will you be able to compromise?

Couple Traits

Along with cohesion, intimacy, control or power, and consensus, two major couple traits include couple communication and conflict resolution skills. Communication, which is the heart of a marriage, determines how well the rest of the marriage is functioning. It involves a loving and cooperative attitude toward a partner and good communication and conflict management skills.

Communication

Communication is a broad topic that includes elements such as listening vs. hearing, types and styles of communication, gender differences, and guidelines for fair fighting. There are three types of communication in which couples engage: *casual talk* when sharing details of life; *conflict talk* when dealing with inevitable disagreements; and *friendship talk*, which builds and maintains intimacy, connection, and security (Markman et al., 2010). Couples often have filters affecting what they hear and say, as well as how they interpret messages. These filters include *distractions* (lack of attention); *emotional states* (moods); *beliefs and expectations* (thoughts and expectations of the relationship); *differences in style* (being expressive or reserved); and *self-protection* (fear of rejection). Everyone has filters, which is not necessarily bad unless they distort communication. The goal is to be aware of filters and not let them hinder communication.

Marital communication is perceived as an important predictor of outcomes for newly married couples, because over time communication difficulties can erode intimate relationships. Using Gottman's four problematic ways of interacting with partners, also known as the "Four Horsemen of the Apocalypse," may be helpful in marriage education programs. They are criticism, contempt, defensiveness, and stonewalling (Gottman, 1994; Gottman, Gottman, & DeClaire, 2006; Gottman & Silver, 1999).

- *Criticism* involves attacking someone's personality or character rather than a specific behavior, usually with blame (e.g., saying "you always" or "never ____").
- *Contempt* focuses on attacking a partner's sense of self with the intent to insult or psychologically abuse him or her and is the worst of the "Four Horsemen" (e.g., name-calling, sarcasm, belligerence).
- *Defensiveness* means seeing oneself as the victim to ward off a perceived attack (e.g., cross-complaining or whining).
- *Stonewalling* involves withdrawal from the relationship to avoid conflict. Partners try to be "neutral," but stonewalling conveys disapproval, distance, separation, and disconnection (e.g., no verbal cues are given that the listener is affected by what he or she hears. In other words, it is like "talking to a stone wall").

A continuing cycle of discord and negative interactions can be difficult to stop without awareness of what is happening. Gottman, who has interviewed and studied numerous couples over the last few decades in the development of his research-based marriage education programs, has found that these behaviors identify those who would divorce with an accuracy of about 90% (Gottman & Gottman, 2017).

Compared to marriages that dissolve, lasting marriages generally have a ratio of five positive interactions between partners for every negative one (Gottman, 1994). Four strategies to facilitate positive communication are suggested: *calm down* when feeling overwhelmed; *speak nondefensively* by listening and not feeling it is necessary to defend yourself; *validation* by letting your partner know that he or she is understood; and *overlearning*—try and try again so that new skills become part of your repertoire. Creating intimacy in your relationship can be facilitated by self-disclosure. When sharing inner thoughts and dreams with a partner, there are opportunities to learn not only about oneself, but also about a partner due to the reciprocal effect of sharing inner thoughts and feelings (Gottman, 2017). Daily compliments to a spouse help to focus on his or her strengths and provide good feelings for each partner. Practicing these skills can help to improve a marriage, as well as spill over to communication styles with children and work colleagues. This is a common topic in RME programs with several exercises for helping partners work on improving their communication skills (Gottman & Gottman, 2017; Markman et al., 2010).

CONFLICT MANAGEMENT

Conflicts are a normal part of relationships, and can actually be positive and constructive, but are easier to manage if people are able to remain physiologically calm (Gottman & Gottman, 2017). Happily married couples behave like good friends and handle their conflicts in gentle, positive ways (Gottman et al., 2006). There are three "conflict blueprints" that can help conflict to be more productive in a relationship (Gottman & Gottman, 2017). The first blueprint is for current conflicts and suggests that both people postpone discussion about the conflict until they are calm and able to listen to the other's perspective. Blueprint 2 refers to the needs for couples to process past conflict or emotional injuries. If left alone, unprocessed issues can continue to cause problems in the relationship. The third blueprint for conflict is for ongoing conflictual issues. These are perpetual issues that are often routed in fundamental personality differences and dreams for the future. These types of conflicts are not necessarily resolvable so the goal is to accept the differences and be able to have a calm discussion about them. In other words, it is important to accept those things about your partner that are likely never to change.

Avoidance of conflict can be facilitated through the use of good communication skills. One suggestion is to begin in a gentle manner and to remain calm. Each conflict has two points of view, so by beginning gently the core of the issue can be reached without defensive barriers. Another recommendation is to use *I statements* rather than *you statements* to share a complaint. This removes blame, disarms the partner, and focuses on the primary issue and emotions of the situation. For example, partners might have a disagreement about household chores. Rather than beginning a statement saying, "You didn't clean up the kitchen after you cooked dinner," an alternative would be, "I get frustrated when I come home from work and the kitchen is not clean." It is also good to describe what is happening without judging; being clear, polite, and appreciative; and not storing things up like bonus miles that are cashed in all at once.

Another skill to learn when communicating about conflict is *active listening*, which is the ability to listen accurately and repeat the message that has been received. It is important to listen when a partner is speaking rather than formulating a response. This will facilitate a better understanding of each partner's point of view. To give participants some practice, a marriage educator might create some situations in order to incorporate a *gentle startup* along with the use of I statements and active listening.

By incorporating meaningful communication and understanding, problems can be identified resulting in a satisfactory outcome for both partners. Using the activity in Box 10.3 on *Conflict Management and Change* in relationships might be helpful in a classroom or between partners.

Box 10.3 Activity: Conflict Management and Change

Have participants fold their arms, as they would normally do. Then ask those who have their left hand pointed upward to stand (the others would have their left hand pointed down). Look around to see how many fold their arms the same way. Ask them to describe how it feels to fold their arms the way that is normal for them. *(They usually describe it as comfortable, safe, relaxed, and the right way to do it.)*

Have participants fold their arms the opposite way and ask them to describe how it feels. *(Usually it is described as uncomfortable, strange, awkward, the wrong way to do it.)*

The point is that "my" way feels right and I will resist doing it "your" way because it feels wrong and uncomfortable. It demonstrates how our differences or preferences can become a point of conflict in relationships. It leads one person to try to change the other because of an individual's perceptions of who is doing something the "right way." With their arms folded the uncomfortable way, ask how they think it would feel if they did it that way for a month. Would it feel different? *(They usually agree that doing it the other way would feel okay if they tried it long enough.)*

The point is that we may be able to change some things for the sake of the relationship if we care enough for the other person. Change is difficult and uncomfortable because it calls us out of our comfort zone, but we can do it. Change also leads to personal growth and growing together as a couple. It is love and commitment that keep a couple together long enough to do the hard work of change.

Areas of conflict for partners often include managing finances, child rearing, sexuality, religion, sharing of household duties, and decision making. For example, how often and when might a couple engage in sexual relations? Will there be separate or joint checking accounts or a combination of both? How will general household chores be approached, such as child care and food preparation? (See Box 10.4 for an activity to stimulate discussion on household chores.)

It can be helpful to set a time and place for discussion, focus only on the problem or issue that is causing tension, and talk about how each person contributes to the problem. Partners should brainstorm, analyze, and evaluate ways to resolve the conflict, agreeing on how each of them will work toward the solution, and then later share individual perceptions about the progress that may have been achieved.

Box 10.4 Division of Labor: Managing Household Tasks

Write various household tasks on ping-pong balls and place them in a box. Some tasks may be written twice as both partners do them, such as working or spending quality time with their spouses and children.

Ask for two volunteers to participate in this activity. They may be two unrelated students in a class or an established couple. Read the following scenario.

> The two individuals in this relationship both have careers. Whereas one partner is an engineer, the other is a firefighter who works varying shifts. They have two children ages 5 and 10.

Select a ping-pong ball from the box, ask which partner will do the task indicated on the ball, and give the ball to that partner. At times, the rest of the participants may also suggest who might perform the task. (*If a ball falls to the floor, a task then "slips through the cracks." Note the task and discuss it, but do not pick up the ball.)* After the balls have all been distributed, provide an additional challenge.

> One partner has a parent living in another city, who is having a health issue and needs assistance. Thus his/her tasks (balls) must be given to the partner remaining at home.

Since it is most likely that the partner who has had to assume all the tasks cannot manage them all as noted by the balls falling to the floor, discuss how they can better manage these tasks by helping each other, eliminating or simplifying tasks, or getting additional assistance. Note the time involved in tasks, sharing of tasks, and gender-related preferences or assignments of tasks.

Examples of Household Tasks Indicated on Ping-Pong Balls

Budget
Pay bills
Make investments
Handle insurance issues
Repair cars
Wash cars
House repairs
Do laundry
Clean house
Vacuum carpets
Mop floors
Do dishes
Yard work or outside work
Purchase children's clothing
Cook breakfast
Prepare lunches
Cook supper
Grocery shopping
Take out garbage
Take care of pets
Plan family entertainment
Children's daily homework
Involvement in children's school activities
Facilitate children's involvement in extracurricular activities
Maintain connections with extended family birthdays, anniversaries
Care for aging parents
Medical appointments for children
Stay home with children when they are sick
Pick children up from school or child care
Bring children to school or child care
Spend quality playtime with children*
Spend quality leisure time with spouse*
Maintain career*
Community involvement
Shop for family presents for birthdays/holidays

*Note asterisk indicates potential duplicate tasks.

CHANGES

Changes occurring in couple and family circumstances can influence marriage education curricula. For example, programs have been created for those who are remarrying and forming stepfamilies, dealing with military deployments, and/or handling stress in their lives.

Changes for Remarried Couples and Stepfamilies

Remarried couples with stepchildren represent a considerable portion of the married population and have unique needs that can be addressed in marriage education programs (Adler-Baeder & Higginbotham, 2020). Among all marriages in 2016, 27% were remarriages, down from 31% in 2008 (Payne, 2018). Although the remarriage rate has declined slightly, there are gender differences with men consistently having higher remarriage rates than women. While 90% of stepfamilies are created after a divorce and remarriage, some stepfamilies evolve from marriages involving a single parent after an out-of-wedlock birth or someone who is widowed. As a result, 42% of adults have a relationship with either a stepparent, a step- or half-sibling, or a stepchild (Parker, 2011). Remarriages are at a slightly greater risk of dissolution compared to first marriages. Compared to first-time married couples, remarried couples used less positive discussion, were much less negative, but were more likely to withdraw from interaction or avoid potentially difficult topics, such as negotiating parenting (Halford, Nicholson, & Sanders, 2007).

Stepfamilies are complex and have developmental differences compared to couples and families in first marriages. Whereas divorce, cohabitation, and serial transitions in and out of marriage are now typical of family life in the US, there are significant consequences for children. The more parental transitions and partnerships children experience, the lower their emotional, psychological, and academic well-being (Amato, 2010; Cherlin, 2009). Moreover, stepfamilies have few institutional supports; may face stigmatization; have issues regarding financial management; and deal with unique issues regarding family rules, boundaries, and parenting decisions. Because the quality of the stepparent-stepchild relationship influences conflicts and relationship quality, priority should be given to the marital relationship and building its strengths (Adler-Baeder & Higginbotham, 2020). Unfortunately, most couples in stepfamilies do not seek premarital education. Furthermore, the unique issues faced by remarried couples are not often addressed in most marriage education courses. Design elements of remarriage courses include the incorporation of a theoretical framework and research-based information; a variety of teaching methods and aides for facilitators and participants; recruitment and implementation materials; and evaluation of programs including the use of control groups and effects over time.

Examples of programs include *Smart Steps: Embrace the Journey* (Adler-Baeder, 2007; www.stepfamilies.info/programs-services/smart-steps), *Supporting Stepfamilies* (Bosh & Strasheim, 2007; extensionpublications.unl.edu/assets/pdf/ec476.pdf) and *Stepping Stones for Stepfamilies* (Olsen, 1999; www.ksre.k-state.edu/families/

topics/stepfamilies/stepping-stones.html). Providing RME to couples forming stepfamilies and giving them additional content specific to their needs can reduce risks for couples and children after divorce.

Changes for Couples Facing Military Deployment

Family separation is common for those serving in the US military and their families and can be due to deployment, permanent change of station, or other circumstances (Mancini, O'Neal, & Lucier-Greer, 2020). While separations have become routine for military couples, they have not prevented military couples from experiencing happy, healthy, and successful relationships. However, it is clear that military relocations, separations, and reunions add stress (Mancini, O'Neal, & Lucier-Greer, 2020). Communication is a critical issue when spouses are deployed. While technology has greatly assisted communication, any lapse of communication can result in concern regarding the well-being of the soldier or family members at home. For some soldiers, access to communications technology may be an issue, while others do not want to communicate for fear that doing so will make them sad or homesick. Knowing what information to communicate or omit, so as not to create worry for the partner, becomes a dilemma. When one spouse is deployed, it creates stress for the spouse at home, who takes on additional roles (Mancini, O'Neal, & Lucier-Greer, 2020). Moreover, when a spouse returns, roles shift to accommodate the returning soldier.

Changes for Couples Facing Stress

Stress, which exists both outside and inside relationships, can influence marital functioning. This can occur both directly and indirectly through the quality of marital communication, the partners' well-being, and the time partners spend together (Bodenmann, Ledermann, & Bradbury, 2007). For example, work, financial, or health stress is known to have a negative influence on marital quality or satisfaction (Kelly, LeBaron, & Hill, 2018). However, this external stress can also influence marital communication, relationship stress, and relationship quality (Ledermann et al., 2010).

The COVID-19 pandemic was a significant external stressor that had considerable impact on relationship quality for many couples, particularly for those who already had lower relationship quality or who were actually in the process of divorcing (Lebow, 2020; Pieh et al., 2020). Other potential negative effects of COVID-19 on couples included reduced sexual intimacy and an increased chance of infidelity (Gordon & Mitchell, 2020; Luetke et al., 2020). Sources of increased stress may be related to both partners working from home along with greater and overwhelming parenting responsibilities; however, some couples found they enjoyed the increased time together and it improved their relationship (Goldberg, McCormick, & Virginia, 2021).

One's own external stress can spill over into a close relationship by intensifying feelings of relationship stress. In other words, low relationship stress and a high level of positive communication are important in relationships. Programs for couples that incorporate stress and coping skills in distress prevention help to manage stress inside the relationship, enhance marital communication, and facilitate long-lasting relationships.

CONTEXT

Knowing the "content" to include in a relationship or marriage education program is not enough; understanding the "context" of teaching is also critical. What does it take to be a *relationship and marriage educator*? What *settings* can be used to teach about relationships and marriage? What *programs, methods,* and *strategies* are helpful? In addition to knowing about marriage and relationships, an educator also needs to know how to develop and teach programs.

Relationship and Marriage Educators

Relationship and marriage educators offer programs, services, and resources to support premarital and married couples and other kinds of intimate partners in building healthy relationships (Stanley et al., 2020). At times marriage educators are also couple facilitators, which means they need to be able to facilitate a discussion about marital issues in a safe and respectful environment. It is important to be mindful of the *Domains of Family Practice Model* (DFP) (Myers-Walls et al., 2011). Relationship and marriage educators are not therapists and should not perceive that their role is to fix people's problems. Participants are there to create solutions for their own problems. Most educators are familiar with the issues of their participants, but also need training to enhance their competence in interacting with them. A relationship and marriage educator needs certain skills, such as making connections between partners, empathizing and validating feelings, staying real and specific (define problem issues so that the couple has something concrete to grasp), exploring different points of view, and recognizing cultural differences. There is increasing emphasis on *facilitation alliance*, which is the connection between the facilitator and program participants, and its impact on program outcomes (Ketring et al., 2017; Quirk et al., 2014). It is important that educators or facilitators be genuine, caring, respectful, and positive, as well as realistic role models. Gender may also be an issue. Some participants, especially men, may respond differently to a male or female educator, so having a male-female team of co-educators is recommended (Ketring et al., 2017). A male-female team should respect each other as equals and be role models for the attitudes, skills, and behaviors being advocated within the program.

The quality of leaders or facilitators is a major key to the success of a relationship and marriage education program, especially with low-income participants. Qualities of relationship and marriage educators or facilitators, which may relate to their personality and training, include individuals who are:

- able to manage group dynamics and handle any negative energy, individuals, or couples who want to monopolize the sessions;
- committed, dependable, prepared, and punctual;
- creative and able to enhance the curriculum through materials and activities;

- energetic and engaging over multiple sessions;
- aware that adults have different learning styles;
- open, honest, and self-aware, as well as able to connect and empathize with participants;
- respectful of boundaries, able to establish ground rules, and keep participants focused on skill building and not problem sharing/solving;
- able to deal with issues and people with a sense of humor; and
- humble about the personal acquisition of skills being a work in progress that continues to evolve (NHMRC, 2007).

While various professionals serve as relationship and marriage educators, some states have laws that indicate who can provide marriage education within specific settings. For example, in Florida individuals electing to participate in premarital education in order to receive a discount on their marriage license need to choose from certain qualified instructors including a licensed psychologist, clinical social worker, marriage and family therapist, mental health counselor, an official representative of a religious institution, or other providers, such as school counselors who are certified to offer these courses (Florida Statutes, 2009). Because each state has different policies regarding whom they perceive as qualified to teach premarital and marriage education courses, attention needs to be given within individual states to promote Certified Family Life Educators for this important role.

Settings for Relationship and Marriage Education

Government initiatives

One of the primary government initiatives for RME is the *Healthy Marriage and Responsible Fatherhood* (HMRF) initiative which is a multimillion-dollar grant program conducted by the Office of Family Assistance. The goal of the program is to promote healthy relationships and marriages, and to strengthen positive father-child interaction (OFA, n.d.). Funding falls under three categories (1) Family, Relationships, and Marriage Education (FRAMEWorks) which funds RME for adult participants; (2) Fatherhood Family-focused, Interconnected, Resilient, and Essential (Fatherhood FIRE) which funds programs promoting responsible fatherhood; and (3) Relationship, Education, Advancement, and Development for Youth for Life (READY4Life) which funds RME for youth ages 14–24 (OFA, n.d.). This funding has resulted in multiple educational initiatives across the country and has helped to build the evidence base for RME.

In many states, legislators and governors have also become involved in efforts to promote premarital education, relationship education in high schools, and covenant marriage. For example, three states (Arizona, Arkansas, and Louisiana) have passed covenant marriage laws to strengthen the marriage bond by promoting premarital education/counseling and making divorce more difficult to obtain (NHMRC, 2010). Only a small percentage of couples (1–3%) choose this controversial option.

COMMUNITY MARRIAGE INITIATIVES

Over the past two decades there has been an explosion of community-based initiatives in marriage education programs and family professionals have become partners in many community initiatives. Often when there are perceived difficulties in marriages and families at local, state, and national levels, various elements of the community, such as business, government, education, and clergy take the initiative to improve marriages and the lives of family members. Some of these nationally visible programs and their goals include (1) *First Things First*, to strengthen families and increase involvement of fathers with their children; (2) the *Oklahoma Marriage Initiative*, to reduce the divorce rate and strengthen families; (3) *Healthy Relationships California*, to teach couples and individuals communication and conflict-management skills with classes available in English, Spanish, Chinese, and Korean; (4) *Stronger Families*, to facilitate life-changing opportunities for couples and families by promoting healthy and loving relationships and providing support at each stage of the marital journey; and (5) *Marriage Savers*, to preserve, strengthen, and restore marriages. There is no one specific plan for individual programs, as they are dependent on the needs of the population, resources available, and expectations of those organizing the program. No single type of organization (e.g., nonprofit, for-profit, education, faith-based, military) is the best option for providing relationship and marriage education, as each has strengths and weaknesses. Therefore, programs that create collaborative partnerships with community-based service providers have an advantage with recruitment, which is essential for voluntary programs (Hawkins & Ooms, 2010). Community marriage initiatives hold considerable promise for the future. Further information on programs in communities in your area can be obtained by contacting the National Association for Relationship and Marriage Education (NARME, www.narme.org).

The Cooperative Extension Service (CES) is another resource for community-based programming. Created by the US Congress, CES has a long history of community-based involvement in family life education and has developed research-based resources in marriage and couples education including fact sheets and programs. More information and resources can be found by visiting the National Extension Relationship and Marriage Education Network (www.NERMEN.org).

ACADEMIC INITIATIVES

High schools and colleges often provide RME programs for their students, with programs for adolescents becoming more frequent as a prevention approach to strengthen current relationships and future marriages. Research indicates that adolescents from diverse backgrounds are interested in relationship education and their intention to access relationship enhancement services in the future increases after participation in a relationship education program (Bradford et al., 2014). Relationship education may be offered to adolescents in middle and high school through family and consumer sciences or health education classes. However, both *nonformal* youth development programs, as well as *formal* relationship education classes should be considered as important delivery options. Offering relationship education programs to younger adolescents who are in middle school can be beneficial in helping them to develop healthy relationship practices at the time that they are starting to explore dating relationships (Futris, Sutton, & Duncan, 2017).

Some examples of programs for youth include *Love U2: Increasing Your Relationship Smarts* (Futris, Sutton, & Duncan, 2017) and *Relationship Smarts Plus* (*RS+*) (Chan et al., 2016). A recent meta-analysis examined 15 studies on youth relationship education programs and found that, overall, these programs are improving basic relationship skills including conflict management and are helping young people to form more realistic attitudes and expectations for romantic relationships (McElwain, McGill, & Savasuk-Luxton, 2017).

College students may have certain advantages, such as education and income, but they experience multiple relationships issues (romantic and nonromantic) that can cause considerable levels of distress (Darling et al., 2007). Various colleges and universities offer academic courses to prepare students to find compatible partners, face challenges, and experience greater relationship satisfaction (Nielsen et al., 2004). Focusing on college students can be constructive, because they are more likely to have some dating experience, are nearing the age when they will seek a life partner, can have more open discussions of sexuality without parental concerns, and have not necessarily begun selecting a partner because marriage is not imminent.

Religious or spiritual initiatives

Relationship, premarital, and marriage education is frequently offered within religious or spiritual communities. In the past, couples often went for an appointment with a clergyperson prior to their wedding ceremony. Whether it was one visit or a few, clergy were often the only persons engaged in guiding new couples in their transition into marriage. The Catholic Church has a long history of premarital education and typically requires all couples getting married in the Catholic Church to participate in such programming (Klausli & Gross, 2021). In addition to communication skills and other content directly related to relationship enhancement, premarital programs delivered within a religious institution often incorporate theology or religion-specific content, such as teaching natural family planning in Catholic-sponsored programs (Klausli & Gross, 2021). However, more programs in other religious settings have developed over the years. *A Lasting Promise: Christian PREP for Couples* is one such program that incorporates Christian teachings about relationships and marriage while integrating research on marriage and relationships. It focuses on teaching couples how to communicate effectively; solve problems; manage conflicts; and preserve and enhance love, commitment, and friendship (prepinc.com/collections/christian-material).

Military initiatives

The military has recognized that the well-being of their soldiers is influenced by the quality of their home life, especially when military couples are at high risk for marital problems that are exacerbated by deployments and combat. Over the past decade, PREP was widely used with married couples in all branches of the military. An adaptation of the PREP entitled *Strong Bonds* was implemented by Army chaplains. Evaluation studies indicated that marriage education has been well received by military couples and can reduce the risk of divorce for those couples completing the program (Stanley et al., 2010). Military couples showed reductions in negative communications and gains in overall confidence in the future of their relationships. Using trained Army chaplains was particularly effective, as they were known and trusted by the couples and could adapt the educational program to their participants with culturally appropriate examples and stories. After deployment, marriage education programs need to help couples renegotiate their relationship, as they may be struggling with communication, balancing responsibilities, decision-making in the relationship, or other mental health problems such as post-traumatic stress disorder (PTSD) or brain injuries (Krill, 2010).

Strategies for Relationship and Marriage Education

There are many organizations providing relationship and marriage education. Whereas some participants may prefer to go to a faith-based institution or school in their vicinity, others may reject going to either of these locations based on negative past experiences. Thus, having seminars and programs in the community, work place, health care centers, or military settings may be helpful in reaching participants who might not engage in marriage education in more traditional settings. On the other hand, while having RME programs on military bases may be convenient, at times soldiers and their spouses or families prefer to go off the base for privacy reasons.

Effective, flexible delivery of relationship education is recommended. Some couples prefer face-to-face relationship education because they value group interaction, whereas others may prefer modes that are more convenient or private, such as online courses, DVDs, and self-directed materials (Duncan & Rogers, 2019; Halford et al., 2004). Relationship and marriage educators need to be flexible and open to find the best educational settings and delivery modes within the societal context of their communities. Even before the COVID-19 pandemic resulted in programs moving to an online or virtual format, online relationship and marriage education programs were becoming more available (Stanley et al., 2020).

RME can occur in individual, dyadic, group, or mass settings. Whether through public awareness spots on television, online courses, or community resource centers, the potential to reach a large number of participants can shape values, attitudes, and behaviors that promote healthy marriages. Teaching strategies should be varied to meet the needs and learning styles of participants. While some may prefer lectures, others value discussion or experiential learning activities. Depending on the culture and age of the audience, some may not want to engage in self-disclosure. Thus, culturally aware educators will need to talk to community members to learn how to best integrate participants' needs into their curriculum. After completion of the program, various modes of contact may be required to sustain the learning that occurred. Using email or social media with participants may facilitate ongoing contact, sharing, and support. There are multiple designs and methods for marriage preparation and enrichment programs that integrate a variety of strategies.

Following a review of implementation research, Briggs, Scott, and Logan (2021) offered these strategies for relationship education for couples:

- Encourage reflection on the relationship and provide practical relationship tools.
- Provide social opportunities with other couples.
- Include case management or family support coaching as a way to create a space for couples to work as a team and practice new relationship skills.
- Recognize that programs for couples need different strategies to recruit, retain, and engage participants than do programs focused on individuals.
- Consider couples' unique strengths and needs to ensure that programming is tailored to your participants.
- Recognize the diversity of the couples served, particularly around sexual orientation, and assess the cultural appropriateness of program content and facilitator training.
- Engage in additional training related to working with couples and managing safety concerns related to interpersonal violence.

CULTURE

Culture should be considered within the context of relationship and marriage education. Marriages or partnerships exist in all societies, in some form, but while it is mainstream in the United States, it may be quite different in other cultures. By exploring the role of culture, not only can different values be found, but a critical examination can also be initiated about how these values influence behaviors, including those in relationships. Globally, many dimensions of marriage and family life have changed over the past century. There has been an increase in the age of marriage, children's involvement in mate selection, premarital sex, and contraceptive use. Fertility rates have declined along with changing relationships between women and men.

People around the world marry for many reasons, including legal, social, emotional, financial, spiritual, and religious. While some cultures place a primary emphasis on the marital bond, others value the parent-child bond. Love, dating, marriage, and divorce vary in different cultures based on religion, as well as patriarchal or matriarchal traditions. While research on other cultural groups is important, we should not draw unwarranted conclusions about individuals based on their group membership. Cultural insight comes from awareness of individual differences within social constructs. Using an ecosystems approach to examine marriages and marital quality can facilitate understanding the systems related to one's individual context, couple context, family background, and sociocultural context (Darling & Turkki, 2009; Duncan, Holman, & Yang, 2007). (See Chapter 8 on the Family Ecosystems Framework.)

Culture is an important source of information about the value of relationships and marriage. Our American culture both values and devalues marriage in several ways. Although our value of marriage may be indicated by a majority of

Americans eventually marrying, there is also a growing number of individuals who have chosen singlehood as a viable lifestyle, as well as couples who cohabit as an alternative to marriage. In addition, many marriages end in divorce. While many couples spend a considerable amount of time, effort, and money on weddings, much less time and energy are spent on preparing for the actual marriage. Often there is a belief that "love conquers all," but certain skills are also needed to maintain a healthy relationship.

■ SUMMARY

As noted by the 5 Cs of Relationship and Marriage Education Model, there are many factors that influence the design and implementation of relationship and marriage education (RME) programs, including knowledge of the consumers, content, changes, context, and culture. While the glamour and excitement of getting married may occupy the thoughts of couples planning for a wedding, working to establish a healthy and stable marriage before and after the ceremony is an important goal. There are several RME programs that can help provide the knowledge and skills needed to sustain a happy and satisfying marriage. RME can empower individuals and couples to form healthy relationships and maintain stable families for the well-being of adults, children, and communities. People may get divorced thinking that they chose the wrong partner, but then remarry and find themselves facing the same problems, but now with a different partner. Thus, it is important to understand the influence of demographic factors and stages of the life cycle, along with personal and relational contexts, individual traits, and couple traits. As cultural influences and the needs and circumstances in life evolve, staying attuned to changes in individuals, relationships, and their environments is critical. Saying "I do" is just the beginning as couple relationships involve a continual process of becoming "us."

■ QUESTIONS AND ISSUES FOR DISCUSSION

1. What are people at your stage of the life looking for in relationships?
2. What can universities, communities, faith communities, and health care centers do to motivate individuals and couples to participate in relationship and marriage education?
3. What other settings could be used to provide relationship and marriage education?
4. Why is it important to have a trained leader for relationship and marriage education programs? Is having a satisfactory marriage sufficient?
5. How would you select a good time to communicate about sensitive issues with a partner? What factors would you consider and what time would you suggest?
6. What messages about marriage, love, and dating are portrayed in the media?
7. What are the laws in your state regarding marriage and divorce? Are there any initiatives for changing these laws?
8. What kinds of messages, traditions, and rituals will you take from your family of origin into your marriage relationship?

9. What are some issues couples might encounter in "Peer Marriages," "Alone Together Marriages," and "Living Apart Relationships"?

ACTIVITIES

1. Invite a panel of engaged couples to class who have participated in premarital education to share their experience and how it influenced their relationship.
2. Invite a panel of couples at different stages of the life cycle to share what is important in relationships.
3. Discuss with a partner your feelings about a current event, an important event from your childhood, and a future goal about which you feel passionate. What did you learn about your partner from sharing these thoughts?

WEB RESOURCES

Marriage Strengthening Research and Dissemination Center (MAST Center)
www.mastresearchcenter.org
The MAST Center conducts research on marriage and romantic relationships in the US and healthy marriage and relationship education (HMRE) programs designed to strengthen these relationships. This research aims to identify critical research gaps, generate new knowledge, and help programs more effectively serve the individuals and families with whom they work. MAST Center research is concentrated in two areas: (1) relationship patterns and trends and (2) program implementation and evaluation.

National Association for Relationship and Marriage Education (NARME)
www.narme.org
NARME is a national association formed to represent the interests and serve the needs of relationship, marriage, and family educators by providing ongoing professional training; hosting an annual conference featuring best practices in the field; disseminating timely and relevant research; facilitating collaboration among healthy marriage, responsible fatherhood, and other family allies; and supporting public policy that strengthens families.

National Extension Relationship and Marriage Education Network (NERMEN)
www.nermen.org
NERMEN provides research-based resources and promotes partnerships to advance the knowledge and practice in relationship and marriage education. It constitutes a nationwide outreach through Extension specialists and educators in partnership with agencies and organizations at the national, state, and community levels that support individuals and couples preparing for, developing, and enriching healthy relationships and healthy marriages.

National Healthy Marriage Resource Center (NHMRC)
www.healthymarriageinfo.org
NHMRC is a clearinghouse for high quality, balanced, and timely information and resources on healthy marriage. The NHMRC's mission is to be a first stop

for information, resources, and training on healthy marriage for experts, researchers, policy makers, media, marriage educators, couples and individuals, program providers, and others.

Smart Marriages

www.smartmarriages.com

Smart Marriages: The Coalition for Marriage, Family, and Couples Education is a special interest group whose members believe that family breakdown can be reduced through education and information. Smart Marriages facilitates a network of marriage professionals that constitutes a coalition for marriage, family, and couples education. Their website contains an archive of the coalition's newsletters, a directory of programming resources, advocacy information, and general articles and information.

■ RESOURCES: PREMARITAL AND MARITAL ASSESSMENT QUESTIONNAIRES

Couple Checkup

www.couplecheckup.com

Couple Checkup is an online couple assessment tool for marriage and relationship enrichment, which can be used alone or in combination with enrichment books, seminars, or marriage retreats. It is a scientifically based assessment that identifies relationship strengths and weaknesses across key relationship areas, including communication, conflict resolution, financial management, relationship roles, affection and sexual relationships, couple closeness and flexibility, family closeness and flexibility, and personality.

PREPARE/ENRICH (Premarital Preparation and Relationship Enhancement)

www.prepare-enrich.com

PREPARE/ENRICH is a customized couple assessment completed online that identifies a couple's strength and growth areas. It is one of the most widely used programs for premarital counseling and premarital education. It is also used for marriage counseling, marriage enrichment, and dating couples considering engagement. Based on a couple's assessment results, a trained facilitator provides 4–8 feedback sessions in which the facilitator helps the couple discuss and understand their results as they are taught proven relationship skills.

RELATE (Relationship Evaluation Questionnaire)

www.relatefoundation.com

RELATE is a comprehensive relationship assessment questionnaire. It is specifically designed to help guide couples to have meaningful discussions about criteria proven to affect relationship satisfaction.

11

Approaches to Parenting Education

> It's 3 a.m. and your 3-week-old son has been crying and fussing since 11 p.m. You have fed him, changed him, and rocked him. You are out of ideas and patience. What does he need?
>
> Your childcare provider pulls you aside and informs you that your 3-year-old has been biting the other children. Is this normal? Why is she doing it? What can you do to stop it?
>
> Your 13-year-old has started to come home after his curfew. He has become sullen and uncommunicative. When he does talk to you, it is usually with disrespect or annoyance. The more you push him, the more he pulls away. What can you do to best deal with the situation?
>
> Your daughter has just started her first year of college at a school 500 miles away. How involved should you be in her daily life? Is it OK to text her every day?

How does a parent best respond to these situations? Are there books that have all the answers, or do parents just "know" what to do? Can you take a class to learn how to be a better parent?

The Importance of Parents and Parenting Education

Being a parent is one of the hardest jobs in the world. Imagine seeing this job description in the paper:

> Wanted: Caregiver to rear one or more children from birth to maturity. The job is a seven-day-a-week, twenty-four-hour-a-day position. No salary or benefits, such as sick or holiday pay and no retirement plan. The caregiver must supply all living expenses for self and children, and in the event of any absence, even for a few minutes with younger children, must supply substitute care. There is no opportunity to meet child or children in advance of taking the position to determine compatibility. Person must provide emotional support, physical care, clean laundry, nutritious food, assistance with school work, and chauffeuring duties. Motivation for the job and satisfaction in it must come from within the applicant, as neither children nor society regularly express gratitude and appreciation. (Adapted from Brooks, 2011)

Despite the challenges, parenting can be one of life's most rewarding experiences, but the knowledge and skills needed for good parenting do not necessarily come naturally. Most parents do not instinctively know how to be a parent or what to do when it comes to discipline, nurturing, toilet training, adolescent mood swings, or any of the many other issues that arise through the child-rearing years. Societal changes have made it more difficult to rely on parenting techniques from the past. The rapid pace at which these changes occur leave children facing issues their parents never imagined. Fortunately, today's parents have the benefit of unprecedented access to parenting resources and supports. There is ample research identifying what children and parents need for optimal development and demonstrating the effectiveness of parent education in supporting and influencing child and parent wellbeing (Morris et al., 2020; National Academies of Sciences, Engineering, and Medicine, 2016). Parenting education can help build the skills of parents. Parents have multiple options for accessing parenting information including books, in-person and online classes, websites, and mobile apps.

Parents have tremendous influence on a child's cognitive, social, emotional, and physical development, making parenting education all the more important. "Children are affected by who their parents *are* (e.g., gender, age, race/ethnicity, intelligence, education levels, temperament); what parents *know* (e.g., child development, normative child behavior); what parents *believe* (e.g., attitudes toward child rearing); what parents *value* (e.g., education, achievement, obedience, interpersonal relationships); what parents *expect* of their children (e.g., age/developmentally appropriate expectations for behavior, achievement expectations); and what parents ultimately *do* (e.g., parenting practices, overall parenting styles) (McGroder & Hyra, 2009). Family characteristics and parenting in the first years of life (including sensitive caregiving, lack of harsh parenting) have been shown to predict prosocial behavior in first grade, with the estimated effects of parenting intersecting with the effects of warm and responsive caregiving in early child care (Brownell & Drummond, 2020).

Parental behavior is directly correlated with outcomes for children (Morris et al., 2017; Reeves & Howard, 2013). Parents who score high on measures of both warmth and control have children who are happier and more competent (Baumrind, 1991). Children are more socially skilled later in life if they have secure attachments to their parents in infancy (Sroufe, 2016). Society benefits from parenting education as well. Effective parenting education programs can provide economic benefits in the form of lower health care costs and tax saving by reducing the need for remedial education and social programs, while increasing productivity provided by a better-prepared workforce (Sampaio et al., 2017).

Federal, state, and local agencies often fund parenting education programs as a way to strengthen families and prevent costly and undesirable outcomes such as child abuse and neglect. The Substance Abuse and Mental Health Services Administration (SAMHSA) funds many family strengthening programs as a way to prevent substance abuse and mental health problems. A review of the Strengthening Families Program (SFP) found significant improvements in youth's behavioral health, including 50% reduction in substance misuse, depression/anxiety, and child maltreatment. Culturally adapted SFP versions have improved family relations and children's behavioral health in 36 countries (Kumpfer & Magalhães, 2018). Similarly, the Office of Juvenile Justice and Delinquency Prevention (OJJDP) invests in parenting education as a way to prevent delinquency (McGroder & Hyra, 2009). These efforts are centered on the prevention of undesirable outcomes. While this is certainly a needed approach, it is important that attention and funding also be provided to programs and approaches that focus on primary prevention and the promotion of positive parenting practices. The primary prevention approach will be discussed in more detail later in the chapter.

Societal Changes and Impacts

The rapidly changing pace of today's society has caused modern-day parents to face challenges unparalleled in previous generations, increasing the need for various types of parenting education. Parenting is more stressful than it was for previous generations (Nomaguchi & Milkie, 2020). Therefore, parenting education needs to shift in response to stressors and also to demographic trends such as delayed childbearing, increased mobility, and co-parenting (Ballard et al., 2018). There are greater influences on children that originate from outside of the home. The media is filled with images of sex and violence and promotes a culture that glorifies celebrity and beauty. Families are impacted by unemployment, substance abuse, and domestic violence. Parents also find themselves seeking guidance on how to explain terrorism and random violence to children following events like school shootings, police brutality, killings of Black individuals, attacks on Asians, and the 2021 US Capitol attack.

Changing demographics have revealed other needs; increasing numbers of grandparents are raising their grandchildren during a time intended for retirement. The mobile nature of our society means that families are more likely to live away from extended family members, which weakens their support network. Work–life balance continues to be a struggle, particularly during the COVID-19 pandemic where many parents teleworked and many children attended school remotely from home. Given all these challenges, it is important to understand the changing demographics and characteristics of the US population and its implications for parent education.

Demographics of Today's Families

In the United States, children aged 0–17 represent almost 22% of the population (ChildStats.gov, 2021). Approximately 67% of these children live with two married parents, while 4% live with their unmarried cohabitating parents. Whereas 21% of the children reside with only their mothers and 5% only their fathers, 4% live with neither of their parents. Of those not living with their parents, most lived with their grandparents (54%) followed by other relatives (22%) and nonrelatives (25%) (ChildStats.gov, 2021). Approximately 6 million children and adults have an LGBTQ+ parent (Gates, 2015).

The racial/ethnic composition of children in the US is 50% White, 26% Hispanic, 14% Black, 5% Asian, 4% more than one race, and 1% Indigenous (Annie E. Casey Foundation, 2020b). The number of children with at least one foreign-born parent rose to 25% in 2020 from 15% in 1994 (ChildStats.gov, 2021). In 2019, 17% of all children aged 0–17 lived in poverty, reflecting little change from 22% in 2010 (Annie E. Casey Foundation, 2020c). In 91% of families with children, at least one parent was employed (US Bureau of Labor Statistics, 2019). These statistics reflect the changing face of America's families. The discussion of family life education audiences in Chapter 3 speaks to the need for family life educators to know and understand the life circumstances and needs of those participating in their programs.

Societal Trends

Parents have always had questions about typical parenting issues, such as child development, discipline and guidance, limit-setting, building self-esteem, health, communication skills, academic achievement, managing work and family, family systems, family transitions, conflict resolution, and parenting children with special needs, but they are also impacted by new and emerging issues that draw media attention and influence culture. It is important for parents to stay attuned to changing issues and trends that influence their children. The press is full of stories about such issues as cyberbullying (e.g., Suciu, 2021), binge drinking (e.g., Murez, 2021), and effects of the COVID-19 pandemic on children's mental health (e.g., Howley, 2021). Some of the more prominent issues in the media today include technology and social media, the issue of indulgent parenting, and fatherhood.

Technology and social media

Technology is revolutionizing family life and became even more influential during the COVID-19 pandemic. As of 2021, 97% of Americans have a cell phone, 85% have smartphones, and 53% of American adults own a tablet computer (Pew Research Center, 2021). Technology and media have impacted both the sources and methods that parents use when seeking advice and how they parent. Parents who are internet and social media users turn to social media sites and online communities, with 40% of parents getting advice from parenting websites or blogs, 29% turning to social media sites, and 19% getting information from online message boards (Auxier et al., 2020).

Parents not only have to manage their own relationship with the internet and mobile devices, but also have to supervise their children's use of and exposure to the same technology. This brings both benefits and challenges. Two-thirds of parents say that parenting is harder today than 20 years ago, with technologies like social media and smartphones being cited as the reason (Auxier et al., 2020). Parents have to cope with both the increased use of technology, the rapid changes in technology, and financial constraints that are hard to manage. A majority of parents (68%) report being distracted by their phones while with their children. In contrast, a small group of parents (9%) indicate that parenting is easier than it was 20 years ago because there is more information and advice for parents and it is easier to keep track of their children. Parents also report the practice of "sharenting," or posting things about their children on social media. While 76% report being able to share information with family and friends as a major reason why they post, 18% do not share things about their children mostly because of privacy-related issues.

Parents have long had mixed feelings about screen time and in what ways it affects children; however, the definition of screen time has expanded beyond television and computers to include gaming systems, smartphones, e-readers, and tablets. While parents recognize that the internet and smartphones can help their children access information and connect to others, they express concern regarding the material to which children are exposed and the fact that online activity results in less face-to-face interaction (Wartella, 2014). There is also concern for children's health and safety, fitness and nutrition, connection with nature, and social and emotional skills in relation to their technology use (Wartella, 2014). However, the COVID-19 pandemic and the resulting dependency on technology for work, school, and social connection intensified parental concerns and forced them to disregard previous screen time rules. For many, COVID-19 exacerbated the digital divide. Families often had multiple demands that didn't match the number of computers in the household or their bandwidth was taxed in order to meet the technology needs of all family members who required computer and internet access for school and work responsibilities.

Parents report that they get screen time advice from doctors or other medical professionals or other parents but guidance on the amount of screen time or the harmful effects of media exposure has never been clear. As the digital landscape has expanded, parents have found themselves asking more nuanced questions such as what age their child should get their own smartphone, join social media, or even if reading an e-textbook is the same as reading a print textbook. There are no clear-cut answers to these questions and parents cannot simply get rid of technology and "screens" in the home. The need for and benefits of technology are great and are an integral part of our society. It is important for parents to learn how to help their children balance screen time with opportunities for face-to-face connection, starting with being a good role model for screen use (Hirsh-Pasek, Evans, & Golinkoff, 2019).

Technology will continue to have a major impact on family life and the parent-child relationship. Therefore, parenting education can provide needed resources and support to help families avoid the pitfalls and take advantage of all that technology has to offer.

INDULGENT PARENTING

Today's parents increasingly practice indulgent parenting, a phenomenon that has received ongoing media attention from news outlets like *Forbes*, *NBC News*, *The New York Times*, and *USA Today* (e.g., Braff, 2020; Francis, 2019; Haller, 2018; Robinson, 2020). Parents indulge their children by giving material goods, attention, and freedom to do what they want and when they want to do it, causing problems for many adolescents. Examples include parents who have been observed ghostwriting homework for their children, making extracurricular decisions for them, preparing application materials for college, arguing with teachers and professors over poor grades, interfering with children's friendship and roommate disputes, and accompanying their children to job interviews. A current parenting issue related to indulgence involves remote learning and the balance between supporting children versus hovering over them as they attempt to learn and helping them with their every move (Braff, 2020). A newsworthy example includes a teenager who killed four people while driving under the influence of alcohol arguing it was not his fault because his parents never said "no" (Amos, 2013). Another example is the "Varsity Blues" scandal in which parents paid money to facilitate their children's admission to college (Joyce, 2019). This parenting behavior undermines the self-efficacy of both their children and other students who were denied admission.

This trend has evolved for various reasons—having fewer numbers of children allows families to provide increased resources for their children; working parents feel guilty about spending less time with their children; parents' own history with indulgence; and the influence of consumerism, media, community, and other people (Cui, Hong, Darling, Janhonen-Abruquah, 2019; Rehm et al., 2017). Moreover, parents with marital difficulties often try to gain an advantage with their spouses or compensate for their divorce/separation by indulging their children.

Parental indulgence has a variety of names including overparenting, helicopter parenting, invasive parenting, hover parenting, concierge parenting, and lawn mower parenting. Although parental indulgence has sometimes been referred to as "over indulgence," in reality indulgence is a continuum with no demarcation between indulgence and overindulgence (Coccia et al., 2012). Indulgent parenting is not limited to the US, since this behavior is noted in Scandinavia as "curling parents" (Hougaard, 2004). Just like the Olympic sport of curling, curling parents sweep obstacles out of the path of their children to make the surface smooth so they can slide to their achieved goal unimpeded. Overparenting exists in other cultures with some cultural differences and similarities. For example, in Finland, a country that encourages independence, helicopter parenting of young adults is not as prominent as in the US. However, in both countries helicopter parenting is related to young adults' depression and life dissatisfaction (Cui, Janhonen-Abruquah, Darling, Chavez, & Palojoki, 2019).

Parental indulgence can be categorized into three types (Clarke, Dawson, & Bredehoft, 2014; Cui, Graber, Metz, & Darling, 2019). *Material indulgence* occurs when parents provide too many things, including time, food, entertainment, or experiences. *Relational indulgence* results from parents who do things for their children that they should do for themselves and are overly protective so that they interfere with opportunities for developing competence or solving problems. *Behavioral indulgence* arises when parents set few expectations for responsible behaviors, fail to enforce rules, teach few skills, or expect too few chores. Thus, parental indulgence is multifaceted, complicated, and more nuanced than the extreme cases highlighted in the news (Wolford et al., 2020).

Adolescents who have been indulged report greater life stress (e.g., irritations, difficulties, and events beyond their control). Although these children are not "at risk" like those who experience harsh parenting, indulgent parenting could be detrimental in other ways that may prevent learning critical skills (e.g., self-regulation) for future competence (Rehm, Darling, Coccia, & Cui, 2017). For example, adolescents who experienced greater parental indulgence were more likely to have unhealthy eating behaviors, such as eating anything they want, having greater fast food intake, and having reduced intuitive food intake which was related to greater fat intake (Coccia et al., 2012; Perez et al., 2018).

While a majority of parents mean well, indulgence does active harm and/or prevents individuals from developing self-efficacy and achieving their full potential. Individuals who have been indulged as children have experienced a range of feelings such as love, confusion, guilt, sadness, and anxiety due to feeling they did not learn how to manage certain tasks or make good decisions in comparison with peers who were not indulged (Clarke, Dawson, & Bredehoft, 2014). Whereas youth may feel satisfaction at the time they are indulged, it can be damaging to their well-being over time, specifically in relation to stress and overall health, as early experiences with stress facilitate the ability to handle stress later in life (Boss, Bryant, & Mancini, 2017). Indulgent parenting in childhood and adolescence has been associated with helicopter parenting in emerging adulthood. As a result, parental indulgence and helicopter parenting can affect college students' mental and behavioral health resulting in anxiety, depression, and life dissatisfaction (Cui, Darling, Coccia, Fincham, & May, 2019; Cui, Darling, Lucier-Greer, Fincham, & May, 2018; Cui, Janhonen-Abruquah, Darling, Chavez, & Palojoki, 2018).

Parental indulgence involves various contradictions and paradoxes. While parents have not generally been indulged, they now indulge their children in a number of ways: lack of rules and daily health routines, few expectations to contribute to household chores, giving in to demands, and solving problems for adolescents rather than allowing them to take responsibility (Rehm et al., 2017). By providing their children with many resources, parents experience increased gratification, while also seeing their children experience satisfaction, but this indulgence can have long-term problematic effects for both parents and children (Veldorale-Griffin et al., 2013). The disproportionate investment of parental emotions, finances, and time devoted to one's children can erode marital bonds and contribute to the potential for divorce. Emotional experiences are often shaped by parents' own perceptions that parenting needs to be effective, but vulnerability occurs when faced with distractions in the family due to internal pressures such as marital disruptions and external stresses of social norms and cultural expectations (Wolford et al., 2020). It can also lead to a destructive culture of parenting that reaches into many societal institutions (Marano, 2008). Overall, parental indulgence is complicated and has important implications for families and children.

Fatherhood

About 6 out of 10 men in the United States are fathers and 46% of fathers have at least one child under the age of 18 (US Census Bureau, 2018a). There has also been an increase in solo fathers with 4% of all children now living with a father only (Livingston, 2018a). Fathers are clearly important in children's lives. Research shows the important contributions that fathers make in children's lives, and in turn, being a father can improve men's well-being (Karberg, Finocharo, & Vann, 2019). Yet, fathers have traditionally been excluded from many parenting education programs. It is important to make sure that parenting education programming is inclusive of both mothers *and* fathers. In addition to including fathers in general parenting education, in recent years there has been an increase in programs that focus specifically on fathers. This increase largely is a result of a national fatherhood initiative with widespread government and community-based support for fatherhood programs that promote positive involvement of fathers with their children.

Fatherhood programs typically fall into three categories: (1) economic support, (2) father involvement, and (3) co-parenting (Fagan & Kaufman, 2015). Many fathers that participate in fatherhood programs may not live with their children. Some of these programs focus on nonresidential fathers in general, but others may have a specific focus such as low-income parenting issues. Fatherhood programs that focus on economic support as a type of care and include work and educational opportunities might be particularly effective with low income fathers (Randles, 2020). Overall, research indicates that fatherhood programs are somewhat effective in reaching desired outcomes, but more research should be conducted.

Definitions and Assumptions

Before moving to the history and practice of parenting education, a discussion of the definition of parenting education is needed. Parent education can be defined as "a service to parents with the goal of improving parenting skills, the parent-child relationship, and communication with children" (Morris et al., 2020, p. 521). Another definition of parenting education provided by the National Parenting Education Network (NPEN) states:

> Parenting education is a process of providing knowledge and skills that parents need to fulfill their role. Parents learn how to establish and maintain a close, nurturing, emotional bond with their children and to foster healthy cognitive, physical, and social/emotional development in their children, teaching the information and skills that children need to thrive. (NPEN, n.d.)

According to NPEN, parents include "key persons who play the central, parenting role in a child's life." This definition recognizes many adults who care for children to whom they are not legally or biologically related.

Assumptions About Parenting Education

Parenting education is influenced by certain assumptions that expand the definitions of parenting education and help to clarify the overall goals of parent education. Assumptions influence the content included in parenting education programs and can also impact how the content is taught or addressed. The following parent education assumptions are adapted from the NPEN model (Smith et al., 1994) and by Campbell and Palm (2018):

- Parents care about their children and want to be good parents.
- Parents are the primary socializers of their children.
- Parenting is a learned skill and parenting education can positively influence attitudes, knowledge, skills, and behaviors.
- All parents have strengths and parent education should build on these strengths.
- Parenting education can effectively address both parent and child needs.
- Parenting education should be respectful and responsive to diverse contexts and cultures.
- All parents can benefit from parent education.
- Effective parenting education may be accomplished by a variety of methods.
- Parenting education is more effective when parents are active participants in and contributors to their parenting education programs.

Brief History of Parenting Education

With these definitions of parenting education in mind, let us review a brief history of parenting education in the United States. Parenting education in the US has some of its earliest roots in the colonial period, when church and state shared the goal of influencing parents to raise their children according to religious mandates (Schlossman, 1976). It can be traced back to fields as diverse as medicine, social work, home economics, education, and psychology. Below is a brief timeline highlighting the progression of parenting education.

- The first magazines for mothers were published in the 1800s such as *Mother's Magazine* in 1832 and *Mother's Assistant* in 1841 (Croake & Glover, 1977).
- In 1897, women gathered at the first National Congress of Mothers, a nationwide parent-education organization known later as the Parent Teacher Association, or PTA (Schlossman, 1976). The PTA grew from that first meeting to an organization of 60,000 members in 1915 to more than 4 million members in 2021. The focus of the PTA shifted through the years to the current mission to "make every child's potential a reality by engaging and empowering families and communities to advocate for all children" (National PTA, n.d.).
- The Child Study Association of America initiated the National Council of Parent Education in 1925, which contributed to the development of instructional materials and sponsored the first university course in parenting education at Teachers College, Columbia, Missouri, in 1925.
- In the mid-1920s the American Home Economics Association began to include parenting education in its educational and lobbying interests. These initial efforts focused on poor families and those considered to be in need (Carter, 1996).
- Following the 1930 White House Conference on Child Health and Protection, a report outlining parent education programs, content, and methods was published in order to guide the growing parenting education movement (Croake & Grover 1977; White House Conference, 1932).
- Benjamin Spock's *Baby and Child Care*, first published in 1946, brought the literature of child care and parenting to the middle class.
- In the 1950s, grassroots parenting groups, such as La Leche League, began to appear and provided parents opportunities to meet with each other. La Leche League is a mother-led group in which women provide support and mentoring with breastfeeding and lactation.
- The federally funded Head Start program, launched in the mid-1960s, acknowledged the value and impact of parents in the education of their children (Carter, 1996). By the 1980s, community-based parenting education programs were joined by state and federally funded programs and a growing number of nonprofit and for-profit organizations.
- The National Extension Parenting Education Model (NEPEM) was developed in 1994 to guide the content needed in parent education programs.
- The National Parenting Education Network (NPEN) evolved from discussions at Wheelock College in 1995 and at the Family Resource Coalition of America conference in 1996. NPEN continues to influence the field of par-

enting education through its work to establish professional standards and competencies, which will be discussed in more detail later in this chapter.

- In 2000, the National Extension Parenting Education Framework (NEPEF) was developed to highlight the process of parenting education.

In summary, parenting education has a long history and has evolved over time. It has moved from informal methods where parents would discuss issues among themselves to more formal methods such as magazines, books, and organizational initiatives. Later various parent education models evolved along with professional standards and competencies for parenting educators.

INCORPORATION OF THEORY

The practice of parenting education is heavily influenced by theory. Theories contribute to our understanding of families and parenting by providing insight and reasonable explanations for individual and family behaviors (see Chapter 8). Theory consists of a set of logically related concepts that seek to describe, explain, and predict behavior within a family and/or parenting context. Many family science students learn about theories in specific courses about theory or when they are incorporated into content-related courses (e.g., family relations, marriage, parenting, child development, sexuality, stress). Therefore, this chapter does not focus on major explanations of theories, but will highlight a few that are relevant to parenting and can provide important frameworks for parenting education programs. Theory can be a guide for our own parenting practices, help us understand our children's behaviors, and enable us to predict outcomes. A key component in parenting theories is the understanding that parents influence children, but also that children can influence parents and that parent socialization strategies are bidirectional (Pardini, 2008). Theories incorporated in parent education classes are often a combination of family theories and child and human development theories, which can integrate various concepts. Family theories such as systems theory, social exchange theory, family development theory, and family stress theory can explain the parent-child relationship in the context of the family.

- *Systems theory* can be used to facilitate understanding boundaries, systems, and subsystems, as well as roles and rules. There is a focus on wholeness (a family is greater than the sum of its parts) and interdependence (what affects one person in a family also influences other members).
- An *ecosystems* approach or *biological ecological* perspective can be used to understand the interaction of various parts of one's ecosystem at different stages of child growth and development. This theory can answer questions about the parent-child relationship taking into consideration other various internal and external systems that interact with the relationship. For example, it can be used to answer the question: What are the roles of parents, peers, schools, childcare workers, employers, culture, and other social systems in the development of children?

- *Social exchange theory* can be used to examine the rewards and costs of having children and parenting them during different stages of their development, such as the rewards and costs of parenting teens with regard to power and independence. Do the rewards of having children outweigh the financial and emotional costs?
- *Family developmental theory* can be used to gain a perspective of individual and family developmental tasks during different stages of the family life cycle, as moving to a different stage is often based on the age of the oldest child. How families are able to handle different life situations depends on whether they are considered "on-time" or "off-time." A situation is considered to be "on-time" if it is consistent with societal views of normal timing, such as graduation from high school. However, an adolescent who becomes pregnant would be considered "off-time."
- *Stress theory* helps people to understand that parents can experience stress that is both *normative* (expected during the lifecycle—e.g., birth of a baby, entering teen years, graduating from high school) and *nonnormative* (unforeseen events or situations—e.g., childhood illness, bullying, substance abuse). See Chapter 8 for further details and references.

Other theories pertinent to parent-child relationships focus on the topics of child-human development and socialization.

- *Piaget's cognitive developmental theory* examines a tendency to create complex cognitive structures or schemes (basic building blocks—organized patterns of thought and behavior to think and act in various situations). Piaget proposed that children adapt to the world and handle information according to two processes—*assimilation* (incorporating new information into existing schemes) and *accommodation* (changing structures to include new information). These steps are balanced through *equilibration*, which is the force that drives the learning process and development. Children have four stages of development: *sensorimotor* (period of rapid growth based on reflexive movements when children use their senses to learn about the world around them); *preoperational* (thinking is intuitive and egocentric, distinguishing between self and the environment using symbols to represent their play and discoveries); *concrete operational* (beginning of logical thought); and *formal operational* (ability to use abstract reasoning) (Phillips, 1981; Piaget, 1950; Piaget & Inhelder, 1969).
- *Erik Erickson's lifespan view of development or psychosocial theory* describes growth as a series of eight stages each with specific physical and psychological needs based on socialization along with a developmental crisis to be met and resolved. These conflicts serve as turning points in the child's development and their capacity to resolve the conflict impacts their ability to develop the specific quality. These stages and the approximate ages include *Basic Trust vs. Mistrust* (0–1); *Autonomy vs. Shame and Doubt* (1–3); *Initiative vs. Guilt* (3–6); *Industry vs. Inferiority* (6–11); *Identity vs. Role Confusion* (adolescence); *Intimacy vs. Isolation* (early adulthood); *Generativity vs. Stagnation* (middle adulthood); *Ego Integrity vs. Despair* (late adulthood) (Erikson, 1950, 1963).

- *Vygotsky's social development theory* suggests that cognitive development occurs through interactions with others and is oriented to the individual's culture and society. There is a *zone of proximal development* (ZPD) in which a child finds a range of tasks too difficult to accomplish alone, but possible with the help of adults or more skilled peers. Using *scaffolding* (similar to ZPD) to help a child learn a new concept helps the child master the task, so the scaffolding can then be removed (Daniels, 1996; Vygotsky, 1978; Wood, Bruner, & Ross, 1976).
- *Attachment theory* examines attachment patterns and a sense of trust that develops with adults who are significant to the child's life. Attachment is thought to be a lasting connectedness between individuals with the infant/caregiver relationship providing the basis for these relationships. There are four types of attachment: *secure, resistant, avoidant*, and *disorganized/disoriented*. The attachment relationship is essential to the child's subsequent cognitive and socioemotional development that will affect their relationships throughout later life by creating an internal working model for individuals as they approach new and existing relationships (Ainsworth, 1973; Ainsworth & Bowlby, 1991; Bowlby, 1969, 1988).
- *Behaviorism* suggests that all behavior is a learned response from the environment and that past experience accounts for all behavior. Desirable outcomes in children can be obtained through conditioning based on consistent reinforcement and punishment (Skinner, 1953, 1957, 1974; Watson, 1925).
- *Social learning theory* proposes that human behavior is learned observationally through modeling without necessarily needing to act in a certain way. Human behavior is explained by continuous reciprocal interactions between the person, behavior, and environment. Bandura (1986) relabeled his approach as "social cognitive theory" in recognition of the more comprehensive nature of his theory than what was traditionally viewed as "learning." (Bandura, 1977, 1986, 1999; Gibson, 2004).

Incorporating theoretical frameworks into parent education courses can provide insight for parents to better understand the development and behaviors of their children, as well as their interactions with them. Some of these theories also have various stages to accommodate different ages and periods of development. Regardless of the setting, incorporating theory is meaningful to the understanding and examination of the parent-child relationship.

Approaches to Parenting Education

The overall goal of parenting education programs is to improve parents' confidence and competence in their parenting, which in turn can foster children's safety and healthy development. Parenting education programs seek to help parents develop appropriate child guidance techniques and gain knowledge and understanding of age-appropriate behaviors. By targeting the knowledge, skills, attitudes, beliefs, and behaviors relevant to effective parenting, parenting education programs can give parents the capacity and confidence to meet their children's developmental needs and prepare them for adulthood (McGroder & Hyra, 2009).

In addition to children's development, parent development is important to include in any discussion about parenting education. A life course perspective can provide a useful framework to examine parenting needs by identifying times of transition that are conducive to parenting education efforts. For example, the transition to parenthood can have a profound impact on the development of both the mother and father. Children's unique development stages or other family transitions are times that parents might be particularly receptive to relevant parenting education programs.

Programs can focus specifically on the parent, child, and/or the parent-child relationship. Some programs focus on the family, community, or environment in which the family lives. Recently there has been an increase in the types of programs that include the entire family and engage both parents and children in skill-building activities. Some programs also offer parents support or referral to services to reduce the stress that makes it difficult for them to be effective parents or focus on unique needs or aspects of parenting. For example, additional parenting challenges arise in relation to issues such as incarceration, divorce, and remarriage (Nomaguchi & Milkie, 2020) and there are parenting education programs designed specifically to meet these challenges.

Using a trauma-informed approach in parent education has received increased attention in recent years (Lindstrom et al. 2018; National Academies of Science, Engineering, & Medicine, 2016; Wagenhals, 2017). Research on adverse childhood experiences (ACEs) has established that trauma during childhood such as abuse or parental incarceration can have a negative impact on parenting behaviors as an adult (e.g., increased chance of child abuse) and in turn on child outcomes (e.g., increased feelings of guilt and shame, difficulty regulating emotion) (Cohen, Hien, & Batchelder, 2008). A trauma-informed approach recognizes the role that trauma plays in parenting and helps to mitigate its effects and reduce chances of re-traumatization (Lindstrom et al. 2018; SAMHSA, 2015). However, there is also recognition that children are resilient. Positive childhood experiences (e.g., safe environments, nurturing relationships) can balance the adverse experiences and be important in shaping future behaviors (Stevens, 2021). This focus on positive experiences and resilience aligns with the strength-based nature of family life and parenting education practices.

There also has been increased attention to factors such as economic status and its effect on parenting (Nomaguchi & Milkie, 2020). The availability of economic resources influences parent needs and may present additional parenting challenges such as housing insecurity and adequate living conditions. Parents with few economic resources may have limited access to parenting resources such as parenting education. It is important for family life educators to reduce barriers to participation and offer accessible culturally appropriate programs that meet the needs of the target population. One approach that can increase access to parenting education resources is to offer programming in conjunction with other social services such as government assistance programs or health care clinics (Knox, Burkhart, & Cromly, 2013; Sanders, Prinz, & Shapiro, 2009).

In order to address these various needs and challenges, parenting education programs can vary in approach and intensity and the particular parenting behaviors or child outcomes being addressed. In general most parenting education programs are preventive in nature, but the focus of the prevention can vary. As discussed in Chapter 1, there are three levels of prevention programs: primary, secondary, and tertiary.

- **Primary prevention** is focused on the protection and education of healthy people from harm *before* something happens.
- **Secondary prevention** involves protection and education *after* problems, conflicts, or risks have occurred so the progress of the problem can be halted or slowed as early as possible.
- **Tertiary prevention** centers around helping people manage complicated, long-term problems to prevent further harm.

The prevention approach used in a parenting education program is often dependent upon the audience addressed. All three levels of prevention programs can involve some level of parenting education. Parenting education programs that operate at the secondary or tertiary level may be referred to as parent interventions or treatments. For example, parenting education programs that use a public health approach have increased in recent years. Using this approach, parenting education is used on a large scale as a treatment for societal issues such as child abuse or reduction of children's behavioral problems (Pickering & Sanders, 2016). However, increased efforts at providing primary prevention to *all* parents beginning prior to birth and continuing throughout the lifespan could reduce the need for programs focusing on secondary and tertiary prevention.

The categories of *universal*, *selective*, and *indicated* reflect the prevention approach applied to each group. Universal prevention programs are designed for the general population and focus largely on primary prevention and the promotion of positive parenting practices. They are designed to inform and prepare parents regarding normative parenting responsibilities and experiences with the intention of preventing problems and promoting optimal development. These programs typically have a lower dosage, or in other words, are shorter in duration and less intensive than selective or indicated programs. A universal prevention program can help to improve general parenting knowledge and skill, but selective and indicated programs may be more effective in helping parents with challenging parenting issues such as disruptive behavior (Leijten et al., 2019).

Selective prevention programs are targeted toward those with higher-than-average risk for problem behaviors by virtue of their membership in a particular population. The goal of selective prevention programs is to prevent the development of serious problems. Selective programs typically have a higher dosage and intensity (Leijten et al., 2019). A selective prevention program might target a particular audience, such as those going through a divorce, as research shows that on average, children with divorced parents score lower on a variety of emotional, behavioral, social, health, and academic outcomes (Amato, 2010). Other examples of selective prevention programs that target particular audiences are programs targeting fathers, adoptive parents, or foster parents.

Indicated programs target those that are already engaged in high-risk behaviors, such as reported child abuse. In such cases, parents may be court-mandated to participate in parenting education programs in order to retain custody of their children (Myers-Walls, 2022). The goal of indicated programs is to end problem behaviors and prevent severe problems. Therefore, indicated programs can be fairly intense and long in duration (Doyle, 2006; McGroder & Hyra, 2009). Problem-focused, indicated programs, should not be confused with therapy. Parenting education differs from therapy in its emphasis on (1) normative development and the prevention of family problems rather than on individual personality and family dysfunction, (2) techniques that provide support rather than conflict and confrontation, and (3) goals that increase self-confidence and satisfaction rather than restructure personality or family dynamics (Myers-Walls et al., 2011).

Common audiences for parenting education programs include parents of infants, toddlers, adolescents, or college-age youth, as well as teen parents, single parents, fathers, stepfamilies, military families, grandparents raising their grandchildren, parents involved in foster care and adoption, parents of children with special needs, and incarcerated parents. Depending upon the situation, the audience might be participating in a universal (all parents), selective (specific populations with unique needs), or indicated (problem-focused) prevention program and the approach taken might be considered primary, secondary, or tertiary prevention. For example, grandparents raising their grandchildren might participate in a program geared specifically for that audience. The approach might be considered primary prevention because the audience is not necessarily considered to be at-risk, but shares a common characteristic or circumstance. Parenting education programs for these audiences can include general parenting education content and discussion of issues unique to that population.

Parenting Education Program Content

When developing or selecting parenting education programs, parenting educators need to be mindful of both the content and the process of delivering this content. Many parenting programs focus on guidance and discipline of young children and the most effective techniques for parents to manage children's misbehavior. Leijten et al. (2019) examined a variety of parenting skills taught in parenting education programs and found that teaching parents to use positive reinforcement, praise, and natural or logical consequences were particularly beneficial in helping parents manage disruptive child behavior.

Although parenting programs exist that focus on a particular topic, such as discipline, Morris et al. (2020) have identified seven common content areas of parenting programs: (1) emotional socialization and communication; (2) minimizing harsh parenting; (3) fostering nurturing, responsive, parent-child interactions; (4) strengthening the parent-child and family relationships; (5) consistent discipline; (6) child and adolescent development; and (7) self-care. These areas align with the six content areas in the National Extension Parenting Educator's Framework (NEPEF) described below.

The National Extension Parenting Education Framework

In 2000, a group of Extension professionals met to outline the critical skills and practices of parenting educators. Their efforts combined the NEPEM "priority practices for parents" with their "priority processes for parenting educators" to create a new structure, the *National Extension Parenting Education Framework*, or NEPEF (DeBord et al., 2006). In the NEPEF, six categories of skills and content practices for parents were recommended: *Care for Self, Understand* (children, their developmental needs, and uniqueness), *Guide, Nurture, Motivate,* and *Advocate.* They are to be used alongside the six processes for parenting educators (*Grow, Frame, Develop, Educate, Embrace,* and *Build*). See Figure 11.1 for these approaches. The NEPEF provides an excellent format in which to consider numerous aspects of parenting education.

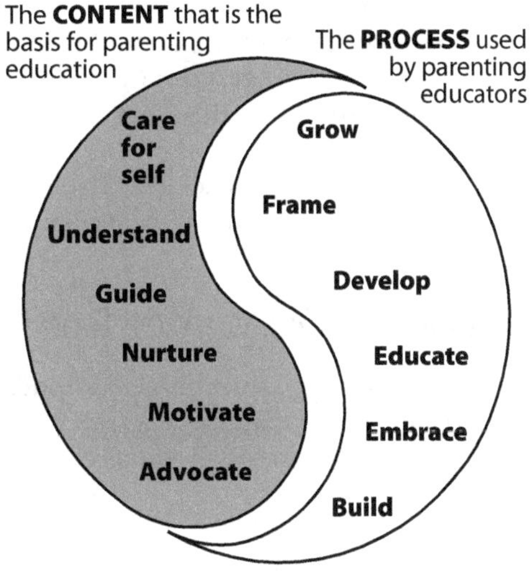

Figure 11.1 Approaches to Parenting Education

Parent Education Core Curriculum Framework

A helpful framework in developing parenting education programs is *The Parent Education Core Curriculum Framework* which provides a guide to planning curriculum for parent education programs (MNAFEE, 2011). The Framework is designed specifically for parents of young children, but it can be adapted to other audiences. The specific goals of the *Parent Education Core Curriculum Framework* are to provide a resource that:

- frames or defines the body of knowledge in the field of parent education;
- is applicable across the field of parent education with any type of parent education program, population, setting, and delivery mode;
- is a planning tool for development and delivery of parent education curriculum and lesson plans;

- identifies the intended content and objectives of parent education (originally designed for Early Childhood Family Education [ECFE] and Even Start);
- provides guidance for parent goal-setting in parent education;
- guides assessment of parent education outcomes and programs;
- promotes accountability in parent education programs and with individual parent educators; and
- informs practice in parent education.

The Framework contains four levels of information including *Domains* (Parent Development, Parent-Child Relationships, Early Childhood Development, Family Development, Culture, and Community); *Components* (areas of content within each domain); *Categories* (units of more specific learning content within each component); and *Indicators* (long-term learning goals in each category for parents participating in parent education). Potential uses of the Framework include developing program curriculum, guiding assessment of program outcomes, or communicating with stakeholders about the importance of parenting education.

The Parent Education Core Curriculum Framework document also includes "Procedures for Using the Parent Education Core Curriculum Framework and Indicators" in curriculum planning and development, as well as implementation. The Framework is an excellent resource for anyone involved in parenting education program development or implementation.

Design and Delivery of Parenting Education

Parenting education is provided in a variety of settings and formats to a number of different audiences. Variations in program goals and the targeted audiences are reflected in the mode of delivery, settings, and strategies used to deliver parenting education.

Mode of Delivery

Three modes of instruction for parenting education are the *individual* mode, the *group* mode, and the *mass* mode (Harman & Brim, 1980). The *individual mode* involves one-on-one interaction. This type of parent education is often carried out via home visiting programs, but increasingly parenting educators are marketing themselves as coaches perhaps to portray an educational approach rather being therapeutic or remedial. Parenting education delivered using an individual mode may also be self-directed in that parents are provided with materials such as DVDs, workbooks, online modules, or other resources, in order to learn the material on their own (Borden et al., 2016). Self-directed programs may include a consultation component with a parenting educator in the form of regular phone calls or video chats to assess progress and answer questions. Self-directed modes of instruction can help reduce barriers to participation and can still provide effective support for parents (Borden et al., 2016).

The *group mode* is a widely used approach through which instruction is delivered to a group of people in classroom settings, workshops, seminars, or support groups. The *mass mode* refers to education provided to the masses, often carried out through the print media such as newsletters, books, and pamphlets; via radio and television programs; and through the internet and technology. Contact through the mass mode can reach a larger audience but may be less personal. The audience is anonymous because there is no direct contact between the educator and the parent. Parent education is increasingly provided in a mass mode through online webinars and learning modules and even through mobile apps.

The COVID-19 pandemic forced parenting educators to quickly adapt parenting education programs for online delivery when they were originally designed to be implemented face-to-face. Suddenly, technology had to be used for all three modes of delivery (individual, group, mass). Programs using individual delivery, such as home visiting as well as those designed for groups, might have switched to a virtual mode of delivery using Zoom, FaceTime, or another virtual meeting platform. Some group delivery might have switched to an asynchronous delivery in which parents could access online material at any time, whereas, others might have continued a synchronous model in which all participants met virtually at a certain time.

Reducing barriers to participation such as transportation or child care is an important aspect of program implementation (Morris et al., 2020) and should also be considered when choosing a mode of delivery. For example, integrating parenting education programs with other social or health care services can help reduce obstacles and increase participation. Other factors to consider when choosing a delivery mode are issues of privacy, accessibility, participant cost, and adequate time to process information and practice skills (Hughes et al., 2015).

Teaching Strategies

Regardless of delivery mode, parent education programs have been found to be most effective in producing behavior change when they incorporate active learning strategies, teach parents positive parent-child interaction skills, and provide opportunities for participants to practice skills through role-playing and other skill-based activities rather than just receiving information (Gross et al., 2018; Leijten et al., 2019; Morris et al., 2020). Parenting educators can provide opportunities for parents to understand relationships and practice skills through role-play scenarios or case studies (Morris et al., 2020). See Box 11.1 for an example of a role play that can provide insight into the parent-adolescent relationship. Other strategies that have been found to be effective in achieving positive outcomes are including the parents as partners in the program, connecting with and building rapport with participants, and facilitating peer support among parents (Morris et al., 2020; National Academies of Science, Engineering, & Medicine, 2016).

Settings

Chapter 4 provided discussion of the many settings in which parent and family life education occur. Similarly, parenting education programs are offered in a number of different settings and through a variety of providers, including schools, Cooperative Extension programs, family and human service agencies,

Box 11.1 **What Do You Hold Dear?**

This role play involves all participants in a parent education program. Ask everyone to stand and find a partner—one will become Person A, the other Person B. (If there is an uneven number of people in the class, suggest one group have 3 members). Ask individuals to think of something each holds dear (e.g., a physical object, person, concept), but not tell anyone. Then ask Person A to make a fist to hold on to what is dear to him/her while Person B tries to get it away from Person A by using any means possible. After a short period of time, reverse the roles of Persons A and B, giving an equivalent amount of time. Following this second interaction discuss their experiences. Were they successful or unsuccessful in getting it away—why or why not? What were participants holding dear? After this discussion, ask what if this was an interaction between a parent and adolescent who was holding dear his or her independence. Would any of the methods used by the participants be effective—why or why not?

neighborhood resource centers, community education, faith communities, and health care settings. In addition, for-profit businesses are increasingly offering programs and services relevant to parenting to employees because they recognize the impact that personal issues and concerns can have on company productivity (Grzywacz & Demerouti, 2013). The government provides parenting education through a variety of programs including Head Start, family support and intervention programs through the child protection system, and programs aimed for military families. As discussed previously, many parent and family education programs are funded through grants, which can create an unstable environment for program planning and implementation. Stable funding sources and continued efforts to present parenting and family life education as an acceptable activity for all families will help to increase the outreach and positive impact of family life education in American society.

Identifying Parenting Education Programs

Multiple parenting education programs cover a broad range of topics and use numerous formats and approaches. Therefore, it can be difficult to find appropriate curriculum or to know if the program will be effective with the intended audience. The ability to adequately evaluate parenting education materials and curricula is an important competency for the professional family life educator. Professional parenting educators must possess the knowledge and skills needed to determine what, if any, theory a program might be based upon and ensure that content is grounded in solid research. The literature regarding the evaluation of parenting curriculum and programs is increasing as the field becomes more firmly established. The Family Life Education Quality Assessment Tool (FLEMat QAT) was designed to help family life educators and those who work with families to judge the quality of written and online materials aimed at families (Myers-Walls, n.d.). See Chapter 7 for a more detailed discussion of evaluation.

Fortunately, there are a number of sources for evidence-based programs focused on multiple audiences, such as *Blueprints for Healthy Youth Development*, which is a registry of evidenced-based parenting education programs (see Chapter 5 for a list of additional resources for evidence-based parent and family programs). Morris et al. (2020) conducted a review of empirically-supported parenting education programs which included, *Nurturing Parenting Programs, Strengthening Families Program, Systematic Training for Effective Parenting (STEP), Parents as Teachers, The Incredible Years, Triple P—Positive Parenting Program, Active Parenting*, and many others. While there are many quality parenting education programs that have not been officially designated as being evidence-based, funders often require supported organizations and agencies to use programs that meet some kind of identified criteria for efficacy.

The Parenting Educator

The role of the parenting educator can vary depending upon the audience, setting, and goals of the group. Therefore, a competent parenting educator should be capable of moving and adapting to whatever role is needed in the particular situation. A parent educator offering a one-day workshop may need different skills than someone facilitating an ongoing group or writing a newspaper column. Those currently working to define and establish the field of parenting education are faced with the difficulty of trying to move the field forward by defining content and competencies while still supporting the broad diversity of the profession.

Competencies for Parent Educators

There is an emerging consensus on the parameters of parenting education and the knowledge and skills needed for effective practice. The discussion surrounding the establishment of parenting education as a field and parenting educators as professionals has led to consideration of competencies. What do parenting educators need to know to effectively practice? What skills should they possess? Campbell and Palm (2018) identified three stages of growth and development (novice, intermediate, and master) for parenting educators in five areas of development: knowledge, group facilitation skills, teaching skills, professional identity and boundaries, and understanding diversity. These levels of professional development provide insight into the depth and breadth of competencies needed by parenting educators as they increase their level of professionalism (see Table 11.1).

Reflective practice, which is relevant to the competencies of a parent educator, is a process of professional growth and development that includes self-assessment as well as assessment of group process and outcomes (Campbell & Palm, 2018). Self-assessment can be a good first step in the reflective practice of a parenting educator and can help to identify knowledge, disposition, and skills. Box 11.2 includes a self-assessment checklist specific to parenting education in group settings.

Table 11.1 Levels of Professional Development for Parent Educators

Novice Level	Intermediate Level	Master Teaching Level
Knowledge		
Aware of basic child development and parenting information. Some apprehension about being able to answer parents' questions.	Possesses broader knowledge base. Aware of a variety of resources on development and parenting issues.	Confident about being able to answer questions and/or able to find resources. Realization of being well-versed.
Aware of basic stages and theories of family dynamics and development.	Able to identify individual families' circumstances in reference to stages and characteristics.	Uses holistic perspective to understand each family's journey. Able to link current challenges and successes to stages and cycles of development. Understands and provides insight into impact of family of origin as well as current family dynamics.
Beginning to understand community resources. Some uncertainty about what is available and how to refer parents to other services.	Aware of basic community services and some comfort with access. Understands referral process.	Able to access information and services easily. Comfortable approaching parents for referrals. Uses a holistic perspective with parents within a collaborative approach.
Group Facilitation Skills Understands group process but feels challenged with group leadership role.	Enjoys group leadership. Focuses primarily on content and plan for session.	Confident as a group leader. Able to blend support and possible intervention with content. Understands behavior and can utilize skills to respond.
Understands dynamics of conflict and behaviors. Uncomfortable dealing with difficult group/individual dynamics.	Has some skills to address challenging behaviors, mostly to defuse them and refocus group.	Is comfortable with addressing challenging or difficult group dynamics. Recognizes and uses "teachable moments." Takes responsibility for healthy group process and development.
Teaching Skills		
Understands adult learning styles.	Plans and executes sessions with a variety of teaching methods but uses discussion as a primary method.	Able to assess parents' needs and styles and match methods accordingly. Shows insight in planning and leading to meet diverse needs of parents.
Able to develop and implement an appropriate parent education session plan.	Able to tailor a plan to an individual group. Able to access ongoing needs of group and modify plan, as needed.	Uses creative and varying strategies for group education and process. Has clear goals and objectives, yet uses flexibility as needed.

Table 11.1 *(cont'd.)*

Novice Level	Intermediate Level	Master Teaching Level
Professional Identity and Boundaries Shows basic self-awareness, but limited understanding of impact on relationship with group and role as facilitator.	Has insight into self, family-of origin experiences, and their impact on the role as a parent educator.	Maturity and life experiences that reflect deeper understanding and self-awareness. Ability to separate biases and strong values from professional role.
Uncertain about skills and abilities as a parent educator.	Growing confidence from positive experiences with parents that affirm abilities as a parent educator.	Quiet confidence in abilities. Leadership role within the parent group, as well as within the profession as a mentor and a guide for other professionals.
Understanding Diversity Shows basic awareness and sensitivity to importance of diversity issues. Not sure how to integrate into practice.	Growing awareness of family and cultural diversity and the impact on family and parenting issues.	Values family structure and cultural diversity in programs. Willing to learn from parents; comfortable addressing differences and facilitating discussion to address differences respectfully.

Source: Campbell, D., & Palm, G. (2018). *Parent education: Working with groups and individuals*. San Diego, CA: Cognella Academic Publishing. Table 14.1, pp. 362–363. Used with permission.

The NPEN Professional Preparation Committee developed a set of core competencies to guide effective parenting education practice (NPEN, 2018). The *NPEN Parenting Educator Competency Model* organizes the knowledge, skills, attitudes, and dispositions needed for effective parent education into four domains, three of which focus on knowledge and one on practice. In addition to the four domains, an addendum includes administration and supervision skills that support the direct provision of parent education programming.

- Domain 1: Knowledge of Human Development Across the Lifespan

  Theories and research on human development and learning across the lifespan

  Diverse influence on human development across the lifespan

- Domain 2: Knowledge of Parent Development, Parenting, Parent-Child and Family Relationships and Other Systems

  Theories and research on parent development, parenting, parent-child and family relationships and other systems

  The parenting role and related responsibilities

  Family, community, and other contextual factors influencing parenting and the parent-child/family relationships

  Diverse community and cultural influences on parenting and the parent-child and family relationships

Box 11.2 Parent Group Leader Competencies: A Self-Assessment Checklist

Instructions: Review each item in each of the three major areas and rate yourself from 1 (Not developed) to 5 (Exemplary).

Knowledge: This area outlines knowledge that is specifically related to understanding group dynamics and facilitating parent learning in a group context.

_____ 1. Understanding the developmental stages of group process as this applies to parent groups.

_____ 2. Understanding different theories of group dynamics and their applications to parent groups.

_____ 3. Understanding the roles and boundaries of the parent group leader.

_____ 4. Understanding the emotional nature of parenting issues and how this influences parent group learning.

_____ 5. Understanding different leadership styles and their effects on parent group behavior.

_____ 6. Understanding multiple ways to assess parent and family strengths and limitations in the context of parent groups.

_____ 7. Understanding a variety of active learning methods to assist parents in solving problems and making decisions.

_____ 8. Understanding and being aware of various community resources for parents and families and how to connect parents to these resources.

_____ 9. Understanding family and community diversity and how diverse values and beliefs influence parenting behavior as well as parent group dynamics.

Dispositions: This category of competencies refers to character traits and emotional attitudes that have been identified as important for parent educators (Auerbach, 1968; Braun et al., 1984; Clarke, 1984). These are different from general personality traits or types such as introvert and extrovert. Each individual will have his or her own unique blend of these dispositions.

_____ 1. *Maturity*: Parent group leader is clear about his or her own identity and able to clearly focus on the needs and issues of parents in the group.

_____ 2. *Caring*: Parent group leader is able to focus on the needs of parents and demonstrate understanding, compassion, and support for parents.

_____ 3. *Nonjudgmentalness*: Parent group leader appreciates the complexities of parenting and accepts parents without blaming them for their problems or mistakes. The focus is on helping parents and understanding that there are no easy answers.

_____ 4. *Sensitivity:* Parent group leader is able to perceive and respond to individual parents' needs and feelings.

_____ 5. *Organization*: Parent group leader is able to express goals clearly and provide direction toward parent learning.

_____ 6. *Flexibility*: Parent group leader is able to change direction as needed and balance between individual and group needs of parents.

_____ 7. *Creativity*: Parent group leader is able to design interesting and engaging parent sessions.

_____ 8. *Enthusiasm/Optimism*: Parent group leader has a positive attitude about people and the subject matter and is able to excite parents about learning.

_____ 9. *Honesty*: Parent group leader is clear about his or her own knowledge and limitations.

_____ 10. *Genuineness*: Parent group leader is honest and open in his or her relationships with parents.

_____ 11. *Humor*: Parent group leader is able to appreciate and express what is humorous without ridiculing people or their problems.

Skills: These are presented in general areas followed by very specific behavioral indicators of each general skill area.

1. Creates a warm and welcoming environment.
   _____ a. Greets each parent or family member in a welcoming manner.
   _____ b. Demonstrates a genuine interest in parent and child well-being.
   _____ c. Uses effective openings for a session—involves parents in an engaging and non-threatening manner.
2. Creates a safe environment for parents to share ideas and feelings.
   _____ a. Helps group establish and implement ground rules.
   _____ b. Elicits a variety of opinions, values, and philosophies from parents.
   _____ c. Affirms parents in a genuine and supportive manner.
3. Guides a discussion, giving it form and structure.
   _____ a. Informs parents of agenda and goals for the session.
   _____ b. Helps parents identify needs and concerns.
   _____ c. Keeps the group focused on the group goals and the topic of discussion.
   _____ d. Asks clarifying questions to better understand parent issues.
   _____ e. Restates and clarifies parent ideas/issues.
   _____ f. Summarizes important ideas/issues.
4. Models acceptance of each individual as someone to be listened to and respected.
   _____ a. Listens carefully to parents.
   _____ b. Gives nonverbal messages of acceptance.
   _____ c. Accepts and acknowledges negative feelings and distress.
   _____ d. Restates and/or acknowledges parent contributions to the discussion.
   _____ e. Addresses diversity and facilitates discussion around differences in values, culture, and family structure.
5. Takes responsibility for establishing a positive and supportive learning environment.
   _____ a. Helps parents to identify and set their own goals.
   _____ b. Invites parent participation using a variety of methods.
   _____ c. Challenges parents to evaluate and reconsider their ideas.
   _____ d. Uses concrete examples to bring abstract concepts to life.
   _____ e. Adapts information to meet different parent capabilities.
6. Fosters relationships and interaction among group members.
   _____ a. Encourages participation of all of the group members.
   _____ b. Connects parent comments and experiences to point out common themes.
   _____ c. Engages the group in problem solving for individual group members.
   _____ d. Addresses conflict directly and respectfully.

Source: Campbell, D., & Palm, G. (2018). *Parent education: Working with groups and individuals*. San Diego, CA: Cognella Academic Publishing. Appendix A, Parent group leader competencies: A self-assessment checklist, pp. 397–401. Used with permission.

- Domain 3: Knowledge of Parenting Education Practice
  Foundations of parenting education
  Adult learning and education
  Educational methodology/instructional design
  Relationships and communication with parents and families
  Working with parents in groups
  Working individually with parents and families (home visits, one-on-one instruction, consultation, coaching)
  Assessment and evaluation
  Professional behavior and development
- Domain 4: Skills for Parenting Education Practice
  Foundations of parenting education
  Adult learning and education
  Educational methodology/instructional design
  Relationships and communication with parents and families
  Working with parents in groups
  Working individually with parents and families (home visits, one-on-one instruction, consultation, coaching)
  Assessment and evaluation
  Professional behavior and development
- Administration and Supervision Addendum
  Program design and evaluation
  Staff supervision
  Policy understanding, development, and management
  Communication and marketing
  Collaboration and referrals with other organizations
  Funding and budget management

Preparation and Training

The qualifications of parenting education providers can range from less than a high school diploma to a graduate degree, specifically in parenting education. Historically, parenting education has been conducted within the domains of a number of different disciplines, including medicine, social work, therapy, home economics, and education, and informally by parent-to-parent advising (Campbell & Palm, 2018). This history has had implications for the formal recognition of parenting education as a profession, as many in the helping professions have been involved in parenting education without the benefit of formal training. For example, parents might ask a pediatrician how best to deal with their toddler's temper tantrums. Although this is not necessarily a medical question, the doctor may be inclined to offer advice. In some circumstances professionals in other related fields provide parenting advice as they are assumed to have expertise in parenting education by virtue of their role. Unfortunately, parenting is seldom directly addressed in training programs for many of the helping professions.

The formal recognition of parenting educators as professionals, and of parenting education as a profession in its own right, is increasing. There have been substantial advances in the identification of the knowledge, skills, abilities, and competencies needed to provide parenting education. There are more opportunities to provide parenting education within the context of education and prevention rather than as embedded within other practices and settings. Professionals in the field are working to formalize training and recognition opportunities for parenting educators, including those working as peer educators and paraprofessionals. Paraprofessional parenting educators have practical parenting knowledge but do not have a higher education degree to prepare them as a parenting educator. They develop parenting education competency through trainings and work experience (NPEN, 2020a).

Peer educators and paraprofessionals

Some parenting programs involve the use of volunteers, usually experienced parents, (sometimes called peer educators or paraprofessionals), who offer support or facilitation. Peer educators share common life experiences with the audience members. Paraprofessionals are generally trained to assist professionals but are not licensed or credentialed themselves. They may have some of the knowledge and skills and may be able to work independently, but do not meet the requirements for recognition as a professional in the field (NPEN, 2020b).

Peer educators are experienced parents who are trained in facilitation techniques and given supporting research-based material on child development and parenting issues. These trained parents then lead parenting groups with new parents. One of the strengths of peer-led programs is the inclusion of parents from the community in leadership roles as group facilitators. These parents often share the same cultural and socioeconomic status as the parents in the rest of the group. This shared background gives the facilitators increased credibility and acceptance and is sometimes used to provide parenting education via home-visiting programs.

There has been substantial work to include peer educators and paraprofessionals within the continuum of parenting education. A comprehensive discussion of the contributions and limitations of the role of peer educators and paraprofessionals can be found on the NPEN website in a white paper on the diverse roles of practitioners in parenting education (Jones et al., 2013).

Program-specific training

Many evidence-based programs provide program-specific training that is required prior to implementation of that program. Those who undergo training may be qualified parent educators or paraprofessionals who do not necessarily have any formal training in child development or parenting. However, they receive a certificate or become certified upon completion of a prescribed training focused on a program's particular approach or curriculum. Continuing education may or may not be required. This approach can be limited, as the provider's expertise is confined to the specific program or materials. Packaged programs can be effective in certain situations or on specific topics, but parenting educators need the ability to deal with a variety of issues and be skilled in adapting to their audience. Training programs for specific curricula may not provide training in issues beyond the content of the program, leaving the educator without the skills needed to deal with unique situations. However, this approach to parent education can be effective, as long as the educator maintains fidelity to the program.

Certificate and degree programs

While parenting education is often included as a topic or course within family and child development degree programs, there are growing opportunities for professionals to be trained specifically in parenting education and to consider parenting education as a primary profession. The number of degree-granting programs in parenting education is increasing throughout the United States. As mentioned in Chapter 2, a number of higher education institutions, such as North Carolina State University, University of Minnesota, and Adelphi University offer graduate certificate programs in parenting education (NPEN, 2021).

Formal Recognition of Parenting Educators

There are several methods of recognition of parenting educators currently available, including state licensure and national certification. Professionals in the field are currently working to identify a formal recognition system.

State licensure and credentialing

Minnesota is currently the only state to require parent and family educators to be licensed. The license is for a specific statewide parenting education program. However, there are several states that offer state-level credentials including North Carolina (NCPEN), Oregon (OPEC), Connecticut (CT-PEN), and New York (NYSPEP).

National certification

Much of the conversation among parenting education professionals regarding professional standards has included the feasibility or need for national certification specifically for parenting educators. The National Council on Family Relations' certification program for family life educators requires knowledge in many of the areas deemed relevant for parenting education. The Certified Family Life Educator (CFLE) designation requires a minimum of a baccalaureate degree and work experience in family life education ranging from 1,600 to 4,800 hours, depending on the level and relevancy of the degree. Some argue that professionals practicing in parenting education should have preparation in the broad areas that make up the CFLE criteria. However many parenting educators who operate as facilitators, paraprofessionals, and volunteers, as well as many that consider themselves to be professional parenting educators, may not be able to meet all of the requirements of the CFLE designation. Others have argued that there is a level and depth of knowledge needed in parenting education that is not included within the CFLE standards.

The idea of required licensure and/or certification of parenting educators has been met with concern by those who support peer-educator/paraprofessional models and other grassroots community-based programs. Establishment of specific academic criteria could prevent many of these parents from practicing as parenting educators.

Framework for Understanding Parent Educator Professional Preparation and Recognition

The NPEN Professional Preparation Committee developed a working draft of the *Framework for Understanding Parenting Educator Professional Preparation and Recognition*. This framework provides a set of core competencies for parenting educators, creates a standard for states that are constructing professional development and recognition systems, and clarifies the roles of peers and paraprofessionals (NPEN, 2020a). The Framework also considers preparation options for individuals entering parenting education from a broad range of experience and educational levels, from a high school education/GED to a doctoral degree. The NPEN website includes resources relevant to the profession of parenting education, competencies, and state and national models.

■ SUMMARY

In this chapter the important role that parents play in the lives of their children has been examined along with the value that parenting education can provide to families and society. In addition to some of the prominent pressures impacting today's families, there was a brief review of the history of parenting education as an approach to societal issues. Relevant theories have been suggested along with the concept of parent development and aspects of parenting education delivery including formats, approaches, audiences, and settings. A number of parenting education models and approaches have been presented. A discussion of parenting education would not be complete without a thorough consideration of the role of the parenting educator, training and preparation options, and competencies for best practice. Finally, existing alternatives for the recognition of parenting education were discussed along with ongoing efforts to bring a more formal and established professional recognition framework to the field.

This is an exciting time for the field of parenting education. The growing number of professionals who consider parenting education to be their primary profession are actively discussing new ideas, approaches, theories, and criteria. Increased recognition of the value and impact of positive parenting on the well-being of individuals and society will no doubt result in continued discussion and growth in this important field.

■ QUESTIONS AND ISSUES FOR DISCUSSION

1. Can parenting educators be effective if they have never had children themselves?
2. Is parenting education a profession or a discipline within the profession of education?
3. Should parenting educators be required to have at least a baccalaureate degree in order to practice?

4. Which term is better: "parent educator" or "parenting educator?" Why?
5. What is an example of a behavior that you modeled after a parent(s)?
6. Which theories related to a child's development seem the most useful?
7. What are some examples of bidirectional influences of parents and children?
8. What are the pros and cons of using an evidence-based parenting education program vs. developing your own program?

■ ACTIVITIES

1. Investigate the availability of parenting education programs in your community. In what settings are they held (health care, community education, Extension)?
2. Use the descriptions of parenting programs, to share the child development theory on which they are based (behaviorism, attachment, social learning, etc.).
3. Scan the internet or social media for emerging issues of concern to parents (e.g., teen sleep, bullying, substance abuse, sexting). What are some ways in which parents can best respond?
4. Identify three ways that you or your friends may have been indulged and three ways that indulgence of children can be harmful to children, families, and society.

12

International Perspectives on Family Life Education

Need for Global Awareness

We live in a complex world where understanding other individuals and cultures is essential. Global awareness is no longer a luxury, but a necessity as we extend our focus to families unlike our own. The need for people to become culturally competent and prepared to work with diverse populations is becoming increasingly important, particularly in the family science field. By incorporating cross-cultural awareness and sensitivity into our classrooms, we can enhance the understanding, appreciation, and acceptance of diverse families and cultures. This increased awareness can enrich our own lives and contribute to the well-being of individuals and families worldwide.

We often hear the terms "global" or "international," but what is the difference? The term *global* is a more holistic term that includes the entire earth or globe and is not just one or two regions. It is synonymous with "worldwide," "universal," and "comprehensive." "Global" means the integration of different nations as a single unit. Therefore, global issues are those that concern and affect the world as a whole and as such must be dealt with by all nations of the world (e.g., global warming, global economy, global pandemics). *International* is smaller in scope and refers to issues and concerns of two or more countries or regions, with additional terms being "foreign" or "multinational." It affects only the countries that are involved, but these countries may function autonomously, such as the focus of individual countries on the degree and emphasis of their family life education programs. It is smaller in scale, although at times some issues may overlap (e.g., international treaties, laws, or health) (Difference Between, 2021; Quora, 2016).

Globalization is the process of the world becoming increasingly connected through trade, ideas, and other aspects of culture along with the transmission of values; economic fragility or stability; and at times cooperation, unrest, or intervention. Information, goods, and services produced in one country are easily available to others in various parts of the world. The clothes we wear, the foods we eat, the music we enjoy, the art we view, the technology we employ, and the natural resources we use are all a result of this global process (You Matter, 2020). Globalization has become a force, changing our world by making it more interdependent and smaller through means of technology and communication.

The trends of globalization and the expanding interrelationships among nations and their peoples have resulted in global diversification, as well as a growing interdependence of the world's population racially, ethnically, culturally, and economically (MBN, 2020). Globalization has not only reduced distance and time, but also has linked countries at opposite ends of the earth resulting in the complex transition of many advanced countries into multiethnic and multicultural societies (Dini, 2000; Foner, 2005; You Matter, 2020).

In general, for over three decades Americans have had a positive view of globalization, because for many years globalization was perceived as *Americanization*, so few adjustments were needed within this paradigm. Now globalization has taken an *Asianization* perspective of people, trade, influence, and ideas (GIS Asie, n.d.; Tay, 2010; World Public Opinion, n.d.). The new leaders of globalization are led by China and India. "Made in China" products fill store shelves, while

Indian software companies run the world's offices. These two most populous countries that had dominated the word economy for over a millennium are regaining status after a brief hiatus.

The increasing globalization and technological development of our world will continue at a rapid pace resulting in anxiety, tension, and conflict for those cultures rooted in more traditional, agrarian, and patriarchal value systems. Some countries have perceived that Western culture is taking a toll on the lifestyle of many teens who copy what appears "cool," such as fashion, drugs, manner of walking, foreign accents, and the way they relate with elders. These trends are spreading through social media, movies, and music and have resulted in ill health, death, a decay in discipline, and disrespect of parents from whom they often steal money to spend on expensive activities (Olga, 2015). As people are exposed to some of the values of Western cultures, societal conflicts are erupting.

Global issues are complex, contextual, and not only influenced by families, but also influence families due to advances in communication, technology, science, and transportation (Smith, 2016). Family ties are of particular importance in an era of globalization where changes in national and global arenas intersect with personal choices and decisions that affect family life (Majeed & Kanwal, 2019). Some positive and challenging consequences of globalization for families include the following: (Majeed & Kanwal, 2019; Mills, 2013; Smith, 2016; Stief, 2020; Thompson, 2019).

- Increased trade has brought economic growth, creativity, innovation, and a higher standard of living for some families. However, if a major shipping route is blocked (e.g., Suez Canal), or there are supply chain issues, the repercussions are felt worldwide.
- Human and family rights (e.g., freedoms and equality), have expanded, as well as education and employment opportunities.
- Increased migration has resulted in greater cultural diversity, ethnic diversity (after several generations), diversity of family structures, and family diversity with more mixed race couples. Because families are stretched across national borders with family members living in different countries, this separation reinforces globalization as more families maintain contact through media and physical visits.
- Greater cultural globalization has resulted in people creating friendship groups within their new countries and through shared interests online and may regard these friendship networks as "family."
- Greater competition in the labor market can increase unemployment and economic stress for workers and families. Economic uncertainties can also influence the strength of family life, as young people are more likely to delay starting a family when there are uncertain conditions in the labor market.
- Immigrants tend to have higher entrepreneurial activity compared to natives and have made significant contributions to innovation (IOM, 2020).
- Intergenerational bonds in migrant families have diminished, as well as collectivism and cultural identity.

- More diversity, choice, and uncertainty have brought about a decline in the number of persons committed to long-term relationships.
- Family challenges have resulted from the break-up of families due to displacement following armed conflicts and turbulence in their countries of origin.
- Family transitions have resulted in changes in family structures, functions, status, and acculturation, which may result in stress, adaptation, resilience, and altered meanings of family.
- Use of online communication allows family members to stay in daily contact with other family members. However, more media usage among children has meant greater exposure to global media events, such as mass shootings, natural disasters, and terrorist attacks, that can have negative effects. This can result in children having more mental health issues and parents becoming more paranoid and restrictive.

There is a worldwide *digital divide* in access to technology. The digital divide involves global gaps in infrastructure; subject matter that is not relevant to people's needs; content that is mostly in English; and economic, social, and cultural obstacles that prevent women's access to, use of, and benefit from information and communications technology (ICT). Some of these constraints include connection costs, computer literacy, and lack of language skills which are often based on socioeconomic disadvantages (Fogel, 2020).

There is also a *gender digital divide* that occurs when women cannot afford ICT because they have less control over their finances. Moreover, the internet can be used not only to perpetuate violence against women, but also to normalize and accelerate exploitation of women, marketing of pornographic material, and facilitation of human trafficking for sexual purposes (Kiran, 2018). Many women in less developed countries of the world do not have access to life-enhancing services for education, health, and financial inclusion. More efficient technological infrastructure across the world allows anyone, but especially women, to connect to much needed familial, social, and financial support. However, some cultural norms prevent women, more than men, from accessing technology—this is especially true for migrants. Closing the gender digital divide is essential during a time when technology plays such a large role in our daily lives and will enable women to better support their families, provide resources and opportunities for their children, bring them closer to family members who live in a different country, and improve their well-being.

Although the functions and structures of families vary by culture, families are still the most important resource in each society. They provide the buffer and protection to keep children and other members safe. However, some families are vulnerable when dealing with health care, economics, environment, and social influences. At times, they cannot manage alone and government steps in to create policies and programs that could affect family structure, education, and financial well-being. These situations afford an opportunity for family life educators to incorporate a preventative and educational approach to individual and family issues by providing necessary life skills.

An international perspective is critical when teaching about families. Many people in the US have an *ethnocentric* view of culture and may judge other cultures by the values and standards of their own culture. Therefore, it is important to provide an alternative perspective. We want to encourage an *ethnorelative* approach where cultures are understood relative to one another and characteristics are regarded as differences with no perception of being good or bad. Whether teaching about family relations, parenting, or marriage, cultural differences and implications can enhance learning, both within our own society, as well as learning about others. We need to create a climate within family science classrooms that fosters thinking not only about family content, but also multicultural understanding. While some family science programs have specific courses in cultural diversity, cultural learning should also be infused into a variety of courses and topics in order to provide and enhance an international perspective to the study of families. Additionally, an ethnorelative approach is important when providing family life education in the community.

Global Issues of Concern to Families

> The family is the natural and fundamental group unit of society and is entitled to protection by the society and the state.
>
> —Article 16(3) of the Universal Declaration of Human Rights (United Nations, 1948)

To better understand the context underlying the development of family life education programs internationally, an awareness of issues of concern to families is essential. These issues vary from country to country. Health concerns provide multiple stressors to families, especially those facing the devastating effects of COVID-19 and HIV/AIDS, which kill far more people than man-made or natural disasters (UNAIDS, 2020c; WHO, 2020b). Various countries have family planning and pregnancy as primary issues and are working to provide education regarding contraceptive options, prenatal care, and parenting. In other countries, marriage education predominates with legislation to assist couples by providing premarital education, whereas some countries are focusing on helping couples with their relationships as they make the transition to parenthood. A number of communities are facing the devastation of war, terrorism, and economic instability that influences individuals and families as they deal with the physical and emotional pain of both the actual events and the accompanying fear.

The world economy was still struggling to recover several years after the past global financial crisis began because countries are inextricably tied to each other's monetary well-being. However, the pandemics of COVID-19 and HIV/AIDS have influenced the global economy and exacerbated the situation. Global unemployment rates remain high, resulting in a synchronized economic downturn that affects both developed and developing countries. While the COVID-19 pandemic will eventually subside, the consequences for jobs and livelihoods around the world will be felt for many years to come. The toll of COVID-19 threatens to undo decades of progress and put millions of people into job insecurity not just today but into the future. People will not be able to afford rent, get an education, visit a doctor, or care for oneself or their family (Ventura, 2020). While there are a numerous global issues confronting individuals and families in various countries and regions of the world, we would like to focus on a few that are central to families: migration, human trafficking, changes in family structure, population and aging, health pandemics, and armed conflicts and turbulence.

Rise of Migration

International migration facilitates global interdependence and unity, but also brings widening demographic, economic, political, and ecological disparities that greatly influence families. While it is most commonly associated with seeking new employment opportunities, individuals and families often migrate due to political and other social reasons. Therefore, viewing families from a global context is not only important to increase our understanding of those beyond our borders, but also to gain insights about those who have recently immigrated to new countries. Because international travel and migration are bringing people of the world together, migration is emerging as one of the major issues of our time.

The number of countries concerned and involved in human mobility is steadily rising. None of the 195 independent states of the world is beyond the reach of migration, being either countries of origin, transit, or destination for migrants, or often all three simultaneously (USDOS, 2020a). Whereas some migration is internal, the rising number of people and families crossing borders is the most reliable indicator of the intensity of globalization. As a result, the traditional boundaries between languages, cultures, ethnic groups, and nations are shifting.

What is meant by the terms *migration*, *emigration*, and *immigration*? *Migration* means to move from one country or region to live in another, but it may be temporary, such as moving for employment, study, medical treatments, or seasonal employment. *Emigration* means to exit and relocate from one's country of origin to live in another on a permanent basis. *Immigration* means to leave one's previous home country to move to, enter, or settle in another country with the intention of permanently living there. The difference between these last two terms is the perspective of which country a person is *leaving* and which country a person is *entering* (Racoma, 2018). Persons emigrate *from* their home country and immigrate *to* a new country.

In 2020, there was an estimated 281 million persons living outside their country of origin, about 3.5% of the world's population, which is similar in size to the entire population of Indonesia—the world's fourth most populous country (UNDESA, 2020). However, the growth of international migration slowed by 27%, or 2 million, migrants due to COVID-19 as borders were closed, along with severe disruptions to international travel and plans to move abroad (UNDESA, 2020). Two-thirds of international migrants live in about 20 countries, with Europe having the largest number of international migrants (about 87 million), followed by North America (about 59 million) and Northern Africa and Western Asia (almost 50 million). India continues to be the largest country of origin for international migrants.

Nearly half of the international migrants are women, most of reproductive age, who either migrate as spouses, family members, or move independently from their families to work abroad as primary breadwinners (UNDESA, 2020). Women are important agents of change as they transform social, cultural, and political norms and promote positive social change across households and communities. However, opportunities for legal migration are limited, so many women who are in undesirable or desperate situations have resorted to unusual forms of migration such as human smuggling, to gain unlawful entry into a country. As a result, many women have experienced gender-specific forms of abuse and exploitation. Much of this migration was due to perceived opportunities for employment, but humanitarian crises also contributed to migration.

International migration has led to a new family form known as *transnational families*, in which the women are the migrants. Transnational families are characterized as having roots in their home countries and simultaneously creating new ties in their host countries. In the process of migration many of these women leave their families and children, which is referred to as "transnational mothering." These women often face criticism at home and abroad due to the perception that they are abandoning their families, however they migrate for the collective well-being of their families and to provide better opportunities for their children (Trask, 2011).

Migration can increase the income and happiness levels of those who move. In addition, migrants often send home money that benefits those left behind, thereby increasing the living conditions and well-being of those family members remaining in their home country. Family members at home also get satisfaction knowing that some family members can realize their potential abroad, which might also increase the opportunities of those left behind to also move abroad. However, having family members abroad is also associated with increased stress and depression for those left behind as the money does not offset these conditions. While money can "buy happiness," it does not relieve the pain of separation (Nikolova, Graham, & Ivlevs, 2018).

The mobility of families can be a concern because it results in family members no longer living in close proximity. When family members move, they often become disconnected from the unifying features of their extended families. While some families maintain communication through the internet and cell phones, quality time may be lost. There may be circumstances due to geography, time, and finances that prevent families from returning home for important family occasions. Thus, family members may not be present for significant family transitions, times of joy and sorrow, or opportunities to resolve family issues and disagreements. The COVID-19 pandemic exacerbated these challenges in maintaining connection. Because of these challenges, younger generations of migrant families may not have opportunities to interact and bond with their relatives as they did when living in their countries of origin.

Human Trafficking

Human smuggling and trafficking are two distinct crimes with overlapping problems (Duong, 2020). *Human smuggling* involves the provision of a service, typically transportation or fraudulent documents to an individual who "voluntarily" seeks to enter a foreign country illegally (HSTC, 2016). *Human trafficking* is the "involuntary" trapping and exploitation of a person using deception, violence, or coercion and is considered the dark underside of globalization (CFR, 2020; HSCT, 2016; USDHS, n.d.). Perceived as "modern slavery," human trafficking is a major issue across international borders. However, at times an act that begins as smuggling turns into trafficking. While smuggling often results in people going their separate ways after the transaction is complete, someone who is smuggled may become exploited en route or upon entering the destination country.

By 2020, the number of persons forcibly displaced across national borders worldwide was 34 million—double the number in 2000. Language barriers and fear of their traffickers and/or of law enforcement frequently keep victims from seeking help, making human trafficking a hidden crime (USDHS, n.d.). It harms adults and children in both wealthy and poor countries and generally takes three forms: *forced labor*, *forced marriage*, and *forced organ removal* (CFR, 2020).

- Forced Labor: Work or service done involuntarily (including sex trafficking) is the most common type of human trafficking, affecting nearly 25 million people worldwide (e.g., domestic work; agriculture; manufacturing; government imposed labor for military service, prisons, or national infrastructure projects; bonded labor to repay loans or inherited debts). Migrants are particularly vulnerable to trafficking, especially forced labor.
- Forced Marriage: Persons compelled to marry without their consent represent more than 15 million people. Forced marriage is defined internationally as occurring when one or both parties are under the age of consent, usually 18 years of age, although some countries permit young people who are 16 or 17 years of age to marry.
- Organ Trafficking: The sale and purchase of organs for transplantation is often the result of economic conditions that force poor and vulnerable individuals to sell their organs to the wealthy. Up to 10% of all transplants are believed to be conducted using illicitly acquired organs, generating between $840 million to $1.7 billion annually.

Women (49%) and girls (23%) make up the majority of all reported human trafficking cases, including 99% of victims of sex trafficking. Men (21%) and boys (7%) make up the majority of those trafficked in male-dominated industries such as agriculture, construction, and manufacturing. The majority of victims of organ removal are also men and boys. Due to COVID-19 there has been a surge in human trafficking due to the large numbers of people who face economic hardship, psychological or emotional vulnerability, natural disasters, or political instability (USDHS, n.d.) Thus, desperate individuals are more likely to accept risky job offers. Additionally, travel bans and isolation resulted in people spending more time on the internet, contributing to an increase of online sexual exploitation—particularly of children (CFR, 2020). Human trafficking is not only an international phenomenon, but also occurs in all 50 states in the US and the District of Columbia (USDOS, 2020b). Many countries around the world, as well as the US, have worked to implement the "3P" paradigm of *prosecuting* traffickers, *protecting* victims, and *preventing* the crime through the passage and implementation of national anti-trafficking laws (USDOS, 2021).

Changes in Family Structure

Many countries are facing accelerated changes that affect individuals, families, and family structure, such as age and stage of adulthood, courtship, marriage or its alternatives, contraception, fertility, parenting, divorce, remarriage, or stepfamilies. However, these changes are hard to quantify globally as countries collect different types of data about families. Minimal data exist about multigenerational households, cohabitation, children born outside of marriage, and with whom a child resides or if they are members of multiple households. Nevertheless, while globally there is a decrease in two parent families, they remain the majority structure around the world (Pasley & Petren, 2016).

In the past, many cultural groups assumed that couples would get married, stay married, have children, and deal with two sets of kin. However, in many societies this has been changing due to migration, cohabitation, contraception, the number of singles and single parents, women joining the labor force, and aging, all of which have altered family structure and the notion of intergenerational relationships. A few highlights of those changes include the following (Furstenburg, 2019):

- The age of first marriage is increasing in most nations of the world. Median ages of marriage are likely to be higher in more developed countries where the age gap between partners tends to be smaller. In developing countries, such as many in Africa, people get married at younger ages with a wider age gap (Buchholz, 2019). Marriage at a later age can imply less family influence on the choice of partner and the options of individuals to form families of their own choosing, including remaining single or cohabitating. Although not uniform, this pattern provides some evidence that the institution of marriage is evolving in response to economic and social change.
- Cohabitation has increased as marriage has become optional, especially throughout the Western world and in Eastern Europe. Cohabitation is more widespread among economically challenged individuals, especially in Latin America and the Caribbean.
- Globally, women are having fewer babies, which may in part be due to the increasing age of first marriage. Fertility rates still remain high in some parts of the world—rural Africa and parts of the Middle East. The global fertility rate, which fell from 3.2 births per woman in 1990 to 2.5 in 2019, is expected to decline further to 2.2 by 2050 (UNDESA, 2019).
- There is a growing trend of families without children, especially in more wealthy nations (e.g., English-speaking nations, Europe, Japan, Korea, Taiwan) where women are electing not to marry or have children.
- Changes in marriage patterns have resulted in more sexual interaction and childbearing outside of marriage (Furstenburg, 2019).
- Divorce has also become more common in most nations. Marriage stability has increased in some countries among those who have more education,

but it has declined for those with less education. As marriage has become more companionate, divorce is more likely to be viewed as acceptable for couples in unsatisfactory relationships.

- The acceleration of women's participation in the labor force in most developing and almost developed countries has resulted in changes in men's and women's domestic roles. The belief in gender equality may have grown faster than its actual practice. Nevertheless, throughout these countries, the push for women's rights has meant that women have far more access to education and labor market participation.
- Due to changes in marriage and work roles, families are less likely to reside in conjoint or complex households, although preferences for intergenerational arrangements continue to prevail in some parts of the world (Furstenburg, 2019).
- Same-sex marriages are now legal in 29 countries. Whereas 20 countries have legalized same-sex marriage through legislation, seven countries have done so through court decisions (*) and two countries have enacted legislation legalizing same-sex marriage after courts mandated them to do so (**). These countries include: Argentina, Australia, Austria*, Belgium, Brazil*, Canada, Columbia*, Costa Rica*, Denmark, Ecuador*, Finland, France, Germany, Iceland, Ireland, Luxembourg, Malta, Mexico*, the Netherlands, New Zealand, Norway, Portugal, South Africa**, Spain, Sweden, Switzerland, Taiwan**, the United Kingdom, and the United States of America*. Five countries support marriage equality in 2020, but have not yet legalized it (e.g., Chile, Czech Republic, Switzerland, Philippines, Thailand) (HRC, 2019).

These changes in family structure are linked with other broader cultural transitions, such as the rise of individualism, secularism, and growth of the welfare state. Thus, some traditional values within a culture have been altered regarding childbearing and the expected ages at which family traditions, such as marriage and childbirth, commonly occur (Mills, 2013; UN, 2019). Moreover, poor economic conditions in some countries have resulted in greater maternal and child mortality. Not only have the composition and structure of families changed in many countries, but also migrants who carried with them the idea of family structure based on their home countries often find that changes in culture and context evolve into further alterations to their families and feelings of uncertainty.

Worldwide Population and Aging

Population growth continues at the global level, but the rate of increase is slowing and the world's population could cease to grow around the end of the century. The global population (almost 7.8 billion) is expected to reach 8.5 billion in 2030, and almost 10 billion in 2050. This assumes a decline of fertility in countries in which large families are still prevalent and a slight increase in countries where women have fewer than two live births, along with continued reductions of mortality for all ages (UNDESA, 2019).

It is important to know why people die to improve how people live. The top global causes of death in order of total number of lives lost are associated with three broad topics: cardiovascular, respiratory, and neonatal conditions. Heart disease, which accounts for 16% of the world's total deaths, has been increasing. Stroke (11%) and chronic obstructive pulmonary disease (6%) are the 2nd and 3rd leading causes of death. COVID-19 has highlighted the importance for countries to invest in vital statistics to allow daily counting of deaths that can affect direct prevention and treatment efforts (WHO, 2020b).

Simultaneously, the world is growing older as global life expectancy (72.6 years in 2019) continues to rise while fertility levels fall. The global median age has increased from 21.5 years in 1970 to over 30 years in 2019 (Ritchie & Roser, 2019). By 2050, one in six people will be 65 years or older. In 2018, for the first time in history, persons aged 65 or older outnumbered children under 5 years of age. Moreover, the number of persons aged 80 or more is projected to triple from 143 million in 2019 to 426 million in 2050 (UNDESA, 2019). However, there has also been a recent decrease in US life expectancy projections due to COVID-19 and the disproportionate impact on Black and Latino populations. This decrease is expected to exceed that of most other high income countries (Andrasfay & Goldman, 2021). Those living in the poorest of countries will live about seven years less than the global average.

The aging of the population will affect everyone and will have a direct bearing on intergenerational and intragenerational relationships. Aging will not only influence the economics of countries, but also family composition, living arrangements, housing, migration, and health and health care. Thanks to medical advances, improved nutrition, and less demanding lifestyles, 65-year-olds in most countries can expect both longer lives and more years in good "physical" health than their parents or grandparents (Ritchie & Roser, 2019).

Aging also brings increased risk of mental health issues related to dementia and Alzheimer's disease. *Dementia*, which is not a normal part of aging, is a syndrome in which there is a deterioration in memory, thinking, behavior, and the ability to perform everyday activities (WHO, 2019a). Worldwide about 50 million people have dementia, with nearly 10 million new cases per year. *Alzheimer's disease* is the most common form of dementia, contributing to about 60% to 70% of the cases. The total number of persons with dementia is projected to reach 82 million by 2030 and 152 million by 2050 (WHO, 2019a). Dementia has a physical, psychological, and economic impact not only on those who have this condition, but also on their caregivers, families, and society at large. Dementia can be overwhelming for the families who have to deal with the situation. Since physical, emotional, and financial pressures can cause great stress, support is needed from health, social, financial, and legal systems (WHO, 2019a).

Health Pandemics: COVID-19 and HIV/AIDS

A *pandemic* is an epidemic of an infectious disease that has spread across a large region (multiple continents or worldwide), affecting a substantial number of people. The COVID-19 pandemic has affected the entire world, regardless of nationality, ethnicity, or faith. COVID-19 does not discriminate, but efforts to prevent and contain it do, as the pandemic has hit hardest the poorest and most vulnerable in our societies. Nearly a year into the pandemic, we face a human tragedy, and a public health, humanitarian, and development emergency (Guterres, 2020). The COVID-19 pandemic has resulted in increasing numbers of infections, deaths, and disruptions to individual and family life. The fluidity of these data makes it difficult to quantify the current situation as this disease continues to rapidly change each day, week, and month. For a number of families, it has meant making big changes in everyday routines due to financial hardships, changes in employment, and the illness or death of a family member(s). Therefore, it is important for family members to stay calm; explain the rationale for social distancing, isolation, and masks to children; receive their vaccinations when available, and remain in touch with friends and family members by electronic communication (Strawn, 2020).

The impact of COVID-19 is a pervasive and current health issue that is intertwined with the HIV/AIDS pandemic, another major world public health concern (HIV.gov, 2020). It is currently estimated that over 5.7 million people have died worldwide from COVID-19, while 1 million people die each year from HIV/AIDS (Johns Hopkins University & Medicine, 2022; Roser & Ritchie, 2019). Whereas 33 million have died since the start of the HIV/AIDS epidemic, 38 million people are living with HIV/AIDS including 1.8 million children under the age of 15. As of 2019, approximately 76 million people have become infected with HIV, with women and girls accounting for about 59% of HIV infections (UNAIDS, 2020b, 2020c).

COVID-19 has not only resulted in increasing numbers of cases and death rates, but it has also disrupted essential health systems and undermined programs to address HIV/AIDS and other global health priorities (HIV.gov, 2020; UNAIDS, 2020b). The status of HIV/AIDS is being affected by the lockdowns and border closures imposed to stop COVID-19 which are impacting both the production and distribution of antiretroviral medicines and leading to increases in cost and supply issues (HIV.gov, 2020). It is predicted that a six-month disruption in HIV treatment could lead to more than 500,000 additional deaths from AIDS-related illnesses.

The United Nations declared its goal to end HIV/AIDS by 2030 with its 90-90-90 policy (UN, 2021; UNAIDS, 2020a). They proposed that 90% of all people living with HIV will know their HIV status; 90% of all people will receive sustained antiretroviral therapy; and 90% of all people receiving antiretroviral therapy will have viral suppression. Of all people living with HIV in 2019, 81% knew their status, 67% were accessing treatment, and 59% were virally suppressed with 12.6 million people still waiting for treatment (UNAIDS, 2020c). The world is approaching the 90-90-90 target, but is not there yet. Nevertheless there are now new proposed targets of 95-95-95 (WHO, 2020a). The progress on the prevention of HIV transmission remains slow with the estimated number of new infections in 2019 being more than three times higher than the UNAIDS 2020 target. While HIV continues to be a major global health issue, because of greater access to effective prevention, diagnosis, treatment, and care, HIV infection prior to COVID-19 had become a manageable chronic health condition enabling people living with

HIV to lead relatively long and healthy lives (WHO, 2020b). AIDS-related deaths have been reduced by 60% since the peak in 2004, but there are still about 5,000 new infections per day (KFF, 2020; WHO 2020a). Because of the increased number of people with HIV receiving treatment in resource-poor countries, deaths have declined and the epidemic has stabilized. However, the setback due to COVID-19 remains unknown.

Over two-thirds of all people living with HIV (38 million) reside in Sub-Saharan Africa (20.7 million), which is the hardest hit region in the world, followed by Asia and the Pacific (5.8 million) (KFF, 2020). Some key populations for infections include men who have sex with men, people who inject drugs, people in prisons and other closed settings, sex workers and their clients, and transgender people (Avert, 2020; WHO, 2020a). While HIV is prevalent in the general population of this region, an increasing number of infections occur among adolescent girls and young women. In 2018, the prevalence of HIV among young women was double that of men. Young women with partners who were 16 or more years older had a three times greater risk of HIV infection compared to those with partners less than 15 years older. Higher levels of spousal physical or sexual violence are also experienced by young women, more than other age group. Young women who experienced intimate partner violence were 50% more likely to have HIV than young women who had not experienced violence (Avert, 2020). Most new victims are women who become infected by their husbands who have both a *home wife* and one or more *traveling wives* as companions when they are away at work. Some women in Africa may not be aware of the ways HIV can be spread and are prevented by cultural norms from insisting on prevention methods when they have sexual relations with their husbands. Gender inequality makes it more difficult for African women to negotiate condom use. Moreover, sexual violence can increase the widespread risk of HIV transmission.

There is also increasing prevalence of HIV in women in Asia, including large epidemics in China and India, due to women's low economic and social position and poor health status. In Asia, injection drug use in conjunction with sexual relations influences the HIV epidemic. As in Africa, gender inequalities and the cultural rules governing sexual relations for men and women are central to this health issue. HIV not only affects the health of individuals, but also families, communities, and the economic development of countries (KFF, 2020).

Armed Conflicts and Turbulence

Trouble spots exist in many parts of the world and when they erupt, suffering and hardship follow. Armed conflicts impact individuals and families in all countries and areas whether it is the country that deploys military personnel to a war zone, suffers the consequences of military expenses and economic warfare, experiences war and terrorism from a distance through the media, or suffers from indoctrination and building of enemy images (Myers-Walls & Myers-Bowman, 2016). Families feel the impact of war even if not in the war zone. Because of their global impact, wars, conflicts, and terrorism are no longer isolated to one or a few countries but affect us all.

War has changed over time as contemporary conflicts try to bring the battle close to the core of the civilian population directly, purposefully, and on a large scale. Families are directly and indirectly affected by war and political violence (Myers-Walls, 2004; Myers-Walls & Myers-Bowman, 2016). Examples include:

- Family members may be killed or injured directly by the turbulence. Their family's lives are disrupted by the loss of income and inability to provide for basic needs.
- Women and girls are particularly targeted by the use of sexual violence as a tactic to humiliate, dominate, instill fear, or forcibly relocate members of the community. Warring groups use rape as a weapon because it destroys communities and punishes men by raping women in their presence (UN, n.d.).
- Many families can be displaced from their homes due to political violence and become refugees or may send their children away for their safety, resulting in family members losing necessary connections with each other. The number of forcibly displaced people globally exceeded 70 million at the end of 2018. This includes 26 million refugees, 3.5 million asylum seekers, and 41 million internally displaced persons (UN, 2019).
- Soldiers going to war experience changes to their families at home related to child care, family lines of authority and responsibility, and stress and anxiety. In addition to the deaths of soldiers, there are visible wounds and amputations, as well as invisible trauma that can last a lifetime (e.g., brain injuries, post-traumatic stress disorder, health issues). Moreover, absence of individuals due to these conflicts and their subsequent reintegration into families can influence the ongoing development of couple and family relationships. Repeated deployments have been related to alcohol abuse, child and domestic violence, and increased divorce.
- Families not directly in the battle zone may be affected by the fiscal choices their countries made to support the war effort and war-time sanctions that result in malnutrition and lack of medical care. Media discussions, videos, and reactions can cause confusion, misunderstandings, and anxiety, especially for children.

Increasingly, the brunt of armed violence and warfare is being borne by children, who suffer in different ways from adults. They are weaker and have more at stake since their physical, mental, and psychological development is heavily dependent on their childhood experiences (Save the Children, 2019). Nearly 420 million (one in five) children worldwide were living in conflict-affected areas in 2017, which was up 30 million from the previous year. Moreover, 142 million are living in high-intensity conflict zones with more than 1,000 battle-related deaths in a year. The countries where children were the most affected are Afghanistan, Yemen, South Sudan, the Central African Republic, the Democratic Republic of Congo (DRC), Syria, Iraq, Mali, Nigeria, Somalia, and Ukraine. One reason for the increased number of children living in areas of conflict is that today's conflicts are more likely to be protracted, urban, and fought among civilian populations. The UN's six disturbing violations against children include (1) being killed, (2) being maimed, (3) being recruited by armed groups or abducted, (4) sexual violence, (5) attacks at school, and (6) denial of humanitarian aid. In many cases, children are specifically targeted (Save the Children, 2019). For the families and children in the world's conflict zones, there are multiple problems for which assistance cannot come soon enough.

THE MEANING OF "FAMILY" THROUGHOUT THE WORLD

What Is a Family?

Family structures and functions vary across countries to reflect varying cultural attitudes about families. (Majeed & Kanwal, 2018; Pesando, 2019). Nevertheless, the family remains a fundamental building block of human societies affecting health, reproduction, and well-being of both present and future generations. Families serve as the basic source of early socialization of children and identification for adults. Family members are engaged with each other in various ways, such as through material, economic, social, and emotional exchanges.

We live in a world of different meanings and contrasting perspectives of family life, so we cannot impose an arbitrary definition of what constitutes a family. Government entities, employers, religions, and individual family members and family groups may view families differently. They may perceive the meaning of "family" as family of origin, family of procreation (biological family), or family of commitment or affiliation. Socially constructed families (family of commitment or affiliation) have been created to serve the nurturance and acceptance needs of the individual, which could be influenced by physical or emotional distance (e.g., migration or perceived lack of support) within the family of origin. Depending on one's culture, family can be perceived as a nuclear family or extended family with multiple generations. Moreover, in some cultures the deceased are still considered as exerting a strong presence in the family. Family can also be defined legally as to who can be married or adopted by law, whereas some perceive taking in a child or nonfamily member as an act of love without the need of legal documentation. Thus, if we impose a single definition of family upon others, we may be sending a message that their family values and structures are not legitimate.

While there is no consensus as to what constitutes a family, particularly across cultures, it could be meaningful to view the family as "a bonded unit of interacting and interdependent individuals who have some common goals, resources, and values, and may share living space for at least part of their life cycle" (Darling, 2005). This nonexclusionary definition of the family embraces differing family bonds, forms, sizes, ages, and role patterns, whether we are discussing same-sex marriages and families, children who divorce their parents, or families who socially open their boundaries to a nonrelative. Such a paradigm facilitates viewing the family as a collection of interdependent, yet independent, individuals whose group entity differs from characteristics of its individual members. When the family is viewed as an interacting group of individuals who are emotionally, physically, and socially interdependent, the focus shifts from the attributes of the group or the individual to the relationships among the family members. In the complex world in which we live, a flexible perspective of families is essential to facilitate the bonds that may have eroded through death, divorce, family separation, or circumstance (Darling, 2005).

Using Theory to Understand International Families

There are multiple theories from various disciplines that can be used to understand international family structures and functions by providing reasonable explanations of individual and family behaviors. Although no single theory is intended to explain everything, especially in countries beyond our border, theory utilizes a certain set of concepts to explain a particular set of phenomena. Because we are affected by our childhood, familial, gendered, cultural, and socialization experiences, the integration of multiple theories is warranted. For example, *exchange theory* can be incorporated to understand the rewards and costs of living in a particular location versus migrating to another country (White, Martin, & Adamsons, 2019). Moreover, immigrants to various new cultures may experience differing levels of adaptation due to the stressors in their lives, availability of resources for coping, and perception of these events. Thus, understanding *family stress theory* and the ABC-X model as it applies to the normative and nonnormative stressors of immigrant families can provide insight into family adaptability, boundary ambiguity, and resilience (Boss, Bryant, & Mancini, 2017; Weber & Branscum, 2020). While families can be analyzed from numerous theoretical frameworks, a few can be highlighted to illustrate how theory can be applied to facilitate greater understanding of international families (see Chapter 8 for further details).

Family systems

Viewing the family as a system provides an important paradigm when analyzing human behavior globally (White, Martin, & Adamsons, 2019). Cross-cultural understanding of intergenerational communications within families, physical and psychological boundaries, feedback in coupled relationships, and parent-child communications can provide insight into interpreting the complex relationships between individuals and their families. Theoretical insights and clarifications can evolve from discussions of boundaries, distance regulation, cohesion, and adaptability in various cultures. What types of cultural boundaries exist for persons of varying ethnic, age, or gender backgrounds? What kinds of expectations for family togetherness and adaptability exist for different ethnic and religious groups? For example, cohesion and enmeshment can have different meanings in cultures that value familism vs. individuality. A discussion of family stories, rituals, and rules can also provide understanding and meaning about differing cultural groups.

Developmental theory

Incorporating a developmental framework, for both individuals and families, can be helpful when trying to understand families across cultures within a perspective of change (White, Martin, & Adamsons, 2019). Whereas change is ever present, gradual, and a part of individual aging, families and society are changing at an even faster rate. Along with media influences, alternate lifestyles, advances in technology and biotechnology, and pandemics, family life has also evolved. Cultural assumptions and beliefs about family life change over time, as do its transitions of getting married, having children, becoming older, and dying. People in diverse cultures develop differently based on the values, economics, norms, and demographics in their cultures, so communicating with individuals from other cultures at varying points in their development can expand insights about family life.

Family ecosystems framework

When studying international families, not only are there many different family customs, but also environments and social contexts for those customs. Some customs, which may seem different to Westerners, include widow inheritance in Africa, living apart together (LAT) in Germany and Sweden, a temporary fixed-period of marriage (*mut'a*) in Iran or places with Islamic law, hymen reconstruction in South Korea and Greek Cyprus, and the subordinate roles of women in many cultures (Francoeur, 2004).

To add an environmental context to international family life education and international family customs and behaviors, the family ecosystems approach can be quite meaningful (Darling, Cassidy, & Rehm, 2017, 2020; Darling & Turkki, 2009). With individual, family, and world issues becoming increasingly complicated, a framework is needed to facilitate our thinking. The reciprocal interactions between environmental influences and families differentiate each country's issues and the preferred mode to ameliorate their concerns. There is increasing awareness that human beings are interdependent creatures and not independent organisms. This is not only true in our relationships with each other, but also with the total environment in which we live. Worldwide population growth, contamination of the environment, pandemics, depletion of energy resources, war, and terrorism have made us aware of our interdependence with each other and with the environment. This holistic view of individuals and groups in their association with the physical, biological, and social conditions and events around them provides a frame of reference that has come to be generally known as *human or family ecology*.

A core value in an ecosystems framework is survival, not just of humans, but other living species as well. This also includes the survival and well-being of the nonliving environment, which is critical for sustaining all life. Most family life educators dealing with international family life education would resonate with the perspective of Bubolz and Sontag (1993), who proposed that the grounding of family ecology theory in values places an important responsibility on scholars and practitioners. We must attend to special problems of groups and subcultures that lack power, self-determination, and access to resources and who experience discrimination and prejudice. These can include racial and ethnic groups, people with disabilities, women, people living in poverty, and the elderly. Attention must be given not only to the "haves," but also the "have nots." The scope of family ecology must be international and address needs of people in developing nations, as well as those that experience fewer privileges in more developed areas of the world. Because human betterment and the quality of the environment are interdependent, the value base of family ecology is grounded in this interdependence.

The major concepts of the family ecosystem involve the *organism* (individual or family) as it *interacts* with its multifaceted *environments*, i.e., natural, human-behavioral, and human-constructed environments (see Chapter 8 for further details). By applying the ecosystems framework, learners and family life education practitioners can examine global issues of family concern and their impact on individuals and family members. This approach can provide an ethnorelative approach to understanding cultural perspectives of families, public policies, and environmental conditions.

What Is Family Life Education—International Perspectives

Although family life education is not yet "global," many countries have their own formal or informal methods for working with and educating families. In general, countries have various programs for families that are funded to different degrees by different sources. Some countries may concentrate their programs on children, while others focus on marriage, parenting, or sexuality. Programs may be part of the educational system or are found in health systems, social welfare, or religious systems.

The differences *within* any country or cultural group may be greater than those *between* groups (Allen & Blaisure, 2015). Culture is the total way of life of people—the customs, beliefs, values, attitudes, and communication patterns that characterize a group and provide a common sense of identity. However, cultural characteristics can change as people are exposed to varying influences over time. Therefore, it is important for family life educators to develop cultural competence, a combination of *awareness*, *knowledge*, and *skills* along with an understanding of the influence of culture on one's life experiences and appreciation of the diverse influences that can shape the lives of others. Expanding awareness of one's own cultural influences, as well as those in other cultures, is an ongoing process. An increase in intercultural sensitivity by recognizing and experiencing cultural similarities and differences, can increase intercultural competence (Bennet, 1993). Diversifying the number of reliable sources of cultural information, can result in greater knowledge and insights. Familiarity of local families, policies, and environmental issues affecting their way of life, along with the cultural nuances of their interactions, can enable practitioners to operate within the context of the local population (Allen & Blaisure, 2015). By incorporating awareness of a culture along with knowledge of cross-cultural interactions, family life educators can use their skills to develop programs and engage families. Programs need to be relevant to the culture and local needs of families to build partnerships between the educator and those whom they will serve. It is important that family life educators do not engage with another culture while perceiving that they know all there is to know about a topic or that culture. In some countries, there is a higher priority on in-country assistance and progress compared to help from outsiders who may not fully understand the culture (Darling & Turkki, 2009). Therefore, educators need to continually learn and appreciate the cultural context of another country to enhance the learning experience for all.

As suggested, diversifying reliable resources helps to gain knowledge and insights. Robila and Taylor's (2018) book is an example of a resource to facilitate understanding diverse international efforts in family life education. It contains contributions of colleagues sharing information about family life education from 24 countries (including the US) representing six continents. While there is an overlap of nine countries between this resource and the information we have included from international colleagues for this text, having a diversity of resources is quite valuable.

Various countries beyond the US have developed extensive programs in family life education and passed new legislation to support family life education (e.g., Singapore, Taiwan). Others have marriage/couples/parent education (e.g., China, Hong Kong, Ireland); sexuality education and a focus on HIV/AIDS (e.g., Australia, Finland, Nigeria, Sweden); and developed academic programs related to family life education (e.g., Hong Kong, South Korea, Taiwan). However, information and communication about the progress of these initiatives worldwide are varied and inconsistent. From an international perspective, family life education exists, but its definition, meaning, goals, and methods can be quite diverse. This is due, in part, to the breadth of the field and the different disciplines involved, especially in the international arena. In fact, a recent Google search for "International Family Life Education" resulted in about 158,000,000 entries. While all these entries may not be applicable to specific programs, family concerns in various countries are resulting in organized programs to assist those in need.

Evolving Status of Family Life Education Internationally

While there are numerous programs dealing with aspects of families and family life education worldwide, we have little comparative data regarding the status of family life education in specific countries. Conducting research internationally has several challenges involving communication, coordination, and interpretation. Nevertheless, it is important to get data from other countries and develop a global network of colleagues to assist each other with issues of professional and social concern.

International Family Life Education—Developmental Context

An exploratory study was conducted through the coordination and support of the National Council on Family Relations (NCFR), an international multidisciplinary professional organization, linking family research with family life education, practice, and policy formation. The purpose of the study was to determine the status of family life education internationally by examining the involvement, interest, and available course work offered in family life education worldwide (Darling & Turkki, 2009). While there can be limitations to interpretation based on the sample, questions, and data collection procedures, it is important to examine the development of FLE in other countries and their family issues of public concern.

The participants in this study consisted of non-US members of four international organizations dealing with family issues. After examining United Nations documents to determine worldwide issues, a survey was developed with the assistance of international colleagues. Although the survey was in English, many family professionals speak English as a second language to facilitate professional communication and collaboration. The final sample consisted of 277 respondents from five continents and 50 countries (Darling & Turkki, 2009). Involvement in family life education was reported by 43.7% of the respondents, whereas 22.6% were involved in parent education and 10.7% considered themselves marriage educators.

These professionals noted that various family issues were of public concern to the people in their countries. The four greatest issues were drug and alcohol abuse, aging, family violence, and adolescent health. Family professionals who reported public interest about family issues believed that the well-being of families was related to the availability of family life education (FLE) courses along with public and legislative attention to FLE. These findings suggested the emerging importance of public consciousness about family matters and family life education in various countries of the world, as well as the need for local family professionals to resolve issues of concern. It is hoped that this public awareness will further a global understanding and education of professionals and students about families (Darling & Turkki, 2009).

Due to the increasing international interest in NCFR's Certified Family Life Educator credential, the respondents were asked to indicate the availability of university-level course offerings in their country that were applicable to NCFR's ten FLE content areas. The responses, which were ranked by their means, resulted from a Likert-type scale ranging from 1 = no coursework to 5 = considerable coursework.

Family Life Education Content Areas	**Mean**
Human Growth and Development Across the Lifespan	3.78
Families and Individuals in Societal Contexts	3.74
Internal Dynamics of Families	3.52
Interpersonal Relationships	3.41
Family Law and Public Policy	3.25
Human Sexuality	3.23
Professional Ethics and Practice	3.16
Family Resource Management	3.15
Parent Education and Guidance	2.94
Family Life Education Methodology	2.77

The most prominent area was *Human Growth and Development* with *Family Life Methodology* having the least preparation. As gratifying as it is to see that so many countries have coursework applicable to family life education, the need for family life education methodology is readily apparent.

International Family Life Education—Current Perspectives

Comments from international family scholars can provide a rich contribution to the perceived status and issues of family life education in various countries. Therefore, in order to provide current information on the perceived development of family life education internationally, non-US members of the National Council on Family Relations and other international family professionals were contacted about the current importance of FLE within their countries, with some of these members recommending other international family colleagues. While the majority of the respondents were in university academic positions, a few were directors of marriage and family centers, research centers, or professional development organizations that support families. They were asked to give their general perceptions and insights about FLE, along with some generic questions that could stimulate their thinking. The responses were from 35 family colleagues, six continents, and 27 countries plus Hong Kong, including: Australia, Brazil, Canada, China plus Hong Kong, Croatia, Denmark, Finland, Ghana, Iran, Jamaica, Japan, Ireland, Israel, Luxembourg, Mexico, Netherlands, Nigeria, Peru, Philippines, Russia, Senegal, Singapore, South Korea (a.k.a. the Republic of Korea), Spain, Sweden, Taiwan, and the United Kingdom.

After a brief explanation of what is meant by FLE, the topics suggested for their input included (1) the existence of structured programs in the public schools or higher education that focus on studying families; (2) availability of community FLE in the public or private sector; (3) public interest in attending FLE programs; (4) promotion of FLE by agencies and policy makers; (5) critical issues facing individuals and families and educational efforts to assist them; and (6) the development of FLE programs in their countries. If family education exits in their countries, is it just beginning, making progress, or doing well? After analyzing the data, some of the resulting themes that evolved were related to perceptions, participation in FLE, and governmental and cultural influences on FLE.

When examining statements from international colleagues, many noted that their comments were "personal opinions" or "uninformed opinions." Others provided qualifying statements such as, "from my point of view," "that I know of," or "as far as I know." **Note**: These were their professional perceptions or based on the perspective of the agency or setting in which they worked. The level of detail was varied as some people shared more about their countries than others. Thus, the following comments should be viewed from this context.

Family life education is perceived as occurring in differing degrees in various countries, as is the need to certify family life educators. An assortment of programs exist in primary and secondary schools, as well as higher education, but family programs vary by length of time and their inclusion within other curricula. While some countries had programs in schools, other countries have government-sponsored programs or programs sponsored by NGO's (nongovernment organizations). These programs are formal or nonformal and are available with varying levels of interest in participation.

A basic issue is whether or not family life education (FLE) or family education (as it is called in some countries) exists beyond the US and to what degree. It should be noted that the respondents might not have thought it occurred in their countries, because it may not be called FLE. Responses ranged from FLE not existing (e.g., Croatia, Finland, Ghana, Iran, Ireland, Israel, Sweden, Russia, the United Kingdom) to being in its infancy or scarcely existing (e.g., Australia, China, the United Kingdom), or being conducted informally by family members in homes or villages (e.g., Ghana), or just beginning, developing, or existing, but insufficient (e.g., Japan, Philippines, Spain). In Australia family education is assumed to be incorporated in learning, but rarely is specifically addressed in formal education.

Progress is being made in some countries (e.g., Canada, Jamaica, Nigeria) and FLE is doing well, developing rapidly, and making good progress in others (e.g., Ireland, Singapore, South Korea, Taiwan). (**Note**: Some respondents from Japan perceived there was no FLE, whereas others indicated that it was just beginning. However, in Japanese there is no word for "family life education," which may account for some of this confusion.) In some countries they have courses linked to "well-being" (e.g., Finland). While some respondents indicated that FLE exists, it is carried out by social workers who support and help families (Denmark). Most likely, programs conducted by those with social work training would not include the preventative approach of FLE.

Certification and certificates in family life education

There has been some initial international interest in certifying family life educators, but it is in its infancy. In 2003, Taiwan's government passed the *Family Education Law* that resulted in approximately 2,700 (in 2019) certified family life educators. Students take 10 courses (five required and five elective courses) and if they get a satisfactory grade or take an exam, they become certified by the government. As a result, the number of Taiwanese family life educators is increasing faster than expected. Singapore hopes to increase the number of family life educators by enhancing training programs and providing certificates in family life education. It has created a FLE certificate to enable the training of new family life educators, develop the capability of existing educators who may not have had training in FLE, and ensure a minimum practice standard for family life educators conducting programs funded by the Ministry.

The South Korean Certified Family Life Educator Program, which has three levels (i.e., second, first, and expert) has been managed by the Korean Association of Family Relations since 1996. There is a requirement of a BA degree in a related field along with courses in family studies, human development, sexuality, family resource management, and FLE, along with a record of participation in FLE programs and ethics education. There are other requirements for non-FS degree graduates or continuing education. This certificate is registered under the Korean Research Institute for Vocational Education and Training as a certificate from private institutes and not the federal government.

School programs at three levels

Family Life Education in Primary School Programs. For varying age levels and to varying degrees, programs in family life education or family education exist in some primary school settings. While there may not be courses specifically focused on FLE, the FLE content is incorporated within other classes. For example, some aspects of healthy relationships, interpersonal relationships, growth and development, and puberty education are taught in general studies and home economics classes (e.g., Australia, Hong Kong, Jamaica, Japan, Philippines, South Korea). At the primary school level in Nigeria, family life education is called sex education, home economics, moral education, civic education, or any name approved by the state or federal education board. To clarify, in Nigeria sex education characterizes the entire structure of a human being and affects behavior.

Moreover, in China parents are required to review FLE programs (child safety, parental involvement, effective schooling) online on a regular basis through the academic year. Some other examples include:

- In Ireland, there is a primary class on Social, Personal and Health Education (SPHE) with a module on *Myself and My Family.* The content varies by age, so children aged 5 should be able to identify and name the people who constitute a family and appreciate that all families are not the same; realize that he/she belongs to a family and that each person has a place and role within the family; explore the things that families do together; realize how families take care of, support, and love each other; and explore and acknowledge many of the things that can be learned in the home.
- In the sixth class, the Irish family module has as its goal that children should be enabled to discuss families and homes and how they can vary in many ways, examine what belonging to a family means, discuss possible changes in family relations, and explore expectations as they grow and mature. Moreover, they can learn how to cope with these changes, and examine some factors that can affect family life (e.g., birth of a baby, addiction, material prosperity, poverty, illness, bereavement, violence, changes in lifestyle, sexual stereotyping). Students should be able to define and discuss behaviors that are important for harmony in family life, critically examine media portrayals of families and family life, and compare and contrast the lifestyles of families in different cultures, both in Ireland and abroad.
- In Jamaica, "Health and Family Life Education" starts in elementary school and runs through middle and high schools. The curriculum is focused on four main themes: (1) Self and Interpersonal Relationships, (2) Sexuality and Sexual Health, (3) Eating and Fitness, and (4) Managing the Environment.
- In Japan, Home Economics Education in grades 5 and 6 of elementary as well as junior and senior high schools includes content about families, but the focus is broad so it is difficult to create suitable lessons for students.
- In Taiwan, the Family Education Law passed in 2003 requires all students K–12 to have at least four hours of family education each year. Each school can arrange the learning experiences according to their needs and resources.
- In South Korea, elementary and middle schools focus on (1) human development and family (e.g., childhood, adolescence, sexuality, family relationships, communication, conflict resolution); (2) family life and safety (e.g., food and nutrition, housing stress, violence); and (3) resource management and independence (e.g., money time, leisure, consumption, work and family, life planning, career).
- In Sweden, FLE is not a part of primary education, however, sex education is mandatory in years 4 to 6 (although only about 10% of teachers have received any training).
- In Peru, the last 5 to 10 years have seen FLE reach more families and become more effective among families with younger children and families in regional/rural areas.

Family life education in secondary school programs. Family life education is taught in some secondary schools, but it is mostly a part of various courses or programs such as Life Society Programs or Liberal Studies (e.g., Hong Kong), Home Economics, Home Science, Family Economics, Health Programs, or Well-Being (e.g., Finland, Ghana, Jamaica, Japan, Senegal, South Korea), Society (e.g., Croatia), or Sexuality Education, Relationships, and Intimate Violence (e.g., Israel). Spain has activities to promote FLE, but they are not provided on a regular basis. While in Ireland it is included in Social, Personal, and Health Education classes, in the United Kingdom it is part of Social or Moral Education. In Japan, both male and female students must take home economics in which studying families is part of the curriculum. This occurs in elementary school (5th to 6th grade), junior high school (7th to 9th grade), and senior high school (10th to 12th grade). However, it all depends on the teacher's perceptions of the importance of studying families, as teachers trained in food and nutrition or clothing may find it difficult to teach about families and family life.

When surveying family life educators throughout the world about their perceptions regarding family life education in their countries, sexuality education was noted by many, even though the topic has encountered resistance in some countries and regions. While family life education is not often explicitly covered in school settings in various countries, one part of FLE, sexuality education, is an important topic for secondary schools. (Note that in some countries it is referred to as "sex" education and in others "sexuality" education; see Chapter 9 for a discussion of these terms.)

- In 1955, *Sweden* made history as the first country in the world to make sex and gender education mandatory in the schools nationwide. Sweden, which is a country where cohabitation has long been an acceptable option for many couples, has compulsory programs in all schools regarding sexuality and living together. This content is continually updated. However, how this topic is integrated into a teacher's lessons is up to the discretion of the school's principal. Two-thirds of secondary schools lack a school-wide sex education system, leaving teachers responsible for planning, developing, and evaluating their own programs. Without adequate training, teachers can find this a daunting task and may skip or under-teach the topic because they are unsure of how to approach it. They propose that because sexuality is natural, it cannot be harmful. The goal in Sweden is to address sexuality according to the age group in a manner more relevant to them. They have an integrated technique so educators incorporate sexuality and diverse lifestyles into traditional curriculum. Similarly, Finland is also considered to have an advanced model of comprehensive sexuality education within Europe.
- In the United Kingdom it is compulsory for secondary schools to provide sex and relationship education from age 11 onward. However, this involves little more than a single weekly session and is unlikely to look anything like adult relationship education programs that focus on reproductive biology and awareness of LGBTQ issues.

- In Ireland, senior high students take a Relationships and Sexuality Education Module in which they learn about self-awareness and personal skills, relationship skills, sexual and reproductive health, sexual identity, parenting, and personal rights and safety.
- In Nigeria, before the widespread initiation of formal schooling, young people were educated informally to prepare them for adult life. However, with the onset of rural to urban migration, they became more involved in risky sexual behaviors. Thus in 2002, a Family Life and HIV Education (FLHE) curriculum was established for primary, secondary, and tertiary levels of education. In Nigeria, the study of sex education has different meanings to different people (e.g., the child, parents, teachers, Christians, or Muslims) and affects how FLE content can be delivered. Sex education in Nigeria, which is often misinterpreted, simply means the knowledge and information about the means of learning the external conditions that aid the development of boys and girls to adulthood. Some included topics are:
  - —Understanding of sexuality as God's gift and comprehension of its procreative meaning and capacity as an expression of love.
  - —Essential biological facts about sexual differences and equality of the sexes.
  - —Discussions of homosexuality and psychosocial development.
  - —Disadvantages of early marriage and advantages of delayed marriage and parenthood.
  - —Information on why people have a need for children and need to be responsible parents.
  - —Understanding natural family planning, modern contraceptives, and alternate methods.
  - —Discussion of the rights of the unborn child, problem of genetic disorders, and supportive attitudes toward "defective" persons.
- In Russia, students receive information about sex from literature, teachers, and priests with mixed results. There are no recommended materials except for some general health statements for 11th grade students. Children can be too embarrassed to ask parents, so they get their information about sex, relationships, and contraceptives from commercials, movies, video games, pornography, and classmates. While sex education was introduced into schools in 2014, there are still no training courses as the government cannot reach a common opinion about this issue. Often times there is underground education when educators and others teach children after school. Students are embarrassed to buy condoms and have a lot of misinformation.

Family life education in university programs. Internationally, university programs vary in name and focus. It is uncommon for universities to have structured programs that deal with families (e.g., Brazil, China, Japan). There are only a few programs that offer majors in family studies and FLE (e.g., more than ten universities in South Korea, six universities in Taiwan, four masters programs in Hong Kong including two in marriage and family therapy, and several family studies/

sociology programs in Canada). In China, there are no structured programs that focus only on families, but there are some Departments of Family and Early Childhood Education. In the Philippines there are courses and degree programs that focus on family studies in colleges and universities (e.g., BS and MS in Family Life and Child Development). At the graduate level in Ireland there are a small number of programs that relate more specifically to families (e.g., Masters in Family Support Studies; Masters in Child, Family, and Community Studies). In Taiwan, the colleges and universities that offer FLE licensure-related courses, provide courses such as Marriage and Family Relations, Introduction to FLE, and Family Development for all students. In Mexico, Catholic universities are beginning to have some programs in family studies, which is quite new.

Many programs infuse family studies content into a variety of courses or programs in child care; social care; social science; family and social policy; home economics; counseling; sociology; social work; education; nursing; anthropology; psychology; personal, social, and humanities education; or women's studies (e.g., Canada, China, Hong Kong, Jamaica, Ireland, Mexico, Taiwan). Thus, a lot of the professional responsibilities related to families are referred to persons with backgrounds in psychology, sociology, and social workers.

In Luxembourg, the focus on family life education within higher education courses and programs varies. At the University of Luxembourg the closest curriculum related to family life education is within the faculty of Humanities, Education, and Social Sciences—namely baccalaureate, masters, or PhD degrees in psychology. Fields of study are broad compared to the US, and subspecialities are uncommon. Thus, those who work with families are primarily psychologists or psychotherapists. There is no distinction between child psychology, adolescent psychology, or gerontology. The primary focus is intervention and not prevention. Professionals rarely specialize in the population with whom they are working. Thus, being a nurse and working in pediatrics does not indicate a background in pediatric nursing. A psychologist may work with children, but did not study "child" psychology.

In Nigeria, family life education is taught at the Universities, Monotechnic institutions, and Colleges of Education. It is not a course of study leading to a degree, but is a component of degrees in Home Economics, Nursing, Psychology, and Primary and Pre-Primary Education programs. Some of the FLE topics covered include the following:

- Explanations of basic concepts—family life education, family planning, and sex education.
- Theories, concepts, and principles of family communication, decision making, and conflict resolution.
- Integration and networking systems in the family and community along with their relationship to the wider society.
- Awareness of the risk of HIV/AIDS and other sexually transmitted diseases.
- Implementation of sexuality and reproductive health education programs at centers of learning, facilitation of awareness of gender differences regarding reproductive concerns, and promotion of communication between spouses on reproductive and sexuality health activities.

- Identification of current problems and solutions for family concerns, such as approaches to male-friendly services. The issue of male participation is of particular interest to family planning in Nigeria as it has been misconstrued to only concern women and children, which affects knowledge, acceptance, participation, and enrollment into family life education programs. A gendered perspective allows a broad view of reproductive education, which can be discussed beyond focusing on women's health issues. Men are encouraged to take equal responsibility for family planning, family life education, and child rearing, and to acknowledge the prevention of sexually transmitted infections as a major factor in the prevention and control of sexually communicable diseases.

Another indicator of university involvement in the study of FLE can be observed by the fact that Japanese colleagues have translated the second edition of *Family Life Education: Working with Families across the Life Span* (Powell & Cassidy, 2007), as well as the third edition (Darling & Cassidy, 2014), and PowerPoint slides of the parable about family life education (see Chapter 1) developed by NCFR's CFLE Advisory Board.

Other family life education programs

Many countries have nonformal programs, such as centers to promote programming related to family life education that were either developed by the government or NGOs (nongovernmental organizations). The number and types of these programs is extensive and variable depending on the country's needs. Some programs exist related to family issues, parenting, new parents, human development, relationships, financial stress, and cultural diversity and can be provided by commercial programs or presented through media.

Family issues

- Singapore has a series of complimentary one- to two-hour family life education programs called FAMILY 365, which are available for the workplace and community touchpoints. The programs cover four key areas—family life, marriage, parenting, and personal work-life. These programs are conducted in English, Mandarin, Malay, and Tamil.
- In Spain, some centers provide parenting programs to families. These programs are less structured and families are invited to attend or may be interested to join on their own.
- In Senegal, there are symposia organized in different cities or villages dealing with family and women's issues. Gender officers from different organizations, as well as professionals are sometimes invited to talk and share their experiences as women in the field.
- Since Filipinos are generally family oriented, there are many private, religious, and NGOs that offer educational programs in the Philippines. EduChild, which stands for "Education for the Upbringing of Children," provides educational seminars for parents and families. Some topics of these seminars include *Beyond I Do, Middle Childhood, Family Visioning Seminar, Parenting Seminar, and School-Based Parenting Seminars.* Other programs

offered by the Catholic Church include sessions to promote strong families, with a variety of topics such as respect and responsibility.

- In Ghana, programs geared toward improvement of family lives are included in ministry programs of various local churches.
- In South Korea, several hundred Family Centers (formerly known as Healthy Family Support Centers (HFSCs) and Multicultural Family Support Centers (MCFSCs) develop, deliver and/or evaluate family life education throughout the country. These are offered through governmental and non-governmental agencies, religious organizations, and universities.
- In Canada, family life education programs are offered by the British Columbia Council for Families, with an emphasis on training for families (e.g., *Parenting Skills* for 0–5, 5–13, and 13–18) and professionals (e.g., *Nobody's Perfect Parenting Facilitators Training, Trauma Informed Practice—Using Creative Process*). There is a fee for these programs.

Programs for new parents

- In China, programs have been established to help parents take care of their new babies and assist mothers with their new bodies and emotions. New parents are interested in these programs.
- In Ireland, all mothers of newborn infants are provided a public health nurse service which involves a few home visits after the baby is brought home and an educational component.
- The Netherlands has a Dutch equivalent of the much used *BookStart* program (BoekStart), which invites the parents of newborns to the public library to receive a book case including a baby book and information on the importance of shared reading.
- In Jamaica, reintegration of school-age mothers into the formal school system is a national policy. The Women's Centre of Jamaica Foundation has served approximately 46,000 teen mothers, many of whom have successfully completed their secondary education.

Programs for parents

- In Singapore, the Ministry of Social and Family Development has been partnering with public schools to deliver two programs. *Signposts* is available only in primary schools and helps parents to understand, prevent, and manage their children's difficult behavior. Another program is the *Positive Parenting Program (Triple P)*, which equips parents with techniques to promote children's psychological, social, and emotional competence.
- In the public sphere in Taiwan, there are Family Education Centers in every city and county that have licensed family life educators and many trained volunteers to help people learn about family issues. While in the private system, there are many associations and foundations offering programs for learners of all ages, most of these family-related associations are Christian organizations that also offer programs for non-Christians. Examples of programs include:

—The *Rainbow Family Life Education Association* trains volunteers to visit classrooms to tell stories to children and encourage them to love their families.

—The *Journey of Intimacy Project* provides training to help with family relations.

—The *True Love Association* offers marriage programs for couples.

—The *GOOD TV* television station offers a variety of programs.

- *Barnardos* is an Irish child-focused charitable organization that conducts parenting courses. These *ParentsPlus* programs are 12-week courses taught by professionals in different services such as Family Resource Centers, Child and Adolescent Mental Health Services, Primary Care Teams, Child Care Communities, and schools. Parent associations in schools arrange lectures for parents on various parenting and family issues—usually at no cost.
- A Chinese program, *Child-Friendly Space*, in collaboration with UNICEF seeks to improve children's well-being with components to involve families through community support and provide children with better living conditions, education, and psychological support.
- In the Philippines, the Catholic Church has many available programs that are offered without charge to members and nonmembers. Topics include respect, responsibility, and dealing with the "blame game," which involves looking to someone or something else to be responsible. Thus, discussions occur regarding expectations, power struggles, control issues, listening, personality differences, childhood issues, emotional baggage, anger, speaking the truth in love, learning how to fight fair, the hurt cycle, forgiveness, and repair and rebuilding trust.
- *VoorleesExpress* (Reading Express) is a Dutch project in which volunteers visit low SES and migrant families weekly over 20 weeks, read to children ages 2–8, and model interactive shared reading experiences to parents while providing information supporting children's literacy development. Another literacy program, Early Education at Home, is delivered to low SES and migrant families by preschool and kindergarten teachers. Families receive activity booklets including a range of parent-child activities for over a three-year period. Parent training also takes place in preschools.
- Parenting classes in Spain are a part of parenting groups in health centers, but attention to parents and families is limited.
- In the United Kingdom, there are some parenting courses that draw about 5,000 couples per year of all ages and stages.
- Peruvian parents get involved with parent-child education and family education through the Parents and Family Association.
- "Fathers Incorporated" is a community-based parenting group established by Jamaican men in 1991 to address negative stereotypes of Jamaican fathers.
- In Brazil, there is a *Happy Child Program* to promote human development by supporting child development in early childhood of families in poverty.

Another program is *Better Early Childhood,* in which there are home visits to families at risk to social vulnerabilities.

Relationships

- In Ireland, voluntary organizations are able to access grants from the Family Support Organization to provide the following types of services: marriage and relationship counseling, marriage preparation courses, child counseling in relation to parental separation called *Rainbows,* and bereavement counselling and support upon the death of a family member.
- Marriage education in the United Kingdom is provided by churches and nonprofits on a small scale because fewer than 1 in 100 have had any kind of marriage education experience. In addition, a limited number of weekend courses such as *Marriage Encounter* exist mainly through community family trusts.
- In Russia, counseling programs in Russian wedding palaces before getting married are popular.

Financial stress

- "Hope Project," which is sponsored by the Chinese Red Cross Foundation and some private foundations, is a program focused on low-resource families in rural areas of China.

Fee-based programs

- In China, parents and children are provided with structured activities (e.g., sports, cooking, exploring nature) aimed at promoting connectedness between parents and children through activities.
- In China, private practitioners (e.g., counselors, life coaches, therapists) provide consultation to assist individuals and families with relationship problems including individual and parent-child problems. Troubled parents who are interested in seeking professional help as a last resort is growing. However, these services are expensive.
- Church groups and professionals in private practice offer FLE programs in Hong Kong.

Cultural diversity

- Multicultural, ethnic, immigration, or new immigrant organizations in Canada emphasize content about families and students with differing backgrounds.

Role of media

- In China, there are several online programs and resources, which are free or require a small payment, that coach people on how to handle relationships, parenting, and family problems. Some online programs provide for an interactive community in which the participants can pose questions, provide feedback, or exchange opinions.
- In Senegal, at times there are TV programs that are promoted in villages about various campaigns by the United Nations, World Health Organization, and local NGOs.

- In Canada, online chat groups and information sources are worthwhile when pertinent information becomes available.
- In Jamaica, radio programs are available, such as: *The Male Box*, *Dadz*, and *Family Time*.
- Media campaigns in Nigeria have been employed to raise awareness of HIV/AIDS and change risky behaviors, since Nigeria has the second largest HIV epidemic in the world and one of the highest rates of new infections in sub-Saharan Africa. Artists, athletes, and other media figures are spokespersons for these campaigns. In addition, due to the recent spike in ownership of cell phones and the need to increase public awareness about HIV/AIDS, text messages with information about HIV/AIDS, as well as reminders to take antiretroviral therapy, have been sent to several million people.

Government programs

Family life education programming, which is often influenced by legislation and various governmental policies, is closely tied to the cultural context of the country. Various countries may have governmental initiatives or motives, but they are not specifically focused on families and their needs or well-being. For example, in Iran it is difficult to advocate for families since there are so many legal and normal challenges in the way of other priorities. Russia is focused on a demographic policy to boost population growth by providing family allowances and benefits of mortgage loans. In regions that awarded family allowances for three or more children, the birth rate increased by 2.4%. In Moscow, mothers who gave birth to triplets received an aid package of $2,400. There is also financial support for mothers who have children and return to work, along with childcare allowances for single mothers of families of three or more children. Of all the areas of spending, family and child support programs have the highest number of allowances and incentives. Some regions of the Russian Federation have tried to introduce programs in the schools to prepare for family life, but they were not successful. The money spent on family and child support programs has been increasing, but still remains comparatively small—never exceeding 5% of the total expenditures.

Other countries have a more comprehensive approach to family programs. An emphasis on children is the major path to improve the well-being of Finnish families. Finland has created a child-friendly country that is a good place to go to school, work, and have a family. By focusing on the lives of Finnish children, Finns believe family well-being can be enhanced. Finland has an extensive program to provide financial and health care assistance to families with children through maternity, paternity, parental leaves and allowances, as well as child benefits and childcare allowances. High quality child care is free in Finland. Programs are developed to have parents actively involved in programs supporting their child's education. Teachers keep parents informed about their children's educational progress by incorporating parent visitation, phone conversations, newsletters, home visits, workshops, and regular communication. Educators are tasked with working as partners in family functioning for the well-being of children. In fact, nearly 90% of parents with young children believe their quality of life to be good or very good. While Finland is child-centered, it also promotes a dignified old age for everyone, so no person is ignored.

Sweden has several social programs to care for families in need, such as (1) early and preventive care so individual and family caring services can cooperate with mothers and childcare centers where advice and support are given to expecting parents; (2) youth centers run jointly with social welfare and medical services that provide advice and support to teen girls and boys on relationships issues, contraception, and drug issues; (3) support groups for single or teen mothers; (4) parent training at antenatal and post-natal clinics; (5) family advice centers where adult relationships can be discussed with counselors and problems resolved; (6) conciliation meetings for those who plan to separate, but need assistance with child custody; (7) group centers for local immigrant groups; (8) support for families who look after a single parent's child for one to two weekends per month to provide the family with a short respite; and (9) monthly income supplements and social allowances.

Family resource centers provide a major service in some countries. For example, the Irish government has 121 Family Resources Centers around the country. Services include establishment and maintenance of groups to meet community needs such as child care, after-school clubs, men's groups, and provision of counselling and support to individuals and groups. The Family Support Agency provides grants to voluntary organizations for marriage and relationship counseling, marriage preparation courses, child counseling in relationship to parental separation, as well as bereavement counseling and support upon the death of a family member. There is also a large parenting support strategy to provide information about parenting and child development. A range of services including a helpline, parenting courses, child contact centers, and counseling services are provided along with the existence of agencies to assist with international adoptions and foster care. All mothers of newborns are provided a public health nurse service which includes an educational component. There is an effort to break the cycle of child poverty where it is most deeply entrenched by providing children with integrated and effective services and interventions.

Australia also has several types of centers to serve families. Some are sponsored by religious organizations such as Natural Fertility Services which is part of the Family Life Services Program of the Archdiocese of Sidney and Parramatta. Others, such as Family Education Australia, is connected with a private foundation while some community organizations receive government funding. These would include programs such as Managing the Teenage Years, Circle of Security, and Triple P (Positive Parenting Programs). There are several governmental agencies that serve families such as the Australian Centre for Child Protection and Families Australia, as well as research institutes (e.g., Australian Institute of Family Studies—the government's key research body, Australian Research Alliance for Children and Youth, University of Sydney, and the Murdoch Children's Research Institute). Families Australia has provided policy advice to the Australian Government and Parliament about how to improve the well-being of Australian families, especially those who are experiencing the greatest marginalization and vulnerability. An important resource is the NSW Child, Family, and Community Peak Aboriginal Corporation, which is a large scale charity to ensure an Aboriginal perspective is included in all high-level policy development and funded programs.

In South Korea, certain content related to FLE is encouraged by law and includes preparation for marriage, parent education, education on family ethics, and education on the realization of the family's value of home life. As a result hundreds of family centers have been created.

While Ireland, Australia, and South Korea have major networks of family support centers, other countries such as Croatia have some public centers. Clients are offered assistance on a variety of topics (e.g., marriage counseling, family relationships, relationships with children, domestic violence). Some successful programs have been developed to treat critical issues among adolescents such as drug and alcohol abuse and peer violence.

In Canada there is a network of community centres that are ethnic based (e.g., Italian Community Centre) while others are community centres for different parts of cities. In addition, there is a network of neighborhood houses that build community within a neighborhood.

Some governments (e.g., Finland, Sweden, Ireland) have broad-based programs for families, while others have a narrower focus. Nigerian national population policy emphasizes the importance of effective and efficient use of contraceptives to achieve a decreased fertility rate. In Nigeria only 10% of women of reproductive age use contraception with an average fertility rate of 5.7 children per woman. While contraceptive methods and services are geared toward women, men are often the decision makers on family size and their spouse's use of family planning. Therefore, spousal disagreement can serve as a deterrent to the increase of family education and family planning.

Other countries have had a focused approach to family issues, such as Singapore, where divorcing families are required to attend the Mandatory Parenting Program (MPP) by the Ministry of Social and Family Development (MSF). The MPP provides consultation for parents before they file a divorce application with the Family Justice Courts. Similarly, relationship counselors in China work in Civil Affairs Bureaus where couples get marriage or divorce certificates. They provide free service to nearly divorcing couples, helping them to become calm before making a final decision. Several UN agencies have programs in Senegal on gender equality, child protection, and nutrition. Some countries, such as Israel, take a health perspective to assess the health of children with regular checkups and possibly some education for children.

In Jamaica, the "Parenting Responsibility and Rights Act" is being written by the National Parenting Support Commission (NPSC), which is a regulatory body that streamlines and coordinates parenting programs. This act focuses on parental responsibility as outlined in the "Child Care and Protection Act." It seeks to hold parents accountable for carrying out commitments for their child's best interests. The NPSC is steadfast in ensuring that Jamaica's parents are afforded the opportunity to know their responsibilities as parents and provide the necessary education to carry out these obligations. The NPSC also encourages the National Parent Sector (a NGO) to submit parent programs to be assessed for accreditation to ensure parents are receiving the best support and education services based on established standards. In addition, the Rural Agricultural Development Authority (RADA) provides training for rural women in home management, parenting, nutrition, and other aspects of family life. Other government organizations that focus on family issues include the Child Protection Agency, Office of the Children's Advocate, Centre for Investigation of Sexual Offences and Child Abuse (CISOCA), and National Council for Senior Citizens.

There are numerous programs for families that are either comprehensive or focused and depend on the government's determination of the financial resources they have to meet family needs. For example, in China, family well-being is not a central concern to agencies and policy makers, as they put more emphasis on economic development and hard sciences vs. social sciences. In Spain, generally agencies and policy makers may promote family life education, but the amount of money dedicated to these programs is very low. Most programs are based on interventions to deal with family issues, concerns, or problems in that country and not the preventative focus of family life education. Canada also focuses more on problems with a social work or counseling emphasis.

The focus of government programs can change over time. For example, policy transitions in the United Kingdom originally supported marriages, evolved to couple relationships, transitioned to parental support, and then changed to the reduction of parental conflict, which is the current remedy that passes for family policy.

Attendance—Family life education programs

Internationally, participation in family education programs is mixed. In some countries people are interested in attending family programs (Jamaica, Spain), especially if they were created to help better understand family challenges and ways to fix them (Senegal). In Australia, people only attend if the program meets their own specific needs or if they have been ordered by the courts to do so. In contrast, in Singapore over 20,000 parents have attended *Positive Parenting Program (Triple P)* programs across 295 schools. They are free along with online versions of one of the parenting programs. The educational programs offered by the *Family Education Centers* in Taiwan are quite popular, but while they are considered important, only some people will attend. It may depend on the topic of the program, as "well-being" is a popular topic with events such as *I Love Me* fairs in Finland. In South Korea there are some fathering programs that focus on males by looking at their roles related to the age of their children (e.g., fathering education focused on infant/toddlers, school-aged, and/or adolescent children). The content of these programs for males varies depending on locations, groups, and other societal needs.

There are various reasons for nonattendance. In some countries there is a stigma of attending family life education programs. In Hong Kong, 652 programs held in 2012 had 80,000 participants and generally there was considerable enthusiasm regarding involvement in parent education seminars and workshops, as well as outings and activities. However, marital family education programs that are remedial in nature tend to have a lower attendance because of the stigma attached. Family education is commonly used by people who are less in need, and these programs are less able to reach those who would benefit the most from them

(Hong Kong). Parenting courses in Ireland are popular, but there is difficulty in engaging hard to reach and vulnerable populations. Some people in the United Kingdom are aware of relationship education, but often are not interested in attending. In a recent survey only 4% of 249 respondents who said they had any relationship problems had attended a relationship education class of any kind.

In Japan, another issue regarding participation in family programs is gender, in that mostly women attend because of their interest in family needs. Males are not only reluctant to participate in family life education programs, but also may not allow their wives to attend any kind of training. In Mexico it is challenging to get women to attend and complete family life education programs. There are many issues, such as lack of transportation or having to schedule programs around the rest of the family (e.g., children's activities and needs). Because people work very long hours, when they are at home their main priority is their children and their needs so attending these programs is considered less essential. Therefore, some programs run by public institutions are tied to physicals or monetary incentives. Similarly, some people in the Philippines attend programs because the government or related institutions have placed these programs as a requirement. For example, a seminar on family planning methods is incorporated as a requirement in securing a marriage license or part of the preparation for marriage especially in the Catholic Church. However, even some of the programs you have to pay for in the Philippines are well attended. Whereas some programs in Nigeria have significant interest (e.g., economic empowerment, health, and nutrition), others have little citizen interest because they conflict with cultural or religious beliefs. For example, programs targeted at human sexuality (in a country with significant HIV/AIDS problems) have often been perceived as inappropriate by some citizens due to misconstrued beliefs that the content will lead to promiscuity.

Family programs: Issues and needs

Countries have similar and different needs and issues based on government support, financial resources, religious views, and cultural beliefs and practices. Some of those issues include the following:

- Representatives from multiple countries express concern regarding issues of violence and abuse—violence prevention, domestic violence, violence against women, parental violence, family violence, child abuse, intimate partner violence, gender inequality, sexual abuse, school violence, peer violence, and cultural violence (e.g., Australia, Brazil, China, Croatia, Finland, Ghana, Ireland, Jamaica, Japan, Mexico, Spain, Ghana, Nigeria). Since the COVID-19 pandemic, Jamaica is experiencing an increase in sexual abuse of young children, teenage pregnancy, and intimate partner violence resulting in homicides. To exemplify the increasing concern about abuse and violence, data from Japan indicated that in 1990 there were 1,101 cases of child abuse. That number increased to 159,850 in 2018. Similarly, domestic violence has increased from 3,608 cases in 2001 to 77,482 in 2018.
- Poverty, homelessness, inequality, and separation of families due to migration are of particular concern in some countries, resulting in complex family issues (Australia, Brazil, Finland, Mexico, Philippines, Senegal, United Kingdom).

- Marriage is also an issue, whether because of an increase in teen marriages in rural areas (Senegal); divorce or instability of relationships (Senegal, United Kingdom); or same sex marriage (Taiwan). Other issues include low birthrate and population aging (Finland), teen pregnancy and general promiscuity (Ghana), drug and alcohol abuse (Australia, Croatia), HIV/AIDS (Nigeria), and female genital mutilation (Senegal).
- Work-family balance and parenting in China are important issues because the country has the highest dual-earner family rates in the world and working adults tend to work long hours. Although new mothers can enjoy three to four months of maternity leave and one year of breastfeeding leave (one hour per day), few other work-family policies are available to working parents.
- In Peru, a critical issue is promoting health awareness due to the COVID-19 pandemic, as well as helping students with special needs and/or learning disabilities.
- In Australia, there is a gap in health and education outcomes between Aboriginal and non-Aboriginal populations. The Australian Human Rights Commission is pushing for funded programs to reduce this gap.
- Foster care in Denmark is a critical issue in regard to communication between the foster carers and the municipality and the lack of preparation to become a foster carer. About 20% of them have not been required to take the initial foster-carer course even though it is a condition to become a foster carer.
- Critical issues in Brazil involve a large income and education inequality and a public system that is very corrupt. Poverty and inequality in Brazil are increasing, although they were decreasing for a time some years ago.
- In South Korea there is a need to increase the number of qualified staff to work in and with various private and public agencies to provide strong FLE programs, continue to diversify the content of FLE to meet the dynamic interests of South Korean families, and provide more long-term advanced-level FLE programs to make positive ongoing changes for families.

Cultural influences in family life education

Family life education programming is closely tied to the cultural context of the country. Countries in the same region or continent may have similar or different political, environmental, and cultural issues and thus different programs are developed. While some issues were reported by multiple countries as general concerns, other countries indicated some specific topics related to their unique cultural context, as noted below.

Japan

- *Karoshi* is death from overwork, most commonly due to a heart attack or stroke resulting from stress. This occurs in young men in their prime years that die suddenly with no signs of previous illness. As a result, some young Japanese are choosing part-time work, contrary to their elder counterparts who work overtime. Consequently, companies and the government are trying to develop a plan for work-life balance.

- *Hikikomori* means pulling inward and seeking extreme isolation. Persons practicing hikikomori, often adolescents or young adults, do not go to school or work, refuse contact with people other than family members, and stay home for more than 6 months. This occurs in about 320,000 households. The number of *Hikikomori* who are 16 to 39 are reported to be 540,000, while the number of *Hikikomori* who are 40 to 60 years old are estimated to be more than 610,000. *Futoko* applies specifically to students who opt out and refuse to attend school.
- The *8050 issue* occurs when parents in their 80s take care of their children in their 50s who live with them. In most cases the children are either not working or earning very little money and therefore depend on their parents' pension money for living.
- Another issue involves a new dimension of the mother-son relationship. Young men in their 20s enjoy being with their mothers and go shopping and dine with them in upscale restaurants. They appear to be a dating couple and the sons do not hesitate to behave like their mother's date and even show off this relationship. A recent news program reported a mother and her 30-year-old son who took a bath together once a week. The question is if this is a new type of relationship or a deviant relationship. Mothers may impair their sons' sexual development. Furthermore, dating among young men and women is in a downward trend.

China

- China has some unique issues related to family relationships. An estimated 61 million left-behind children live alone or with grandparents or elderly relatives. They have to endure separation from their parents who left to work in more wealthy cities thousands of miles away and earn a better life for their family. The typical family structure is two working parents, two grandparents, and one to two children. Grandparents help out and play an important role in child rearing. But, the well-being of seniors is a critical issue in contemporary China although little attention is being paid to this concern.
- Fathers who are the sole support of their family work long hours and have less involvement in parenting. Lack of emotional support is a critical issue for Chinese mothers who complain and call it *widowed parenting*. Social media attacks on Chinese fathers are common, blaming them for lazy parenting, not loving their wives, and not knowing how to interact with their children. A wife and her in-laws living together under the same roof can cause conflicts—a typical Asian phenomenon.
- Chinese culture highly values the role of parents in their children's development. If a child does not behave, it is perceived as the parents' fault. Parents of only one child have more resources to provide for their child's living and education. Chinese parents place high expectations on their children's academic accomplishments and career achievements and tend to be overly involved in their children's lives during adolescence and emerging adulthood. They keep a close eye on children's schooling and romantic relation-

ships. However, parents are now paying more attention to children's healthy emotional development.

Australia

- There is growth of *fly-in/fly-out employment* in the mining industry, in which workers fly to remote locations to work for 10 to 15 days before returning home for 3 to 5 days. The ongoing absence of one partner has a significant cumulative impact for marital and parental relationships.

Nigeria

- Nigeria is a multilingual, multiethnic, and multireligious society with three different legal systems operating simultaneously—civil, customary, and Islamic. Therefore, the degree to which citizens participate in programs to improve family life often depends on the extent to which program activities and goals align with the beliefs and practices of select groups, as well as the public trust.

The Role of Religion in Family Life Education

Religious context impacts the role of family life education in several countries. However, as globalization and migration continue and other cultural influences infiltrate these regions, some of the beliefs, values, and practices related to these religiously traditional countries will be moderated. Some examples include:

- Family education in the Confucian tradition has a long history in China and Hong Kong dating back to the fifth century AD. FLE is considered an essential component of socialization of Chinese culture, upholding the significant role of the family as a socialization agent in transmitting core virtues and values to the next generation.
- In an Islamic culture like Iran, there is no public education about families except for what is depicted on television programs or in short snapshots in schools which focus on the Islamic version of family structure.
- In Ghana, programs focused on improvement of family lives are included in ministry programs of various local churches. The increasing divorce rate and negative impact on children are being addressed by some churches through mandatory premarital counseling, but the impact is not significant. While there is a compulsory premarital counseling program in churches for 12 to 24 weekly sessions, there are no marriage enrichment or parenting programs.

Geographical Variations in Family Life Education

The development and status of family life education programs varies by country, region, and continent. Within certain geographical areas (continents as categorized by the United Nations), there are both similarities and differences. For example, there are similarities in family education in Japan and China pertaining to being at the beginning stages of development of FLE, while Singapore and Taiwan have made considerable progress in legislation, governmental policies, and family education programming. Although Hong Kong is a part of China, there are notable differences. Hong Kong schools offer masters programs in family education and intervention, as well as marriage and family therapy. Moreover, family education programs have a large number of participants. According to Xia and Creaser (2018), mainland China may benefit from the success of Hong Kong to further develop FLE curriculum and practice. In China, professionals in childhood education, women's studies, social work, and psychology provide family education. Chinese society emphasizes child education, especially academic education, with family studies being infused into various educational programs. Whereas Middle Eastern countries are considered part of Asia, they are dissimilar to countries such as China, Japan, and Taiwan with respect to family education, because family studies courses, faculty, and programs are few in number and based on individual faculty interests (e.g., Israel, Iran). In Europe, countries such as Finland, Sweden, and Ireland have multiple programs for families, but Russia and Croatia do not.

The perceptions of international family professionals provide insight into the status of family programs and family life education in various countries. However, *family life education* is not a common term used internationally and may be called *parenting education* or *parent training* in some countries. Some programs that focus on *well-being* are becoming more prominent and recognizable than FLE. Many family centers and programs that have been developed are more focused on family services and intervention rather than prevention—the core of FLE. Hopefully the field of FLE internationally will become more prominent when countries realize that the preventative health and relationship programs and services they provide are synonymous with family life education. Formal and nonformal programs are offered within different settings, curricula, and lengths of time, along with the varying preparation of teachers. However, there was little mention of evaluation of these programs. Schools, governments, and family professionals are addressing family issues to some degree, but those countries with governmental support via legislation, policies, and funding seem to be making more progress with family education programs in all kinds of settings.

Additionally, there is an increase in evidence-based programs that have a global reach (Ballard et al., 2018). For example, the *Triple P Positive Parenting Program* is an evidence-based parenting education program which was developed in Australia. In addition to Singapore, which was mentioned earlier in the chapter, the program has been implemented extensively across the US as well as over 25 other countries. The *Strengthening Families Program* and the *Prepare/Enrich* premarital education program were both developed in the US but now are offered in multiple countries. Sufficient support and funding are essential for programs to establish longevity and make a long-term impact on individuals and families.

While no one solution or program can meet all the needs of people in these countries, our awareness of the issues and challenges they face, along with their efforts to ameliorate family concerns are important for our understanding of the status of family well-being and family life education internationally. By understanding world families and international efforts in family life education, family professionals can promote multicultural understanding both at home and abroad.

Implications for Public Policy

In the public arena for social justice, family life educators need to be aware of differences in policies, norms, and laws in some countries. Women who have been raped and then courageously named their assailants have triggered international protests when they were tried and convicted of fornication and sentenced to death by stoning. Moreover, some countries still force abortions, infanticide, child abandonment, and female genital mutilation. Gender inequality is pervasive in India and a significant factor for malnutrition among women and adolescent girls. Early marriages and adolescent pregnancies are also common in some parts of India, resulting in low birth weight and chronic malnutrition in their children (Bhangaokar & Pandya, 2018). Whereas some of these government policies are being relaxed, they still exist in many cultures. Family life educators need to consider what they can do to promote equal legal rights for all regardless of their age, gender, race, ethnicity, religion, or sexual orientation.

Women are perceived to be a huge untapped economic resource and are taking more of a public stance for gender equality. Moreover, women are surpassing males in educational achievement and aspiration. Patriarchy will not disappear overnight, but there is a shift toward equality. Gender issues are evident when considering health, family structure, and violence. However, increasing the status of women does not necessarily decrease family violence, since often an increase in violence occurs when men feel threatened by a loss of power. Therefore, educators need to thoughtfully design curricula, texts, media presentations, and other activities to promote gender equality as part of cultural change.

There is an increasing need to incorporate a family lens when creating public policy. While progress is slow, family life educators should take notice of the passage of a "Family Education Law" in Taiwan on January 7, 2003. The Ministry of Education sought a legal means for promoting family education and the integration of work from all levels of governments, nongovernmental organizations, and educational organizations to actively empower people of all ages to have a better family life. This legislation was to promote preventative education by improving family education knowledge, strengthening psychological and physical development, and improving family and social harmony. They define family education as all kinds of education activities for furthering family relations and functioning including parent education, filial education, sexuality education, marriage education, ethical education, education about family resources and management, and other family education matters. This legislation made Taiwan the first country in the world to pass a national bill regarding family life education, effectively rewriting world history regarding FLE (Hwang, 2003; Hwang, 2005; Hwang, 2018). As previously noted, not only has Singapore become involved in legislation and family programming, but Saudi Arabia has also passed legislation to promote family life education programming (Almalki & Ganong, 2018).

The South Korean government implemented the Framework Act on Healthy Families in 2003 and the Multicultural Family Support Act in 2008. Under the supervision of the Ministry of Gender Equality and Family, local family centers and other private nongovernmental family centers have provided various services including FLE. In addition, there have been various FLE programs provided by the Ministry of Health and Welfare (e.g., early childhood development and parent education, adoption education programs through support centers for early child care). Other governmental agencies and the legal system have also provided programs such as the Ministry of Education (e.g., parenting education for families with school-aged children), the Ministry of Labor (e.g., work-family balance education), and family courts (e.g., parenting education for divorcing parents).

Families have a profound impact on their members. However, when they cannot provide for the healthy nurturance of members, the effects reverberate across their lives and are ultimately felt by society. As a result, there is a need for family life education aimed at strengthening family ties and relationships and preventing some of these problems. As the interest in family life education expands, we will also have to work on creating a variety of approaches that can be used by multiple countries, professions, and individuals.

Educational Methods to Enhance Cross-Cultural Awareness

Opportunities for Professionals

Preparation of family professionals to work with culturally diverse populations and increase their global awareness is becoming increasingly important. Family professionals can get involved in international conferences, meet with groups of international families within their own communities or universities, or become involved in international travel. While there are various exchange programs for students and professionals, the Fulbright Scholar Program is quite exceptional for providing cross-cultural understanding. As a Fulbright Scholar, one has an opportunity to be a cultural ambassador for the United States, while having a large array of experiences from which cross-cultural learning can be acquired. There are a number of Fulbright programs for both students and professionals, although the more familiar one provides travel and living allowances for US scholars to teach or conduct research abroad (www.cies.org). One should not be discouraged if you cannot find "family life education" in the list of academic disciplines for potential exchange programs. Family life educators are welcomed in a variety of disciplines and professions, such as education, family and consumer sciences, or the social sciences. Whereas human development and family science departments are prominent in the US, the study of family is located within various other programs depending on the country of interest.

Opportunities for Students

Travel programs: Cross-cultural study

Future family professionals have numerous opportunities to get involved in cross-cultural study programs to learn about international families. These options exist at various colleges and universities, often led by individual professors who engage with a smaller group of participants in their major to provide experiential opportunities to help learners develop an appreciation for families and cultures that are different from their own. The sessions can be short-term or a full semester. Contacting a university study-abroad office or a department administrator can be helpful in planning cross-cultural learning experiences. Rather than merely visit a country, participants become immersed in the culture by visiting museums, cultural and educational centers, government offices, or related community groups involving care for children or older adults. Programs may be short-term (2–3 weeks) or longer-terms (1–2 semesters). They may be able to have contact with families in the host culture that can involve home stays, ethnographies, and/or service projects as a part of their course work. Participants can become involved in activities of daily living, such as eating meals with the family, spending time with children, or becoming involved in family-related events. In addition, they can take an active part in these cross-cultural experiences by reading required books, writing papers, and planning their participation in field trips. Being in a different environment can be a life-changing experience when confronting living standards different from one's own, realizing the importance of language in understanding others, being aware of looking different, facing one's own ethnocentricity, and observing similarities and differences in family life. Cross-cultural experiences related to families provide excellent opportunities for exposing participants to some of the content areas for NCFR's Certified Family Life Educator Program (see Appendix A), such as families in society, internal dynamics of families, family resource management, parent education and guidance, interpersonal relationships, and human sexuality.

Classroom activities for students

Classroom activities can be incorporated to facilitate cross-cultural understanding. Some examples include global virtual exchange, brief reports, electronic portfolios, circular role play, and an activity called Barnga (see Box 12.1).

Global virtual exchange. Travel to other countries may be cost prohibitive for many students, along with curtailed study-abroad programs and other international travel opportunities due to COVID-19. In an effort to overcome these obstacles, enhanced technology options have resulted in an increase in global virtual exchange. Global virtual exchange programs provide an opportunity for sustained, real-time interaction with peers in another country with a goal of increased global competence. For example, a course might include a virtual exchange in which students are able to partner with students in another country for virtual discussions or collaborative projects.

Brief reports. Since cross-cultural travel and virtual exchange experiences are not always feasible, activities can be created to integrate cross-cultural learning into the classroom. These vary in complexity and depth of exposure. Individually or in small groups, participants can investigate a country by using international references on families (Adams & Trost, 2005) and particularly international family life education (Robila & Taylor, 2018). Through sharing with class members how families function in other countries and how culture has influenced the attitudes, behaviors, and family life education endeavors of the people in that country, learners can become aware of the differences in families and family issues in diverse cultures.

Electronic portfolios. Classroom projects can be expanded by having learners create electronic portfolios about various countries using technology and research to prepare an in-depth examination of a country and its families (Subramaiam, 2006). They can examine the geography; lifestyles; political and economic systems; family structure and culture; economic data; financial management; and information on housing, health, and consumption patterns. As a group they prepare an electronic portfolio by creating a PowerPoint presentation using charts, tables, clip art, and video clips, along with the development of a website. Several internet sources can be provided, such as the *Central Intelligence Agency: World Fact Book*; *International Database*; *Population Reference Bureau*; *United Nations Population Fund*; and *United Nations Educational, Scientific, and Cultural Organization.* Learners are not only able to enhance their research skills on the internet, but also have a meaningful, in-depth learning experience about families in other cultures.

Circular role-play. In order to better understand and enhance a cross-cultural perspective in family science courses, a circular role-play learning experience can be implemented using any topic of interest, such as marital interaction, sibling relationships, or parent-child communication. By varying the focus, this activity can facilitate the infusion of cultural learning into a variety of courses and topics. While a family life educator can utilize any teaching method in different cultures for the purpose of comparison and cross-cultural sharing, Darling and Howard (2006, 2015) described a circular role-play technique, applying it to parent-youth communication about sexuality within three different cultural contexts (United States, Costa Rica, and Finland). In this experience, participants were asked to engage in the role of a parent and then an adolescent daughter (or son) by listening to a scenario and then thinking through how they might react or what they might say from the perspective of both the parent and adolescent in that situation. The following steps were involved in this activity.

- Participants were asked to bring a paper and pencil/pen and join others in a small circle.
- The following scenario was read to the class about a potential dilemma for parent-youth interaction regarding sexuality.
- Anna, who is age 14, is going to stay home while her parents leave for the weekend to visit a relative in another town. Anna prepares dinner, does her homework, and then invites her boyfriend to the house to watch TV. However, Anna's parents encounter some bad weather and return home. While one parent is putting the car in the garage the other parent comes into the living room to find Anna and her boyfriend on the couch in a nude embrace.
- Respondents were asked to write what as a parent they would they say in their initial response to this issue.
- The response was passed to the person on the right who, as a teenager, responded to the parental statement.
- The response of the teenager was passed back to the person role-playing the parent for a response to the adolescent statement.
- The second response of the parent was passed to the teenager on the right, who again responded to this parent.

Thus, each individual simultaneously played the roles of a parent and adolescent in two different hypothetical family scenarios. The parent and adolescent characters each wrote multiple responses depending on time limitations.

After the exchange of statements between pairs of participants, the parent-youth communication patterns were discussed from the perspective of the culture in which the activity was being conducted. Reactions from other cultures to the same scenario were then shared with participants who were amazed at the differences in parental reactions. For example, in the US a common response was "OMG," anger, and threats, whereas in Costa Rica there was denial saying, "not my daughter," and in Finland the typical parental response was an apology for the intrusion. While this teaching method could be used with any topic, the statements from participants in these three cultures can be shared with participants to illustrate cross-cultural differences in parent-youth interactions related to sexuality (Darling & Howard, 2006). This learning experience, along with the discussion of the results from other cultures, stimulated cross-cultural learning and understanding about the purposes and processes underlying family behaviors. By looking at cultural evidence from three countries, this learning experience facilitated the exploration of the richness and diversity of parent-youth communication concerning sexuality issues from a cross-cultural perspective. Considering variations from others' experiences facilitates putting our own culture's parenting and sexual understandings in perspective.

Barnga. A good activity to better understand inter- and cross-cultural awareness is Barnga. It is a simulation game depicting how cultural groups may have some problems assimilating into other groups especially if they have language difficulties and do not understand the cultural rules, local behaviors, interactions (see Box 12.1).

Box 12.1 **Barnga**

Barnga facilitates awareness of intercultural awareness, and can be used to promote the realization that various cultures perceive things differently and play by different rules, requiring family life educators to understand and reconcile these differences in order to function effectively in cross-cultural groupings (Thiagarajan & Thiagarajan, 2011).

Barnga involves a card game. Participants are placed in groups and provided with the rules of the game (which vary for each group). Each group participates in a few rounds to understand how to play the game, and then the instructions are removed. After that, the only word that can be spoken is "Barnga," although participants are permitted to gesture or draw pictures with no written words. After each round, the winner and loser from each group move to another group and the game resumes (Pittenger & Heimann, 1998).

The success lies in the discussion after the game in which a variety of questions can be posed, such as (1) What were their reactions while playing the game before and after the rules changed?; (2) After they realized something was different how did they deal with it?; and (3) How did not being able to speak contribute to their feelings?; and (4) What were their thoughts about working with people from other groups who behaved differently? Why are cross-cultural communication and understanding important?

Future Directions for International Family Life Educators

What does the future hold? Globalization and struggles with interdependence will continue along with inherent issues related to family adaptations to the stress of migration and acculturation. Family life educators will need to become increasingly culturally competent and recognize the unique challenges they face when teaching in diverse settings both in the US and abroad. *LEADER: A strengths based cultural competence model for FLE* (Mallette et al., 2022) links cultural competence to practice (see Figure 12.1). This model suggests that culturally competent family life educators need to have the necessary *motivation*, *awareness*, *knowledge*, and *skills* to develop competency in FLE practice.

Before any individuals or educators can move toward greater cultural competence, they must be *motivated* to do so either by personal experience or exposure to other cultures and their similarities and differences. *Motivation* represents the perceptions by educators that it is important to enhance their own backgrounds or interests of their participants in cross-cultural learning. Earlier in this chapter we presented some background *knowledge* for family life educators in regard to various global changes affecting families. This was enhanced by the comments from international family colleagues describing the educational accomplishments, matters of concern, and cultural issues they experience. These statements provide an *awareness* to family life educators of what individuals and families in these countries are facing and what family life educators need to understand. Finally various *skills* (FLE methods) are essential to facilitate learning in a cross-cultural environment. The leadership competencies of *learning*, *self-evaluation*, *assessment*, *development*, *engagement*, and *reflection* build on cultural learning and allow family life educators to move from learning to modifying the behaviors that they needed to practice with diverse audiences. While some elements in the model are already part of our cultural milieu and discussed in earlier chapters, they become even more important in cross-cultural learning environments. The final section of the model includes the tasks in which family life educators will engage as they move to the practice of FLE. Conducting a needs assessment; choosing, adapting, and developing FLE curricula; applying ethical principles; advancing social justice and public policy; connecting and engaging with participants; implementing culturally appropriate FLE programming; and monitoring and evaluating effectiveness are all important to successful programs.

With increasing numbers of educators who are teaching, studying, or doing research abroad, along with learners who are taking courses, becoming involved in study trips, or conducting research, there is a definite need for developing innovative methods and materials that are culturally sensitive to people living in other countries. One cannot use family life education methods that work in the US and assume that they are universal. The following are some suggestions for working with other cultures that provide examples relative to the LEADER model.

- Examine how different cultures perceive and value marriage, family, gender, aging, children, and parenting, as well as the roles of education, government, and religion. This knowledge can be gained from talking to individuals, families, and colleagues; attending seminars and classes; reading cross-cultural

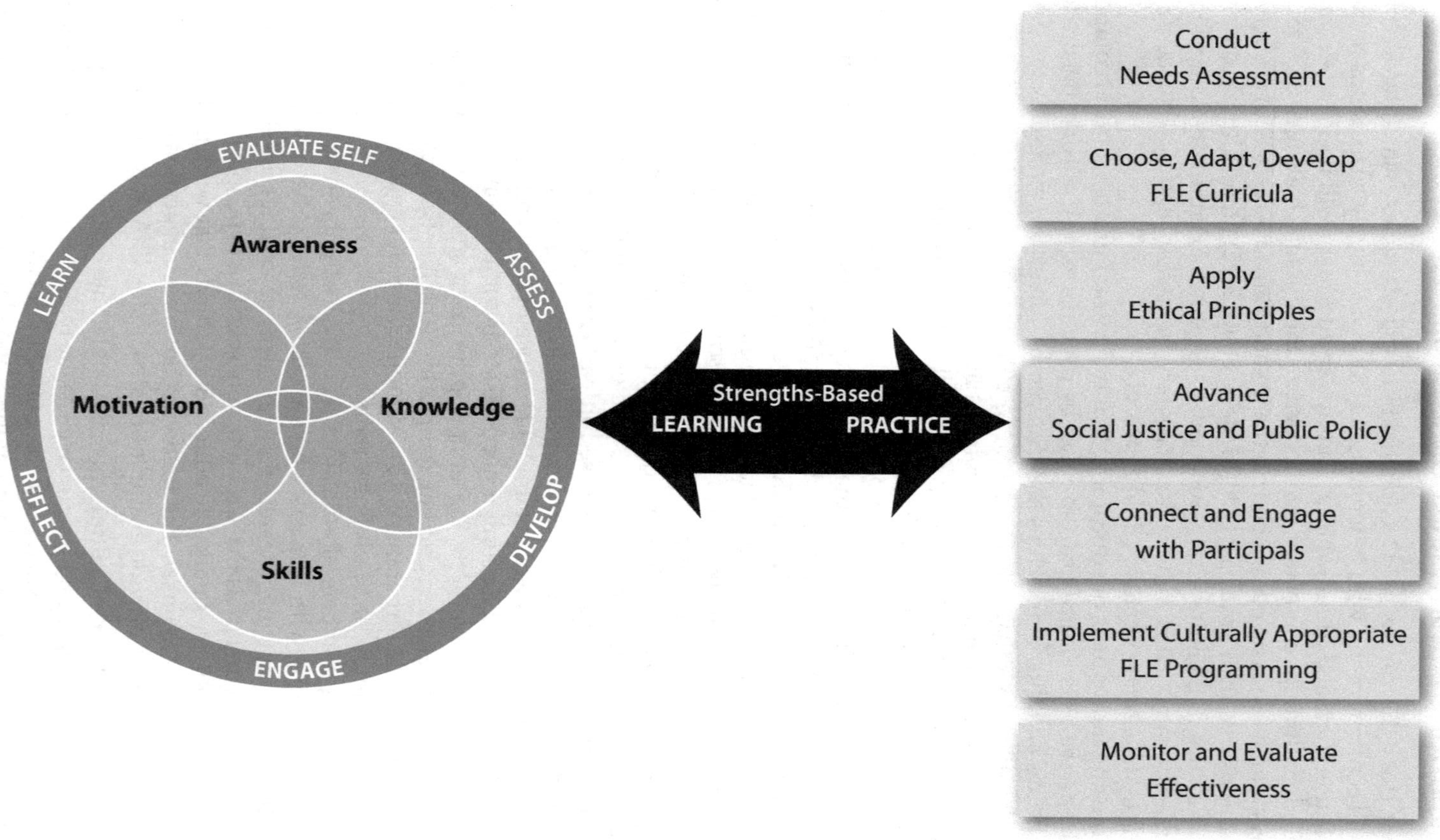

Figure 12.1 LEADER: A Strengths-Based Cultural Competence Model for FLE

Source: Mallette, J, Baugh, E., Ballard, S., & Taylor, A. (2022). A cultural competency model for family life education. In S. M. Ballard & A. C. Taylor (Eds.), *Family life education with diverse populations* (pp. 19–39). San Diego, CA: Cognella Academic Publishing. Used with permission.

literature; conducting cross-cultural research; and studying public policies from other countries. We need to understand what is taught to whom and the differences in cultural perceptions of family structure, composition, and life stages.

- Understand personal assumptions, values, and biases regarding cultural diversity, in general, and specifically to the cultural group to be taught. Then assist family life education participants to further understand their beliefs about culture. Using Bennett's "Model of Cultural Competency" can facilitate development of cultural sensitivity by moving from ethnocentrism to ethnorelativism (Bennett, 1993).
- Use current culturally relevant research to support the content of the program. If you have not personally conducted such research, make contact with researchers in a country of interest. By incorporating research, you can display an understanding of the circumstances of the people in other countries and a willingness to connect with relevant family and child issues. You can meet some of these international colleagues at professional conferences in the US and abroad.
- Incorporate applicable theory into your content. Theory helps participants of all ages to understand the knowledge, attitudes, and behaviors being integrated into the course. However, some theories that are quite usable in Western culture may not work in other cultures, or may have to be altered for different circumstances. For example, using developmental theory in some cultures may be difficult because developmental transitions or milestones may vary in timing, definition, and importance. However, one can use developmental theory to examine transition points in family lives to see the similarities and differences across cultures (e.g., child birth, adolescent issues, marriage, aging).
- Build rapport with participants by learning some phrases in their native language and pronouncing their names correctly. Attempts to speak their language and embrace their culture are appreciated.
- Be aware that some verbal and nonverbal communications may have different meanings in various cultures. Touch, hand gestures, or eye contact that might be acceptable in one country could be offensive in another. Therefore, be sensitive to various gestures and body language that can cause distress and misunderstandings when traveling abroad, interacting with international students and colleagues, or teaching individuals and families in a cultural context beyond your own.
- Use culturally appropriate metaphors that relate to the country of interest. If using sports examples to communicate a concept, use soccer, rugby, cricket, or cycling rather than baseball or football depending on the popularity of a sport in that country.
- Attempt to understand the family boundaries, rituals, cohesion, and adaptability of cultures and apply metaphors to assist with learning abstract concepts. One example relates to Asians, who appreciate metaphors when

discussing love, anxiety, and boundary issues. Therefore, a teacher could use Post-it Notes and tell them that "healthy love is like Post-it Notes—a little sticky, but not too sticky" (Hwang, 2005, p. 171).

- Be considerate of cultural norms since some content could put learners at increased risk. In Asian countries women can be emotionally or physically harmed when they "speak their minds" (Hwang, 2005). Awareness of multiple contexts in a culture is important. While some members of a culture may follow the traditional practices and views of a culture, others are more modern in their approaches. Thus, integrating theory and research may vary depending on the target audience in the country of interest.
- Experience the world around you and contrast the similarities and differences that exist. Seek opportunities to travel and study in other countries such as international conferences, participating in study-abroad programs, and collaborating with researchers in other countries. If you are unable to travel abroad, talk with people who are from a different culture, perhaps through a global virtual exchange program. Engage in a meaningful conversation and find out something about them and how they see the world.
- Be patient. Finding simple answers to complex problems can take time. Americans do not always endure delays in progress, but building and learning cross-cultural rapport requires tolerance and persistence without appearing frustrated.

One way to gain multicultural understanding of families worldwide and the issues and changes they encounter is to pay attention to the anniversaries of *International Year of the Family.* The UN General Assembly proclaimed 1994 as the International Year of the Family (IYF) with its theme of "Family Resources and Responsibilities in a Changing World" (UNDESA, 1994). They proposed that the family constitutes the basic unit of society and therefore warrants special attention. This event was followed by anniversaries of IYF in 2004 and 2014, which were designed to highlight the role of families and increase awareness of family issues among governments and the private sector, as well as stimulate efforts to respond to family problems and improve collaboration among national and international nongovernmental organizations. The current focus is on the *International Day of Families,* which is held yearly on May 15 to honor the importance of families—both traditional and nontraditional—as the foundation of society. This day celebrates the importance of families, people, societies, and cultures around the world (UN, 2020a).

Families can join the celebration by doing a project in their community to benefit families, organize a family picnic, or build a family tree in which they invite multiple generations to provide valuable information about themselves or relatives they have not met. They will appreciate being asked about their knowledge of family history and enjoy telling stories of family members (National Today, n.d.).

Some suggestions from international colleagues to celebrate international families include the following:

- meetings with families and students from other cultures, with an opportunity to hear their concerns

- academic symposia on various topics such as wellness of families, child care and work, worldwide gender equality, national health insurance, family violence, parenting, HIV/AIDS and the teenage population, and the impact of war on family life
- media presentations on family issues and family programs
- celebrating National Family Days as well as the International Day of Families
- International Family Strengths Conference
- development of fact sheets on family issues
- provision of new support services for international families
- cross-cultural entertainment presentations

In order for family professionals to have a place in the evolving international importance of family education as a profession, it is essential to develop an exchange of ideas and practices regarding the content and direction of various countries' approaches to family life education. We need to be internationally aware of the needs and concerns families experience and the environmental contexts of their ecosystems. If we cannot be engaged to think globally, we will fail to connect with the context in which families live. Including research, learning experiences, and textbooks from the US is not a viable approach when teaching in other cultures. Culturally-relative and sensitive methods and materials need to be incorporated for both classroom use and for professional development to assist teachers, leaders, and administrators in their work with families. It is important to both help individual families and sensitize public opinion on family-related issues. Since we are dealing with complex issues, we will need complex solutions to provide a preventative approach to assisting families. Thus, it will take a multinational, multicultural, and multidiscipline network of family professionals working together to enhance family well-being worldwide.

■ SUMMARY

This chapter examined the need for awareness and understanding of global issues of concern to families including migration, human trafficking, changes in family structure, population and aging, health pandemics, policy, and armed conflicts and turbulence. Family has different meanings and definitions in each culture, but using theory helps us to understand families and their interactions with multifaceted environments. Whereas family life education is evolving worldwide as demonstrated by the comments shared by international family professionals, we share many of the same family issues that are still unresolved. Since current and future family life educators often partake in international educational experiences, it is important to be cognizant of various cultures and use educational methods that will be sensitive and effective with others. A strengths-based cultural competence model for family life educators is a helpful guide. While the teaching methods may vary, the global concerns that affect families affect us all no matter where we live.

■ QUESTIONS AND ISSUES FOR DISCUSSION

1. What have you learned about children and families from foreign travels and visitors from other countries? What insights did you receive about your own culture?
2. In what country beyond the US would you like to live? How would your life be different in regard to your family life, school experiences, gender opportunities, dating, extracurricular activities, or employment?
3. What are some cultural traditions in which you and your family participate either from US culture or another cultural group? What traditions might you take with you into the next generation?
4. What are the biggest challenges facing our planet? What impact can families make?
5. How can you enjoy a good quality life without causing problems for future generations?
6. How does globalization impact various elements of interest to families (e.g., marriage, family functions, parenting, child care, education, aging and retirement, family structure)?
7. What are three examples of cultural differences and/or family life education or family programs in other countries that interested or surprised you?

■ ACTIVITIES

1. Using the ecosystems approach or any other theory mentioned in this chapter or text, analyze a global issue facing families.
2. Examine a global issue related to our environment (e.g., water supply, worldwide food supply, hazardous waste, pandemic, sustainable development, rising of the sea level, overconsumption) and analyze how this environmental resource impacts families and their ecosystems.
3. Experience a cultural environment unlike the one with which you are familiar. This could be a cultural celebration, restaurant with specialized cultural foods, or religious setting. How does it feel to be different in this setting? What feelings might you have if you were to become a permanent or semipermanent resident within this culture? What did you learn about this culture?

■ WEB RESOURCES

Confederation of Family Organizations in the European Union (COFACE)
www.coface-eu.org
COFACE links family organizations across Europe to discuss and work on issues such as balancing work and family life, children's well-being, solidarity between generations, migrant families, disabled and dependent persons, gender equality, education, parenting, health issues, and consumer affairs.

European Society for Family Relations (ESFR)

www.esfr.org

ESFR is an interdisciplinary scientific association for European research on families and family relations. Its purpose is to serve as a network, support and link family research, and exchange results. While ESFR was established as a federation of family researchers and family research institutes within Europe, it also welcomes researchers and institutes outside of Europe as affiliates.

International Federation for Home Economics (IFHE)

www.ifhe.org

The International Federation for Home Economics is the only worldwide organization concerned with Home Economics and Consumer Studies and serves as a platform for international exchange within the field of Home Economics. IFHE provides opportunities for global networking among professionals, promotes the recognition of home economics in the everyday lives of individuals and families, promotes continuing education in home economics, and provides opportunities through practice, research and professional sharing that can lead to improving the quality of everyday life for individuals, families, and households worldwide. IFHE is an International Nongovernmental Organization (INGO), having consultative status with the United Nations (ECOSOC, FAO, UNESCO, UNICEF) and with the Council of Europe.

National Council on Family Relations (NCFR)

www.ncfr.org

The National Council on Family Relations is a professional association for the multidisciplinary understanding of families. NCFR provides an educational forum for family researchers, educators, and practitioners from around the world to share in the development and dissemination of knowledge about families and family relationships, establish professional standards, and work to promote family well-being. NCFR is a nonpartisan, nonprofit, and international professional organization that links family research with policy formation and practice.

APPENDIX A

The Family Life Education Framework

This framework expands on definitions of family life education by specifying major content for broad, lifespan family life education programs. It reflects current conceptual development and empirical knowledge in each content area, and gives attention to relevant knowledge, attitudes, and skills. The framework is not intended as curriculum, but as a guide for program development, delivery, and assessment. It is assumed that practitioners would select the most appropriate organization of concepts and kinds of methodologies in order to meet the needs of their specific audiences. Communication, decision-making, and problem-solving have not been treated as separate concepts and should be incorporated into each content area.

Areas Addressed in FLE Programs for Stages of Childhood, Adolescence, Adulthood, and Later Adulthood

Families and Individuals in Societal Contexts

Internal Dynamics of Families

Human Growth and Development Across the Lifespan

Human Sexuality

Interpersonal Relationships

Family Resource Management

Parent Education and Guidance

Family Law and Public Policy

Professional Ethics and Practice

Family Life Education Methodology

Families and Individuals in Societal Contexts

Childhood

- Describe jobs, employment, housing, transportation and the family
- Comprehend reciprocal influences on the family (economical, political, technological, environmental)
- Develop programs that support individuals and families
- Understand the importance of families, neighborhood, and the community
- Encourage families, schools, and other support organizations to work together
- Recognize and appreciate differing spiritual beliefs and practices
- Develop skills to negotiate risk and opportunity in external environments
- Understand individuals' and families' relationship to media and technology

Adolescence

- Examine families and the workplace
- Comprehend reciprocal influences on the family (economical, political, technological, environmental)
- Support education as preparation for the future
- Promote education throughout the lifespan
- Encourage individual and family responsibility in the community
- Recognize and appreciate the influence of religion and spirituality on families
- Support families with special needs and problems
- Understand the role of family in society
- Access supportive networks (family, peers, religious institutions, community)
- Negotiate risk and opportunity
- Foster resiliency
- Understand individuals' and families' relationship to media and technology

Adulthood

- Support family participation in the education of children
- Utilize the education system
- Recognize and appreciate the influence of religion and spirituality on families
- Use supportive networks (family, peers, religious institutions, community)
- Understand and obtain community support services
- Promote life-long learning
- Understand population issues and resource allocation
- Comprehend reciprocal influences on the family (economical, political, technological, environmental)
- Address economic fluctuations and their impact on families
- Understand the interrelationship of families, work, and society

- Encourage individual and family responsibility in the community
- Understand the role of family in society
- Foster resiliency
- Understand individuals' and families' relationship to media and technology

Later Adulthood

- Promote life-long learning
- Support the educational system
- Recognize and appreciate the influence of religion and spirituality on families
- Promote healthy development throughout the lifespan
- Encourage relationships with adult children, extended family, and peers
- Understand and obtain community support services
- Comprehend reciprocal influences on the family (economical, political, technological, environmental)
- Address economic fluctuations and their impact on aging families
- Knowledge of population issues and resource allocation (health care, transportation, housing)
- Address social issues (age discrimination, elder abuse prevention, caregiving)
- Understand the role of family in society
- Understand individuals' and families' relationship to media and technology

Internal Dynamics of Families

Childhood

- Recognize the individuality and importance of all family members
- Learn how to get along in the family (e.g., problem-solving)
- Express feelings in families
- Develop awareness of personal family history
- Appreciate family similarities and differences
- Realize the impact of internal and external change on families
- Understand the responsibilities, rights, interdependence of family members
- Increase awareness of family rules
- Distinguish families as sources of protection, guidance, affection, and support
- Recognize families as possible sources of anger and violence
- Acknowledge the presence and nature of family problems

Adolescence

- Navigate the transition to adulthood
- Increase awareness of changes in family composition (birth, marriage, divorce, illness, death)
- Manage and express feelings in families

- Cope with internal change and stress in the family
- Describe the interaction of friends and family
- Exhibit communication in families
- Identify interaction between family members
- Clarify different needs and expectations of family members
- Understand the responsibilities, rights, interdependence of family members
- Determine family rules (overt and covert)
- Increase awareness of intergenerational relationships
- Observe the influence of family background
- Take note of family history, traditions, and celebrations
- Distinguish families as sources of protection, guidance, affection, and support
- Recognize families as possible sources of anger and violence
- Clarify family differences (membership, economic level, role performance, values)

Adulthood

- Clarify individual development in the family
- Define individual and family roles
- Take note of intimate relationships in the family
- Identify sources of stress and coping with stress
- Distinguish lifestyle choices
- Adapt to changing needs and expectations of family members
- Negotiate intergenerational dynamics throughout the lifespan
- Understand the responsibilities, rights, and interdependence of family members
- Learn to navigate family transitions (birth, marriage, remarriage, divorce, illness, death)
- Consider value of family history, traditions, and celebrations
- Comprehend factors affecting marital and family relationships
- Give and receive affection
- Be aware of power and authority in the family
- Understand the effects of family on self-concepts of its members
- Distinguish families as sources of protection, guidance, affection, and support
- Clarify family differences (membership, economic level, role performance, values)
- Recognize families as possible sources of anger and violence
- Increase awareness of varying influences on family interaction patterns (ethnic, racial, gender, social, cultural)
- Determine family rules (overt and covert)

Later Adulthood

- Clarify individual development in the family
- Define individual and changing family roles
- Adapt to changing needs and expectations of family members
- Navigate family transitions (marriage, divorce, remarriage, illness, retirement, death)
- Understand the responsibilities, rights, interdependence of family members and productivity
- Nurture intimate relationships in the family
- Understand the effects of family on self-concepts of its members
- Comprehend factors affecting marital and family relationships
- Give and receive affection
- Be aware of the changes in power and authority in the family
- Identify sources of stress and coping with stress, diseases, and disabilities
- Determine family rules (overt and covert)
- Distinguish families as sources of protection, guidance, affection, and support
- Distinguish lifestyle choices and changes (retirement planning, retirement)
- Consider the value of family history, traditions, and celebrations
- Negotiate intergenerational dynamics throughout the lifespan
- Increase awareness of varying influences on family interaction patterns (ethnic, racial, gender, social, cultural)
- Recognize families as possible sources of anger and violence
- Clarify family differences (membership, economic level, role performance, values)

Human Growth and Development Across the Lifespan

Childhood

- Understand physical, cognitive, affective, moral, personality, social, and sexual development
- Take responsibility for keeping healthy (nutrition, personal health, exercise, sleep)
- Recognize the uniqueness of each person
- Identify similarities and differences in individual development
- Appreciate people with special needs
- Clarify perceptions about older people (adolescents, adults, elderly)
- Identify social and environmental conditions affecting growth and development

Adolescence

- Accept individual differences in development
- Take responsibility for personal health (nutrition, personal health, exercise, sleep)

- Understand the effects of chemical substances on physical health and development
- Comprehend and differentiate between types of development (physical, cognitive, affective, moral, personality, social, sexual)
- Distinguish the interaction among types of development
- Recognize patterns of development over the lifespan—conception to death
- Evaluate stereotypes and realities about adulthood and aging
- Describe developmental disabilities
- Identify social and environmental conditions affecting growth and development

Adulthood

- Understand the transition to adulthood
- Recognize factors influencing individual differences in development
- Comprehend and differentiate between types of development (physical, cognitive, affective, moral, personality, social, sexual)
- Distinguish the interaction among types of development
- Take responsibility for personal and family health
- Promote development in self and others
- Recognize patterns of development over the lifespan—conception to death
- Evaluate myths and realities of adulthood and aging
- Adjust to developmental disabilities
- Identify social and environmental conditions affecting growth and development

Later Adulthood

- Recognize factors influencing individual differences in development
- Comprehend and differentiate between types of development (physical, cognitive, affective, moral, personality, social, sexual)
- Distinguish the interaction among types of development
- Adjust to developmental disabilities
- Recognize patterns of development over the lifespan—conception to death
- Adapt to and cope with physical changes in later adulthood
- Take responsibility for personal health and safety
- Adjust to grief and loss
- Evaluate myths and realities of aging
- Identify social and environmental conditions affecting growth and development

Human Sexuality

Childhood

- Respond to children's curiosity about their bodies
- Label physical and sexual development

- Clarify body privacy and protection against sexual abuse
- Conceptualize similarities and differences in individual sexual development
- Define aspects of human reproduction (prenatal development, birth, puberty)
- Expand the child's perceptions about sexuality
- Become aware of social and environmental conditions affecting sexuality

Adolescence

- Label physical and sexual development (sexual identity, sexual orientation, etc.)
- Explain interaction among types of development
- Clarify body privacy and protection against sexual abuse
- Communicate about sexuality (personal values and beliefs, shared decision making)
- Teach characteristics of healthy and ethical sexual relationships
- Understand the choices, consequences, and responsibility of sexual behavior
- Explain the transmission and prevention of sexually transmitted diseases and infections
- Describe human reproduction and conception
- Affirm the normality of sexual feelings and sexual responses
- Expand knowledge of interpersonal dynamics of intimacy
- Identify stereotypes and realities about human sexuality
- Increase awareness of varying family and societal beliefs, myths, and realities about sexuality

Adulthood

- Demonstrate responsible sexual behavior (choices, consequences, shared decision making)
- Affirm normality of sexual feelings and sexual responses
- Communicate about sexuality (personal values and beliefs, shared decision making)
- Observe characteristics of healthy and ethical sexual relationships
- Knowledge of interpersonal dynamics of sexual intimacy
- Explain the transmission and prevention of sexually transmitted diseases and infections
- Comprehend reproductive health (contraception, infertility, and genetics)
- Prevent sexual abuse
- Increase awareness of varying family and societal beliefs, myths, and realities about sexuality

Later Adulthood

- Understand human sexual response and aging
- Affirm normality of sexual feelings and sexual responses

- Clarify body privacy and prevention of sexual abuse
- Communicate about sexuality (personal values, beliefs, shared decision making)
- Observe characteristics of healthy and ethical sexual relationships
- Value sexuality education in later adulthood
- Define sexual expression and intimacy
- Explain the transmission and prevention of sexually transmitted diseases and infections
- Develop appreciation of sexual needs in adult living situations
- Increase awareness of varying family and societal beliefs, myths, and realities about sexuality

Interpersonal Relationships

Childhood

- Respect for self, others, and property
- Share feelings constructively
- Express emotions
- Develop, maintain, and end relationships appropriately
- Build self-esteem and self-confidence
- Identify and enhance personal strengths
- Communicate with others
- Share friends, possessions, and time
- Act with consideration for self and others
- Develop problem-solving and conflict management skills
- Accurately assess how one's words and behaviors affect others
- Appreciate diverse individuals, cultures, and communities

Adolescence

- Respect for self, others, and property
- Change and develop one's thoughts, attitudes, and values
- Deal with success and failure
- Accept responsibility for one's actions
- Assess and develop personal abilities and talents
- Communicate information, thoughts, and feelings
- Manage and express emotions
- Initiate, maintain, and end friendships
- Build self-esteem and self-confidence
- Assess compatibility in interpersonal relationships
- Act with consideration for self and others

- Understand the basis for choosing a family lifestyle (values, heritage, religious beliefs)
- Understand the needs and motivations involved in dating
- Recognize factors that influence mate selection (social, cultural, personal)
- Understand the dimensions of love and commitment
- Explore the responsibilities of marriage
- Discover where one fits in relation to others (the "me" among the "we")
- Appreciate diverse individuals, cultures, and communities

Adulthood

- Establish personal autonomy
- Build self-esteem and self-confidence
- Achieve constructive personal changes
- Communicate effectively
- Manage and express emotions
- Develop, maintain, and end relationships
- Exercise initiative in relationships
- Recognize factors associated with quality relationships
- Take responsibility and make commitments in relationships
- Evaluate choices and alternatives in relationships
- Act in accordance with personal beliefs with consideration for others' best interest
- Understand the effects of self-perceptions on relationships
- Recognize influences on roles and relationships (ethnic, racial, gender, social, cultural)
- Understand types of intimate relationships
- Create and maintain a family of one's own
- Be aware of changes in intimate relationships over time
- Manage and cope with crises
- Find meaning and purpose in relationship to others
- Appreciate diverse individuals, cultures, and communities

Later Adulthood

- Build self-esteem and self-confidence
- Understand the effects of self-perceptions on relationships
- Exercise initiative in relationships
- Continue intimate relationships
- Recognize factors associated with quality relationships
- Take responsibility and make commitments in relationships

- Evaluate choices and alternatives in relationships
- Act in accordance with personal beliefs with consideration for others' best interest
- Be aware of changes in intimate relationships over time
- Maintain relationships with one's own family
- Communicate effectively
- Manage and express emotions
- Recognize influences on roles and relationships (ethnic, racial, gender, social, cultural)
- Manage and cope with crises
- Share interpersonal wisdom and experiences with future generations
- Cope with stress
- Appreciate diverse individuals, cultures, and communities

Family Resource Management

Childhood

- Take care of possessions
- Help with family tasks
- Learn about time and schedules
- Learn to choose (develop decision-making skills)
- Understand how to earn, spend, and save money
- Develop awareness of space and privacy
- Develop talents and abilities
- Select options for food, clothing, and play
- Use, save, and manage human and non-human resources
- Describe the influences on consumer decisions (personal values, costs, media, peers)

Adolescence

- Allocate time for work, school, and leisure
- Negotiate privacy and independence
- Select resources to meet personal needs (food, clothing, recreation)
- Use personal resources
- Understand how to earn, spend, and save money
- Participate in personal and family decision-making
- Take responsibility for decisions
- Develop leisure interests
- Clarify values as basis for choices
- Choose long- and short-term goals

- Explore career choices
- Assessment of and changes in personal and family resources
- Describe the influences on consumer decisions (personal values, costs, media, peers)

Adulthood

- Expend human energy
- Develop personal resources
- Develop personal resources through career choices
- Clarify values as basis for choices
- Develop leisure interests
- Recognize the varying needs of family members for privacy and independence
- Use resources to meet basic needs of family (food, clothing, shelter)
- Classify differing views about uses of family resources
- Establish long- and short-term goals
- Develop a financial plan
- Practice resource consumption and conservation (material and non-material)
- Balance family and work roles
- Describe the influences on consumer decisions (personal values, costs, media, peers)
- Plan for retirement and long-term care

Later Adulthood

- Clarify values as basis for choices
- Establish a plan for the distribution of resources and management if incompetent (will, living will, and advance health care directives)
- Use personal resources
- Expand leisure interests
- Balance life patterns of retirees with work roles of children
- Recognize the varying needs of family members for privacy and independence
- Practice resource consumption and conservation (material and non-material)
- Use resources to meet basic needs of family (food, clothing, shelter)
- Classify differing views about uses of family resources
- Establish long- and short-term goals (e.g., long-term care)
- Manage financial resources in retirement
- Describe the influences on consumer decisions (personal values, costs, media, peers)

Parent Education and Guidance

Childhood

- Know the responsibilities of parents and caregivers
- Identify the rewards and demands of parenthood
- Develop awareness of varied parenting situations (single parenting, co-parenting, step-parenting, adoption, LGBTQ, parents who live away from children)
- Compare differing parenting styles and behaviors
- Meet children's needs at different stages of development
- Foster appropriate play and interaction with infants and young children
- Express caring and compassion
- Promote developmentally and individually appropriate guidance strategies for young children
- Cultivate caregiving skills
- Demonstrate safety, health, and the feeding of children
- Teach responsibilities of children in parent-child relationships
- Encourage communications with parents
- Teach problem-solving and conflict resolution
- Identify sources of help for parenting (family, neighborhood, community)
- Note problems of family violence, abuse, neglect
- Help parents cope with the stresses of parenting

Adolescence

- Teach responsibilities of parents and caregivers
- Identify the rewards and demands of parenthood
- Develop awareness of varied parenting situations (single parenting, co-parenting, step-parenting, adoption, LGBTQ, parents who live away from children)
- Understand marital, parenting, and children/youth roles in the family
- Comprehend factors to consider in deciding if and when to become a parent
- Compare differing parenting styles and behaviors
- Develop awareness of influences on parenting (ethnic, racial, gender, social, cultural, community)
- Observe and meet children's needs at different stages of development
- Respond to individual differences in children
- Promote developmentally and individually appropriate activities for children
- Foster appropriate play and interaction with infants and young children
- Express caring and compassion to children
- Promote developmentally and individually appropriate guidance strategies
- Guide and supervise access with media and technology
- Demonstrate safety, health, and nutrition for children

- Teach life skills of (self-sufficiency, safety, decision-making)
- Teach responsibilities of adolescents in parent-child relationships
- Encourage communications with parents
- Teach decision-making, problem-solving, and conflict resolution in the family
- Identify sources of help for parenting (family, neighborhood, community)
- Note problems of family violence, abuse, neglect

Adulthood

- Encourage care of self and adult relationships
- Recognize and build family and individual strengths for parenting
- Identify rewards and demands of parenthood
- Stress intentional parenting (goals, values, and traditions)
- Comprehend factors to consider in deciding if and when to become a parent
- Recognize changing parent-child relationships over the lifespan
- Observe and meet individual needs of children and adolescents at different stages of development
- Prepare for birth and parenthood
- Change parental responsibilities as children become independent
- Support youth in transition to adulthood
- Develop awareness of varied parenting situations (single parenting, co-parenting, step-parenting, adoption, LGBTQ, parents who live away from children)
- Understand marital, parenting, and children/youth roles in the family
- Compare differing parenting styles and behaviors
- Recognize importance of communications regarding child-rearing practices and decisions between parents, grandparents, and other caregivers
- Develop awareness of influences on parenting (ethnic, racial, gender, social, cultural, community)
- Provide and monitor a safe and healthy environment for children and youth
- Express care and compassion
- Promote developmentally and individually appropriate guidance strategies
- Guide and supervise access with media and technology
- Teach life skills to children and adolescents (self-sufficiency, safety, decision-making, problem-solving, and conflict resolution)
- Promote developmentally and individually appropriate activities for children
- Foster appropriate play and interaction with infants and young children
- Create learning environments and involvement in education of children and adolescents
- Encourage parent-child communications
- Receive and give support for parenting

- Identify sources of help for parenting (family, neighborhood, community)
- Prevent and respond to family violence, abuse, and neglect

Later Adulthood

- Encourage care of self and adult relationships
- Recognize and build family and individual strengths for grandparenting
- Value the importance of family stories and traditions
- Develop awareness of changing parent-child roles and relationships in later life
- Negotiate adult relationships with adult
- Identify demands and rewards of grandparenthood, including the possibility of rearing and caring for grandchildren
- Knowledge of intergenerational and diverse households (strengths, roles and challenges)
- Adapt to the complexities of varied parenting situations (blended families, single parenting, step-parenting, care-taking of disabled children, return of adult children to the household, parents and grandparents who live away from children, LGBTQ families)
- Express care and compassion to grandchildren and their parents
- Encourage grandparent-grandchild communication
- Stress the importance of communications between parents and grandparents regarding parenting styles, parenting decisions, and values
- Evaluate the role of media and technology in family relationships
- Receive and give support for parenting and grandparenting
- Identify sources of help for parenting (family, neighborhood, community)
- Teach decision-making, problem-solving, and conflict resolution in the family
- Note problems of family violence, elder abuse, and neglect

Family Law and Public Policy

Childhood

- Understand and respect the law
- Develop, evaluate, and implement laws and policies affecting families
- Formulate children's legal rights
- Advocate for resources that support the development of parent education
- Develop, evaluate, and implement public policy as it affects families with children (taxes, civil rights, social security, economic support laws, regulations)

Adolescence

- Respect the civil rights of all people
- Understand legal definitions and laws affecting families
- Comprehend individual and family legal protection, rights, and responsibilities

- Evaluate and comprehend laws relating to marriage, divorce, family support, child custody, child protection and rights, and family planning
- Describe family conflict and legal protection of and for family members
- Define the interaction of families and the justice system
- Understand families with incarcerated adolescents
- Identify the impact of laws and policies on families
- Develop, evaluate, and implement public policy as it affects families with children (taxes, civil rights, social security, economic support laws, regulations)

Adulthood

- Transmit values regarding education, justice, and the law
- Understand and influence laws and policies
- Evaluate and comprehend laws relating to marriage, divorce, family support, child custody, child protection and rights, and family planning
- Describe family conflict and legal protection of and for family members
- Develop, evaluate, and implement public policy as it affects families with children (taxes, civil rights, social security, economic support laws, regulations)

Later Adulthood

- Transmit values regarding education, justice, and the law
- Understand and influence laws and policies
- Protect the civil rights of all people
- Evaluate and comprehend laws relating to marriage, divorce, family support, protection and rights of vulnerable individuals, property, wills, estate planning, and living wills
- Describe family conflict and legal protection of and for family members
- Develop, evaluate, and implement public policy as it affects families with children (taxes, civil rights, social security, economic support laws, regulations)

Professional Ethics and Practice

Childhood

- Take responsibility for actions
- Understand consequences of actions for self and others
- Honor spiritual ideas and beliefs
- Respect persons who are different
- Gain new rights and responsibilities with age
- Understand that rights are for all persons

Adolescence

- Develop a personal code of ethics
- Explore personal spirituality

- Connect personal autonomy and social responsibility
- Become aware of the interrelationship of rights and responsibilities
- Understand ethical principles as one kind of value
- Become aware of ethical implications of social and technological change
- Understand ethical dilemmas and conflicts

Adulthood

- Establish an ethical philosophy of life
- Act in accordance with personal beliefs with consideration for others
- Continue growth in spirituality
- Balance personal autonomy and social responsibility
- Become aware of the interrelationship of rights and responsibilities
- Understand ethical principles as one kind of value
- Use ethical values as a guide to human social conduct
- Assist others in the formation of ethical concepts and behavior
- Become aware of ethical implications of social and technological change

Later Adulthood

- Balance personal autonomy and social responsibility
- Continue growth in spirituality
- Act in accordance with personal beliefs with consideration for others
- Become aware of the interrelationship of rights and responsibilities
- Understand ethical principles as one kind of value
- Use ethical values as a guide to human social conduct
- Review quality of life and end of life issues
- Develop awareness for protection from exploitation
- Consider ethical implications of social and technological change
- Share life's wisdom and ethical experiences with future generations

This framework was originally developed by the National Council on Family Relations' Standards and Certification Committee (1984), building upon the earlier work of the Texas Council on Family Relations (1977).
It was further revised and edited in 1997 by David J. Bredehoft, PhD, CFLE, Chair of Social and Behavioral Sciences, Concordia University, St. Paul, MN.
This current version was edited by David J. Bredehoft, PhD, CFLE, and Michael J. Walcheski, PhD, CFLE, Associate Vice President of Graduate Studies and Dean of the College of Human Services and Behavioral Sciences, both of Concordia University, St. Paul, MN.
Special thanks to members of the original committee and members of the 1995–96 and 2010 Focus Groups for their input. Permission to reprint this article was granted by the National Council on Family Relations.

APPENDIX B

Family Life Education Content Areas

Content and Practice Guidelines (2020)

These guidelines represent the content from the National Council on Family Relations (NCFR) *University and College Curriculum Guidelines* and the *Competencies for Family Life Educators*, which were developed by faculty at Weber State University. It represents the knowledge, skills, and abilities identified as necessary for attainment of the Certified Family Life Educator (CFLE) credential. These content areas include theory, research, and practice within the field of Family Life Education. Examples of some of these core theories/frameworks/perspectives include family systems, ecosystems, individual and family development, exchange, symbolic interaction, conflict, feminist, and stress.

The content areas are illustrated in the *Lifespan Family Life Education (FLE) Framework* (Bredehoft & Walcheski, 2011), which outlines all ten content areas specific to four age groups: childhood, adolescence, adulthood, and later adulthood. The four age groups demonstrate the principle that FLE is relevant to individuals and families across the lifespan. The fact that FLE is inclusive of all audiences is represented by the words *Value; Diverse Cultures, Communities, and Individuals;* and *Justice*, that are woven throughout the framework. Additionally, FLE has a foundation in systems thinking (both family systems and larger ecosystems) and this systems approach is represented by the words "within the context of the family system" and "reciprocal interactions between family and ecosystem" that also are woven throughout the framework.

In 2007 and again in 2014 NCFR, along with Schroeder Measurement Technologies (SMT) (now SMT/Prometric), conducted a job analysis survey which was distributed to current Certified Family Life Educators who were asked to rate the importance of each knowledge, skill, and ability in the content outline to competent practice. The results of the surveys were used to update the content outline which represents the foundation of the CFLE credential as assessed through both the CFLE-approved program and exam processes. In 2020 the content outline was further revised to align content area objectives with Bloom's Taxonomy.

There are two parts to each of the following 10 FLE content areas. The first is "Content" which gives an overview of the subject matter included within each content area. The second component includes "Practice" which relates to the tasks expected of an entry-level CFLE. The "Practice" segment serves as the basis for questions on the CFLE exam. It also provides guidance to academic programs as they develop course objectives and learning outcomes.

I. Families and Individuals in Societal Contexts

Content: An understanding of families and their relationships to other institutions, such as the educational, governmental, religious, health care, and occupational institutions in society.

e.g., Research and theories related to: Structures and Functions; Cultural Variations (family heritage, social class, geography, ethnicity, race & religion); Dating, Courtship, Marital Choice; Kinship; Cross-Cultural & Minority (understanding of lifestyles of minority families & the lifestyles of families in various societies around the world); Changing Gender Roles (role expectations & behaviors of courtship partners, marital partners, parents & children, siblings, & extended kin); Demographic Trends; Historical Issues; Work/leisure & Family Relationships; Societal Relations (reciprocal influence of the major social institutions & families, i.e., governmental, religious, educational, health care, & economic).

Practice—A CFLE is prepared to:

- Describe the characteristics, diversity, and impact of local, national, and global social systems on individuals and families
- Explain factors (e.g., media, marketing, technology, economics, social movements, war, natural disasters, epidemics, environment, sustainability) influencing individuals and families from both contemporary and historical perspectives
- Describe factors that influence the relationship between work, personal, and family life
- Articulate social and cultural influences affecting various aspects of family life (e.g., dating, courtship, partner/marital choice and relationships, family composition, divorce, and dying/death).
- Exemplify the reciprocal interaction between individuals, families, and various social systems (e.g., workplace, health, legal, educational, religious/spiritual)
- Assess the impact of demographics (e.g., class, race, ethnicity, religion, generation, gender, sexual orientation) on contemporary families

II. Internal Dynamics of Families

Content: An understanding of family strengths and weaknesses and how family members relate to and interact with each other.

e.g., Research & theories related to: Internal Social Processes (including cooperation & conflict); Communication (patterns & problems in couple relationships & in parent-child relationships, including stress & conflict management); Conflict Management; Decision-making and Goal-setting; Normal Family Stresses (transition periods in the family life cycle, three-generation households, caring for the elderly, & dual careers); Family Stress & Crises (divorce, remarriage, death, economic uncertainty & hardship, violence, substance abuse); Special Needs in Families (including adoptive, foster, migrant, low income, military, & blended families as well as those members with ambiguous loss, chronic illness and/or disabilities).

Practice—A CFLE is prepared to:

- Recognize and describe healthy and unhealthy characteristics pertaining to:
  - —Family relationships
  - —Family development
- Analyze family functioning using various theoretical perspectives
- Analyze family dynamics from a systems perspective
- Compare and contrast family dynamics in response to normative and non-normative stressors
- Assess family dynamics in response to stress, crises, and trauma
- Facilitate and strengthen communication processes, conflict-management, and problem-solving skills
- Describe, develop, and/or reinforce strategies that help families function effectively

III. Human Growth and Development Across the Lifespan

Content: An understanding of the developmental changes (both typical and atypical) of individuals in families across the lifespan. Based on knowledge of physical, emotional, cognitive, social, moral, and personality aspects.

e.g., Research and theories related to: Prenatal; Infancy; Early and Middle Childhood; Adolescence; and Adulthood (early, middle, and late).

Practice—A CFLE is prepared to:

- Explain developmental stages, transitions, elements, and challenges throughout the lifespan
- Illustrate reciprocal influences:
- Individual development on families
- Family development on individuals
- Describe and exemplify the impact of individual health and wellness on families
- Assist individuals and families in effective developmental transitions
- Apply appropriate practices based on theories of human growth and development to individuals and families

- Compare and contrast various socio-ecological influences on human development across the lifespan (e.g., sexual/gender identity, trauma, etc.)

IV. Human Sexuality Across the Lifespan

Content: An understanding of the physiological, psychological, and social aspects of sexual development across the lifespan, to achieve healthy sexual adjustment.

e.g., Research and theories related to: Reproductive Physiology; Biological Determinants; Emotional and Psychological Aspects of Sexual Involvement; Sexual Behaviors; Sexual Values & Decision-Making; Family Planning; Physiological & Psychological Aspects of Sexual Response; Influence of Sexual Involvement on Interpersonal Relationships.

Practice—A CFLE is prepared to:

- Describe the biological aspects of human sexuality (e.g., sexual functioning, reproductive health, family planning, sexually transmitted infections)
- Explain the psycho-social aspects of human sexuality:
  - —Characteristics of healthy and unhealthy sexual relationships
  - —Interpersonal dynamics of sexual intimacy
  - —Risk factors (e.g., substance abuse, social pressures, media)
- Address human sexuality from value-respectful position
  - —Apply best practices associated with sexuality education programming

V. Interpersonal Relationships

Content: An understanding of the development, maintenance, and dissolution of interpersonal relationships among friends, roommates, coworkers, neighbors, as well as family members.

e.g., Research and theories related to: Self and Others; Communication Skills (listening, empathy, self-disclosure, decision making, problem-solving, and conflict resolution); Forms of Intimacy, Love, and Romance; Relating to Others with Respect, Sincerity, and Responsibility.

Practice—A CFLE is prepared to:

- Describe the impact of personality and communication styles
- Explain the developmental stages of relationships
- Analyze interpersonal relationships using various theoretical perspectives
- Develop, implement, and assess relationship enhancement and enrichment strategies
- Develop, implement, and assess communication, problem solving, and anger and conflict management strategies
- Describe the impact of violence and coercion in interpersonal relationships

- Exemplify the influence of unhealthy coping strategies (e.g., substance use, disordered eating, avoidance) on interpersonal relationships

VI. Family Resource Management

Content: An understanding of the decisions individuals and families make about developing and allocating resources including money, time, energy, space, material and health assets, and networks of support to meet their goals.

e.g., Research and theories related to: Goal Setting and Decision-Making; Development and Allocation of Resources; Social Environment Influences; Life Cycle and Family Structure Influences; Consumer Issues and Decisions.

Practice—A CFLE is prepared to:

- Explain the multiplicity of resources families need, acquire, and manage (e.g., personal, familial, professional, community, environmental)
- Recognize and facilitate the reciprocal relationship between individual/family/community choices and resources
- Exemplify and facilitate effective decision-making processes (e.g., assessment of individual and family needs, identification and evaluation of options and resources, implementation of decision, evaluation of outcomes)
- Explain the impact of values and goals in the decision-making process
- Apply organizational and resource management strategies to a variety of circumstances
- Apply basic management tools and principles to a variety of contexts
- Inform individuals and families of consumer rights, responsibilities, and choices of action/advocacy
- Assist families as they cope with the loss of valued resources
- Apply best practices associated with financial literacy programming

VII. Parenting Education and Guidance

Content: An understanding of how parents teach, guide, and influence children and adolescents, as well as the changing nature, dynamics and needs of the parent-child relationship across the lifespan.

e.g., Research and theories related to: Parenting Rights and Responsibilities; Parenting Practices/Processes; Parent-Child Relationships; Variation in Parenting Solutions; Changing Parenting Roles Across the Lifespan.

Practice—A CFLE is prepared to:

- Promote healthy parenting from systems and lifespan perspectives
- Promote healthy parenting from a child's and parent's developmental perspective
- Apply child guidance strategies based on the child's age/stage of development to promote effective developmental outcomes

- Explain different parenting styles and their associated psychological, social, and behavioral outcomes
- Articulate best practice associated with high quality parent education
- Analyze and assess various parenting programs, models, and principles
- Evaluate the effectiveness and appropriateness of various parenting strategies
- Exemplify various parenting roles (e.g., father/mother, grandparents, and other caregivers) and their impact on and contribution to individuals and families
- Articulate parenting strengths and challenges within various family structures (e.g., single, blended, same sex)
- Describe the impact of societal trends on parenting (e.g., technology, substance abuse, media)
- Exemplify the influence of cultural differences and diversity on parenting practices
  —Compare and contrast strategies to support children in various settings (e.g., schools, legal system, health care
- Illustrate the various pathways to parenting and their associated issues and challenges, (e.g., assisted reproduction, adoption, childbirth, blending)

VIII. Family Law and Public Policy

Content: An understanding of legal issues, policies, and laws influencing the well-being of families.

e.g., Family and the Law (relating to marriage, cohabitation, divorce, family support, child custody, child protection and rights, and family planning); Family and Social Services; Family and Education; Family and the Economy; Family and Religion; Policy and the Family (public policy as it affects the family, including tax, civil rights, social security, economic support laws, and regulations); and Roles for Family Life Educators.

Practice—A CFLE is prepared to:

- Understand the following policy processes (e.g., policy formation, policy implementation, policy assessment and evaluation)
- Identify current and proposed laws, public policies, and initiatives that regulate and influence professional conduct and services
- Identify current and proposed laws, public policies, and initiatives that affect families (e.g. intended and unintended consequences)
- Distinguish between lobbying, policy evaluation, analysis, education, and advocacy
- Analyze policy resources for evidence of bias (e.g., unintended, inherent, political, self-interest)
- Inform families, communities, and policy makers about public policies, initiatives, and legislation that affect families at local, state, and national levels

- Facilitate opportunities for family and community members, professionals, and policy makers to discuss family issues and propose possible remedies.

IX. Professional Ethics and Practice

Content: An understanding of the character and quality of human social conduct, and the ability to critically examine ethical questions and issues as they relate to professional practice.

e.g., Research and theories related to: Formation of Social Attitudes and Values; Recognizing and Respecting the Diversity of Values and the Complexity of Value Choice in a Pluralistic Society; Examining Value Systems and Ideologies systematically and objectively; Social Consequences of Value Choices; Recognizing the Ethical Implications of Social and Technological Changes, Ethics of Professional Practice

Practice—A CFLE is prepared to:

- Demonstrate professional attitudes, values, behaviors, and responsibilities to clients, colleagues, and the broader community, that are reflective of ethical standards and practice
  - —Describe the domains and scope of practice for Family Life Educators and the role of collaboration
  - —Establish and maintain appropriate personal and professional boundaries
  - —Recognize and deconstruct personal biases
  - —Devise and implement a personal ethics plan to support/reflect the standards of the profession
  - —Maintain current knowledge and skills in the field
- Evaluate, differentiate, and apply diverse approaches to ethical issues and dilemmas
- Identify and apply appropriate strategies to deal with conflicting values
- Choose approaches that demonstrate respect for diverse cultural values

X. Family Life Education Methodology

Content: An understanding of the general philosophy and broad principles of Family Life Education in conjunction with the ability to plan, implement, assess, and evaluate such educational programs.

e.g., Research and theories related to: Planning and Implementing; Assessment and Evaluation (materials, program outputs, implementation & effectiveness); Instructional Techniques; Sensitivity to Others (to enhance educational effectiveness); Sensitivity to Community Concerns and Values (understanding of the public relations process).

Practice—A CFLE is prepared to:

- Employ a variety of strategies to identify and meet the needs of different audiences

- Utilize appropriate techniques and technologies to promote application of information in the learner's environment
- Create learning environments that are respectful of individual vulnerabilities, needs, and learning styles and demonstrate sensitivity to diversity and community needs, concerns, and interests
- Apply best practices in group process, facilitation, and coaching skills
- Develop and implement culturally competent educational materials and learning experiences
- Identify and utilize appropriate sources for evidence-based information
  - —Understand basic research and evaluation methods (i.e., survey/questionnaire, interview, focus group, observation)
  - —Recognize and locate reliable sources of information (i.e., scholarly journals, governmental agencies, etc.)
  - —Evaluate sources of information
  - —Interpret basic demographic and other data sources
  - —Translate research-based information into plain language appropriate for the public
- Implement evidence-based programs
- Design educational experiences that include the following:
  - —Needs assessment
  - —Knowledge of audience
  - —Goals, objectives, and/or learning outcomes
  - —Content development
  - —Implementation/means of delivery (i.e., activities, teaching strategies)
  - —Assessment measures and evaluation of process and outcomes
- Promote and market educational programs
- Adhere to principles of adult learning and education when working with individuals, parents, and families
  - —Apply best practices of program evaluation (i.e., needs assessment, theory of change/logic model, process evaluation, outcome/impact evaluation, cost efficiency analysis) as appropriate throughout the development and implementation of educational programs

REFERENCES

Bredehoft, D. J. & Cassidy, D. (Eds.) (1995). *Family Life Education curriculum guidelines*. Minneapolis: National Council on Family Relations.

Bredehoft, D. J. & Walcheski, M. J. (Eds.). (2011). The Family Life Education framework poster and PowerPoint. Minneapolis, MN: National Council on Family Relations.

National Council on Family Relations. (2020). Family life education content areas. Minneapolis, MN: National Council on Family Relations. Retrieved from https://www.ncfr.org/cfle-certification/what-family-life-education

National Council on Family Relations Certified Family Life Education Advisory Board. (2018). Family Life Education content areas. Content and practice guidelines. In *Tools for ethical thinking and practice in family life education* (4th ed., pp. 35–41). Minneapolis, MN: National Council on Family Relations.

APPENDIX C

Certified Family Life Educator (CFLE) Code of Professional Ethics

Preamble

Family Life Education focuses on healthy individual and family functioning within a family systems perspective and provides a primarily educational/preventive approach. Application of knowledge about healthy individual and family functioning can prevent or minimize many societal problems.

The skills and knowledge needed for healthy functioning across the lifespan are widely known: knowledge of human development, good decision-making skills, effective parenting, strong communication skills, and knowledge of healthy interpersonal relationships. The goal of Family Life Education is to teach and foster this knowledge and these skills to enable individuals* and families to function optimally within the context of their environments.

Family Life Education professionals consider societal issues—social justice, economics, education, discrimination, family policy, poverty, and more—within the context of families and through a strengths-based perspective. Family Life Educators are inclusionary in practice, recognizing diverse individual and family identities and structures.

Professionals that are Certified Family Life Educators (CFLEs) have demonstrated knowledge of the following 10 content areas:

1. Families and Individuals in Societal Contexts
2. Internal Dynamics of Families
3. Human Growth and Development across the Lifespan
4. Human Sexuality
5. Interpersonal Relationships

*The term "individual" is used in this document to include children, youth, and adults, with the understanding that there are unique and qualitatively different stages of development for each of these groups.

6. Family Resource Management
7. Parent Education and Guidance
8. Family Law and Public Policy
9. Professional Ethics and Practice
10. Family Life Education Methodology

The CFLE Code of Professional Ethics identifies guidelines for professional behavior. These guidelines show the public and members of the profession the principles and values that guide professional practice for Family Life Educators. The following core values are reflected in the ethical principles: do no harm, respect diversity and practice cultural competence, engage in ethical decision-making, practice with integrity, recognize and build on individual and family strengths, and practice with humility and warmth.

Ethical Principles

A. Relationships with Individuals and Families

The Family Life Educator will:

1. be aware of the influence we have and avoid practices that harm or exploit.
2. respect cultural beliefs, backgrounds, and differences, and engage in practice that is responsive to diversity.
3. respect individuals' and families' right to privacy, and maintain confidentiality at all times, except when disclosure is necessary to prevent harm.
4. treat individuals and families with warmth, respect, and sensitivity to their needs and rights as developing persons.
5. regard individuals and families as complex, interactive systems.
6. strive to understand individuals, families, and communities within their contexts.
7. practice with humility from a strengths-based perspective.
8. support healthy interpersonal relationships.
9. engage individuals, families, and communities as partners in problem solving and decision-making.
10. advocate in partnership with individuals, families, and communities.
11. communicate respectfully and clearly in our work with individuals, families, and communities.
12. communicate openly and truthfully about the nature and extent of Family Life Education services provided.
13. provide services and program environments that are safe and nurturing.
14. collaborate with individuals, families, and communities in the design, implementation, and evaluation of Family Life Education programs and services.

15. support individuals, families, and communities as they make decisions about the use of resources to best meet their needs.
16. encourage individuals, families, and communities to reflect upon their values, and promote their healthy development and well-being.
17. support the right of all individuals and families to have access to quality education, health, and community resources.
18. acknowledge and strive to maintain professional boundaries and not exploit families or individuals when multiple relationships exist.
19. openly acknowledge potential conflicts of interest.
20. strive to ensure that all individuals, families, and communities have access to and are encouraged to participate in Family Life Education.

B. Relationships with Colleagues and the Profession

The Family Life Educator will:

1. value and promote diversity and work collaboratively with colleagues.
2. demonstrate integrity and strive to make ethical decisions.
3. recognize the difference between personal and professional values in our professional interactions.
4. define our role as Family Life Educators and practice within our level of competence.
5. engage in current, evidence-informed practice.
6. be committed to ongoing professional development to enhance our knowledge and skills.
7. obtain informed consent when providing services or conducting research.
8. use policies and support systems for addressing difficult situations.
9. follow the mandatory reporting of abusive behavior in a respectful and prudent manner.

C. Relationships with Community/Society

The Family Life Educator will:

1. be knowledgeable about community resources and make and accept informed, appropriate referrals.
2. be aware of the boundaries of our practice and know when and how to use other community resources for the benefit of individuals and families.
3. communicate clearly and cooperate with other programs and agencies in order to best meet individuals' and families' needs.
4. advocate for laws and policies that empower individuals, families, and communities and reflect our changing knowledge base.
5. respect and uphold laws and regulations that pertain to our practice as Family Life Educators and offer expertise to legal authorities based on professional knowledge.

By my signature below, I verify that I have read these ethical principles and that I will use the principles to guide my professional practice as a Certified Family Life Educator (CFLE).

Printed Name Signature Date

This signed document must be submitted along with the CFLE-approved program application, the CFLE exam application, or as part of the recertification or upgrade processes.

Adapted from the Minnesota Council on Family Relations Ethical Thinking and Practice for Parent and Family Life Educators (2016) by members of the Certified Family Life Educator (CFLE) Advisory Board Ethics Subcommittee: Dorothy Berglund, PhD, CFLE; Dawn Cassidy, MEd, CFLE; Bryce Dickey, MS, CFLE; Susan Meyerle, PhD, CFLE; and Ahlishia Shipley, PhD, CFLE. Approved by the CFLE Advisory Board in May 2018.

National Council on Family Relations | 661 LaSalle Street, Suite 200 | Saint Paul, Minnesota 55114
888-781-9331 | 763-781-9331 | Fax: 763-781-9348 | info@ncfr.org | www.ncfr.org

APPENDIX D

Career Opportunities in Family Science

Setting	Employment Opportunities
Business, Consumer, and Family Resources Services	Employee Assistance Specialist Corporate Childcare Administrator Family Financial Counseling and Planning Consumer Protection Agencies Family Resource Management Food Assistance Programs Child and Family Poverty Research Research on Work and Families Family Business Consultant
Community-Based Social Services	Youth Development Programs Adoption Agencies Foster Care Programs Teen Pregnancy Counselor Family Preservation Worker Welfare Assistance for Low-Income Families Vocational Rehabilitation and Job Training Adult Day Care Providers Gerontology Programs
Early Childhood Education	Childcare Centers Head Start Programs Preschools Montessori Schools Child Development Consultant
Education	Public School Teaching in Family and Consumer Sciences (Certification) Cooperative Extension University Teaching and Research in Family Science Departments Family Life Education Sexuality Education Programs in Parish and Community Settings Parent Educators Family Peace and Justice Education Children's Museum Education Marriage and Family Enrichment Facilitators High School Guidance Counselor

(continued)

Setting	Employment Opportunities
Faith-Based Organizations	Clergy Family Mentor Family Life Educator Parent Educator Youth Worker
Family Intervention	Individual and Family Therapy Case Manager for Family Treatment Plans Crisis and Hotline Services Court-Mandated Parent Education Programs Divorce Mediation Abuse Protection Services Sexual Violence Drug and Alcohol Prevention Counselors Residential Treatment Programs Victim/Witness Support Services
Government and Public Policy	Family Policy Analyst Advocate/Lobbyist on Behalf of Children, Women, and Family Well-Being Cooperative Extension Specialist Military Family Support Services Departments of Child and Family Services Juvenile Justice
Health Care and Family Wellness	Public Health Programs and Services Hospital Family Support Professionals Nutrition Education and Counseling Prenatal and Maternity Services Holistic Health Centers Long-Term Care Administrator Hospice Programs
International Education and Development	International Family Policy Analyst Peace Corps and NGO Leadership Global Family Planning Programs Community and Sustainable Development International Human Rights Advocacy Immigration and Migrant Families Services
Research	Grant Proposal Writing Academic and Government-Related Research in Family Science Content Areas Population Studies and Demographic Research Community-Based Research for Non-Profit Family Agencies Program Evaluation and Assessment
Writing and Communication	Curriculum and Resource Development Public Service Radio and TV Programming Newspaper and Magazine Journalism on Social Issues Affecting Children and Families

Careers in Family Science. (2009). Minneapolis: National Council on Family Relations. Permission to reprint this material was granted by the National Council on Family Relations.

APPENDIX E

Program Evaluation

The Five-Tiered Approach

Level/Title	Purposes of Evaluation	Audiences	Tasks	Kinds of Data to Collect/Analyze
Tier 1—Needs Assessment	1. To document the size and nature of a public problem 2. To determine unmet need for services in a community 3. To propose program and policy options to meet needs 4. To set a data baseline from which later progress can be measured 5. To broaden the base of support for a proposed program	1. Policymakers 2. Funders 3. Community stakeholders	1. Review existing community, county, and state data 2. Determine additional data needed to describe problem and potential service users 3. Conduct "environmental scan" of available resources 4. Identify resource gaps and unmet needs 5. Set goals and objectives for intervention 6. Recommend one program model for range of options	1. Extant data on target population; services currently available 2. Interviews with community leaders 3. Interviews or survey data from prospective participants 4. Information about similar programs in other locations
Tier 2—Monitoring and Accountability	1. To monitor program performance 2. To meet demands for accountability 3. To build a constituency 4. To aid in program planning and decision-making 5. To provide a groundwork for later evaluation activities	1. Program staff and administrators 2. Policymakers 3. Funders 4. Community stakeholders 5. Media	1. Determine needs and capacities for data collection and management 2. Develop clear and consistent procedures for collecting essential data elements 3. Gather and analyze data to describe program along dimensions of clients, services, staff, and costs	1. MIS (management information system) data; collected at program, county, and/or state level 2. Case material; obtained through record reviews, program contact forms, etc.
Tier 3—Quality Review and Program Clarification	1. To develop a more detailed picture of the program as it is being implemented 2. To assess the quality and consistency of the intervention 3. To provide information to staff for program improvement	1. Program staff and administrators 2. Policymakers 3. Community stakeholders	1. Review monitoring data 2. Expand on program description using information about participants' views 3. Compare program with standards and expectations 4. Examine participants' perceptions about effects of program 5. Clarify program goals and design	1. MIS monitoring data 2. Case material 3. Other qualitative and quantitative data on program operations, customer satisfaction, and perceived effects; obtained using questionnaires, interviews, observations, and focus groups

Level/Title	Purposes of Evaluation	Audiences	Tasks	Kinds of Data to Collect/Analyze
Tier 4—Achieving Outcomes	1. To determine changes, if any, have occurred among beneficiaries 2. To attribute changes to the program 3. To provide information to staff for program improvement	1. Program staff and adminis-trators 2. Policymakers 3. Community stakeholders 4. Funders 5. Other programs	1. Choose short-term objectives to be examined 2. Choose appropriate research design, given constraints and capacities 3. Determine measurable indicators of success for outcome objectives 4. Collect and analyze information about effects on beneficiaries	1. Client-specific data; obtained using ques-tionnaires, interviews, goal attainment scaling, observations, and functional indicators 2. Client and community social indicators 3. MIS data 4. Comparable data for comparison group(s)
Tier 5—Establishing Impact	1. To contribute to knowledge development in the field 2. To produce evidence of dif-ferential effectiveness of treatments 3. To identify models worthy of replication	1. Academic and research com-munities 2. Policymakers 3. Funders 4. General public	1. Decide on impact objectives based on results of Tier 4 evaluation efforts 2. Choose appropriately rigorous research design and comparison group 3. Identify techniques and tools to measure effects in treatment and comparison groups 4. Collect and analyze information to identify program impacts	1. Client-specific data; obtained using ques-tionnaires, interviews, goal attainment scaling, observations, and functional indicators 2. Client and community social indicators 3. MIS data 4. Comparable data for control group(s)

Source: Adapted from Jacobs, F. H. (2003). Child and family program evaluation: Learning to enjoy complexity. *Applied Developmental Science, 7*(2), 62–75.

References

Abma, J., & Martinez, G. (2017). Sexual activity and contraceptive use among teenagers in the United States, 2011–2015. *National Health Statistics Reports*, 104, 1–23. Retrieved from www.cdc.gov/nchs/products/databriefs/db366.htm

Adams, B. N. (2004). Families and family study in international perspective. *Journal of Marriage and Family*, 66, 1076–1088.

Adams, B., & Trost, J. (2005). *Handbook of world families*. Thousand Oaks, CA: Sage.

Adams, P. (2006). Exploring social constructivism: Theories and practicalities. *Education*, 34, 243–257.

Adler-Baeder, F. (2001). *Smart steps for adults and children in stepfamilies*. Lincoln, NE: Stepfamily Association of America, and Watertown, NY: Cornell Cooperative Extension of Jefferson County.

Adler-Baeder, F. (2002). Understanding stepfamilies: Family life education for community professionals. *Journal of Extension*, 40(6). Retrieved from www.joe.org/joe/2002december/iw2.php

Adler-Baeder, F., & Higginbotham, B. (2004). Implications for remarriage and stepfamily formation for marriage education. *Family Relations*, 53, 448–458.

Adler-Baeder, F., & Higginbotham, B. (2020). Efforts to design, implement, and evaluation community-based education for stepfamilies: Current knowledge and future directions. *Family Relations*, 69, 559–576.

Adler-Baeder, F., Kerpelman, J., Schramm, D., Higginbotham, B., & Paulk, A. (2007). The impact of relationship education on adolescents of diverse backgrounds. *Family Relations*, 56, 291–303.

Adler-Baeder, F., Robertson, A., & Schramm, D. (2010). Community education programs serving couples in stepfamilies: A qualitative study of format, content, and service delivery. *Journal of Extension, 48*(5). Retrieved from https://tigerprints.clemson.edu/joe/vol48/iss5/16/

Administration for Children and Families (ACF). (2005). *Healthy marriage matters*. Washington, DC: Author.

Ads, M., & Blume, L. B. (2022). Family life education with Arab immigrant families. In S. M. Ballard & A .C Taylor (Eds.), *Family life education with diverse populations* (2nd ed., pp. 333–360). San Diego, CA: Cognella Academic Publishing.

Ahmed, R. (2005). Egyptian families. In J. Roopnarine & U. Gielen (Eds.), *Families in global perspective* (pp. 151–168). Boston: Pearson.

Ainsworth, M. (1973). The development of infant-mother attachment. In B. Caldwell & H. Ricciuti, (Eds.), *Review of child development research* (Vol. 3, pp. 1–94). Chicago: University of Chicago Press.

Ainsworth, M., & Bowlby, J. (1991). An ethological approach to personality development. *American Psychologist*, 46, 331–341.

Alford, S. (2008). *Science and success: Sex education and other programs that work to prevent teen pregnancy, HIV & sexually transmitted infections* (2nd ed.). Washington, DC: Advocates for Youth.

Allar, I., Elliott, E., Jones, E., Kristjansson, A. L., Taliaferro, A., & Bulger, S. M. (2017). Involving families and communities in CSPAP development using asset mapping, *Journal of Physical Education, Recreation & Dance*, 88, 7–14.

Allemand, M., Steiger, A., & Hill, P. (2013). Stability of personality traits in adulthood: Mechanisms and implications. *The Journal of Gerontopsychology and Geriatric Psychiatry*, 26, 3–13.

Allen, W., & Blaisure, K. (2009). Family life educators and the development of cultural competency. In D. Bredehoft & M. Walcheski (Eds.), *Family life education integrating theory and practice* (2nd ed.). Minneapolis, MN: National Council on Family Relations.

Allen, W., & Blaisure, K. (2015). Family life education and the practice of cross-cultural competence. In M. Walcheski & J. Reinke (Eds.), *Family life education: The practice of family science* (pp. 27–37). Minneapolis, MN: National Council on Family Relations.

Allen, S., Duncan Perrote, D., & Feinman, S. (2022). Family life education with Indigenous families. In S. M. Ballard & A. C Taylor (Eds.), *Family life education with diverse populations* (2nd ed., pp. 263–308). San Diego, CA: Cognella Academic Publishing.

Allen, K., & Henderson, A. (2017). *Family theories: Foundations and applications*. Sommerset, NJ: John Wiley & Sons.

Allen, K., & Huff, N. (2015). Family coaching: An emerging family science field. In M. Walcheski and J Reinke (Eds.), *Family life education: The practice of family science* (pp 61–72). Minneapolis, MN: National Council on Family Relations.

Allen, K., & Lavender-Stott, E. (2020). Preparing the educators who teach about families: Engaging family science in the university setting. *Family Relations*, 30. doi: 10.1111/fare.1241

Alliance for Work Life Progress (AWLP). (2005). The categories of work-life effectiveness. Retrieved from www.awlp.org/pub/work-life_categories.pdf

Almalki, S., & Ganong, L. (2018). Family life education in Saudi Arabia. In M. Robila & A. Taylor (Eds.), *Global perspectives on family life education* (pp. 33–48). Cham, Switzerland: Springer International Publishing.

Amato, P. (2000). The consequences of divorce for adults and children. *Journal of Marriage and the Family*, 62, 1269–1287.

Amato, P. (2010). Research on divorce: Continuing trends and new developments. *Journal of Marriage and Family*, 72, 650–666.

Amato, P. (2011a). Marital quality in African American marriages. Retrieved from www.healthymarriageinfo.org/resource-detail/index.aspx?rid=3929

Amato, P. (2011b). Divorce among African Americans. Retrieved from www.healthymarriageinfo.org/resource-detail/index.aspx?rid=3929

Amato, P., & Cheadle, J. (2005). The long reach of divorce: Divorce and child well-being across three generations. *Journal of Marriage and Family*, 67, 191–206.

Amato, P., & Hays, L. (2014). "Alone together": Marriages and "living apart together" relationships. In A. Abela & J. Walter (Eds.), *Contemporary issues in family studies: Global perspectives on partnerships, parenting and support in a changing world*. Malden, MA: John Wiley & Sons.

Amato, P., Booth, A., Johnson, D., & Rogers, S. (2007). *Alone together: How marriage in America is changing*. Cambridge, MA: Harvard University.

Amato, P., Kane, J., & James, S. (2011). Reconsidering the "good divorce." *Family Relations*, 60, 511–524.

American Academy of Pediatrics et al. v. Clovis Unified School District. (2015). 12CECG02608.

American Association of Sexuality Educators, Counselors, and Therapists (AASECT). (2019). *AASECT position statement on consent and sexual violence*. Retrieved from www.aasect.org/aasect-position-statement-consent-and-sexual-violence

American Association of University Women (AAUW). (2011). *Crossing the line: Sexual harassment at school*. Washington, DC: Author.

American Evaluation Association (AEA). (n.d.). *What is evaluation?* www.eval.org/About/What-is-Evaluation

American Sexual Health Association (ASHA). (n.d.). *What is sexual health?* Retrieved from www.ashasexualhealth.org/sexual-health

Amnesty International. (n.d.). *Armed conflict*. Retrieved from www.amnesty.org/en/armed-conflict

Amos, D. S. (2013). Was it "affluenza" or permissive parenting? *Jacksonville Times-Union*. Retrieved from www.jacksonville.com/story/news/education/2013/12/27/was-it-affluenza-or-permissive-parenting/15804521007/

Anderson, M., & Jiang, J. (2018). Teens, social media, & technology 2018. *Pew Research Center*. www.pewresearch.org/internet/2018/05/31/teens-social-media-technology-2018

Anderson, L., & Krathwohl, D. (2001). *A taxonomy for learning, teaching, and assessing: A revision of Bloom's taxonomy of educational objectives*. Boston: Allyn & Bacon.

Andrasfay, T., & Goldman, N. (2021). Reductions in 2020 US life expectancy due to COVID-19. *Proceedings of the National Academy of Sciences (PNAS)*. Retrieved from www.pnas.org/content/118/5/e2014746118

Annie E. Casey Foundation. (2016). A shared sentence: The devastating toll of parental incarceration on kids, families and communities. *Policy Report: Kids Count*. https://assets.aecf.org/m/resourcedoc/aecf-asharedsentence-2016.pdf

Annie E. Casey Foundation. (2020a). 2020 Kids count data book. *Kids Count Data Center*. https://assets.aecf.org/m/resourcedoc/aecf-2020kidscountdatabook-2020.pdf

Annie E. Casey Foundation. (2020b). Child population by race in the United States. *Kids Count Data Center*. https://datacenter.kidscount.org/data/tables/103-child-population-by-race?loc=1&loct=1#detailed/1/any/false/1729,37,871,870,573,869,36,868,867,133/68,69,67,12,70,66,71,72/423,424

Annie E. Casey Foundation. (2020c). Children in poverty (100 percent poverty) in the United States. *Kids Count Data Center*. https://datacenter.kidscount.org/data/tables/43-children-in-poverty-100-percent-poverty?loc=1&loct=1#detailed/1/any/false/1729,37,871,870,573,869,36,868,867,133/any/321,322

Arcus, M. E., Schvaneveldt, J. D., & Moss, J. J. (1993). The nature of family life education. In M. E. Arcus, J. D. Schvaneveldt, & J. J. Moss (Eds.), *Handbook of family life education: Foundations of family life education* (Vol. 1, pp. 1–25). Newbury Park, CA: Sage.

Arcus, M. E. (1995). Advances in family life education: Past, present, and future. *Family Relations*, 44, 336–343.

Arditti, J. (2008). Parental imprisonment and family visitation: A brief overview and recommendations for family friendly practice. In T. LaLiberte & E. Snyder (Eds.), *CW 360: A comprehensive look at prevalent child welfare issue: Children of incarcerated parents* (pp. 16, 32). St. Paul: University of Minnesota. Retrieved from www.cehd.umn.edu/ssw/cascw/attributes/PDF/publications/CW360_2008.pdf

Arnett, J. (2000). Emerging adulthood: A theory of development from the late teens through the twenties. *American Psychologist*, 55, 469–480.

Arnett, J. (2004). *Emerging adulthood: The winding road from the late teens through the twenties.* New York: Oxford University Press.

Arnett, J. (2007). Emerging adulthood: What is it and what is it good for? *Child Development Perspectives*, 1, 68–73.

Asay, S., Younes, M., & Moore, T. (2006). Transformation in higher education: The impact of international study tours on college students. In R. Hamon (Ed.), *International family studies: Developing curricula and teaching tools* (pp. 85–99). Binghamton, NY: Haworth Press.

ASPE—Office of the Assistant Secretary for Planning and Evaluation. Office of Human Services Policy. (2013). *Key implementation considerations for executing evidence-based programs: Project overview.* Washington, DC: US Department of Health and Human Services. Retrieved from www.aspe.hhs.gov/hsp/13/keyissuesforchildrenyouth/keyimplementation/rb_keyimplement.pdf

Australian Council of Professions. (2003). *What is a profession?* Retrieved from www.professions.org.au/what-is-a-professional/

Auxier, B., Anderson, M., Perrin, A., & Turner, E. (2020). Parents' attitudes-experiences-related to digital technology. *Pew Research Center.* Retrieved from www.pewresearch.org/internet/2020/07/28/parents-attitudes-and-experiences-related-to-digital-technology/

Avert. (2020). *HIV and AIDS in East and Southern Africa Regional Overview.* Retrieved from www.avert.org/professionals/hiv-around-world/sub-saharan-africa/overview

Avery, C. (1962). Inside family life education. *The Family Life Coordinator, 11*(2), 27–39.

Bailey, S., & Gentry, D. (2013). Teaching about family science as a discipline. In G. W. Peterson & K. R. Bush (Eds.), *Handbook of marriage and the family* (pp. 861–883). New York: Springer.

Baldwin, K. E. (1949). *The AHEA saga*. Washington, DC: American Home Economics Association.

Ballard, S. M., Cassidy, D., Taylor, A. C., & Robila, M. (2018). Family life education in the United States. In M. Robila & A. C. Taylor (Eds.), *Global perspectives on family life education* (pp. 195–215). New York: Springer.

Ballard, S., & Morris, L. (2003). The family life education needs of midlife and older adults. *Family Relations*, 52, 129–136.

Ballard, S. M., & Taylor, A. C. (2012). A framework for best practices in family life education. *Certified Family Life Educator Network, 24*(4), 12–13.

Ballard, S. M., & Taylor, A. C. (2022a). Best practices in family life education. In S. M. Ballard & A.C. Taylor (Eds.), *Family life education with diverse populations* (2nd ed., pp. 1–18). San Diego, CA: Cognella Academic Publishing.

Ballard, S. M., & Taylor, A. C. (Eds.). (2022b). *Family life education with diverse populations* (2nd ed.). San Diego, CA: Cognella Academic Publishing.

Ballard, S. M., Tyndall, L., Baugh, E., Bumgarner, C., & Littlewood, K. (2016). Framework for best practices in family life education: A case study. *Family Relations*, 65, 393–406.

Ballard, S. M. (2020). The process of evaluation: Toward an implementation framework. *Family Relations*, 69, 461–478.

Bandura, A. (1977). *Social learning theory.* New York: General Learning Press.

Bandura, A. (1986). *Social foundations of thought and action.* Englewood Cliffs, NJ: Prentice-Hall.

Bandura, A. (1999). Social cognitive theory: An agentic perspective. *Asian Journal of Social Psychology*, 2, 21–41.

Barnes, C., Stanley, S., & Markman, H. (2004). Christian PREP: The prevention and relationship enhancement program. *Marriage & Family: A Christian Journal*, 7, 63–76.

Barroso, A., Parker, K., & Bennett, J. (2020, May 27). As millennials near 40, they're approaching family life differently than previous generations. *Pew Research Center.* Retrieved from www.pewresearch.org/social-trends/2020/05/27/as-millennials-near-40-theyre-approaching-family-life-differently-than-previous-generations/

Baugh, E., & Coughlin, D. (2012). Family life education with black families. In S. Ballard & A. Taylor (Eds.), *Family life education with diverse populations* (pp. 235–254). Thousand Oaks, CA: Sage.

Baugh, E., Ballard, S. M., Carter, L., Tyndall, L., Nolan, M., & Littlewood, K. (2017). The county-wide dissemination of Triple P Parenting Program: An implementation study. *Progress in Community Health Partnerships: Research, Education, and Action*, 13, 73–81.

Baugh, E. J., & Rajaei, A. (2022). Family life education with Black families. In S. M. Ballard & A. C. Taylor (Eds.), *Family life education with diverse populations* (2nd ed., pp. 239–262). San Diego, CA: Cognella Academic Publishing.

Baumrind, D. (1991). The influence of parenting style on adolescent competence and substance abuse. *Journal of Early Adolescence*, 11, 56–95.

Bean, R., Perry, B., & Bedell, T. (2001). Developing culturally competent marriage and family therapists: Guidelines for working with Hispanic families. *Journal of Marital and Family Therapy*, 27, 43–54.

Beavers, R., & Hampson, R. (2000). The Beavers systems model of family functioning. *Journal of Family Therapy*, 22, 128–143.

Bedi, R. (2012, February 27). Indian dowry deaths on rise. *The Telegraph*. Retrieved from www.telegraph.co.uk/news/worldnews/asia/india/9108642/Indian-dowry-deaths-on-the-rise.html

Beecher, C. E. (1858). *A treatise on domestic economy* (3rd ed.). New York: Harper & Brothers.

Bennett, M. (1993). Toward ethnorelativism: A developmental model of intercultural sensitivity. In R. M. Paige (Ed.), *Education for the intercultural experiences* (pp. 21–71). Yarmouth, ME: Intercultural Press.

Benson, J. J., & Donehower, A. K. (2020). Best practices in family life education programming for midlife and older adults. *Family Relations*, 69, 577–594.

Biden, J. R. (2021). Executive order on preventing and combating discrimination on the basis of gender identity or sexual orientation. *The White House*. Retrieved from www.whitehouse.gov/briefing-room/presidential-actions/2021/01/20/executive-order-preventing-and-combating-discrimination-on-basis-of-gender-identity-or-sexual-orientation

Bigfoot, D. (2008). Cultural adaptations of evidence-based practices in American Indian and Alaska native populations. In C. Newman, C. Liberton, K. Kutash, & R. Friedman (Eds.), *A system of care for children's mental health* (pp. 69–72). Tampa, FL: University of South Florida, Louis de la Parte Florida Mental Health Institute.

Billings, D. (2004). Primary colors personality text. Retrieved from www.dawnbillings.com/main/personalityHow

Bishop, M., Ioverno, S., & Russell, S. (2019). Promoting school safety for LGBTQ and all students in Texas. *The Stories and Numbers Project*. Retrieved from http://utw10886.utweb.utexas.edu/wp-content/uploads/2019/03/stories-and-numbers-policy-brief-full-report.pdf

Bhangaokar, R., & Pandya, N. (2018). Family life education in India: Policies and prospects. In M. Robila & A. Taylor (Eds.), *Global perspectives on family life education* (pp. 75–89). Cham, Switzerland: Springer International Publishing.

Blase, K., & Fixsen, D. (2013). Core intervention components: Identifying and operationalizing what makes programs work. *Office of the Assistant Secretary for Planning and Evaluation Research Brief*. Retrieved from https://aspe.hhs.gov/reports/core-intervention-components-identifying-operationalizing-what-makes-programs-work-0

Bloom B. (1956). *Taxonomy of educational objectives, handbook I: The cognitive domain*. New York: Longman.

Blumberg, S. J., Kogan, M. D., & Boyle, C. A. (2019). Prevalence and trends of developmental disabilities among children in the United States: 2009–2017. *Pediatrics*, 144, e20190811.

Bodenmann, G., & Shantinath, S. (2004). The couples coping enhancement training (SSET): A new approach to prevention of marital distress based upon stress and coping. *Family Relations*, 53, 477–484.

Bodenmann, G., Ledermann, T., & Bradbury, T. N. (2007). Stress, sex, and satisfaction in marriage. *Personal Relationships*, 14, 551–569.

Bond, J., Galinsky, E., & Hill, E. (2004). *When work works: Flexibility—A critical ingredient in creating an effective workplace*. New York: Families and Work Institute.

Bookwala, J. (2005). The role of marital quality in physical health during the mature years. *Journal of Aging and Health*, 17, 85–104.

Borden, L. M., Gunty, A., Lu, Z., Mischel, E., Otto, M., & Richmond, A. (November). Enhancing child outcomes through high-quality parent education. A partnership between The Military REACH Team, The Center for Research and Outreach (REACH), and The University of Minnesota. Retrieved from https://assets.reachfamilies.info/reachfamilies.umn.edu/files//rdoc/ParentEducation_040517.pdf

Bornstein, M. H. (Ed.). (2002). *Handbook of parenting, Vol. 1: Children and parenting* (2nd ed.). Mahwah, NJ: Lawrence Erlbaum.

Bosley, A., and Ranck, A. (2019). Increased—For better or for worse? Transgender individuals, couples, and families in the 21st century. In K. Lyness & J. Fischer (Eds.), *Gender, sexual identity, and families: The personal is political*. Ann Arbor, MI: Michigan Publishing, University of Michigan Library.

Boss, P. (1999). *Ambiguous loss: Learning to live with unresolved grief*. Cambridge, MA: Harvard University Press.

Boss, P. (2006). *Loss, trauma and resilience: Therapeutic work with ambiguous loss*. New York: W.W. Norton & Co.

Boss, P., Bryant, C., & Mancini, J. (2017). *Family stress management. A contextual approach*. Thousand Oaks, CA: Sage Publications.

Bouchet, S. (2008). *Children and families with incarcerated parents*. Baltimore, MD: Annie E. Casey Foundation. Retrieved from www.f2f.ca.gov/res/pdf/ChildrenAndFamilies.pdf

Bouchet, S., Torres, L., & Hyra, A. (2013). Understanding Hispanic diversity: A "one size" approach to service delivery may not fit all. *Office of Planning, Research, and Evaluation, Administration of Children and Families*. Retrieved from www.acf.hhs.gov/sites/default/files/opre/hmmi_hispanic.pdf

Bowlby, J. (1969). *Attachment and loss: Vol. 1. Attachment*. New York: Basic Books.

Bowlby, J. (1988). *A secure base: Parent-child attachment and healthy human development*. New York: Basic Books.

Boyd, L., Hibbard, C., & Knapp, D. (2001). *Market analysis of family life, parenting, and marriage education for the National Council on Family Relations*. Alexandria, VA: Human Resources Research Organization.

Boyer, J. (2018). New name, same harm: Rebranding of federal abstinence-only programs. *Guttmacher Policy Review*, 21, 11–16.

Bradford, A. B., Adler-Baeder, F., Ketring, S. A., & Smith, T. A. (2012). The role of participant–facilitator demographic match in couple and relationship education. *Family Relations*, 61, 51–64.

Braff, D. (2020). The new helicopter parents are on zoom. *The New York Times*. Retrieved from www.nytimes.com/2020/09/28/parenting/helicopter-parent-remote-learning.html

Braithwaite, S., Delevi, R., & Fincham, F. (2010). Romantic relationships and the physical and mental health of college students. *Personal Relationships*, 17, 1–12.

Bramlett, M., & Mosher, W. (2002). Cohabitation, marriage, divorce, and remarriage in the United States (Series 22, No 2). *Centers for Disease Control and Prevention*. Retrieved from www.cdc.gov/nchs/data/series/sr_23/sr23_022.pdf

Bray, J., & Kelly, J. (1998). *Stepfamilies: Love, marriage, and parenting in the first decade.* New York: Broadway.

Bredehoft, D. J., & Walcheski, M. J. (Eds.). (2011). *The family life education framework poster and PowerPoint.* Minneapolis, MN: National Council on Family Relations.

Brick, P., & Lundquist, J. (2003). *New expectations: Sexuality education for mid and later life.* New York: SIECUS.

Brick, P., & Taverner, B. (2001). *Positive images: Teaching abstinence, contraception, and sexual health.* Morristown, NJ: Planned Parenthood of Greater Northern New Jersey, Inc.

Brick, P., Davis, N., Fischel, M., Lupo, T., MacVicar, A., & Marshall, J. (1989). *Bodies, birth, and babies: Sexuality education in early childhood programs.* Hackensack, NJ: Planned Parenthood of Bergen County.

Brickman, P., Rabinowitz, V., Karuza, J., Jr., Coates, D., Cohn, E., & Kidder, L. (1982). Models of helping and coping. *American Psychologist*, 37, 368–384.

Bridgeman, R. P. (1930). Ten years' progress in parent education. *Annals of the American Academy of Political and Social Science*, 151, 32–45.

Brim, O. (1959). *Education for child rearing.* New York: Russell Sage Foundation.

Bristor, M. (2010). *Individuals and family systems in their environments.* Dubuque, IA: Kendall Hunt.

Brock, G. (1993). Ethical guidelines for the practice of family life education. *Family Relations*, 42, 124–127.

Brock, G. W., Oertwein, M., & Coufal, J. D. (1993). Parent education theory, research, and practice. In M. E. Arcus, J. D. Schvaneveldt, & J. J. Moss (Eds.), *Handbook of family life education* (Vol. 2, p. 88). Newbury Park, CA: Sage.

Bronfenbrenner, U. (1979). *The ecology of human development.* Cambridge, MA: Harvard University Press.

Bronfenbrenner, U. (2005). *Making human beings human: Bioecological perspectives on human development.* Thousand Oaks, CA: Sage.

Brooks, J. (2011). *The process of parenting* (6th ed.). New York: McGraw-Hill.

Brotherson, S., & Duncan, W. (2004). Rebinding the ties that bind: Government efforts to preserve and promote marriage. *Family Relations*, 53, 459–468.

Brown, A. (2020). Nearly half of U.S. adults say dating has gotten harder for most people in the last 10 years. *Pew Research Center.* Retrieved from www.pewsocialtrends.org/2020/08/20/nearly-half-of-u-s-adults-say-dating-has-gotten-harder-for-most-people-in-the-last-10-years/

Brown, S. (2018). Many professors have to report sexual misconduct. How should they tell their students that? *The Chronicle of Higher Education.* Retrieved from www.chronicle.com/article/many-professors-have-to-report-sexual-misconduct-how-should-they-tell-their-students-that/

Brown, S., & Taverner, B. (2001). *Streetwise to sex-wise: Sexuality education for high-risk youth.* Morristown, NJ: Planned Parenthood of Greater Northern New Jersey, Inc.

Brownell, C. A., & Drummond, J. (2020). Early childcare and family experiences predict development of prosocial behaviour in first grade. *Early Child Development and Care*, 190, 712–737.

Bruess, C., & Schroeder, E. (2018). *Sexuality education: Theory and practice.* Scotts Valley, CA: ETR.

Brunner, R., Craig, P., & Watson, N. (2019). Evaluability assessment: An application in a complex community improvement setting. *Evaluation*, 25, 349–365.

Bubolz, M., & Sontag, S. (1993). Human ecology theory. In P. Boss, W. Doherty, R. LaRossa, W. Schumm, & S. Steinmetz (Eds.), *Sourcebook of family theories and methods: A contextual approach* (pp. 419–448). New York: Plenum Press.

Buchholz, K. (2019). This chart shows the age that people get married across the world. *World Economic Forum*. Retrieved from www.weforum.org/agenda/2019/09/when-people-get-married-around-the-world/

Buckley, R. R. (2016). Principle of least interest. In C. L. Shehan (Ed.), *Encyclopedia of family studies*. doi: 10.1002/9781119085621.wbefs288

Burnette, C. E., & Renner, L. M. (2016). A pattern of cumulative disadvantage: Risk factors for violence across Indigenous women's lives. *The British Journal of Social Work*, 47, 1166–1185.

Burnes, T. (2017). Flying faster than the birds and bees: Toward a sex positive theory and practice in multi-cultural education. In R. K. Gordon et al. (Eds.), *Challenges associated with cross-cultural and at-risk student engagement* (pp. 170–187). Hershey, PA: ICI Global.

Buston, K., Wight, D., Hart, G., & Scott, S. (2002). Implementation of a teacher-delivered sex education programme: Obstacles and facilitating factors. *Health Education Research*, 17, 59–72.

Bryant, C. M. (2020). Studying marital relationships using family systems as a guide. In A. G. James (Ed.), *Black families: A systems approach* (pp. 124–131). San Diego, CA: Cognella Academic Publishing.

Byrne, A., & Carr, D. (2005). Caught in the cultural lag: The stigma of singlehood. *Psychological Inquiry: An International Journal for the Advancement of Psychological Theory*, 16, 84–91.

Calasanti, T., & Keicolt, K. (2007). Diversity among late-life couples. *Generations: Journal of the American Society on Aging*, 31, 10–17.

Campbell, D., & Palm, G. (2018). *Parent education: Working with groups and individuals*. San Diego, CA: Cognella Academic Publishing.

Canadian Evaluation Society. (2015, July 14). What is evaluation? https://evaluationcanada.ca/sites/default/files/definition_of_evaluation_20150714-1_en.pdf

Carroll, J., & Doherty, W. (2003). Evaluating the ineffectiveness of premarital prevention programs: A meta-analytic review of outcome research. *Family Relations*, 52, 105–118.

Carroll, C., Patterson, M., Wood, S., Booth, A., Rick, J., & Balain, S. (2007). A conceptual framework for implementation fidelity. *Implementation Science*, 2, 1–9.

Cassidy, D. (2003). The growing of a profession: Challenges in family life education. In D. Bredehoft & M. Walcheski (Eds.), *Family life education: Integrating theory and practice* (pp. 44–55). Minneapolis, MN: National Council on Family Relations.

Centers for Disease Control and Prevention. (2011). Youth risk behavior surveillance—United States, 2011. *Morbidity and Mortality Weekly Report*, 61, 1–168. Retrieved from www.cdc.gov/mmwr/pdf/ss/ss6104.pdf

Centers for Disease Control and Prevention (CDC). (2013). *Adverse childhood experiences (ACE) study*. Retrieved from www.cdc.gov/violenceprevention/aces/about.html

Centers for Disease Control (CDC). (2019a). Vital signs: Adverse childhood experiences, (ACEs). *Vital signs*. Retrieved from www.cdc.gov/vitalsigns/aces/modules/VS_ACE.pdf

Centers for Disease Control and Prevention (CDC). (2019b). *HIV: Youth*. Retrieved from www.cdc.gov/hiv/group/age/youth/index.html

Central Intelligence Agency: *World fact book (Database)*. Retrieved from www.cia.gov/the-world-factbook/

Chalmers, L., & Milan, A. (2005). Marital satisfaction during the retirement years. *Canadian Social Trends*, 76, 14–17.

Charles, P., Kerr, M., Wirth, J., Jensen, S., Massoglia, M., & Poehlmann-Tynan, J. (2021). Lessons from the field: Developing and implementing an intervention for jailed parents and their children. *Family Relations*, 70, 171–178.

Cherlin, A. (2010). Demographic trends in the United States: A review of research in the 2000s. *Journal of Marriage and Family*, 72, 403–419.

Cherlin, A. (2009). *The marriage-go-round: The state of marriage and the family in America today.* New York: Alfred A Knopf.

ChildStats.gov (2021). America's children: Key national indicators of well-being, 2021. *Forum on child and family statistics.* Retrieved from www.childstats.gov/americaschildren/

Chin, H., Sipe, T., Elder, R., Mercer, S., Chattopadhyay, S., Jacob, V., Wethington, H., Kirby, D., Elliston, D., Griffith, M., Chuke, S., Briss, S., Ericksen, I., Galbraith, J., Herbst, J., Johnson, R., Kraft, J., Noar, S., Romero, L., & Santelli, J. (2012). The effectiveness of group-based comprehensive risk-reduction and abstinence education interventions to prevent or reduce the risk of adolescent pregnancy, human immunodeficiency virus, and sexually transmitted infections. *American Journal of Preventive Medicine*, 42, 272–294.

Cilluffo, A., & Cohn, D. (2019). 6 demographic trends shaping the U.S., and the world in 2019. *Pew Research Center.* www.pewresearch.org/fact-tank/2019/04/11/6-demographic-trends-shaping-the-u-s-and-the-world-in-2019/

Clarke, J. (1998). *Who, me lead a group?* Seattle, WA: Parenting Press, Inc.

Clarke, J., Dawson, C., & Bredehoft, D. (2014). *How much is too much?* Boston, MA: DeCapo Press.

Clauss, B. (2005). Syllabus objective guide. In M. Walcheski & N. Gonzalez (Eds.), *Teaching family life education: A syllabus collection* (pp. 7–8). Minneapolis, MN: National Council on Family Relations.

Coccia, C., Darling, C., Rehm, M., Cui, M., & Sathe, S. (2012). Adolescent health, stress, and life satisfaction: The paradox of indulgent parenting. *Stress and Health*, 28, 211–331.

Cohen, J., Byers, E., Sears, H., & Weaver, A. (2004). Sexual health education: Attitudes, knowledge and comfort of teachers in New Brunswick Schools. *The Canadian Journal of Human Sexuality*, 13, 1–15.

Cohen, L. R., Hien, D. A., & Batchelder, S. (2008). The impact of cumulative maternal trauma and diagnosis on parenting behavior. *Child Maltreatment*, 13, 27–38.

Collins, C., Alagiri, P., & Summers, T. (2002). *Abstinence only vs comprehensive sex education: What are the arguments? What is the evidence? Policy monograph.* San Francisco: AIDS Research Institute. Retrieved from ari.ucsf.edu/science/reports/abstinence.pdf

Collins, W. A. (2003). More than myth: The developmental significance of romantic relationships during adolescence. *Journal of Research on Adolescence*, 13, 1–24.

Collins, C. (2018). What is White privilege, really? *Teaching Tolerance Magazine*, 60, www.learningforjustice.org/magazine/fall-2018/what-is-white-privilege-really

Concordia Publishing House. (n.d.). *Learning about sex complete set* (set of 11). St. Louis, MO: Author. Retrieved from www.cph.org/p-6917-learning-about-sex-complete-set-setof-11.aspx

Connell. J. (2012). *Parenting 2.0 summary report: Parents' use of technology and the Internet.* Minneapolis: Minnesota Agricultural Experiment Station. Retrieved from www.cehd.umn.edu/fsos/projects/parent20/pdf/p20summaryreport-july2012.pdf

Consumer Financial Protection Bureau. (n.d.). *Financial education placemats.* Retrieved from www.consumerfinance.gov/practitioner-resources/resources-for-older-adults/financial-education-placemats/

Coontz, S. (2005). *Marriage, a history: From obedience to intimacy or how love conquered marriage.* New York: Viking.

Correa, N. P., Hayes, A. K., Bhalakia, A. M., Lopez, K. K., Cupit, T., Kwarteng-Amaning, V., Keefe, R. J., Greeley, C. S., & Van Horne, B. S. (2021). Parents' perspectives on the impact of their incarceration on children and families. *Family Relations*, 70, 162–170.

Costa, T., & McCrae, R. (2003) *Five factor model of personality.* Lutz, FL: Psychological Assessment Resources, Inc.

Council on Foreign Relations (CFR). (2020). Human trafficking in the global era. *World 101*. Retrieved from https://world101.cfr.org/global-era-issues/globalization/human-trafficking-global-era

Coyne, J., Rohrbaugh, M., Shoham, V., Sonnega, J., Nicklas, J., & Cranford, J. (2001). Prognostic importance of marital quality for survival of congestive heart failure. *American Journal of Cardiology*, 88, 526–529.

Croake, J. W., & Glover, K. E. (1977). A history and evaluation of parent education author. *The Family Coordinator*, 26, 151–158.

Cross, T., & Cross, A. (2015). Working with American Indian and Alaska Native individuals, couples, and families: A toolkit for stakeholders. *National Resource Center for Healthy Marriage and Families*. Retrieved from www.fatherhood.gov/sites/default/files/resource_files/e000003170.pdf

Cui, M., Darling, C., Coccia, C., Fincham, F. D., & May, R. W. (2019). Indulgent parenting, helicopter parenting, and well-being of parents and emerging adults. *Journal of Child and Family Studies*, 28, 860–871.

Cui, M., Darling, C. A., Lucier-Greer, M., Fincham, F. D., & May, R. W. (2018). Parental indulgence: Profiles and effects on young adults' emotional and behavioral problems. *Journal of Child and Family Studies*, 27, 2456–2466.

Cui, M., Hong, P., Darling, C., & Janhonen-Abruquah, H. (2019). A cross-cultural perspective on the role of parents in university students' mental health. In D. Esteves, D. Scarf, P. Pinheiro, H. Arahanga-Doyle, & J. Hunter (Eds.), *Global perspectives on university students* (pp. 81–108). Hauppauge, NY: Nova Sciences Publisher.

Cui, M., Janhonen-Abruquah, H., Darling, C. A., Chavez, F. L., & Palojoki, P. (2018). Helicopter parenting and young adults' well-being: A comparison between United States and Finland. *Cross-Cultural Research*, 53, 410–427.

Dahl, G. (2010). Early teen marriage and future poverty. *Demography*, 47, 689–718.

Dail, P. (1984). Constructing a philosophy of family life education: Educating the educators. *Family Perspective*, 18, 145–149.

Daniels, H. (Ed.). (1996). *An introduction to Vygotsky*. London: Routledge.

Darity, W. (Ed.). (2008). Marriage. In *International encyclopedia of the social sciences*. Farmington Hills, MI: Gale, Cengage Learning.

Darling, C. A. (2005). Families in a diverse culture: Changes and challenges. *Journal of Family and Consumer Sciences*, 97, 8–13.

Darling, C., & Cassidy, D. (1998). Professional development of students: Understanding the process of becoming a Certified Family Life Educator. *Family Science Review*, 11, 106–118.

Darling, C., & Cassidy, D. (2014). *Family life education: Working with families across the lifespan*. Long Grove, IL: Waveland Press.

Darling, C. A., Cassidy, D., & Rehm, M. (2017). Family life education: Translational family science in action. *Family Relations*, 30, 742–752.

Darling, C., Cassidy, D., & Rehm, M. (2020). The foundations of family life education model: Understanding the field. *Family Relations*, 69, 427–444.

Darling, C., Fleming, M., & Cassidy, D. (2009). Professionalization of family life education: Defining the field. *Family Relations*, 58, 330–372.

Darling, C. A., & Howard, S. (2006). Cultural lessons in sexuality: Comparison of parent-child communication styles in three cultures. In R. Hamon (Ed.), *International family studies: Developing curricula and teaching tools* (pp. 41–98). Binghamton, NY: Haworth Press.

Darling, C., & Howard, S. (2015). Human sexuality across the lifespan. In M. Walcheski & J. Reinke (Eds.), *Family life education: The practice of family science* (pp. 177–188). Minneapolis, MN: National Council on Family Relations.

Darling, C. A., & Mabe, A. (1989). Analyzing ethical issues in sexual relationships: An educative model. *Journal of Sex Education and Therapy*, 15, 234–246.

Darling, C., McWey, L., Howard, S., & Olmstead, S. (2007). College student stress: The influence of interpersonal relationships on sense of coherence. *Stress and Health*, 23, 215–219.

Darling, C., Senatore, N., & Strachan, J. (2012). Fathers of children with disabilities: Stress and life satisfaction. *Stress and Health*, 28, 269–278.

Darling, C. A., & Turkki, K. (2009). Global family concerns and the role of family life education: An ecosystemic analysis. *Family Relations*, 58, 14–27.

Das, A., Waite, L., & Laumann, E. (2012). Sexual expression over the life course. In L. Carpenter & J. DeLamater (Eds.), *Sex for life: From virginity to Viagra, how sexuality changes throughout our lives* (pp. 236–259). New York: University Press.

Deal, R. (2006). *The smart stepfamily: Seven steps to a happy family.* Bloomington, MN: Bethany House Publishers.

DeBord, K., Bower, D., Myers-Walls, J. A., Kirby, J. K., Goddard, H. W., Mulroy, M., & Ozretich, R. (2006). A professional guide for parenting educators: The National Extension Parenting Educator's framework. *Journal of Extension*, 44. Retrieved from https://archives.joe.org/joe/2006june/a8.php

DeBoer-Moran, J. (2015). Social media and family life educators. In M. Walcheski & J. Reinke (Eds.), *Family life education: The practice of family science* (pp. vii). Minneapolis, MN: National Council on Family Relations.

DeLamater, J., & Hyde, J. (1998). Essentialism vs. social constructionism in the study of human sexuality. *Journal of Sex Research*, 49, 69–77.

Demick, J. (2002). Stages of parental development. In M. H. Bornstein (Ed.) *Handbook of parenting Vol. 3: Being and becoming a parent* (2nd ed.). Mahwah, NJ: Lawrence Erlbaum.

Demir-Dagdas, T., Isik-Ercan, Z., Intepe-Tingir, S., & Cava-Tadik, Y. (2017). Parental divorce and children from diverse backgrounds: Multidisciplinary perspectives on mental health, parent–child relationships, and educational experiences. *Journal of Divorce & Remarriage*, 59, 469–485.

DeNavas-Walt, C., Proctor, B., & Smith, J. (2012). Income, poverty, and health insurance coverage in the United States: 2011. Report number P60-243. US Department of Commerce, Economics and Statistics Administration. Retrieved from www.census.gov/library/publications/2012/demo/p60-243.html

Denford, S., Abraham, C., Campbell, R., & Busse, H. (2017). A comprehensive review of reviews of school-based interventions to improve sexual health. *Health Psychological Review*, 11, 33–52.

DePanfilis, S. (2018). *Child protective services: A guide for caseworkers*. Washington DC: Department of Health and Human Services. Retrieved from www.childwelfare.gov/pubPDFs/cps2018.pdf

DePaulo, B., & Morris, W. (2013). The unrecognized stereotyping and discrimination against singles. *Personality & Social Psychology Bulletin*, 39, 237–249.

Devine, J. E., & Ortman, J. M. (2014). Nation to become a plurality, but some areas already are. *Census Blogs*. United States Census Bureau. Retrieved from www.census.gov/newsroom/blogs/random-samplings/2014/06/nation-to-become-a-plurality-but-some-areas-already-are.html

Devor, H., & Dominic, K. (2015). Trans* sexualities. In J. DeLamater & R. Plante (Eds.), *Handbook of the sociology of sexualities* (pp.181–199). Switzerland: Springer International Publishing.

Dew, J., Dean, L., Duncan, S. F., & Britt-Lutter, S. (2020). A review of effectiveness evidence in the financial-helping fields. *Family Relations*, 69, 614–627.

DeYoung, C., Quilty, L., & Peterson, J. (2007). Between facets and domains: 10 aspects of the big five. *Journal of Personality and Social Psychology*, 93, 880–896.

Dib, C. (1988). Formal, nonformal, and informal education: Concepts/applicability. *Cooperative Networks in Physics Education, Conference Proceedings*. 173rd American Institute of Physics, New York: American Institute of Physics (pp. 300–315). Retrieved from www.techne-dib.com.br/downloads/6.pdf

Dickinson, H. E. (1950). *The origin and development of the aims of family life education in American secondary schools*. Unpublished doctoral dissertation. Nashville, TN: George Peabody College for Teachers.

Difference Between. (2021). Difference between global and international. Retrieved from www.differencebetween.net/language/words-language/difference-between-global-and-international/

Dimok, M. (2019). *Defining generations: Where Millennials end and Generation Z begins*. www.pewresearch.org/fact-tank/2019/01/17/where-millennials-end-and-generation-z-begins/

Dini, L. (2000). An Italian statement on international migration. *Population and Development Review*, 26, 849–852.

Dion, M. (2005). Healthy marriage programs: Learning what works. *Future of Children*, 15, 139–156.

Doherty, W. J. (1995). Boundaries between parent and family education and family therapy: The levels of family involvement model. *Family Relations*, 44, 353–358.

Doherty, W. J. (2000). Intentional marriage: Your rituals will set you free. Presentation at Annual Smart Marriages Conference, Denver, Colorado. Retrieved from www.smartmarriages.com/intentionalmarriage.html

Doherty, W., & Anderson, J. (2004). Community marriage initiatives. *Family Relations*, 53, 425–432.

Doherty, W., & Lamson, A. (2015). The levels of family involvement model: 20 years later. In M. Walcheski & J. Reinke (Eds.), *Family life education: The practice of family science* (pp. 39–46). Minneapolis, MN: National Council on Family Relations.

Donaldson. J., & Franck, K. (2016). Needs assessment guidebook for Extension professionals. *The University of Tennessee Extension Publications*. PB 1839. Retrieved from https://extension.unr.edu/publication.aspx?PubID=3557

Dooley, D. (2017) Parenting tips on golden empire transit buses and shuttles [Web log post]. Retrieved from www.acesconnection.com/blog/parenting-tips-on-golden-empire-transit-buses-and-shuttles

Dorri, A., Mallory, A., Bishop, M., & Russell, S. (2019). *What research says about comprehensive and inclusive sexuality education*. Austin, TX: The Stories and Numbers Project.

Doss, B., Rhoades, G., Stanley, S., Markman, H., & Johnson, C. (2009). Differential use of premarital education in first and second marriages. *Journal of Family Psychology*, 23, 268–273.

Doyle, J. (2006). Prevention and early intervention. Issue 1 Addendum. Retrieved from www.emqff.org/wp-content/uploads/Prevention-and-Early-Intervention-Issue-1-Addendum-03-07-06.pdf

Drucker, P. (1954). *The practice of management*. New York: Harper & Brothers.

Duncan, S., Holman, T., & Yang, C. (2007). Factors associated with involvement in marriage preparation programs. *Family Relations*, 56, 270–278.

Duncan, S. F., & Goddard, H. W. (2016). *Family life education: Principles and practices for effective outreach*. Thousand Oaks, CA: Sage.

Dunlap, A. (2016). Changes in coming-out milestones across five age cohorts. *Journal of Gay & Lesbian Social Services*, 28, 20–38.

Duong, K. (2020). Human trafficking and migration: Examining the issues from gender and policy perspectives. In J. Winterdyk & J. Jones (Eds.), *The Palgrave international hand-*

book of human trafficking (pp. 1819–1833). Cham, Switzerland: Palgrave Macmillan. Retrieved from https://link.springer.com/referenceworkentry/10.1007%2F978-3-319-63058-8_131

Duvall, E., & Miller, B. (1984). *Marriage and family development* (6th ed.). New York: HarperRow.

Duvall, E. M. (1950). *Family living*. New York: Macmillan.

Duvall, E. M., & Hill, R. (1945). *When you marry*. New York: Heath.

Eberly Center. (n.d.). *Grading and performance rubrics*. Pittsburgh, PA: Carnegie Mellon University. Retrieved from www.cmu.edu/teaching/designteach/teach/rubrics.html

Eddy, J., & Poehlmann, J. (2010). *Children of incarcerated parents: A handbook for researchers and practitioners*. Washington, DC: Urban Institute Press.

Edin, K., & Kefalas, M. (2005). *Promises I can keep: Why poor women put motherhood before marriage*. Berkeley: University of California Press.

Elflein, J. (2021). COVID-19 deaths worldwide as of February 26, 2021 by country. *Statista*. Retrieved from www.statista.com/statistics/1093256/novel-coronavirus-2019ncov-deaths-worldwide-by-country/

Ellenwood, S. (1998). *The art of loving well: A character education curriculum for today's teenagers*. Boston: Boston University Press.

Erikson, E. (1950, 1963). *Childhood and society*. New York: W.W. Norton.

Ertmer, P., & Newby, T. (1993). Behaviorism, cognitivism, and constructivism: Comparing critical features from a design perspective. *Performance Improvement Quarterly*, 6, 50–72.

Everson, R., Darling, C., & Herzog, J. (2013). Parenting stress among U.S. army spouses during combat-related deployments: The role of sense of coherence. *Child and Family Social Work*, 18, 168–178.

Fagan, J. (2009). Relationship quality and changes in depression symptoms among urban, married African Americans, Hispanics, and whites. *Family Relations* 58, 259–274.

Fagan, J., & Kaufman, R. (2015). Reflections on theory and outcome measures for fatherhood programs. *Families in Society: The Journal of Contemporary Social Services*, 96, 135–142.

Fairchild Bridal Group. (2002). American weddings: Fairchild bridal infobank American wedding study. Retrieved from www.sellthebride.com/documents/americanweddingsurvey.pdf

Families & Schools Together, Inc. (FAST). (2020). https://www.familiesandschools.org/

Family and Youth Services Bureau (FYSB). (2020). Title V state sexual risk avoidance education: Fact sheet. *FYSB: An Office of the Administration for Children & Families*. Retrieved from www.acf.hhs.gov/fysb/resource/title-v-state-sexual-risk-avoidance-education-fact-sheet-0

Fawcett, E., Hawkins, A., Blanchard, V., & Carroll, J. (2010). Do premarital education programs really work? A meta-analytic study. *Family Relations*, 59, 232–239.

Fein, D. (2009). Spending time together: Time use estimates for economically disadvantaged and nondisadvantaged married couples in the US. *Office of Planning, Research, & Evaluation, Administration for Children and Families*. Retrieved from www.mdrc.org/sites/default/files/full_507.pdf

Fein, D., Burstein, N., Fein, G., & Lindberg, L. (2003). The determinants of marriage and cohabitation among disadvantaged Americans: Research findings and needs. *Marriage and family formation data analysis project*. Bethesda, MD: Abt Associates, Inc. Retrieved from www.acf.hhs.gov/sites/default/files/documents/opre/determinants_findings_fin2_opt2.pdf

Felitti, V., Anda, R., Nordenberg, D., Williamson, D., Spitz, A., Edwards, V., Koss, M., & Marks, J. (1998). Relationship of childhood abuse and household dysfunction to many of the leading causes of death in adults: The adverse childhood experiences (ACE) study. *American Journal of Preventive Medicine*, 14, 245–258.

Fileborn, B., Lyons, A., Hinchliff, S., Brown, G., Heywood, W., & Minicheliello, V. (2017). Learning about sex in later life: Sources of education and older Australian adults. *Sex Education*, 17, 165–179.

Fincham, F., & Beach, R. (2010). Marriage in the new millennium: A decade in review. *Journal of Marriage and Family*, 72, 630–649.

Fincham, F., Stanley, S., & Rhoades, G. (2011). Relationship education in emerging adulthood: Problems and prospects. In F. Fincham & M. Cui (Eds.), *Romantic relationships in emerging adulthood* (pp. 293–316). Cambridge, MA: Cambridge University Press.

FindLaw. (2013). State-by-state marriage "age of consent" laws. Retrieved from www.family.findlaw.com/marriage/state-by-state-marriage-age-of-consent-laws.html

Fink, L. (2005). A self-directed guide to designing courses for significant learning. *Instructional Development Program, University of Oklahoma*. Retrieved from www.deefinkandassociates.com/GuidetoCourseDesignAug05.pdf

Fisher, H. (2004). *Why we love: The nature and chemistry of romantic love*. New York: Henry Holt and Company.

Fisher, T. (2012). *What sexual scientists know about gender differences and similarities in sexuality*. Whitehall, PA: Society of Scientific Study of Sexuality.

Flores, A. R., Herman, J. L., Gates, G. J., & Brown, T. N. (2016). How many adults identify as transgender in the United States? *UCLA School of Law, Williams Institute*. Retrieved from https://williamsinstitute.law.ucla.edu/publications/trans-adults-united-states/

Flores, D., & Barroso, J. (2017). 21st century parent-child sex communication in the U.S.: A process review. *Journal of Sex Research*, 54, 532–548.

Florida Statutes. (2011). Marriage fee reduction for completion of premarital preparation course. *The Florida Senate*. Retrieved from www.flsenate.gov/laws/Statutes/2011/741.0305

Foa, U., & Foa, M. (1974). *Societal structures of the mind*. Springfield, IL: Charles C. Thomas.

Fogel, R. (2020). The digital divide: Gender and technology in an unequal world. *University of Washington*. Retrieved from https://depts.washington.edu/urbanuw/news/the-digital-divide-gender-and-technology-in-an-unequal-world/

Foner, N. (2005). *In a new land: A comparative view of immigration*. New York: University Press.

Fong, T. (2008). *The contemporary Asian American experience: Beyond the model minority* (3rd ed.). Upper Saddle River, NJ: Prentice-Hall.

Fournier, A. B. (2018). Why the brain is our most important sex organ. *She Knows*. Retrieved from www.sheknows.com/health-and-wellness/articles/1137738/brain-most-important-sex-organ/

Francis, M. (2019). Helicopter parenting and bulldozer parenting are bad for everyone—including parents. *NBC News*. Retrieved from www.nbcnews.com/think/opinion/helicopter-parenting-bulldozer-parenting-are-bad-everyone-including-parents-ncna1065266

Francoeur, R. (2004). Foreword. In R. Francoeur & R. Noonan (Eds.), *The continuum complete international encyclopedia of sexuality* (pp. ix–x). London, England: Continuum International Publishing Group.

Francoeur, R., & Noonan, R. (Eds.). (2004). The continuum complete international encyclopedia of sexuality. London: Continuum International Publishing Group.

Friedman, E. (2009). Kids born to unwed moms hit record high. *ABC News*. Retrieved from www.abcnews.go.com/Health/WomensHealth/story?id=7575268&page=2#.UYbylIKC3u1

Fry. R. (2013). A rising share of young adults live in their parents' home. *Pew Research Center*. Retrieved from www.pewsocialtrends.org/2013/08/01/a-rising-share-of-young-adults-live-in-their-parents-home

Fry, R., Passel, J. F., & Cohn, D. (2020). A majority of young adults in the U.S. live with their parents for the first time since the Great Depression. *Pew Research Center.* www.pewresearch.org/fact-tank/2020/09/04/a-majority-of-young-adults-in-the-u-s-live-with-their-parents-for-the-first-time-since-the-great-depression/

Furstenberg, F. (2019). Family change in global perspective: How and why family systems change. University of Pennsylvania Population Center Working Paper (PSC/PARC), 2019-22. Retrieved from https://repository.upenn.edu/psc_publications/22

Future of Sex Education Initiative (FoSE). (2020a). National sex education standards: Core content and skills, K–12 (2nd Ed.). Retrieved from https://advocatesforyouth.org/wp-content/uploads/2020/03/NSES-2020-web.pdf

Future of Sex Education (FoSE). (2020b). National teacher preparation standards for sexuality education. Retrieved from https://advocatesforyouth.org/wp-content/uploads/2019/09/teacher-standards-1.pdf

Gagnon, J. (1990). The explicit and implicit use of the scripting perspective in sex research. *Annual Review of Sexual Research*, 1, 1–44.

Gagnon, J., & Simon, W. (1973). *Sexual conduct: The social origins of human sexuality.* Chicago: Aldine.

Ganong, L., & Coleman, M. (2004). *Stepfamily relationships: Development, dynamics, and interventions.* New York: Kluwer Academic.

Gardener, H. (2006). *Multiple intelligences: New horizons.* New York: Basic Books.

Gardener, H. (2011). *Frames of the mind: The theory of multiple intelligences.* New York: Basic Books.

Gardiner, K., Fishman, M., Nikolov, P., Glosser, A., & Laud, S. (2002). State policies to promote marriage. *Assistant Secretary for Planning and Evaluation.* Retrieved from www.aspe.hhs.gov/hsp/marriage02f

Gardner, S., & Howlett, L. (2000). Changing the focus of interventions: The need for primary prevention at the couple level. *Family Science Review,* 13, 96–111.

Gardner, S., Giese, K., & Parrott, S. (2004). Evaluation of the connections: Relationships and marriage curriculum. *Family Relations,* 53, 521–527.

Garst, B. A., & McCawley, P. F. (2015). Solving problems, ensuring relevance, and facilitating change: The evolution of needs assessment within cooperative extension. *Journal of Human Sciences and Extension*, 3, 26–47.

Gartrell, N., & Bos, H. (2010). US national longitudinal lesbian family study: Psychological adjustment of 17-year-old adolescents. *Pediatrics*, 126, 1–9.

Gates, G. (2013). LGBT parenting in the U.S. *UCLA School of Law, The Williams Institute.* Retrieved from https://williamsinstitute.law.ucla.edu/publications/lgbt-parenting-us/

Gay & Lesbian Advocates & Defenders (GLAD). (n.d.). Marriage—A history of change. *GLAD Answers*. Retrieved from www.glad.org/wp-content/uploads/2017/01/marriage-history-of-change.pdf

Geiger, A. W., & Livingston, G. (2019). 8 facts about love and marriage in America. *Pew Research Center.* www.pewresearch.org/fact-tank/2019/02/13/8-facts-about-love-and-marriage/

Gelles, R., & Perlman, S. (2012). *Estimated annual cost of child abuse and neglect in the United States.* Chicago, IL: Prevent Child Abuse America.

Gerbner, G. (2009). Cultivation theory. In E. Griffin (Ed.), *A first look at communication theory* (7th ed., pp. 353–354). New York: Frank Mortimer.

Gibbs, N. (2009). The growing backlash against overparenting. *Time*. Retrieved from http://content.time.com/time/subscriber/article/0,33009,1940697-7,00.html

Ginicola, M., Smith, C., & Filmore, J. (2017). *Affirmative counseling with LGBTQIA+ people.* Alexandria, VA: American Counseling Association.

GIS Asie. (n.d.). Globalization or asianization. *French Academic Network on Asian Studies.* Retrieved from www.gis-reseau-asie.org/en/globalization-or-asianization

Global Advisory Board (GAB). (2020). Who we are. *Global sexual health & well-being*. Retrieved from www.gab-shw.org/about/who-we-are/

Goddard, H. W., & Olsen, C. (2004). Cooperative extension initiatives in marriage and couples education. *Family Relations*, 53, 433–439.

Goldenberg, H., & Goldenberg, I. (2013). *Family therapy: An overview* (8th ed.) Belmont, CA: Brooks/Cole.

Goldberg, A., McCormick, N., & Virginia, H. (2021). Parenting in a pandemic: Work-family arrangements, well-being, and intimate relationships among adoptive parents. *Family Relations*, 70, 7–25.

Goldberg, S., Rothblum, E., Russell, S., & Meyer, I. (2020). Exploring the Q in LGBTQ: Demographic characteristic and sexuality of queer people in a U.S. representative sample of sexual minorities. *Psychology of Sexual Orientation and Gender Diversity.* Advance online publication. https://doi.org/10.1037/sgd0000359

Goldfarb, E. (2003). What teachers want, need, and deserve. *SIECUS Report*, *31*(6), 18–19.

Goldfarb, E., & Lieberman, L. (2020). Three decades of research: The case for comprehensive sex education. *Journal of Adolescent Health*, 68, 13–27.

Gordon, L. (2000). *PAIRS for peers: Practical exercises enriching relationship skills*. Westin, FL: PAIRS Foundation.

Gore, A., & Gore, T. (2002). *Joined at the heart: The transformation of the American family.* New York: Henry Holt.

Gottman, J. M. (1994). *What predicts divorce: The relationship between marital processes and marital outcomes*. Hillsdale, NJ: Erlbaum.

Gottman, J. M., Gottman, J. S., & DeClaire, J. (2006). *10 lessons to transform your marriage.* New York: Three Rivers Press.

Gottman, J. M., & Silver, N. (1999). *The seven principles for making marriage work.* NewYork: Crown Publishers.

Gottman, J. S. (2007). *Loving couples loving children*. Seattle, WA: The Gottman Relationship Institute.

Gray, J. (1992). *Men are from Mars, women are from Venus: A practical guide for improving communication and getting what you want in your relationships*. New York: Harper Collins.

Gross, K. H., & Ballard, S. M. (2013). The ABCs of evaluation. *CFLE Network*, NCFR.

Gross, P. (1985). *On family life education. For family life educators* (2nd ed., rev.). Montreal: Concordia University Centre for Human Relations and Community Studies.

Gross, P. (1993). *On family life education: For family life educators* (3rd ed.). Montreal: Concordia University Centre for Human Relations and Community Studies.

Gross, T., Mason, W. A., Parra, G., Oats, R., Ringle, J. L., & Haggerty, K. (2018). Adherence and dosage contributions to parenting program quality. *Journal of the Society for Social Work Research*, 6, 467–489.

Grzywacz, J. G., & Demerouti, E. (Eds.). (2013). *New frontiers in work and family research.* New York: Psychology Press.

Guerrero, L., Andersen, P., & Afifi, W. (2007). *Close encounters: Communication in relationships*. Thousand Oaks, CA: Sage.

Guterres, A. (2020). Coronavirus global health emergency. *United Nations*. Retrieved from https://www.un.org/en/coronavirus

Guttmacher Institute. (2013). *State policies in brief: Sex and HIV education*. New York: Author. Retrieved from www.guttmacher.org/statecenter/spibs/spib_SE.pdf

Guttmacher Institute. (2017). *Abstinence-only-until-marriage programs are ineffective and harmful to young people.* New York: Author. Retrieved from www.guttmacher.org/news-release/2017/abstinence-only-until-marriage-programs-are-ineffective-and-harmful-young-people#

Guttmacher Institute. (2019). *Adolescent sexual and reproductive health in the United States*. New York: Author. Retrieved from https://www.guttmacher.org/fact-sheet/american-teens-sexual-and-reproductive-health#

Guttmacher Institute. (2020). *Sex and HIV education: State laws and policies*. New York: Author. Retrieved from http://www.guttmacher.org/state-policy/explore/sex-and-hiv-education

Halford, W. K., Markman, H., & Stanley, S. (2008). Strengthening couples relationships with education: Social policy and public health awareness. *Journal of Family Psychology, 22*, 497–505.

Halford, W. K., Markman, H., Stanley, S., & Kline, G. (2003). Best practices in relationship education. *Journal of Marital and Family Therapy, 29*, 385–406.

Halford, W. K., Moore, E., Wilson, K., Farrugia, C., & Dyer, C. (2004). Benefits of flexible relationship education: An evaluation of the couple CARE program. *Family Relations, 53*, 469–476.

Halford, W. K., Nicholson, J., & Sanders, M. (2007). Couple communication in stepfamilies. *Family Process, 46*, 472–483.

Halford, W. K., O'Donnell, C., Lizzio, A., & Wilson, K. (2006). Do couples at high risk of relationship problems attend premarriage education? *Journal of Family Psychology, 30*, 160–163.

Haller, S. (2018). What type of parent are you? Lawnmower? Helicopter, attachment? Tiger? Free-range? *USA Today*. Retrieved from www.usatoday.com/story/life/allthemoms/2018/09/19/parenting-terms-explained-lawnmower-helicopter-attachment-tiger-free-range-dolphin-elephant/1357612002/

Hammond, R., & Cheney, P. (2009). *Sociology of the family*. Released under a Creative Commons License of Attribution (BY).

Hanover Research. (2016). Best practices in engaging diverse families. http://www.pthvp.org/wp-content/uploads/2016/10/Engaging-Diverse-Families.pdf

Harcourt-Medina, K. T., & Mulroy, M. (2022). Family life education with incarcerated persons and their families. In S. M. Ballard & A. C Taylor (Eds.), *Family life education with diverse populations* (2nd ed., pp. 69–100). San Diego, CA: Cognella Academic Publishing.

Harwood, R., Miller, S., & Vasta, R. (2008). *Child psychology: Development in a changing society*. Hoboken, NJ: John Wiley & Sons.

Hawkins, A., Blanchard, V., Baldwin, S., & Fawcett, E. (2008). Does marriage and relationship education work? A meta-analytic study. *Journal of Consulting and Clinical Psychology, 76*, 723–734.

Hawkins, A., Carroll, J., Doherty, W., & Willoughby, B. (2004). A comprehensive framework for marriage education. *Family Relations, 53*, 547–558.

Hawkins, A. J., Clyde, T. L., Doty, J. L., & Avellar, S. (2020). Best practices in family life education program evaluation. *Family Relations, 69*(3), 479–496.

Hawkins, A., & Ooms, T. (2010). *What works in marriage and relationship education? A review of lessons learned with a focus on low-income couples*. Littleton, CO: National Healthy Marriage Resource Center. Retrieved from www.archive.acf.hhs.gov/healthymarriage/pdf/whatworks_edae.pdf

Heatherington, E. (2005). Divorce and the adjustment of children. *Pediatrics in Review, 26*, 165–169.

Hellmich, N. (2013). One in ten high school seniors are extreme binge drinkers. *USA Today*. Retrieved from www.usatoday.com/story/news/nation/2013/09/16/extreme-binge-drinking-seniors/2809739/

Hennon, C., Radina, M., & Wilson, S. (2013). Family life education: Issues and challenges in professional practice. In G. Peterson & K. Bush (Eds.), *Handbook of marriage and the family* (3rd ed., pp. 815–843). New York: Springer.

Hildebrand, V., Phenice, L., Gray, M., & Hines, R. (2008). *Knowing and serving diverse families* (3rd ed.). Columbus, OH: Merrill.

Hill, R. (1949). *Families under stress*. New York: Harper & Brothers.

Hines, S. (2006). Intimate transitions: Transgender practices of partnering and parenting. *Sociology*, 40, 353–371.

Hirsh-Pasek, K., Evans, N., & Golinkoff, R. M. (2019). Screen time for children: Good, bad, or it depends? *Brookings Institute*. https://www.brookings.edu/blog/education-plus-development/2019/02/06/screen-time-for-children-good-bad-or-it-depends/

HIV.gov. (2020). The global HIV/AIDS epidemic. Retrieved from www.hiv.gov/hiv-basics/overview/data-and-trends/global-statistics

Hodapp, R. M., & Krasner, D. V. (1994). Families of children with disabilities: Findings from a national sample of eighth-grade students. *Exceptionality*, 5, 71–81.

Hofschneider, A. (2013, August). Bosses say "pick up the phone." *The Wall Street Journal*. Retrieved from http://online.wsj.com/news/articles/SB10001424127887323407104579036714155366866

Holman, T., Busby, D., Doxey, C., Klein, D., & Loyer-Carlson, V. (1997). RELATionship evaluation. Provo, UT: The RELATE Institute.

Holmes, E. K., Galovan, A. M., Yoshida, K., & Hawkin, A. J. (2010). Meta-analysis of the effectiveness of resident fathering programs: Are family life educators interested in fathers? *Family Relations*, 59, 240–252.

Holmes, L. (2021). Comprehensive sex education for youth with disabilities: A call to action. *SIECUS*. Retrieved from https://siecus.org/resources/comprehensive-sex-education-for-youth-with-disabilities/?eType=EmailBlastContent&eId=1fa863cc-da55-4b83-b0b3-25454e9740ff

Hougaard, B. (2004). *Curlingföräldrar och servicebarn* [Curling parents and service children]. Stockholm: Prisma.

Howe, G., Levy, M., & Caplan, R. (2004). Job loss and depressive symptoms in couples: Common stressors, stress transmission, or relationship disruption? *Journal of Family Psychology*, 18, 639–650.

Howley, E. (2021). Children's mental health crisis could be a next "wave" in the pandemic. U.S. *News and World Report*. Retrieved from www.usnews.com/news/health-news/articles/2021-03-04/childrens-mental-health-crisis-could-be-a-next-wave-in-the-pandemic

HUD. (2020). HUD releases 2019 annual homeless assessment report. Retrieved from www.hud.gov/press/press_releases_media_advisories/HUD_No_20_003

Hughes, J. (2020, February 13). Getting to know Generation Alpha: 10 takeaways for higher ed. *Keystone Academic Solutions*. www.keystoneacademic.com/news/getting-to-know-generation-alpha-10-takeaways-for-higher-ed

Hughes, R., Bowers, J., Mitchell, E., Curtiss, S., & Ebata, A. (2012). Developing online family life prevention and education programs. *Family Relations, 61*(5), 711–727.

Hughes, R., Jr., Ebata, A. T., Bowers, J., Mitchell, E. T., & Curtiss, S. L. (2015). Strategies for designing online family life education programs. In M. J. Walcheski & J. S. Reinke (Eds.), *Family life education: The practice of family science* (pp. 131–140). Minneapolis, MN: National Council on Family Relations.

Human Rights Campaign (HRC). (2019). Marriage equality around the world. Retrieved from www.hrc.org/resources/marriage-equality-around-the-world

Human Smuggling and Trafficking Center (HSTC). (2016). Human trafficking vs. human smuggling. Fact Sheet. Retrieved from https://ctip.defense.gov/Portals/12/Documents/HSTC_Human%20Trafficking%20vs.%20Human%20Smuggling%20Fact%20Sheet.pdf?ver=2016-07-14-145555-320

Hwang, N. (2003). Family education law in Taiwan. Paper presented at the annual meeting of the National Council on Family Relations, Vancouver, BC, Canada.

Hwang, S. (2012). Family life education with Asian immigrant families. In S. Ballard & A. Taylor (Eds.), *Family life education with diverse populations* (pp. 187–209). Thousand Oaks, CA: Sage.

Hwang, S. (2018). Family life education in Taiwan. In M. Robila & A. Taylor (Eds.), *Global perspectives on family life education* (pp. 49–62). Cham, Switzerland: Springer International Publishing.

Hwang, S. H. (2022). Family life education with Asian immigrant families. In S. M. Ballard & A.C. Taylor (Eds.), *Family life education with diverse populations* (2nd ed., pp. 361–394). San Diego, CA: Cognella Academic Publishing.

Hwang, W. (2005). An Asian perspective on relationship and marriage education. *Family Process*, 44, 161–173.

Hyde, J., & DeLamater, J. (2020). *Understanding human sexuality.* New York: McGraw-Hill.

International Organization for Migration (IOM). (2020). World Migration Report 2020. Retrieved from https://publications.iom.int/system/files/pdf/wmr_2020.pdf

It's That Easy! Collaborative. (2016). *It's That Easy! A Guide to Raising Sexually Healthy Children*. St Paul, MN: Minnesota Department of Health. Retrieved from http://itsthateasy.net/

Jackson, G. (2009). Sexual response in cardiovascular disease. *Journal of Sex Research*, 46, 223–236.

Jackson, L. J., & Fife, S. T. (2018). The impact of parental divorce: The relationship between social support and confidence levels in young adults. *Journal of Divorce & Remarriage*, 59, 123–140.

Jacobs, F. H. (2003). Child and family program evaluation: Learning to enjoy complexity. *Applied Developmental Science*, 7, 62–75.

Jacobs, F. H., & Kapuscik, J. L. (2000). *Making the count: Evaluating family preservation services*. Medford, MA: Family Preservation Evaluation Project, Tufts University.

James, J., & Lewis, M. (2020). Theorizing about Black families. In A. G. James (Ed.), *Black families: A systems approach* (pp. 2–11). San Diego, CA: Cognella Academic Publishing.

Jayakody, R., Thornton, A., & Axinn, W. (2008). *International family change: Ideational perspectives*. New York: Lawrence Erlbaum.

Jayson, S. (2009). Family life, roles changing as couples seek balance. *USA Today.* Retrieved from http://usatoday30.usatoday.com/news/health/2009-04-18-families-conf_N.htm

Jelen, E. (2005). The family in Argentina: Modernity, economic crisis, and politics. In B. Adams & J. Trost (Eds.), *Handbook of world families* (pp. 391–413). Thousand Oaks, CA: Sage.

Jiang, C. (2013). Why Chinese couples are divorcing before buying a home. *Time*, 181(19). Retrieved from http://world.time.com/2013/04/29/why-chinese-couples-aredivorcing-before-buying-a-home/

Johns Hopkins University & Medicine. (2022). COVID-19 dashboard by the Center for Systems Science and Engineering (CSSE) at Johns Hopkins University (JHU). Retrieved from https://coronavirus.jhu.edu/map.html.

Johnson, B. (2013). Sexually transmitted infections and older adults. *Journal of Gerontological Nursing*, 39, 53–60.

Joyce, A. (2019). The college admissions scandal is more proof that helicopter parenting hurts kids. *The Washington Post*. www.washingtonpost.com/lifestyle/2019/03/12/college-admissions-scandal-is-more-proof-that-helicopter-parenting-hurts-kids/

Juvenile Justice Evaluation Center. (2003). *Evaluability assessment: Examining the readiness of a program for evaluation*. Program evaluation briefing series, #6. Washington, DC: Author. Retrieved from www.jrsa.org/pubs/juv-justice/evaluability-assessment.pdf

Kacher, K. (2013). Work-life matters. *Minnesota Business Magazine*. Retrieved from http://minnesotabusiness.com/article/guest-column-work-life-matters

Kahn, K., Arino, J., Hu, W., Raposo, P., Sears, J., Calderon, F., Heidebrecht, C., Macdonald, M., Liauw, J., Chan, A., & Gardam, M. (2009). Spread of a novel influenza A (H1N1) virus via global airline transportation. *New England Journal of Medicine*, 361, 212–214.

Kaiser Family Foundation (KFF). (2004). Sex education in America. Retrieved from https://www.kff.org/hivaids/report/sex-education-in-america-summary/

Kaiser Family Foundation (KFF). (2018). Abstinence education programs: Definition, funding and impact on teen sexual behavior. Retrieved from www.kff.org/womens-health-policy/fact-sheet/abstinence-education-programs-definition-funding-and-impact-on-teen-sexual-behavior/

Kaiser Family Foundation (KFF). (2020). The global HIV/AIDS epidemic. Retrieved from https://www.kff.org/global-health-policy/fact-sheet/the-global-hivaids-epidemic/

Kamper, C. (2003). *Connections + PREP: Relationships & marriage interpersonal relationship program for secondary students: Instructor's manual*. Berkeley, CA: The Dibble Fund for Marriage Education.

Kamper, C. (2011). *Connections: Relationships & marriage*. The Dibble Institute. Retrieved from www.dibbleinstitute.org/connections-relationships-marriage/

Kapinus, C., & Johnson, M. (2003). The utility of family life cycle as a theoretical and empirical tool: Commitment and family life cycle state. *Journal of Family Issues*, 24, 155–184.

Karberg, E., Finocharo, J., & Vann, N. (2019). Father and child well-being: A scan of current research. *National Responsible Fatherhood Clearinghouse*. https://fatherhood.gov

Karoly, L. A., Kilburn, M. R., Cannon, J. S., Bigelow, J. H., & Christina, R. (2005). *Many happy returns: Early childhood programs entail costs, but the paybacks could be substantial*. Santa Monica, CA: Rand Corporation. Retrieved from www.rand.org/publications/randreview/issues/fall2005/returns.html

Kelly, J. (2002). Psychological and legal interventions for parents and children in custody and access disputes: Current research and practice. *Virginia Journal of Social Policy and Law*, 10, 129–163.

Kelly, J., & Emery, R. (2003). Children's adjustment following divorce: Risk and resilience perspectives. *Family Relations*, 32, 252–262.

Kelly, T. (2004). Ireland. In R. Francoeur & R. Noonan (Eds.), *International encyclopedia of sexuality* (pp. 569–580). New York: Continuum.

Kemp, G., Segal, J., & Robinson, L. (2013). Guide to step-parenting & blended families. *Helpguide*. Retrieved from www.helpguide.org/mental/blended_families_stepfamilies.htm

Kempner, M. (2004). More than just say no: What some abstinence-only-until marriage curricula teach young people about gender. *SIECUS Report*, 32, 2–4.

Kennedy, S., & Bumpass, L. (2008). Cohabitation and children's living arrangements: New estimates from the United States. *Demographic Research*, 19, 1663–1692.

Kenny, L., & Sternberg, J. (2003). Abstinence-only-education in the courts. *SIECUS Report*, 31, 26–29.

Kerckhoff, R. (1964). Family life education in America. In H. T. Christensen (Ed.), *Handbook of marriage and the family* (pp. 881–911). Chicago: Rand McNally.

King, V., & Scott, M. (2005). A comparison of cohabiting relationships among older and younger adults. *Journal of Marriage and Family*, 67, 271–285.

Kirby, D. (2007). *Emerging answers: Research findings on programs to reduce teen pregnancy and sexually transmitted diseases*. Washington, DC: National Campaign to Prevent Teen and Unplanned Pregnancy. Retrieved from http://www.urban.org/events/thursdayschild/upload/Sarah-Brown-Handout.pdf

Kirby, D. (2008). The impact of abstinence and comprehensive sex and STD/HIV education programs on adolescent sexual behavior. *Sex Research and Social Policy*, 5, 18–27.

Kirby-Wilkins, J., Taner, E., Cassidy, D., & Cenizal, R. (2014). *Family life education: A profession with a proven return on investment (ROI).* White Paper. St. Paul, MN: National Council on Family Relations.

Kiran, Q. (2018). Gender digital divide: Does it exist? *Digital (In)Equality.* Retrieved from https://wpmu.mah.se/nmict181group1/gender-digital-divide/

Kirkendall, L. (1973). Marriage and family living, education for. In A. Ellis & A. Abarbanel (Eds.), *The encyclopedia of sexual behavior* (2nd ed). New York: Hawthorne.

Kline, G., Stanley, S., Markman, H., Olmos-Gallo, P., St. Peters, M., Whitton, S., & Prado, L. (2004). Timing is everything: Pre-engagement cohabitation and increased risk for poor marital outcomes. *Journal of Family Psychology,* 18, 311–318.

The Knot. (n.d.). Wedding money: What does the average wedding cost? Retrieved from http://wedding.theknot.com/wedding-planning/wedding-budget/qa/what-does-the-average-wedding-cost.aspx

The Knot. (2012). Results of largest wedding study of its kind. Retrieved from www.prnewswire.com/news-releases/theknotcom-and-weddingchannelcom-revealresults-of-largest-wedding-study-of-its-kind-surveying-more-than-17500-brides-195856281.html

Knox, M., Burkhart, K., & Cromly, A. (2013). Supporting positive parenting in community health centers: The ACT Raising Safe Kids program. *Journal of Community Psychology,* 41, 396–407.

Kohler, P., Manhart, L., & Lafferty, W. (2008). Abstinence-only and comprehensive sex education and the initiation of sexual activity and teen pregnancy. *Journal of Adolescent Health,* 42, 344–351.

Kolb, D. (1984). Experiential learning: Experience as the source of learning and development. Upper Saddle River, NJ: Prentice-Hall.

Koohang, A., Riley, L., Smith, T., & Schreurs, J. (2009). E-learning and constructivism: From theory to application. *Interdisciplinary Journal of E-Learning and Learning Objectives,* 5, 91–109.

Krathwohl, D. (2002). A revision of Bloom's Taxonomy: An overview. *Theory into Practice,* 41, 212–218.

Krathwohl, D., Bloom, B., & Masia, B. (Eds.). (1973). *Taxonomy of educational objectives: The classification of educational goals. Handbook II: Affective domain.* New York: David McKay.

Kreider, R. (2005). Number, timing and duration of marriages and divorces: 2001. *Current Population Reports,* 70–97. Washington, DC: US Census Bureau.

Kreider, R., & Ellis, R. (2011). Living arrangements of children, 2009. *Current Population Reports.* Washington, DC: Government Printing Office. Retrieved from www.census.gov/prod/2011pubs/p70-126.pdf

Krill, S. (2010). When one spouse returns from deployment: Tips for MRE practitioners working with military couples. *National Healthy Marriage Center.* Retrieved from www.healthymarriageinfo.org/resource-detail/index.aspx?rid=3129

Krouse, A., & Howard, H. (2009). *Keeping the campfires going: Native women's activism in urban communities.* Lincoln: University of Nebraska Press.

Krueger, R. A., & Casey, M. A. (2015). *Focus groups: A practical guide for applied research* (5th ed.). Los Angeles, CA: SAGE Publications.

Kumpfer, K. (2020). Strengthening families program. https://strengtheningfamiliesprogram.org/

Kumpfer, K., & Magalhães, C. (2018). Strengthening families program: An evidence-based family intervention for parents of high-risk children and adolescents. *Journal of Child & Adolescent Substance Abuse,* 27, 174–179.

Kumpfer, K. L., Scheier, L. M., & Brown, J. (2018). Strategies to avoid replication failure with evidence-based prevention interventions: Case examples from the strengthening families program. *Evaluation & the Health Professions*. Advance online publication. doi: 10.1177/0163278718772886

Kuperberg, A. (2014). Age at coresidence, premarital cohabitation, and marriage dissolution: 1985–2009. *Journal of Marriage and Family, 76*, 352–369.

Kyler, S. J., Bumbarger, B. K., & Greenberg, M. T. (2005). *Technical assistance fact sheets: Evidence-based programs*. Pennsylvania State University Prevention Center for the Promotion of Human Development.

Lake Placid Conference on Home Economics proceedings of the first, second, and third conferences. (1901). Geneva, NY: American Home Economics Association.

Lange, J., Ali, A., Brush, C., Corbett, A., Kelley, D., Kim, P., & Majbouri, M. (2018). *Global Entrepreneurship Monitor United States Report 2017*. Babson Park, MA: Babson College.

Larson, J. (2002). *Consumer update: Marriage preparation*. Washington, DC: American Association for Marriage and Family Therapy. Retrieved from www.aamft.org/imis15/Content/Consumer_Updates/Marriage_Preparation.aspx

Larson, J. (2003). *The great marriage tune-up book*. San Francisco: Jossey-Bass.

Larson, J. (2004a). Innovations in marriage education: Introduction and challenges. *Family Relations*, 53, 421–424.

Larson, J. (2004b). Premarital assessment questionnaires: Powerful tools for improving premarital counseling. *Marriage & Family: A Christian Journal*, 7, 17–28.

Laszloffy, T. (2002). Rethinking family development theory: Teaching with the systemic family development (SDF) model. *Family Relations*, 51, 206–214.

Ledermann, T., Bodenmann, G., Rudaz, M., & Bradbury, T. (2010). Stress, communication, and marital quality in couples. *Family Relations*, 59, 195–206.

Leijten, P., Gardner, F., Melendez-Torres, G. J., van Aar, J., Hutchings, J., Schulz, S., Knerr, W., & Overbeek, G. (2019). Meta-analyses: Key parenting program components for disruptive child behavior. *Journal of the American Academy of Child & Adolescent Psychiatry*, 58, 180–190.

Leinwand Leger, D. (2013). Overdoses attributed to club drug "Molly" increase. *USA Today*. Retrieved from www.usatoday.com/story/news/nation/2013/09/25/club-drug-molly-abuse-increases/2868811/

Lenhart, A., Madden, M., Smith, A., Purcell, K., Zickuhr, K., & Rainie, L. (2011). *Teens, kindness and cruelty on social network sites*. Pew Internet & American Life Project. Retrieved from www.pewinternet.org/Reports/2011/Teens-and-social-media.aspx

Letiecq, B. L. (2019). Surfacing family privilege and supremacy in family science: Toward justice for all. *Family Relations*, 11, 398–411.

Levin, I. (2004). Living apart together: A new family form. *Current Sociology*, 52, 223–240.

Levine, M. (2010). Raising successful children. *The New York Times*. Retrieved from www.nytimes.com/2012/08/05/opinion/sunday/raising-successful-children.html?pagewanted=all&_r=0

LGBTQ Nation. (2015). Gender-neutral prefix "Mx." is now in the *Oxford English Dictionary*. Retrieved from https://www.lgbtqnation.com/2015/08/gender-neutral-prefix-mx-is-now-in-the-oxford-english-dictionary/#:~:text=On%20Thursday%2C%20The%20Oxford%20English%20Dictionary%20officially%20announced,into%20the%20lexicon.%20Their%20definition%20reads%20as%20follows%3A

Lichter, D., & Qian, Z. (2008). Serial cohabitation and the marital life course. *Journal of Marriage and Family*, 70, 861–878.

Lindau, S., Schumm, L., Lauman, E., Levinson, W., O'Muircheartaigh, C., & Waite, L. (2007). A study of sexuality and health among older adults in the United States. *The New England Journal of Medicine*, 362, 762–774.

Lindstrom Johnson, S., Elam, K., Rogers, A. A., & Hilley, C. (2018). A meta-analysis of parenting practices and child psychosocial outcomes in trauma-informed parenting interventions after violence exposure. *Prevention Science* 19, 927–938.

Livingston, G. (2018a). About one-third of U.S. children are living with an unmarried parent. *Pew Research Center.* www.pewresearch.org/fact-tank/2018/04/27/about-one-third-of-u-s-children-are-living-with-an-unmarried-parent/

Livingston, G. (2018b). The changing profile of unmarried parents. *Pew Research Center.* www.pewresearch.org/social-trends/2018/04/25/the-changing-profile-of-unmarried-parents/

Lobo, S. (2009). *Urban clan mothers, keeping the campfires going: Native Women's activism in urban communities,* (pp. 1–21). Lincoln, NE: University of Nebraska Press.

Loper, A., Clarke, C., & Dallaire, D. (2019). Parenting programs for incarcerated fathers and mothers: Current research and new directions. In J. M. Eddy & J. Poehlmann-Tynan (Eds.), *Handbook on children with incarcerated parents* (pp. 183–203). Cham, Switzerland: Springer International Publishing.

Lopez, M., Hofer, K., Bumgarner, E., & Taylor, D. (2017). Developing culturally responsive approaches to serving diverse populations: A resource guide for community-based organizations. *National Research Center on Hispanic Children and Families.* Publication #2017-17.

Lopez, M., Krogstad, J., & Passel, J. (2020). Who is Hispanic? *Pew Research Center.* Retrieved from www.pewresearch.org/fact-tank/2020/09/15/who-is-hispanic/

Lucier-Greer, M., & O'Neal, C. (2022). Family life education with military and veteran families. In S. M. Ballard & A.C. Taylor (Eds.), *Family life education with diverse populations* (2nd ed., pp. 141–172). San Diego, CA: Cognella Academic Publishing.

Luo, S., & Klohnen, E. (2005). Assortative mating and marital quality in newlyweds: A couple-centered approach. *Journal of Personality and Social Psychology,* 88, 304–326.

MacInnes, M. (2008). One's enough for now: Children, disability, and the subsequent childbearing of mothers. *Journal of Marriage and Family,* 70, 758–771.

Majeed, M., & Kanwal, S. (2019). The global integration and transmission of social values: A case of family ties. *Social Indicators Research,* 141, 703–729.

Mallette, J. K., Baugh, E. J., Ballard, S. M., & Taylor, A. C. (2022). A cultural competency model for family life education. In S. M. Ballard & A. C. Taylor (Eds.), *Family life education with diverse populations* (2nd ed., pp. 19–40). San Diego, CA: Cognella Academic Publishing.

Mancini, J. A., O'Neal, W., & Lucier-Greer, M. (2020). Toward a framework for military family life education: Culture, context, content, and practice. *Family Relations,* 69, 644–661.

Manning, W., & Cohen, J. (2012). Premarital cohabitation and marital dissolution: An examination of recent marriages. *Journal of Marriage and Family,* 74, 377–387.

Marano, H. E. (2008). *A nation of wimps.* New York: Random House.

Market Business News (MBN). (2020.) What is global interdependence? https://marketbusinessnews.com/financial-glossary/global-interdependence-definition-meaning/

Marketing Charts. (2007). Teen market to surpass $200 billion by 2011, despite population decline. *The Teens Market in the U.S. Report.* Retrieved from www.marketingcharts.com/wp/traditional/teen-market-to-surpass-200-billion-by-2011-despite-populationdecline-817/

Markman, H., Stanley, S., & Blumberg, S. (2010). *Fighting for your marriage* (3rd ed.). San Francisco: Jossey-Bass.

Marquardt, E., Blankenhorn, D., Lerman, R., Malone-Colon, L., & Wilcox, W. (2012). *The president's marriage agenda for the forgotten sixty percent. The state of our unions.* Charlottesville, VA: National Marriage Project and Institute for American Values. Retrieved from www.stateofourunions.org/2012/SOOU2012.pdf

Martin, E. (2017). Hidden consequences: The impact of incarceration on dependent children. *NIJ Journal*, 278. Retrieved from https://nij.gov/journals/278/Pages/impact-ofincarceration-on-dependent-children.aspx

Mauer, L. (2022). Family Life Education with lesbian, gay, bisexual, transgender, and queer (LGBTQ) families. In S. M. Ballard & A. C Taylor (Eds.), *Family life education with diverse populations* (2nd ed., pp. 199–238). San Diego, CA: Cognella Academic Publishing.

Mbwana, K., Terzian, M., & Moore, K. (2009). What works for parent involvement programs for children: Lessons from experimental evaluations of social interventions. *Child trends fact sheet* #2009–47. Washington, DC: Child Trends. Retrieved from www.childtrends.org/wp-content/uploads/2009/12/What-Works-for-Parent-Involvement-Programs-for-Adolescents-February-2010.pdf

McAllister, S., Duncan, S. F., & Hawkins, A. J. (2012). Examining the early evidence for self directed marriage and relationship education: A meta-analytic study. *Family Relations*, 61, 742–755.

McDermott, D. (2011). What do parenting educators need to know and do? PowerPoint presentation at the National Forum on Professional Preparation Systems in Parenting Education.

McGee, J. (n.d.). Teaching millennials. https://www.scribd.com/document/381902050/Teaching-Millennials

McGee, M. (2004). Talking with kids about pleasure. *Planned Parenthood Federation of America Educator's Update*, 8, 1–6.

McGroder, S., & Hyra, A. (2009). Developmental and economic effects of parenting programs for expectant parents and parents of preschool-age children. *Partnership for America's Economic Success*. Retrieved from www.readynation.org/docs/researchproject_mcgroder_200903_paper.pdf

Merriam-Webster Dictionary. (n.d.). Definition of profession. Retrieved from www.merriam-webster.com/dictionary/profession

Mikulincer, M., & Shaver, P. (2012). Adult attachment orientations and relationship processes. *Journal of Family Theory & Review*, 4, 259–274.

Miller, J., & Seller, W. (1990). *Curriculum perspectives and practices*. New York: Longman.

Miller, P. M. (2011). Homeless families education networks: An examination of access and mobilization. *Educational Administration Quarterly*, 47, 543–581.

Miller, S., Miller, P., Wackman, E., & Nunnally, D. (n.d.). Couple communication. Retrieved from http://www.couplecommunication.com/index.html

Mills, M. (2004). Globalization and family life. In A. Abela & J. Walker (Eds.), *Contemporary issues in family studies: Global perspectives on partnerships, parenting, and support in a changing world* (pp. 249–261). Chichester, UK: Wiley-Blackwell.

Mills, M. (2014). Globalization and family life. In A. Abela & J. Walker (Eds.), *Contemporary issues in family studies: Global perspectives on partnerships, parenting and support in a changing world*. Malden, MA: John Wiley & Sons.

Minnesota Association for Family and Early Education (MNAFEE). (2011). *Parent education core curriculum framework*. St. Paul, MN: Author. Retrieved from https://www.mnafee.org/uploads/1/3/7/0/13709464/core_curriculum_2011.pdf

Minnesota Council on Family Relations (MCFR). (1997). *Ethical thinking and practice for parent and family educators*. Minneapolis, MN: Ethics Committee, Parent and Family Education Section.

Minnesota Council on Family Relations (MCFR). (2009). Ethical thinking and practice for parent and family life educators. In D. Bredehoft & M. Walcheski (Eds.), *Family life education: Integrating theory and practice* (pp. 233–239). Minneapolis, MN: National Council on Family Relations.

Minnesota Council on Family Relations (MCFR). (2018). *Ethical thinking and practice for parent and family life educators. Tools for ethical thinking and practice in family life education* (4th ed.). Minneapolis, MN: National Council on Family Relations.

Mitchell, K., Ybarra, M., Korchmaros, J., & Kosciw, J. (2014). Accessing sexual health information online: Use, motivations, and consequences for youth with different sexual orientations. *Health Education Research*, 29, 147–157.

Modo, I. (2005). Nigerian families. In B. Adams & J. Trost (Eds.), *Handbook of world families* (pp. 25–46). Thousand Oaks, CA: Sage.

Mohr, K. A. J., & Mohr, E. S. (2017). Understanding Generation Z students to promote a contemporary learning environment. *Journal on Empowering Teaching Excellence*, 1, Article 9.

Montfort, S., & Brick, P. (1999). *Unequal partners: Teaching about power and consent in adult-teen relationships*. Morristown, NJ: Planned Parenthood of Greater Northern New Jersey, Inc.

Moor, A. (2019). What each of the letters in LGBTQIA+ mean. *Bestlife*. Retrieved from https://bestlifeonline.com/what-lgbtqia-means/

Moore, T., & Asay, S. (2013). *Family resource management*. Thousand Oaks, CA: Sage.

Morris, A. S., Robinson, L. R., Hays-Grudo, J., Claussen, A. H., Hartwig, S. A., & Treat, A. E. (2017). Targeting parenting in early childhood: A public health approach to improve outcomes for children living in poverty. *Child Development*, 88, 388–397.

Morrison, E., & Price, M. (1974). *Values in sexuality: A new approach to sex education*. New York: Hart Publishing.

Movement Advancement Project and SAGE. (2017). Understanding issues facing LGBT older adults. www.lgbtmap.org/policy-and-issue-analysis/understanding-issues-facing-lgbt-older-adults

Mulroy, M. (2012). Family life education with prison inmates and their families. In S. M. Ballard & A. C. Taylor (Eds.), *Family life education with diverse populations* (pp. 41–59). Thousand Oaks, CA: Sage.

Murez, C. (2021). No drop in teens' use of pot, binge drinking despite pandemic lockdowns. *US News & World Report. Health Day News*. Retrieved from www.usnews.com/news/health-news/articles/2021-06-25/no-drop-in-teens-use-of-pot-binge-drinking-despite-pandemic-lockdowns

Myers-Walls, J. (n.d.). *Family life education materials: Quality assessment tool*. Lafayette, IN: Purdue Extension. Retrieved from www.extension.purdue.edu/purplewagon/FLEMat-QAT/FLEMat-QAT.htm

Myers-Walls, J. (1998). *What is your parent education approach?* Lafayette, IN: Purdue University Cooperative Extension Service.

Myers-Walls, J. (2004). Children as victims of war and terrorism. *Journal of Aggression, Maltreatment, & Trauma*, 8, 41–62.

Myers-Walls, J. (2012). Family life education with court-mandated parents with families. In S. M. Ballard & A. C. Taylor (Eds.), *Family life education with diverse populations* (pp. 61–90). Thousand Oaks, CA: Sage.

Myers -Walls, J. (2020). Family life education for families facing acute stress: Best practices and recommendations. *Family Relations*, 69, 662–676.

Myers-Walls, J. (2022). Family life education with court-mandated parents and families. In S. M. Ballard & A. C. Taylor (Eds.), *Family life education with diverse populations* (2nd ed., pp. 101–139). San Diego, CA: Cognella Academic Publishing.

Myers-Walls, J., Ballard, S., Darling, C., & Myers-Bowman, K. (2011). Reconceptualizing the domains and boundaries of family life education. *Family Relations*, 60, 357–372.

Myers-Walls, J., & Myers-Bowman, K. (2016). War and families. *Encyclopedia of family studies*. Retrieved from https://onlinelibrary.wiley.com/doi/full/10.1002/9781119085621.wbefs529

Nadal, K. L. (2008). Preventing racial, ethnic, gender, sexual minority, disability, and religious microaggressions: Recommendations for promoting positive mental health. *Prevention in Counseling Psychology: Theory, Research, Practice and Training*, 2, 22–27.

Nakonezny, P., & Denton, W. (2008). Marital relationships: A social exchange theory perspective. *The American Journal of Family Therapy*, 36, 402–412.

National Academies of Sciences, Engineering, and Medicine. (2016). *Parenting matters: Supporting parents of children ages 0–8*. Washington, DC: The National Academies Press.

National Adult Protective Services Association (NAPSA). (2021). *Academy for Professional Excellence: Core competency areas*. Retrieved from https://theacademy.sdsu.edu/programs/apswi/core-competency-areas/

National Center for Family & Marriage Research (NCFMR). (2010). *Remarriage rate in the U.S. 2010*. Retrieved from http://ncfmr.bgsu.edu/pdf/family_profiles/file114853.pdf

National Center for Health Statistics (NCHS). (2017). Over half of the U.S. teens have had sexual intercourse by age 18. *Centers for Disease Control and Prevention*. Retrieved from www.cdc.gov/nchs/pressroom/nchs_press_releases/2017/201706_NSFG.htm

National Commission on Family Life Education. (1968). Family life education programs: Principles, plans, procedures. A framework for family life educators. *The Family Coordinator*, 17, 211–214.

National Council on Family Relations (NCFR). (n.d.-a). Family life education PowerPoint. Retrieved from http://www.ncfr.org/cfle-certification/what-family-life-education

National Council on Family Relations (NCFR). (n.d.-b). Degree programs in family science. Retrieved from http://www.ncfr.org/degree-programs

National Council on Family Relations (NCFR). (1984). *Standards and criteria for the certification of family life educators, college/university curriculum guidelines, and an overview of content in family life education: A framework for life span programs*. Minneapolis, MN: Author.

National Council on Family Relations (NCFR). (2003). Assessing the future: Family life education. *NCFR Fact Sheet*. Minneapolis, MN: Author.

National Council on Family Relations (NCFR). (2009a). Family life educators code of ethics. Retrieved from www.ncfr.org/sites/default/files/downloads/news/cfle_code__of_ethics_2012.pdf

National Council on Family Relations (NCFR). (2009b). *Family life education content areas: Content and practice guidelines*. Minneapolis, MN: Author. Retrieved from www.ncfr.org/sites/default/files/downloads/news/cfle_content_and_practice_guidelines_2014.pdf

National Council on Family Relations (NCFR). (2013). Standards and criteria: Certified family life educator program. Retrieved from www.ncfr.org/sites/default/files/2017-01/standards_2013.pdf

National Council on Family Relations (NCFR). (2014). *2014 job analysis survey summary*. Clearwater, FL: Schroeder Measurement Technologies, Inc.

National Council on Family Relations (NCFR). (2018a). CFLE code of ethics. Retrieved from www.ncfr.org/sites/default/files/2018-06/CFLE-Code-of-Ethics.pdf

National Council on Family Relations (NCFR). (2018b). *Tools for ethical thinking and practice in family life education* (4th ed.). Minneapolis, MN: Author.

National Council on Family Relations (NCFR). (2019). Certified family life educator (CFLE) employer work experience assessment and verification form. Retrieved from www.ncfr.org/sites/default/files/2018-12/2019_Employer%20Assessment%20and%20Verification%20Form.pdf

National Council on Family Relations (NCFR). (2020). Utah law recognizes family life educators. Retrieved from https://www.ncfr.org/news/utah-law-recognizes-family-life-educators

National Education Association (NEA). (2003). Guide to teaching online courses. Retrieved from http://www.nea.org/technology/images/onlineteachguide.pdf

National Healthy Marriage Resource Center (NHMRC). (2007). Become a marriage and relationship educator. Retrieved from www.healthymarriageinfo.org/educators/become-educator/index.aspx

National Healthy Marriage Resource Center (NHMRC). (2010). Covenant marriage: A fact-sheet. Retrieved from www.healthymarriageinfo.org/download.aspx?id=329?

National Institutes of Health (NIH). (2011). Why population aging matters: A global perspective. *US Department of Health and Human Services*. Retrieved from www.nia.nih.gov/sites/default/files/2017-06/WPAM.pdf

National Institutes of Health (NIH). (2019). HIV undetectable = untransmittable (U=U, or treatment as prevention). *National Institute of Allergy and Infectious Diseases*. Retrieved from www.niaid.nih.gov/diseases-conditions/treatment-prevention

National Marriage Project & Institute for American Values (NMP & IAV). (2012). The state of our unions: Marriage in America 2012. *University of Virginia and Center for Marriages and Families Institute*. Retrieved from www.stateofourunions.org/2012/SOOU2012.pdf

National Parenting Education Network. (2018). Parenting education competencies: A resource document for the field of parenting education. Retrieved from https://npen.org/Professional-Parenting-Educator-Competencies

National Parenting Education Network. (2020a). Paraprofessional parenting educator competencies: A resource document for the field of parenting education. Retrieved from https://npen.org/Paraprofessional-Parenting-Educator-Competencies

National Parenting Education Network. (2020b). Framework for understanding parenting educator professional preparation and recognition. Retrieved from https://npen.org/professional-preparation

National Parenting Education Network. (2021). Parenting educator professional preparation and recognition. Retrieved from https://npen.org/professional-preparation

National Prevention Council. (2011). National prevention strategy. Washington, DC: US Department of Health and Human Services, Office of the Surgeon General. Retrieved from http://www.surgeongeneral.gov/initiatives/prevention/strategy/report.pdf

National PTA. (n.d.). About PTA. Retrieved from www.pta.org/home/About-National-Parent-Teacher-Association

National Stepfamily Resource Center (NSRC). (2013). Stepfamily FAQs. Retrieved from www.stepfamilies.info/about/

National Today. (n.d.). International family day. Retrieved from https://nationaltoday.com/international-day-families/

Neff, L., & Karney, B. (2004). How does context affect intimate relationships? Linking external stress and cognitive processes within marriage. *Personality and Social Psychology Bulletin*, 30, 134–148.

Neff, L., & Karney, B. (2007). Stress crossover in newlywed marriage: A longitudinal and dyadic perspective. *Journal of Marriage and Family*, 69, 594–607.

Newberger, C. M. (1980). The cognitive structure of parenthood: Designing a descriptive measure. *New Directions for Child and Adolescent Development*, 7, 45–67.

Newman, B., & Newman, P. (2007). *Theories of human development*. Mahwah, NJ: Lawrence Erlbaum.

Nielsen, A., Pinsof, W., Rampage, C., Solomon, A., & Goldstein, S. (2004). Marriage 101: An integrated academic and experiential undergraduate marriage education course. *Family Relations*, 53, 485–494.

Niklova, M., Graham, C., & Ivlevs, A. (2018). International migration: What happens to those left behind? *Brookings Institution*. Retrieved from www.brookings.edu/blog/future-development/2018/09/13/international-migration-what-happens-to-those-left-behind/

Nilson, L. (2003). *Teaching at its best: A research-based resource for college instructors* (2nd ed.). Bolton, MA: Anker Publishing.

Nixon, E., Greene, S., & Hogan, D. (2012). Negotiating relationships in single-mother households: Perspectives of children and mothers. *Family Relations*, 61, 142–156.

Noe-Bustamante, L., Mora, L., & Lopez, M. H. (2020). About one-in-four U.S. Hispanics have heard of Latinx, but just 3% use it. *Pew Research Center.* www.pewresearch.org/hispanic/2020/08/11/about-one-in-four-u-s-hispanics-have-heard-of-latinx-but-just-3-use-it/

Nomaguchi, K., & Milkie, M. A. (2020). Parenthood and well-being: A decade in review. *Journal of Marriage and Family*, 82, 198–223.

Nygren, P., Green, B., Winters, K., & Rockhill, A. (2018). What's happening during home visits? Exploring the relationship of home visiting content and dosage to parenting outcomes. *Maternal and Child Health Journal*, 22, 52–61.

Olga, I. (2015). Influence of western works on teens should be checked. *The New Times.* Retrieved from https://www.newtimes.co.rw/section/read/194905

Olsen, C. (1999). Stepping stones for stepfamilies. *The Forum for Family and Consumer Issues*, 4. Retrieved from http://ncsu.edu/ffci/publications/1999/v4-n3-1999-winter/showcase-usa.php

Olson, D. (2000). Circumplex model of marital and family systems. *Journal of Family Therapy*, 22, 147–167.

Olson, D., & DeFrain, J. (2006). *Marriages and families: Intimacy, diversity, and strengths.* New York: McGraw-Hill.

Olson, D., DeFrain, J., & Olson, A. (1999). *Building relationships: Developing skills for life.* Minneapolis, MN: Life Innovations.

Olson, D., Fournier, D., & Druckman, J. (1996). *PREPARE.* Minneapolis, MN: Life Innovations.

Olson, D., & Gorall, D. (2003). Circumplex model of marital and family systems. In F. Walsh (Ed.), *Normal family processes: Growing diversity and complexity* (3rd ed., pp. 514–548). New York: Guilford Press.

Olson, D., Larson, P., & Olson-Sigg, A. (2009). Couple checkup: Tuning up relationships. *Journal of Couple & Relationship Therapy*, 8, 129–142.

Olson, D., & Olson, A. (2000). *Empowering couples: Building on your strengths.* Minneapolis, MN: Life Innovations.

Olson, D., Olson-Sigg, A., & Larson, P. (2012). *The couple check-up.* Nashville, TN: Thomas Nelson.

Olson, D., Russell, C., & Sprenkle, D. (1989). *Circumplex model: Systemic assessment and treatment of families.* Binghamton, NY: Haworth Press.

Olson-Sigg, A. (2004). Premarital education programs for youth: Investing in prevention. *Marriage & Family: A Christian Journal*, 7, 123–129.

Ooms, T. (2002). Strengthening couples and marriage in low-income communities. In A. Hawkins, S. Wardle, & D. Coolidge (Eds.), *Revitalizing the institution of marriage for the twenty-first century: An agenda for strengthening marriage* (pp. 79–100). Westport, CT: Praeger.

Ooms, T., & Hawkins, A. (2012). *Marriage and relationship education: A promising strategy for strengthening low-income, vulnerable families. The state of our unions.* Charlottesville, VA: National Marriage Project and Institute for American Values.

Ooms, T., & Wilson, P. (2004). The challenges of offering relationship and marriage education to low-income populations. *Family Relations*, 53, 440–447.

Osborne, C. (2005). Marriage following the birth of a child among cohabiting and visiting parents. *Journal of Marriage and Family*, 67, 14–26.

Owen, J., Rhoades, G., Stanley, S., & Fincham, F. (2010). Hooking up: Relationship differences and psychological correlates. *Archives of Sexual Behavior*, 39, 553–563.

Oyserman, D. (2017). Culture three ways: Culture and subcultures within countries. *Annual Review of Psychology*, 68, 435–463.

Paik, S. J., Rahman, Z., Kula, S. M., Saito, L. E., & Witenstein, M. A. (2017). Diverse Asian American families and communities: Culture, structure, and education (Part 1: Why they differ). *School Community Journal*, 27, 35–66.

Palm, G. (2015). Professional ethics and practice. In M. Walcheski & J Reinke (Eds.), *Family life education: The practice of family science* (pp. 61–72). Minneapolis, MN: National Council on Family Relations.

Palm, G. (2018). Professional ethics and practice in family life education. In *Tools for ethical thinking and practice in family life education* (pp. 1–10). Minneapolis, MN: National Council on Family Relations.

Palm, G., & Cooke, B. (2021). *Ethical principles for parent and family life educators* (Webinar). National Council on Family Relations.

Pardini, D. (2008). Novel insights into long-standing theories of bidirectional parent-child influences: Introduction to the special section. *Journal of Abnormal Child Psychology*, 36, 627–631.

Parker, K. (2011). A portrait of stepfamilies. *Pew Research Center*. Retrieved from www.pewsocialtrends.org/2011/01/13/a-portrait-of-stepfamilies/

Pasley, K., & Petran, R. (2015). Family structure. *Encyclopedia of Family Studies*. Retrieved from https://onlinelibrary.wiley.com/doi/full/10.1002/9781119085621.wbefs016

Patton, M. Q. (2012). *Essentials of utilization-focused evaluation*. Los Angeles: Sage.

Patton, G., Coffey, C., Cappa, C., Currie, D., Riley, L., Gore, F., Degenhardt, L., Richardson, D., Astone, N., Sangowawa, A., Mokdad, A., & Ferguson, J. (2012). Health of the world's adolescents: A synthesis of internationally comparable data. *The Lancet*, 379, 1665–1675. Retrieved from https://www.thelancet.com/journals/lancet/article/PIIS0140-6736(12)60203-7/fulltext

Payne, K. K. (2019). Children's family structure, 2019. *Family profiles*, FP-19-25. Bowling Green, OH: National Center for Family & Marriage Research. Retrieved from https://doi.org/10.25035/ncfmr/fp-19-25.

Pearson, M. (2004). Love U2: *Getting smarter about relationships*. Berkeley, CA: The Dibble Fund for Marriage Education.

Pearson, M., Stanley, S., & Kline, G. (2005). *Within my reach*. Greenwood Village, CO: PREP for Individual, Inc.

Pendergast, D. (2006). Sustaining the home economics profession in new times—A convergent moment. In A. Rauma, S. Pollanen, & P. Seitamaa-Hakkarainen (Eds.), *Human perspectives on sustainable future* (pp. 3–39). Joensuu, Finland: University of Joensuu.

Pendergast, D. (2009). Generational dynamics: Y it matters 2 u & me. *International Journal of Home Economics*, 2, 67–84.

Perez, A., Cui, M., Darling, C., & Coccia, C. (2018). The effects of helicopter parenting on eating behaviors of college students. *Journal of the Academy of Nutrition and Dietetics*, 118, A80. doi: 10.1016/j.jand.2018.06.075

Permenter, C. (2013). Telecommuting an attractive option for millennials. *USA Today*. Retrieved from www.usatodayeducate.com/staging/index.php/career/telecommuting-an-attractive-option-for-millennials

Pesando, L. (2019). Global family change: Persistent diversity with development. *Population and Development Review*, 45, 133–168.

Peters, R. A. (2013). Don't turn your child into a praise junkie! *The Today Show.* Retrieved from www.today.com/id/12648314/ns/today-parenting_and_family/t/dont-turn-your-child-praise-junkie/

Peterson, B. (2004). *Cultural intelligence: A guide to working with people from other cultures.* Yarmouth, MA: Intercultural Press.

Peterson, C., Florence, C., & Klevens, J. (2018). The economic burden of child maltreatment in the United States, 2015. *Child Abuse and Neglect*, 86, 178–183.

Peterson, G., Hennon, C., & Knox, T. (2010). Conceptualizing parental stress with family stress theory. In S. Price, C. Price, & P. McKenry (Eds.), *Families & change: Coping with stressful events and transitions* (pp. 25–49). Thousand Oaks, CA: Sage.

Peterson, J., & Hyde, J. (2010). A meta-analytic review of research on gender differences in sexuality: 1993–2007. *Psychological Bulletin*, 136, 21–38.

Peterson, C., Kearns, M., McIntosh, W., Estefan, L., Nicolaidis, C., McCollister, K., Gordon, A., & Florence, C. (2018). Lifetime economic burden of intimate partner violence among U.S. adults. *American Journal of Preventive Medicine*, 55, 433–444.

Petkus, J. (2015). A first-hand account of implementing a family life education model: Intentionality in Head Start home visiting. In M. Walcheski & J. Reinke (Eds.), *Family life education: The practice of family science* (pp. 325–331). Minneapolis, MN: National Council on Family Relations.

Petri, A., & Slotnik, D. (2021). Attacks on Asian-Americans in New York stoke fear, anxiety and anger. *The New York Times*. Retrieved from www.nytimes.com/2021/02/26/nyregion/asian-hate-crimes-attacks-ny.html

Pew Research Center. (2013a). A survey of LGBT Americans: Attitudes, experiences, and values in changing times. Retrieved from www.pewsocialtrends.org/2013/06/13/a-survey-of-lgbt-americans/9/

Pew Research Center. (2013b). Cell phone ownership hits 91% of adults. Retrieved from https://www.pewresearch.org/fact-tank/2013/06/06/cell-phone-ownership-hits-91-of-adults/

Pew Research Center. (2015). The American family today. Retrieved from www.pewsocialtrends.org/2015/12/17/1-the-american-family-today/

Pew Research Center. (2021). Mobile fact sheet. www.pewresearch.org/internet/fact-sheet/mobile

Phillips, J. (1981). *Piaget's theory: A primer.* San Francisco: Freeman.

Piaget, J. (1950). *The psychology of intelligence.* London: Routledge & Kegan Paul.

Piaget, J., & Inhelder, B. (1969). *The psychology of the child.* New York: Basic Books.

Pickering, J. A., & Sanders, M. R. (2016). Reducing child maltreatment by making parenting programs available to all parents: A case example using the Triple P-Positive Parenting Program. *Trauma, Violence, & Abuse*, 17, 398–407.

Pizzigati, K., Stuck, E., & Ness, M. (2002). *A child advocacy primer: Experience and advice from service providers, board leaders, land consumers.* Washington, DC: Child Welfare League of America Press.

Popenoe, D., & Whitehead, B. D. (2003). *The state of our unions, 2003.* New Brunswick, NJ: National Marriage Project, Rutgers University.

Population Reference Bureau (Database). (n.d.). Informing a smarter world. Retrieved from https://www.prb.org/about/

Poth, C., Lamarche, M., Yapp, A., Sulla, E., & Chisamore, C. (2014). Towards a definition of evaluation within the Canadian context: Who knew this would be so difficult? *Canadian Journal of Program Evaluation*, 29, 87–103.

Powell, L., & Cassidy, D. (2007). *Family life education: Working with families across the lifespan.* Long Grove, IL: Waveland Press.

Prensky, M. (2001). Digital natives, digital immigrants. *On the Horizon*, 9, 1–6.
Prinz, R. J., Sanders, M. R., Shapiro, C. J., Whitaker, D. J., & Lutzker, J. R. (2016). Addendum to "Population-based prevention of child maltreatment: The U.S. Triple P system population trial." *Prevention Science*, 17, 410–416.
Professional Standards Council. (n.d.). What is a profession? Retrieved from www.psc.gov.au/what-is-a-profession
Proulx, C., Helms, H., & Buehler, C. (2007). Martial quality and personal well-being: A meta-analysis. *Journal of Marriage and Family*, 69, 576–593.
Puckett, J., Woodard, E., Mereish, E., & Pantalone, D. (2015). Parental rejection following sexual orientation disclosure: Impact on internalized homophobia, social support, and mental health. *LGBT Health* 2, 265–269.
Purvis, M. (2013). Paternal incarceration and parenting programs in prison: A review paper. *Psychiatry, Psychology and Law*, 20, 9–28.
Quigley, E. (1974). *Introduction to home economics* (2nd ed.). New York: Macmillan.
Quist, B. (2015). Misperception of work-life balance: The five secret strategies for family life educators. In M. Walcheski & J. Reinke (Eds.), *Family life education: The practice of family science* (pp.107–115). Minneapolis, MN: National Council on Family Relations.
Quora. (2016). What is the difference between the terms global and international? Retrieved from www.quora.com/What-is-the-difference-between-the-terms-global-and-international
Racoma, B. (2018). Immigration, emigration, and migration: What are the differences? *Day Translations*. Retrieved from www.daytranslations.com/blog/all-migration-terms/
Randles, J. (2020). The means to and meaning of "being there" in responsible fatherhood programming with low-income fathers. *Family Relations*, 69, 7–20.
Rasmussen, W. D. (1989). Taking the university to the people. Ames, IA: University Press.
Ratnam, G. (2020). Generation Alpha characteristics and parenting tips. *First Cry Parenting*. https://parenting.firstcry.com/articles/generation-alpha-characteristics-and-parenting-tips/
Raymond, M., Bogdanovich, L., Brahmi, D., Cardinal, L., Fager, G., Frattarelli, L., Hecker, G., Jarpe, E., Viera, A., Kantor, L., & Santelli, J. (2008). State refusal of federal funding for abstinence-only programs. *Sexuality Research and Social Policy*, 5, 44–55.
Rea, A. (2020). How serious is America's literacy problem? *Library Journal*. www.libraryjournal.com/?detailStory=How-Serious-Is-Americas-Literacy-Problem.
Reeves, R. V., & Howard, K. (2013). The parenting gap. *The Brookings Institution*. Retrieved from www.brookings.edu/research/papers/2013/09/09-parenting-gap-social-mobility-wellbeing-reeves
Rehm, M., Darling, C., Coccia, C., & Cui, M. (2017). Parents' perspectives on indulgence: Remembered experiences and meanings when they were adolescents and as current parents of adolescents. *Journal of Family Studies*, 23, 278–295.
Resilient Educator. (2021). Trauma-informed strategies to use in your classroom. Retrieved from https://resilienteducator.com/classroom-resources/trauma-informed-strategies/
Ritchie, H., & Roser, M. (2019). Age structure. *Our World in Data*. https://ourworldindata.org/age-structure
Robert Wood Johnson Foundation. (2017). Comprehensive risk reduction education. Retrieved from www.countyhealthrankings.org/take-action-to-improve-health/what-works-for-health/strategies/comprehensive-risk-reduction-sexual-education
Roberts, B., & Mroczek, D. (2008). Personality trait change in adulthood. *Current Directions in Psychological Science*, 19, 31–35.
Roberts, B., Kuncel, N., Shiner, R., Caspi, A., & Goldberg, L. (2007). The power of personality: A comparative analysis of the predictive validity of personality traits, SES, and IQ. *Perspectives on Psychological Science*, 2, 31–35.

Robila, M., & Taylor, A. (Eds.). (2018). *Global perspectives on family life education*. Cham, Switzerland: Springer International Publishing.

Robinson, B. (2020). New study shows how perfection and anxiety can lead to helicopter parenting. *Forbes*. Retrieved from www.forbes.com/sites/bryanrobinson/2020/10/03/new-study-shows-how-perfection-and-anxiety-can-lead-to-helicopter-parenting/?sh=106a4f7a4f83

Roehl, A., Reddy, S., & Shannon, G. (2013). The flipped classroom: An opportunity to engage millennial students through active learning strategies. *Journal of Family & Consumer Sciences*, 105, 44–49.

Rohrbaugh, M., Shoham, V., & Coyne, J. (2006). Effect of marital quality on eight-year survival of patients with heart failure. *American Journal of Cardiology*, 98, 1069–1072.

Roopnarine, J., & Gielen, U. (2005). Families in global perspective: An introduction. In J. Roopnarine & U. Gielen (Eds.), *Families in global perspective* (pp. 3–13). Boston: Pearson.

Rosenbaum, J. (2009). Patient teenagers: A comparison of the sexual behavior of virginity pledgers and matched nonpledgers. *Pediatrics*, 123, 110–120.

Roser, M., & Ritchie, H. (2019). HIV/AIDS. *Our World in Data*. Retrieved from https://ourworldindata.org/hiv-aids

Royse, D. (2001). *Teaching tips for college and university instructors: A practical guide*. Needham Heights, MA: Allyn & Bacon.

Ruey, S. (2010). A case study of constructivist instructional strategies for adult online learning. *British Journal of Educational Technology*, 41, 706–720.

Russell, S., Mallory, A., Bishop, M., & Dorri, A. (2020). Innovation and integration of sexuality in family life education. *Family Relations*, 69, 595–612.

Ryan, C., Russell, S., Huebner, D., Diaz, R., & Sanchez, J. (2010). Family acceptance in adolescence and health of LGBT young adults. *Journal of Child and Adolescent Psychiatric Nursing*, 23, 205–213.

SafeSchools. (2019). Sexual harassment prevention in schools. *Vector Solutions*. Retrieved from www.vectorsolutions.com/resources/blogs/sexual-harassment-prevention-in-schools/

Sakaluk, J., Kim, J., Campbell, E., Baxter, A., & Impett, E. (2020). Self-esteem and sexual health: A multilevel meta-analytic review. *Health Psychological Review*, 14, 269–293.

Salazar, L., Davenport, R., & Hancock, D. (2014). New healthcare reform developments and strategies (Webinar). Retrieved from http://tcbmag.com/Industries/Insurance/Wells-Fargo-Webinar.

Sampaio, F., Jan, J., Barendregt, J. J., Feldman, I., Lee, Y. Y., Sawyer, M. G., Dadds, M. R., Scott, J. G., & Mihalopoulos, C. (2018). Population cost-effectiveness of the Triple P Parenting Programme for the treatment of conduct disorder: An economic modelling study. *European Child & Adolescent Psychiatry*, 27, 933–944.

Sanders, M. R., Prinz, R. J., & Shapiro, C. J. (2009). Predicting utilization of evidence-based parenting interventions with organizational, service-provider and client variables. *Administration and Policy in Mental Health and Mental Health Services Research*, 36, 133–143.

Santelli, J., Kantor, L., Grilo, S., Speizer, I., Lindberg, L., Heitel, J., Schalet, A., Lyon, M., Mason-Jones, A., McGovern, T., Heck, C., Rogers, J., & Ott, M. (2017). Abstinence-only-until-marriage: An updated review of U.S. policies and programs and their impact. *Journal of Adolescent Health*, 61, 273–280.

Santrock, J. W. (2017). *Life-span development* (17th ed.). McGraw-Hill.

Sassler, S. (2010). Partnering across the life course: Sex, relationships, and mate selection. *Journal of Marriage and Family*, 72, 557–575.

Satcher, D. (2001). The surgeon general's call to action to promote sexual health and responsible behavior. *Office of the Surgeon General: Office of Population Affairs*. Retrieved from https://www.ncbi.nlm.nih.gov/books/NBK44216/

Save the Children. (2019). Stop the war on children. Retrieved from stop-the-war-on-children-2019.pdf

Sawyer, W., & Wagner, P. (2020, March 24). Mass incarceration: The whole pie 2020. *Prison Policy Initiative*. www.prisonpolicy.org/reports/pie2020.html

Schick, V., Herbenick, D., Reece, M., Sanders, S., Dodge, B., Middlestadt, S., & Fortenberry, J. (2010). Sexual behaviors, condom use, and sexual health of Americans over 50: Implications of sexual health promotion for aging adults. *The Journal of Sexual Medicine*, 7, 315–329.

Schlossman, S. L. (1976). Before home start: Notes toward a history of parent education in America, 1897–1929. *Harvard Educational Review*, 46, 436–467.

Schmitt, E., Hu, A., & Bachrach, P. (2008). Course evaluation and assessment: Examples of a learner-centered approach. *Gerontology and Geriatrics Education*, 29, 290–300.

Schramm, D. G., & Becher, E. H. (2020). Common practices for divorce education. *Family Relations*, 69, 543–558.

Schvaneveldt, P. (2022). Family life education with Latino/Latina immigrant families. In S. M. Ballard & A. C. Taylor (Eds.), *Family life education with diverse populations* (2nd ed., pp. 395–426). San Diego, CA: Cognella Academic Publishing.

Schvaneveldt, P., & Behnke, A. (2012). Family life education with Latino immigrant families. In S. M. Ballard & A. C. Taylor (Eds.), *Family life education with diverse populations* (pp. 165–186). Thousand Oaks, CA: Sage.

Schwartz, P. (1994). *Love between equals: How peer marriage really works*. New York: Free Press.

Schwartz, P. (2001). Peer marriage: What does it take to create a truly egalitarian relationship? In A. S. Skolnick & J. Skolnick (Eds.), *Families in transition* (pp. 182–189). Boston: Allyn & Bacon.

Schwartz, P. (2006). *Finding your perfect match*. New York: Penguin.

Scommegna, P. (2020). Changing race and ethnicity questions on the U.S. census form reflect evolving views. *Population Reference Bureau*. Retrieved from www.prb.org/changing-race-and-ethnicity-questions-on-the-u-s-census-form-reflect-evolving-views/

Seefeldt, K., & Smock., P. (2004). Marriage on the public policy agenda: What do policymakers need to know from research? *National Poverty Center*. Retrieved from http://www.npc.umich.edu/publications/workingpaper04/paper2/04-02.pdf

Seibel, N. L. (2011). *Using evidence-based programs to support children and families experiencing homelessness*. An initiative of the Conrad N. Hilton Foundation, in partnership with The National Center on Family Homelessness, National Alliance to End Homelessness and ZERO TO THREE: National Center for Infants, Toddlers and Families.

Sesame Street. (2013). Coping with incarceration. Retrieved from https://sesamestreetincommunities.org/topics/incarceration/

Sex Education Collaborative. (2018). Professional learning standards for sex education. Retrieved from https://siecus.org/resources/professional-learning-standards-for-sex-education/

Sexuality Information and Education Council of the United States (SIECUS). (n.d.-a). Abstinence only until marriage programs. Retrieved from www.siecus.org/index.cfm?fuseaction=Page.viewPage&pageId=523&parentID=477

Sexuality Information and Education Council of the United States (SIECUS). (n.d.-b). Comprehensive sexuality education. Retrieved from www.siecus.org/index.cfm?fuseaction=page.viewPage&pageId=514&parentID=477

Sexuality Information and Education Council of the United States (SIECUS). (n.d.-c). Talk about sex: What is sexuality. Retrieved from www.seriouslysexuality.com/index.cfm?fuseaction=Page.ViewPage&pageId=1071

Sexuality Information and Education Council of the United States (SIECUS). (1998). *Filling the gaps: Hard to teach topics in sexuality education*. New York: Author.

Sexuality Information and Education Council of the United States (SIECUS). (2004). *Guidelines for comprehensive sexuality education: Kindergarten through 12th grade* (3rd ed.). New-York: Author. Retrieved from www.siecus.org/_data/global/images/guidelines.pdf

Sexuality Information and Education Council of the United States (SIECUS). (2007). On our side: Public support for comprehensive sexuality education. Retrieved from www.siecus.org/_data/global/images/public_support.pdf

Sexuality Information and Education Council of the United States (SIECUS). (2008). Sex respect review. Community Action Kit. Retrieved from www.communityactionkit.org/index.cfm?fuseaction=page.viewpage&pageid=990

Sexuality Information and Education Council of the United States (SIECUS). (2009). In their own words: What abstinence-only-until marriage programs say. *SIECUS Public Policy Office*. Retrieved from www.siecus.org/index.cfm?fuseaction=Page.ViewPage&PageID=1199

Sexuality Information and Education Council of the United States (SIECUS). (2018a). A history of federal funding for abstinence-only-until-marriage programs. Retrieved from https://siecus.org/wp-content/uploads/2018/08/A-History-of-AOUM-Funding-Final-Draft.pdf

Sexuality Information and Education Council of the United States (SIECUS). (2018b). On our side: Public support for sex education. Retrieved from https://siecus.org/wp-content/uploads/2018/08/On-Our-Side-Public-Support

Sexuality Information and Education Council of the United States (SIECUS). (2018c). Policy brief: Sex ed & parental consent opt-in vs. opt-out. Retrieved from https://siecus.org/wp-content/uploads/2018/09/Policy-Brief-Opt-in-v.-Opt-out-Redesign-Draft-09.2018.pdf

Sexuality Information and Education Council of the United States (SIECUS). (2019). Trump attempts to shift TPPP to promote abstinence-only ideology. Retrieved from https://siecus.org/resources/trump-shifts-teen-pregnancy-prevention-program/

Sexuality Information and Education Council of the United States (SIECUS). (2020). 2020 sex ed state legislative mid-year report. Retrieved from https://www.siecus.org/wp-content/uploads/2020/09/SIECUS-2020-Mid-Year-Report_FINAL.pdf

Sexuality Resource Center for Parents (SRCP). (2020). A definition of sexuality. Retrieved from http://www.srcp.org/for_all_parents/definition.html

Sexuality Resource Center for Parents (SRCP). (2021a). For parents of children with developmental disabilities. Retrieved from http://www.srcp.org/for_some_parents/developmental_disabilities/index.html

Sexuality Resource Center for Parents (SRCP). (2021b). Sexual development from 0–18. Retrieved from https://opnff.net/Files/Admin/Sexual%20Development%20from%200-18%20Years%20Old.pdf

Shah, A. (2011). Health issues. Global issues: Social, political, economic and environmental issues that affect us all. *Global Issues*. Retrieved from www.globalissues.org/issue/587/health-issues

Sharman, C. (2005). The problem with drinking. *Perspectives in Health: Magazine of the Pan American Health Organization*. Pan American Health Organization. Retrieved from www.paho.org/English/DD/PIN/Number21_article04.htm

Sheng, J. (2005). Chinese families. In B. Adams & J. Trost (Eds.), *Handbook of world families* (pp. 99–128). Thousand Oaks, CA: Sage.

Shlafer, R., Gerrity, E., Ruhland, E., & Wheeler, M. (2013). Children with incarcerated parents—Considering children's outcomes in the contexts of family experiences. *Children's Mental Health eReview*. St. Paul, MN: University of Minnesota Extension, Children, Youth, and Family Consortium.

Shor, L., & Freire, P. (1986). *A pedagogy for liberation: Dialogues on transforming education*. South Hadley, MA: Bergin & Garvey.

Silliman, B., & Schumm, W. (2004). Adolescents' perceptions of marriage and premarital couples education. *Family Relations*, 53, 513–520.

Simon, S., Howe, L., & Kirschenbaum, H. (1972). *Values clarification: A handbook of practical strategies for teachers and students*. New York: Hart Publishing.

Simon, W., & Gagnon, J. (1984). Sexual scripts. *Society*, 22, 53–60.

Simovic, D. (2019). 39 entrepreneur statistics you need to know in 2020. *SmallBizGenius*. Retrieved from www.smallbizgenius.net/by-the-numbers/entrepreneur-statistics/

Simpson, E. (1972). *The classification of educational objectives in the psychomotor domain: The psychomotor domain* (Vol. 3). Washington, DC: Gryphon House.

Singh, J. (2005). The contemporary Indian family. In B. Adams & J. Trost (Eds.), *Handbook of world families* (pp. 129–166). Thousand Oaks, CA: Sage.

Skinner, B. (1953). *Science and human behavior*. New York: Macmillan.

Skinner, B. (1957). *Verbal behavior*. New York: Appleton-Century Crofts.

Skinner, B. (1974). *About behaviorism*. New York: Knopf.

Skogrand, L., Reck, K., Higginbotham, B., Adler-Baeder, F., & Dansie, L. (2010). Recruitment and retention for stepfamily education. *Journal of Couple & Relationship Therapy*, 9, 48–65.

Slonim, G., Gur-Yaish, N., & Katz, R. (2015). By choice or by circumstance?: Stereotypes of and feelings about single people. *Studia Psychologica*, 57, 35–48.

Small, S., & Memmo, M. (2004). Contemporary models of youth development and problem prevention: Toward an integration of terms, concepts, and models. *Family Relations*, 53, 3–11.

Small, S. A., Cooney, S. M., & O'Connor, C. (2009). Evidence-informed program improvement: Using principles of effectiveness to enhance the quality and impact of family-based prevention programs. *Family Relations*, 58, 1–13.

Small, S., & Huser, M. (2015). Principles for improving family programs: An evidence-informed approach. In M. J. Walcheski & J. S. Reinke (Eds.), *Family life education: The practice of family science*. Minneapolis, MN: NCFR.

Smith, A. (2013). Smart phone ownership 2013. *Pew Internet*. Retrieved from http://pewinternet.org/Reports/2013/Smartphone-Ownership-2013/Findings.aspx

Smith, C. A., Cudaback, D., Goddard, H. W., & Myers-Walls, J. (1994). *National extension parent education model*. Manhattan, KS: Cooperative Extension Service.

Smith, T. (2016). Global family life education. *National Council on Family Relations, CFLE Network*. Retrieved from www.ncfr.org/cfle-network/current-issue/global-family-life-education

Smith, W. M., Jr. (1968). Family life education—Who needs it? *The Family Coordinator*, 17, 55–61.

Somerville, R. (1971). Family life and sex education in the turbulent sixties. *Journal of Marriage and the Family*, 33, 22–35.

Southwick, E. (2011a). All about happiness. Retrieved from www.allabouthappiness.com/about/

Southwick, E. (2011b). Happiness and life success coaching with Edward Southwick, Jr. Retrieved from www.youtube.com/watch?v=y-oOMQ86Jvk

Spigner-Littles, D., & Anderson, C. (2010). Constructivism: A paradigm for older learners. *Educational Gerontology*, 25, 203–209.

Spoth, R, Guyll, M., & Day, S. (2002). Universal family-focused interventions in alcohol-use disorder prevention: Cost-effectiveness and cost-benefit analyses of two interventions. *Journal of Studies on Alcohol and Drugs*, 63, 219–235.

Squires, N., & Smith, R. (2006). What is marriage education. *Married for good*. Retrieved from http://www.marriageeducation.ca/philosophy.html (Site discontinued)

Sroufe, L. A. (2016). The place of attachment in development. In J. Cassidy & P. R. Shaver (Eds.), *Handbook of attachment theory, research, and clinical applications* (3rd ed., pp. 997–1011). New York: The Guilford Press.

Staats, C., Capatosto, K., Tenney, L., & Mamo, S. (2017). State of the science: Implicit bias review. *The Ohio State University Kirwan Institute for the Study of Race and Ethnicity.* www.KirwanInstitute.osu.edu. http://kirwaninstitute.osu.edu/wp-content/uploads/2017/11/2017-SOTS-final-draft-02.pdf

Stangler-Hall, K., & Hall, D. (2011). Abstinence-only education and teen pregnancy rates: Why we need comprehensive sex education in the U.S. *PLOS ONE* 6, e24658.doi:10.1371/journal.pone.0024658. Retrieved from http://www.plosone.org/article/info:doi/10.1371/journal.pone.0024658

Stanley, S. (2001). Making the case for premarital education. *Family Relations*, 50, 272–280.

Stanley, S. (2002). What is it with men and commitment, anyway? Keynote address to the 6th Annual Smart Marriages Conferences. Washington, DC.

Stanley, S., Allen, E., Markman, H., Saiz, C., Bloomstrom, G., Thomas, R., Schuum, W., & Bailer, A. (2005). Dissemination and evaluation of marriage education in the army. *Family Process*, 44, 187–201.

Stanley, S., Amato, P., Johnson, C., & Markman, H. (2006). Premarital education, marital quality, and marital stability. Findings from a household survey. *Journal of Family Psychology*, 20, 117–126.

Stanley, S., Markman, H., & Jenkins, N. (2004). *Marriage education using PREP with low income and diverse clients*. Denver, CO: PREP.

Stanley, S., Markman, H., Jenkins, N., & Blumberg, S. (2009). *PREP version 7.0b leaders manual*. Greenwood Village, CO: PREP Educational Products.

Stanley, S., Rhoades, G., & Markman, H. (2006). Sliding versus deciding: Inertia and the premarital cohabitation effect. *Family Relations*, 55, 499–509.

Stanley, S., Whitton, W., & Markman, H. (2004). Maybe I do: Interpersonal commitment levels and premarital or non-marital cohabitation. *Journal of Family Issues*, 25, 496–519.

Statista. (2021). Number of single-person households in the United States from 1960–2020. Retrieved from www.statista.com/statistics/242022/number-of-single-person-households-in-the-us/

Staton, J., & Ooms, T. (2012). *"Something important is going on here!" Making connections between marriage relationship quality and health: Implications for research and health care systems, programs and policies*. Fairfax, VA: National Healthy Marriage Resource Center (NMHRC). Retrieved from www.healthymarriageinfo.org/resource-detail/index.aspx?rid=3984

Steck, P. (2009). Addressing changes in family structures. *International Social Security Administration (ISSA)*. Retrieved from www.issa.int/content/download/75658/1435994/file/2TR-29.pdf

Steele, M. (2005). Teaching students with learning disabilities: Constructivism or behaviorism? *Current Issues in Education*, 8, 6–16.

Sternberg, R. (1986). A triangular theory of love. *Psychological Review*, 93, 119–135.

Stevens, J. (2021, March 16). We've changed our name to PACES Connection. *PACES Connection*. www.acesconnection.com/blog/we-ve-changed-our-name-to-paces-connection

Stevenson, B., & Wolfers, J. (2013). Where do you stand in the global love ranking? *Bloomberg*. Retrieved from www.bloomberg.com/opinion/articles/2013-02-14/where-do-you-stand-in-the-global-love-ranking-

Stief, C. (2020). Globalization in the modern world. *ThoughtCo.* Retrieved from www.thoughtco.com/globalization-positive-and-negative-1434946

Stokes-Eley, S. (2007). Using Kolb's experiential learning cycle in chapter presentations. *Teacher Development*, 13, 26–29.

Strawn, J. (2020). Effects of COVID-19 on families. *UC Health*. Retrieved from https://www.uchealth.com/en/media-room/COVID-19/effects-of-COVID-19-on-families

Stulhofer, A. (2015) Medicalization of sexuality. *The International Encyclopedia of Human Sexuality*. Retrieved from https://onlinelibrary.wiley.com/doi/abs/10.1002/9781118896877.wbiehs297

Subramaiam, A. (2006). Creating an electronic portfolio to integrate multiculturalism in teaching family economics. In R. Hamon (Ed.), *International family studies: Developing curricula and teaching tools* (pp. 487–514). Binghamton, NY: Haworth Press.

Substance Abuse and Mental Health Services Administration (SAMHSA). (2012). Nonresearcher's guide to evidence-based program evaluation. *SAMHSA's NREPP*. Retrieved from www.nrepp.samhsa.gov/Courses/ProgramEvaluation/resources/NREPP_Evaluation_course.pdf

Substance Abuse and Mental Health Services Administration (SAMHSA). (2015). Trauma. www.samhsa.gov/trauma-violence

Suciu, P. (2021). Cyberbullying remains rampant on social media. *Forbes*. Retrieved from https://www.forbes.com/sites/quora/2017/03/14/cyberbullying-among-teens-prevalence-impact-and-the-path-forward/?sh=570699167189

Sue, D. (2010). *Microaggressions in everyday life: Race, gender, and sexual orientation*. Somerset, NJ: Wiley and Sons Inc.

Tamminen, S. (2003). *Making sense of the Finns—A cross-cultural training program*. Helsinki, Finland: Cultrane Ky.

Taverner, B., & Montfort, S. (2005). *Making sense of abstinence: Lessons for comprehensive sex education*. Morristown, NJ: Planned Parenthood of Greater Northern New Jersey, Inc.

Taverner, B. (2006). Tips for emerging sexology professionals: Networking and nurturing. *Contemporary Sexuality*, 40, 1–8.

Tay, S. (2010). America's call to globalization. *Forbes*. Retrieved from www.forbes.com/2010/09/22/asia-america-globalization-markets-economy-book-excerpt-simon-tay.html?sh=3ae776514bca

Taylor, C., & Taylor, G. (2003). Designing dynamic stepfamilies: Bringing the pieces to peace. Video series. Retrieved from designingdynamicstepfamilies.com

Taylor, P., Funk, C., & Clark, C. (2007). As marriage and parenthood drift apart, public is concerned about social impact. *Pew Research Center*. Retrieved from www.pewresearch.org/social-trends/2007/07/01/as-marriage-and-parenthood-drift-apart-public-is-concerned-about-social-impact/

Taylor, P., Funk, C., & Craighill, P. (2006). Are we happy yet? *Pew Research Center*. Retrieved from www.pewresearch.org/social-trends/2006/02/13/are-we-happy-yet/

Tennant, J. (1989). Family life education: Identity, objectives, and future directions. *McGill Journal of Education*, 24, 127–142.

Thiagarajan, S., & Thiagarajan, R. (2011). *BARNGA*. Boston: Intercultural Press.

Thomas, J., & Arcus, M. E. (1992). Family life education: An analysis of the concept. *Family Relations*, 41, 3–8.

Thomas, R. (1996). Reflective dialogue parent education design: Focus on parent development. *Family Relations*, 45, 189–200.

Thomas, R., & Footrakoon, O. (1998). What curricular perspectives can tell us about parent education curricula. *Parenthood in America*. Retrieved from http://parenthood.library.wisc.edu/Thomas/Thomas.html

Thompson, K. (2019). Globalisation and the family. *Revise Sociology*. Retrieved from https://revisesociology.com/2019/04/13/globalisation-family/

Thurber, A., & DiAngelo, R. (2018). Microaggressions: Intervening in three acts. *Journal of Ethnic & Cultural Diversity in Social Work*, 27, 17–27.

Tieffer, L. (2004). *Sex is not a natural act and other essays* (2nd ed.). Boulder, CO: Westview Press.

Timmerman, G. (2009). Teaching skills and personal characteristics of sex education teachers. *Teaching and Teacher Education*, 25, 500–506.

Torino, G. C., Rivera, D. P., Capodilupo, C. M., Nadal, K. L., & Sue, D. W. (2018). Everything you wanted to know about microaggressions but didn't get a chance to ask. In *Microaggression theory: Influence and implications* (pp. 3–15). John Wiley & Sons.

Torstendahl, R., & Burrage, M. (1990). *The formation of professions: Knowledge, state and strategy.* London: Sage.

Trask, B. (2011). Globalization and families: Meeting the family policy challenge. Presentation to United Nations. Retrieved from www.un.org/esa/socdev/family/docs/egm11/Traskpaper.pdf

Trenholm, C., Devaney, B., Fortson, K., Quay, L., Wheeler, J., & Clark, M. (2007). *Impacts of four title V, section 510 abstinence education programs*. Final report. Princeton, NJ: Mathematica Policy Research Group.

Trevor Project, The. (2020a). *Coming out: A handbook for LGBTQ young people*. New York: The Trevor Project. Retrieved from www.thetrevorproject.org/wp-content/uploads/2019/10/Coming-Out-Handbook.pdf

Trevor Project, The. (2020b). *2020 national survey of LGBTQ youth mental health*. New York: The Trevor Project. Retrieved from www.thetrevorproject.org/survey-2020/

Tschofen, C., & Mackness, J. (2012). Connectivism and dimensions of individual experience. *International Review of Research in Open and Distance Learning*, 13, 124–143. Retrieved from http://search.proquest.com/docview/1140135888?accountid=4840

Umberson, D., Williams, K., Powers, D., Liu, H., & Needham, B. (2006). You make me sick: Marital quality and health over the life course. *Journal of Health and Social Behavior*, 47, 1–16.

United Nations (UN). (n.d.). Rape: Weapon of war. Retrieved from https://www.ohchr.org/EN/NewsEvents/Pages/RapeWeaponWar.aspx

United Nations (UN). (1948). Universal Declaration of Human Rights—Article 16(3). Retrieved from www.un.org/en/documents/udhr/

United Nations (UN). (2008). Divorces and crude divorce rates by urban/rural residence: 2004–2008. Demographic yearbook, 2008. Retrieved from http://unstats.un.org/unsd/demographic/products/dyb/dyb2008/Table25.pdf

United Nations (UN). (2013). Global issues: Family. Retrieved from www.un.org/en/globalissues/family/index.shtml

United Nations (UN). (2019). Peace, dignity and equality on a healthy planet. www.un.org/en/sections/issues-depth/migration/index.html

United Nations (UN). (2020). International Day of Families 15 May. Retrieved from https://www.un.org/en/observances/international-day-of-families

United Nations (UN). (2021). World leaders in General Assembly adopt political declaration pledging urgent, transformative action to stop global AIDS epidemic by 2030. June 8, 2021. Retrieved from www.un.org/press/en/2021/ga12333.doc.htm

UNAIDS. (2020a). 90-90-90: An ambitious treatment target to help end the AIDS epidemic. Retrieved from www.unaids.org/en/resources/909090

UNAIDS (2020b). COVID-19 and AIDS. Retrieved from www.unaids.org/sites/default/files/media_asset/20200909_Lessons-HIV-COVID19.pdf

UNAIDS. (2020c). Global HIV & AIDS statistics—2020 fact sheet. Retrieved from www.unaids.org/en/resources/fact-sheet

UN Department of Economic and Social Affairs (UNDESA). (1994). The international year of the family (IYF) 1994. Retrieved from http://social.un.org/index/Family/InternationalObservances/InternationalYearoftheFamily.aspx

UN Department of Economic and Social Affairs (UNDESA). (2013a). Twentieth anniversary of the international year of the family, 2014. Retrieved from www.un.org/development/desa/family/twentieth-anniversary-of-the-international-year-of-family-2014/resolutions-and-reports.html

UN Department of Economic and Social Affairs (UNDESA). (2019). World population prospects, 2019. Retrieved from https://population.un.org/wpp/Publications/Files/WPP2019_Highlights.pdf

UN Department of Economic and Social Affairs (UNDESA). (2020). International migration highlights, 2020. Retrieved from https://www.un.org/development/desa/pd/sites/www.un.org.development.desa.pd/files/undesa_pd_2020_international_migration_highlights.pdf

United Nations Educational, Scientific, and Cultural Organization (UNESCO). (Database). Retrieved from https://en.unesco.org/about-us/introducing-unesco

United Nations Educational, Scientific, and Cultural Organization (UNESCO). (2020). Switched on—Sexuality education in digital space. Retrieved from https://en.unesco.org/events/switched-sexuality-education-digital-space

UN Population Fund (UNFPA). (n.d.). Database. Retrieved from www.unfpa.org/

UN Population Fund (UNFPA). (2008). Migration. Retrieved from www.unfpa.org/pds/migration.html

UN Statistics Division (UNSD). (2008). Minimum legal age for marriage without consent. Retrieved from http://data.un.org/Data.aspx?d=GenderStat&f=inID:19

United Way Worldwide. (2009). Focusing on program outcomes: A guide for United Ways. www.unitedwaynems.org/wp-content/uploads/2018/02/Outcomes_Guide_Final-08.28.09.pdf

US Bureau of Labor Statistics (BLS). (2013). 2012–2013 occupational outlook handbook. United States Department of Labor. Retrieved from www.bls.gov/ooh/

US Bureau of Labor Statistics (BLS). (April 21, 2020). Employment characteristics of families—2019. www.bls.gov/news.release/famee.nr0.htm

US Census Bureau. (2013). Asians fastest-growing race or ethnic group in 2012. Retrieved from www.census.gov/newsroom/releases/archives/population/cb13-112.html

US Census Bureau (2018a). Fatherly figures: A snapshot of dads today. www.census.gov/library/ visualizations/2018/comm/fathers-day.html

US Census Bureau (2018b). U.S. Census Bureau releases 2018 families and living arrangements tables. https://www.census.gov/newsroom/press-releases/2018/families.html

US Census Bureau. (2020). Quick facts United States. Retrieved from www.census.gov/quickfacts/fact/table/US/IPE120219

US Census Bureau. (2021). International database: World population estimates and projections. Retrieved from www.census.gov/programs-surveys/international-programs/about/idb.html

US Department of Defense (USDOD). (2009). Plans for the department of defense for the support of military family readiness. Retrieved from www.militaryonesource.mil/12038/MOS/Reports/FY2009_Report_MilitaryFamilyReadinessPrograms.pdf

US Department of Defense (USDOD). (2018). 2018 demographics: Profile of the military community. Office of the Deputy Assistant Secretary of Defense. Retrieved from https://download.militaryonesource.mil/12038/MOS/Reports/2018-demographics-report.pdf

US Department of Homeland Security (USDHS). (n.d.). What is human trafficking? Retrieved from www.dhs.gov/blue-campaign/what-human-trafficking

US Department of State (USDOS). (2020a). Independent states of the world. Retrieved from www.state.gov/independent-states-in-the-world/

US Department of State (USDOS). (2020b). U.S. trafficking in persons report: United States. Retrieved from www.state.gov/reports/2020-trafficking-in-persons-report/united-states/

US Department of State (USDOS). (2021). National slavery and human trafficking prevention month. Retrieved from www.state.gov/national-slavery-and-human-trafficking-prevention-month/

van Bergen, D., Wilson, B., Russel, S., Gorgon, A., & Rothblum, E. (2020). Parental responses to coming out by lesbian, gay, bisexual, queer, pansexual, or two-spirited people across three age cohorts. *Journal of Marriage and Family*, 83, 1116–1133.

Veldorale-Griffin, A., Coccia, C., Darling, C., Rehm, M., & Sathe, S. (2013). The role of parental indulgence and economic stress in life satisfaction: Differential perceptions of parents and adolescents. *Journal of Family Social Work*, 16, 205–224.

Ventura, L. (2020). Unemployment rates around the world 2020. *Global Finance Magazine*. Retrieved from www.gfmag.com/global-data/economic-data/worlds-unemployment-ratescom

Vespa, J., Medina, L., & Armstrong, D. M. (2020). Demographic turning points for the United States: Populations projections for 2020 to 2060 (P25-1144). *US Census Bureau*. www.census.gov/library/publications/2020/demo/p25-1144.html

Vogt, S. (n.d.). What makes marriage work: Common values. Retrieved from www.foryourmarriage.org/everymarriage/what-makes-marriage-work/common-values/

Vuletich, H. A., & Payne, B. K. (2019). Stability and change in implicit bias. *Psychological Science*, 30, 854–862.

Vygotsky, L. (1978). *Mind in society: The development of higher psychological processes*. Cambridge, MA: Harvard University Press.

Wagenhals, D. (2017). Increasing awareness of trauma in family life education. *CFLE Network*, 29, 1.

Wages, S., & Darling C. (2004). Evaluation of a marriage preparation program using mentor couples. *Marriage & Family: A Christian Journal*, 7, 103–121.

Walker, S. (2016). Creating the future we want: A framework for integrating family and consumer sciences research, practice, and policy on technology use. *Journal of Family and Consumer Sciences*, 108, 7–19.

Walker, S. (2017). Creating parentopia: Design-based research to develop an interface for parent learning communities and networks. In B. K. Smith, M. Borge, E. Mercier, & K. Y. Lim (Eds.), *Making a difference: Prioritizing equity and access in CSCL, 12th International Conference on Computer Supported Collaborative Learning (CSCL)*, Vol. 1. Philadelphia, PA: International Society of the Learning Sciences. https://repository.isls.org//handle/1/253

Walters, A., & Hayes, D. (2007). Teaching about sexuality. *American Journal of Sexuality Education*, 2, 27–49.

Walters, J., & Jewson, R. (1988). *The National Council on Family Relations: A fifty-year history, 1938–1987*. Minneapolis, MN: National Council on Family Relations.

Wartella, E., Rideout, V., Lauricella, A. R., & Connell, S. L. (2013). *Parenting in the age of digital technology: A national survey.* Report of the Center on Media and Human Development, School of Communication, Northwestern University.

Wartella, E., Rideout, V., Lauricella, A., & Connell, S. (2014). *Revised parenting in the age of digital technology: A national survey.* Report of the Center on Media and Human Development, School of Communication, Northwestern University.

Watkins, R., Meirs, M., & Visson, Y. (2012). A guide to assessing needs: Essential tools for collecting information, making decisions, and activity development. *The World Bank*. Retrieved from https://openknowledge.worldbank.org/handle/10986/2231

Watson, J. (1925) *Behaviorism*. New York: W.W. Norton.

Waxman, H. (2004). *The content of federally funded abstinence-only education programs*. Washington, DC: U.S. House of Representatives Committee on Government Reform.

Weahkee, R. (2010, June). Message from the director, division of behavioral health. *Indian Health Service Headquarters Division of Behavioral Health Newsletter*, 1–12.

Webb, F. J., & Gonlin, V. (2019). Questions and concerns regarding family theories: Biracial and multiracial family issues. In N. Roy & A. Rollins (Eds.), *Biracial families: Crossing boundaries, blending cultures, and challenging racial ideologies* (pp. 33–57). Springer.

Weber, J., & Branscum, A. (2020). *Individual and family stress and crises*. Austin, TX: Sentia Publishing Company.

Weigley, E. (1976). The professionalization of home economics. *Home Economics Research Journal*, 4, 253–259.

Weiss, E., & Lee, G. (2009). Parenting education is economic development. Partnership for America's economic success. *Council for a Strong America*. Retrieved from www.readynation.org/uploads/20090708_PAESParentingBriefFinal.pdf

Whitchurch, G. (2005). Walking the walk: Teaching systems theory by doing theory. In V. Bengston, A. Acock, K. Allen, P. Dilworth-Anderson, & D. Klein (Eds.), *Sourcebook of family theory & research* (pp. 573–574). Thousand Oaks, CA: Sage.

White, J., Martin, T., & Adamsons, K. (2019). *Family theories: An introduction*. Thousand Oaks, CA: Sage.

Wilcox, B. (2010). *When marriage disappears: The retreat from marriage in middle America. The state of our unions 2010*. Charlottesville, VA: National Marriage Project and Institute for American Values.

Wilkenfeld, B., & Ballan, M. (2011). Educators' attitudes and beliefs towards the sexuality of individuals with developmental disabilities. *Sexuality and Disability* 29, 351–361.

Williams, L. (2004). The meaning of marriage: Two churches, one marriage. University of San Diego. Retrieved from https://sites.sandiego.edu/interchurch/religious-differences/

Williams, L., & McBain, H. (2006). Integrating gender on multiple levels. A conceptual model for teaching gender issues in family therapy. *Journal of Marital and Family Therapy*, 32, 385–397.

The Williams Institute. (2019). LGBT demographic data interactive. UCLA School of Law. Retrieved from https://williamsinstitute.law.ucla.edu/visualization/lgbt-stats/?topic=LGBT#density

W. K. Kellogg Foundation. (2004). *Using logic models to bring together planning, evaluation, and action. Logic model development guide*. Battle Creek, MI: Author. Retrieved from www.wkkf.org/knowledge-center/resources/2006/02/wk-kellogg-foundation-logic-model-development-guide.aspx

Wolford, S., Darling, C. A., Rehm, M., & Cui, M. (2020). Examining parental internal processes associated with indulgent parenting: A thematic analysis. *Journal of Child and Family Studies* 29, 660–675.

Wood, D., Bruner, J., & Ross, G. (1976). The role of tutoring in problem solving. *Journal of Child Psychology and Child Psychiatry*, 17, 89–100.

Wood, M. (2003). Experiential learning for undergraduates: A simulation about functional change and aging. *Geriatrics & Geriatrics Education*, 23, 37–38.

Wood, R., Avellar, S., & Goesling, B. (2008). Pathways to adulthood and marriage: Attitudes, expectations, and relationship patterns. US Department of Health and Human Services. Retrieved from http://aspe.hhs.gov/hsp/08/pathways2adulthood/index.shtml

Woods, S. (2020). Covid-19 and ambiguous loss. *Psychology Today*. Retrieved from www.psychologytoday.com/us/blog/in-sickness-and-in-health/202005/covid-19-and-ambiguous-loss

Woodworth, J. (2020). Students with disabilities (9). *National Center for Education Statistics*. https://nces.ed.gov/programs/coe/indicator_cgg.asp

World Association for Sexual Health (WASH). (2008). *Sexual health for the millennium: A declaration and technical document*. Minneapolis, MN: World Association for Sexual Health.

World by Map. (2010). Median age of the world. Retrieved from http://world.bymap.org/MedianAge.html

World Health Organization (WHO). (2010). Global health observatory: HIIV/AIDS. Retrieved from http://www.who.int/gho/hiv/en/index.html

World Health Organization (WHO). (2017). *Sexual health and its linkages to reproductive health: An operational approach*. Retrieved from http://www.who.int/reproductivehealth/publications/sexual_health/sh-linkages-rh/en/

World Health Organization (WHO). (2019a). Dementia. Retrieved from www.who.int/news-room/fact-sheets/detail/dementia

World Health Organization (WHO). (2019b). Sexual health. Retrieved from www.who.int/health-topics/sexual-health#tab=tab_1

World Health Organization (WHO). (2020a). HIV/AIDS. www.who.int/news-room/fact-sheets/detail/hiv-aids

World Health Organization (WHO). (2020b). The top 10 causes of death. Retrieved from www.who.int/news-room/fact-sheets/detail/the-top-10-causes-of-death

World Population Review. (2020a). Teen pregnancy rates by state 2020. Retrieved from www.worldpopulationreview.com/state-rankings/teen-pregnancy-rates-by-state

World Population Review. (2020b). What percentage of the population is transgender 2020. Retrieved from www.worldpopulationreview.com/state-rankings/transgender-population-by-state

World Public Opinion. (n.d.). Globalization. Retrieved from www.americans-world.org/digest/global_issues/globalization/culture.cfm

Xia, Y., & Creaser, C. (2018). Family life education in China. In M. Robila & A. Taylor (Eds.), *Global perspectives on family life education* (pp. 33–48). Cham, Switzerland: Springer International Publishing.

Xia, Y. R., Do, K. A., & Xie, X. L. (2013). The adjustment of Asian American families to the U.S. context: The ecology of strengths and stress. In G. W. Peterson & K. R. Bush (Eds.), *Handbook of marriage and the family* (pp. 705–722). New York, NY: Springer.

Yarber, W., & Sayad, B. (2019) *Human sexuality; Diversity in contemporary society*. New York, NY: McGraw Hill.

You Matter. (2020). Globalization: Definition, benefits, effects, examples—What is globalization? Retrieved from https://youmatter.world/en/definition/definitions-globalization-definition-benefits-effects-examples/

Youcha, G. (1995). *Minding the children: Childcare in America from colonial times to the present*. New York: Scribner.

Zablotsky, B., Black, L. I., Maenner, M. J., Schieve, L. A., Danielson, M. L., Bitsko, R. H., Blumberg, S. J., Kogan, M. D., & Boyle, C. A. (2019). Prevalence and trends of developmental disabilities among children in the United States: 2009–2017. *Pediatrics*, 144, e20190811.

Zarra, E. J., III. (2017). *The entitled generation: Helping teachers teach and reach the minds and hearts of Generation Z*. Lanham, MD: Rowman & Littlefield.

Index